ISAAC BASHEVIS SINGER

The Magician of West 86th Street

ISAAC BASHEVIS SINGER

The Magician of West 86th Street

A Biography by
PAUL KRESH

THE DIAL PRESS
NEW YORK

Published by
The Dial Press
1 Dag Hammarskjold Plaza
New York, New York 10017

Manufactured in the United States of America

First printing

Design by Karin Batten

Grateful acknowledgment is made for permission to use the following copyrighted material:

Library of Congress Cataloging in Publication Data

Kresh, Paul.
Isaac Bashevis Singer, the magician of West 86th
Street

Bibliography: p.
Includes index.
1. Singer, Isaac Bashevis, 1904–   —Biography.
2. Authors, Yiddish—United States—Biography.
I. Title
PJ5129.S49Z74   839'.09'33 [B]   79-18589
ISBN 0-8037-3696-7

To Penrod

Contents

Acknowledgments

The author would like to acknowledge the cooperation of the many individuals and institutions for whose help he is grateful.

First and foremost, to Isaac Bashevis Singer, who gave so much of his time and attention in the course of countless interviews, and to Alma, his wife, whose warmth and enthusiasm were always a source of assurance. To Isaac's son, Israel Zamir, and his family, for their hospitality at Kibbutz Bet Alpha in Israel. To Chaim Vinitsky, director of the United Jewish Appeal in Israel, who worked out the logistics of that visit. To Dvorah and Abraham Menashe, who have provided so much information and guidance. To Claire Miller, the Executive Vice-president of Miller-Brody Productions, whose invitation to prepare the script for a Newbery Award educational filmstrip about Isaac Singer inspired this book. To Anne Knauerhase, formerly of The Dial Press, whose patience, interest, and editorial advice were of so much help and inspiration during the early stages; and to Juris Jurjevics, who took up where she left off. To Richard Marek, the former editor-in-chief at Dial, and Joyce Engelson, who responded so encouragingly to the proposal; to Helen Meyer, then president of Dial, who seconded it; to Britt Bell, managing editor at Dial, Sharon Mazur, and Johanna Tani for their help in seeing this manuscript through the vicissitudes of production; and especially to Cary Ryan for her astute and steadfast editorial guidance, which has been of incalculable importance.

To Howard Moss, for his sympathetic interest and practical help. To Roger W. Straus, Jr., who provided much useful information and advice, generously supplied many of the books needed for research, and so graciously granted permission to quote from the many volumes published by Farrar, Straus and Giroux. To the many other publishers and publications who gave similar permissions, and to Carole Stoddard for her help in obtaining these clearances.

To Joseph Singer, who answered hard questions and provided valuable insights. To the editors, translators, critics, and friends of Isaac Singer, who granted interviews, including: Aaron Alperin; Paul Berkowsky, the associate producer of Yentl on Broadway; Robert Brustein; Arthur A. Cohen; Laurie Colwin; Bruce Davidson; Tovah Feldshuh; Harvey Gardner of Fawcett Publications; Mirra Ginsburg; Elaine Gottlieb; Irving Howe; Lila Karpf; Rachel MacKenzie, fiction editor of The New Yorker; Samuel L. Schneiderman; Zvee Schooler; Elizabeth Shub; Dorothea Straus; Eve Roshevsky of Doubleday; and Simon Weber, editor of the Jewish Daily Forward. To the MacDowell Colony and the Virginia Center for the Creative Arts, which provided the happy environments where revisions could be made amid tranquil surroundings. To Leta Cromwell, who made her home in St. Thomas available for additional work on the manuscript.

To Robert Fulford of the Canadian Broadcasting Company, who allowed the use of broadcast materials. To the Jewish Theological Seminary; Yivo; the American Jewish Committee; and other organizations and their libraries, which furnished background materials. To the staff of the United Jewish Appeal–Federation of Jewish Philanthropies Joint Campaign, especially to Ernest W. Michel, executive vice-president, and Robert I. Smith, public relations director, for their understanding and forbearance during the period when the preparation of this book required so much of my attention and energy. And to Stephen Potter for his critical advice and unfailing support.

To Dr. Justus Rosenberg of Bard College, who permitted the author to sit in on Mr. Singer's classes and lectures. To Bernice Belth and Ethel Press, who conducted countless hours of research, as well as to Ms. Press for her translations of Yiddish manuscripts. To Robert Lesher, Isaac Singer's agent, for his benign influence and suggestions, and to Robert P. Mills, my own, for many hours of consultation and guidance. Lastly, to Fay Miller, without whose help in readying this manuscript for publication the whole effort might still remain a stack of uncorrelated pages; and to Robert Barth, for his cheerful assistance in getting these pages ready for submission.

Introduction

Isaac Bashevis Singer and I first really got to know one another in the summer of 1966. It was at a *hagigah*, a festival of the arts, sponsored by the National Federation of Temple Youth in a camp near Warwick, New York, operated by the Union of American Hebrew Congregations. The *hagigah* was an experimental program of study and "creativity." There were classes for drama, writing, painting, sculpture, literature, music, and dance; there were seminars with leaders in every field of the arts, performances on Jewish themes by actors and opera singers and modern dancers, and original religious services, some accompanied by jazz and rock. At the same time the Summer Institute for the Creative and Performing Arts in Judaism had attracted some forty especially talented college students and an unusual number of outstanding performers.

I had come as the editor of the UAHC's official publication, *American Judaism*, to cover these events and take part as a teacher in the creative writing seminars. I arrived one evening to find Mr. Singer, our most distinguished literary guest, holding forth before a small group of faculty members in the lounge.

We had met briefly a few times before. One day a member of the magazine's staff had come into my office, filled with enthusiasm, insisting that I get hold of the latest issue of *Esquire*, which contained one of Singer's stories. At the time I resisted the suggestion, asking why anybody would want to read nostalgic tales about Jewish life in Poland anymore. Who needed it? Who wanted to go back to the *shtetls* and the little shabby *shtiebele* sidestreet synagogues and the airless lives of stifling people in depressing ghettoes? It seemed to me it was high time to leave all that behind. But after sampling a few of Isaac's stories I realized what I had been missing. Nostalgic tales indeed! Here was the real thing: the kind of vigorous writing I had been looking for in Jewish fiction and had seldom found. We published several of Isaac's stories and essays in *American Judaism* after that, and I became so dedicated a convert that I wound up lecturing about his work at sisterhood luncheons and in temple sanctuaries on the Reform Jewish circuit. Once, during a visit to my office, Isaac had even listened to a portion of a taped lecture and commented graciously that I seemed to understand what he was doing. But my first real encounter with him was in Warwick that summer evening. There he sat, in the midst of a group of camp counselors in their sportshirts and jeans, wearing his uniform of dark business suit, white shirt, and whisper-quiet tie, his blue eyes twinkling in his chalk-white face, teasing us about the absurdities of modern art, obscure poetry, and novels that perversely refused to tell a story.

"Mr. Singer," I began, about to protest one of his disparaging remarks about the obliquity of modern verse.

"Call me Isaac," he interjected, and I have called him that ever since.

Isaac attacked all my idols at once but did so with such good humor that I couldn't find it in me to feel offended. We talked and joked far into the night, and the next day Isaac made a round of appearances at outdoor classes and seminars, at indoor readings and consultations with fledgling authors. I remember him lounging under the willow trees by the lake, warning students—as he still does—that "a writer must have roots . . . an address . . . a Jewish writer must first of all be a good writer."

He lectured about his own work and fielded questions with the wit and verve I have since seen him display countless times. In the afternoons he would sit in a field going over a manuscript of his own or lie in the sun for a snooze. He seemed always ready to talk and made himself accessible to everyone fortunate enough to find a place by his side. His jokes could be barbed, but along with the charm for which he is famous, he generated an aura of kindness.

We put on a one-act opera based on his most celebrated story, "Gimpel the Fool," for which I had written the libretto and Charles Davidson had composed the music. I am sure Isaac was aware of every weakness in the libretto, the music, and the rather rough performance we were able to stage in the camp auditorium, but he said he loved every minute of it.

Later that summer news came from home that my dog had died, and when I came away from the telephone, I felt unspeakably lonely and bereft. Others dismissed my grief with the reminder that it was "only a dog" who had died, after all, not a person, but Isaac understood. He was kind and comforting. I knew I had made a friend.

Later Isaac described his experiences at the *hagigah* in an article published in *American Judaism*. A slightly more satirical version appeared, I was told, in Yiddish in the *Jewish Daily Forward*.

"It is needless to say," he wrote, "that most of these young people nurse creative ambitions. Every other *hagigahnik* wants to be either a writer, a painter, a sculptor, or a musician. One of the campers told me a year ago that he wanted to become a 'creative rabbi.' As if this weren't enough, this same movement organized something this past summer it calls the Summer Institute for the Creative and Performing Arts in Judaism. If one had to be gifted to be invited to the *hagigah*, one actually had to be a *Wunderkind* or a bit of a genius to participate in the Institute. The fact is, the *hagigahniks* and those attending the Institute were so intermixed that until the very end I could not tell which were which. Those taking part in the Institute should have been a bit older, but to my eyes they all seemed terribly young. Quite frequently, it was difficult for me to differentiate between the students and the professors.

"Here I am chatting with this admiring youth. He asks for my autograph and I pinch his cheek. But soon it comes out that he is a famous rabbi and a university professor into the bargain. I made a vow to myself to pinch no more cheeks in this youthful domain where even the old appear young."

At Warwick, Isaac wrote, it would have been possible to go without eating, but "it was physically impossible to run away from culture. . . . the moment you walk away from one cultural effort you instantly fall into another. If you don't want instructions in sculpture from Nehemiah Mark you must take a class in literature from Rabbi Dan Isaac, Paul Kresh, Leslie Fiedler, Muriel Rukeyser, Joseph Landis, or Henry Rago. If you grow tired of literature you fall into the clutches of such musicians as Paul Ben-Haim, Lazar Weiner, Yehudi Wyner, Jack Gottlieb (an assistant to the celebrated Leonard Bernstein), Herbert Fromm, Charles Davidson, the cantor and musician Raymond Smolover, or Alan Rich, the music critic of the *Herald Tribune*, may it rest in peace. You try to escape from music and lurking in ambush for you are such painters as Moses Soyer, Irving Amen, Gideon Shacknai, and Nissan Engel. Here, people dance—there, they compose poetry; here, they discuss Maimonides—there, Martin Buber; here, the future of Yiddish—there, the fate of Israel. Where is there escape when in every hall, on every meadow, under every tree, and beneath every shrub something is being taught or debated?

"Not only did the young people not run away, but they in fact ran after every creative person who had something to say, to recite, to sing, to teach, or to narrate. Those who like to decry the materialism of Jewish youth in America and its devotion to the almighty dollar should spend at least three days in Warwick. There were moments when I felt as if I had fallen in among zealous Hasidim at some rabbinical court. I saw distinguished rabbis performing the work of waiters and errand boys. . . ."

American Judaism is no more, and I am no longer with the Union of American Hebrew Congregations, but since those days I have pursued a rewarding friendship with Isaac that has meant much to me both personally and professionally. He has always been ready to read one of his stories aloud on a radio program, grant an interview, attend a dinner, share a lunch in one of his favorite haunts on the Upper West Side, or lend his name to a good cause. When the idea of writing this book came up, he agreed not only to cooperate on the project but to forego the right to see the manuscript, so that the portrait could be drawn as objectively as possible. We have spent innumerable hours at his apartment in New York and in his Miami Beach condominium talking about his life, his work, his opinions. With patience and forbearance he has allowed me to sit in on his classes at Bard College, to follow him around to lectures and parties and readings, to interview his son and daughter-in-law and grandchildren on their kibbutz in Israel. There have been days, with his staggering schedule of work and appearances, when he was simply too exhausted to talk to me, but his generosity with his time and attention has been remarkable.

Yet, even with all these advantages, how does one write a book about a living man, who is active, pursuing his star as an author and as a person? One cannot properly call such an effort a biography in the conventional sense at all. I have tried in the pages that follow to paint a living, tentative picture of Isaac's life and work. I have talked to dozens of his friends, his translators, his publishers, his editors, his critics, his secretarial assistant, his wife, his nephew Joseph. I have reread all his books, including some unpublished manuscripts—and his brother's books, for without an understanding of the achievements of Israel Joshua Singer I think it is impossible to appreciate those of Isaac Bashevis Singer. I have plodded through a great many essays and book reviews of widely varying quality and significance, interviews, and transcriptions of radio and television appearances. Not being versed in Yiddish, a language my parents resorted to when they didn't want me to understand what they were saying (so that I never really learned it), I have had to rely on the authority of others to discuss Isaac's mastery of Yiddish style and to provide rough translations of material that has not yet appeared in English.

Isaac's wife, Alma, asked me once how—as an American Jew who had virtually no Yiddish at his command and who had not lived the Jewish experience of pre-Hitler Warsaw—I could possibly hope to understand, let alone treat in a book, the life and work of a man like her husband. I can only reply now, as I did then, that perhaps my very ignorance sets me closer to the viewpoint and position of the vast majority of Isaac's English-speaking readers, whose sensibilities and general view of the world are akin to mine, whose interests and experiences tend to parallel mine, and who might be likely to ask the same questions that would occur to me. Certainly those *landsmen* from Central Europe who speak the *mamalushen* and grew up much as Isaac did have not shown the deepest sympathy for him—nor the profoundest insight into his work.

Isaac has had his own apprehensions at times about what his "biographer" was up to and what I meant when I told him at the outset that I wanted to paint an "honest" portrait of him. It seems to me that there are aspects of almost every life that should not, by any common standard of decency, be discussed publicly during the subject's lifetime. Yet where is one to draw the line? It has been the struggle of my own conscience in writing this book to walk the precarious boundary between candor and simple decency. I am not much of a gossip writer and must confess that I am somewhat weary of the tendency in contemporary biography to offer endless views of clay feet while neglecting the rest of the idol.

All things considered, some questions, for the moment, are perhaps better left unanswered. People often ask about "Singer's women"—all those intense, libidinous daughters of Eve who wreak so much havoc in his pages.

They wonder whether those spicy amorous adventures he describes in his fiction are based on his own experiences. I would refer them to a hilarious article by Tova Reich called "The Mistresses of Singer" (*Harper's*, May, 1979). Mrs. Reich, the author of the novel *Mara*, claims that all over Israel, Eastern Europe, and America women have been coming forward to announce that they were once Isaac's mistresses. "These women," she writes, "range in age from their mid-fifties to their early nineties, and all of them, if you care to look closely, possess at least one feature—a cynical mouth, a poignant wrist, a melancholy eye—that startles your attention and impels you to consider." Even their own husbands boast that these women have been involved with Isaac and that "the reflected glory of the laurel wreath embraces their heads as well, concealing, even for a moment enhancing, the cuckold's horns." According to Mrs. Reich, her own Aunt Henny in Tel Aviv, who wears "tinselly-tinkly earrings," counts herself among the chosen, and there's a ninety-three-year-old lady living in "an alley off Krochmalna Street" who claims to be the oldest among them and to have served as the model for Wanda in *The Slave*. Every year, Mrs. Reich asserts, the American mistresses get together for a convention in Miami or on the Upper West Side of Manhattan ("I live on the West Side," Isaac once told a reporter, "because that's where my women are."). When it was announced that Isaac was to receive the Nobel prize for literature in October 1978, Mrs. Reich adds, a motion was put on the floor at one of their meetings that they all go with the laureate to Stockholm. They decided, however, to defer to Alma. "In public it is as it has always been. The wife gets all the credit." Mrs. Reich clearly labeled her piece "a fantasy." So let it stand.

The better I have come to know him and his work, the more I have cherished and admired Isaac Bashevis Singer. Not everyone who is acquainted with him, to be sure, *does* love him or is entirely susceptible to his charm; nor do all his readers share my high estimate of what he has accomplished. These people too are given their say in these pages. At any rate Isaac Singer has trusted me, and I do hope when he reads this volume, if he does, he will enjoy the experience and find his trust in me and his patience with me justified. I told him once that I would rather have a friend than a book; I still feel that way.

After one wearying session, when I was going over some aspect of his youth for the umpteenth time in order to clear up a few matters that were still woolly in my mind, Isaac fixed upon me with those keen, cool, azure eyes of his and said, "Listen, my dear friend, you have milked this cow for all that is in it, and if you cannot make cheese out of this, from now on that is your problem." I pray that what I have set out here has turned to cheese.

Isaac, who at the time of this writing is approaching his mid-seventies, has, in his own inimitable way, and with a skill no other writer could presume to emulate, been unfolding the episodes of his life in his own books of memoirs. Yet even in these memoirs Isaac is the storyteller first and the autobiographer second, seldom (as some reporter once put it) allowing a few facts to stand in the way of a story. Nor are the facts always as clear as they might be: It is doubtful that Isaac himself is sure where life ends and literature begins, although both the life and the literature are his own. Even so, I hope that in the pages that follow I have disentangled fact from fable where possible and caught some measure of this extraordinary man.

"What are writers?
The same kind of entertainers as magicians.
As a matter of fact, I admire someone
who can balance a barrel on his feet
more than I do a poet."

—Celia Chentshiner in SHOSHA

PART 1

"An Author
Must Have Roots"

T he world of Isaac Bashevis Singer unfurls like a great mural across the pages of his writings. Here are the vanished *shtetls* of Radzymin and Bilgoray, with their devout rabbis, steeped in piety, observing to the letter the precepts of their faith, ready to wrestle with the Devil and lock him in a cage if he shows his face, defending traditional values, suspicious of all that is secular and *tref*. Here are the sensual eaters and carousers, the womanizers, the self-indulgent. Indoors, pale beneath their yarmulkes, sit the yeshiva students, with one eye on the Torah and the other on the tempting shapes that spur their lust. Demons cavort in this world, and witches. The scene is Warsaw, shivering under bitter winds and snows.

Rough coachmen drive their droshkies over cobbled streets to grimy stations; trains depart in clouds of steam, huffing and chugging through peasant villages and pine forests. In the comfortless cars jeering snub-nosed Poles in shabby uniforms threaten Jews. And then there are the animals, the animals that are "the wonder of God's creation"—the patient dogs, usually named Burak, goats with full udders and innocent eyes, horses patient under whips and curses, twittering parakeets and canaries filling the gloomy air of the ghettoes with their song.

Through long winter nights in poorhouses old men distract one another from the bites of lice and the cold with fantastic tales of mismatched lovers, of women who turn into fishes, and of latter-day saints who try to renounce all earthly pleasures but somehow succumb just the same. Small-time Spinozas suddenly yield to instinct as reason gives way to the hungers of the flesh; a foppish *shlemiel* of a baker, on the other hand, can metamorphose into a worldly-wise philosopher. All in this world is exactly what it seems, yet all is also an illusion, a *trompe l'oeil* joke on our gullible, pitifully limited senses, a magician's sleight-of-hand trick.

In this world the ice freezes harder and the sun shines hotter than in other places; the stars stare out from a heaven where the very spheres are engaged in celestial copulation. Yet there is room in the scheme of things for Aunt Yentl to tell her stories of bygone days, for lovers to wander over the cobbled streets of old cities, for prostitutes to lurk in the gateways of courtyards, for little boys to ask impossible questions about the nature of existence. There is room for the chorus of gossips, the greedy merchant, the prudent farmer. Housewives wring the necks of chickens, and ritual slaughterers cut the throats of beasts, while the reverent cling to abstinence and intone their prayers. Dybbuks enter the bodies of innocent girls to spew out filth and mockery even as virgin brides allow their heads to be shaved, don wigs, and turn into matrons overnight.

There is room too in this world of Isaac's for a number of the earth's great cities, where sophisticated bluestockings puff on cigarettes and pine for their lost loves, and refugees whose souls have long since died patrol the earth as ghosts uprooted from the past. Just as there is room for small-town shops and cottages, where the scene is set eternally with the rude artifacts of the past and ills are cured by cupping and bleeding (all doctors in this world are quacks).

Here Jews are granted bodies as well as minds and souls, bodies that itch and palpitate and squirm in their implacable yearning for affection and fulfillment. And here there is poverty, with all its afflictions, but there are boisterous weddings and holiday celebrations too, gargantuan festivities as well as funerals where floods of tears are shed, as when the Vistula overflows its banks in early spring. It is a vulnerable world, invaded one day by the Russians, the next by the Austrians or the Germans, but life goes on despite the upheavals, the pogroms, the droughts, the plagues—despite every manner of natural and man-made catastrophe.

Here enlightenment is constantly at war with ignorance, but as often as not the ignorant and the fools prove wiser than the prodigies and scholars. For all of them temptation lies in wait; one false step and a man or woman can forfeit all the joys of this life and the next: "It is one small step from the study house to the house of prostitution." Poverty may grind men down, but riches are illusory. Revolutionaries are nothing more than dupes of the greedy powers they would supplant; their ideals, when they win, inevitably become the ideologies of new and crueller despotisms. Only the pious avoid the pitfalls of this world and reap the benefits of the hereafter, for the old values are the only ones to be trusted; the rest is a snare and a delusion devised by the Evil One.

There are no lies in this illusionist's world, for eventually all things, even lies, come true. Afflictions lurk everywhere in wait for man. Betrayals sour friendship, even love. Laughter turns suddenly to dread, and sticks in the throat. Capricious fortune makes beggars of millionaires. It is easy to get lost amid chimerical landscapes, even on familiar streets: A safe-looking boulevard twists without warning into a nightmare of alleys and dead ends; a trip to a lecture at a university can become an ordeal of terror. The dead come back, sometimes to comfort the living, but just as often to unhinge and destroy them. Gossips spread malice and troglodytes seize power while the sensitive, the intelligent, the wonder-struck, the would-be wise, survive from moment to moment in constant peril.

Behind the tenement walls there lurks a Jewish underworld, a subcity of thieves and criminals; and beneath that, the dark unmapped terrain of Gehenna itself. Only the few who fast enough and pray enough, who are strong enough to withdraw from all that is worldly, attain that peculiar paradise in which the reward for piety is an eternity of study in a celestial university where angels make music and a man's wife is privileged to serve until the end of time as his footstool. Even so, every inch of Isaac's world, from the prehistoric mountains of *The Slave* to the cafeterias of New York's Lower East Side, where decaying journalists lament old failures over their tea and rice pudding, is pulsing with life, with suspense, with the twinkle of mischief that age cannot extinguish from this author's eyes. It is a world so persuasively constructed that within its confines even the unreal seems real, the cushions on chairs still warm from the recent press of living bodies, the air breathable, the rain moist, the ice cold enough to freeze the reader's flesh.

Over it all presides that God with whom Isaac, like Job, has his quarrels, but in whom he has never ceased truly to believe—gazing down on the ingenious complexities whereby men trap themselves, holding forever His enigmatic, exasperating silence. Why does He keep His peace with the unjust and the wicked? Is it for the sake of the thirty-six "hidden saints" who are said to justify the existence of the world in God's eyes by their goodness? Is it in the hope that His people will yet come to obey His six hundred and thirteen holy commandments? Isaac's God never speaks, yet the sky is covered with signs that attest to His truths; the very stars are letters of fire aflame in the heavens to convey his meanings. Above the voices of the articulate, aggressive women, the blaspheming dybbuks, the gabbling gossips, the mumbling *rebbes*, the murmuring lovers, the chattering demons and shrill witches, the garrulous philosophers and truculent revolutionaries, can be heard always the sound of His silence. He has other worlds on his mind besides this one, has created others and destroyed others; storytellers may spin their tales until their tongues go dry, but He will have the final word: "The whole earth, all the stars, all the planets, all the comets," as Isaac Singer writes in *The Slave*, "represent within them one divine history, one source of life, one endless and wondrous story that only God knows in its entirety."

In this world of Isaac's there exists one special street, which lives eternally through his work—even though its onetime residents have long since vanished into the graves and crematoria of the Holocaust, and their homes have been replaced by the grim, gray houses of contemporary Warsaw. This was Krochmalna Street, the street on which the Singers—or Zyngers, as it was spelled then—lived when Isaac was a boy: Isaac's practical, rational, skeptical mother, Bathsheba, with her fiery red hair and stinging tongue; his mystical, unworldly, ultrapious father, Pinchas Mendel, who scarcely made a living as the neighborhood rabbi but whose wisdom was respected by every Jew on the block; his rebellious, idealistic, impious older brother, Israel Joshua; his neurasthenic, high-strung sister, Hinde Esther; his dreamy-eyed kid brother, Moishe, destined, like his father, to enter the rabbinate—but too religious, when the final cruelties closed in, to sustain the flesh that housed his spirit; and Isaac himself, red hair aflame and blue eyes twinkling in the pallid face of a cheder child, a little boy "in search of God" who was to become a young man "in search of love," seeing and hearing everything, forgetting nothing, setting it all down to build a bridge between our world and a precious, obliterated past.

❅

Isaac is impatient this morning. Where is that girl? Where is Dvorah? She was supposed to be here at nine o'clock sharp, and it's ten after. Time to be on the highway instead of standing here on the corner of Eighty-sixth Street and Amsterdam Avenue, waiting.

Early fall sunlight is awash over Manhattan, turning the cityscape tawny against a clear sky at the start of a busy weekday morning in October 1975. Isaac looks at his watch again. He's due at Bard College for a one o'clock seminar, must get there by noon if there's to be time for a bite of lunch before class. Where's Dvorah? She's never late, he can't understand it. Isaac hates to be late, hates to be kept waiting like this, standing around. Never mind, it's in the hands of the Almighty. If she doesn't show up soon, he'll take a cab to Grand Central, the train to Rhinecliff, New York.

A car approaches, a big blue comfortable-looking sedan. Dvorah waves. She's a pretty girl, with a face as fragile and unblemished as the shell of an egg. Her intense blue eyes are darker than Isaac's, her hair a rich brown and clipped close. She is breathless, eager, disarming. He cannot resist her apologies. The traffic . . . oh, yes . . . One sidelong smile from Dvorah and Isaac is in good spirits. He never stays angry for long, anyhow. She gets out and opens the door for him so he can sit up front next to her.

Dvorah is twenty-one. Isaac is fifty years older. A few months ago he agreed to take on this assignment, teaching two days a week at Bard College in Annandale-on-Hudson, a two-hour drive from New York. A seminar on literature one day, a class in short-story writing the next. Today he's combining the two so he can get back to the city and keep an appointment early tomorrow.

Dvorah is a new friend, a fresh face in Isaac's busy life. A Bard student from Brooklyn, she had admired Isaac's work long before she met him. Her mother, shortly before her death, had urged her to go see Singer: "Tell him you want to be a writer yourself and he must help." Instead Dvorah sent him a Jewish New Year's card, telling him how much she liked his work and asking whether they might meet. She couldn't go on studying at Bard at eight hundred dollars a course, she said, but if she could be his chauffeur, ferry him up there and back, maybe he would let her sit in on his writing class. A couple of days later he phoned her and said, "Well, will you take me?"

This is their eighth trip up. The car maneuvers through the heavy city traffic, wheels out onto the highway. The Hudson sparkles below in the bright sunlight. After a while there are trees lining the landscaped parkway, their leaves just turning saffron and flame-red and umber, the sky a strong blue. Isaac asks Dvorah to turn off the car radio. He's feeling talkative this morning. Playful. She glances at him with smiling eyes that delight in him. Removing his battered brown felt hat, he reveals a scattering of sparse white hair above the pale pink dome of his head, and white ears, pointed, like an elf's. He takes off his raincoat, holds it in his lap. How thin his neck and shoulders are, frail, vulnerable. His voice, with the distinctly Polish-Yiddish accent that over four decades in America have not obliterated, quavers a little with age. Yet when he turns to talk to Dvorah, the pale blue eyes shimmer, and there is energy as well as affection in the low voice.

"You're still working at the academy, Dvorah?"

"Yes. The Academy of American Poets."

"Poets. And what do you do there?"

"I'm a reader. I read manuscripts from poets."

"And they pay you for that? For reading poetry?"

"I also do a little filing."

"At least it's money."

"Will you sing me a *nigun* today? You promised to sing me a Hasidic song, and you never have."

"I could only sing for you if I was hiding in a dark place where nobody could see me, in a closet."

"We can go into the woods this afternoon, and you can sing for me."

"It would frighten away the nightingales."

"Even Jewish nightingales?"

"Well, if they were Jewish nightingales maybe it wouldn't frighten them."

"My grandfather used to sing me beautiful Yiddish songs from the Ukraine."

"My songs are from the Polish Hasidim. They're different."

"Come on. Sing one."

"If you'll bring me a fiddler, I'll climb up on a roof and sing you a *nigun*."

"Why not now?"

"I'm too shy. Besides, my dear, if I could sing like a crow even, I would consider myself a good singer." He chuckles.

"What's funny?"

"I once got an invitation. It was addressed to Isaac Bashevis comma Singer. They wanted me to come to some meeting and sing folk songs."

Dvorah laughs boyishly. With her short haircut, her black turtleneck with the silver chain, her tiny white hands controlling the oversized car with complete assurance, she might be the perfect model for the girl in Isaac's story "Yentl the Yeshiva Boy," which is going to open on Broadway as a play in a couple of weeks.

Dvorah, in fact, used to attend a yeshiva in Flatbush. She left at the age of nine when her family moved to Great Neck, where she went to public elementary school and later high school. She then enrolled at Bard but left after two years to travel in Scotland, where she performed with a pantomime troupe. After that she went to Israel to study. Back in New York, she married Abraham Menashe, a young photographer, a Jew from Egypt. He makes a living taking pictures at weddings and bar mitzvahs so that he can pursue his craft, photographing Hasidic life in Brooklyn. He and Isaac are collaborating on a picture book. Dvorah sees her father, a surgeon, even less now than she did before her mother's death. They don't get along too well. She thinks of Isaac as the father she always wished she'd had. This suits him, especially during the long drives up to Bard.

"Do you ever sing for Alma?" Dvorah asks.

"Alma is a wonderful woman, but she's too practical. Every day she gets up and tells me that the price of cottage cheese is thirty cents more than it was twenty years ago."

"What do you say?"

"After thirty-eight years of marriage, what can I tell her? She is interested in all kinds of things, in the theater, in movies, in literature—on which she has very fine opinions—but at breakfast she prefers to talk about cottage cheese. She is an enlightened woman, but recently when somebody said to her, 'You are a liberated woman,' she became insulted."

The sun climbs toward noon.

"Tell me," Dvorah says, turning again to her passenger, "if you had your choice between a bore and a bitch, which would you take?"

"I'd take the bitch."

The Bard campus looks like some colonial-village restoration project financed by the Rockefellers, with its red brick, white wooden porticoes, rolling lawns, and ivy rippling against building walls in the light wind. The sun is even warmer now, the sky a profound blue. The breeze ruffles the grass like a hand stroking a dog's fur. In this eighteenth-century *mise-en-*

scène the students look incongruous in their jeans, legend-bearing T-shirts, and plastic jackets, as though somebody had lowered the wrong backdrop behind them.

Isaac usually goes to the little apartment kept for him about half a mile off campus, but there isn't time now. Only about a half hour for lunch in the cafeteria, then on to Professor Justus Rosenberg's seminar on literature.

In the cafeteria students are lining up with their trays for low-priced lunches. Dvorah goes into the sun-splashed dining room to save a table, then gets on line to put together a vegetarian lunch for Isaac, who eats neither meat nor fish nor fowl—not even chicken soup. Several students speak to him. One comes up to the table. Isaac beams, looks up, and greets her.

"Hi. My name is Debbie. I just wanted to tell you I love your work."

Debbie wears heavy-rimmed glasses, her black hair in bangs that practically hide the lenses. She has just returned from a visit to Israel. Isaac is glad to hear it. He was in Israel himself during the summer.

A boy arrives at the table to ask Isaac whether he could get into the short-story writing class.

"Why not? You're welcome to join. Of course."

Isaac continues to be genial, but when Dvorah brings the tray, he concentrates on his food. Soon she gets up again to fetch him a glass of milk and a second helping of beets.

After lunch Dvorah says good-bye, promising to wait for him in front of the building where his afternoon seminar will end at two.

The seminar classroom has harsh yellow walls and a worn carnation-red carpet, but the room is spacious, and light filters down agreeably through a high oval window in one wall and tall french windows at the back. School-room chairs with ungainly, paddle-shaped armrests are lined up in rows. Near the front desk a young man is tinkering with a tape recorder, trying to coax it to work so that this session in the seminar series on literature can be preserved for the archives along with the rest. When the room is about half filled, a large dog of doubtful breed wanders in, sniffs, decides that this course is not for him; Bard is an informal place. The students come mainly from middle-class backgrounds, but the college has a reputation in the arts, and many of these young men and women are planning careers as painters, actors, dancers, writers; a sprinkling of them are prospective scientists and mathematicians.

Dr. Justus Rosenberg, the English professor who has persuaded Isaac to teach at Bard this semester, joins him at the front desk and announces that today's subject is folklore in literature. The students have been asked to read three of Isaac's stories: "Gimpel the Fool," "The Spinoza of Market Street," and "Yentl the Yeshiva Boy." Dr. Rosenberg would like to start off with a discussion of "Yentl."

Isaac tells the group that he originally sold the story for twenty dollars. He never dreamed that someday it would become a topic for classroom discussion.

A young woman at the back suggests that "Yentl" is more modern than most of the author's tales. The story, written in Yiddish in the 1950s, first appeared in English in the magazine *Commentary* in 1962 in a translation by Marion Magid and Elizabeth Pollet. It was reprinted in the collections *Short Friday* and *An Isaac Bashevis Singer Reader.* This fable about a Polish rabbi's daughter who says she has "the soul of a man and the body of a woman" and who thirsts so much for learning that she disguises herself as a boy so she can enter a yeshiva has especially intrigued these young readers.

Why does Yentl want to be a man? Isaac points out that many women have wished that they were men. "I once heard a girl say to me, 'If I would be a man, I would seduce another woman every day.' When the story first came out in Yiddish, many readers protested. What kind of a story was this for a Yiddish writer to publish? In Talmudic law, for a girl to disguise herself as a man is a sin. A man is not allowed to put on the dress of a woman, nor a woman the garments of a man. Yentl's act was a sin—but a sin committed for the sake of being able to study Torah—a kind of contradiction. For if you believe in the Torah, how can you do something which is against it?"

The Yiddish critics were not patient with this paradox. And they complained that the topic was unsuitable for Yiddish literature, "which has," Isaac says, "always dealt with men and women in terms of such problems as a rich girl falling in love with a poor man, very simple topics, very traditional."

One woman in the class wants to get down to cases. Does Yentl have lesbian tendencies, yes or no? Isaac says he supposes she must, "because after all she does marry the beautiful Hadass in the course of the tale," but that he has left the sexual question ambiguous. "Otherwise, I would have had to describe their wedding night, and this I did not want to do." There will, however, be such a scene in the stage version.

Another woman raises her hand. How could Yentl get away with the marriage? How could one woman fool another like that?

"You'd be surprised how people can cheat one another. Strong characters can hypnotize weak characters. We are hypnotized all the time."

A young man asks whether Isaac had the rights of women in mind when he wrote "Yentl." He replies that he was thinking at the time about the restrictions Judaism imposes on women. "A woman is not to study the Torah. There are a number of commandments which are only for men, not women. There is a benediction which the Orthodox say every day: 'I thank you, God, that you did not create me a woman.' These things have been seething in Jewish history for two thousand years. But this was not my main reason for writing the story. The human soul is full of contradictions. In

Warsaw I once saw a man steal a *tallis*—a prayer shawl. To steal a prayer shawl is sheer nonsense, because you are breaking the law of the Almighty, who said, 'Thou shalt not steal.' But in the thief's mind there was no contradiction. So Yentl breaks the law in order to be able to study the law. Yes, it is a modern story, but I think, personally, that if the story is right, all stories are modern stories."

Isaac cites the *Iliad* and the *Odyssey* as timeless stories. If Homer had imposed psychological and philosophical commentaries on the action, these epics would be obsolete. In *Point Counter Point* Aldous Huxley tries to explain his characters in Freudian terms, he says, and this dates the book. "A story need never become dated. Only the commentary becomes dated."

But why did Isaac pick a strange girl like Yentl as the heroine of his story?

"I am interested always in the exception—you might say, almost, in freaks. Because through the exception we can learn more about ourselves, about normal people."

Isaac wants everybody with a question to have a turn. A young man points out that Yentl's mother is dead when the story starts and that her father laments that Yentl isn't proficient in domestic matters and says God should have made her a boy. How could a father say such a thing to his own daughter? Isaac says he has heard fathers say such things to their children. He has known parents so eager to have a girl that when a boy was born they dressed him as a girl and gave him a girlish name. Dr. Rosenberg points out that Rilke was made to dress like a girl until the age of puberty and ended up a homosexual. Isaac reminds the class that his story is set in a period when it would have taken enormous courage for a woman to dress in a man's clothes, to pass herself off as a boy and actually enroll in a yeshiva, because if she was caught it would be no laughing matter.

"What would they have done to her?" one of the students asks.

"Well, I will tell you. Since the Jewish people didn't have any power, they wouldn't have killed her, she wouldn't be put to death; and they didn't have a prison to put her in either in the little town where this story takes place. All they could do, they could call her a sinner. But that in itself would be enough. Her reputation would be ruined. Completely. And naturally, an adventurous girl like Yentl would have to go to another town where nobody would persecute her, because in those days, if you committed a sin in Yonkers, they wouldn't know about it in Poughkeepsie. It was easier to hide. But at the same time it was very difficult. And because of the kind of father she had, so strict in his ideas, for her it was even more difficult."

"Did you write the story as a protest against puritanism?"

"I wrote the story to show that behind all the strict behavior, behind the long skirts and the rules and regulations, human nature was still there. So many things can keep a person captive because of a fear of losing one's reputation, but our passions are still there."

Isaac has the class's hushed attention as he talks about his novel *Satan in*

Goray, set in the time of Sabbatai Zevi, when the Jews of Poland were expecting the Messiah momentarily. A preacher told them that the Messiah
would come to redeem them only if they sinned. "And there was no lack of
volunteers. People who were supposed to be saints in their behavior came
out and even indulged in incest to hasten the coming of the Messiah. The
preacher had given them the green light. . . ."

The discussion turns from *Satan in Goray* to the philosopher Spinoza,
"who believed that emotions are always wrong. According to Spinoza every
man or woman who falls in love is crazy. Insane. A kind of insanity like any
other kind of insanity. But somehow humanity rejected this part of Spinoza.
We still think that love is a beautiful thing. And so it is with art. I would say
that in art it is better to do what your emotions tell you than what your
reason tells you, because reason is not the most important element in art. In
science, perhaps, yes. If your reason tells you that by making such and such
a calculation you will reach the moon, and you want to reach the moon,
you have to listen to logic, to mathematics, and to the computer. You will
not get to the moon by your emotions."

Dr. Rosenberg points out the struggle in Isaac's work between natural impulses and the mysterious workings of fate, between instinct and conscience,
"always pitted against each other . . . which makes for tension and for ambiguity."

Isaac agrees about the struggle within his characters. The voice of nature
tells us one thing while the Commandments of Moses tell us to curb our
natural impulses; so obeying those apparently simple Commandments is not
an easy thing.

Isaac reiterates his faith in the emotional approach, simplicity, and clarity. The professor cites Ezra Pound, James Joyce, the painter Miró, and the
composer Schoenberg as artists who have followed more complex routes to
the essential truths. Isaac retorts that you shouldn't have to consult a dictionary or acquire a special skeleton key to unlock the meaning of a work of
art. It seems evident that Isaac's opinions about art and literature arise from
his own predilections, champion the strong points of his own work, and might
just possibly be a kind of apologetic for his approach to storytelling, as opposed to more experimental methods.

"A story shouldn't need explanations," he says. Ambiguity is one thing,
obscurity is another. He would hate to think of a world where people would
have to read *Finnegans Wake* or nothing.

Dr. Rosenberg says maybe it's a matter of developing certain tastes—a
taste for Ezra Pound, for example—of making the leap, for instance, from
representational to abstract art, or from program music to atonal music.

Isaac, who has little interest in music except perhaps for the simple Hasidic tunes he has promised to sing someday for Dvorah, wonders about this.
"People can be hypnotized. People can get accustomed to dictatorship—

even to sitting in prison. I once had a friend who was a leftist. They put him in prison, and he sat there for years. When he got out, he told me he missed being in jail."

Dr. Rosenberg thinks maybe it is time for the students to get back to the subject they were supposed to discuss in the first place—the role of folklore in literature. He speaks of folkloric influences on such writers as Gogol and Pushkin, of the folk sources from which the classical Yiddish writers drew, from which Isaac himself draws in his tales for children.

Isaac says, "I will tell you, Dr. Rosenberg, how I feel about folklore. I feel that God has given talent to only a few people in each generation, but there is such a thing as a collective talent, and this is what creates folklore. You see here the work of a hive of bees. And why are people interested in folktales? Because we are limited, not only by governments, by fashions, by laws, by other people, but also by the laws of nature. If you walk in the street you know that you are not invisible, you are going to be seen. If you have no wings, you know you cannot fly. But folklore gives you wings, gives you the little cap that makes you invisible, gives you little boots so you can walk seven miles in a second. This appeals immensely to our human emotions. Folklore doesn't give a hoot about the mind. It works only for your feelings. And this to me is the essence of art. . . . In my case I use Yiddish folklore—the folklore I heard in the house where I grew up."

Isaac treats the class to a story from Russian folklore, the story of a man and wife who never have to work because their dog brings them everything: "Milk, meat, bread—such a dog! But the dog becomes old, he cannot provide for the family anymore, so they throw him out." Any man, says Isaac, can read such a story and recognize the dog as the symbol of himself as the breadwinner, see in the dog's tragic fate his own possible end: " 'If I would stop making a living they would throw me out.' Folklore does in a few drops what art has to add a lot of water to do."

The hour and a half has flown. The professor reminds the students to prepare for next week, and the seminar is over. Dvorah is waiting outside as she promised she would be, fresh as the air of the deepening autumn day. The sun is still shining; the colors of the leaves seem even more extravagant this afternoon. From a chapel comes the sound of Bach on an organ.

Dvorah goes up to an office to answer a letter requesting Isaac's appearance at the Lotos Club in New York to accept still another literary award. He sits on a bench in the sun, stooping a little over a local newspaper as he waits for her in his dark suit and white shirt with the quiet tie, the wisps of his white hair blowing in the drowsy breeze, birds chirping all around him to the orderly strains of Bach.

Dvorah comes back with a draft of the letter, and Isaac's face lights up. He goes over the text with her. "I wish I had ten daughters like you," he says.

Now Dvorah takes Isaac by both hands and pulls him up from the bench. He must go with her to see the waterfall. "It's only twenty minutes from here."

They are walking through the fields, the young woman and the man in his seventies, past clumps of early autumn flowers and stretches of long late-summer grass, then through a dense grove where leaves are falling gently, turning the forest floor underfoot into a rich mosaic. Suddenly the woods end. There is a stream ahead, and the roaring waterfall. Isaac doesn't say a word about the beauty of the afternoon, the birdsong all around, the water-fall they have come to see. He only says, almost curtly, "All right, so we've seen it. Let's go back and have some tea." Yet if anyone has ever really seen this place—sensed it, drunk it in, experienced its beauty—it is surely Isaac.

In the opposite direction from the waterfall Campus Road leads to Isaac's apartment—a tiny kitchen, a bath, and two rooms crowded with cots, a dormitory chair, a simple desk. When Isaac walks inside, he sees that the window sill is lined with dead flies. "I should say *kaddish*," he tells Dvorah, pointing to the corpse of a fly. "This fly is better than I am. I am less than this fly. His death is more important than mine would be."

Isaac says there is a ghost in the apartment, though it has not yet shown itself. He would like to meet the ghost. Usually Isaac stays overnight in the apartment, but today there is scarcely time to sit down and have a cup of tea. Isaac dozes for a few moments, and then it is time to walk back to the cafeteria to eat before the six o'clock class in short-story writing.

For supper Isaac has vegetables and tea. Then, through the smoky, deepening twilight, he and Dvorah walk to a colonial building where several students are standing on a balcony waving to them as they arrive.

Upstairs they enter a high, narrow, immaculately white room with tall windows and a curved ceiling—the sort of room in which eighteenth-century statesmen might have gathered to deliberate on the fate of the Thirteen Colonies. The students in Isaac's short-story class, eleven of them, dressed in worn shirts and jeans and denim skirts, look incongruous in this austere, rather formal setting.

Isaac sits at the head of the table and tells his young writers that he is eager to hear what they have written since their last class. Copies of each story under consideration are passed out so that all can follow the text while the author reads it aloud.

Clio, a thin young woman with long, straight blond hair, pinches a paper clip with her pale fingers as she reads her story, "The Interface."

When she is done, a young man says he feels that Clio has used too many contemporary references that will be meaningless in a couple of years. Isaac suggests that if there are dated references the publishers can always add footnotes explaining them, and gets a laugh. A woman complains that there are so many characters in Clio's story that it is difficult to keep track of them.

Another says that the style seems to change in the final pages, to grow suddenly and unexpectedly lyrical. One man thinks the story could have been improved by a greater use of dialogue.

As the class continues and the comments grow more frank and heated, one gets the feeling of being at a kind of group therapy session, where the patients are stories instead of people. After hearing his students out for a while, Isaac speaks up. "The writing is good, the language is good, the details are good." But Clio hasn't provided enough material "to make us feel that her girl belongs nowhere—a very important statement." The story, he says, is about alienation. But to interest us it must be "a bad case of alienation." A "light case" is not important, because after all everyone is a little bit alienated. "To think of not having any address, of not belonging, is terrible. To bring this out you need strong events." Isaac suggests that the story be rewritten to describe "stronger events," with the sense of alienation growing "stronger from page to page and from sentence to sentence" until the reader is convinced that the girl's alienation is not just a passing state of mind but a real and distressing condition. "You have made a real beginning, but you'll have to build it up."

A thin, intense young man named Lee reads his story, "Some Kind of Solitude," next. Isaac says this story too is about alienation. Dvorah thinks that maybe here again the story has switched styles in the final paragraphs and lost "the beautiful simplicity" of its opening. Some of the students find Lee's hero too cynical and "unlikeable." Isaac says there is no law in literature that the hero of a story can't be cynical or that he must be likeable. He says the trouble is that even a master would be hard put to tell such a story in so few pages. We ought to know more about the hero—who he is, what kind of person he is. "We know that he is a lonesome man and doesn't get along with others and wants to be alone, but it is not enough."

Then Isaac says maybe he has delivered his verdict too quickly. He wants to know what the others think. One young woman defends the length of the story; if that's the length the author decided upon, why must it be longer? Isaac replies, "You are right. But to write a very short story you must have a very light touch. I think sometimes you young people are in a way too lazy to write more. I would like to see some of you overwrite rather than underwrite. If you overwrite, it can always be edited."

The next story, by a boy named Tom, is called "Interview with Silas Bodenham." The first criticism of Tom's effort comes from a woman who feels Silas is too articulate for the tobacco-chewing backwoodsman he is apparently supposed to be. Isaac says, "I will tell you how I feel about it. I feel it's what they call in Europe a *feuilleton*." There is some discussion about how to translate the French term. An anecdote? A sketch? Not quite that, says Isaac. "It has the form of fiction, but it is really not fiction. . . . But I liked the little story. If I would be an editor in a small town, I would publish

it immediately." Still, Isaac wonders why Tom's piece couldn't have been a
little longer. "You are all very stingy about paper. Is there a special dearth of
paper here at Bard?"

The last story of the evening is read by Laurie, a young woman with a
low, throaty voice. Though she is reticent, she has an undefinable poise and
ease. Quickly, with almost no expression, she reads a tale about a retired
railroad man. Everyone in the room is excited about the story—impressed
by how well Laurie has brought off the Dickensian trick of describing a
character exclusively through the objects that surround him.

Isaac in particular is elated. He says he feels privileged to be in the presence of a genuinely promising young talent. "If I would be an editor of a
magazine, I would edit it a little bit and publish it. And since it is a good
story, we will finish this evening with it. Next week bring me more stories. I
am hungry for stories."

❀

Isaac Bashevis Singer holds eleven honorary degrees* ("You'll have to call
me Doctor, Doctor, Doctor, Doctor, Doctor, Doctor, Doctor, Doctor, Doc-
tor, Doctor, Doctor now," he says), has twice won the National Book
Award, and in 1978 was awarded the Nobel prize in literature. He is
regarded as one of America's most distinguished writers. And yet this author
of eight published novels, seven books of short stories, four books of memoirs, twelve books for children, and hundreds of short stories and articles has
never had a college education and writes all his work in Yiddish, a language
the majority of his readers don't understand.

Isaac was born on Bastille Day ("or November 21," he says; "I have two
birthdays") in 1904 in a tiny Polish town called Leoncin, in the province of
Warsaw, the second son of Pinchas Mendel Singer, an impoverished Hasidic rabbi from the town of Tomaszow, and Bathsheba Zylberman, the
daughter of the rabbi of Bilgoray, in the province of Lublin. The contradictions in Isaac's own nature and in the characters he writes about—the
conflicts between the rational and the irrational, the innocent and the
worldly, the demonic and the cherubic, the real and the fantastic, the
romantic and the conservative—can all be traced to the marriage of his
parents and the legacy of a Polish-Jewish past.

---

* By the end of 1978 Isaac Bashevis Singer had received doctorates from the Hebrew University, Jerusalem; Brandeis University; St. Michael's College, Winooski, Vermont; Texas Christian University; Sacred Heart University, Connecticut; Hebrew Union College-Jewish Institute
of Religion, Cincinnati, Ohio; Spertus College, Philadelphia, Pennsylvania; Bard College;
Long Island University; University of Connecticut; and Uppsala College, Uppsala, Sweden.

Isaac's father's father was one Reb Samuel, an assistant rabbi in the town of Tomaszow. The family claimed they could trace their lineage to a disciple of Rabbi Israel Ben Eliezer, the Baal Shem Tov himself—the revered sage of the Ukraine who founded Hasidic Judaism. Reb Samuel's father was still another rabbi, Isaiah Konsker, a Hasid and a scholar, although he never had a congregation. Isaiah's father in turn was Reb Moshe, who was known in his time as "the sage of Warsaw." From him the line went back to Reb Tobias, the rabbi of Sztektcin, and beyond him to Reb Moshe, the rabbi of Neufeld. It was this Reb Moshe who is supposed to have been the disciple of the Baal Shem Tov. His father was Reb Zvi Hirsch, the rabbi of Zhorker. The Singers, in fact, would have been a little like Pooh Bah in *The Mikado*, who could trace his ancestry back to a "primordial atomic globule," had the globule in question shown a vocation for the rabbinate.

Isaac's grandfather, Reb Samuel, however, refused for years to become a rabbi, devoting himself instead to the Cabala, the body of Jewish mystical literature that was to have so great an influence on Isaac's ideas and work. Not only did Reb Samuel fast a great deal; as Isaac says in his book of memoirs *In My Father's Court*, he sweated so much when he prayed that "his wife had to give him a fresh shirt every day—an unheard of luxury in those days."

As for the women in Pinchas Mendel's family, they were stalwart personalities indeed. Isaac's paternal grandmother was a woman named Temerl, whose mother, Hinde Esther, had supported her husband by selling jewelry. Temerl supported hers too. Jewish women in Poland in those days bore children, cooked, and ran their households while their men were out studying the Torah, and supported them if necessary. "Rather than complain," Isaac recalls, "our grandmothers praised God for providing them with husbands who were scholars." It was only when Isaac's grandmother could no longer earn a living that her husband, Reb Samuel, agreed to enter the rabbinate.

Isaac's great-grandmother, Hinde Esther, was celebrated because a famous rabbi had once offered her a chair when she was taken to visit him. Her daughter, Temerl, wanted nothing more than to see her sons study the Torah. In the case of her youngest, Pinchas Mendel, she certainly got her wish. Not only did he devote himself to religion and Jewish scholarship; he shunned worldly interests completely. He sported sidelocks and a neck kerchief, and continued to wear long hose and the traditional half-shoes even after they had gone out of style. His childhood hope was to become a saint. He had no friends among boys his age, shared none of their interests. According to Isaac he was "superior and aloof." Temerl hoped that Pinchas Mendel would marry young, although she insisted that his bride come from a rabbinic line. But the bride he chose died before their wedding day.

Soon afterward Pinchas Mendel was called up for conscription into the army of Czar Alexander III, the King of Poland as well as Autocrat of all the

Russias. His only way out would have been to wound himself, but his mother wouldn't hear of it. The sole effort he made to evade conscription was to pray that it wouldn't happen. And, in fact, as a recruit, he drew a high number in a lottery and was excused from service. By then he was twenty-one, but with his quaint Hasidic clothes, the sash about his loins, the skull cap under his velvet hat, and his full red beard, he looked much older. The other young men, who wore polished boots and gold-rimmed glasses, made jokes about this venerable-looking boy who wanted to be a "wonder rabbi." Pinchas Mendel's concern for the purity of his soul sprang from his ardent hope that one day he would be able to perform miracles.

In the meantime, however, Pinchas Mendel acceded to his mother's wishes and agreed to marry the daughter of the rabbi of Bilgoray.

Close to the Austrian border, the town of Bilgoray was bustling with Cossak officers who danced with the Russian women, played cards for hours on end at the local military clubs, and trotted through the streets on horseback cracking their riding whips. Tomaszow, Pinchas Mendel's home town, was a sleepy village by comparison. But if the Jews of Bilgoray regarded themselves as more sophisticated than the Jews of other towns in the area, Jacob Mordecai Zylberman, the Bilgoray rabbi, was himself infinitely austere. Once, when a troupe of actors came to town to perform, he put on his coat, stormed out to the barn where they were giving their show, and ordered them off the premises as blasphemers, sending the audience along with them. This formidable man was an expert not only in Hebrew and Hebrew grammar but in mathematics as well. He had two sons whose reputations in town were based on their keen wits and adder-sharp tongues. His wife, Hannah, was a dour woman with a skeptical turn of mind that had transmitted itself to their daughter, Bathsheba. Hannah was also known for her stinging sarcasm.

Jacob Zylberman was a man who thought long and hard about the eternal questions. He had no patience with petty things, small talk; he hated gossip. He would hand down his religious interpretations and legal decisions conscientiously, but he never got too close to his congregants. In every way he was a Mitnagged—a member of that European Jewish sect that put the emphasis on learning and the law, in complete antithesis to the Hasidic approach to Judaism and life in general, which stressed emotion, zeal, and mysticism. For the Hasidim, singing and dancing, miracles and marvels; for the Mitnagdim, a sane and rational faith the wisdom of which was to be sought in scholarship, not in folklore. In the genius of Isaac these two strains were to join, in a not always harmonious combination.

Rabbi Zylberman was fond enough of his two clever sons, Joseph and Itche, but his daughter, Bathsheba, was the apple of his eye. Her eyes were blue, her skin fair, her hair—like Pinchas Mendel's beard—bright red. She had a thin nose, a pointed chin, a rather frail body. According to the

Bilgoray cobblers she wore the smallest shoes in town. "When she left the house," Isaac recalls, "she would polish those shoes a hundred times with a brush or an old stocking."

Despite this small vanity, if custom had permitted it Bathsheba might almost have been a model for Isaac's Yentl, for the rabbi's daughter was something of a scholar. She was self-taught in both the Hebrew language and the reading of the holy books. She is said to have known the entire Jewish Bible practically by heart.

Where to find a husband for a girl like that? Her most promising prospect was a wealthy young man from Lublin, but her father hoped to locate a man who was at once learned enough and wise enough in the ways of the world to make a good living as a rabbi, maybe even in a decent-sized city. The matchmakers were not long in informing Reb Jacob that there was just such a paragon in the nearby town of Tomaszow. Pinchas Mendel was, after all, the son of Reb Samuel, Tomaszow's assistant rabbi. But the Zylbermans were to get only half of what they bargained for. Learned enough Pinchas Mendel surely was, at least in matters concerning his faith, but wise in the ways of the world he would never be.

Temerl arrived in Bilgoray for the signing of the articles—a custom among the Jews of Poland, which brought the prospective in-laws together— wearing a satin dress that, according to Isaac, hadn't been stylish for a hundred years. The high-spirited Temerl and the gloomy Hannah were worlds apart. When Hannah asked Temerl how her impractical young dreamer of a son was going to support a wife, Temerl responded airily that God would provide. As for Pinchas Mendel himself, he looked, Isaac was told later, "more like a father-in-law" than a prospective bridegroom. He couldn't speak Russian or Polish or write down the address where he lived "in gentile letters." When his in-laws-to-be talked about real estate or politics, he was at a complete loss. He knew about spirits, demons, and goblins; he knew even more about serving God. But he was certain the world this side of eternity was an evil place, and he would never change his mind about that.

It was when Bathsheba heard Pinchas Mendel discussing religious matters with her father that she made up her mind. And after the Shavuoth holiday late that spring, in the year 1889, Pinchas Mendel Singer, twenty-one, married Bathsheba Zylberman, seventeen, and the two rabbinical families were joined together. Shavuoth is the spring harvest festival that commemorates the giving of the Ten Commandments to Moses on Mount Sinai. It is also the holiday when the Book of Ruth—the story of the marriage of Ruth the Moabite into the House of David—is read in the synagogue. There were those who felt that the union of a Hasidic man and a Mitnagged woman was practically an intermarriage in itself.

The wedding in Bilgoray was a noisy occasion, a chance for the girls of the village to try out the latest dances. And everyone was in step, it seemed, except the bridegroom. Although it was a warm day, he was wearing his fur coat because it was the finest article of clothing he owned.

What was to be done to speed the new son-in-law on his way to a rabbinical career? Reb Jacob offered to support him for five years while he learned Russian and passed the necessary examinations. Pinchas Mendel had little difficulty with the rabbinical code, but he developed a block against learning Russian that lasted all his life. His father-in-law hired a Russian tutor for him and did everything he could to guide him into practical paths. But Pinchas Mendel went his own way. Instead of concentrating on his Russian textbooks, he passed his time in the Hasidic study house or went off to visit his parents or cronies or the rabbinical court on the other side of the Austrian border. An incurable visionary, he wrote his own commentaries on the Gemara, the body of Jewish oral law, but he never got rid of his broad Polish-Yiddish accent. He defeated the efforts of tutor after tutor. Finally, despite the fact that by now he and Bathsheba had two children, Hinde Esther, born in 1891, and Israel Joshua, born in 1893, and had buried a third who had died in infancy—he left his family and went back to Tomaszow to live with his parents, who asked nothing of him. And he might have stayed there for good had Bathsheba not gone to Tomaszow to try to bring her husband to his senses.

Pinchas Mendel agreed that he had to do something to earn a living. He tried to sell subscriptions to a prayer book he had translated into Yiddish, and he began giving sermons in small Jewish towns. One day, in the town of Leoncin, he gave such a powerful sermon that the people asked him to stay and be their rabbi. The town was small enough so that the fact that he had not passed the proper examinations could be overlooked. They declared him their rabbi, and their rabbi he was to be. In 1897 he went back and got his wife and children and brought them to Leoncin. There he made four rubles a week and whatever else he could pick up from handling lawsuits and presiding at weddings and other rabbinical functions, while his wife, Bathsheba, got the yeast-selling concession for the local Sabbath loaves. And it was there in Leoncin, in 1904 (not in Radzymin, as Isaac has sometimes stated), that Isaac Singer was born.

One must try to imagine a town dotted with tiny houses, birds nesting in their sloping shingle roofs, the unpaved streets covered with white sand from the nearby banks of the Vistula. There were painted signs above the drygoods shop and the grocery, pictures of pots and pans over the hardware store, cutouts of tomcats wearing leather boots and smoking cigarettes in holders in the tobacconist's windows. Bakeries, tailor shops, and a cobbler's shop marked by a sign showing a pair of boots lined the streets. Leoncin had one factory—the only two-storied building in town—which turned out a bottled beverage called *kvass*. Nearby was a warehouse containing farm machinery. In town there were two shops run by gentiles—one selling pork, the other beer and whiskey. Beyond, near a meadow, stood the local house of worship and the ritual bath. In the meadow itself cattle and horses grazed while ducks swam in the pond where the animals came to drink.

The family only lived in Leoncin until 1907, when Isaac was three years old, but he has some vivid memories of the place. "Our house was a poor house," he recalls. "We were a rabbi's house. Very little furniture but many books. I remember how sandy the town was, and I remember the animals. Every week there was a market, and many peasants would come to the town bringing livestock. Once I saw a peasant beating a pig. Maybe it had been squealing. I ran in to my mother to tell her the pig was crying and the man was beating it with a stick. I remember this very vividly. Even then I was thinking like a vegetarian!

"My brother, Israel Joshua," he says, "was eleven years older than I, and my sister, Hinde Esther, was thirteen years older. Between the time of Joshua's birth and my own there were two other children, but they died of scarlet fever."

Isaac remembers his father's striking countenance—his dark hair, his blue eyes, the bright-red beard. After her wedding his mother's red hair was cropped close and hidden under a *sheitl*—the wig all devout Jewish married women were required to wear. "But there was a sharpness in her eyes. My father's eyes expressed goodness itself."

He recalls being terrified when the ram's horn was blown to announce the arrival of the Jewish New Year. And he remembers coming into the house with his face all grimy from playing in the sand, his mother scrubbing him vigorously, complaining all the while, "Look at this boy, look at him—he looks like a chimney sweep!" In fact, one night he did see a chimney sweep on the roof of the house across the way and imagined with dread that the sooty lad wanted to catch him and lift him to the roof.

About the prayer house, which was usually empty except in the evenings and on the Sabbath, Isaac says, "I used to go there, into this empty little synagogue, and there was a *meshugeneh*, a crazy fellow called Dulcha—and he used to shake one of his legs and nod his head in a crazy way, and I used to imitate him." In the play *Yentl* there is a character much like Dulcha who appears in the synagogue scene during the first act.

Isaac's brother Israel Joshua tells many stories of the family's early days in Leoncin in *Of a World That Is No More: A Tender Memoir*. These stories reveal that the children, despite their strict religious upbringing, lived close to nature. Even as a little boy Joshua would sneak out of the house to play in the fields with his friends. He loved animals, especially horses. He also had a gift for mimicry and would do imitations of the teachers at the cheder, the religious school, where he unwillingly spent a good ten hours of each day. He was a rebel almost from infancy, oppressed by religious ritual, the drabness of the study house, and the opacity of the religious books he was forced to read. This brought him into early conflict with his father, and the strain between them increased as Joshua grew older.

Moishe, the youngest son, was born in 1906, at a time when the Jews of Poland were subject to sanctioned hatred, pogroms, an attempted revolution. During the Russo-Japanese War many Jews in Leoncin had become convinced that the arrival of the Messiah was imminent. But the year of the expected coming, the Jewish year 5666 (1906), went by without the Redeemer showing himself.

Pinchas Mendel would go to visit his parents in Tomaszow, and days and weeks would pass before his wife and children saw him again. Once, when Isaac was three, Pinchas Mendel went off to see about the possibility of resettling in a village called Radzymin, for he wasn't doing too well on his meager income in Leoncin, and he wasn't happy there. While he was gone a longstanding feud between Leoncin's artisans and peddlers and the town's wealthier Hasidim came to a head, with the two groups trying to drown out each other's prayers in the prayer house. Both sides blamed the hostilities on Pinchas Mendel's trips; and on his return they presented him with a list of demands: He must not go off traveling again—or if he did, he must let the community know in advance, so that a substitute could be found; he must stop accepting gifts of snuff; he must desist from hanging about the prayer house after services and go directly home.

Soon afterward the Singers put all their possessions in a wagon and left for Radzymin. Isaac describes the journey in *In My Father's Court*: "All the Jews in town came to bid us good-bye, and the women kissed Mother. Then we rode through fields and forests and passed windmills. It was a summer evening, and the sky seemed to blaze with glowing coals, fiery brooms, and beasts. There was a buzzing, a humming, and the croaking of frogs. The wagon halted and I saw a train—first a large locomotive with three lamps like suns, then freight cars trailing behind in a slow, preoccupied way. They seemed to come from nowhere and to go to beyond the end of the world where the darkness loomed. I began to cry. Mother said, 'Why are you crying, silly? It's just a train.' I know exactly what I saw at the time—a train with cars—but there was a sense of mystery about it that still remains with me."

To a Mitnagged a train is a train. To a Hasid it can be a mystery. To Isaac Singer at three it was both at once.

❊

At Bard, on the way back to the car with Dvorah, Isaac is talking about Laurie and her story. He says he enjoys his class in short-story writing, with original work on paper to be considered and talked about, more than the afternoon seminar with its questions and abstract discussions.

Dvorah sets the big car speeding toward New York through the starry October night. She reaches out her right hand and offers Isaac's left one a daughterly squeeze. Isaac begins to talk of the Cabala and an idea that has always fascinated him—that the whole of the cosmos is engaged in a kind of universal copulation of the spirit. He recalls his young manhood in Warsaw, when he first began to meet women—how shy he was with them, what a gulf there was between his early fantasies and the awkwardness of his first self-conscious sexual advances. He says he can understand almost anything that happens between human beings except when one tries to hurt the other physically. "But you know," he continues, "it's harder for me to imagine some things than others. I can imagine sex with perhaps two women, but with a man and a woman—that's harder for me to imagine."

If all the laws ever legislated by men were to be wiped out, he says, and all that was left were the Ten Commandments, it would be enough. There would be enough messages for mankind for the next ten thousand years. But the Seventh Commandment, he says, has always been the most difficult for him to manage. "I don't think I am naturally a monogamous person. Yet when I try to talk to Alma about all the possibilities—all the directions love can take, all the conceivable byways of human passion, she doesn't want to hear about it. She's a conventional woman. I love her. A wonderful woman, but conventional."

As the car turns into the block where Isaac lives, Alma herself can be glimpsed racing around the corner from Amsterdam Avenue to the huge arched entrance of the old-fashioned stone apartment building so that she will be there when Isaac comes home. He might be hungry and want something to eat. He might be tired after the long day and want to go straight to bed. He might be lonesome or elated and want to tell her about it.

Isaac says goodnight to Dvorah, pats her cheek, helps himself out of the car with surprising agility, his raincoat on, his old brown hat in place. He hasn't seen Alma hurrying into the house ahead of him, but she will be there waiting for him when he gets upstairs.

❀

Pinchas Mendel's duties in Radzymin were to act as head of the local yeshiva and to serve, without a salary, as secretary to Rabbi Yekele. A wonder-working Hasidic rabbi who cured the sick and made barren women fertile by means of special amber charms and coins, Rabbi Yekele had a round, fat belly and a long yellow beard. Two women dominated his life.

One was his mother, the other his wife. His mother had a red face and wrinkles, a fuzz of white beard, and eyes that Isaac recalls as eternally angry. His wife had a pretty face and brown eyes. Her wig was made of silk, she wore laces and satins and jeweled rings on her fingers, and she had the manners of an aristocrat. The rabbi's mother disapproved of her, felt the *rebbitzin* put on airs. Besides, she was unable to bear children, a topic for jokes among the populace—especially since the rabbi himself was so shy that he took his baths in private rather than use the ritual bath set up for the public.

Despite Rabbi Yekele's shyness, he was something of a coarse man. When he prayed he screamed. On the Sabbath, Isaac remembers, Rabbi Yekele was especially demonstrative, shutting his eyes tight as he recited from the Torah, clapping his hands as he screamed his prayers, stamping his feet. And when the Sabbath meal was served on a long table, a beadle would remove his boots and walk over the tablecloth to pour out the wine. But when Isaac's brother Joshua would imitate the rabbi's histrionic style of worship, wailing and rolling his eyes, Pinchas Mendel would blame Bathsheba, saying she encouraged this insolence by speaking disrespectfully of Rabbi Yekele. Even Isaac's sister, Hinde Esther, he complained, was beginning to lose her piety with all the mockery that was going on.

Rabbi Yekele's mother was always making trouble for Pinchas Mendel. It was bad enough that Pinchas Mendel received no wages, but this angry-eyed woman begrudged him even the few rubles handed out to him now and again. Three-year-old Isaac had heard about her stinginess, and although she, like the *rebbitzin*, spoiled him, he was wary of her. But he loved the rabbi's wife, and Rabbi Yekele's court and life-style appeared marvelous to him.

Visits to the rabbi's house were a joy to Isaac. A red staircase led to a parlor, where the floor was covered with carpets. There were heavy draperies on the windows, tapestries on the walls, objects of gold and silver and ivory and mother-of-pearl on display in cases, leather-bound books on polished shelves. The rabbi's wife would welcome Isaac's mother as though receiving a member of nobility. For Isaac there would be cakes and wine or sweet brandy, candies, and toys. Once, when he admired a bead on the *rebbitzin*'s cloak, she snipped it off and gave it to him. But soon after Isaac and his mother had arrived, the two women would go off and huddle together, discussing secret matters exclusive to women—over, Isaac recollects, many a sigh and tear.

Some days it would be Isaac's father who would take him up the staircase to that sumptuous parlor. Then Rabbi Yekele's wife would smile and kiss Pinchas Mendel and say, "Welcome, Leoncin rabbi." When those two talked, it was about religion, sometimes even about the deplorable state of the world. Isaac's mother was jealous of those visits.

The Singers didn't live on the same scale as the Yekeles. They rented an apartment in a small house in town. Their possessions were few, their existence spartan.

When Isaac was still three years old, he was enrolled in the local cheder. The school consisted of a single room with a kitchen and a big table surrounded by benches for the children. It was a typical small-town Polish cheder, in fact, except for one thing—there were girls in the class.

The teacher was a very old man: "He was so old, that teacher," Isaac recalls. "His name was Reb Fischel, and he taught us the alphabet—the *aleph bes*. He had a pointer, and he used to point at the blackboard and make us repeat after him, '*Aleph, bes, gimmel, daled . . .*' The next day we would have forgotten everything, and he'd have to start all over again. Reb Fischel screamed too—how he screamed! Radzymin was a town of screamers. But his wife—she was soft-spoken, and she used to say to him, defending me, 'What do you want from the baby?' "

Isaac remembers bouts of terror at cheder, when he would suddenly be overcome with fear. "The other children would ask me why I was afraid," he says. "I told them it was because the teacher was a frog. Often people seemed like frogs to me when I was little. But this frog taught me the Hebrew alphabet, after all, and there were plenty of times when I felt other emotions besides fear. I remember there was an older boy named Benjamin, who was my friend, and a girl named Leah and another girl—Esther. When we weren't in class, we all used to play together outside the school. Benjamin and I were fathers, the girls mothers. We had no toys, but in a pile of dirt in the rabbi's courtyard you could always find broken dishes, papers, boxes, boards. Once I played for days with a dried palm branch I found there.

"One of the little girls—it was Leah or maybe her name was Sheindl—used to pretend that she was my wife. I would go off to synagogue, and she would cook my supper—sand and water. When we didn't have water, we would urinate in the sand to create some. So when I came back from prayers, this little girl used to have my supper ready.

"Of course the prayers I had been praying weren't real prayers. I just used to shake back and forth and make up words that sounded like Hebrew prayer words, and then Sheindl would get out a broken plate and put mud in it and hand me a spoon and say here was my supper, and I would pretend to eat it. . . ."

The real food Isaac ate during the cheder recess was a substantial, starchy lunch his mother used to pack up for him before he set out in the morning: a container of soup stock with potatoes, rice, or noodles, and perhaps a chunk of meat. And water to drink.

One day Isaac got into a terrible battle with his "wife": "She tried to take a piece of paper away from me and I was furious. I hit her with some object and blood began to come out of her nose. My parents punished me. My father called me a murderer. I have felt guilty about that episode all my life."

But Isaac's most vivid memory of Radzymin is of a fire that broke out in Rabbi Yekele's house on a Friday afternoon just before the Sabbath. Isaac describes the fire in *In My Father's Court*: "I remember it as if it were yesterday. Mother, emptying her slop pail, saw two heavy columns of smoke. 'Woe is me,' she cried.

"Packing our possessions in sheets, we carried them into the garden. My sister, who was seventeen at the time, took my younger brother and myself by the hand, moaning in a singsong voice, 'Where shall I take the children?' There were many places to go, the town wasn't surrounded by flames, but my sister enjoyed drama.

"My brother Joshua fetched water from a well and helped extinguish the fire. I felt deliriously happy. People were running about, carrying parcels; someone led horses, a trumpet was blowing; Jews carried sacred books and scrolls of the Law. It was like a holiday. I had heard people speak of the Messiah, of God, Gehenna, and Paradise, and it seemed to me that I was experiencing it all at one time. The sun shone and flames leaped at the sky. People ate their meal outdoors. Gentiles and Jews mixed together. An elderly man approached me, asking, 'Who am I?'

" 'I'm afraid of you,' I said.

" 'Why?'

" 'Because you're a frog.'

" 'Why a frog?'

" 'Just because.'

"I found myself in a strange house where people asked me all kinds of questions and laughed at my answers. I tried to hide behind the stove, and crawled under the bed. I was half crazed with excitement."

While Isaac was in his first year at cheder his brother Joshua, a year past his bar mitzvah, was spending much of his time reading the Talmud in the local study house. But he had also started reading storybooks. His father would denounce him for reading these *tref* books, for to Pinchas Mendel, as Isaac has said, "everything that was not the Bible or the books of commentary about the Bible was *tref*. That included the writings of Sholom Aleichem, Isaac Loeb Peretz—everybody."

Isaac himself was beginning to ask the kind of questions he would someday weave into the fabric of his own prose: "Where is the end of the world? Why do birds fly and worms crawl?" Pinchas Mendel had only one answer for all such questions: "That's how the Lord made it." And when Isaac asked where the Lord lived, what He looked like, and whether he could visit Him, his father would explain that Isaac couldn't see the Lord, the Ruler of the Universe was invisible.

A God you couldn't see? Yet you had to say a prayer to Him before you could eat so much as a cookie? Once Isaac pointed to a cloud and demanded of his father, "Is that Him?"

Pinchas Mendel was at a loss, exasperated. A cloud was a cloud. It took up water and gave out rain. How could a cloud be mistaken for the God of all creation?

In 1908, after a year and three months in Radzymin, Pinchas Mendel grew weary of the borderline existence they were eking out and decided he would try his luck in the big city, Warsaw. So Isaac, Hinde Esther, Moishe, and their parents set out once more, this time by train, while Joshua rode in the wagon that carried the household furniture. Isaac looked out the train window and stared with fascination at the trees, the buildings, the people going by in the wrong direction. He describes the journey in *In My Father's Court:* "A horse-drawn wagon had wheels that seemed to move in reverse. Cows were grazing and horses nuzzled each other in meadows. It all seemed mysterious. . . ."

After the long trip the Singers got off the train and climbed into a droshky. Soon they were crossing the bridge that led into Warsaw. "A broad river with the sky in it stretched beneath us. Ships floated by. Over the bridge, which had intricate ironwork columns, trolleys and omnibuses raced. We came upon tall buildings, crooked roofs, ironwork balconies. It looked as if there was always a fire raging in Warsaw, because people kept running and shouting. It seemed like an endless holiday. . . ."

❧

American friends of the Hebrew University in Westchester County request the pleasure of your company at the Golden Jubilee Tribute Dinner in honor of Isaac Bashevis Singer, who will receive the S.Y. Agnon Gold Medal presented by H. E. Simcha Dinitz, Ambassador of Israel to the United States. . . .

A fall evening in 1975. Chilly, topcoat weather. The Golden Jubilee Tribute Dinner is being held at the Rye Town Hilton, in Rye, New York, one of those exurban Hiltons trying to look as much as it can like a country inn but still looking like a Hilton. A well-dressed crowd throngs into the reception hall outside the ballroom. Westchester County's wealthiest and most prominent Jews are on hand. The Hebrew University in Jerusalem, according to the press release, is "the world's largest Jewish institution of higher learning." And the Agnon medal is the highest honor the American Friends bestow.

There is no more fitting recipient of the S.Y. Agnon Gold Medal in American life today than Isaac Bashevis Singer.

Through his novels and short stories, I.B. Singer has recreated a world of characters and personalities, ideas and ideals, without which much of the flavor and unique qualities of European Jewish life before the Holocaust would be lost forever. . . .

But I.B. Singer is a modern man. A contemporary of the late Shmuel Yosef Agnon, the first Israeli Nobel Laureate, Singer relates the passions and agonies of worlds in flux and an era of whose growing pains we are all a product. . . .

The American Friends of the Hebrew University take great pride in presenting the S.Y. Agnon Gold Medal to Mr. Singer on the occasion of the Hebrew University's Gold Jubilee and the publication of his latest book, *Passions*. In receiving the medal, Isaac Bashevis Singer will become one of only ten Americans thus honored.

Who's here? Who isn't! The honorary chairmen for the event are two of the area's most active "lay leaders" in Jewish causes—Laurence A. Tisch and the Honorable Herbert Tenzer. The chairman is Leon L. Gildesgame, another respected Jewish leader. The co-chairman is Isaac's publisher, Roger W. Straus, Jr., of Farrar, Straus and Giroux.

And where is I. B. Singer himself? Ah, here he is, spruce in a dark suit and sober tie, lean, wiry, springy, his hair a thin white halo about his head, his face slightly creased with age but flushed with health, his pale blue eyes missing nothing as he roams through the throng with cheerful aplomb, beaming, nodding, shaking hands, murmuring modest acknowledgments of the words of praise pouring in on him from every side.

Before a set of french doors leading to a garden Isaac sits down at a table to autograph copies of *Passions*. The line is long, but the author is indefatigable.

"Please . . . sit down. What is your name? Hillel? Like Hillel!"

"Yes. We are all giving you so much trouble."

"No trouble."

"Good evening, Mr. Singer. I just read *Enemies*. I thought it was a marvelous book. I came to Westchester just to meet you."

"Thank you. How do you spell your name?"

"I've been reading your books to my children as they grow up. That's the only way they'll ever know about the *shtetl*."

"Thank you very much."

"I've been waiting on line all this time to meet you, and now I've lost my tongue."

"Sit down, my friend, and don't worry. What is your name? How do you spell it? What would you like me to write here?"

"You're going to have a sore arm by the end of the evening, Mr. Singer."

"Not at all. Don't worry about it."

After a while Isaac is called to his feet to have his picture taken with various VIPs, presidents of universities and philanthropic organizations, members of boards of trustees, and their wives and sisters-in-law.

Alma, wearing a fashionable long gown, has retired to a corner table to finish her plate of hors d'oeuvres and her drink and to get out of the limelight. Her handsome face looks rather drawn tonight. When she looks worried, she is usually worried about Isaac.

"Does he look tired to you? I'm afraid he will wear himself out if he goes on like this."

Roger Straus doesn't think so. "He's thriving on all the recognition. It's good for him. He waited a long time for it."

The lights in the reception hall are flashing. Time for dinner in the ballroom. "Hatikvah" and "The Star-Spangled Banner," then the invocation: ". . . Isaac Bashevis Singer, whom we honor this day . . . honors *us* in spirit, mind, and heart as he paints for us a picture of a world that is gone. . . . May the Holy One reward him in this world and the world which is outside. . . ."

After the inevitable fruit cup, thick kosher roast beef, and synthetic kosher ice cream with cherry syrup have been served, Leon Gildesgame introduces the president of the American Friends of the Hebrew University, Max W. Kampelman, who in turn introduces Simcha Dinitz. The ambassador proceeds to reveal himself as a fan of the guest of honor's work: "I have learned to appreciate not only his wisdom, his wit, but his great humility. . . ."

Under the bright lights on the dais Isaac blinks his milky blue eyes.

The ambassador presents the sculpted gold Agnon medal to Isaac. By the time the Honorable Avraham Harmon, president of the Hebrew University in Jerusalem, introduces the guest of honor, the night has begun to wear on.

Isaac acknowledges the award, reminding the audience that "many great writers have never gotten any honors, any medals, any doctorates—and they remain great."

He tells an anecdote about his maternal grandfather, the rabbi of Bilgoray, who "once asked his audience a question: Why is the Almighty so eager that Jews should pray three times a day? If a Jew misses a prayer, he's already going to Gehenna. He's a great God, he has many planets, he is praised by the angels all the time. Why is he so eager that a little Jew in a little village should pray to him three times and also in addition say prayers over everything he gets and everything he eats? The Almighty, my grandfather explained, does not need such praise at all. The only thing, he knows from experience that when people stop praising him, they will start to praise one another. And he doesn't like it."

Laughter.

Isaac apologizes for the lateness of the hour and says he is going to dispense with the speech he was planning to deliver: "I wouldn't want to keep you." The audience will have none of this and applauds until Isaac rescinds the decision and proceeds to talk about what makes a Jewish writer. "Must he necessarily write in Yiddish or Hebrew? Can he also write in another language? Does the fact that he is a Jew qualify him as a Jewish writer? Must he write only about Jewish life?"

The first condition for being a writer, "Jewish or Turkish," Isaac says, is that he have talent. The question of what constitutes talent can be argued, but he will present his own ideas on the subject: "Talented writers are always informative. . . . They say something new. . . . They portray characters which may not be new but which seem new, which appear in a new light. The reader . . . always has the feeling that he is visiting a new place, meeting a new person, undergoing a new experience, physical or spiritual or both. . . ."

Then Isaac sounds a theme that is fundamental to his views on writing: "A writer must have roots. The deeper a writer's roots, the greater his capacity for achievement. . . . Every artist must have an address." But if a writer must have roots in his environment, he "must not be entirely of it. . . . He must at the same time be an insider and an outsider. Otherwise, his work will be provincial. The true artist is simultaneously a child of his people and its stepchild"—a member of the family yet "profoundly alien" from it.

Another condition: "The creative person . . . cannot reconcile himself either to God's injustice or to man's. His conscience is shocked by the laws of life. Every artist has to keep asking the eternal question; they never let him rest."

At last Isaac returns to the questions he originally asked about the Jewish writer: "Theoretically, Jewish literature may be written in every language of the world. Nevertheless, it is a fact that Jewish art is strongest when the Jews lead their own distinct life, speak their own language, cultivate their own customs, and maintain their own traditions from generation to generation. The richer the soil, the stronger the plant . . ."

"Assimilation is a poor soil for creative work. No one has yet written a great work of art about assimilationists. . . . even if a creative writer succeeds in portraying an assimilationist, he must never be one himself."

A writer must be able to trace his lineage. "He must have a home; he cannot be a man trying to break out of his own skin. . . . The great authors were all deeply bound to the culture of their people. They knew each other's language, their habits, their weaknesses and strengths. Talented artists have often waged war on their people, on their environment, but they have never succeeded in breaking away from them."

No great artist has been produced by a people "still in the process of formation. . . . Great masters have emerged only when their people were ripe in maturity and saturated with tradition . . . solidly rooted." Thus the achievements of Sholom Aleichem, of S.Y. Agnon, of Isaac Loeb Peretz. Someday, perhaps, when Jews have lived in America or England as long as they have in Russia, Poland, or Galicia, this country may produce "full-blooded" Jewish writers. Meanwhile "the Yiddish-speaking writer in America is in fact living the past, both in his language and in his thinking. The soil for Yiddish here is becoming ever thinner."

And what of Israel? "The ground is not yet completely right, but at least there is great hope. The Jews in Israel have an address.

"Of one thing I am certain. Talent can never spring from a spirit which is satisfied with itself, which feels at home on the earth, which is sure of its convictions and does not unceasingly ask the eternal questions. . . . The creative man . . . is a mutation of his kind—an experiment in the divine laboratory . . . the embodiment of human sorrow, human wonder, human protest. This is why, no matter how deep his roots among his own, he'll be pursued by all mankind."

The response in the dining room is uproarious. As the applause dies down Alma and Isaac slip out of the crowd to the windy parking lot, where friends are waiting to drive them home to the city. Isaac is really tired now but beaming. Recognition of this sort has been so long in coming that it still has the charm of novelty for him.

❀

The city of Warsaw has been the capital of Poland since the sixteenth century. Records show that there were Jewish families paying taxes in Warsaw as early as 1423. In fact, there were Jews in Poland as early as the tenth century, when the country was first consolidated. Legend has it that a Jewish merchant named Abraham Prochownik was offered the crown of Poland at that time. And in fact, until the sixteenth century, Polish Jews enjoyed special privileges and immunity from the sort of persecution that decimated the Jewish population of Western Europe after the outbreak of the Black Death. But in the seventeenth century Bohdan Chmielnicki, the leader of the Cossacks, terrorized Poland's Jews, torturing and murdering them wholesale.

In 1772, in the first of three partitions of Poland, large areas of the country were annexed by Russia, Austria, and Prussia. As this added several million Jewish subjects to the Russian empire, Russia established the newly ceded territory as the Pale of Settlement and forbade Jews to live outside the area for fear that their "evil" influence might corrupt the Russian masses. In 1882 laws were passed forbidding Jews to live even in rural areas inside the Pale. Occasionally students and merchants were able to obtain special permission to reside in cities outside the Pale, but for the most part they were confined to towns within its limits. Life within the Pale, which after 1815 included Warsaw, was cruel indeed. From 1772 to 1917 Jews were excluded from Russian commerce and culture. Educational opportunities were extremely limited. And then there were the boycotts, the high taxes, the pogroms. Whatever the Jews of the Pale had by way of education and a cultural life they built for themselves, among themselves, on the foundations of their own ancient past. Hasidism, with its emphasis on emotion and mysticism, had spread rapidly in Warsaw. Most of the approved synagogues and prayer houses were Hasidic. Only toward the end of the eighteenth century had the sober, rational Mitnagdim—the Litvaks, or Lithuanian Jews—arrived in large enough numbers to be taken seriously.

Warsaw remained a part of Poland until 1795, when it was annexed by Prussia in the third partition of Poland, which wiped that country off the map. In 1792 there had been 6,750 Jews in Warsaw—about 10 percent of the total population. Some were active in commerce, some ran taverns, some were craftsmen or involved in industry, others worked as laborers or domestics. Even so, their non-Jewish neighbors spared them no love. For years they had been subject to expulsion, attacked in the streets, reviled, shunned. And under Prussian rule only Jewish residents were allowed to stay on in the city, and even they were under constant threat of attack by their neighbors. In 1802 a "German synogogue" was established. But in 1805 there were new attacks on the Jews of Warsaw. Even so the Jewish population, swelled by immigration from neighboring countries, continued to increase; in 1810 Jews made up about 17 percent of Warsaw's population.

When Napoleon created the Grand Duchy of Warsaw as a buffer state between Russia and Prussia, the Jews of Warsaw enjoyed a year of comparative tranquility, from 1807 until 1808, when the French emperor imposed new restrictions on Jewish rights. In 1809 a Jewish quarter was established in the city. Only prosperous Jews—real-estate owners, merchants, manufacturers, bankers—were allowed to stay, provided that they dressed as Europeans, spoke and wrote in Polish, German, or French, and sent their children to secular schools. In 1813 the city fell to the Russians.

In 1815 the Congress of Vienna created "Congress Poland," a nominally independent kingdom under the personal rule of the Czar, with Warsaw as the capital. (Prussia retained the western provinces, while Austria held Galicia.) By 1816 the Jewish community of Warsaw was the largest in Europe; numbering 15,600, it represented 19.2 percent of the total population. But its status deteriorated, and Jews were hated more virulently than ever. Then the Russians crushed a series of insurrections, and for a while things were better for the Jews of Warsaw, many of whom took part in these anti-Russian uprisings, just as they had in 1772. But the pendulum swung once more, and at the end of the 1870s there was a renewal of anti-Jewish feeling, and a pogrom broke out in the city in the wake of similar pogroms in Russia. Somehow, even with all this adversity, by the middle of the nineteenth century half the people engaged in the city's commerce were Jews. Yet this half represented a mere 2 percent of the Jews in Warsaw; the rest struggled along as peddlers, artisans, and laborers. Only slightly more than 1 percent made it into the professions.

By the end of the nineteenth century many Jews had gained a foothold in Polish trade and found themselves competing more and more with non-Jews. But most were still artisans or laborers or worked in little shops, and the professional class among Jews remained minuscule.

Many Jews hoped and worked for Polish independence, believing that with the end of the Russian yoke would come the end of anti-Semitism. A good many wanted to assimilate—though the masses of poor Jews would have nothing to do with the idea. The Enlightenment was spreading through Europe, sweeping ignorance and superstition away, proclaiming a new era of education, equality, and freedom of thought and awakening Jewish hopes everywhere for liberation and acceptance; but it somehow passed Warsaw by.

In 1910 there were more than three hundred thousand Jews living in Warsaw—more than a third of the Polish-Jewish population. They had suffered severe repression, only gradually eased in the previous fifty years. Yet, despite ostracism, pogroms, and segregation, an increasing number of them were playing a part in the world of Polish finance, commerce, and industry. They were still in a small minority, however. Most of Warsaw's Jews were just managing to scrape by.

Isaac Singer was still an infant when Isaac Loeb Peretz, Poland's great Yiddish voice of the Enlightenment in Jewish literature, was at the height of his fame. Sholom Aleichem—the pen name of Solomon Rabinowitz, the Russian born storyteller who had established Yiddish as a literary language in Europe—would soon be leaving Russia for America to live out his days in New York.

When the Singers arrived in Warsaw in 1908, Jewish life there was in ferment. There were those who, inspired by the example of the German Jews, were seeking to assimilate. There were more Jewish converts to Christianity in Warsaw than in any other city of Eastern Europe. There were also Zionists, for the most part students and young people who believed that the only hope for Jews lay in migration to Palestine. And there were Socialists and members of workers' circles who eventually consolidated into the Bund, a group that organized strikes and demonstrations and was active in the pursuit of Yiddish culture. Warsaw was also the center of Hebrew publishing, with a number of daily and weekly Yiddish newspapers that printed the work of journalists, poets, scholars, and authors.

This, then, was the Jewish Warsaw into which the droshky brought the

Singers, passing by the prosperous neighborhoods to deposit them and their few possessions in a poverty stricken district at Number 10 Krochmalna Street.

The Singers moved their meager belongings into the second-floor apartment at Number 10. The neighborhood was really a slum, the apartment a tenement. Gone were the fields and meadows of Leoncin, the visits to the posh parlor of the rabbi's home in Radzymin. The cramped apartment was sparsely furnished. The family of six lived in three rooms—a. living room, a bedroom, and a kitchen. The living room doubled as a study, where Pinchas Mendel kept his books and held his court. The entire family, as Isaac recalls, slept in the bedroom.

There were no pictures on the walls, no figurines or statuary. Isaac would see such things in the apartments of neighbors but never at home. To display them would have been to flout the Second Commandment: Thou shalt not make unto thee any graven image, or any likeness of any thing that is in heaven above, or that is in the earth beneath.

The pantry was never stocked with food; Bathsheba would go down and buy only what they needed for a single day, for there was seldom enough money on hand to pay for more.

For light in the evenings there were kerosene lamps. Pinchas Mendel would sit up late at night studying holy books by that light. Heat was supplied by coal, which had to be dragged upstairs in heavy containers.

There was a single outhouse in the courtyard, shared with the local rodent population as well as the neighbors. Isaac remembers that outhouse with horror—a dark, filthy place. Because of it many children were stricken with constipation.

The staircase was almost as bad. Some of the children in the building used it instead of the outhouse, and some of the women treated it as a garbage dump. The janitor, who was supposed to keep lamps lighted on the staircase, seldom got around to it, and even when he did, the smoking lamps gave so little light, as Isaac says in *In My Father's Court*, "that the darkness seemed to thicken around them."

When he had to go up the staircase, Isaac believed that he was pursued by "all the devils, evil spirits, imps of whom my parents spoke," as he said in *In My Father's Court*. These may well be the very imps and devils who turn up in the pages of Isaac's fiction. And then there were the cats. To Isaac their wails were like the wailing of the spirits of the dead. Sometimes there would actually be a funeral procession waiting at the gate of the courtyard when Isaac was coming home. He would be out of breath and nearly out of his mind with fear by the time he reached the apartment door. Often at night he would wake from nightmare-haunted sleep, drenched in sweat.

Even so the apartment cost only twenty-four rubles a month (about twelve dollars then), and the Singers were hard enough put to meet even that rental. And the flat had one feature that redeemed its dingy quarters for

Isaac—a balcony where he loved to spend his time. This refuge above the
street was Isaac's television set, his movie house, his theater in the round.
When he looked down from his perch on the second floor, he felt close to
life, close to the teeming action on the sidewalk. There he would spin out
his daydreams and think about the questions that never ceased to plague
him: Why was the sky blue? How deep was the earth beneath the flagstones?
Why did men and women love each other? Where was this God his father
talked about so much?

It took a hot summer night to get Pinchas Mendel out onto that balcony.
To him the appendage to the apartment was part of the street and the sav-
agery of the whole *tref* world outside. The children of a king, he would say,
should confine themselves to the palace. And all Jews were children of a
great king.

Inside the bare, dark rooms Pinchas Mendel presided as the rabbi of
Krochmalna Street. As in Leoncin, he had no official right to his status, but
the people on the street quickly came to respect his judgments. He would
preside over his rabbinical court—the *beth din*—relying on what gifts and
fees his clients brought him to support his family.

In the descriptions Isaac and Israel Joshua offer of their mother in their
memoirs she emerges as a person of great piety and at the same time a level-
headed, sober woman who served throughout their childhood as a coun-
terweight to the otherworldly, impractical man who ruled the household.
Although her red hair was hidden by the obligatory wig and her gray eyes
were often clouded by the practical problems that beset the Singers, Bathsheba was undoubtedly a striking woman with a penetrating mind. Not that
she ever flaunted her sophistication; according to Isaac, she was the most
conscientious of wives and mothers, and when relatives descended on the
household, Bathsheba unquestioningly cooked their meals and cared for
their practical needs. But she surely found the gossip and petty concerns of
her neighbors restricting. Her reading seems to have consisted of her books
of morals—*Duty of the Heart, The Rod of Chastisement, The Good Heart*—
and other simplistic religious tracts deemed suitable at that time for women
of her class. But (unlike Isaac) both Israel Joshua and his nephew, Maurice,
feel that she was not only a gifted storyteller (Isaac says that he absorbed the
plots of many of his children's tales on her knee) but could also write, and
even completed an autobiography, which she destroyed out of false modesty.

In *Of a World That Is No More* Israel Joshua called the marriage between
Bathsheba and Pinchas Mendel a "mismatch" and wrote that "they would
have been a well-mated couple if she had been the husband and he the
wife. . . . Father was short and round, with a soft, fine, delicate face, warm
blue eyes; full rosy cheeks; a small chiseled nose, and plump feminine
hands. If not for the great reddish-brown beard and corkscrew sidelocks, he
would have resembled a woman. Mother, on the other hand, was tall and
somewhat stooped, with large, piercing, cold-gray eyes, a sharp nose, and a

jutting pointed chin like a man's." According to Hinde Esther the two were just as different in spirit. Pinchas Mendel was a devoted scholar but "more a creature of heart than of intellect," while Bathsheba, who took after her father, was "an accomplished worrier, a fretter, a doubter; totally devoted to reason and logic; always thinking, proving, pondering, and foreseeing. She brooded about people, about the state of the world, about God and His mysterious ways. She was, in short, the complete intellectual." She knew the Torah by heart, along with the books of the prophets and the Hagiographa, and when her husband wanted to find a passage in one of those volumes, it was Bathsheba who would locate it for him. In Leoncin, according to Joshua, Bathsheba "didn't have a friend in town." She was withdrawn with strangers and often "lonely, depressed, alienated."

Bathsheba's realm was the kitchen, where she was often expected to rustle up glasses of tea and snacks for her husband's clients.

Isaac recalls her meals with affection, although Joshua claimed that she only went through the motions of cooking and that her meals were less than distinguished. For breakfast she would serve a piece of bread and butter with farmer cheese, sometimes a piece of herring for a treat. The *fleisheck*, or meat meal, served at noon, was soup with potatoes and onions, or rice and beans, a small piece of meat, sometimes noodles, and puddings or home-baked cakes or strudel. Supper was a light meal—noodles again, or rice and milk, or bread with sour milk, or bread and herring—served at about eight in the evening. ("Children," Isaac recalls, "did not go to bed especially early. They were sent to sleep at almost the same time as their parents. The whole business of making such a big distinction between grown-ups and children did not exist. A child was considered just a small grown-up.")

According to Joshua, Bathsheba was no better at housework than she was at cooking. Yet when funds were short in Leoncin, she made yeast and sold it to help support the family. She was a devoted wife and mother, and if the kitchen was not the world she would have chosen for her sphere, she made the best of her relegation to it, as so many Jewish women had done for centuries.

To the end of her days, despite a life of hardships, grueling chores, wartime hunger, a draining daily routine, and the unremitting demands of everyone around her, Bathsheba somehow maintained a balance between her skeptical practicality and her unswerving faith. More than once this faith was severely tried by the bitterness of events, but Isaac is confident she never lost it.

After the family's midday meal on Saturdays Pinchas Mendel would send Isaac to buy hot water at Itchele's grocery store at Number 15 Krochmalna Street. The store had quarters in the back where Itchele lived with his wife, Shprintza, a tireless woman who bore children, worked in the store, picked cucumbers, minded the Sabbath kettle, and also found time for charity. One of her sons went to cheder with Isaac.

Itchele spent more time praying than he did tending to business. He was always arranging banquets for Hasidim in the neighborhood, studying the law, and reciting from the pages of that mystical book the *Zohar*.

When Isaac visited, Shprintza would be dressed for the Sabbath in her wig and holiday clothes, while Itchele wore a satin capote—a long coat worn by the Jews of Eastern Europe—and a hat edged with fur. They had two daughters, and every Saturday the girls would ask Isaac which one of them he would like to marry. He'd point to the younger and, when pressed for an explanation, would declare that the older one was too big for him.

In his story "Reb Itchele and Shprintza" Isaac tells how he would walk in and ask for hot water for his parents' tea (a pious Jew is not allowed to heat water on the Sabbath), and Itchele would tease him, demanding why he bothered to ask when everybody already knew the nature of his errand. Itchele would then demand to know whether Isaac intended to continue in his father's footsteps, praising Pinchas Mendel as "a wonderful man" and "a sage." He would urge Isaac to study with his own son, Noah, and quiz him about his Torah studies, complaining all the while about the lack of piety in the younger generation. Leaving the cozy atmosphere of Itchele's store, Isaac would wonder if there really might ever come a time when the Messiah would arrive and it would always be the Sabbath.

The rabbinical court Pinchas Mendel conducted was an institution that goes back to Talmudic times. "The *beth din*," Isaac has explained in *In My Father's Court*, "was a blend of a kind of court of law, synagogue, house of study, and, if you will, a psychoanalyst's office where people of troubled spirit could come to unburden themselves." And come they did, day in and day out, seeking justice. When the litigants in a case were ready to accept the rabbi's judgment, they would touch the corners of a handkerchief, signifying their willingness to accede. They were not bound by the rabbinical verdict. Their acquiescence was voluntary, based on deep faith and trust in Pinchas Mendel's vigorous sense of justice.

"Out of my father's mouth," Isaac wrote, "spoke the Torah, and all understood that every word was just. I was often witness to how my father, with his simple words, routed pettiness, vain ambition, foolish resentment, and conceit."

Isaac would eavesdrop on his father's cases, eye to the keyhole, ear to the door, taking in everything—all to be put down someday in *In My Father's Court*. The book was first published in English translation in 1966, when Isaac was in his sixties, but it had been many years in preparation and, like so many of his works, was printed in Yiddish, in installments in the *Jewish Daily Forward*, even as he was writing it. In the pages of that book Isaac recounts anecdotes about the *beth din*, along with other tales about his childhood in Warsaw, with typical economy and a fierce attention to physical detail. Never cluttered with historical notations or explanations, these episodes hold up the bright illumination of a modern understanding to the events of a vanished past. The lapidary descriptions are at once more tender and more fanciful than the vivid, sharply focused, factual recollections of the earlier years Israel Joshua set down in *Of a World That Is No More*, even though Joshua subtitled his book "A Tender Memoir." Each episode is a self-contained unit with its own story line and denouement. For Isaac is above all a storyteller, never a mere reporter. Yet even where he has altered or reordered the events of his childhood in fashioning these miniatures, it is certain that they—like everything he has ever put down on paper—are faithful to the essential truth of actual experiences.

And what experiences they were. All Krochmalna Street is there to see, hear, smell, and touch. As in Isaac's novels and short stories, there is a kind of chorus on the outskirts of the action, a motley assortment of gossips, boasters, busybodies, and troublemakers whose function is to carry tales back and forth and make malicious observations—often quite penetrating—on the actions and motivations of the protagonists, like a chorus in a Greek play or a Gilbert and Sullivan operetta. It is the chorus that supplies the comedy and the ironic perspective on recollected events; the author himself keeps out of it.

In *In My Father's Court* we see Pinchas Mendel in his court receiving wealthy clients and poverty-stricken ones, distraught women seeking divorces, guilt-ridden mothers of abandoned children, greedy businessmen, cuckolded husbands, victims of injustices large and small as well as chronic injustice-collectors.

An elderly couple who shared the house on Krochmalna Street arrived one day to ask the rabbi to grant them a divorce. They were simple people with married children, but the wife had discovered that her husband was involved with a younger woman, and she didn't want to stand in his way. She only wanted to see him happy. He promised her that after a hundred and twenty years she would lie next to him in the cemetery, and that was enough for her. "I will be his footstool in Paradise," she said. Pinchas Mendel not only arranged the divorce but presided at the wedding of the old man and his new bride. When the old man died at last, both women cried at his funeral.

Another divorce case involved a local haberdasher who had fallen ill. He seemed to need a doctor more than a divorce, but he didn't want to deprive his wife of the freedom to live her own life and marry again without having to wait for him to die. Sometime after the couple's visit to Pinchas Mendel, Isaac passed the man's store and saw his wife measuring out a length of silk, seemingly unaffected by her husband's imminent demise or the touching gesture he had made. This was a revelation to young Isaac, who had been rather upset about the situation. "I, a stranger, was suffering, while she, his wife, appeared unmoved. Later in life, I was to have the same experience many times—to lose sleep over people I hardly knew though their closest relatives remained indifferent. I had learned for the first time that there are people so stolid that no misfortune can affect them." The divorce was granted, and the woman remarried. Years later she died in a typhoid epidemic. Soon there was not only a strange man in the haberdashery but a strange woman—*his* new wife.

The father of a no-account young man who had broken off his engagement to his fiancée came to see Pinchas Mendel to find out whether it was all right for his son to keep the engagement gifts. As the case developed it came to light that the fiancée was a gold digger who would always order the most expensive item on a restaurant menu and who ran with her engagement ring from one jeweler to another to have it appraised. The rabbi's ruling, however, was that the greed of the young man's father was more deplorable than that of the girl. She was allowed to keep the gifts.

One day a salesman arrived, sporting a trim beard and striped trousers and speaking Yiddish with a German accent. At first the salesman impressed Pinchas Mendel with his learning. Then, after several visits, the rabbi abruptly ordered him out of the house. What was the offense? It seems his aim was to sell Pinchas Mendel a share in life eternal for a hundred rubles cash. He'd been all over Warsaw selling shares in Paradise. The rabbi washed his hands, then turned to Isaac, admonishing the child, "Let this be a lesson to you."

A tinsmith named Moshe Blecher used to come see Isaac's father to set him impossible Talmudic questions. Moshe worked high up on the crooked roofs above the tenements, and Isaac would often peer up at him, worrying that he might fall to the gutter. Moshe's principal interest in life was the Holy Land. He wanted more than anything to go there. And one night, to everyone's astonishment, a big wagon drew into Krochmalna Street, and Moshe Blecher and his wife and children departed for Palestine, the entire neighborhood cheering him on his way. There was no news of them at first, and when the news did trickle back, it wasn't good: Moshe couldn't find work in the Promised Land. His family was going hungry, living on rice and water. All Krochmalna Street took up the tinsmith's cause, and on the eve of the Day of Atonement the biggest subscription ever raised on the block was taken up for the Blechers. Years later Moshe came back, sunburned, swarthier, and with a strange gleam in his eye that especially impressed young Isaac. He went back to plying his trade high above the cobblestones of Krochmalna Street, but it seemed to Isaac that he was still searching for something, even up there on the roofs. And eventually he went back to Palestine, although this time there were no crowds to send him on his journey. Nobody ever found out what became of him.

Moshe's adventures did little to interest Pinchas Mendel in the idea of moving to the Middle East. Isaac's father didn't approve of Zionism or of its founder, Theodor Herzl. He didn't believe that the land of Israel could be redeemed by the efforts of pioneers draining swamps to obliterate malaria; he thought they would only bring contamination to the Holy Land. The Jews would return to their ancient homeland only in God's good time, when the Lord of the Universe willed it, he felt.

Once, even though Pinchas Mendel had a reputation throughout the neighborhood as a naive, unworldly man, a wealthy couple laid an important lawsuit in his lap. Bathsheba served the litigants tea and cookies while they sat and talked about credit, net value, gross income, account books, ledgers, interest, notes. It took days just to present the case. Isaac was sent running to buy refreshments for them—apples, cakes, sausages, cold cuts, cigarettes, cigars, a Polish newspaper, a tin of sardines. And all the while the case grew more and more complicated. Pinchas Mendel began to wish he had never become involved, for it was taking up too much of his time, interfering with his studies. But two rabbis, worldly men versed in business affairs, were called in as negotiators, and at length Isaac's father handed down the verdict: a compromise, which the negotiating rabbis resisted at first but finally agreed to honor. Before Pinchas Mendel knew it, the case had won him a quite a reputation. But he waved the celebrity aside, reminding his son of the Lamed-Vov Tzaddikim, the thirty-six hidden saints whose presence in the world is said to justify its continued existence in the eyes of God—"simple Jews, tailors, shoemakers and water carriers," poor, humble, seemingly ignorant men. But "one contrite heart," Pinchas Mendel told Isaac, "is worth more to the Almighty than thirty silk gaberdines." A worldly reputation, he warned, meant nothing.

One case that had a disturbing effect on Isaac involved a woman who had abandoned an illegitimate child, leaving it in a basket on the steps of a church. She had changed her mind and come back for the infant, but basket and baby were gone. Had demons made off with it? Had the baby been taken to a foundling home? The woman went on with her life, married, and had other children. She was a grandmother when guilt began to torment her. The father of her first child had been a gentile, and she began to imagine that every gentile she passed on the street was her son. Isaac's father dealt with this case by ordering the woman to abstain from meat on weekdays, fast on Mondays and Thursdays, recite psalms, and give alms.

The incident had serious side effects on young Isaac. One day there was a fire across the street from the Singers'. The firemen came in their shiny helmets, rolled out their hoses before the gathering crowd, and went up their ladders. Watching them, Isaac got it into his head that one of the firemen, a fellow with a long face and a dark moustache, must be this woman's long-lost son. "Should I go down and tell him the truth? Perhaps I should throw down a note. But he would not know Yiddish. I stared at him until it seemed that he felt my gaze." But when the fireman did look up, he raised a threatening fist (not an unusual gesture for a gentile to make in Warsaw in those days toward a Jewish child).

A few days later Isaac began to think that maybe he too had been abandoned as an infant. Perhaps he had been placed in his mother's cradle by a servant who was his real mother. The thought that he was really a stepchild brought a lump to his throat and tears to his eyes. At last he could bear it no longer and went to his mother. "Mama, am I really your son?" Bathsheba opened her eyes wide. "God have mercy!" she said. "Have you gone crazy?" She shook her head in despair. The boy was growing up like a wild animal.

"My father," Isaac has said, "was a man for whom Jewishness was the very essence of life. The Torah, the Talmud, Cabala, Hasidism, this was his very life. He knew almost nothing about the world, really nothing. He didn't read newspapers, he knew that the gentiles had some scholars, he had heard of them, that they created airplanes and built guns and automobiles, but it was as if you would hear that something happened on the planet Mars. This was my father.

"It never occurred to him that a man could lie. One day he had sixty rubles. This was his whole capital, and for a poor man it was a huge sum of money. A man came to him and said, 'I have a daughter who is already over eighteen and should be married, but I cannot marry her off because she has no dowry.' My father took his entire capital and gave it to this man. My mother reproached my father about that. She said, 'Look at this man, he gives his last sixty rubles to somebody who told him a story. Maybe he didn't even have a daughter. Maybe he was just a beggar in the street. . . .'

"All my father's beliefs, all his thoughts, were connected with religion, with the Jewish religion—the hope that the Messiah will come. He believed not only in the Torah and the Talmud but in every little law which the rabbis had added through the generations. . . .

"To prove that there is a God he told all kinds of stories, not only stories about miracles but about demons and imps, because if there are demons there are also angels."

Isaac absorbed these stories his father told—just as he did his mother's skepticism. "The net result," he says, "is that I remained both a doubter and a man of faith."

In the house on Krochmalna Street, where religion was the very air the family breathed, where Pinchas Mendel seemed to spend his every spare moment writing commentaries on the works of earlier commentators on Jewish law, recreational facilities were severely limited. There were no Victrolas in the homes of the religious Jews who lived on the street, certainly none in the Singer household. It was considered sacrilegious to have such things in one's possession. "There was only one measure for everything," Isaac says. "Was it religious or anti-religious?" Machines were antireligious, and to this day Isaac is uneasy in their presence.

To amuse himself Isaac would play with colored pencils or fill a tiny bottle with water and hold it over a page to magnify the letters. Sometimes he would hold the bottle up to the light and thrill to the colors when the water split the sunlight into a rainbow.

When other children were playing with toys, the Singer children were playing with the books in their father's library. One day Isaac and his little brother Moishe were playing bookstore. Moishe was running the store; Isaac was the customer. Moishe took down book after book until Isaac saw one that interested him.

"How much is this book?" he asked.

"A million rubles [about half a million dollars]," Moishe replied.

"I can't afford so much," Isaac told his brother.

"How much can you pay?"

"How about a groschen [about half of a penny]?"

Isaac bought his brother's half-million-dollar book for less than a penny.

Isaac has always been strangely reticent about Moishe. Although Moishe was only two and a half years younger than Isaac, he does not figure largely in the stories of Isaac's childhood. Isaac describes him as "a most beautiful child, with large blue eyes, a skin as white as alabaster, blond hair—very blond—almost gold." Moishe had a sweet disposition and a sense of humor. He was the only son in the family to become a rabbi, and he remained pious until his tragically premature death.

Isaac's blue-eyed, pale-skinned older brother—Isaac usually refers to him simply as Joshua—was always taller, more physical and more athletic than Isaac, and more concerned with the real world and what was going on in it than anyone else in the family. He had begun to rebel against his father's orthodoxy as a small boy, hating the cheder and the oppressive teachers in the little town of Leoncin, drawing an obscene caricature in that pious book *The Rod of Chastisement*, the pages of which his mother salted with tears while she read of the dire punishments awaiting sinners in the next world.

"In our house," Joshua wrote in *Of a World That Is No More*, "everything was a sin. Calling my teacher, Reb Mayer, crazy was a sin. Catching flies on the Sabbath was a sin. Drawing was a sin. Running was also a sin, since it did not befit Jews to run, only gentiles. No matter what one did or didn't do, chances were it was sinful. Doing absolutely nothing was certainly a sin. 'Why are you wasting time?' Father would complain each time he caught me looking out the window. 'A Jew must never be idle. He must study instead.'"

Even the Sabbath brought no respite from the tyranny of the Torah under Pinchas Mendel's rule. There were treats at Sabbath meals—fish, meat, carrot stews, raisin wine—but so much of the day was spent in the prayer house that by the time the family got home, the food would be cold. And soon after they had eaten, the time for naps would come. If Joshua didn't want a nap, he would be expected to read about the world's vanities in a grim volume called *The Book of Morals,* all the while longing for the great outdoors. Often enough he would simply take off into the sunlit countryside to escape "the prison of the Torah, the awe of God and Jewishness."

Isaac's sister, Hinde Esther, was something else again. Isaac recalls her in the pages of *In My Father's Court* as rather beautiful in her youth, but in photographs her features are heavy, she looks stout, and there is a kind of lethargy in her expression. Not that she was lethargic; on the contrary, Hinde Esther was high-spirited, hyperactive, and high-strung. Whereas her mother was steady and practical, she was mercurial and emotional to the point of instability. She was sentimental, given to exaggerating almost everything that happened in her life, while her mother's tendency was to understate things. The two women didn't get along well: "Although my mother loved her, she just could not stand her. My sister took after my father." The smallest things could set her off. One day she came home and told her mother that she wanted to buy an artificial braid for her hair to keep in step with the fashion. Bathsheba was against it. "If you have hair, why do you need artificial hair?" was her typically practical reaction. Their quarrels became more and more frequent. However, Pinchas Mendel, usually so austere, was loving and indulgent with his daughter.

Hinde Esther showed some talent for writing as a child and later tried her hand at it, but her emotional instability ultimately proved to be her downfall. Isaac feels that she inherited her temperament, along with her affectionate nature and eccentricities, from the Hasidic side of the family. "Had she lived in another era," he says in *In My Father's Court,* "she might have become a female saint. . . . Our great-grandmother, whose namesake my sister was, used to wear ritual fringes and visit the Belz rabbi like a man. My sister was akin to all the saintly female *rebbitzins* who fasted and made pilgrimages to Palestine to pray at ancient graves. Hers was a life of holidays, hymns, hope and exultation. She was a Hasid in skirts." Isaac describes her as suffering from hysteria and mild attacks of epilepsy, "chattering, singing, and laughing all day long," heaping praise on those she liked and unrestrained abuse on those she considered her enemies. She would alternate between jealousy of her brother Israel Joshua and the lavish bestowal of kisses. Everything in her life was important: a mash note from a barber across the street was regarded as a prelude to neighborhood gossip that would destroy her life. Isaac goes so far as to say that "at times, she seemed possessed by a dybbuk." Undoubtedly her personality served as a model for the religious hysteric Rechele in Isaac's first novel, *Satan in Goray.*

Isaac himself took after both sides of the family. As Irving Buchen said in *Isaac Bashevis Singer and the Eternal Past,* ". . . the ease with which [Isaac] moves in his work from the synagogue to the brothel, from heavenly seraphim to satanic imps, may largely have its roots in the confluence of parental legacies. But it is important to stress that Singer does not fuse the mystical and rational. Rather, he brings them together in a durable and responsible antithesis, which results in a vision that is simultaneously responsive to and skeptical of everything celestial and terrestrial, freakish and familiar."

In the Singers' home there was often talk about the supernatural, about dead spirits coming back to take over the living, souls returning in the form of animals. Hobgoblins took over houses. Demons haunted cellars. Isaac feels that his father encouraged this kind of talk because he wanted his children to realize that there are more things in heaven and earth than are dreamed of in a realist's philosophy. Isaac's mother was more clear-eyed about such matters. He illustrates her skepticism in the chapter "Why the Geese Shrieked" in *In My Father's Court*. One day a woman came to the apartment carrying two dead geese in a basket. She claimed that even though the geese had been slaughtered according to Jewish law and all their internal organs removed, they kept on shrieking woefully. Isaac recalls that he and his father went white with fear, but his mother insisted that dead geese don't shriek. Even after the woman demonstrated that these headless and disemboweled geese did indeed shriek when hurled against each other, Bathsheba smiled, remaining composed and skeptical. Pinchas Mendel felt that here surely was proof of God's existence, but Isaac's mother simply laughed and asked the visitor whether she had removed the geese's windpipes. No, the windpipes were still inside the geese. "Take them out," Mrs. Singer predicted, "and the geese will stop shrieking." The woman did so. "Everything hung in the balance," Isaac writes. "If the geese shrieked, Mother would have lost all: her rationalist's daring, her skepticism, which she had inherited from her intellectual father." Isaac himself was praying that the geese *would* shriek, as they probably would have done if he had invented the tale. But they didn't. "Dead geese don't shriek," Isaac's mother repeated, summing things up.

Isaac was so frightened by the stories he heard on Krochmalna Street about devils, demons, and werewolves that he hated to go out and stayed indoors as much as he could and read. The Singers, however, had a neighbor named Basha with three daughters—two-year-old Teibele; Yppe, who was five; and Shosha, who was nine, a year older than Isaac. He first writes of her in *A Day of Pleasure* in the chapter called "Shosha." Sometimes during the long winter nights Isaac would get tired of reading and go to visit Shosha. On the way to her apartment he had to pass through a dark hallway, but when he got there and saw the fair-skinned girl with blond braids and blue eyes before him, he stopped being scared.

Shosha and Isaac used to tell each other stories and play with her toys, which "consisted of articles discarded by grown-ups; buttons from old coats, a tea-kettle handle, a wooden spool with no thread left, tinfoil from a package of tea. . . ." Isaac used to draw people and animals for Shosha with his colored pencils. He'd listen to the cricket behind her hearth, imagining the insect was telling "a story that would never end." Shosha had a house imp too who used to play tricks, such as putting her shoes and stockings on the table when she was asleep, braiding her hair, and causing the shadows she made on the wall with her fingers to leap about. One night, Isaac claims, a shadow goat actually leaped off the wall and butted her. The house imp also caused her to lose a coin her mother had given her to buy fresh rolls.

Once Isaac asked Shosha to elope with him to Berlin, but she was a practical girl and talked him out of it. When the Singers moved to Number 12 Krochmalna Street some years later, Isaac had to stop paying those nocturnal visits to Shosha. It was "not fitting for a Hasidic boy, a student of the Talmud, to play with girls." But he missed her. Much later, just before Isaac was to leave Warsaw for the United States, he went to see Shosha. Her story is the subject of Isaac's next-to-last novel, which ran as a series in the *Jewish Daily Forward* and was published in English in 1978 by Farrar, Straus and Giroux.

Throughout Isaac's boyhood most of his life revolved around the cheder, where the principal subject—practically the only subject—was the Jewish religion. Before a boy could understand Judaism, he had to learn Hebrew, so reading and writing in that ancient language were taught—in the same alphabet used for Yiddish—while the children studied the Pentateuch, the first five books of the Bible. Later they would go on to the Talmud, the collection of Jewish laws replete with case histories, fables, examples, precepts, and rulings on every conceivable human action, from the most grandiose to the most quotidian. Still later there would be classes in the Biblical commentaries, including the kind of commentaries *on* the commentaries that Isaac's father spent so much time writing.

In the chapter of *In My Father's Court* called "The Strong Ones," Isaac deplores the cheder as a kind of airless prison where tyrannical, ill-tempered teachers made innocent children suffer. But the situation was not limited to the cheder. "What was wrong with society," he writes, "was wrong with the cheder."

Isaac's first cheder in Warsaw was at Number 24 Krochmalna. At first a tutor took him to school and brought him home again. His classmates included the inevitable bully, surrounded by "assistant bullies and sycophants," and a boy who posed as a saint, doing everybody favors and smiling cherubically, pretending to sympathize with the bully's victims—while, in fact, he sided with the bully. There was also a liar who boasted that his family was rich and famous and constantly entertained celebrities. He was always promising the other boys gifts from home of dates and figs, but nothing would come of it. And there was a miniature businessman, right out of *Catch-22*, always making trades of buttons for nails, a pencil for a bit of putty, a piece of candy for a roll. He would lend money on interest and "half the cheder was indebted to him."

"From my seat in the cheder I saw everything, and even though the bully had punched me, I presented him with neither smiles nor gifts. I called him an Esau and predicted that his hereafter would be spent on a bed of nails. He hit me again for that, but I didn't weaken. I would have nothing to do with the bully, the priggish saint, the moneylender or the liar, nor would I pay them compliments."

This attitude made Isaac anything but popular. The boys would snitch on him to the teacher, snub him, threaten to break his leg. Even the teacher's wife began making cutting remarks about him. Then everything changed. One day the bully picked on a new boy with the courage to hit back. He ended up, "like Haman," being punished for his sins—with a sound whipping. A parent complained about the usurious practices of the moneylender, and the "saint's" hypocrisy was unmasked. The other boys started talking to Isaac again.

Isaac made one real friend in cheder, a boy a year older than himself named Mendel. "He was a fine, decent person without social ambitions. We studied from the same Pentateuch, walked with our arms about each other, and learned to write Yiddish. Others, jealous, intrigued against us, but our friendship remained constant. We were like David and Jonathan. Even after I left the cheder, this friendship persisted."

Isaac and his new friend, along with a few other boys—Mottel and Abraham—went around together for a while, but eventually there was a falling out. Isaac, they felt, was too bossy. They began to cut him dead. They would turn away when he came along and whisper among themselves. Isaac was deeply disturbed. "Friendships with me are not casual," he says. "I cannot make new friends easily."

Isaac couldn't figure out what he had done to alienate the other cheder boys. He began to find ways to pass the time by himself. If he got hold of a groschen somehow, he would spend it on a piece of candy or on colored pencils to draw pictures with. ("What I can draw today," Isaac says, "is exactly what I drew when I was five years old.") He also bought Yiddish storybooks, which were sold by the neighborhood peddlers for a groschen. These books had little morals about the power of prayer or the price of succumbing to temptation, but they were also adventure stories with plenty of suspense. Isaac once told his mother that if he had a million rubles he would spend the whole thing on storybooks. She told him he was silly—there weren't enough storybooks published in Yiddish in Warsaw to use up even ten rubles. Isaac says that these stories he read in his childhood, like those he heard from his mother about the fools of Chelm and animals and merchants traveling through Polish ghettoes, had a strong influence on the children's stories he started to write himself late in his life.

During the long summer days Isaac, who had scribbled what he liked to think were words on paper even before he could write, began to make up his own tales. He would cover both sides of a sheet of paper with the beginnings of a fairy tale about a king with one wicked son, one foolish son, and one jolly son, but never got much further. He would sketch strange, freakish-looking humans and outlandish animals.

During the period when he was banished from the company of his friends Isaac loved best of all to sit on the balcony of the family apartment, watching, absorbing, pondering eternal questions, letting his imagination run free. One day he looked down from that privileged eyrie above the street to see other boys running, chattering, playing games, and he felt a terrible pang of envy. He thought perhaps he would go mad from loneliness. Maybe he would jump off the balcony. Maybe he would relieve his feelings by spitting on the cap of the janitor below; it made him feel better just to think about it.

Soon afterward the friends who had been shunning Isaac sent one of their number as a go-between to arrange a truce. They wanted Isaac to make the first move toward reconciliation, but in his boyish pride he refused. Later the friends capitulated, sending him a letter telling how much they missed him.

Reinstated among his companions, young Isaac rewarded them by making up fantastic tales that held them spellbound for hours. He boasted that he was writing a book. And indeed he was. Before he was ten he discovered the stories of Edgar Allan Poe and Arthur Conan Doyle in Yiddish editions. He was enthralled. There also was a series of Yiddish detective stories that amused him, with a hero by the name of Max Spitzkopf. Isaac had begun to write his own Spitzkopf stories. He became so involved with the character that one day, playing detective, he followed a strange man down the street. Eventually the stranger turned around and glared at him. "Little boy," he demanded, "why are you following me?" Isaac melted out of the scene as gracefully as he could. After that he confined himself to writing about Spitzkopf rather than impersonating him.

Meanwhile, Warsaw itself—the great city beyond the ghetto—beckoned to the imaginative boy. He loved to see the big boats floating down the Vistula, the trolleys rumbling over the cobblestoned streets, the monument of King Zygmunt, held up by four stone mermaids, cleaving the Polish sky. He would watch the grown-up couples in their finery strolling through the Saxony Gardens, envying the rich who lived in tall, spruce apartments with ironwork terraces or fine homes with courtyards where gaslight spread a bluish glow in the evening and shrubs and flowers decked the private gardens.

In "A Day of Pleasure," the most charming of all Isaac's stories about his childhood, he tells of the time when he went on an errand for his father in connection with a *din torah*, a legal matter, involving a shoemaker and was rewarded for his effort with a ruble tip. To Isaac, who got a two-groschen piece—a kopeck (about a penny)—a day from his parents and promptly invested it in chocolates, jelly beans, ice cream, or colored crayons, this was a windfall indeed,. Most of the time he was in debt to a classmate and had to pay a groschen a week for each four groschen he had borrowed. A steep interest rate. But now he had a ruble all his own—a hundred kopecks.

With his new wealth Isaac decided to indulge "in the pleasures of the world." He hailed a droshky, gave the driver the ruble, got four forty-groschen pieces in change, and was off on a wild ride through town. The driver cracked his whip, and Isaac almost fell out of his seat as the vehicle went plunging past trolley cars, delivery vans, carts, other droshkies. But the driver ordered him off the seat and threatened him with the whip if he didn't go when the ride was only half over. But Isaac still had his change. He went into a sweetshop, where a girl, seeing the little boy with the red earlocks sticking out from under his black velvet hat, cried out, "Look at that little Hasid!" The little Hasid didn't care. He was busy buying out the store. He went to a park, sat down on a bench, and gobbled up all he could, feeding the rest to the swans in a lake. He took another droshky, giving an address in a fancy neighborhood. There the janitor chased him away. He comforted himself with another purchase at a fruit store. The fruit made him thirsty, but by now he was broke. He had to walk home with a nail inside his boot. Glutted with sweets and overcome with guilt, he reached the apartment at dusk, lied about where he had been, and made for the water faucet. His mother wrung her hands, sighed and said—as she so often had occasion to say in those days—"Just look at that child. . . ."

Another time—Isaac describes it in *In My Father's Court*—Reb Asher, the local dairyman who sold the Singers their milk, butter, and cheese, let Isaac ride next to him in his wagon on a trip to the train depot. This meant several hours of bliss for Isaac. He could think of no greater ecstasy than to own a horse and wagon, and here he was riding through the city as a guest in the most wonderful of all conveyances. "Soldiers marched; policemen stood guard; fire engines, ambulances, even some of the automobiles that were just beginning to appear on the streets of Warsaw rushed past." Reb Asher with his whip could protect him from all harm. Isaac felt the whole of Warsaw must be jealous of the little boy in the velvet cap riding through the city in the milk wagon.

From then on Reb Asher took Isaac on many such rides. When he went off to fetch milk cans from the train, Isaac would guard the wagon and hold the reins. Sometimes the horse would turn and seem to stare at him in disbelief. Isaac would sit there, growing increasingly uneasy as the minutes passed. What if the horse should suddenly dash off and wreck the wagon with him in it? What if one of the big strong gentiles passing by should take it into his head to turn on Isaac and hit him, or pull his earlocks, which was considered great sport among the Poles? But of course Reb Asher would come back, and all would be well. Isaac's greatest desire at the time was to ride with Reb Asher day and night, through field and forest, all the way to Africa, to America, to the ends of the earth, "always to watch, to observe all that was going on around me."

But it was always back to Krochmalna Street in the end. Still, life for Isaac was not all drab, even there. For one thing, there were the holidays. Every Jewish holiday is a time for remembering, for linking the present with the past through rituals, special foods, and recitations. Even the feast days are joyous celebrations. Chanukah, the Feast of Lights, is especially a children's holiday. During Chanukah there was cheder for only half a day. Isaac's mother would make potato pancakes every night, and there were special songs and dances and games with a *dreidl*—a top with Hebrew letters. Every child would get a groschen or two extra every day for the whole of the eight-day period, and every night a candle was added to the menorah to commemorate the miracle that occurred after the Maccabees recaptured the Temple in Jerusalem from the tyrant Antiochus: They found only enough oil in the Eternal Light above the Ark to burn for one day, but the light burned for eight days.

The winter when Isaac turned seven Warsaw froze in the grip of a cold spell that lasted for weeks. Nonetheless he had to go to cheder every morning. In his story "A Hannukah Eve in Warsaw," which appears in his collection of children's stories *Naftali the Storyteller and His Horse, Sus,* Isaac recalls the way he looked on his way to school that freezing winter: "Mother wrapped me in two woollen vests, two pairs of socks, and gloves. She stuck a hood on my head which covered my red hair and earlocks; when I looked in the mirror I couldn't recognize myself and stuck my tongue out at the stranger." On the eve of Chanukah he was supposed to go home earlier than usual. He assured his teacher, who normally saw him home, that he could find his way alone. The older cheder boys teased him, yelled, made faces, threw snowballs, until he got away from them.

Darkness fell early. Isaac looked at the Christmas decorations in shop windows. He watched the lamplighter with his long pole, lighting the gaslights in the streets. He passed women hawking their wares in doorways— potato cakes, chickpeas, hot lima beans, bagels. He was growing hungrier and hungrier. He started to imagine all the food he would buy if he had a million rubles. Snow started to fall, mixed with sleet. Isaac ran. Several times he fell. He found himself in an unfamiliar neighborhood where the streetlights were electric instead of gas and the trolley was electric instead of horse-drawn. He knew he was lost.

Suddenly a "man in a long coat and black beard turned white from the snow and frost" shouted at Isaac. Didn't the boy realize he had nearly been run over by a trolley? In his panic Isaac told the man he was an orphan who lived with his grandfather and was on his way to say *kaddish* for his parents.

The man took him to a restaurant, where Isaac could not stop himself from elaborating on his lies—until one of the customers recognized him. When the man who had brought him let go of his hand, Isaac ran out of the restaurant. He considered taking a train to Berlin, but then he began to think about his parents and his friend Shosha. Instead of going home, he headed for Shosha's place. Meanwhile the Singers were waiting for Isaac before lighting the Chanukah candles. Isaac's mother had guessed where he was and finally came to fetch him. He expected a severe punishment. Instead, his father smiled and gave him a present—"a prayer book from the Land of Israel."

"I took the prayer book," Isaac writes, "with joy and trepidation. I had never before held an object that stemmed from this distant and sacred land. It seemed to me that this prayer book exuded the scent of figs, dates, carob beans, cloves, cedar. All the stories from the Scriptures suddenly came to mind: of Sodom, of the Dead Sea, of Rachel's Tomb, of Joseph's dreams, of the ladder the angels climbed up to and down from heaven, as well as of King David, King Solomon, the Queen of Sheba."

Hinde Esther didn't think Isaac ought to have been given the book at all. Why should the worst dog get the best bone? And Bathsheba warned Pinchas Mendel that he would spoil the boy and cause him to grow up "completely wild." Pinchas Mendel replied that a holiday was a holiday. "With the Almighty's help, he'll grow up a decent man. . . . Pray from this book," he told Isaac. "Everything that comes from the Land of Israel is holy. The Wailing Wall is a remnant of the Holy Temple, which the evildoers demolished. The Divine Presence reigns there forever. Jews sinned; that's why the Temple was destroyed. But the Almighty is all merciful. He is our Father and we are his children. God willing, the Messiah will come and we'll all go back to our homeland. A fiery Temple will descend upon Jerusalem. The dead will be resurrected. Our grandfathers, grandmothers, great-grandfathers, and all the generations will live again. The light of the sun will be seven times brighter than now. The saints will sit with crowns upon their heads and study the secrets of the Torah."

"Mama, the potato pancakes are getting cold," Hinde Esther commented.

Jewish life on Krochmalna Street moved to the rhythms of the seasons, each with its holiday customs and traditions. During the joyous yearly spring festival of Purim—a celebration recalling how the Jewish Queen Esther persuaded her husband the Persian king to spare the Jews when they were about to be slaughtered by his wicked prime minister Haman—the neighbors would send gifts to the Singer family. Messengers would come all day long with wine and meats and oranges and cakes and cookies. One well-wisher would send the rabbi of Krochmalna Street a can of sardines, another a smoked salmon, still another a sweet-and-sour fish. Visitors would throng the little apartment, bringing apples in tissue paper, figs, and dates.

Outside, the street would be alive with maskers wearing helmets on their heads and children carrying cardboard shields and swords covered with gold and silver paper. The sweetshops were filled with cookies in the shapes of Queen Esther, the evil Haman, the Persian King Ahasuerus, and Queen Vashti—the wicked queen succeeded by Esther in the story. From the bakeries and the ovens in the Jewish kitchens wafted the scents of cinnamon and saffron and rich chocolate, of fresh-baked cakes and sweets.

"The kids," Isaac recalls in "The Purim Gift" in *In My Father's Court,* "were always swallowing Esther's head or biting off Haman's leg, and the noisemakers would make a merry clamor with their groggers," which they twirled to drown out the sound of Haman's name every time it was mentioned. Isaac was in his glory on Purim.

Purim was also a time when boys and girls who were going together sent each other gifts. One Purim a girl on the block got a silver box from her boyfriend. When she opened it, she found a dead mouse inside. Amid the screeches of the other girls she had to be revived with compresses of cold water and vinegar. In revenge she sent the prankster a cake filled with refuse. In reprisal he forwarded a live mouse. It began to turn into something of a war between the sexes, with everybody on the block taking sides and the families of both youngsters descending on Pinchas Mendel's court like Jewish Capulets and Montagues. They shouted and hurled insults at one another even while he pored over his books trying to find a solution to the problem. In the end Pinchas Mendel denounced both sides. Food, which God had created to dispel man's hunger, had been defiled, he said. Everyone concerned had acted badly. Since the case did not amount to a real *din torah,* the rabbi never got paid for handling it. But soon afterward the boy and girl made their peace, and there was talk of fixing a wedding date.

On the Sabbath following that Purim, when he had finished eating the *cholent*—the Sabbath stew—Isaac went out onto his beloved balcony. The air was mild. The snow had long since melted, and the pavements were dry. Streamlets in the gutters reflected the glittering gold sun and the blue sky. Young couples were setting out on their Sabbath walks. Suddenly came the two who had quarreled and caused such a commotion.

"A boy and a girl quarreled. What of it? I stood on the balcony in my satin gaberdine and my velvet hat and gazed about me. How vast was this world! And how rich in all kinds of people and strange happenings. And how blue was the sky way above the rooftops. And how deep the earth beneath the flagstones. And why did men and women love each other? And where was God, who was constantly spoken of in our house? I was amazed, delighted, entranced, I felt that I must solve this riddle. I, alone, with my own understanding."

Passover was another holiday celebrated on Krochmalna Street, but this spring festival was a more serious occasion than Chanukah or Purim. Days beforehand the family would busy itself getting rid of everything they had that was *chumetz*—tainted with leaven. Because the Jews had no leaven to bake their bread during their sojourn in the Sinai Desert, every bit of food made with leavening had to be banished from the house. A special set of pots and dishes were brought out for the week of the holidays, and those used during the year were stowed out of sight or, among the most devout, gotten rid of permanently.

Isaac looked forward to Passover as a time when he could enjoy the luxury of an egg; because the family was poor, eggs were seldom eaten during the rest of the year. What made the Singers really conscious of their poverty, however, was their clothing. Isaac can remember his mother wearing the same dress year in and year out, taking such good care of it that it would continue to look almost new. A pair of shoes had to last three years. One Passover brought the Singers an unexpected windfall. Isaac's father was able to sell all their leavened bread, flour, kneading boards, rolling pins, and other kitchen utensils to their gentile janitor. Rich Jews disposed in this way of such luxuries as whiskey and cherry brandy and preserves; the Singers had only the humblest staples and pots and pans. Yet the revenue from this sale, combined with an offer from a tailor named Jonathan, who had just moved to Warsaw from Leoncin, spelled good luck for Isaac. Jonathan agreed to make a capote for the boy on credit, and the Singers decided to use the money to complete the outfit.

While Isaac went to Jonathan's house to be fitted for the satin capote— and grilled on his knowledge of Hebrew—his mother went out and bought him a brand-new pair of boots. Meanwhile a seamstress was sewing new shirts for him, and a new hat made of real velvet was purchased and put away on a closet shelf to await its debut on the eve of the Festival of Freedom.

Isaac, who had never been much interested in clothes, kept imagining himself as he would appear on Passover eve, the envy of all his contemporaries as he strode into the study house with his father. But Isaac knew even as he dreamed this dream that the material world was full of traps. Something was bound to go wrong.

The following day, as the sun was setting, Isaac put on his new outfit. Imagining himself the scion of a line of millionaires, he could scarcely wait to get to the study house to show off his new wardrobe. But when father and son arrived, the door was locked. A sign hung on it: "Gas out of order. Closed until after the holiday." They had to go to another study house for the Passover prayers, a place where not a single boy knew Isaac or deigned to admire him in his resplendent array. "It was a harsh blow," Isaac comments in "The Satin Coat" in *In My Father's Court*, "and a lesson not to get involved in worldly vanities."

❀

An evening in early spring—Purim, 1976. Isaac is about to speak at the
Northern Valley Temple in Closter, New Jersey, a modern structure with
wall-to-wall carpeting. In the lobby there is a Bicentennial display featuring
life-size molded figures of American Jews of Colonial days in wigs and silk
suits. The theme: Jewish contributions to early American life.

The lecture hall is a modern multipurpose room suitable for dances, bar
mitzvahs, and communal meals, as well as lectures. At the back of the room
Isaac is already autographing copies of his books, which are on sale to the
members of the audience.

The host for the evening is a tall man with a rather military bearing, active in the synagogue, involved in local Jewish causes. He looms over the
lectern, introducing Isaac as "our greatest living Jewish writer." Isaac's pink
head appears above the lectern. He wants to know if there is any water. A
glass and pitcher are located behind him. Isaac fills the glass. "I don't drink
it," he says, "but I like to know it's there."

The lecture for this evening is on folklore and literature. Isaac reads
swiftly from a prepared text, as though communicating important news. At
one point he reads aloud the words "in this country," then interrupts himself to explain that this talk was first given at the Hebrew University in
Jerusalem, and for a moment he imagined he was still in Israel. Looking out
on this audience, he thinks he might still be there. Laughter.

After the lecture there are questions and answers. "I will answer any question I can. But I promise you that if you ask a question and I don't know the
answer I will answer with another question."

A young man raises his hand. He wants to know if Isaac's novel *The Family Moskat* was once serialized on the radio in New York. "The answer to
this difficult question is yes," says Isaac. (*The Family Moskat* was serialized
over WEVD in New York in the late forties; Isaac himself wrote the scripts
in Yiddish.)

An older man informally outfitted in bright colors rises to ask whether
Singer thinks that the culture of the Diaspora is part of Jewishness. Isaac affirms that he does. In that case, the man wants to know, which period in
Jewish history should he single out for the attention of his children as
representing essential Jewishness? Isaac replies that for the thousands of years
since the Jews were dispersed from their homeland they have worried about
their survival as a people and the survival of their religion. There were many
disasters that seemed enough to destroy the Jews, but somehow they were
survived. "Meanwhile, whole empires of other peoples have risen and
fallen." This response does not seem to satisfy the brightly clad gentleman.
His neighbors are signaling him goodnaturedly to sit down, but he persists.

Isaac avoids giving him a direct answer. The questioner, when he resumes his seat at last, murmurs, "He's smart, he's smart."

A woman rises now to ask about *Yentl*—the familiar gambit about whether the author intended the play to have feminist overtones. "I did not mean that every girl is a Yentl," Isaac responds, indicating that the woman who worked on the play with him added the feminist component. But he goes on to say that Yentl's yearning to study the Torah is an expression of the well-known yearnings of Jewish women for learning of all kinds. And he adds that if *Yentl* is a feminist play even though he didn't intend it as such, he won't argue with it.

A man who describes himself as a pious Jew says he was horrified by the frontal nudity in the play. Isaac counters, "If you were such a pious Jew, why were you at the play altogether?" Maybe someday, he adds, for devout Jews who insist on attending the theater, there will be chorus girls who are really rabbis in *payiss* (earlocks) . . .

Isaac, spry and delighted, seems content to go on into the night replying to questions, but the chairman finally calls a halt, thanks the speaker, and adjourns the meeting.

Isaac and Alma accompany their host and hostess for the evening back to their home for tea and a few *hamantaschen*.

❀

There were no trees on Krochmalna Street except for one Isaac remembers in front of the cheder. Some people kept potted plants, but Isaac's parents regarded this as a pagan practice. Remembering the fields and orchards and animals of Radzymin and Leoncin, Isaac longed for the country. But as he says in *In My Father's Court*, he seldom saw much of nature in Warsaw. There it was a thrill even to see a leaf on the stem of an apple. "I would sniff at it and carry it home until it wilted."

Isaac had heard his friend Moshe (called Boruch-David in his memoirs) talk so often about the countryside beyond Warsaw, where, he insisted, there were such creatures as cows, that early one summer morning when Isaac was about eight years old the two boys set out to see the world beyond the city. Isaac was amazed enough at the sight of Krochmalna Street, which he'd never seen so early in the morning: stones damp with dew, which he thought fell only in the Holy Land; peasants bringing chickens, geese, ducks, freshly laid eggs, and vegetables to market; pomegranates and bananas being set out in the market stalls, luxuries destined for the tables of rich Christian families.

The boys walked until they got to open country. "I saw broad meadows covered with grass and all sorts of flowers, and mountains of a kind I had never known to exist." They saw and smelled the scents of earth and grass mingled with the smoke of locomotives, looked around at the blooming trees and the clouds above the sun-dappled land. "This then was the world God had created."

Later in the day Isaac and Moshe climbed a hill and looked down at the green and silver waters of the Vistula. They followed a path to the river and went wading in the cold water, Isaac worrying all the while that a fish might bite him. Suddenly Isaac looked up and beheld what was for him a startling sight—men working long poles in the water, pushing rafts made of logs downstream toward Danzig. One of the men had a beard and wore a skull cap. A Jewish merchant!

Before the day was over, Isaac saw a man and woman lying on the grass making love and wondered whether this was a fit sight for a Hasidic boy to witness in a Polish Garden of Eden. The boys never did see a cow that day, but by the time Isaac got home, his head was filled with the sights of the world beyond the city, where nature had not been obliterated by stone and squalor.

One day, more than half a century later, a gentleman came to see Isaac. "Don't you recognize me?" he asked. Isaac looked closely. He could hardly believe his eyes. It was Moshe. The two had been friends for years in Warsaw, until they'd had a falling out, and Isaac had often wondered what had become of him. Moshe said he had left Warsaw to pursue a career as a journalist and might have made a name for himself as a newspaper correspondent had it not been for his fatal flaw: he was extremely quarrelsome. He'd quarreled with every boss he'd ever had and lost one job after another. No matter how hard he tried to control his temper it would flare up sooner or later, and disaster would follow. Then Isaac remembered that as a child too this Moshe had always been ready to pick an argument. In fact, it was for this very reason that Isaac had ended their friendship. Still Isaac was delighted to see Moshe again and eager to resume their acquaintance. But pretty soon Moshe began to irritate Isaac just as he'd done before. Even in his old age he could not prevent himself from picking fights, and once more the friendship dissolved.

When Isaac was around ten, his best friend was Mendel, whom he describes in his story "The Mysteries of the Cabala" in *A Day of Pleasure*. Mendel was tall and dark, with "hair so black it had a bluish tinge," and wore "a tattered gaberdine and torn boots." His whole family lived in one room at 13 Krochmalna Street.

In those days Isaac's pockets bulged with the storybooks he rented two for a groschen, and he had begun to investigate his father's book of the Cabala, drawing angels, two-headed animals, and "demons with horns, snouts, snakes' bodies, calf's feet," on the end papers. The Singers were sure he would grow up to be a crazy philosopher, "like that professor in Germany who pondered and philosophized for years, until he arrived at the conclusion that a man should walk with his head down and his feet up."

Mendel and Isaac spent a great deal of time making up stories and telling them to each other. One day Mendel had a secret to confide: His father was not really a coal porter but a millionaire in disguise who made his money as a robber, digging tunnels into banks and removing the gold to his palace in the forest. He only pretended to be a porter in order to fool the police. When Mendel grew up, he intended to become a robber too and marry a princess.

Isaac told Mendel that he himself was studying the Cabala and stunned him with tales of the magic he could perform. Finally Isaac admitted that he was lying, but when he went home, he asked his father to teach him the cabalistic mysteries.

Pinchas Mendel reminded Isaac that a man had to be thirty before that was permitted. Besides, he said, the Cabala was only for "strong brains." Isaac's brains were too young and weak. When he grew up and married, it would be different.

The ten-year-old felt himself growing sadder and sadder. Then he realized why: The street was full of girls, but there was no way for him to know which one he was going to marry. Perhaps his father could look into the Cabala and tell him the answer.

"What do you have to know for?" Pinchas Mendel asked. "They know in heaven and that is enough." Then he stooped down and kissed Isaac's forehead.

To marry off Hinde Esther, "the Hasid in skirts," was one of her mother's dearest ambitions, but it didn't look as though it would be easy. One day, however, as Isaac tells it in *In My Father's Court*, a Reb Gedaliah Kreitman came to see the family. His sons had somehow avoided the draft and gone off to Belgium, where they were making money as diamond cutters. Even so, Reb Gedaliah, who was in charge of the funds collected for a certain yeshiva in Palestine, still controlled them. He brought out a picture of a handsome young man with a round beard, dressed in worldly garb. He assured the Singers that his son Abraham was pious, ate only kosher food, knew his Talmud, and would make an excellent husband. Bathsheba didn't care for the idea of her daughter's going beyond the Polish frontier, but she would be relieved to have the irritable, irrational, argumentative girl out of the house. So the wedding was set to take place in Berlin. This made Bathsheba more nervous still, but Reb Gedaliah had reassuring things to say about the world beyond Poland. There were lots of Jews in Antwerp; the Jews of Berlin also had ritual baths and prayer houses; even in Paris he had visited a rabbi . . .

Hinde Esther showed quite a literary flair in the letters she wrote to Abraham, and the long-distance courtship between Hinde Esther and young Kreitman continued apace. Pinchas Mendel borrowed money from a loan company for her trousseau. The girl, however, insisted her mother was sending her away because she hated her, and she had frequent fainting spells. Nonetheless, shortly before World War I, Hinde Esther went off to her wedding in Berlin and her married life in Antwerp, and things quieted down for a while at the apartment on Krochmalna Street.

Meanwhile, Joshua had been bringing home paper, pencils, charcoals, and paints, smuggling in secular books in Yiddish, and impressing Isaac immeasurably with tales of pioneers in Palestine, revolutionaries in Russia, and millionaires "richer than Rothschild" in New York. Everything Joshua told Isaac was, as he wrote in *In My Father's Court*, "embedded in my brain. Closing my eyes as he talked, I saw shapes and colors that I had never seen before which kept shifting into designs and forms. Sometimes I saw a fiery eye, brighter than the sun and with a weird pupil. To this day, when I try to do so, I can still see this radiant eye."

Now Isaac began to scribble in earnest on sheets of paper filched from his father's drawer. "I was so eager to indulge in this infantile writing that I could scarcely wait for the Sabbath to terminate so that I could get back to it." His father wasn't pleased. For that matter, neither was his mother. She didn't think "normal boys" acted like that.

"When I remember the days of my early childhood in Leoncin and Radzymin," Isaac says, "it seems to me that it was always summer. Like Florida, like the tropics, although in reality the winters must have been severe. But when I remember Warsaw I remember winter—always bitter cold."

One snowy Sabbath night when Isaac's father was haranguing his disciples on the evils of worldly pleasure and extolling "the joys of the pious in heaven, seated on golden chairs with crowns on their heads, as the mysteries of the Torah were unravelled," a visitor entered the study. As Isaac recounts the story in *In My Father's Court*, the man wanted to know if he could ask the rabbi a question; the question turned out to be whether it was permissible for a man to sleep next to his dead wife. It seemed the man and his wife had shared the only bed in their flat at 13 Krochmalna Street. The wife had died, and her corpse was in the bed. Since the premises were infested with rats, the man was afraid to sleep on the floor. When the story came out, Isaac, for the first time ever, saw his father's face wet with tears—eyes, cheeks, henna beard, and all.

As a member of the priestly caste, Pinchas Mendel was not allowed to enter a room where a corpse was lying, but Isaac followed a group of neighbors to the icy basement room where the dead woman lay. There Isaac's teeth chattered not only from the cold but from terror. The room was like a cave, the walls black, the scene dim in the light of flickering candles. Fear and curiosity struggled in the boy. Even though there would be nightmares as a penalty, he brought himself to look at the corpse. After that he was afraid to go home alone, but one of the neighbors saw him safely back. Isaac's father gave the poor man part of the Singers' household money for the week to help survive the squalor of his situation.

There was plenty of squalor on Krochmalna Street. Isaac saw it for himself and describes it in the chapter in *In My Father's Court* called "The Collector." His father hired him to go after the sums that were owed by various clients because one collector after another had been dilatory at the job or kept more than the 20 percent commission allotted on sums collected. When things got so bad that the landlord was threatening to toss the Singers out of their apartment and auction off their furniture, and the groceryman was refusing to allow them any more credit, Isaac was appointed the new collector. At first he was ashamed of the assignment, but after his first two hours on the job his coat pockets were swelled with copper and silver coins, and he had to stuff money into his breast pocket and his trousers. The women in the places he visited would give him fruit, cookies, and candy, and the men would pinch his cheeks.

As he made the rounds he began to sort out the people who lived in the neighborhood—tailors, cobblers, furriers, brushmakers, artisans. In one house girls were stringing colorful coral beads, which gleamed in piles all over their apartment, on tables, chairs, and beds. To Isaac the room looked like an enchanted palace. In another flat he saw dead animals heaped on the floor, and screamed. (The tenant, he later learned, bought hares from a hunter and sold them to neighborhood restaurants.) In some places people sat around playing cards. In one room an old woman prayed from a holy book while a white-haired man planed a board, letting the chips fall. In the apartment of a bookbinder Isaac saw workers trampling over holy books. In still another he caught a glimpse of a strange female with a head that "almost came to a point" and the great eyes of a calf, who grunted at him. Once he saw a paralyzed man with a sallow face lying on a shelf and dribbling food spooned up to him by a woman.

He climbed up a filthy stairway past children playing with gobs of mud and stumbled with a pounding heart through the inky tenement corridors. He lit a match to get his bearing, opened one of the unnumbered apartment doors, and found himself staring at a corpse wrapped in a sheet lying on the floor, "a pair of candles at its head and a woman beside it on a footstool, weeping, wringing her hands, and crying out." He fled from the place, tearing his gaberdine, threw up, and shivering uncontrollably, decided he did not want to be a collector anymore. Soon afterward things got so bad that Isaac's mother went off to Bilgoray to get help from her father. And Isaac, for the first time in his young life, began to take an active interest in his studies.

❊

In *An Isaac Bashevis Singer Reader,* published in 1971 by Farrar, Straus and Giroux, Isaac and his editor, Robert Giroux, decided to include four chapters that "for technical reasons" had been left out of the 1966 edition of *In My Father's Court.* The chapters are entitled "My Father's Friend," "Dreamers," "Wedding," and "Had He Been a Kohen."

"My Father's Friend" tells about how Isaac's father used to save up money to publish his own Biblical commentaries and recounts the religious conversations between Pinchas Mendel and another rabbinical scholar, Reb Nachman.

"I loved to be present when Father and Reb Nachman conversed. They both had red beards and blue eyes, but Reb Nachman was a kind of Hasidic dandy, with a dazzling alpaca capote, gold-rimmed glasses dangling from a black ribbon and polished boots. A fine, intelligent person."

One day Pinchas Mendel sent Isaac on a minor errand to see Reb Nachman, who having heard that Joshua had become "corrupted" by the secular life he was leading, warned Isaac about heresy. Reb Nachman brought up evolution, asking young Isaac whether an ape could "come from itself" and citing all the nonsensical things scientists said in order "to keep from admitting that there is a Creator." In the midst of the conversation Russian policemen knocked on Nachman's door. They had come to arrest Nachman for his part in an illegal cigarette-selling business, started because the man could not make enough money from his writings and editing assignments.

Young Isaac was terrified. He had seen the Pawiak prison in Warsaw and thought his own turn to be jailed had come. Suddenly everything became "inexpressibly dear to me: the Warsaw streets, our home, the summer day." Isaac's host was saved from incarceration by the arrival of his own son, who made a deal with the Russians. But the incident shook Isaac profoundly and made him realize how precarious the status of Warsaw's Jews was. Perhaps God would protect them in the long run. "But what if the heretics were right?"

"Dreamers" is about another Jewish denizen of the district, Reb Ezekiel, who taught Isaac how to play chess but had to sell fish for a living ("How could such a man, who was always looking into books, fool around with fish?") and other wistful men who used to visit the Singers on Krochmalna Street. One, a failed merchant, spent all his savings on the train fare for a visit to a wonder rabbi. He returned months later with his clothes in tatters but with a strange light of faith in his eyes—and in the end divorced his practical wife, who wanted only to live "like other people." Another "dreamer" was a young man engaged to teach Isaac the Torah, who longed to renounce the world, immerse himself in Judaism, and travel on foot to Palestine. He was suddenly called by a telegram announcing his wife's death in another town, and Isaac never found out what became of him. These men left Isaac with "a longing for distant places, mysterious saints, and caves where cabalists in white silk gaberdines ponder the secrets of the Torah."

"A Wedding" is a memoir about the houses of ill repute on Krochmalna Street. Here Isaac conjures up a remembered streetscape of whores, thieves, and pimps, the kind of underworld figures who have always fascinated him and who figure in his novel *Yarme and Kayle*.

He writes that when a prostitute gave him a piece of chocolate, he threw it away, knowing that it was forbidden to look at prostitutes, for "the mere sight is defiling," even though he had as yet no idea what they did that was so objectionable.

The chapter winds up with a wedding between a mild young man of the neighborhood and a whore—a marriage sanctioned, to Isaac's surprise, by his own father. The description of the wedding itself, attended by a crowd of the most disreputable elements in town, is a marvel of compassionate observation. The experience quickened in Isaac the desire to "grow up quickly and to learn all the secrets of heaven and earth from which young boys were barred."

In "Had He Been a Kohen" Isaac tells about the time a wild-eyed young woman came to his father to demand a divorce because her husband had gambled away their stove. Pinchas Mendel refused to grant the divorce on such flimsy grounds. The couple obtained one from another rabbi, but eventually the man came back to Pinchas Mendel to ask if he could remarry his former wife. Since the man was not a Kohen, a member of the priestly caste, Isaac's father was able to grant the permission, and the man and woman, who really loved each other, were reunited. This is a touching vignette that offers a glimpse of the true liberality beneath Pinchas Mendel's stern exterior.

In 1914, when Isaac was nine years old, the Singers moved next door to Number 12 Krochmalna Street. This was a step upward for the family. Gone now were the nightmare journeys in the dark to the outdoor toilet, the ill-lit, foul-smelling staircases, the cramped, tiny rooms. Even though the apartment at Number 10 cost only twenty-four rubles a month and the new place rented at twenty-seven rubles, the family decided the move might change their luck. Besides, the house manager was a friend of Pinchas Mendel's.

Moving in itself was no easy task. As the Singers loaded their possessions into a wagon some things broke. A huge wardrobe like an oaken fortress, decorated with the heads of lions and weighing about a ton, seemed reluctant to leave for the new quarters at all. Yet it had somehow been dragged from Radzymin years before, and the family had no intention of leaving it behind now.

When they moved in, the place was freshly painted. At last they had the conveniences of indoor plumbing and gaslight instead of smoky kerosene. You put a four-groschen piece into a meter and behold!—gaslight. Moreover, Number 12 had a gate that led to Mirowska Place and the bazaars beyond. Isaac's father would now be rabbi not only of Krochmalna Street but of Mirowska Place as well. There would be new lawsuits, weddings, and divorces to help pay the difference in rent. In *In My Father's Court* Isaac describes Number 12 as a city in itself: it "swarmed with Torah, prayer, commerce, and toil." There were three big courtyards, two Hasidic study houses, even a synagogue for Jews who opposed Hasidism. From the bakery across the way came the smells of freshly baked bread, caraway seeds, rolls, and bagels. Some apartments even had telephones. There was no carrying coal or lighting kindling to make tea here—you pressed a match and a blue flame sprang from the oven jet.

But 1914, the year World War I broke out, was a fateful one for the Singers as well as for the world. For years Joshua had scoffed at his father's unworldly ways and rebelled against the rigidities of Hasidic ritual. Though he still dressed like a Hasid, he spent more and more of his time painting, reading secular books, arguing with his mother about Copernicus and Darwin. Kitchen seminars would last far into the night, Joshua denigrating the orthodoxy he regarded as primitive superstition, Pinchas Mendel expressing skepticism about the idea that the Christians and the Turks might allow the Jews to turn Palestine into a homeland, denouncing the "sweetened poison" of Peretz's prose, belittling the hope that socialism would lead to Utopia. Finally the relationship between Pinchas Mendel and Joshua, whom he termed "an unbeliever, an enemy of Judaism," grew so tense that Joshua went off to live with another family, returning only for visits, dressed—to his father's mortification—in contemporary Polish fashion.

Just before he moved, Joshua gave Isaac a copy of Dostoevsky's *Crime and Punishment* in a Yiddish translation. The boy only half understood what he was reading, but he was utterly fascinated with the character of Raskolnikov, who went his own way and lived in a world of his own devising. Isaac has since spoken often of his interest in the freaks of the world—the exceptions who prove the rule—and Raskolnikov was the first "freak" whose acquaintance he made in literature. He began to wonder who the men were who wrote books such as *Crime and Punishment* and whether he might grow up to be one of them. He wondered too about the philosophers of whom Joshua so often spoke, and where one might obtain books by them. In his second book of memoirs, *A Little Boy in Search of God*, he describes his boyhood visit to Bresler's library on Nowolipki Street in Warsaw to hunt them up. There he told the librarian that he was interested in finding out "the secret of life." He came away with two volumes, one in Yiddish, the other in Hebrew. The Yiddish book devoted a few pages to each of the best-known philosophers—Plato, Aristotle, Democritus, Schopenhauer, Locke, Hume, Kant, Spinoza. Isaac read quickly and secretly for fear his father would find him out and take the volume away from him. He was especially struck by the theories of the Dutch philosopher Baruch Spinoza, whose Portuguese-Jewish parents emigrated to Amsterdam, where their son made a living grinding lenses while he devoted his mind to theology and philosophy. Isaac was the more intrigued since his father felt the philosopher's name should be "blotted out." He thought he could see a connection "between the Cabala and Baruch Spinoza. Both felt that everything in the world is a part of God, but while the Cabala rendered to God such attributes as will, wisdom, grandeur, mercy, Spinoza attributed to God merely the capacity to think. The anguish of people or animals did not concern Spinoza's God in the slightest. He had no feelings at all concerning justice or freedom. The Baal Shem and the murderer were of equal importance to Him. He Himself wasn't free but had to act according to eternal laws. Everything was preordained, and no change whatsoever could effect Spinoza's God or the things that were part of Him. Billions of years ago he knew that someone would assassinate the Austrian archduke and that Nikolai Nikolaevich would have an old rabbi in a small Polish town hanged for being an alleged German spy.

Later on Isaac was to read more on this subject and find himself thrilled by Spinoza's concept of God, but at this early encounter he felt chilled by the idea of a God without compassion, a God who cared nothing for justice or freedom, who was Himself restricted by eternal laws, for whom all things were preordained. Spinoza, the book said, felt that God should be loved with a rational love—*amor Dei intellectualis*. But how to love a God who felt no concern for the starving and the suffering, the tortured and the exiled? And how could Spinoza be sure that "God has no will or compassion? He, Spinoza, was no more than blood and flesh himself, after all."

By the time Isaac returned the two library books, he had come to the conclusion that all the philosophers were saying was what he had been hearing all his boyhood from his mother—"that the ways of God (or nature or of Substance or of the Absolute) were hidden."

Isaac has never stopped thinking about Spinoza, but he has always come around again to a certain exasperation with the notion of a God who can think but not feel. For to Isaac "the problem of problems is still . . . the suffering of people and animals."

❀

Tonight, a rainy night late in November 1975, Isaac is speaking at the Ninety-second Street YMHA on Manhattan's Upper East Side, in that paneled auditorium of dark wood that has long been a kind of temple where poets of renown read their poems, celebrated operas and plays are performed, and great authors and thinkers from all over the world deliver lectures. He is at home here, having read his children's stories and lectures to capacity audiences from the stage above which gilt letters proclaim the names of the greatest Jews of all: MOSES, MAIMONIDES, HERZL, EINSTEIN.

Isaac, wearing dark glasses, is introduced by a representative of Tel Aviv University, the institution sponsoring this event. The house is packed. The audience includes a sprinkling of physicians, students, psychologists, social workers. The subject is Isaac's own idea of God.

Isaac declares that he himself has no clear idea of the aims or expectations of God. He has never been able to come to terms with the Spinozan idea of a God whose infinite intellect is not balanced by compassion. After nearly a lifetime of pondering the matter he is sure that his God is not Spinoza's God. He can only conceive of a God who cares, a personal God who keeps watch over the world.

Perhaps, Isaac goes on, his concept of God is determined by his own tastes, limited by his own experiences and imagination—though Isaac protests, "He is not a product of my imagination." And as the lecture goes on Isaac's God begins more and more to resemble the author. For to Isaac God is an artist whose "acts of creation are works of art." He is "not a perpetually wound up clock but creative, dynamic, full of wisdom, and not cruel." Isaac talks—as he often does—of the cabalistic conception of the universe as involved everywhere in "divine copulation." Every day Isaac's God brings into being a whole new batch of angels. Like all artists, He loves to experiment. "But true art is not chaotic. God's creation is not chaotic. He works in light and shade, in harmony and disharmony. Like every true artist, He is constantly surprising himself. He makes artistic errors and then corrects them. Everything He does has meaning. He is not like a modern poet. His whole existence is one struggle. Sometimes He has to do a whole work over. He needs endless time to do His work. One eternity is not sufficient for Him."

This God of Isaac's is also a playwright who needs an audience, "a big public." He doesn't discuss His work. He never explains it. He never grants interviews, "and in this, how right He is!" Isaac has said elsewhere that God is a great novelist engaged in writing the story of Creation and that most of us cannot wait to wake up every morning to find out what happens in the next chapter. Now he expands this idea: God also demands a lot from His readers. Some might feel that His novel is too long. But "we are the actors in God's theater, His library, His museum."

Now Isaac turns back to the idea of Spinoza. Spinoza's notion of God's nature still puzzles him, still puts him off. How can everything be predetermined? "Freedom to me is a divine attribute." God leaves men free to choose between good and evil. Ritual fringed garments, phylacteries, animal sacrifices—the myriad customs of religion are interchangeable, but always the issue is between discipline and temptation. Still and all, God Himself is not entirely free. Sometimes He may regret having created Man but, like any author, once embarked on the first chapter, He no longer feels free to scrap the book. The universal novel of creation is, in Isaac's view, "finally a love story"; God is capable of infinite love, which he expresses through creation; God is a lover in love with what he creates. This God of creation, this struggling artist God, is not a static being, but always growing, expanding like the expanding universe, turning intentions into deeds.

Isaac concludes his lecture with a magical description of a summer night in the country from his novel *The Slave*.

As always, questions follow. The first is from a man who wants to know if the Devil is also a creative artist. Before he answers, Isaac exchanges his sunglasses for a regular pair. "See, I have a special pair of glasses for answering questions." Then he tells the man that the reason there is a Devil is that God needs critics. "In fact, he creates his own opposition."

A woman springs up. She is in a fury. Singer has completely distorted the ideas of Spinoza, on whose life and theories she, by her own description, is an authority. When Isaac answers her frivolously, she stalks out of the hall.

There follow the inevitable questions this season about *Yentl* and women's lib. When these are disposed of, a young man wants to know how Isaac feels about mystical matters—psychical research, clairvoyance, apparitions.

Isaac admits that he is susceptible in this area. "I read all the books and magazines of the crackpots. I consider myself one of the crackpots. But I don't believe that Buddha is ready to appear every time a couple of men and women in Brooklyn call him. I have no ax to grind. There may be such things as premonitions and psychic experiences. Yet I cannot really tell you that I saw a ghost."

It becomes evident that Isaac is of two minds on the subject, as he is on so many subjects. Asked if he practices meditation, he replies, "I meditate every day but never between one and two." The auditorium rings with laughter. A woman asks him if he believes in reincarnation. "I find myself full of faith and also doubt." He reminds his listeners that he is first and foremost a storyteller. "I am a fiction writer and so I am accustomed to lying."

When somebody up in the balcony wants to ask another question, Isaac raps out instantly, "Wait, first we will take the lower sphere—then the higher."

Another questioner wants to know more about Singer's concept of God. In his reply he mentions that God incorporates both the male and female principles.

Somebody asks him how he feels about Blake, whether Blake has influenced him? Instantly he retorts: "Blake stole all his ideas from me."

Spinoza comes up again. Isaac says Spinoza simply didn't allow God "enough attributes. Catholics have given God ten attributes. And ten are not enough."

One man wants to know what Singer means when he says he's a Jew. Answer: "First of all I come from a long line of rabbis. Maybe I'm not a hundred percent Jewish but at least one percent. My father frequently called me a *goy*, but even he admitted that there must be something Jewish about me."

A woman leaps to her feet. She wants to talk about *Yentl*—the frontal nudity once more. Isaac, accustomed for several months now to this one, counters, "It may come as a surprise to you, but our grandmothers who went to the *mikvah* were all naked—and this is not my fault."

Laughter, then a sober silence as a dignified fellow gets up to demand that Isaac try to define his God in the light of the Nazi Holocaust.

"If God gives man a knife to cut bread, to peel an apple, it is not His fault if the knife is used to cut people. God is not an Indian giver. God hopes against hope."

When the question period is over, Isaac opens a manuscript and reads aloud, to the delighted audience, his story "Sabbath in Gehenna."

❀

At the outbreak of World War I relations between Poles and Polish Jews were almost at the snapping point. Many of the Jews who had leaned toward assimilationism turned to the idea of Jewish nationalism instead. At the same time, as the war progressed thousands of Jewish refugees began pouring into Warsaw. By 1917 there were 343,400 Jews in the city—41 percent of the total population. German forces had entered Warsaw in 1915, raising the hopes of Jews that they would be spared the worst excesses of Russian cruelty. The Polish nationalists fervently backed the Polish legions as they fought alongside Austria and Germany against Russia. These legions were commanded by Joseph Pilsudski, the Polish general and politician who had been exiled to Siberia in 1887 for a supposed attempt on the life of the czar but who returned in the early 1900s to lead the struggle for Polish liberation. In 1916 Germany and Austria proclaimed Poland an independent kingdom, but Germany actually occupied the country and controlled the government.

The Germans in particular seemed anxious to win the Jews of Poland over to their side. A notice was posted in Warsaw by the occupying Germans: "Jews, do not let yourselves be misled by false promises. Did not the Czar in 1905 promise equal rights for Jews? How did he fulfill his promise? Remember the expulsion of the Jewish masses from the long established settlements!" The notice went on to recall Kishinev and Bialystok, scenes of hundreds of bloody pogroms conducted by the Russians.

It was true that under German occupation the Jews of Poland enjoyed more liberty than they had ever had under the Russian rulers. They even began to rebuild long dormant Jewish institutions and to publish experimental literary journals such as *Kaliastre*. But they remained divided. Most of them knew that neither the Germans nor the Russians were really interested in improving conditions for Jews.

In 1917 Pilsudski refused to support the Central Powers in their demand for increased Polish participation in the war and was sent to prison. The independence movement transferred its headquarters to Paris. Only when the Austrians and Germans were defeated in 1918, while the Russians were preoccupied with their revolution at home, did Poland regain its independence. After that Pilsudski returned to power and proclaimed himself chief of state. But for the vast majority of the Jews of Poland, and for the Singers in Warsaw, all these power struggles only spelled hunger, the dangers of being drafted to fight for a cause that could not possibly be their own, and different degrees and varieties of humiliation and hardship.

❈

When the war came, Joshua was ordered to report for conscription in Tomaszow. He decided to go to Tomaszow and enlist, even though the trip would be dangerous (at that time Jews were being driven out of their villages as a result of a new wave of anti-Semitism promulgated by the czar's uncle). He refused to maim himself, as many another young Pole did to avoid service. When his father urged him to do so, he said, "Haven't we enough cripples already?"

As Isaac describes it in *In My Father's Court*, one night after Joshua's departure there was a knock at the Singers' door, and there stood Joshua, sporting a blond beard, a derby hat. Pinchas Mendel lit the gas, but Joshua ordered him to put it out. His grandfather, the Bilgoray rabbi, he explained, had tried to get him exempted from service but had failed. He had advised desertion. So Joshua had gone into hiding rather than report for conscription. He was traveling with a false passport under the name of Rentner. He did not dare to stay in the apartment for long, for the authorities might be searching for him. In the morning he let his father wind phylacteries about his arm, mumbled a prayer, ate a crust of bread, and vanished.

Afterward news came that Joshua was living in an artist's studio on Twarda Street that belonged to a well-known sculptor named Ostrzego. Isaac went to visit his brother there, climbing five flights of stairs to find himself in "a fantastic hall with a large skylight and landscapes, portraits, and nude paintings on the wall." There were statues covered with sacks, which to Isaac looked like shrouded corpses. In the next room sat his older brother, surrounded by other young men and women. Among these bohemians Isaac felt embarrassed by his earlocks and his gaberdine. One of the painters asked him to pose for a sketch. When it was done, the others quibbled over its merits, which reminded Isaac of a visit to a clinic where the doctors had poked at him. The door to the studio kept swinging open, and more and more colorful young people walked in. Isaac stared at them as though they were creatures from another planet, astonished by these people who ate milk with meat, never prayed or studied holy books, and posed for portraits in the nude. He visited his brother several more times, and each time was amazed by what he saw—especially the naked breasts on the statues of women.

"This was quite a change," he wrote, "from my father's study, but it seems to me that this pattern has become inherent to me. Even in my stories it is just one step from the study house to sexuality and back again."

Meanwhile, life at Number 12 Krochmalna Street was growing harder. There was little money for food, and Isaac's appetite seemed to increase in inverse proportion to the available supplies. Storekeepers on the street were hiding goods and raising prices, demanding gold and silver instead of inflated paper notes. Everyone who could was hoarding food. German cannons became audible in Warsaw. There was news of the burning of synagogues. Jews were divided in their loyalties—some for Germany, others for Russia.

Isaac's mother would lie awake listening to the sounds of cannon fire and rain and wind. His father covered sheets of paper with Biblical commentaries and read newspapers, demanding to know what a machine gun was, what a grenade was. Isaac read the papers too, and wondered, as he read of soldiers falling in battlefields, whether God was really as merciful as he had been told. He hoped to find the answer before his bar mitzvah.

❦

A Sunday afternoon in early December 1975. Bleak skies, a bitter wind. Isaac is speaking before the Society for the Advancement of Judaism, a Reconstructionist group, on West Eighty-sixth Street in Manhattan. The topic for today: Literature and the Yiddish Language. Isaac is introduced by the spiritual leader of the society, Rabbi Allen Miller: "He is original both in his use of Jewish traditional materials and in his modernistic attitude toward it. . . . it is my pleasure to present to you, a legend in his own life-time. . . . "

. Isaac peers out over his audience. Mostly middle-aged people, trying to settle themselves comfortably, their overcoats draped over the backs of the institutional auditorium seats. A surprising number of young people too.

"I don't know," Isaac begins. "Should I speak to you in Yiddish, in English, or half Yiddish, half English? I cannot make up my mind. How many of you speak Yiddish?" A mixed response. "All right. I will speak in all languages." He reads aloud a page of "Yentl the Yeshiva Boy" in Yiddish ("Yentl der Yeshive Bocher"), then a few pages in English. After a while he stops. "I think that many of you have seen the play, so there's perhaps no need to read the whole story to you—you know already what happens."

After the intermission Isaac goes on to read his story "Sabbath in Gehenna." It is about how the souls in Hell behave when the fires there are turned off every Saturday. What do they talk about? How to make a better Gehenna, of course. The story is a satire on the ways of radical reasoning. The sinners discuss various panaceas. Each soul, they agree, must stop thinking about its own suffering and join with the others to demand improved conditions. But here the consensus ends. Some want an extra day off from punishment every week, some want a six-week holiday every year; others want to practice free love with the female sinners. There are protests against the hot coals they have to pick up with their naked fingers, against the lashings, the tortures. Others are more concerned with the absence of culture. One sinner proposes publishing a revolutionary magazine, *The Gehenna Week*. After all, there are lots of writers in Hell. But they disagree on the nature of the proposed publication. One soul warns that at the high temperatures in Gehenna such a magazine would only catch fire. Wouldn't it be better to organize opera productions or a theater group? Maybe a play about a love affair between a sinner and a saint . . . Finally the politically oriented sinners dismiss the cultural schemes, demanding the formation of a political party "built on democratic principles" to fight for reforms. In fact, for revolution. Only the revolutionaries cannot agree either. Nor can the sinners who think money would solve Gehenna's problems, nor those who would slip up to Heaven and kill a few saints. At the close of the episode the Sabbath ends, the fires flare up again, the punishments are resumed, and the cries of the sinners are heard once more.

The question period begins. A woman wants to know whether Isaac has read Erica Jong's *Fear of Flying*. He hasn't. A man asks whether Isaac is trying to "penetrate the psychology of a transvestite" in "Yentl." No. "I'm not a didactic writer."

Another questioner wonders whether Isaac has ever thought of going back to Poland and visiting the scenes of his childhood. "Some may go. I myself decided never to go back. I'd rather live with the memories I know than to go to a place which is like a cemetery as far as the Jewish people are concerned."

A man asks in Yiddish whether, even though Isaac is opposed to ending any story with a moral or a message, some message might not usually be implied. If a story has a meaning, Isaac answers, different readers will find different messages in it. And yes, there may be hidden messages in his stories. "Yentl," for him, has a kind of "cabalistic meaning"—that sins, for example, can serve to "lift up the soul."

A young man wants to know what conditions are necessary for Isaac to write a story. "Three conditions. First, I must have a story. A story with a plot. Second, I must have a desire or passion to write that story. Third, I must have the happy illusion that I am the only one who could write this particular story."

A woman asks whether the author has his plot in his mind when he sits down to write. "I imagine that I know exactly, but the moment I have written the first twenty lines, changes begin to occur." In writing a novel his plans are upset even more completely.

Another woman would like to know whether Isaac's personal experiences are the basis of his work. "I would say that all my writing is full of personal experiences—except that they are so changed that I don't recognize them myself any longer."

A man asks whether there are any new writers writing in Yiddish. "There are very few. . . . the younger generation doesn't know Yiddish. . . . Yiddish is a sick language. On the other hand, when I came to this country, I told the editor of the *Jewish Daily Forward*, where I applied for a job, that I would like a steady job. He didn't see how this was possible, since in five or ten years Yiddish would be gone. Then he gave me an assignment, and it's already forty years since I asked for that job, and the paper is still there and we still have Yiddish readers and young people are studying Yiddish. From a logical point of view Yiddish should have been dead two hundred years ago. But from the same point of view not a thread should be left of the Jewish people. Just the same, here we are, our language is here, and only in the last fifty years Hebrew, which was considered a dead language, has revived."

The last question comes from a woman who asks whether there is still scorn for Yiddish in Israel. Isaac replies that Yiddish and respect for Yiddish are both coming to life in the Jewish state. Yiddish is being taught at the Hebrew University in Jerusalem. One of Isaac's books has just appeared in that country in the original Yiddish. "They don't spit in the face of their mother anymore. Only once in a while they make a face."

When the lecture is over, Isaac and Alma hurry across town to the East Side, where a psychiatrist connected with the society is giving a cocktail party in their honor. Isaac is soon ensconced on a sofa with a pretty young admirer, answering all her questions and taking in her youth and beauty along with a finger sandwich and a reviving cup of steaming tea.

❀

After the Germans occupied Warsaw in 1915, the hunger in the city grew worse. Isaac could not help thinking that if they had stayed at Number 10 Krochmalna Street, endured the lack of indoor toilets and gaslight, things would have gone better for them. As it was, the broth grew thinner, and the men who poured over the holy books in the study house were starving. It was a cold winter as Isaac recalls in "Hunger" (*In My Father's Court*), and there was no fuel in the ovens. Isaac's father went to see the wife of the Radzymin rabbi, who was now living in Warsaw. She lent him her diamond ring to pawn, and out of that came flour, bread, and groats; meat was too expensive to buy.

What Isaac remembers most clearly that year was the terrible cold. The Singers couldn't afford to heat their apartment. Frozen pipes made the indoor toilet unusable. Icicles hung from the window frames. "When I was thirsty," Isaac remembers, "I broke off an icicle and sucked it."

Through the long nights the boy would lie shaking as the wind crept past the panes. Mornings were so cold that the family would sleep late—except for Pinchas Mendel, who would scrape the window panes with his hands and put a pan of ice on the stove. He had given up cigarettes, sugar, all luxuries—except for the tea he kept in front of him as he studied and wrote out his commentaries with numb fingers.

Under German occupation Joshua no longer had to hide or conceal his identity, and he came home to live, sleeping on a table in his father's study. His mother would cover him with anything she could get her hands on. All winter he and his father quarreled, although Joshua tried to assuage Pinchas Mendel by putting on phylacteries in the mornings and pretending to pray. And one day, as the winter dragged on through a series of drab meals of half-frozen potatoes and cabbage in cocoa butter with no meat or fish, Joshua helped to repair a German bridge and was paid with a huge loaf of bread, to the boundless joy of the family, who lived on that wheel-shaped loaf for weeks.

Although money was scarce, Isaac's father had always dreamed of seeing one of his books of commentaries published, and when a visiting cousin was able to get his relatives to send fifty marks from Austria, Pinchas Mendel withheld thirty as a down payment on getting a book put into print. Isaac went with him to the print shop, which was fascinating with its cases of type and wooden trays. For thirty marks the printer agreed to set thirty-two pages and send Pinchas Mendel the galley proofs. The twenty marks remaining for food and expenses went fast. Pinchas Mendel got back his galleys and corrected them, but there was no money for the next installment.

To add to the family's misfortunes that winter, Moishe came down with typhus. A carriage took the blond child away to a hospital, and the authorities came to disinfect the house. Pinchas Mendel and Joshua went into hiding, but Isaac and his mother, suspected of being exposed to typhus, were taken off to an institution, where they were separated. First they cut off Isaac's red earlocks, and then, when he was too self-conscious to strip in front of a female guard, they tore the clothes from him, bathed him and showered him, and dressed him in hospital garb. When he looked in the mirror, shorn of his earlocks and his Hasidic clothes, Isaac thought maybe he wasn't Jewish any longer. When he was finally reunited with his mother, he discovered that she too was wearing different clothes and her head was bound in a kerchief.

Isaac and Bathsheba stayed in the institution for twelve days. Isaac, as he recalls in *In My Father's Court*, was pale and terribly thin, and he had a dry cough that wouldn't go away. His mother insisted that he eat even though the food wasn't kosher. "I ate double portions, Mother's and mine, savoring the nonkosher taste. Mother shook her head over me, having hoped that I would be at least a little reluctant, but corruption had begun in me long before." Bathsheba herself grew so frail from living on dry bread that she had to spend most of the time on her back, and she worried constantly about Moishe and Hinde Esther, who, during the invasion of Belgium in 1914, had fled Antwerp for London with her husband. There had been practically no word from her since. News finally came that Hinde Esther was all right, and after a fortnight the rest of the family was back together again. But life under the Germans only grew worse. By 1917 typhus and typhoid fever raged through the city, and the Germans were ordering the populace to disinfect themselves in public baths. People were staying alive by eating potato peelings and rotten chestnuts. Hunger and sickness were everywhere.

One night Bathsheba had a dream—her father in Bilgoray was dead. She received no letters, but she was sure the dream was true. They would have to go to Bilgoray.

Because of the hardships that year Isaac's bar mitzvah—his coming of age at thirteen in accordance with the Jewish tradition—wasn't much of an occasion. Isaac was given a pair of phylacteries by his father—not even a new pair but a hand-me-down. There was no party, no ring or watch or fountain pen as a present. But there was a compensation—the trip Isaac and Moishe were to take with their mother to Bilgoray.

Pinchas Mendel felt he could not abandon his rabbinical duties in Warsaw to make the trip, especially since the rabbi of Radzymin had hired him to do some editorial work and helped him get an appointment as head of a yeshiva in the neighborhood. Joshua did not want to go to Bilgoray either. He had met Genia, the girl he was going to marry, had found a job with an educational journal called *Hayamir*, and had begun to publish articles and stories in the Yiddish press. He was not about to be torn away from Warsaw.

Bathsheba, Joshua, and Isaac took turns waiting in line day after day before the Austrian consulate to obtain the visas that would enable Isaac, his mother, and Moishe to travel to Austrian-occupied Bilgoray. All their efforts did them no good. Only those ready to bribe the guards—often more than once—got anywhere. The soldiers would spit out "Verflutchte Juden"—damned Jews. The Kafkaesque gates of the consulate stayed closed. While Isaac waited on the line that led nowhere he studied a German textbook. German came easily to him because it was like Yiddish. A few years later his knowledge of German would help him pay the rent, but studying it now led no nearer to Bilgoray. The Singers were just about ready to give up hope when Joshua came home waving his mother's passport. Inside were visas for Isaac and Moishe as well. Somehow Joshua had managed to get hold of thirty marks and bribe a German guard at the consulate to obtain these precious documents.

Isaac recalls the time of the trip in "The Journey" in *In My Father's Court.* Months of hunger had eroded the family's morale, but now Isaac danced for joy. He would soon be traveling on a train once more. But Bathsheba saw no reason for frivolity. She decided that she was committing a sin by leaving her husband and oldest son behind. Isaac couldn't understand all the breast-beating and endless arguments over whether they were doing the right or the wrong thing. He could only think of being on that train, watching through an enchanted window as the world raced past.

During their last days in Warsaw, Isaac was sent to a cobbler to get his boots resoled. He walked downstairs into a cellar littered with shoes and rags. A newborn infant lay "in the midst of its own filth." The dust and foul odors were suffocating. "I was overcome with a sense of the injustices in the world, of young men going off to die or be wounded, of people whose constant work would not earn them a piece of bread, a shirt, or a baby crib. The cobbler, I knew, could not continue to struggle indefinitely. Sooner or later he would come down with typhus or consumption. And how could the baby flourish amid the smoke, dust, and stench?" Isaac was long pursued by guilt over the lot of the cobbler, who ever since, he says, has symbolized for him the injustices of society.

One summer day in 1917 Joshua took Bathsheba and the two boys down to the Danzig station. Soon after they boarded, a whistle screeched, and the train began to move. The figure of Joshua grew smaller, shrinking with the station platform. The world of Warsaw receded: "houses, trees, wagons, entire streets revolving and drifting backward as if the earth were a huge carousel."

Isaac's mother took a bottle of milk and cookies from a satchel, and as he ate Isaac forgot the retreating city—the war, the hunger, the illness—and gave himself up to the ecstasy of travel.

For three days and nights Bathsheba and her sons were borne through a green world of tiny villages, orchards, and fields where women and girls worked and peasants mowed hay. Once Isaac saw a scarecrow, and he and his brother were more unnerved by it than any crow would have been. They saw windmills too, and sheep and cattle, and it occurred to Isaac that the land they were passing through must somehow resemble Israel: "The world seemed like an open Pentateuch. The moon and the eleven stars came out, bowing before Joseph, the future ruler of Egypt."

The first evening, their train pulled into the Ivangorod station on the Austrian border. Isaac was astonished to see Jews in uniform among the soldiers. Two of them started to teach Isaac and Moishe how to play chess. Another let Moishe try on his cap and even hold his sword.

On the third day, as the train sped past burnt-out forests marking the Russian retreat, Isaac continued to stare with unwearying fascination at the fields and forests and villages rushing by. The scent of pine needles was intoxicating, the sight of hares and squirrels exciting, exotic. At length the Bilgoray passengers were transferred to flatcars attached to a tiny locomotive, where they sat on benches during the final leg of the journey. "Everyone in the car looked sunburned, their clothes had a sun-faded appearance. Many of the men had red beards and were dressed in gaberdines, and I felt related to them."

Somebody called out "Bathsheba!" And soon Isaac's mother was surrounded by women who confirmed the dream that had brought her on this journey: Her father was indeed dead—as were others in the family: her mother, a sister-in-law, two nieces, and a nephew.

The poor woman gave way to tears. Isaac wanted to cry with her, but he couldn't. "I cheated, wetting my eyes with saliva."

Suddenly the cars of the little train jumped the track. There was a long wait while men with poles set them right again. Even then, the trip was far from over. The train kept stopping for one passenger to get a drink of water or another to answer a call of nature in the bushes or for the engineer to deliver a parcel.

During one of these long pauses a woman came out of a shack and handed Isaac's mother a present of blackberries. Bathsheba could scarcely touch the food, but pretty soon the tongues, lips, and hands of the two boys were thoroughly stained.

At last they arrived in Bilgoray, which was even prettier and more serene than Isaac had imagined it would be, with its gardens, orchards, giant chestnut trees, and smells of fresh milk and warm dough.

The Bilgoray branch of the family came pouring out of Isaac's grandfather's house to welcome the travelers, ushering them into a huge kitchen with an oven as big as any Isaac had ever seen in a bakery. The boys were offered prune cake.

Isaac gazed at the trees and wild flowers in the garden, heard the sounds of birds and crickets and chickens clucking as they waddled through the grass. When he looked up, he could see the Bilgoray synagogue and, beyond it, fields that rambled all the way to the forest.

"I wished I could stay here forever. . . ."

———

In Bilgoray, Isaac at last met his mother's family, who up till then had been unreal to him—among them, his frail but sprightly Uncle Joseph, who was now the rabbi of Bilgoray, and Joseph's third wife, Yentl. Yentl was a simple woman whose biggest tragedy was that she was barren. All the wonder-working rabbis in Poland had been unable to change that. Her husband made cruel fun of her for it frequently. Joseph may have been witty enough, and he often seemed lost in what passed for deep thought, but Isaac didn't think much of his intellect; most of his remarks struck the boy as inane. And evidently the Jews of Bilgoray shared this sentiment. Joseph lacked his father's competence in dealing with legal problems, and he was never much of a scholar.

Among his new found cousins Isaac saw many a redhead like himself. Joseph's oldest daughter, Frieda, was off living in Russia with her mother's relatives. She was rumored to be bright and well-educated, but wrote infrequently and was spoken of as something of a legend. Joseph's oldest son, Avromele, who was twenty-two, seldom opened a book and spent most of his time performing chores, fetching well-water, and chopping wood. His younger sister Brocha, who had pale skin and yellow hair, spent her days sitting at a sewing machine, filling orders for clothes for local customers. Next came the fiery-haired Taube, a tall girl who, as Isaac recalls her in "Bilgoray" (*In My Father's Court*), "twitched and squinted" and worked hard between bouts of illness that the local doctor diagnosed as "nerves." Samson—the only one of the children to survive the Holocaust—was Isaac's age. Though he feared his father, he studied as infrequently as Avromele and also spent most of his time doing household chores. The youngest, eight-year-old Esther, who was her father's favorite, wore her hair in braids and went to an Austrian school in the town.

In addition to Joseph and Yentl's family, Isaac met the brood belonging to his dark-haired, blond-bearded Uncle Itche, a man whose piety was mitigated by the celebrated "streak of skepticism" that ran through the clan, and Itche's wife, Rochele, a rabbi's daughter who believed in ghosts and the power of amulets and charms. Itche and his wife had become melancholy after the death of their younger son in an epidemic and fussed over their remaining boy, Moshele, to the point of stifling him, worrying that he was never dressed warmly enough, warning him not to get overheated or catch cold, plying him with milk and cookies, and generally spoiling him rotten.

Nearby, in the village of Tarnogrod, there were more relatives. And in Bilgoray there were still others.

Almost every Jew in Bilgoray said his prayers three times a day. The Jewish women cut their hair, covering their heads with bonnets or kerchiefs rather than wigs. Even the relatively enlightened men still wore their long gaberdines, and there were frequent fast days. Close as they were to the railroad, many of the townspeople had never boarded a train. Isaac Loeb Peretz had come from this area, but almost nobody had heard of him.

Jewish holidays in Bilgoray were a revelation to Isaac. The customs had not altered for centuries. In the old synagogue the floor was covered with hay. A metal vase contained the foreskins of circumcised infants. The matzoh to be eaten at the end of the Passover holiday, the *afikomen*, hung from the synagogue walls. A book of penitential prayers, of a kind no longer published, lay open on the lectern.

"In this world of old Jewishness I found a spiritual treasure trove," Isaac says in "Bilgoray." "I had a chance to see our past as it really was. Time seemed to flow backward. I lived Jewish history."

Yet slowly Zionist ideas, Socialist propaganda, and talks of strikes and demonstrations were beginning to infiltrate even into Bilgoray. Economic conditions for the Jews of Bilgoray were not good. A thriving business in exporting sieves to Russia had gone bad when the Russian market closed. Many local young men were working on a railroad the Austrians were constructing. Two Jewish sisters had opened a brothel near the Jewish cemetery and did a thriving business with the visiting soldiers.

Of late, evening parties in the town had been enlivened by arguments about which kind of Utopia the Jews ought to be promoting. A play called *Shulamit* was produced in Yiddish at the local firehouse by a stock company from Warsaw. And an old bachelor lawyer named Jonah Ackerman had opened a Yiddish library of worldly books in his home—though he was so respected a citizen that nobody dared smash his windows in reprisal.

Isaac feels that were it not for the years in Bilgoray he might never have been able to write his first novel, *Satan in Goray,* for the atmosphere of the fictional town in that book was drawn from his experience of Bilgoray—just as the characters of Rechele and the Orthodox Rabbi Benish in that novel were based in part on his own Aunt Rochele (along with his sister, Hinde Esther) and his Uncle Joseph.

Isaac's first summer in Bilgoray was as pleasant as he had imagined it might be in his most extravagant daydreams. The weather was warm, and he never went hungry. Perhaps best of all, he was sent to the Turkish study house, which had been founded by the Hasidim under his grandfather. There, with his cousin Samson and another boy named Benjamin Brezel assigned to him as students, he began studying the Talmud—although actually he spent more time telling his pupils about the wonders of Warsaw than anything else.

Late in the summer, however, as he recollects in "Old Jewishness" (*In My Father's Court*), Isaac came down with a fever that proved to be typhus. He was treated by a Czech military doctor. The boy, who had begun to have sexual dreams that allowed him no peace and in which his cousin Esther frequently played a role, had a hallucination during his illness that three women were "tied around my neck and weighing me down." His mother tried to tell him his high fever was causing him to imagine things, but he was not reassured.

It was months before Isaac recovered his strength and was able to go back to his studies and his reading. Meanwhile news came that Joshua too was ill with typhus in Warsaw. It was not an easy summer for Bathsheba. Hinde Esther and her husband had been separated when the English turned Abraham over to the Russians so that he could report for military duty. And Pinchas Mendel had decided to go back to Radzymin, where, the Radzymin rabbi assured him, he could earn a better living than in Warsaw.

As it turned out, Isaac, his mother, and Moishe remained in Bilgoray for nearly four years. When winter came, there were rumors of a new revolution in Russia. But Isaac almost never saw a newspaper there. He only knew that there was hunger in the town because a new soup kitchen had opened and long lines formed. When the Germans captured Lithuania and the Ukraine, many Polish Jews came back to Bilgoray, some bringing with them the new Bolshevik ideas. A professional preacher named Ansel Shur brought his children home to Bilgoray speaking modern Hebrew. Isaac made friends with one of them, a boy named Mottel, whom he tells about in "New Friends" (*In My Father's Court*).

The talkative Mottel was short and wide and, with his "small nose, light eyes, heavy lips," looked like a Russian. He disparaged the grammar, pronunciation, and fanaticism of the students at the Turisk study house. He also lent Isaac books of stories and poetry, primers and grammar texts, which Isaac approached "with incredible passion." For weeks Isaac spent several hours a day studying Hebrew. He discovered the Hebrew poetry of Chaim Bialik and soon began to write poems and stories in Hebrew himself. Some of them he sent to a local Hebrew newspaper, which published them.

When Mottel read Isaac's first poem, he couldn't believe his eyes. He accused his friend of plagiarism. And when he realized the poem was original, he grew jealous and began to boast that it was his lessons that were responsible for Isaac's facility.

As soon as word got around that Isaac was reading and writing heretical literature, he was up to his neck in trouble. Though he went on studying every morning and afternoon at the Turisk study house, the Hasidim no longer had much use for him, and Bathsheba accused him of trying to humiliate her family. On the other hand, the relatively enlightened citizens of Bilgoray began to take an interest in what the young author was putting down on paper.

In "The New Winds," the closing chapter of *In My Father's Court*, Isaac recalls walking about in those days with the melancholy air of a pre-Raphaelite poet. He tried to convince two of his friends, Notte Shverdsharf and Meir Hadas, that suicide was the noblest act a man could commit. But instead of committing suicide his friends became involved with new groups promulgating zionism and bolshevism.

Isaac, who had begun to weary of solemn religious tracts, began to read in omnivorous fashion, absorbing the works of Mendele Mocher Sforim, Sholom Aleichem, Isaac Loeb Peretz, Sholem Asch, and Jacob Cohen. He would sit under the apple tree in the family garden, or up in the attic of the house, devouring stories, plays, essays, novels. When the Americans began sending Yiddish translations of European books along with sacks of flour, he proceeded avidly to Strindberg, Turgenev, Tolstoy, de Maupassant, and Chekhov. Some time later he discovered a book by Stupnicki about Spinoza and this time went into a turmoil over Spinoza's ideas. He realized that as a young boy he had missed the point of Spinoza's concepts. "As I read this book, I felt intoxicated, inspired as I never had before. It seemed to me that the truths I had been seeking since childhood had at last become apparent. Everything was God—Warsaw, Bilgoray, the spider in the attic, the water in the well, the clouds in the sky, and the book on my knees. Everything was divine, everything was thought and extension. A stone had its stony thoughts. The material being of a star and its thoughts were two aspects of the same thing. Besides physical and mental attributes, there were innumerable other characteristics through which divinity could be determined. God was eternal, transcending time. Time, or duration, controlled only the modi, the bubbles in the divine cauldron, that were forever forming and bursting. I too was a modus, which explained my indecision, my restlessness, my passionate nature, my doubts and fears. But the modi were created from God's body, God's thought, and could be explained only through Him."

Spinoza may have haunted the maturing Isaac's thoughts, but it was the bodies of women that haunted his dreams. "I thought I was going crazy, or was possessed by a dybbuk. Desires and fantasies became all-consuming. I resolved to fast. But fasting had no effect."

Isaac accepted a job teaching Hebrew in private homes to "beginning" students, only to discover that his pupils were not boys and girls but young men and women. The women came dressed in their best clothes. "I faced them in a long gaberdine, a velvet hat, and with dangling sidelocks. How, since I am naturally shy, I had the nerve to accept this assignment I do not know, but it has been my experience that shy persons are sometimes unusually bold."

One of Isaac's Hebrew students was the attractive daughter of an enlightened Jewish watchmaker named Todros. Like Isaac, Todros was interested in philosophy and science, and he subscribed to some of the scientific journals printed in Warsaw. He and Isaac had many long conversations. From Todros, Isaac learned about the theories of Einstein and Planck and got the latest scientific news on the nature of the atom. They would sit up nights discussing science, Isaac arguing in a Talmudic singsong about whether the electron was really the smallest unit of matter. All the while he would be thinking secretly about the watchmaker's daughter, with whom he had fallen in love. She would bring glasses of tea from the kitchen, and he would stare, smitten, at her pale face and coal-black eyes.

Isaac's efforts to teach Hebrew to the "worldly" boys and girls of Bilgoray gained him something of a reputation in the town, but his mother and her relatives were scandalized. They wanted him to concentrate on studying for the rabbinate and to stay with his "own kind." Nevertheless, he stubbornly continued to associate with the non-Hasidic students and to yearn for the watchmaker's daughter, with her "indescribable smile." He was ready to start living life rather than reading and thinking about it. He was also ready to return to Warsaw, for he had begun to feel cramped in the parochial town of Bilgoray. He was to get his wish, but in a rather different manner from what he had hoped.

❀

In 1918 Poland, under Pilsudski, declared its independence and reclaimed Western Galicia for the Austrians. Russia contested Poland's claim to Eastern Galicia, but Poland secured the territory and was confirmed in its possession by the Treaty of Riga with Russia in 1921.

In 1920, when Isaac was sixteen, Pinchas Mendel decided to leave Radzymin to accept an appointment as rabbi in the little Eastern Galician town of Dzikow, a *shtetl* not far from Bilgoray. Bathsheba wanted to move to Dzikow to join her husband, but Isaac would have no part of the plan. He was intent on returning to Warsaw. After much argument it was agreed that he would go to the city—providing that he entered a seminary and pursued his studies for the rabbinate. And so, in 1921, Isaac went to Warsaw and enrolled in the Tachkemoni Rabbinical Seminary.

The following year—as it turned out, Isaac's only year at the seminary—was what he has called "one of the worst times of my life." He had no permanent address but lived like an itinerant beggar, sleeping now in one place, now in another, and he often went hungry. He was also impatient with the school curriculum, which seemed to him to cover ground he was already familiar with. As he could not muster any interest in religious books, he started reading Knut Hamsun's *Hunger*, which, he feels, had as much of an influence on his own development as it did on that of twentieth-century fiction.

❀

"Animals," says Isaac, "are the wonder of God's creation." Dvorah, who has been working for him as part-time secretary in recent months, and has heard him say this often, has decided to take him at his word and invite him to go with her to the zoo.

"By all means," Isaac says, "absolutely, we'll go to the zoo."

It's a chilly day in April 1976 when they set out for The Bronx Zoo. They meet in front of Isaac's favorite restaurant on West Seventy-second Street in Manhattan. Dvorah is driving—this time a Datsun that she and her husband Abraham have just acquired, white with a shiny blue interior, looking and smelling extremely new. Isaac is in a splendid mood, relaxed and tranquil. He is pleased to find that admission to the zoo is free for people over sixty-five. He wants to pay for the parking in the lot at the entrance, but Dvorah won't let him.

They go first to the bird house. Isaac is entranced. The birds here are on display in settings that approximate their natural habitats. Isaac stops in front of every display, carefully reading the printed captions, wanting to know the name of each bird before he examines it. He stares for a long time at each exhibit.

"These are God's creatures," he tells Dvorah, "happy, contented, tranquil. How can we not believe that there is a higher power who has shaped these birds?" He is particularly impressed by the large exotic birds with their fantastically colored feathers and headdresses, birds with ornate crowns on their heads, wading birds with long spindle-thin legs, toucans with outsized, flamboyantly colored beaks. Once he stops to watch two birds mating.

"See? They don't need a *ketubah* [a marriage contract]. No guilt. They behave exactly as God wants them to behave. They do as nature tells them to do."

When they leave the bird house, Isaac eagerly reads the clusters of signs leading to other kinds of animals. On their way to the wolves, they pass a huge ostrich. Isaac stops to stare, reminded somehow of the women he knew in his youth in Warsaw. He talks about one in particular, who was much older than he, not mentioning her name but obviously remembering her vividly and the fact that she was something of a masochist. She used to like to be urinated on.

"Repulsive," Dvorah says. Isaac shrugs. People have their ways. What is the use of judging them?

Arriving at the wolf compound, Isaac comments, "You see how these animals are—completely out for themselves."

"People are that way too," Dvorah says.

"Not always. Sometimes people are interested in each other, kind to each other."

People pass the girl of twenty-one and Isaac, ever closer to seventy-two, wearing his standard winter outfit—a dark hat, overcoat, and suit, a blue shirt, a self-effacing tie. Dvorah has on a long-sleeved blouse, black trousers.

Around her shoulders is a heavy white shawl her grandmother knitted for her. A woman passes, comments to a friend, "How nice—the grand-daughter taking such good care of her grandfather, spending time with him."

"These wolves are mainly interested in their territorial rights," Isaac observes. He stands for a while, reading about the wolves.

When Isaac has had enough, he and Dvorah contemplate the deer, and Isaac shakes his head in wonder at their gentleness. Then they pass a troupe of peacocks.

"They are not of this earth," Isaac concludes. "They are queens from somewhere else in the universe, with jewels on their backs."

The day grows increasingly chilly, cloudy. Isaac admires the polar bears wading in their pool, never feeling the chill. He stands for a long time watching them in silence, looking pensive.

Suddenly he brightens and offers to buy Dvorah popcorn. They share the bag of popcorn and some Stardust sweets, chewy, cherry-flavored candies. Isaac wants to go back to the peacocks. They find a bench near the gaudy birds.

After a long while they get up and read a sign with arrows pointing in various directions to worlds of monkeys, gorillas, and tigers. They head for the tigers, but suddenly it is almost five o'clock, and everything is closing.

On their way to the car Isaac, looking pensive once more, speaks of Runya, the woman who bore his son, and whom he has not seen for more than forty years. He talks of the *meshugassim* of people—their private luna-cies, eccentricities. "But when you get into their minds," he tells Dvorah, "they don't seem to be so crazy. Raskolnikov, in *Crime and Punishment*— once you understand him, you can see it all from his point of view."

When they get to the parking lot, Isaac wants to sit in the car for a moment, warming up from the chill of the afternoon, looking at the bare trees that in a matter of weeks will be putting out leaves. "Let's not go yet," he says. Unknowingly echoing Whitman, he says he thinks he could live with the animals. Dvorah says they'll come back again another time. They'll see the thunderstorm staged in the rain forest in the bird house early every afternoon. They'll ride the tram high above the grounds, visit the giraffes . . .

Everyone has left. The park is closed. It's getting dark. Dvorah starts the motor and drives a musing Isaac home.

❀

Israel Joshua as a young man has been described by his nephew, Maurice Carr (in his own youth Maurice changed his name from Kreitman to Carr when he decided to become a journalist) as "masterful and handsome, with an erect bearing, a powerfully domed, balding skull, a stubbornly upturned little chin and huge eyes, blue pools sparkling with stern authority, with pristine *joie de vivre* and bitter disillusionment."*

When he was eighteen, Joshua had wanted to be a painter. He tried in vain, despite his connections with the art world of Warsaw, to make his way in that discipline. At the same time he pursued his bent as a writer.

In 1915, when he was twenty-two, he published his first stories about Hasidic life in Poland in a magazine called *Dos Yiddishe Vort*. In 1918 he married Genia Kupferstok, the girl he had been courting, a simple, honest woman, the daughter of a landowner in the town of Krasmobrod. That year, seeking new horizons, Joshua took Genia to German-occupied Kiev, where he found a job as a proofreader. There he was soon writing for the daily newspaper *Di Naye Tsayt* and contributing pieces to the magazines *Oyfgang* and *Baginen*. He was at first influenced by the writers of the city who were known as the Kiev group, but soon began to develop a style entirely his own.

Soon after the birth of their first son, Yasha, in 1919, Joshua and Genia went to Moscow, where Joshua became a full-fledged Bolshevik, as enthusiastic about the cause as his hero would be in the final chapter of the novel he was soon to write. It wasn't long, however, before he experienced a disillusionment as profound as his initial fervor. This change of heart was no doubt connected with the fact that the editors in Russia would publish his stories and then, when he came around to collect his fees, refuse to pay him.

In 1921 Joshua brought Genia and the two-year-old Yasha back to Warsaw. Joshua had no job, and the family had to live with Genia's parents, but Joshua was working on some well-planned short stories, and his writing was going well. Isaac himself had done some writing while studying at the seminary, and he showed his work to his older brother. Joshua was more pleased with the efforts than Isaac was.

In Warsaw Joshua found himself in the midst of the literary, philosophical, and political ferment among Yiddish writers there. It was hard for a writer to hear his own voice, let alone establish its identity. Yet Joshua had already freed himself of fashionable Russian influences and was now able to put his own stamp on his prose. A number of his works soon saw publication, among them a symbolist play called *Erd-Vey* (*Earth-Cry*). His fame spread beyond Poland when, in 1923, *Erd-Vey* was produced by the Yiddish Art Theater in New York. By then he had published a book of short stories called *Perl un Andere Dertailungen* (*The Pearl and Other Tales*). The title story won him praise among Warsaw's Jewish intellectuals, who saw the miserly old gem merchant in the tale as a symbol of a society in decay—a stubborn survivor who refuses to die. Despite the fact that the story was

---

* Maurice Carr, "My Uncle Yitzhak," *The Jerusalem Post*, July 4, 1975.

about injustice and ugliness, it was told in the most lyrical of styles. Joshua, who constantly admonished Isaac to exclude all commentary—even stylistic commentary—from his fiction, resolved thereafter to adhere to his own advice. Yet the powerful personality he tried so hard to keep out of his prose continued to express itself in his writing. Despite his best efforts, his scorn for ignorance and anger at cruelty would pervade the family novels that were later to win him a considerable literary reputation.

In 1925 another of Joshua's short-story collections, *Oy Fremder Erd* (*Oh, Strange World*) was published. Across the Atlantic Abraham Cahan, the publisher of the *Jewish Daily Forward*, was so impressed with Joshua's work that in 1927 he sent him to the Soviet Union as a *Forward* correspondent. From there Joshua dispatched a series of articles describing Jewish life under Stalin, unsentimental firsthand reports that reflected the austerity and harshness of life for Jews in the Soviet "paradise." These were later published by B. Kletzkian in Vilna in 1928 as the collection *New Russia*. In 1927 Kletzkian published the novel *Shtol un Ayzn*, which Joshua had just completed—a book that was to reach the English-speaking public eight years later under the title *Blood Harvest*, published by Alfred A. Knopf. It was reprinted in 1969 by Funk and Wagnall as *Steel and Iron*—a literal equivalent of the Yiddish.

The protagonist of *Steel and Iron* is a Jewish deserter hiding out from the Russian army in Warsaw during World War I—much as Joshua himself had done. After nine months at the front Benjamin Lerner flees the infantry to take cover in his Uncle Baruch Joseph's apartment. There he falls in love with his cousin Gitta, but his uncle has other plans for her and makes life so unpleasant for Benjamin that he flees the house without identification papers or a kopeck in his pocket and wanders through the streets of Warsaw. Here the novel offers a vivid picture of the wartime city. Benjamin sees carts crammed with refugees, prisoners with shaven skulls driven through town on their way to Siberia, soldiers carousing with syphilitic whores, bridges dynamited by Russian troops. He joins a group of bohemians dodging conscription in a sculptor's studio. Later in the book he joins a corps of German army engineers and becomes Number 301, laboring from dawn until late at night "like a drayhorse" to move logs for a bridge. Life is dominated by the whistle of an inexorable siren; the soup is ugly brown slop he can scarcely bring himself to eat; the crowded barracks stink. Conditions are worse than at the front. Benjamin feels he can only earn respect with his fists and does so when he cracks open the face of a Pole egged on by his fellows to "kill the Jewboy."

As the story unfolds in the unsparingly bleak manner of so many proletarian novels of the thirties the landscape grows ever more drab, the action more brutal, flickering like the scenes in some gray silent-screen melodrama. Eventually Benjamin helps organize a revolt of the oppressed laborers against their German overseers and has to flee through fields and

forests for his life. He finds his cousin Gitta again and takes her with him to
join a newfound friend, a curiously idealistic war profiteer named Aaron
Llovish, who is working to restore a country estate as a haven for Jewish refugees. In the end, however, the little Utopia is taken over by the Germans,
who rape Gitta and send Benjamin off to prison. But Benjamin is soon free
and off to Russia, where he arrives opportunely in the midst of the assault
on the Winter Palace. The book closes as, rifle in hand, the eternal outcast
leads a detail of brave comrades in a night attack.

Steel and Iron is choppily episodic, relentlessly mirthless, and above all
ugly, piling up descriptions of all that was sordid and degrading in tormented wartime Warsaw. Its lugubrious tone is suffocating, its hero a bitter,
preposterous forerunner of Ari ben Canaan in Leon Uris's *Exodus*. Had this
been I. J. Singer's only novel, he might well have remained a blurred figure
in the faded group portrait of forgotten authors of outdated proletarian fiction. Even so, the book has a crude power, which proceeds from its passionate attention to revealing detail and the hatred that smoulders between
the poker-faced Brechtian detachment of its lines, and its author's skill at literary construction hints that there will be more persuasive things to come
than this story of a cardboard hero's doomed conflict against inexorable steel
and merciless iron.

❁

In 1922 Isaac fled the Tachkemoni Rabbinical Seminary and returned to
Bilgoray, where he was able to scrape out an income giving Hebrew lessons.
Eventually, however, he fell ill and went to live with his family in Dzikow,
the "half bog, half village" where Bathsheba and Moishe had joined Pinchas
Mendel and where Moishe was studying for the rabbinate.

Isaac found Dzikow even more stultifying than Bilgoray had been. Perhaps the one redeeming event was Moishe's discovery of the works of a
Hasidic mystic named Nachman Bratzlaver. Isaac read Rabbi Bratzlaver's
stories and essays with fascination, attempting to reconcile this Hasid's
thinking with Spinoza's—to make sense of a God who, according to Spinoza, was a power without feeling but who, according to Bratzlaver, was all
love and benevolence.

Writing in the 1960s of Isaac's teen-age years in Bilgoray, Irving Buchen
would comment: "Singer's adolescence is a study in strain. He walks a tightrope between two ages and worlds; he is on the way to becoming both a
modern man and a transmigrated soul. While he pours and puzzles over
Spinoza he unknowingly hums an old Hasidic melody. He reads Dostoevsky
and studies the Cabala until the two begin to counterpoint and coincide

with each other. Determined to pursue free inquiry, he resists the Orthodox surrender of eternal questions to God's jurisdiction. And yet he is aware even at this point that although the secular philosophers are intoxicating and profound, they neither provide answers to the eternal questions nor offer peace."*

In 1923, after the birth of his second son, Joseph, Joshua was hired as co-editor of *Literarishe Bletter* (*Literary Pages*), a journal that was published on newsprint and looked like a tabloid but read like a university literary magazine. Soon after he got the job, he wrote to Isaac in Dzikow, offering him work as a proofreader on the magazine's staff.

Opening the letter, Isaac could scarcely believe his good fortune. The nine months with his family in Dzikow had begun to oppress him like some rainy, unending twilight from which there would never be an escape. It was all he could do to wait out the days before he boarded the train for Warsaw.

Aboard that train Isaac saw Jewish paupers cursed by a band of hooligans who boarded the third-class carriage and harangued the Jewish passengers as Bolsheviks, Trotskyites, Soviet spies, and Christ-killers. They pushed the poor Jews and their bundles and crates off the seats, yanked at their beards, tore the wig off an old lady, stomped on the Jews' ragged possessions, taunted them with requests for Sabbath hymns.

"I stood there," Isaac says in *A Little Boy in Search of God,* "frightened, in a corner of the carriage near the toilet, gripping a bundle that consisted entirely of manuscripts and the few books I possessed. . . . I knew full well that what I was seeing now was the essence of human history. Today the Poles tormented the Jews; yesterday the Russians had tormented the Poles. . . . It was entirely possible that had I had a pistol or poison with me at that time, I would have killed myself."

After a while the Polish tormenters grew bored and tired, lolled in their seats, and started snoring.

The Warsaw Isaac reached at last was now a part of the five-year-old Polish republic. In Russia Stalin was already a force to reckon with, and Hitler was launching his first unsuccessful *putsch* in Germany, while Mussolini was busy administering castor oil to his opponents. Although the typhus epidemic had reduced Warsaw's population considerably, it was still difficult to find an apartment, since people from the provinces were swarming into the city in search of work.

Joshua, Genia, and the children were already cramped in a tiny one-room apartment, and had no room for Isaac. But one of the editors of *Literary Pages*, Melech Ravich, offered to share his own attic apartment on the fifth floor of a run-down building with Isaac.

In *A Little Boy in Search of God* Isaac describes Ravich as a tall, stout man, eleven years Isaac's senior, fluent in Polish and German, and a con-

* *Isaac Bashevis Singer and the Eternal Past.*

vert to vegetarianism (which Isaac would embrace much later in his life), who believed with an unshakable faith that an age of justice was on its way, that men would soon be brothers—and vegetarians. He foresaw a future in which "There would be no Jews, no gentiles, only a single united mankind whose goal would be equality and progress." He believed that the world of letters would help to bring about this Utopian state of affairs.

The staff of *Literary Pages* too was in a ferment about the redeeming powers of socialism, literature, and sociology. According to Isaac, the publication was filled with bad poetry, bad articles, and "false criticism."

When Isaac wasn't proofreading for *Literary Pages* ("the kitchen of literature," he calls proofreading) or listening with quiet contempt to the theories of its writers and editors, he was tossing and turning in his attic bed, tormented by feverish fantasies of passion that assailed him "like locusts." He had still not been to bed with a woman, but in his imagination, as he writes in *A Little Boy in Search of God*, he "had already committed all the excesses that could only be fancied. I wanted to write and to study but ninety percent of my spiritual energy was squandered on yearning for the forbidden." Sometimes he imagined himself speeding at a thousand times the velocity of light to far galaxies, sometimes as a magician luring "all the beauties of the world to my bed through magic." Meanwhile he suffered from hunger and illness and, as the winter drew on, from the aching cold.

There were two places of refuge from the torment and turbulence of Isaac's life. One was the Writers' Club, where the waitresses sometimes allowed him credit for the food at the buffet table, where every few evenings he could listen raptly to a lecture, and where he met other aspiring young writers who were equally impoverished and equally scornful of all the poems, articles, and stories published by established writers. The other was the library, where he could browse for hours and devour books on philosophy, psychology, biology, astronomy, and physics. When he came across a book on psychical research, he became so entranced with the subject that he sat up far into the nights reading, forgetting the tattered state of his clothes, his skimpy meals, the bedbugs in his unheated room.

Isaac's salary at *Literary Pages* was supposed to come to about six dollars a week, which was considered a decent sum at the time. He was never sure, though, whether he would collect it or not. Some weeks he'd get the equivalent of a dollar and a half, some weeks, two. His brother helped him with meals, clothes, and patient advice.

To supplement his income Isaac began to take on work as a translator, turning pulpy novels into Yiddish serial stories for Warsaw newspapers. Later he turned this newfound skill as a translator to more serious purposes. He translated two novels by Knut Hamsun into Yiddish. He worked on Yiddish versions of Stefan Zweig's *Romain Rolland* and Erich Maria Remarque's *The Way Back* and *All Quiet on the Western Front*. Putting to work the German he had started to learn while waiting on line for that visa in front of the Austrian consulate, he prepared a Yiddish version of Thomas Mann's *The Magic Mountain*. (When an interviewer asked him once how he had dealt with the French passages in that book, he replied, "Since it was bad French, I translated it into bad Yiddish."*) Then he began to gain a footing with his own prose. At first he tried to write in Hebrew, but nothing he created in that language satisfied him. He seemed unable to breathe life into the sacred tongue. When he turned back to Yiddish, he was still disappointed. He would tear to shreds every manuscript he attempted.

"The themes employed by Yiddish writers and the writing itself struck me as sentimental, primitive, petty," he says in his third book of memoirs, *A Young Man in Search of Love*. "Too often it had to do with a girl whose parents wanted an arranged marriage while she really loved someone else. Quite often the girl came from a wealthy family and the youth was the son of a tailor or shoemaker." Isaac wondered if it would be possible to describe in Yiddish the kinds of sexual experiences he had started to have since his return to Warsaw. For Yiddish literature seemed to him more and more "provincial and backward," while Hebrew, the language in which he had first tried to write, "lacked words used in day-to-day conversation." Writing in that ancient tongue had meant consulting dictionaries and aping the language of the Scriptures. On the other hand, "Yiddish literature reminded me of my father's courtroom, where almost everything was forbidden"—and this despite the taboo themes that had been taken up by Sholem Asch.

Yet in his early twenties Isaac did come to grips with the problem of writing fiction in Yiddish and was able to complete several stories to his own satisfaction. In 1927—the same year in which Israel Joshua's *Steel and Iron* appeared—Isaac saw his first short story in print. It was called "Oyf der Elter" ("In Old Age") and appeared in Issue Number 60 of *Literary Pages*. In *A Young Man in Search of Love* Isaac describes the qualifications with which that story was accepted, foreshadowing the kind of reservations with which his work was to be greeted by Yiddish-speaking readers for years to come: "I . . . submitted it to the editor of the magazine of which I was the proofreader. He promised to read it and if it pleased him, to publish it. After a while he informed me that he had read the story and even though he found it flawed, he would print it. I asked him what these flaws were and after some lengthy deliberation he said that the piece was too pessimistic, that it lacked problems, and that the story was negative and almost anti-Semitic. Why write about thieves and whores when there were so many decent Jewish men and devoted Jewish wives? If such a thing were translated into Polish and a gentile read it, he might conclude that all Jews were depraved. A Yiddish writer, my editor argued, was honor-bound to stress the good in our people, the lofty and sacred. He had to be an eloquent defender of the Jews, not their defamer.

---

* *Isaac Bashevis Singer and the Eternal Past.*

"I didn't have the opportunity to answer him since the telephone rang at that moment and he stayed on it for a long time, but his comments irked me. Why did a story have to be totally optimistic? What sort of criterion was this? And what did it mean that it 'lacked problems'? Wasn't the essence of the world and of the human species one enormous problem? And why must a Yiddish writer be a defender of his people? Was it the Yiddish writer's obligation to conduct an eternal dialogue with the anti-Semite? Could a work written in this vein possess any artistic value? The Scriptures on which I had been raised didn't flatter the Jews. Quite the contrary, they spoke of their transgressions. Even Moses didn't emerge pure. I didn't have too high an opinion of this editor and his contentions."

Isaac had signed his story "Tse," the first in a series of pseudonyms he was to adopt over the years to distinguish what he regarded as journalism from serious fiction. Later that year, in the same publication (Issue Number 80), there appeared another story called "Vayber" ("Women") under the signature "Isaac Bashevis." The "Bashevis" was derived from his mother's first name—Bas-Sheva—which is the Yiddish form of the name Bathsheba. Isaac says he took the name so that his readers would not confuse him with his brother. He did not wish to trade on Israel Joshua's reputation. But, in fact, not long after the publication of these two stories the Yiddish-reading public of Poland discovered who this Bashevis was and realized that there was a second Singer in the family who must be taken seriously as a writer.

❄

May 25, 1976

Samuel L. Shneiderman, a Yiddish journalist, translator, and author, worked with Isaac on *Literary Pages* in the 1920s and has since renewed the acquaintance in New York. He is a stout, fiery fellow, with keen, flashing eyes and a vehement way of putting things. He sits at a table by a window in his comfortable apartment on the Lower West Side of Manhattan, surrounded by bookcases filled with tomes in Yiddish, Hebrew, and English. With a scowl Sam recalls his days as an interviewer for *Literary Pages*, when he first knew Isaac.

"There was never such a weekly magazine in America," he explains. "It was a literary publication devoted to literature and problems concerning literature. There were short stories, poetry, theater reviews, interviews with writers, and articles about them. *Literarishe Bletter*—" Sam's wife, Eileen, interrupts to explain that the word *Bletter* is a sardonic pun; it means not only "pages," or "leaves," but also "blot." "Anyhow," Sam goes on, "it was the center of literary and cultural life for Warsaw's Jewish intellectuals, and the foremost Yiddish writers in Poland were among the contributors. At first it came out in a big format—like a newspaper, like *The New York Times.* Later it looked more like a magazine."

When asked why Joshua Singer resigned as co-editor soon after Isaac joined the staff, Sam reflects. "There were all kinds of conflicts. After the time he had spent in the Soviet Union, he found all Communists especially repugnant. He hated it when one of the other editors or anybody would call him *chaver*—comrade. And one of the reasons he left was that he was disturbed by what he considered leftist influences in the publication."

Sam recalls Isaac in those days: ". . . very thin—skinny, with flaming red hair and those mischievous eyes. I remember that wall in the Writers' Club where he used to sit to keep warm. A big room where lectures were given, and there were always discussions and arguments going on. And Isaac, always making jokes, doing imitations of the editor and especially of one critic whose way of telling an anecdote Isaac could mimic to perfection. He used to come down to the print shop, where the printers were two brothers Isaac happened to find especially comical. He once wrote a story about them. I asked him afterward if he was afraid to come down to the print shop, where we used to read proofs together, for fear they had recognized themselves in the story and were laying for him. He shrugged this off; they either never knew about the story or deliberately didn't mention it.

"Isaac's humor was only one aspect of his personality and his abilities. He is basically a serious man, always was. The number of things he knows, the extent of his interests are amazing. Yet somehow he stays outside things. He is a mystic, for instance, with a healthy suspicion about things mystical. He knows literature, he has read an enormous amount, but in his own work he started right away to depart from all he had read. In Joshua's work you can find a continuation of the tradition of the great European novelists, detect the influence of the Russians, the Poles. But in Isaac the pattern is broken. Of course when you read his work in Yiddish, you can appreciate it much more. Even his early reviews and articles show a mastery of the mother tongue, of its rhythms and potentialities, and that biting wit which especially can express itself so well in the Yiddish idiom.

"His style—ah, that style. From the beginning it was the envy of other Yiddish writers. His mastery of transition, for example—how gracefully he glides from description to dialogue, from the ambiance of a place to the action happening there. What a storyteller! The literary world of Warsaw saw it right away—the richness of the language, the imaginative blending of the absolutely real and the totally fantastic—all absolutely new in Yiddish writing.

"I never visited him at home—there was no home to visit. Just a succession of rooms where he never invited anyone. We were never, in fact, close friends. Isaac has had very few close friends. I remember he even looked like a hermit, but a special kind of hermit. A hermit with a lust for living, a passion for women, a strong desire to travel, to know the world."

As to the neighborhood where Isaac grew up, "Krochmalna Street, you know, was not all poverty, the way Isaac describes it in his memoirs. There were some quite well-to-do people living there, and not everybody on the street was a Jew. As a matter of fact, the street is remembered especially because of an orphange that was located there, run by a man named Janus Korczak, who was also a leading Polish-Jewish writer and educator. When the Nazis rounded up the children and sent them to an extermination camp, the Gestapo was willing to free him, and the Poles to hide him, but he went with his charges to Treblinka and died with them. Krochmalnagasse is remembered for the martyrdom of Janus Korczak.

"It is all gone now, of course. A vanished world, as Joshua called it in his book *Of a World That Is No More*. I have visited Warsaw many times since the end of World War Two, and there's hardly a trace of the life that once was there. When Isaac looked down from his balcony at the children playing, where the shops and the markets and the taverns were and where Isaac's father held his *beth din*, where once there were restaurants and nightclubs and *shinks*—that's what they called the bistros—there are now gray rows of Soviet-style apartment complexes, all the same, all modern and severe, all drab. The Germans razed everything after the Warsaw ghetto uprising, they leveled it completely, and the Poles rebuilt the area as a residential neighborhood. But no shops now, no taverns, no markets, no bakeries, no prayer houses. Only here and there you can see a house where a *mezuzah* was once fastened to the doorway, and the traces of it are there to tell you this was once a Jewish house. There is a Yiddish theater in the neighborhood, where the Poles come and listen to simultaneous translations over earphones in the same building that houses all Warsaw's remaining Jewish institutions. There are the offices of the *Folkshtimme*, the only Yiddish paper in all Poland. Well, there are only six or seven thousand Jews in Poland altogether—and their numbers in Warsaw you can count in the hundreds. In Tomaszow or Bilgoray or Leoncin you might still find a trace of the old flavor. But the Jewish section of Warsaw, Grzybow, is Jewish no longer. There is still a Krochmalna Street, but Isaac would never recognize it. The orphanage has been rebuilt and named for Janus Korczak, but otherwise he would find no trace of the life he has described."

Isaac has never gone back to Poland; he says he never will.

In the four years between his return to Warsaw in 1923 and the publication of his first stories, Isaac's will to survive was sustained by his undiminished curiosity and sense of wonder, by a growing interest in science that balanced his preoccupation with the occult and the mystical, by an indomitable sense of humor that counteracted his pessimism, and by the friendships and adventures that colored what might otherwise have been an oppressively drab existence. He had shaved off the earlocks and abandoned the traditional gaberdine of the Hasid and was eager to savor the ways of the secular world, test out his newly liberated mind and body. This did not take long. During the spring of 1924, he recalls, in A *Little Boy in Search of God*, he met "a man and a woman who came to influence my whole life."

The man was Aaron Zeitlin, a literary idol of Isaac's whom he met one spring day in 1924 when the two were standing in the only warm place in the Writers' Club, near a wall heated by an oven in the restaurant next door. Isaac knew the work of Aaron's father, the writer Hillel Zeitlin, a mystic with a strong interest in cabalism who believed that the Jews would stay united only if they kept their faith along with their hopes for a return to the Jewish homeland. Isaac had read his book *The Problem of Good and Evil* in Bilgoray and found in its pages "more philosophy . . . than in all the other books of this kind put together." His son Aaron was a religious poet—a great poet, Isaac still believes, admiring the depth and clarity of his work. Books meant everything to Aaron, whereas Isaac was beginning to think more about women and less about books. But they shared other interests. Both scorned the sentimentality of a Yiddish literature content to propagandize for social justice or nationalism. Both were interested in psychical research. Both believed in God as well as in "demons, evil spirits, in all kinds of ghosts and phantoms." And both regarded most of the Yiddish literati of Warsaw as provincial. The Yiddish critics disparaged young Zeitlin's work, just as later some of them would Isaac's. The only thing that dampened Isaac's admiration for Hillel was the poet's tendency to soften his opinion of any critic who spared him a bit of praise.

Isaac met the woman who was to influence his life at a time when he was torn by guilt, frustration, and confusion after some hasty, fumbling sexual experiments conducted "in an atmosphere of fear." It also seemed to Isaac that some occult force was at work, robbing everything he wrote of its importance, and he would tear up one manuscript after another in rage at what he regarded as total failure. "A day didn't go by," he says in A *Little Boy in Search of God*, "that I didn't contemplate suicide."

To make matters worse, Isaac was once again looking for a room. Everywhere he looked the rent was too high or there wasn't enough light or the place was damp and cold. The search became an endless climb up flights of stairs. There came a day when the idea of room-hunting was too much for him. He got up late and decided to go to the Writers' Club instead. He couldn't wait to get to the wall at the club, where the heat would stop his shivering. Once there, he sat down by his wall with a book on the occult. Suddenly his reading was interrupted by a young poet, who began jeering at the book in his hands as "opium to lull the masses." After a while the conversation took a more practical turn. Was Isaac still looking for a room? As it happened, the poet had a relative who wanted to give up hers. He described her as the daughter of a rabbi who had apparently lost her senses; a frustrated writer and painter who had gone through three husbands. Nevertheless the poet felt that Isaac really ought to look her up. Isaac put away his book and set out in search of her. The address the poet had given him was near the Jewish cemetery on Gesia Street. On his way there Isaac resolved that whatever he did, he would *not* get involved with this mad divorcée with her unwritten books and unpainted pictures. Still in his early twenties, he longed for a girl as pure and virginal as a drawing for a fairy tale, who would find out "about love" from him.

The courtyard he came to at last reminded him of Number 10 Krochmalna Street. The walls were peeling, there was a huge garbage bin in the middle of the court, and an old man was shouting "I buy clo' " at the ragged children. Isaac thought he could detect the odor of corpses. Soon he was climbing stairs again—three flights to a scabrous brown door. No one answered his knock. Then he heard a woman's voice behind him, turned, and saw the "lady of the house," a woman approaching her forties or maybe already in the midst of them. She wore a black dress that stretched to her ankles, and her red hair, wound into an unfashionable chignon, was topped by a black silk hat that would have been the last word in style half a century earlier. She had the whitest skin, and her eyes were green with flecks of yellow. "Her cheeks were sunken, her chin was narrow, her nose thin, her neck long, her red hair faded." Isaac was sure she had once been beautiful. She asked what Isaac wanted. He took out the piece of paper with the name the poet had scribbled on it: Gina Halbstark is the name Isaac gives her in his memoirs.

Gina (Isaac still prefers not to disclose her real name) opened the door to her tiny apartment, disappeared into the shadows of the windowless flat, and came back wearing a housecoat, her face freshly powdered. She granted that she wanted to let the room but pointed out that it was so dark it would only be suitable for a bat.

"I'm a bat," Isaac assured her.

One minute Isaac and Gina were strangers, the next they were as intimate as old friends. It turned out that they had read the same authors—not only the Yiddish writers Mendele Mocher Sforim, Sholom Aleichem, and Isaac Loeb Peretz, but also the novels of Tolstoy, Dostoevsky, Lermontov, and Knut Hamsun, the plays of Strindberg, and the works of Mickiewicz and such now forgotten Polish authors as Slowacki, Wyspiaski, and Przbysszewski. Gina had even read the writings of Israel Joshua Singer. She was also interested in the occult. Her bookshelves contained magazines and one book after another on the subject. Somehow the two of them did finally get around to the question of the rent, and it was arranged that he was to pay whatever he felt he could afford.

To complete a perfect morning Gina made lunch for Isaac, after which she accompanied him to the hall, where they embraced and kissed "with the fervor of reunited lovers," Gina whispering, "I know you from an earlier life." On a spring afternoon in Warsaw Isaac had found both a room and a woman to share it with him.

In Isaac's description of Gina in his memoirs one can discern the lineaments of many of the women who people his books—the faded beauty, the "genteel seediness," the impassioned nature, the penetrating intellect streaked with irrationality, the enthrallment with the occult. And as his own heroes so often do, Isaac began to fear that he would lose "the world to come" by his involvement with her. When they were making love, Gina would weep and sing and scream loud enough to wake the neighbors. She confided to him that she felt the desire to sleep with all her former husbands at the same time. Alternately she incited in him throes of lust and spasms of revulsion. He hated her and loved her. In succumbing to his passion for her, he felt he was forsaking his mission as a Jew, of "vanquishing nature and harnessing it in such a way that it served the Ten Commandments." Nature, instead, was vanquishing Isaac.

Gina told Isaac that when she had caught typhus during the war and the doctors had tried to poison her, her dead grandmother had come to her in a dream and forbade her to take the medicine they prescribed. And when she had lain ill with the flu, this same grandmother had cured her by magically filling a glass at her bedside with warm milk. Isaac found it hard to accept these tales, but she assured him that if he stayed with her he would see for himself that such things were true. She also told him that her dead grandmother had informed her that she and Isaac were going to collaborate on a book. Gina was obsessed with death and kept talking about a burial plot she wanted them to buy. She insisted on taking him to visit a Russian cemetery in Warsaw, where he was reminded by the legends on the gravestones how many had died young in the war. There she spoke to him of eternal life—inviting him home, in the next breath, for a plate of noodles and onions. Amid the rows of graves, with their faded photographs of the deceased, she put her mouth to his.

Gina and Isaac had just enough money to keep them alive. They would walk for miles, for even a streetcar was too expensive. They would buy food in cheap markets where black army bread sold for half price.

Then one day in 1924 Isaac got a notice to report for conscription. The idea of spending two years in the company of tough, ignorant peasants, away from books and the opportunity to write, away from Gina, horrified him. For Isaac, as he says in *A Little Boy in Search of God*, "a barracks represented a much harsher punishment than prison." It was above all his passion for privacy—and the shyness that pursued him into his adult life—that made Isaac hate the idea of the army. If he was drafted, he decided, he would kill himself. In the meantime he would starve himself until he was simply too weak to serve.

Hunger, according to Isaac, seemed to make him weak in every way but sexually. It also induced strange visions of giants in antique clothing who marched in a "cosmic funeral procession," and dreams of murders and pogroms. Yet when he woke up, it was always with lust recharged. He and Gina would stir at the same instant, and fall "upon one another with a hunger that astounded us."

Isaac's examination for conscription, which he describes in the opening pages of *A Young Man in Search of Love*, was an ugly experience. Christian conscripts denounced the Jews, who tried to appease them with chocolate, cigarettes, and compliments, and taunted Isaac when he undressed—in itself an agony for him: "My skin was unusually white and my hair as red as fire. Somebody gave me a slap in the rear, another flicked my nose, a third called me 'slob, jerk.' "

The military doctors who examined Isaac suspected he had been deliberately starving himself, but they deferred him for a year. Isaac couldn't believe his luck.

Back out on the street, Isaac stared at himself in the window of a furniture store and thought he looked like a consumptive or somebody who had just narrowly escaped death. Free of his anxiety about conscription, he began to think about his writing and to wonder how much longer he could go on as a failure. Passing a bookstore crammed from floor to ceiling with books, he wondered why the world needed another writer anyhow.

When he finally arrived home after a detour to the Writers' Club, an aggrieved Gina awaited him. It was true that her dead grandmother had already informed her about the deferment, but why hadn't he phoned her with the news? She had made him lunch, but it had grown cold. Alternately she scolded and kissed him. But Isaac fell into a deep sleep, and neither her kisses nor her insults could wake him.

In the spring of 1924 a new owner took over *Literary Pages*, and Isaac got a raise, so that he was able to pay Gina his share of the rent. Summer approached, and night came later and later. Warsaw sweltered in a heat wave. Isaac would lie awake while Gina tried her hand at automatic writing or mumbled the Hebrew prayers she still recited at bedtime. He would listen in the night for a revelation that didn't come. Then, one night, the formula did arrive, in a dream: "That which we called death was life, and that which we called life was death. The stone in the street lived and I was a corpse. The stone didn't hope or suffer; for it, time, space and causality didn't exist. It didn't have to eat; it needed no apartment; it was part of the mighty, extensive life that was the universe. That which we called life was a kind of nuisance, a poisonous toadstool that grew on old planets. The earth suffered from an eczema of its skin. From time to time it scratched itself, causing an earthquake or a flood, but there was no danger of this eczema penetrating any more deeply or infecting other planets. The prognosis was a favorable one. All that was required was that for a few minutes the earth should grow a few hundred degrees hotter or colder on its outer surface. The earth could easily manage this, but the eczema was so light and the earth so involved with its activities that she neglected to do this, since the eczema might one day vanish of its own. The symptoms of this eczema were quite familiar to the cosmic medicine—a little dust on the surface became ill and became transformed into consciousness, which in God's dictionary was a synonym for death, protest, goals, suffering, having, asking countless questions and growing entangled in endless contradictions." It was a theme Isaac would express later in his writing and which would culminate in the final chilling line of his second novel, *The Family Moskat:* "Death is the Messiah."

In the morning Gina came to Isaac fresh and cool to wake him from his cosmic dream and tell him that she wanted to have a child by him. Isaac didn't think he wanted to be the father of Gina's child; he was growing weary of her. He describes his disenchantment in *A Young Man in Search of Love*. She wanted him to marry her, to build her life around him. She became jealous and possessive. She even began to deny the affairs she had claimed she had had in earlier years and to assume a posture of virtue. Isaac decided to look for a room of his own and move out. He wanted a place to write and freedom to see other women.

One night, to get away from Gina, he walked through a neighborhood haunted by streetwalkers and examined the local denizens—a gaunt girl with a narrow face and sunken cheeks, a tall redhead wearing green boots and a yellow dress, a berouged but resigned young whore "obviously waiting patiently till the other two were engaged and her turn came. . . .

"Certainly it would be crazy, having Gina, to go with one of them and risk venereal disease. I barely had enough in my pocket to pay for a meal if I decided to eat out. But somehow, my pace slowed. I was seized by an urge for a strange body, for unheard words spoken by a different voice. 'Why fear syphilis?' a voice within me asked. 'You're not long for this world anyhow.' "

Isaac decided to follow the redhead into a narrow hallway—where he was nearly annihilated by a gigantic pimp who lurked in the shadows. With pounding heart and parched throat he escaped to the street and "vowed never to defy Him again." Half a century later this nether world of Jewish Warsaw would find its way into Isaac's novel *Yarme and Kayle*.

During the summer of 1924 Isaac fantasized about writing a novel in which the hero was in love with a number of women, but for a time he remained promiscuous only in his imagination. Then, in the fall of 1924, Isaac found a clean room with an elderly doctor and his wife on Dzika

Street, a sunny place with a view of the street. When Gina heard he was moving out, she grew hysterical, swore to end her life, and seemed suddenly to age as she cursed her lover and mocked her own misfortune. "For the first time," Isaac writes in *A Young Man in Search of Love*, "I grasped the fact that love was no game. Love killed people." Although Isaac continued to see Gina, the series of love affairs that followed left him little time for her.

Most of the women he responded to, then and later, were fiery creatures. He says he adored them all. "I always felt that two girls were better than one and three were better than two." Even so, no matter how many women there were in his life, each was to him an individual to be cultivated and pursued beyond the simple gratification of desire. Isaac could never have gone along with Louis-Ferdinand Céline's dictim, "Put a bag over their heads and they're all the same."

Isaac describes the women in his life in Warsaw in some detail in *A Young Man in Search of Love*, although he freely admits that he has changed their names and some of the events as well. First, there was Marila (as with most of the women in Isaac's memoirs, this was not her real name), a Polish girl who was a servant in the Dzika Street apartment. She was "tall with a high bosom and round hips," muscular calves, and pale blue eyes that "exuded a peasant strength." This girl with a "mouthful of wide teeth and dimples" who made up Isaac's bed every day and kept his room in order was not to be resisted for long. Marila was ready to oblige him with more than an occasional glass of tea.

Then there was "Miss Stefa" Janovsky. Isaac met her at a time when his brother Joshua had persuaded him that he really ought to go to Palestine. Things got to the point where the Palestine Bureau in Warsaw actually issued Isaac a certificate of immigration to Palestine, but since such a certificate was meant to be good for an entire family, the bureau stipulated that Isaac must marry first—either authentically or in name only. There were many marriages of convenience for this purpose. There would have to be a ceremony with a woman in Warsaw; they could divorce after they reached Palestine. Isaac had made such a strong resolve never to marry that "even a marriage in name only frightened me somewhat." But the bureau soon put him in touch with the Janovsky family, and he was interviewed by Stefa, a tough-minded woman a few years older than Isaac, with a snub nose, boyishly cut blond hair, and a preoccupied expression. Her lover, she explained, lived in Palestine, and she wanted Isaac to marry her so she could join him there. When she and Isaac got to Palestine, they could arrange for a divorce. As things turned out Isaac never did marry Stefa or become her lover, either, although he fantasized about the possibility—for one day she found out that her lover in Palestine was already married. She then confessed to Isaac that the same lover had left her pregnant. Now in her fifth month, she wanted Isaac to marry her anyhow. Thinking back on the affair,

Isaac believes he would have gone through with the marriage, mostly to save the woman's reputation, had she not met a rich textile merchant in Warsaw and married him instead. Isaac has always hated to disappoint anybody.

❀

March 25, 1976

Dear Friend John Reiss,

I certainly intend this time to keep my word, God willing. I'm going to California for a conference for writers of children's books, but I will see to it that I'm back home May 3rd. And I intend to leave for Winooski on the morning of May 4th. The only thing I would like to know is, how do you get from New York to Burlington? Perhaps I should go from Los Angeles to Boston and from Boston to Winooski? Please let me know how to go there because I have asked many people and they don't know where Winooski is . . .

When May 4 arrives, Isaac is off as promised on the plane to Burlington, Vermont, where he is to be met and escorted to Winooski for a day of appearances as guest lecturer at St. Michael's College.

At the tiny Burlington airport Professor John Reiss, Professor Ellen Cannon, and another young professor are waiting for him. Reiss wants to take Isaac to his home in Winooski to have dinner with his wife and six children. Instead Isaac insists on taking everybody to a restaurant in a local hotel and treating them all to dinner.

During dinner Ellen Cannon, a plainly, even rather severely dressed woman with a prominent nose, intense dark eyes, and brown hair worn in bangs, keeps saying to Isaac, "I really can't believe you're here." Although there are some Jewish students and faculty members at St. Michael's, Ellen feels isolated. She teaches political science but is deeply interested in literature, especially Jewish literature, and has written a thesis on the subject, which she would like Isaac to look over. He assures her he will do so before he leaves. John Reiss is a light-skinned, dark-haired man, middle-aged yet young-looking, quiet and serious, with a mild, attentive manner. His wife is a round-faced, friendly woman. The children, ranging in age from five up into the teens, are a well-behaved lot. John and Isaac are getting along quite well.

Suddenly a bat appears in the restaurant, sending the customers into a panic. Somebody springs up, grabs a broom a waiter brings, and kills the bat with the broom. Isaac is profoundly depressed. It is a long time before he can say anything at all. When he speaks, it is in sorrow, which he finds hard to conceal, over the loss of a creature who has died needlessly just because it couldn't open a window and escape. Crushed to death, like an insect . . . and one shouldn't even kill an insect.

The next morning Isaac delivers an open lecture attended by a large crowd of students. The subject is Yiddish—is it dead or merely sick? The students, as most students are, seem delighted with Isaac's lecture, especially with its humor, and linger on to ask him questions about his books and stories. Then he goes off with Professor Reiss and another professor, a published poet, to the local television station for an interview. By the time the interview is over Isaac feels rather tired but tries his best not to show it. After lunch, even though it's a cloudy day and a chill wind is blowing through the streets of Winooski, he is anxious to go for a walk. He turns down a country road, stopping to pat a large sleepy dog and talk to him. Isaac is beginning to feel sleepy himself and returns to his room at the Ramada Inn for a nap. When he wakes up, he leafs through a book of poems one of the professors has left with him. As he reads he grows more and more disturbed. Why, these poems are all about hunting animals! He cannot bear to look at any more and puts the book aside.

Before his evening appearance in the college auditorium Isaac attends a dinner in his honor in a softly lighted room where a fire is roaring in an open fireplace. At the candle-lit table Isaac chats easily with honor students and selected faculty members as he eats the vegetable plate prepared especially for him. He works in a few digs against the obscurity of modern novels and poems and answers questions quietly and affably. After dinner, though, as the time for his appearance nears, Isaac tenses up. He has given this particular lecture on folklore and literature many times, yet the prospect of a formal appearance still unnerves him. A professor of Latin who has gone out of his way to be friendly at dinner keeps trying to put him at ease, but it is impossible for Isaac to relax until his performance is over.

The lecture is read before a hushed audience and followed by a reading of "Sabbath in Gehenna" and the inevitable question period, with Isaac adroitly fielding familiar queries.

Afterward he stands about at a reception where wine and cheese are served, tired out but bravely maintaining an appearance of interest in all that the faculty members who have gathered around him—mostly women—have to say. As soon as he can he goes back to his room, where he turns the heat up as far as it will go. It is still rather early, but Isaac is soon sound asleep.

He is up at seven the next morning to have breakfast and keep his promise to Ellen Cannon, going over her thesis on Yiddish literature with her and making suggestions for revisions, a process that takes several hours. He also suggests to Ellen that maybe she should accept a job she has been offered in Boston, where she would have a better chance of finding a husband.

At the little airport John Reiss and his entire family turn up to see Isaac off. Isaac opens his suitcase and finds a chocolate peanut-butter cup he brought along in case he got hungry late at night. He hands it to John Reiss's five-year-old daughter, who is delighted. He is still playing and talking with the little girl when his flight is called.

Why did Isaac go to all this trouble? From California to New York to a little town in Vermont with no time to rest up or attend to his own writings? To Ellen Cannon's house when the sun was scarcely up, helping a woman he didn't know with a paper on a subject that was all too familiar to him?

"I hate to disappoint anyone."

❀

As he tells it in the pages of A *Young Man in Search of Love,* Isaac had taken a leave of absence from his proofreading job in order to marry Stefa, but when he found out about her marriage, he went back to work. The authors whose proofs he corrected were beginning to complain about the errors he overlooked, which they attributed to "spite and indifference." He was impatient with the rhetoric, the banality, and the Communist sentiments of the "trash" he had to proofread and was suffering headaches from the material he had to go through.

Gina, meanwhile, began to hint that her days were numbered. She grew thinner and weaker and became less interested in a sexual relationship. But there were other women to fill that need for Isaac. Many young women came to the Writers' Club to "strike up acquaintances with the writers and launch illicit affairs with them." Some of them, Isaac recalls, were married. Some wrote poems in Yiddish or Polish. Some were Zionists dreaming of Palestine, others.Communists longing for life in the Soviet Union. Some offered to translate the works of the Yiddish writers into Polish, some were actresses. Among them was the beauty Isaac calls "Miss Sabina" in A *Young Man in Search of Love.* She was "small and plump, with a high bosom, a short neck, a hooked nose, full lips and a pair of brown eyes that reflected the merriment of those who have little to hope for." Sabina smoked cigarettes, told jokes and racy stories, and typed manuscripts for the club members on a Yiddish typewriter. She supported a mother and two younger brothers. Isaac thought most of her stories were lies but later came to believe they might have been true. She spoke of an older writer who had been her lover, an impotent fellow with one lung and one kidney who had died shortly before Isaac took up with her. It turned out there really had been such a writer, and he had kept "a whole harem of mistresses." She also told Isaac that her mother, who rented rooms to aging bachelors, had once taken in a cousin, a girl who was supposed to be the daughter of a rabbi but turned out instead to be a Russian agent. One night police came to the house and arrested the cousin. According to Sabina, the girl managed to escape, got herself smuggled into the Soviet Union, and ended up as a high Soviet official. This remarkable cousin, it seemed, also had a voracious appetite for men and had carried on with all the old bachelors who rented rooms from Sabina's mother. Isaac couldn't help comparing Sabina's vivid tales with the naive and primitive provincialism of Yiddish literature. "The same writers who told astounding stories at the Writers' Club trembled the moment they took pen in hand lest, God forbid, they slip into melodrama."

For Isaac it was quite a year. While conducting an affair with Sabina and still occasionally seeing Gina, he also managed to visit the *zaftig* serving girl Marila in the kitchen where he rented his room "when the household was asleep"—even while he was still pledged to go through with the wedding to the pregnant Stefa.

When Isaac wasn't working at his job as a proofreader, visiting the Writers' Club, or spending time with one of his women friends, he haunted libraries, reading occult literature, alternating between skepticism and the hope that "sooner or later the truth would reveal itself to me." He had chosen two idols to serve—"the idol of Literature and the idol of Love" while his colleagues at the Writers' Club continued to worship "the idol of World Betterment." Sabina shared in this worship, although she hadn't yet decided whether she was a Stalinist, a Trotskyite, "or maybe an anarchist."

Sabina wanted Isaac to move in with her and her family. He hesitated to become more deeply involved with her, but he was making so little money that he could no longer afford his room on Dzika Street. It would be a practical step to move into Sabina's place, where the rent would be cheaper. But when he told his landlady he was leaving, she was disconsolate, and Marila was so hurt that he became filled with remorse and said he would keep the old room too.

How was Isaac going to pay for two rooms when he could scarcely afford one? In his memoirs he relates that at that crucial moment he was offered a job translating novels of suspense into Yiddish for the Warsaw newspaper *Radio*. This turned out to involve more than mere translation: For the Yiddish reader in Warsaw the actual locale of a novel had to be transposed to Warsaw; and if the characters were Germans, they had to be converted into Jews before *Radio*'s subscribers would read about them. Isaac met all the editorial requirements.

For some time Isaac continued to live with Sabina and her mother, sleeping at night in "a tiny room with a window facing a blank wall" in a house without electricity. Sabina and Isaac lived together as lovers, although she scorned romantic love and never spoke of marriage—and her mother served him lunches. Meanwhile, Isaac still had a key to Gina's apartment in Warsaw and saw her from time to time. In the summer of 1925, with Warsaw broiling in a merciless heat wave, Gina asked him to join her in a villa she had rented in the woods just outside the summer resort of Otwock. The idea of swimming and sunbathing on the shore of the Schvider River there didn't appeal to Isaac; his white skin would only blister and the sun's glare would hurt his eyes. He turned down Gina's invitation though he knew that she was ill, perhaps seriously, and his conscience bothered him.

Remaining in the city, Isaac saw less and less of Sabina and began to sleep alone in the room on Dzika Street. "I would waken in the night and give my imagination free rein." He thought about God and God's "divine attribute of creativeness." He decided that "creation is coupling and God must come together with his female aspect to produce birth." He dreamed of demons and evil spirits and "wild cruelties and scenes of horror words cannot describe" and would wake up "with a lust that astounded me." He would literally feel "the earth revolving on its axis, rotating around the sun," and he thought, "I am the earth, I am the sun, I am the galaxy; I am a letter or a dot in God's infinite book. Even if I am an error in God's work, I cannot be completely erased." He tried to communicate with Gina telepathically, begging her not to die.

That summer Isaac wrote a story called "In the World of Chaos." The hero was a corpse who didn't know he was dead but went wandering around Poland visiting country fairs and calling on rabbis, one of whom revealed to him that he was no longer alive. "Unbutton your gaberdine and you'll see that you're wearing shrouds," the rabbi told him. This story was never published in English, but Isaac was to write several others on the same theme, notably "Two Corpses Go Dancing." The theme certainly reflects his state of mind during the hot summer of 1925 in Warsaw.

Isaac relates in *A Young Man in Search of Love* how one afternoon he stopped by at Gina's apartment to see if there was any mail and found a letter from his father: "To my dear son, the scholar and man of substance, long may he live. . . . After I've wished you peace, I inform you that I must come to Warsaw to see a doctor since I am, may it not happen to you, not in the best of health. I'm suffering from stomach trouble as well as hemorrhoids and may the Almighty take pity and grant complete recovery to all the ailing of Israel. I've been away from Warsaw so long that I don't know if any of my old friends are still alive, since all kinds of misfortunes and plagues occurred during the war, heaven protect us, and I haven't received any letters from them in a long time. 'Thou knowest not what a day may bring forth.' I heard that a Dr. Sigmund Frankel is a great healer and they are all, as it is known, emissaries of God. I therefore ask you to get me an appointment for a visit with this Doctor and to meet me at the train that will leave, God be willing, on the evening of the 12th day of Tammuz and arrive in Warsaw on the morning of the 12th at 10 A.M. at the Danzig Depot . . ." Pinchas Mendel added that he feared there was "some growth, God forbid, that must be attended to."

Isaac didn't know what date it was. He finally got hold of a Yiddish newspaper and realized that it was already the twelfth of Tammuz, the very day his father was to arrive. In the letter his father had asked him to find a room where he could stay. It was too late to do anything about that now. Finally he leaped aboard a moving streetcar. The conductor snarled at him. He prayed that his father would still be at the station, and he was. Luckily he had run into the "rabbi from Kupiecka Street," an old crony, who had persuaded him to wait around for Isaac.

Looking at his father, Isaac found Pinchas Mendel older, his once-red beard now gray, his forehead "sallow and wrinkled as parchment," his back stooped. It was arranged for him to stay at the home of the Kupiecka Street rabbi. On the short ride there Isaac noticed that the houses had gone to seed. The rabbi's apartment reminded him of his childhood home on Krochmalna Street, smelling of chicory, onion, moldy bread, and gas. He left the two old friends to "discuss learned matters" and went off to arrange an appointment with the doctor.

Pinchas Mendel had brought along the manuscript he had been working on for years, his book of commentaries, which he called *The Righteousness of Rashi.* Joshua, now in America and working on the *Forward,* had been sending money home to his father, who hoped he had enough to publish his manuscript. But there wasn't much interest in such scholarship in the Warsaw of the twenties.

In *A Young Man in Search of Love* Isaac describes a walk through Warsaw with his father during the week before he went to see his doctor. Passing the windows of a secular bookstore, Isaac could sense his father's disapproval of the books on display and the sons he had fathered who would write more such stuff. But what could one expect with a Mitnagged mother? At least his sons had studied the Torah, and young Moishe was studying for the rabbinate. While they walked Pinchas Mendel looked with surprise at the groups of Jewish boys going by dressed in tunics and short pants and wearing the Star of David on their caps. The girls too wore short dresses that showed their legs. And they all sang—in Hebrew. When Isaac explained that these were young Zionists, his father's astonishment grew. Didn't they know they must wait for the Messiah?

As father and son continued their walk they passed a poster advertising a Yiddish operetta from America, and Pinchas Mendel commented: "That which we are seeing are the pangs preceding the deliverance." They went by a group of convicts sweeping a gutter in front of a prison, and this led to talk of good and evil, punishment and suffering. These things, Pinchas Mendel told his son, were riddles even Job and Moses couldn't solve. Then he asked Isaac whether there was a synagogue nearby; it was time for the evening prayers.

Isaac's father was not able to publish his manuscript, and the prescriptions he got from Dr. Frankel in Warsaw didn't seem to help him much. He was to die four years later in Dzikow. Meanwhile it was Bathsheba's hope that after her husband died Moishe would be able to take over his post. But a rabbi must marry, and she was having difficulty arranging the right sort of match for the intensely pious Moishe, whom his own father described as a saint among saints. Moishe at nineteen was even more unworldly than Pinchas Mendel himself. He "wore a wild beard and earlocks dangling to the shoulders, a gaberdine to the ankles, an unbuttoned shirt, and old-fashioned slippers." He was "tall, even taller than . . . Joshua; blond; with a rare white skin, big blue eyes, and well-formed limbs. He looked like the image of Jesus Christian artists had created. The gentiles in Father's town considered Moishe a holy man and that's what he actually was. Had there existed such an institution as a Jewish monastery, Moishe would have surely become a monk."

In their letters from Galicia, Isaac's parents kept telling him to get married, "but I was no better suited to be a husband than was Moishe." When he lived with Gina, she had darned his socks and sewed on buttons; now "I went about messy and buttonless. . . . I went days without shaving. My hair started to fall out."

The autumn of 1925 came, and Gina was still in the country. Then the secret came out: She was consumptive and anemic. A woman who lived nearby took care of her. When he visited her, Isaac slept on a cot. Gina no longer talked of bearing him a child. She said she had come to this place in the woods to die. But a friend of hers, another consumptive woman who came to visit, hinted that Gina was not as sick physically as she thought.

In any case Isaac went back to Warsaw.

Then he met Runya and fell in love. "She wasn't really a beauty according to the measures of our time," he says. "She was kind of short, and on the fat side, but she had a lot of life in her. She was a passionate woman."

Of their courtship Isaac has little to say. He does not even refer to Runya by her real name. He has not disclosed when he met her, and he is not willing to talk about the years he spent with her. In his fourth book of memoirs, *Lost in America*, there appears a young woman who bears Isaac a child, but she does not seem to resemble Runya much. Were Sabina and Runya really the same person? It's possible. Again, Isaac isn't saying.

What is certain is that Runya was the mother of Isaac's only child, his son Israel, born in 1929, the year of Isaac's father's death. Were they husband and wife? "Runya and I were never married by a rabbi," Isaac says. "But she was my wife. We were very progressive in those days."

Isaac describes Runya as a woman of exceptional vivacity but of mercurial temperament. They frequently fought, and when they did, it was more often than not on the subject of politics. Runya was a fervent Communist, whereas Isaac had been skeptical about Utopias from childhood (as he still is). Several times while he was living with her Runya was arrested on political charges. So many of her friends were Communists that Isaac was afraid he would be arrested too. And one day he was. He says he forgets now exactly how it came about. "I think I was supposed to go and be a witness about her Communist activities, or maybe to get in touch with the district attorney, and I neglected to do so, or didn't receive the message." At any rate Isaac was carted off to jail and spent a whole day behind bars—for the first and only time in his life. It is not a memory he cherishes or an adventure he would care to repeat. "It felt terrible to be there—just terrible. I was sitting with a few thieves at first, and then they put in a few Communists, and the Communists held a cell meeting on the spot and talked about saving humanity. I never wanted to go into politics, and that experience only confirmed my feelings about it."

Over the years Isaac and Runya lived together intermittently. They quarreled and made up many times. Finally Isaac moved out permanently. "It was dangerous to live in that house." That was not the end of their relationship, but monogamy was becoming more and more of a problem for him. He wanted to be free to consort with what women he chose. The song of the sirens rose up from the Vistula, and Isaac was unable to resist their tempting music.

Isaac, of course, did not devote all the time and energy of his young life to women. He devoted much of both to reading, some to writing, and when he wasn't reading or writing, to pondering the moral, religious, and philosophic questions that had plagued him since childhood—and continue to do so in his later years.

At twenty-one, he says in *A Young Man in Search of Love*, he bought an account book from a pushcart salesman and made in it all sorts of notations about everything from plots for novels and plays to "rules of physical and spiritual hygiene." He even recalls trying to put together in those pages a revised version of the Ten Commandments, which he expanded to twelve. He still remembers some of his improvements: "Do not kill nor exploit the animal, don't eat its flesh, don't flail its hide, don't force it to do things against its nature." His amendment to "Thou shalt not murder" reads "Control the birth of man and beast—He who said 'Thou shalt not kill' should have also said: 'Thou shalt not overly procreate.'" To the Seventh Commandment, Thou shalt not commit adultery, which he says has given him much trouble throughout his adult life, Isaac added that no marriage ought to last longer than fifteen years. "Right next to this piece of audacity I drew a creature with the antlers of a deer, the scales and fins of a fish, and the legs of a rooster." The pages of the book were also filled with calculations of how much money he would need if he were not to starve to death or have to sleep in the street or ask Joshua for help. But Isaac's mental life, for all his irrepressible playfulness and concern for quotidian practicalities, went deeper than that.

His reading had always been wide and varied. He had grown up, despite his father's disapproval, with the works of the great Yiddish storytellers. As a child he had read the *Book of the Covenant* in his father's bookcase, which described the theories of Newton and Copernicus. As he grew older he had read books on physics and astronomy. He went on to the cosmological theories of Kant and Laplace. From the books on religious philosophy he borrowed in childhood from the local library he had proceeded to test his mind on such difficult works as Maimonides's *Guide for the Perplexed* and Judah Halevi's defense of Jewish thought in the *Khuzari*. He had pursued his reading of Spinoza in Bilgoray. And during his proofreading period in Warsaw he had found Aaron Zeitlin a man with whom he could discuss philosophy.

Isaac had read Shakespeare in Yiddish along with the Russians—Gorki, Andreyev, Tolstoy, Dostoevsky. He knew the works of Mann and Hamsun and Romain Rolland, and now he became familiar with the works of Darwin and Marx. And he began to question given opinions about these writers.

Indeed in his proofreading days in Warsaw, as he describes them in *A Young Man in Search of Love*, Isaac started wondering about popular opinion on many subjects. He engaged in mental arguments with God, with the prophets, with organized religion and philosophy, even as he scrutinized the literary values he had up to then taken for granted: Was Shakespeare really such a great genius? Were Gorki and Andreyev such "pillars of literature"? Had Hegel really anything new to say? Those Yiddish household gods, Sforim, Peretz, Aleichem—were they really so wonderful? Had the species truly originated as Darwin claimed they had? Was there any substance to the assertions of Marx, Lenin, Bukharin? Was democracy indeed the best system? Could a Jewish state in Palestine really solve the Jewish question? Did the words *equality* and *freedom* really mean something, or were they merely rhetoric? "Was it worthwhile to go on living and struggling in this world, or were those who spat upon the whole mess right?"

On his visits to the Writers' Club in Warsaw Isaac would get into heated discussions about these matters with the Yiddish journalists who hung out there. "Nearly everyone here at the Writers' Club bore some passion and was blinded by it. The young writers all aspired to become literary geniuses and many of them were convinced they already were, except that the others refused to acknowledge the fact. The Communists waited impatiently for the social revolution to start so that they could exact revenge upon all the bourgeois, Zionists, Socialists, petit-bourgeois, the *Lumpen-proletariat*, the clergy, and most of all the editors who refused to publish them. The few women members were convinced that they were victims of male contempt for the female sex." Listening to them talk, Isaac decided that he was an anti-feminist.

Even when he recalls those days of youthful cynicism, iconoclasm, and bitterness, when he doubted more and more that the world was headed for a Utopian condition and claimed to foresee not only a second world war but "a third, a tenth," the playfulness in Isaac's nature will bubble up unexpectedly: "I came to doubt every belief that was fashionable—even theories of the day on raising children, or whether they ought to be raised at all. My sister-in-law, Genia, Joshua's wife, often consulted with her sister, Bella, and with neighbors about which would be best for Josele—to breast feed him or give him a bottle, to use this formula or that. But something within me asked, 'What for? Why? Why slaughter chickens, slaves, and kids and bring up people?' "

Coming to the conclusion that the "babble about a better tomorrow" simply masked the inescapable truth that might makes right, Isaac wondered how he could think of becoming a writer at all: "I no longer believed that God had issued the Torah on Mount Sinai along with all the innovations and restrictions that commentators and exegetes had added in every generation. Whether God was a substance with infinite attributes, or the absolute, or blind will, or whatever the philosophers chose to call Him, you couldn't depend on His justice and providence. I could never forget the tens of millions of people who had perished in the World War, in the Bolshevik Revolution, in the pogroms, the famines, the epidemics. Millions of peasants in Russia had been labeled kulaks and exiled to Siberia. Whole villages had been starved out. There was fighting in China, in Manchuria. In generation after generation people sacrificed their lives in battle, but nothing was ever realized. How did one become a writer in such a universal slaughterhouse? How could I write about love while millions of innocent creatures writhed in the clutches of butchers, slaughterers, hunters and vivisectionists of every ilk?"

Isaac had heard his brother say that nature "demonstrated no religion." Obviously nature cared nothing about the massacring of Armenians and Bulgarians, let alone pogroms against Jews.

Yet the old questions went on plaguing him: "Well, but how had nature become that which it was? Where did it get the power to watch over the farthest stars and over the worms in the gutter? What were those eternal laws by which it acted? What was light? What was electricity? What went on deep inside the earth? Why was the sun so hot and bright?"

On a chair next to his bed in those days Isaac kept a "history of philosophy and a number of other books which might help me restore order to my disturbed spirit." They lay in a pile—borrowed collections of Tolstoy's moral stories and essays, Spinoza's *Ethics*, Kant's *Critique of Pure Reason*, Schopenhauer's *The World as Will and Idea*, Nietzsche's *Thus Spake Zarathustra*, a book by the pacifist Foster, Payot's *The Education of the Will*, and volumes on hypnotism, autosuggestion (Coué, Charles Bedouin) and who knows what else—all of them works that touched on the essential. "I had even bought *The Path of the Righteous* by Reb Moshe Haim Luzzato and The Book of Deuteronomy, which I had considered the wisest work ever created by man."

Rummaging in bookstores, he came across still other books "that steered me in the direction I was to follow later." He discovered the works of a Professor Kraushaar, dealing with the false messiah Jacob Frank and his disciples. He read everything he could about the era of Sabbatai Zevi, whose example Frank had followed. He found books that described the punishments inflicted on witches; books about dybbuks. "In these works I found everything I had been seeking—hysteria, sex, fanaticism, superstition." Isaac was becoming something of a mystic.

Isaac had promised his father that he would live as a Jew. How could he reconcile all he had been reading and thinking with Jewishness? In *A Young Man in Search of Love* he sums up the conclusions he reached while still in his twenties: "The Jew personified the protest against the injustices of nature and even those of the Creator. Nature wanted death, but the Jew opted for life; nature wanted licentiousness, but the Jew asked for restraint; nature wanted war, but the Jew, particularly the Diaspora Jew (the highly developed Jew) sought peace. The Ten Commandments were in themselves a protest against the laws of nature. The Jew had taken upon himself the mission of vanquishing nature and harnessing it in such a way that it served the Ten Commandments. Because the Jew went against nature, it despised him and took revenge upon him. But the victory lay on the side of the Jew. Even if he had to wage war against God, the Jew would not desist. According to the Talmud, even a voice from heaven should be ignored if it is not on the side of justice. When the Jew knew that something was right, he dared oppose the Almighty Himself."

Recalling Spinoza's view that anything could become a passion, Isaac resolved "to become a narrator of human passions rather than of a placid lifestyle," to write about Jews, their sufferings, problems, trials, and aspirations, but to write about them as three-dimensional human beings with flesh-and-blood bodies as well as souls, appetites as well as minds.

"Contemplating what I knew of history and my own nature, I had [in my childhood] come to the conclusion that human beings are in constant need of adventure, change, risk, danger, challenge. The fear of boredom is as great and often greater than the fear of death. But is there a base for ethics in the face of that biological necessity? Aren't all commandments just wishful thinking? Can there be as much adventure in curbing the emotions as in letting them have their way? Can there be as much hazard in building as in destroying? Can man ever learn to indulge in the whims and excitements of his nature without hurting other people and animals? Many times I had decided that this was impossible, but I kept on returning to this problem of all problems which had been bothering me from my childhood. I still hoped against hope that science, art, technological advance, and permanent study of how to have fun without doing evil to others may replace the lust for murder, rape, treachery, revenge, and all the other destructive passions for which mankind pays such a terrible price. I was dreaming not only of a new philosophy, a new religion, a new social order, but also of new ways of amusing people and giving them the tension which they must have to be themselves."

"In later years," Isaac has admitted, "the suspense in my life and in my writing fused in such fashion that I often didn't know where one began and the other ended."

In any case, out of the contradictions in Isaac's character—his leaning toward the occult; his natural skepticism and sense of irony, and his keen, caricaturist's perception of human frailty, pettiness, and spite; his yearning for a world free of meanness and cruelty—there had already begun to emerge a storyteller's voice that was entirely his own. In that voice he would tell, ever more skillfully, suspenseful fables about people he had known and lived among since childhood, people who were in the thrall of their passions, who inhabited a country subject not only to the laws of nature but to the caprices of unseen powers—whether those powers dwelt in the Gehenna feared by the pious or in the unconscious part of the mind, the geography of which was even then being mapped by psychologists.

❀

July 20, 1976.

Scientists are jubilant over the news that the robot spacecraft Viking I has landed safely on the planet Mars 212 million miles away, and so is Isaac. He has been talking about it all afternoon, even since he saw the word MARS in giant letters on the front page of the *New York Post* with a picture of the desert Plain of Chryse where the Viking landed.

Isaac has scrutinized the story of the landing and is waiting anxiously for the next edition of the paper. "Ach," he says at first, "they're only going to find rocks there." After he has thought about it awhile, though, he expresses the idea that the planet Mars itself must be alive. After all, the earth is alive. It produces so much life—even Einsteins, Tolstoys—how can one think of it as dead? And if the earth is alive and Mars is alive, perhaps the two planets are lovers, as the Cabala suggests.

Maybe the scientists will find microbes with their experiments. But after all, what are we if not mere microbes? The human mind is only a tiny mirror and can reflect only tiny things. When microbes travel, naturally they search for other microbes. They conceive of the cosmos in microbial terms. We are miserable little germs taking nourishment from the earth, the living earth. Like tiny fleas living on the body of a dog, assuming in their narrowness that the dog must be dead because it is not a flea.

As the day goes on Isaac reveals his knowledge of astronomical distances—how far the earth is from the sun, and the distances between planets. All afternoon he can talk of nothing but the news from Mars. A fellow writing an article for a literary magazine arrives for an interview. Isaac virtually ignores his questions—questions he has answered countless times until he knows the entire routine by heart—and will talk to him only of Mars.

An aspiring photographer working as a model for Raphael Soyer (who is illustrating A *Young Man in Search of Love*) arrives to take Isaac's picture. He tries without success to engage her too in conversation about the scientific news and its meaning. Women, he says, seem to have no curiosity about these things.

Alma has gone off to Switzerland, is waiting for him to join her next week in the mountain village of Wengen, where they spend time each summer. In the evening Dvorah phones to tell him that if he will turn on his television set—he hasn't touched it since the two hours he spent recently watching the Democratic Convention—he will be able to see pictures transmitted through space by Viking I. Isaac fiddles with the set for a while but can't find the program. Impatiently he switches off the machine.

"Ach, they will only find rocks."

❁

What were Isaac's relations with Joshua during the decade after his brother got him the job as a proofreader in Warsaw? In his memoirs Isaac talks gratefully of the financial help and moral support his brother offered him. He writes of him always with admiration, even with reverence. Yet he also avoided seeing much of him.

When Abe Cahan appointed Joshua as Polish correspondent for the *Jewish Daily Forward*, his salary came to about fifty dollars a week, but this amounted to a considerable sum when exchanged for Polish zlotys, and "literary and journalist Warsaw," Isaac says, "seethed over my brother's salary." "One day he was a pauper," Isaac writes in A *Young Man in Search of Love*, "the next he was already considered rich by the indigent literary community. He wanted to help me, but I had resolved to live on my earnings. I actually avoided him, and the reason for this was my shyness. Known writers and young women who were admirers of literature used to congregate at his home. Most of these young women came from affluent homes, were fashionably dressed, smoked cigarets, spoke a good Polish, laughed loudly and kissed the men, and I was ashamed before them with my cheap clothes, my broken Polish, and my Yeshiva-studentlike bashfulness. They were older than I and they discussed me as if I were some curiosity."

During the hot summer of 1925, when Isaac refused Gina's invitation to join her in Otwock and stayed alone in Warsaw, there was a second invitation that he turned down—to be the guest of Joshua and his family in another resort called Schvider, not far from Otwock. Isaac explains why he refused: "My brother Joshua had gone to Schvider for the summer along with his wife and children, Yasha and Josele, or Joziek, as his mother called him. My brother had rented a villa from the Yiddish writer Alter Kacyzna. Other Yiddish writers and journalists were also vacationing in the area. From earliest childhood I had felt a powerful urge to be with my brother. Now that I had begun to write I was anxious to show him my work and consult with him. My brother was more than willing to help me, but I was somehow ashamed to face him both on account of my dealings with women and because of my writing."

There was more to it than that. The two men were very different. Photographs of Israel Joshua Singer taken in the late 1920s disclose a formidable figure, with cropped hair, burning eyes, a jaw as firm and square as a patriarch's, gazing solemnly into the camera. He was large-framed and still husky and muscular from the activity of those early years in the countryside of Leoncin. Next to him, the drawn, pale Isaac looks almost emaciated. Isaac's outlook on the world in those days was scarcely the same as his brother's. "He was far from an optimist, but he wasn't as pessimistic as I. He had a wife and children. Like many other liberals he hoped that despite all its insanities, mankind would move forward, not backward. But I spoke like a nihilist and a suicide, and more than once I evoked his anger." Isaac felt that his pessimism would cause his brother embarrassment. And there was his own embarrassment to think about—for the wives of the writers who frequented Joshua's villa "whispered about me and slandered me among themselves."

There also seems to have been a measure of envy in Isaac's attitude toward Joshua that he has never openly admitted in talking about him; envy not only of the stability of Joshua's life but of his literary achievements. When he was writing *Steel and Iron*, Joshua had shared the manuscript with Isaac, but Isaac had not shown Joshua beforehand either of the stories he published the same year in *Literary Pages*. When Joshua was working on his next book, *Yoshe Kalb*, in the early thirties, he again shared the experience with Isaac, who by that time was paying more frequent visits to him and Genia in their apartment on Leszno Street. "Once in a while," Isaac says, "he asked me for advice." Isaac would comb the libraries for texts of old incantations his brother wanted for the book while Joshua threw himself into the task of gathering and assembling background information on nineteenth-century life in Galicia. "In this," Isaac observes, "he resembled all the great realist writers, who never feel that they can know enough." Even then, however, Isaac did not return the compliment by showing his own work to Joshua. He feared that his brother would only laugh at what he was doing.

Yet Joshua's own literary development was going far from smoothly. After *Steel and Iron* he decided that he no longer wanted to write in Yiddish and created a scandal by sending off a letter to several Yiddish newspapers declaring that the attempt to create literature in Yiddish was demeaning for a writer. What point was there in writing in a dying dialect for a narrow-minded readership? He thought for a while of adopting Hebrew but was frustrated by the limited vocabulary of the ancient tongue, which had not yet—as it has today—found equivalents for twentieth-century objects. Joshua also tried French and German, but no books came of these experiments. Then, in 1932, he went back to Yiddish and wrote the novel *Yoshe Kalb* (*Yoshe the Loon*), which was an immediate success.

The richly colored, crowded canvas of *Yoshe Kalb* represented a startling change from the stark, war-ravaged atmosphere of *Steel and Iron*. In *Yoshe Kalb* the reader is drawn back into the nineteenth-century Galician town of Nyesheve in Austrian Poland. The town's sensual, cigar-puffing Rabbi Melech wants to marry off his plump, dull-witted thirteen-year-old daughter, Serele, to Nahum, the frail, nervous son of the austere and illustrious rabbi of Rachmanivke in Russia—so that he himself will be free to take his fourth wife, an orphan girl named Malkah. Despite the resistance of Nahum's mother, the wedding is arranged.

Joshua describes the heady Hasidic excesses that lead up to the wedding ceremony in vivid detail: the crowds of Hasidim singing, dancing, trading stories, praying; young Talmudic students donning the rotting Cossack uniforms that are stored from one wedding to the next and riding emaciated nags to greet the pale, shy bridegroom; and the ceremony itself, after which Serele wolfs down her broth while her terrified fourteen-year-old husband stares dumbly at his plate. Alone at last in the bridal chamber with Serele, Nahum can only mouth silently the word "Mama!" The celebrants have all but given up hope for the marriage by the time the petrified boy finally consummates the union.

Soon afterward Rabbi Melech weds the fiery, neurotic Malkah (in whom we recognize many of the traits of Hinde Esther). Living up to her nickname, Spitfire, Malkah refuses to shave her head, stubbornly withholds her body from her new husband, and throws one hysterical tantrum after another. Bored with life at the rabbi's court, she conceives a passion for Nahum—at once the man she has yearned for and the child to whom she has longed to give birth. By devious methods she seduces the inhibited young man and at last arranges a tryst with him in a moonlit forest glade.

But on her way to the rendezvous she snatches a candle from a lamp in a barn and flings it into a heap of straw—and as she lies with her lover, the Nyesheve synagogue burns to the ground.

When Malkah dies bearing Nahum's child, Nahum leaves town. His wanderings take him finally to the far-distant village of Biologura, where the beadle of the synagogue takes him in tow and sets him to work sweeping, fetching wood, and drawing water. He nicknames the withdrawn, seemingly imbecile boy Yoshe the Loon. Virtually the beadle's slave, the abjectly penitent Nahum spends what little time he has to himself reciting prayers, fasting, and mortifying his flesh.

Nahum ignores the advances of the beadle's half-witted daughter, Zivyah, a vast fleshy woman with matted hair who wants Nahum "in a simple, shameless, animal way," but Zivyah persists, telling the villagers that Nahum is her husband. Eventually, however, she finds an outlet for her lust elsewhere. When she discovers that she is pregnant, Nahum is blamed; it is his sin, the villagers believe, that has caused the epidemic fever that is killing their children, and they force him to marry Zivyah.

Soon afterward Nahum flees the town. And fifteen years later he returns to Nyesheve to reclaim Serele. But the Biologura tribunal catches up with him, and he is tried. Is he, the tribunal asks, Nahum, Serele's husband, or Yoshe, Zivyah's husband? A wise man in the village answers: "You are Nahum and you are Yoshe; you are a scholar and you are an ignoramus; you appear suddenly in cities and you disappear suddenly from them; you wander in the cemeteries in search of your own kind and you steal through fields at night; and wherever you come you bring with you disaster, terror, pestilence; you unite yourself with women; you flee from them and you return. You know not what you do; there is no taste in your life or in your deeds, because you are nothing yourself, because—hear me!—you are a dead wanderer in the chaos of the world!" The next day, Nahum-Yoshe disappears from Nyesheve, now indeed a dead soul and a wanderer, reviled, rejected, dispossessed forever.

No two heroes could be more different than the activist, extroverted Benjamin Lerner of *Steel and Iron* and the hermetic, self-mortifying, introverted Nahum of *Yoshe Kalb,* yet both are misfits who can find no place for themselves in the world, both rejects of rigid societies that cannot accommodate them.

In contrast to *Steel and Iron,* with its bitter, rigid prose and two-dimensional characterizations, *Yoshe Kalb* is a hypnotically compelling work, glowing with color, life, and suspense, and peopled with whole, convincing characters drawn in a sharp, unflinchingly realistic focus quite new to Jewish literature at that time. It is as though in writing *Steel and Iron* Joshua had purged himself of his anger at man's inhumanity to man and thus freed himself to accept life as it is—and to present it as it is, with the objectivity of the true storyteller. *Yoshe Kalb*, like Joshua's memoirs, is both a fascinating book and a reliable record of a vanished world, portrayed in all its convoluted piety and coarse vitality.

With the publication of *Yoshe Kalb* Joshua became something of a literary celebrity. He sent the manuscript to Cahan at the *Jewish Daily Forward* in New York, and Cahan accepted it, beginning the long tradition of publishing the brothers Singer in serial form. Chapter after chapter held the *Forward* readers fascinated, and soon the Yiddish Art Theater decided to adapt the book as a play. Maurice Schwartz negotiated for the rights himself, made the adaptation, and played the part of Rabbi Melech. It was, in fact, as a play rather than as a novel that *Yoshe Kalb*, produced for Yiddish-speaking audiences in a number of countries and eventually in English on Broadway, won world-wide popularity. But Joshua heard (and would soon see for himself) that Schwartz's adaptation had turned the story into something of a spectacle, with a great deal of emphasis on production and stagecraft and very little on the interpretation of character—rendering it a pageant rather than a serious drama. From then on Joshua would adapt his novels for the stage himself.

In 1933 the New York publishing firm of Liveright brought out *Yoshe Kalb* in English. Unfortunately, as Isaac points out in his introduction to the 1965 reprint, Liveright decided to call it *The Sinner*, "an insipid title that robbed the book of many of its chances for success, since thousands of readers knew of the book only as *Yoshe Kalb*." (It was reissued in 1965 by Harper and Row under its original title.) He recalls that the English-language version of the play was a failure too, "perhaps because all those who wanted to see the play could still see it in Yiddish. I was not in America yet, but my impression was that Broadway tried to turn *Yoshe Kalb* into vaudeville, with dancing girls and songs." Even the success of the original with the Yiddish-reading and theater-going public was not unmixed. The book's serialization in the *Forward* drew scores of letters praising the achievement, the play ran on and on to packed houses, but left-wingers attacked the novel and the *Forward* in the same breath for publishing it. The Stalinists, as Isaac has commented, "seemed to consider this one newspaper and its writers the only major obstacle to the coming of the revolution."

Cahan now wanted Joshua to come with his family to America, and they decided to take him up on the invitation. And so in 1933 Joshua, Genia, Yasha, and Josele packed to go to the States. But a deep shadow fell across their elation over this forthcoming move. Shortly before they departed Yasha fell ill with pneumonia. Suddenly, at fourteen, he was dead. It was a terrible blow on the eve of venturing forth to start a new life in a new land. The grief-stricken couple and ten-year-old Joseph left for New York in a state of shock and gloom.

Isaac too, left behind in Warsaw, was plunged into melancholy. Although he had not shown Joshua any of his new work, he still regarded his older brother as his mentor. Without him, he recalls, "I was a limp man without a crutch."

Isaac read the letters Joshua sent from America and his articles in journals from abroad with wonder and perhaps more than a twinge of envy. The staff of the *Forward*, Yiddish theatrical circles, and a worshipful public were paying homage to Joshua as a genius, while back in Warsaw Isaac was still struggling along with his articles and translations.

In truth, Isaac was doing more than that. With his friend Aaron Zeitlin he had started a magazine called *Globus*, and in its pages they published a number of Isaac's short stories. More important, Isaac had been busy all that year writing a novel of his own.

❀

In his first novel, *Satan in Goray*, Isaac's preoccupation with mysticism, his grounding in Hasidism, and his admiration for the works of Dostoevsky and Poe converged in the creation of a Gothic tale of demonic possession unlike any other in Yiddish literature. The story begins in 1648, when the Ukrainian Cossack hetman Chmielnicki is leading a revolt against the Polish gentry, slaughtering men, women, and children. Men are flayed alive, and women are tortured by peasants who rip open their bellies and sew cats inside—a gruesome image that recurs in a number of Isaac's tales. At the same time, just as the Holocaust and the rebirth of Israel will occur in symbolic conjunction centuries later, the celebrated cabalist Sabbatai Zevi announces that he is the Messiah and that the millennium is due in 1666.

A number of years after the Chmielnicki pogroms, the Jews of Goray return to their ravaged city. Among the survivors are Rabbi Benish Ashkenazi, the descendant of a long line of rabbis who is "reckoned among the most brilliant men of his day," and Reb Eleazar Babad, once the leader of the Jewish community and its richest citizen, who returns with his only remaining daughter, the seventeen-year-old Rechele, a girl with black hair down to her waist, large dark eyes, a lame left foot, and a greenish complexion. Rechele is one of those astonishing women who so frequently inhabit the pages of the books of both Singer brothers. When there is a storm, she screams and hides under a bed. When neighbors come to visit her, she turns them away with total indifference. She sits alone knitting or reading Hebrew books. When we learn more about Rechele's background, we are not surprised at her eccentricites or even at the hysteria that is to overtake her later.

Born in Zamosc in 1648, the very year of the Chmielnicki pogroms, Rechele was taken in flight from the slaughter, in her mother's arms, to Lublin. When she was five, her mother died, and she was adopted by her uncle, a ritual slaughterer named Zeydel Bur, and raised by his mother-in-law, a ninety-year-old deaf hag "with a waxen, shriveled face, full of moles and clumps of yellowish hair." This woman told Rechele frightful tales of ghosts and demons, wild beasts, and cannibals roasting children on spits, beat her, and administered other sadistic punishments: "Every Friday afternoon the old woman would force Rechele to put her head into the trough, now filled with hot water, and Rechele would scream until she was hoarse." Rechele spent much of her time locked inside a dusty bedroom listening to the scratching of mice and "other small sounds, as though a hand groped its way through the darkness." She even saw the same sort of chimney sweep who frightened Isaac in his childhood, grimacing "blackly, like a devil," his eyes "all white as though the eyeballs were turned up."

Her uncle, a tall man with heavy eyebrows and black beard that reaches all the way to his waist, makes his entrance into the story in a coat covered with blood and feathers, holding a knife in the corner of his mouth. In the courtyard where he does his slaughtering stands a bucket of blood. "Butcher boys in red-spattered jackets, with knives thrust in their belts" move through the courtyard shouting. Slaughtered chickens still flap their wings after death. Dying calves smite the earth with their hoofs. Rechele sees two boys skinning a goat, which lies there "with eyeballs protruding in amazement and white teeth projecting in a kind of death-smile." Sometimes Rechele sees her uncle testing his blade with his index finger.

This theme of the horror of slaughter is to recur in Isaac's writings again and again, a stark answer to the question of why he turned early from eating meat, or even wearing a fur collar on a winter coat.

When the neurotic Rechele grows up, she is reunited with her father, Reb Eleazar. Back in Goray with him, she is courted by a devout ascetic named Itche Mates, who fasts a great deal and hardly ever sleeps. Rechele consents to wed Itche, but he is unable to consummate the marriage.

Itche, a fervent cabalist, believes—as do many of Goray's Jews—that Sabbatai Zevi is the Messiah and that the apocalypse is imminent. Rabbi Benish rejects this view and forbids his congregation to study Sabbatai Zevi's mystical commentaries. This arouses the wrath of his chief enemy in town, Reb Mordecai Joseph, who denounces Benish as a heretic, plunging the old man into a melancholy that leads him to forsake his congregation—and ultimately to desert Goray. Then another man, Reb Gedaliya, in every way the opposite of the abstinent, ascetic Itche Mates, and like Rechele's uncle, a ritual slaughterer, arrives from Zamosc to urge the citizens of Goray to serve God through joy, overthrowing their ancient customs and indulging their senses. Reb Gedaliya sets the pace by seducing as many of the local women as he can. If Itche is the soul of abstinence, Gedaliya is his opposite. He passes off impure animals as kosher, encourages sin, plunges the whole community into promiscuity and self-indulgence.

One June night in the midst of the general saturnalia Rechele is awakened by the voice of an angel. She rises from her bed and proceeds to the study house, where she falls on her face, and a strange voice issues from her throat prophesying that the Messiah is to reveal himself that very autumn at the time of the Jewish New Year.

License and hysteria soon reach a fever pitch, and those who so far have doubted that Sabbatai Zevi is the Messiah are converted, or intimidated into silence. Both Mordecai Joseph and Itche leave Goray to bear the good tidings to far-off places. The licentious Reb Gedaliya is the hero of the hour. As Rechele lies in bed reading holy books whose pages turn of their own accord, he comes to her naked, "wearing only a skull cap," lifts her white silk gown, kisses her feet, and tells her, "Rechele, it is midnight. The heavens are parting. The Divine Parents are coupling face to face. Rechele, be of good cheer. This is the hour of union. . . ."

The Messiah does not appear that fall, but as the Feast of Tabernacles follows the New Year, Goray is deluged with disasters. Icy winds tear shingles from the roofs; children fall ill, mainly from eating the meat that Gedaliya has foisted on the town; an oily yellow vapor rises from a swamp; darkness overtakes the sky on a holiday morning; hail falls, thunder peals, and lightning flashes; and a fault is discovered in the prayer-house wall. Mordecai Joseph and Itche return to Goray in rags and report that Sabbatai Zevi has gone to Constantinople and converted to Islam. Reb Gedaliya says they are lying.

Now Goray is divided. It becomes "a den of robbers, an accursed town": The children play macabre jokes, and hoodlums try to rape an old woman. There is famine in the town. Houses burn down, polecats bite infants, bears and boars lurk in the roads, thieves run rampant.

In the final chapters, spun out in the archaic language of an apocryphal Biblical tale, Rechele is entered by Satan and possessed by a dybbuk. Reb Gedaliya abandons her. At last the dybbuk is driven out, and Rechele dies exhausted.

Satan in Goray is a universal parable, to which all readers everywhere can respond. Its moral? Isaac, who is never to do so again, spells it out clearly on the final page: "Let none attempt to force the Lord: to end our pain within the world: the Messiah will come in God's own good time." Rabbi Benish Ashkenazi, who is driven out of Goray by reason of his piety, sanity, and moderation, provides the only example worth following. Itche, with his self-flagellation, and Gedaliya, with his self-indulgence, are pied pipers who can only lead their followers to disaster.

Much has been made of the symbolism in Isaac's first novel, but the magic of the tale is less in its symbolic meaning than in its telling. Through the skillful use of evocative detail the author has transformed what might have been an abstract fable into an experience. Not only is *Satan in Goray* rich in vivid, convincing descriptions of things, places, and people—characters, unlike Joshua's, who are fully human from the waist down as well as from the waist up; it is haunting in its imagery: Long after the reader has forgotten the plot, he will remember the smell of poverty in the hovel in Lublin where Rechele grows up, the odor of death in a graveyard, and the perfume of nature on a summer evening. And unlike Joshua's work, *Satan in Goray* is enriched by fantasy. While the fantastic phenomena in the novel might well be the products of the deranged minds of its characters, Isaac makes it clear that they are to be understood as objectively real events: Rechele's history is certainly fertile ground for hysteria, but the dybbuk that possesses her is a real dybbuk. Isaac would cease to insist on the objective reality of demons, witches, and dybbuks in his family novels, but he was to return to it later, always with increasing control of material that in less certain hands would have been absurd.

If *Yoshe Kalb* is a richly embroidered, closely worked tapestry, *Satan in Goray* is more like a series of tableaux etched in luridly colored glass and set out for our inspection in a long narrow gallery of dark-glassed Gothic windows.

It is interesting to compare the bored, spiteful, malevolent, and impassioned Malkah of *Yoshe the Loon* with *Satan in Goray*'s Rechele. Isaac grants that both of them were inspired in part by Hinde Esther but feels there is more contrast than similarity between them: "Malkah is sane but greedy for life, for enjoyment, while Rechele is a nervous wreck with a kind of sexiness which hysterical, neurotic women sometimes suppress in themselves." Certainly both women are startling, even terrifying creatures to encounter in Yiddish fiction contrived by the sons of a Hasidic rabbi in Poland; their true emotional sisters—Jael, Jezebel, perhaps Delilah—may be found in the pages of the Old Testament but never in the tales of Isaac Loeb Peretz, Israel Zangwill, or Sholom Aleichem.

Although he did some research before writing *Satan in Goray*, Isaac asserts that not too much was necessary, since he had grown up with the subject matter. In *Of a World That Is No More* Joshua tells of a time in Leoncin, while Isaac was still an infant, when news came of pogroms in Russia and the unspeakable atrocities committed: infants tortured, patriarchs hacked to death by axes, the bellies of pregnant women slit open. When a scroll that had disappeared from the local prayer house turned up in a pond, the Jews of the village became convinced that the nadir had been reached and the Messiah was on his way. The Russo-Japanese War, the pogroms, the revolutions—all the omens were right. Pinchas Mendel set about searching for symbols and portents in his holy books while Bathsheba looked on with cool skepticism. Scholars checked Pinchas Mendel's interpretations and found them "irrefutable." The Jews of Leoncin stopped studying, attending to business, and mending their roofs. "Flushed, beaming, exultant, Father painted the coming world in vivid, glowing pictures to hushed crowds in the house of worship." There was no certainty as to the exact manner in which the Messiah would arrive, but he would come in the Jewish year 5666 (1906). Some thought a huge cloud would appear, and the Jews would board it and take off for Israel. Others insisted that the great Temple destroyed in Jerusalem by the Romans would descend from the heavens, miraculously restored, that Judaism's saints would be brought back to life, and that men would spend their days in rapt study of the Torah. Those who were looking forward to an end of their poverty and spending the remainder of their days contemplating their newfound riches, riding around in carriages and attending banquets, found this vision disappointing. Joshua himself would rock Isaac's cradle, imagining it was a wagon that would take the family—including their little sisters dead from scarlet fever—to the Holy Land: "I steered the cradle so recklessly that more than once I dropped Isaac on his head, with who knows what dire results."

As the final month of the year 5666 approached, the townspeople watched every cloud in the sky for a portent. But the year passed without the Messiah's materializing. It was a terrible disappointment. Joshua himself was "enraged and embittered." All that came to Leoncin after the Days of Awe in the year 5667 were torrential autumn rains and economic hardships.

Having heard about all this, along with the disputes that broke out continuously during his childhood about other claimants to the title of Messiah—including one local rabbi actually suspected of being a secret disciple of Sabbatai Zevi—Isaac did not need to look far to find the ingredients of his tale.

Aaron Zeitlin serialized *Satan in Goray* in 1934 in the magazine *Globus*. By the time it appeared in book form, issued by the Warsaw P.E.N. Club in 1935, Yiddish readers in Warsaw were well acquainted with it. The reviews were largely favorable, although some critics expressed a certain puzzlement over the strong element of sensuality in the tale, and complaints soon started coming in from readers (they have never ceased) that Isaac's writing was too preoccupied with sex and matters of the flesh. Many also let it be known that they would have preferred a more flattering portrait of Jews and Jewish life.

In an article in *Commentary* for June 1960 Irving Howe noted that the Jewish reading public in Warsaw was uneasy about the "grotesquerie," the sexuality, and the fascination with false messiahs in Isaac's writing. Yiddish literature, says Howe, "is a literature devoted mainly to humanism, to rationalism. It tends to be a little puritanical in regard to sexual matters. And here comes along a writer like Isaac Bashevis Singer, who populates his novels with imps, with devils, with Satans, with seizures, epileptic fits, false Messiahs—all kinds of strange creatures that a nice Jewish mother wouldn't let into her house. The Yiddish reading public has always been uneasy with him—admiring him and yet recognizing that there's a very great spiritual distance between them and him."

For all Isaac's shyness about showing Joshua any part of the manuscript of *Satan in Goray*, his brother proved to be one of the book's strongest champions. He thought quite highly of it.

By 1934 Isaac's life with Runya in Warsaw was coming to an end. She wanted him to move to the Soviet Union with her and their son, Israel, but Isaac wouldn't hear of it. He had never felt any enthusiasm for communism, especially the Russian brand. He reminded Runya that when *Yoshe Kalb* came out, the Stalinists had promptly attacked it as a roadblock on the highway to world revolution. The Soviet Union would prove to be a hell, not a Utopia. And so the quarrels between Isaac and Runya grew ever more bitter and more political. Then, early in 1935, Isaac received an invitation from his brother to join him in America and start a new life there, and the prospect seemed infinitely more attractive than continuing life with Runya. And there seemed little else to keep Isaac in Poland, for he had all but lost touch with his family. His brother Moishe, at thirty-one, was now a rabbi. Before his death in 1929 Pinchas Mendel, who had not deigned to comment on Joshua's writings when they appeared, had never so much as mentioned Isaac's stories in his letters or congratulated him on their publication. And Hinde Esther and her son, Maurice, were off in England. Then too, Isaac, who had traveled much in Poland (to Lublin, Cracow, and the Baltic Sea in his twenties), visited Denmark, and gone by boat to Sweden, wanted to see more of the world. Poland was beginning to seem like a prison to him. Perhaps most compelling, the shadow of Hitler was lengthening across Europe, and Isaac foresaw imminent disaster for Poland's Jews. He opted for America.

Before he could leave, there were forms to fill out, interviews with officials to get through, the usual red tape. Joshua sent an affidavit guaranteeing that Isaac would be taken care of in New York. The P.E.N. Club in Warsaw helped him to obtain a passport. Before this document was his, he had to assure an official that he would be able to support himself in the States: "I told him I would be writing books, making speeches, living like a celebrity. I thought at the time I was lying to him, but later it all came true."

In early spring 1935 Isaac set out for Paris on the first leg of his journey westward, and Runya, as Isaac once told Irving Buchen,* "took my son and went off to that new haven which turned out to be a butcher shop."

Runya was later expelled from the Soviet Union, accused of fomenting Zionist activities, which was as strongly discouraged in Stalin's Russia as it is in Brezhnev's. Worse might have happened to her, but relatives who had once done time in Polish jails for Communist activity were able to intervene

* *Isaac Bashevis Singer and the Eternal Past.*

on her behalf. Exiled, she fled with her son to Turkey and later to Palestine, where her mother lived. And, in Isaac's words, "There she and my son stayed. I did not see my son again until twenty years later."

❀

The Lotos Club is housed in a comfortable old townhouse in the Sixties, just east of Manhattan's Central Park. A winding staircase leads to the reception room and library where the P.E.N. Club usually holds its cocktail parties honoring the publication of new books by its members. On this winter afternoon in 1975 at the start of a cold December the bar outside the library is thronged with members of New York's literary establishment. Six authors are being honored today, and their books, as is customary, are displayed on a table: *Foresights*, by Gerald Sykes; Hortense Calisher's *Collected Stories*; Jean Dalrymple's *From the Last Row*; David Dempsey's *The Way We Die—An Investigation of Death and Dying in America*; *A Kind of Order, a Kind of Folly*, a book of essays and comments by the poet Stanley Kunitz; and *Passions*, the latest collection of short stories by Isaac Bashevis Singer.

In the library itself, lined on all sides with books written by members of the club, a wall-to-wall crowd of authors, editors, publishers, and their friends are indulging in their favorite occupation of literary gossip. The room is spacious but warm and cozy in the mellow lamplight. Poet Muriel Rukeyser, current president of P.E.N., goes over to Isaac, who is beaming as he chews on a cheese-covered cracker and holds court before a well-dressed circle of admirers. Isaac, who has told Muriel more than once that he is very fond of her but can't understand a word of her poetry, accepts her congratulations, shakes hands, and asks slyly, "Are you still mixed up in leftist causes?"

"He always needles me like this," Muriel says. She decides this time not to rise to the bait, inquiring only whether he's enjoying himself.

Isaac finishes his cracker and waves a glass of ginger ale expansively. "I'm thriving," he says, "on adulation."

❀

July 27, 1975

The road winds north from Tel Aviv through the eastern Jezreel Valley in Galilee to Kibbutz Bet Alfa at the foot of Mount Gilboa. Bet Alfa, which was founded in 1922 by Jewish pioneers from Poland, lies serene under the hot July sun, its sprawling fields, acres of vegetables, flowering gardens, and rows of one- and two-story buildings arranged in neat patterns. The Bet Alfa settlers grow wheat, olives, grapefruit, and cotton, raise fish, and keep cows and chickens. There's even a factory where elderly residents manufacture thermostats for refrigerators. The feeling here is one of lush growth, of peace and prosperity. Yet Kibbutz Bet Alfa is close to the borders of Jordan and Syria, and only a week ago several terrorist infiltrators from Jordan eluded capture here. Even so, only the sounds of lawnmowers and the shouts of playing children disturb the stillness.

In this voluntary agricultural community, where there is no such thing as private wealth and the kibbutz itself is responsible for meeting the needs of its members, lives Israel Zamir (Hebrew for "singer" or "songbird"), the only child of Isaac Bashevis Singer. Israel, his wife, Aviva, and their four children occupy a two-room apartment in a group of modest buildings surrounded by tree-dotted lawns. Their flat is furnished simply in functional modern style, flooded with light, and surrounded by grass and flowers. The living room has coffee-colored walls, windows with green curtains and yellow shutters, a bright-orange Danish rug, and a smaller, waterproof carpet for the baby, Yuval. The walls are decorated with paintings by friends.

Israel Zamir—whose nickname is Srool—has the blue eyes and red hair that run in the family, a pink, freckled face, a blunt nose. His stocky but trim figure is decked out for the country in a blue sport shirt and orange shorts.

On this Sunday afternoon the apartment is crowded with children—three of Israel and Aviva's and three more who belong to Aviva's sister and brother-in-law—all here for a birthday party in honor of Israel and Aviva's fourteen-year-old daughter, Mirav. The festivities are over now, and Mirav has gone off to visit friends in Haifa. Her brothers, Noam, eleven, and Elan, five, and the baby, Yuval, born six months ago, are blond and good-looking. The blond hair comes from the Singer side of the family. Aviva, a strapping, down-to-earth, high-spirited woman who exudes good health and good humor, is dark-haired.

Sunday is important to the children, for it is only on weekends that they get to live full-time with their parents. The time is also precious to Israel, who spends four days a week in Tel Aviv editing the weekend magazine section of the newspaper *Al Ha-Mishmar*. Even though he travels hundreds of kilometers a day from Bet Alfa to Tel Aviv and back so as to spend his nights with his family, he longs all during the week for his weekends with his kids.

"It's different on a kibbutz," Israel says. "You have to gain the love of your children. Our son Noam, for instance, is here every day from four thirty in the afternoon until seven thirty in the evening. But he comes of his own accord. He could get his food and sleep in the children's house with the others, so you see, it is an honor that he visits us. We have to talk with him, play with him, supply him with toys, pay attention to him if we want him to keep coming every day. I have to earn his love."

Four mornings a week Israel leaves Bet Alfa after breakfast at about 5:30 A.M. It takes several hours to drive to his office. He covers feature assignments personally, edits the copy of the several reporters and editors who assist him, reads proofs, goes over the graphics with his staff artist, Leah. He writes much of the copy himself: "Everything not signed is mine." Thursdays he spends in the composing room, putting together the two-color, twenty-four-page supplement. In addition Israel has translated his father's novel, *Enemies, A Love Story*, into Hebrew. He has also prepared the Hebrew versions of more than a score of his father's short stories. And he does some writing of his own, including fiction, although at this point he feels (and his father tends to agree) that he has more of a talent for journalism than for literature.

One day a week Israel works in his garden. Sometimes he serves in the communal kitchen or helps out with other community chores. Several years back he held the highest post at Bet Alfa—secretary of the community. Today his responsibilities are more peripheral.

How did this forty-six-year-old son of Isaac Singer get to Bet Alfa in the first place? "I was five years old when my mother took me to the Soviet Union. We went there in part because she had a sister over there. And she was interested in the Soviet experiment. But while there she translated some literary work into Russian that displeased the authorities, and she spoke up about Jewish affairs, and was denounced as a Zionist, so one day we were given just twenty-four hours to get out of the country.

"We went to Istanbul, without papers, without a visa. My grandmother—my mother's mother—was living in Palestine and after eight months was able to send the papers that made it possible for us to come to this country. We went to Tel Aviv, and for the next two years we lived with my grandmother. I went to religious school.

"Later, when we moved to Jerusalem in 1940, to please my grandmother, who was quite religious—in fact, my mother's brother was a rabbi—I was enrolled in a yeshiva. Then, in 1942, I was sent to a children's farm run by a woman named Shaeyar who worked for the Hadassah organization. It was a lovely place in the country, cool, kind of like a park. In 1944 I graduated from the school there and went to Tel Aviv, where I hoped to learn a trade. For a year I went to electrician's school. I was not very good at it. I spent more time with the Haganah, the group that was struggling for Israel's independence, than I did studying.

"In 1946 my mother decided to send me to this kibbutz. I was sixteen. I went through the tenth and eleventh grades here at Bet Alfa. My mother still lived in Jerusalem then. When the war of liberation began, after the UN partitioned Palestine and the Arabs invaded us, I stopped going to school. Meanwhile my mother met a businessman who lived in Haifa. They married and went to live in Haifa, where she had another child. She has lived in Haifa happily with her husband ever since then. She never saw my father again. She doesn't want to see him. She's not angry at him, but they are not friends."

In the 1948 War of Independence, Israel fought with a unit whose mission was to secure the kibbutzim in the western Negev and to control the water lines to those settlements. Particularly vivid in his memory is a battle that took place near the Gaza Strip, over a hill known as Hill Number 86. "There I was," Israel remembers, "in army uniform, in the Negev, dividing my time between manning a machine gun against the enemy and serving in a Negev hospital."

In 1955 Israel went to America to see his father for the first time since he was five years old. Isaac tells about that meeting in his story "The Son," written in 1962 and published in English in his short-story collection *A Friend of Kafka and Other Stories* in 1970: The ship from Israel was due in at noon, but it was late. The day was hot, and it was raining. It seemed to the waiting father that every Jew in the world was down at the dock, expecting some passenger or other: ". . . assimilated ones, and rabbis with long beards and sidelocks; girls with numbers on their arms from Hitler's camps; officers of Zionist organizations with bulging portfolios; yeshiva boys in velvet hats, with wildly growing beards; and worldly ladies with rouged faces and red toenails. I realized I was present at a new epoch in Jewish history. When did the Jews have ships?—and if they did, their ships went to Tyre and Sidon, and not to New York. . . ."

The ship didn't get in until evening. The father, waiting all that time, recalled how the mother of the boy had taken him off to Russia all those years ago. The son had sent a snapshot, but it was blurred. Was he tall or short? Was his hair still light, or had it turned dark? The boy spoke only Hebrew; it would be necessary to look up words in a dictionary in order to converse with him. Then suddenly the son appeared, and "something screamed in me . . . a fatherly love awoke in me."

Father and son embraced on the dock, "and his stubble rubbed my cheek like a potato grater. He was strange to me, yet I knew at the same time I was as devoted to him as any other father to his son. We stood still with that feeling of belonging together that needs no words. In one second I knew how to treat him." The father was amazed at his own memory of Hebrew words. As they rode home in a taxi through the New York night the father felt he could read his son's thoughts. "As if to try out my telepathic powers, I said to him, 'There are no accidents. If you are meant to live, you have to remain alive. It is destined so.'

"Surprised, he turned his head to me. 'Hey, you are a mind reader!' "

Writing of that reunion in *The New York Times* on April 17, 1970, Israel Shenker disclosed that Israel Zamir had written and published his own story about that meeting and the correspondence preceding it in *Al Ha-Mishmar*.

In that account Israel said he had known his father over the years only from letters and from what his mother had told him. When they met, Israel observed that "he wanted to come close to me and he found that he was offending me. His Hebrew was strange, a mixture of Talmudic language and the Hebrew of the Enlightenment." Israel had been embarrassed by his father's style and had destroyed his letters. "Sometimes for Rosh Hashanah or for a birthday he would send me a few dollars, possibly when he was overcome by a feeling of fatherhood or guilt."

Up to this crucial hour Israel had felt little affection for his father. When he thought about him at all, he imagined him as "one of those American tourists who come to the kibbutz, with a very luxurious car, and through the window you can see the back of a fat neck. . . . the man stays for a short while, praises everything in a loud voice, spreads boyish smiles all over the place, and leaves as he came, in a cloud of dust, amid the children's dreams about the magical life across the ocean."

Landing in New York, Israel noticed a group of Hasidim chanting songs and wondered whether his father had reverted to being a Hasid with a long beard.

During the taxi ride home on that rainy night flashes of lightning mingled with the glare of neon signs. Israel was oppressed by the silence that hung between them. A cold sweat ran down his arms, and he wanted to explode the "rocks of silence, to tear down the barrier." But he didn't want his father to know how he felt.

Israel recalled his harrowing flight out of Russia and the cheap hostelries where he had stayed in Istanbul, and how it felt to be without a country, without papers, without money. Then, upon learning that during World War II his distant father had been beset by nightmares in which he saw his wife and son being sent off to Auschwitz in a convoy, he forgave his father for having failed to send money when he and his mother needed it, for the years of separation, for all of it.

What did Isaac think of the story? He told Israel Shenker that his son had some good phrases but that he tended to mix his metaphors, writing, for example, that a boat made its way like a blind man and shook like a drunkard. "I say either you compare the ship to a blind man or to a drunkard. You cannot do the two things together. He writes that there was 'an abyss' between him and his father. I say 'an abyss' is not exact. If you say 'abyss' it should be a real abyss. He says 'a mountain of strangeness.' In literature, a mountain is a mountain." Isaac has always been suspicious of metaphors.

And what does Israel Zamir think of his father's writing? "His first novel, *Satan in Goray*, was translated into Hebrew and was not a big success in this country. It didn't make a big impression on me either. Then in 1959 I read *The Slave*. I was shocked by it, by how different it was from the first book, and I came to admire his writing." He has never read his father's work in Yiddish. "I can read the letters, of course, since they are the same as

Hebrew, but I don't understand the language. I tried to learn it but couldn't; I had to give up."

Now, in the waning July afternoon at Kibbutz Bet Alfa, Israel and Aviva have said good-bye to her sister and brother-in-law and their children. The air is drenched with the smell of flowers and sweet grass. The family moves outside to the lawn. Noam climbs up into the branches of a tree. In her plain summer dress Aviva relaxes on the lawn with the baby Yuval in her arms.

Israel is speaking of his first visit to America. He stayed in New York for two years, working for a Zionist youth organization that prepared American youngsters for life in Israel. When he returned to Israel, he went back to Bet Alfa, where he was asked to prepare himself for a career as a teacher. "I didn't want that at first, but afterwards I agreed, and I went to study in a seminary for teachers near Haifa." It was there that he met Aviva, who came from a kibbutz called Magen in the Negev. She too had been sent to the Haifa seminary to pursue a teaching career. They were married eight months later.

In 1967 Israel went to America once more to work for the Jewish Agency. At the same time he sent back dispatches as a correspondent of *Al Ha-Mishmar*, reporting on the civil rights movement, the death of John F. Kennedy, the thriving rock culture—sending back reports on the American scene as he saw it.

After three years in the United States Israel returned to Bet Alfa. "They asked me to teach Hebrew in a little town. I taught American youths and, later, Russian youths. I kept on writing too—features, what you call human-interest stories."

Israel went to Germany in 1974 with a group of newspapermen, but it made him uneasy. "I had always felt that the gates of Germany were the gates of Dachau. And when I got to Germany, as a matter of fact, the first thing I did was to visit Dachau. I went alone. The rest of the time in Germany I kept realizing that we must establish relations with the Germans again but . . . it is hard to forget. I can see another holocaust, maybe not from the Germans, and once again nobody will give a damn."

After a time Israel, who says he hasn't spoken so much English in years, returns to the subject of his visit with his father in 1955: "You know, he wasn't so famous yet in those days. And I had fought in a war, I considered myself a *mensch*. How could I accept the authority of this man? But it turned out that from the beginning we treated each other not as father and son but as friends."

Israel has indeed made friends with his father and come to admire him ("I think he is a great writer") and is pleased though not overwhelmed by Isaac's fame. One gets the feeling that there is very little life might devise that could overwhelm Israel Zamir.

A walk through Bet Alfa in the deepening twilight. The whole of the kibbutz is a tamed garden, almost an Eden compared with some of the raw and primitive settlements elsewhere in this country. Summer breezes blow down from the mountains, and only the twittering of birds breaks the stillness. In the public dining hall Israel eats a dinner made up mainly of vegetables grown here on the land. He admits that sometimes he gets bored with kibbutz life, but he sees enough of the hectic city, and the life here is ideal for the children. "The education they get here is wonderful. All day my son, for example, is involved in constructive activities. And then there are the hours he spends with us—voluntarily. He couldn't have such a life in a big city. He won't get fed up with his parents the way so many American children do. And he isn't spoiled."

Back at the apartment Aviva talks a bit about herself. She was born in Tel Aviv and spent a number of years in Israel's youth movement. The group she grew up with went to the army together and later shared life on a kibbutz. After she married Israel, she was able to fulfill some of her dreams of travel—they went to New York together and later to Paris. Aviva enjoys painting and reading. She and Israel have had a television set for about six months, but they don't watch it very often. They like documentaries, news shows, and historical programs about the pioneering days in Israel. They never attend services at the synagogue on the kibbutz, although they do celebrate the Jewish holidays at home with the children and join the rest of the kibbutzniks in dancing and singing at Jewish festivals such as Purim and Chanukah.

Aviva sees certain similarities between her husband and his father: "They both have the red hair, of course, and the same eyes. They both have strong characters and a sense of humor. Israel jokes a lot, and people like to joke with him. With his father it's hard to tell when he's joking and when he's being serious."

Despite the twinkle in his blue eyes and his interest in writing, Israel does not seem as much like his father as Aviva says. He is sober, serious, stable almost—but not quite—to the point of stolidity. He enjoys his family and would rather be at home with his children than anywhere else. He is fond of facts. Neither whimsy nor fantasy appeal to him particularly. He is at ease in the world of Bet Alfa, indeed in the world of modern Israel, and does not give the impression that he ever thinks of himself as an alien or an outcast. He believes wholeheartedly that his people have a future, but that they will have to fight for it on their own, with little help from others. He is a gentle man, and on the surface seems—as Isaac does sometimes—a simple man. But it is evident from what he says and what he writes that he too sees through appearances, that he shares his father's wariness of all that is glib and facile in human nature. He is certainly an Israeli—pragmatic, skeptical, matter-of-fact, down-to-earth; at the same time, he is informed, alert, sensitive, and capable of great kindness to those who win his trust.

It is dark now, after a plum-red Galilee sunset, and time to leave Bet Alfa. Israel says, "By the way, I have a message for you from my father. [Isaac has recently been there on one of his twice-yearly visits.] Before he left he asked that you please do not try to get in touch with my mother in Haifa. But when you get back to Tel Aviv, you should call my cousin Maurice Carr. Incidentally, he had an article about my father published in *The Jerusalem Post* earlier this month. If I can find my copy, I'll be glad to give it to you . . . Yes, here it is. Perhaps you can read it before you get in touch with him. Here's his number."

❀

Maurice Carr, the son of Hinde Esther, doesn't wish, as it turns out, to talk about his Uncle Isaac. Over the telephone in Tel Aviv, speaking with a brisk, clipped British accent, he says, "This subject no longer interests me," and hangs up abruptly.

Isaac left Israel a few weeks ago rather peeved with his nephew Maurice. The Hebrew University had invited Isaac to Jerusalem to receive an honorary degree. He had arrived with Alma as an honored guest, only to be confronted with a copy of *The Jerusalem Post* for July 4, containing "an intimate pen-portrait of the popular Yiddish writer . . . written by his nephew, Maurice Carr."

Maurice, writing in a brilliant if somewhat ornate style, starts off his "pen-portrait" by declaring that he believes if Isaac had his way he wouldn't be anybody's uncle, brother, son, husband, father, or grandfather. He then describes what he calls a "prenatal memory" of his "Uncle Yitzhak lying somewhat shamefacedly in bed with a young woman, with his mind on a story and the air thick with demons." The young woman is his own mother, whom he is comforting because she has seen evil spirits in the dark. Later in the article Maurice—who was born in 1913 and grew up in London—describes a visit to Warsaw in 1926, where he sees his "Uncle Shiya" [Joshua] and "his Uncle Yitzhak" [Isaac], then twenty-two and already "fought over by the girls." Isaac takes Hinde Esther and the thirteen-year-old Maurice to see a Yiddish play, where Isaac "looks away from the stage; the foolishness it offers is not for him." They return to spend the night in Joshua's apartment. "Early in the morning two girls turn up, one plump, the other scraggy. They have a tug-of-war over [Isaac]. Each girl grabs a hand and pulls for all she is worth. He stands there, arms spreadeagled in a silent crucifixion, and on his face a curious grimace of taunting anguish.

"I feel sorry for him. I needn't worry. Yitzhak is an escape-artist, the sex-Houdini. The plump girl gets herself pregnant. He has to go and live with her. It is as if she had fettered him in chains, locked him away in a cell behind bars. But he wriggles out and is off, off to the next liaison and the next. . . ."

Not one to leave things half said, Maurice describes the character of Yasha Mazur in his uncle's novel *The Magician of Lublin* as "a variant of Yitzhak himself, a genius, an agonized prankster, tricky, fickle," and goes on to disclose that in the summer of 1969 Isaac paid a visit to "a cherished mistress, a Holocaust survivor," in Israel. He describes Alma as a "lovely, highly cultured, long-suffering wife." He quotes Isaac as saying "If a father wants to sleep with his daughter, why shouldn't he? We are all governed by our passions." He also quotes his uncle as telling him that "nothing brings two men so much together as sharing the same woman."

Not all the article in *The Jerusalem Post*, to be sure, is devoted to such scandalous revelations. There is a charming description of a search party's hunt for Isaac, who has disappeared into a pine wood during a stay at a summer bungalow outside Warsaw. They find him "sitting high in a tree. With the agility of a monkey, he clambers down from his favourite retreat." There are glimpses of Isaac doing impersonations of "one Yiddish writer after another" for the entertainment of a summer crowd, the disclosure that Joshua once nursed Isaac back from incipient tuberculosis, and recollections of interviews Isaac gave during one of his visits to Israel "in the press, on radio and television," of his invitation "to the table of President Zalman Shazar," and of his lectures at the Hebrew University.

The article also reports on a reunion between nephew and uncle in Paris in 1947. Maurice remembers Isaac "traipsing around with a violin which he has bought as a gift, but will not deliver for years yet" to his son in Israel. They talk of the Holocaust, and Maurice quotes Isaac as responding "as it were, with the Kaddish, the prayer for the dead, which ignores death and exalts life. Instead of lamenting the six million dead, he speaks of life triumphant: 'There is going to be a Jewish State, and thanks to Jewish intelligence, and Jewish diligence, it will be the most advanced country in the Middle East.' "

What prompted Maurice to compose so frank and undiplomatic a "pen-portrait" of his uncle, timed for publication just when Isaac was to be in the country to be honored by a university? Perhaps it was a Rosh Hashanah visit in Maurice's home one fall when Isaac said to his nephew, "à propos of nothing, 'Your mother was mad as a bat.' " There's no way of knowing; at the moment Maurice refuses to be interviewed.

Maurice Carr does agree to an interview a year later, in the spring of 1976, when the Canadian Broadcasting Company is preparing a special radio feature on Isaac Singer. On that occasion he points out that the family really had more than two talented writers. Pinchas Mendel was a writer;

Moishe was a writer as well as a rabbi; and Hinde Esther wrote an autobiographical book called *Der Shaidim Tantz* (*The Demon's Dance*), of which her son thinks highly. Even Bathsheba, he tells the CBC, was more than the storyteller Isaac describes; she too could write. During a visit in Warsaw "she confided to my mother that she had written her autobiography, she had taken years doing it. But in the end she had destroyed it because she felt it was profane. As a deeply religious woman, she felt this was the right thing to do."

Maurice tells his CBC interviewer that Hinde Esther was not terribly impressed with Isaac as a child, because "he was very small" and "very taciturn." She described him to Maurice as "terribly pale . . . a wisp of a child . . . freckled, with red sidelocks hanging down to his shoulders," following everyone about, eavesdropping behind doors, and "saying nothing." Not everyone, however, was unimpressed with Isaac as a boy. The day he was found up in a tree reading a book, Hinde Esther remembers somebody saying in a stage whisper, so that Isaac would be sure to hear, "Isaac is really the great man of the family. He's going to surpass his brother."

Speaking of Isaac's work, Maurice, who has been one of his uncle's many translators and works as a correspondent in Tel Aviv, expresses the belief that Isaac's ability as an entertainer sometimes "interferes with his quality as a writer."

He goes on to talk about Joshua's relationship with Isaac: "It was not so much the relationship of an elder brother to a younger but [that of] a wise father to a lost child. And Isaac, I believe, smarted under that but accepted it, because he is, at bottom, a very practical man. He knew that I. J. Singer was terribly vain. He also knew that people were trying to spoil the relationship between himself and I. J. Singer. . . . And he was very, very careful to play second fiddle . . . to accept the role of the lost child who is listening to the wisdom of his father. He was even, I think, ready to flatter I. J. Singer, because his older brother had wonderful qualities, but he also had one quality that marked the entire Singer family with the exception of the father—my grandfather—and that was tremendous vanity. Isaac has his vanity, but he's able to mask it. I. J. Singer had this vanity, but he was not able to mask it. And Bashevis was very, very careful to keep on the right side of I. J. . . . very, very careful indeed.

"Not until I. J. Singer's death [in New York in 1944] did Isaac's talent really blossom forth. It was as if some kind of clamp had been taken off him spiritually and he was free and he was able to develop.

"I don't want to give the impression that Isaac did not love his elder brother . . . but within this love there were all sorts of complex emotions and fears and jealousies and attachments and enslavements."

Maurice also points out that Isaac, although he gave up the earlocks and the Hasidic way of dressing and living while still on the threshold of manhood, has never really broken with traditional Judaism. "He had not rejected his upbringing; he had simply outgrown it. If he meets a man on the street on a dark night, and if he knows that this man believes as a Jew and believes in God, he'll feel a hell of a lot safer than if he thinks that this man is a Jew and an unbeliever. He is still very much part of the Jewish tradition—we see it in his work."

Maurice agrees with Isaac that Hinde Esther was plagued all her life by bad luck—in Maurice's words, "as if truly haunted by demons, which so arranged things that at the very moment she was born a black cat threw a litter of kittens at the foot of her bed." Isaac, he says, once noted that even when he dedicated his book *The Seance and Other Stories* to his sister, the inscription was misprinted "In memory of my beloved sister Minda Esther." When they talked about this, Maurice says his uncle smiled like "a Jewish mephisto" and declared: "God does not bother with the speck we live on; it's just a trivial speck in the universe to him. He has delegated the management to a petty functionary, an angel with clipped wings, who is a first-class muddlehead and messer. What can you do about it?"

Hinde Esther's life does seem to have been lived under the influence of some sort of curse. It was never easy for her, and it was hell for her son. In a letter to Isaac dated January 14, 1952, when Maurice was nearly forty and living in Paris, he describes the epileptic fits from which his mother suffered for some twenty years. In the early 1940s, he says, these fits gave way to attacks of panic, which developed into delusions of persecution. At times she seemed in perfect possession of herself, and Maurice wondered whether the illness might be feigned. But he soon realized that it was not so, and he refused to give up the hope that her condition could be cured. He took her to great specialists in Paris and London, who confirmed she was severely neurotic but not psychotic. She also lost the sight of one eye from a cataract but refused to undergo an operation for its removal. Maurice says he could not bring himself to urge the operation on her, since her heart was weak and there was no telling whether she would survive the anesthetic.

Maurice reminds Isaac that Bathsheba was little more than a child when Hinde Esther was born. He says he does not know why, but for some reason Bathsheba took an instant dislike to her first-born. The baby was placed in the home of a wet-nurse, an overcrowded environment where she was kept in a crib under a table. Maurice believes that dirt from the underside of the table got into Hinde Esther's eyes, blinding her for a time and causing the condition that in later years produced the convulsions—always preceded by fits of blinking—and ultimately the cataract. According to Maurice, Bathsheba told Hinde Esther that she had left her with the wet-nurse for three years, visiting her only once a week and never picking her up.

Maurice claims that when he was thirteen, on a visit to Poland with his mother, he overheard Bathsheba say, "I now see you're a very pretty woman, Hindele. I wonder why I used to think you uglier than Yenta?" (Yenta was the village idiot in Leoncin.)

Maurice also tells Isaac that he believes Hinde Esther's parents simply married her off to a man on whom they had not set eyes until twenty-four hours before the wedding. His mother, he is certain, never really cared for his father, Abraham, and they grew further apart as time went on. Abraham was a healthy man, but life was turning out to be bitter for him too. His alienation from Hinde Esther left the burden of her care on Maurice's shoulders. Until Maurice married at twenty-six, he lived at home with his parents, and his mother's needs took priority over everything else in his life. Among other things, he translated her novel. He sacrificed his youth and his own dreams on her behalf, trying all the while to keep his suffering to himself.

Maurice's marriage was a blow to Hinde Esther. On whom could she lean now? Maurice and his wife, Lola, lavished all their love and attention on their daughter, Hazel. And out of concern for the child's peace of mind, Maurice felt he could not move his family into Hinde Esther's home. Nor could he imagine bringing his mother to Paris to live with them. He had suggested that she spend part of her time in Paris, part in London, and part at some seaside resort, but this didn't suit her. When she put up at a Paris hotel or at a beach resort in England, her feelings of persecution only increased. Maurice writes that he has just returned from a visit with her in London, where, he discovered, she was as unhappy as ever.

Maurice goes on to thank his uncle for the money he has forwarded him from time to time. He speaks of a job he has taken with the *London Jewish Chronicle* and additional work with two small Israeli journals. He hopes that the income will make it possible for him to provide his mother with a regular allowance. And what does he want from Isaac? If his uncle is planning to make another visit to Israel during the forthcoming summer, could he please stop in London to visit Hinde Esther, and perhaps make time to come to Paris, so that he and Maurice can discuss her condition.

Hinde Esther Kreitman died in the 1960s. Her husband is still alive.

❀

"My visits to Israel," Isaac says on his return from Bet Alfa, "refresh my spirits. I see my son there, my grandchildren, and that is most rewarding. At first I also used to travel all around the country, but now I am content to spend most of my time in Tel Aviv. It is enough for me to stroll through the streets and look at the faces of the people—I never tire of watching them."

On one of his visits to Bet Alfa Isaac gave a lecture on Yiddish. "People say that Yiddish is dead, but a big crowd attended the lecture, and people wanted me to come again and again. On one trip to Israel I made a speech about Yiddish and the part Yiddish played in the Zionist movement, as well as uniting Jewish people everywhere in Europe. How can you forget a language that was a vital part of five hundred years of your history? There's a Yiddish newspaper today in Israel called *De Letze Newes* [*The Latest News*]. It's selling well. It's the only paper outside of *Ha'aretz* that gets no subsidy from the government. *De Letze Newes* supports itself."

In Israel, Isaac also lectured on Jewish literature. Immigrants from the Soviet Union were in the audience. "I met Joseph Kurler and his wife after the lecture. Kurler is something of a symbol of the Jews who have left Russia in recent years. He is a poet. He spent six years in a labor camp—for no sin except that he is a Yiddish writer, a Yiddish poet. Now, all these writers who have come from the Soviet Union know only one language that matters to them: Yiddish. They can speak some Russian, but they've no use for that language, especially in Israel. Immediately they try to publish something in Yiddish. The labor organization Histadruth publishes a magazine called *Die Goldener Keit* [*The Golden Chain*]. These intellectuals from the Soviet may well bring about a revival of interest in Yiddish as a legitimate, living language. And why not? Aramaic isn't quite forgotten—and didn't the Jewish people speak Aramaic as long as they've spoken Yiddish? Aramaic is actually a part of the Hebrew language."

Isaac was not surprised to learn that many of the new immigrants were reluctant to settle in outlying areas. "Baron de Hirsch tried to persuade Jews from Russia to found farm colonies in Argentina, and I can understand how they felt. Only in Israel have Jews ever been persuaded to love villages and settlements. But a Jew must be able to visit a city often—even from the moon."

While he is on the subject of cities Isaac says that it seems to him Tel Aviv is becoming more and more like New York. "Every time you cross Ben Yehuda Street you take your life in your hands. True, on Yom Kippur you don't see a car in sight. But New York streets are pretty empty on Yom Kippur too. If you didn't see all the Hebrew signs in Tel Aviv you might think you were on Delancey Street or even upper Broadway. There's so much enterprise—the kind of initiative that, in fact, built New York. If only there would be peace, they would work miracles."

Some of the indications that Israel is a modern nation please Isaac—the fact, for instance, that the young men of Tel Aviv wear their hair and dress "just like the younger generation in Paris, London, Rome, or New York." But he is alarmed that there are robberies and murders in Israel, even though Theodor Herzl is supposed to have said that a nation is not really a nation until it has its own thieves. "These are not patriotic thieves who steal just to show that Israel has thieves like any other country. They don't care

about Israel, these thieves, only about their pockets. And I don't like it when
the ultra-Orthodox throw stones at people riding in cars on the Sabbath either. A man who throws stones at a car is not really a religious man. But
Israel, with or without special laws being passed in the Knesset, is a deeply
religious country."

Isaac believes that the political events of recent years, from the hostility of
the Soviet Union to the hijacking of Israeli planes, terrorist massacres, and
anti-Israel developments in the United Nations, have caused the "evapora-
tion of leftism" in the Jewish State. "You don't see pictures of Lenin in the
kibbutzim; nobody thinks communism is going to save the Jews, or anybody
else."

Israeli culture, Isaac feels, will grow and deepen under the influences of
the intellectuals who have poured in from Eastern Europe. "After all, a
country in the process of formation, under the constant threat of war, is not
such a good soil for the development of talent. This will happen later.
Much of the culture in Israel today is borrowed culture. I went to the opera,
but it was an Italian opera. Eventually what is produced in Israel will be
uniquely its own contribution."

Isaac is confident that courtesy, like culture, will develop in the Promised
Land in time. "In restaurants today, the waiters are just as rude as the kind
that used to stand over the customer in Jewish eating places on the Lower
East Side, telling you what to eat. Manners—that will come also."

And the women of Israel? "They're not idlers, and since they serve in the
army, they're not softies. But I will tell you, in Tel Aviv you see plenty of elegant women; Israeli women are not masculinized, but they're not *yentes* either. Russian women find the adjustment easier than other newcomers
exactly because they're used to holding jobs."

Isaac is skeptical about the existence of demons in the Promised Land.
"The climate is so beautiful and there is so much sunshine I think they
would have great difficulty in Israel. They like overcast skies, old houses. I
have looked for demons in the Jewish State, but I have found very few.
Someday, when Tel Aviv is older, the houses will be suitable for demons. In
Haifa, perhaps never. . . . In Safed, that town in the mountains founded
by the medieval mystics, there they would be at home. But Safed has a big
population of angels too. The demons wouldn't like that."

Demons or no, and even with the thieves he reads about in the Israeli
press, Isaac feels safe in Israel. "I was never afraid to walk the streets at
night. Israel is the only country—even under the constant threat of war—
where a Jew can feel completely safe, completely at home.

"America is my country. I wouldn't trade my American citizenship for all
the money in the world. But in Israel, I will tell you, I feel good. The lives
of Israel's Jews are a part of my life. I can only sleep well if I know they are
sleeping well."

Mostly, Isaac says, when he is in Israel, "I like to stay in my hotel room and write. Israel is a wonderful place to do literary work. It inspires me—something in the climate and in the air is stimulating to a writer."

If, as Maurice Carr alleged in his article in *The Jerusalem Post*, Isaac really had a "cherished mistress" in Israel who took up his time when he was there on previous occasions, he certainly isn't talking about it. Whose business is it, anyhow?

In that wildly uneven, cantankerous chronicle of his travels, *Eastward Ha!*, S. J. Perelman describes how, when he was disconsolate in Jerusalem, his spirits were lifted one day by an encounter with Isaac in the "clamant coffee shop" of the King David Hotel. They spent five happy hours together, during which Isaac confided to Perelman that at one time his dream in life was to build a replica of Captain Nemo's submarine, "complete with player piano and five hundred rolls," and retrace the underseas peregrinations of Verne's hero. "Luckily for his readers, of whom I am the most devoted," Perelman comments, "that dream evaporated."*

❁

Lunchtime on a cloudy weekday afternoon in July 1976. Isaac is ushering a young woman to the door of his apartment, a copy of his latest book, *A Little Boy in Search of God*, jutting out of her capacious shopping bag. She thanks him for the time he has given her and for the book, flashing a farewell smile.

"A nun," Isaac sums up the visitor, without further explanation, when she is gone. "They don't wear uniforms anymore."

Before leaving the house Isaac wants to show off a new feature of the apartment—a study he has fixed up, the walls lined with bookcases of various sizes, shapes, and kinds of wood, jampacked with volumes of every description. Several desks and chairs have been moved into the room, and the floor has been covered with a faded figured carpet. Every inch of the white walls above the bookcases is covered with awards, certificates, citations, documents, some in wooden frames, some laminated in plastic, some sporting gleaming medals affixed to the framed panels. Here are his National Book Awards for the illustrated children's version of his early memoirs, *A Day of Pleasure* (1970), and the short-story collection *A Crown of Feathers* (1975); the Newbery Honor Awards for his children's books, including *Zlateh the Goat and Other Stories*; the certificates for honorary degrees; assortments of texts, printed, illuminated, silk-screened, hand-engraved, calligraphed in elaborate scripts—all testifying to the variety and excellence of Isaac's literary achievements.

* S. J. Perelman, *Eastward Ha!* New York: Simon and Schuster, 1977.

It looks like rain outside. Isaac goes to get his dark raincoat and umbrella. He walks rapidly down upper Broadway in search of a place to eat that is not too crowded and that will serve his vegetarian needs. Not rapidly enough, however, to avoid the substantial obstacle of a well-dressed middle-aged couple.

The woman greets Isaac warmly and introduces her husband. "You'll come to dinner tonight," she tells the author. "We're expecting a wonderful crowd. I'm sure you'll enjoy yourself." She doesn't mention Alma, seeming to know somehow that Isaac's wife has just gone off to the Swiss resort town of Wengen, where he'll be joining her the following week for their annual summer vacation.

"My dear lady," Isaac answers, backing off a step or two. "I would love to accept your kind offer, but this evening I'm afraid it would be impossible."

She detains him a bit longer, trying to cajole him into changing his mind. At last she lets him go.

Isaac inspects several coffee shops before discovering one with a free booth. In none of these places is he known, as he is in his favorite haunt on Seventy-second Street. Nobody here fusses over him, stares at him, treats him like somebody special. He seems to enjoy the anonymity, greeting the waitress who seats him with deferential courtesy, taking a long time over the menu.

The Democratic Convention has been on television for days, and Isaac has been watching it. He wants to know more about this man Mondale, whether Jimmy Carter is worth taking seriously as a presidential candidate, whether there is really any difference between him and Gerald Ford.

Isaac decides on a fried-egg sandwich and a cup of coffee. He's not too hungry today. He opens his *New York Times*, purchased at a stand along the way, and looks down through the index on the split page to see what's been going on. The daily newspaper is at once his addiction and his despair. He shakes his head over it. He wonders whether it will ever be possible to govern the United States properly.

Suddenly the sky outside the glass walls of the coffee shop darkens from leaden gray to ominous black. It's pouring. "I don't understand Him," Isaac says, indicating with a gesture the Power behind the clouds. "Why does He change the weather like this? Who is He punishing? My only sins have been with women."

The downpour is delaying Isaac's trip to the bank a few blocks away; he waits patiently, talking about his attempts to make order out of his papers, his letters, his manuscripts, his life. Dvorah has been trying to organize as much as she can, but he still can't put his hands on everything he wants. How can one ever rescue from chaos so great an accumulation of papers, pictures, books, correspondence, documents, possessions? He says all this cheerfully. One senses it is not a problem that really oppresses him.

Isaac has other things on his mind. He has been writing a new play—*Old*

Love—dictating it to Dvorah, although he is never comfortable writing anything unless he can put it down in Yiddish first. A woman named Eve Friedman is working on another play, based on his story "Teibele and Her Demon." Bruce Davidson reports progress in raising money for the production of the movie version of *Enemies, A Love Story*. And there is a new project that has captured Isaac's imagination—a book for children about the great philosophers.

The rain shows no sign of letting up. The pages of the *Times* yield no special revelations, although Isaac does pause carefully to read the front-page story about Mondale's convention appearance. "Is he a radical? Ah, a liberal. They're all the same, all these politicians."

Isaac gets up quickly, tired of waiting, puts on his raincoat with a boy's eagerness. He plunges into the heavy rain, hurrying to reach the bank, complete his business there, get on with the day. Half-walking, half-running, he waves good-bye.

❀

A few days later Isaac is packing for the trip to Wengen. Dvorah is doing her best to help him. The problem is shoes. Isaac buys countless pairs of them. Whenever he goes into a shoestore, he buys a pair, because he cannot bear to disappoint the salesman after putting him through the trouble of taking down boxes so he can try on various styles. Actually, he always ends up buying black loafers. But when it comes to getting dressed, he invariably has trouble finding a pair that match. The missing shoe always turns up in the same place—under his bed, which is where Dvorah finds it today.

Dvorah comes back with the shoe into the room where Isaac is piling clothes into a suitcase, to find him standing there with one sock on and one sock off. Yet the chore of packing doesn't seem to irritate him at all. He takes time out to teach Dvorah a Yiddish song, clapping hands with her pattycake style:

> *Patch, patch kicheleh, mame vet keifen shichele, Shichele vul di mame keifen, un in cheder vet dos kind loffen.*

> Knead, knead the dough, the mother will buy the shoes, Shoes the mother will buy, to cheder the child will run.

It takes almost all day to get Isaac packed, clean out the refrigerator, make order out of accumulated mail and papers, lock up the apartment. Dvorah would like to help him organize the suits and sweaters and underwear for his trip; Isaac refuses. All he wants to do is play pattycake and teach her Yiddish songs. As the day goes on the words of the songs become more serious, the melodies more melancholy. Isaac switches to songs in Polish—marching songs with a military beat. And he marches up and down as he sings until Dvorah collapses laughing. Late in the afternoon Dvorah helps get Isaac and his luggage into a cab and rides out to the airport with him. Now he would like Dvorah to return the compliment by teaching him some songs in English. She tries out Simon and Garfunkel on him—"Bridge Over Troubled Water." He is more intrigued with the calypso song made famous by Harry Belafonte: "Mama, look a booboo."

Isaac gets out of the cab at Kennedy Airport in excellent spirits, singing "Mama, look a booboo" as he waves good-bye to Dvorah and follows a porter who is wheeling his bags to the check-in counter.

❀

In Wengen Alma and Isaac live quietly for a month or so every summer. There are no phone calls, no lectures, no cocktail parties at the P.E.N. club, no ladies in search of literary advice, no autographs to sign in bookstores, no dinners to attend, no speeches to deliver. They stay in a little hotel with a view of a snow-covered Alp. They take long walks, sip tea, linger over long dinners, talk, and relax. Isaac's favorite reading in Wengen is the *International Herald Tribune*, where he feels he can find as much news in a few pages as in the entire poundage of the Sunday *New York Times*. Isaac takes his work with him and spends a few hours every day covering lined pages in composition notebooks with his precise Yiddish script. In the fall he will return to the complicated schedule of a literary celebrity again, his calendar crowded with appointments, the phone ringing incessantly, the mail piling up in stacks at his apartment door. Sometimes he wonders whether it wouldn't be best for him and Alma to buy a house in the country somewhere and forget about living in New York. It is not the same city he came to half a lifetime ago. He is beginning to hate the dirt, the crime, the deteriorating services. But he feels that if he did move out of New York he would still have to have easy access to it. His career, his friends, his interests, are there—and have been, ever since he left Warsaw to start a second life on the other side of the world.

PART 2

"An Address"

Oⁿ his way to New York from Warsaw in the spring of 1935 Isaac Singer stopped over in Paris. "I wore a stiff collar and cuff links," he remembers. "My eyes were still blue, but the red hair had started already to vanish. My winter suit with the padded shoulders was too warm for Paris in April—it was years before I owned a summer suit."

Traveling under the name of Icek-Hersz Zynger, as he was identified in his passport, Isaac arrived in Paris by train. "I spent three days there. The only other city outside of Warsaw where I had ever spent any real time was Copenhagen. But Paris! I had told myself that I would not fall in love with this city the way other writers always did, I was not going to let myself be hypnotized. But I did fall in love with Paris just the same, the minute I got there. Paris in 1935 looked to me like one big carnival—a Purim carnival. Yes, in Paris it seemed to me it was always Purim, always a holiday. Full of life, of songs, of freedom and sheer nonsense. I called it Purim to myself instead of Paris."

While there he went to a Yiddish theater to see a performance of *Yoshe Kalb*. He met with Aaron Alperin—who since 1928 had been editor of tne *Pariser Haint*, a Yiddish newspaper published in Paris—to discuss the syndication of his work.

"Our publisher, Yashkant," Alperin says, "who was one of the pioneers of Yiddish journalism in Europe, predicted even then that Isaac Singer would become more famous than his brother." Alperin remembers Isaac as an impassioned young man "with more than the usual appetite for life and living."

Isaac, at thirty, traveled tourist class to America on the *Champlain*. He remembers being rather lonesome during the eight-day crossing. He did run across the American labor leader David Dubinsky on board, and the two were able to converse in Yiddish, for although Dubinsky was by then president of the International Ladies Garment Workers Union, he had started out as a baker in his father's shop in Lodz. But there were few other

Yiddish-speaking passengers aboard. "Besides, I was shy. I don't to this day make acquaintances quickly. I was gloomy about the future. I felt that Yiddish was on its deathbed. My Polish publisher had gone bankrupt. I said to myself, I have left a place where people speak Yiddish, but the situation of Yiddish even there is miserable. I am going to the United States, where Yiddish is dying. My language is dying. In Poland, half-dead. In the United States, three-quarters dead." Standing on the deck of the *Champlain*, staring down at the indifferent waves as the liner sped him to a country that for him might just as well have been another planet, he thought of himself as finished, not only as a writer but as a person. He had left behind all his relations but Joshua, his friends, his women. Would he ever see his son again? Would he really be able to get a job on the *Jewish Daily Forward*?

Isaac's spirits lifted when he saw his brother waving from the North River pier. It was the first of May, May Day. Joshua and a colleague of his named Leon Kreskin, another writer on the *Forward* staff, helped him get his luggage into a car. On the way to Sea Gate, the community in the Coney Island section of Brooklyn where Joshua and his family lived, they passed the *Forward* building. Isaac noticed that all ten floors were draped in red banners. "I asked my brother, 'The government allows a thing like this?' He answered me, 'Yes, this is a free country, and after all it's May Day.' A free country. 'So why the red? Why not the American flag?' "

Genia welcomed her brother-in-law with a warm embrace. There was no extra room, but he could sleep on a sofa in the living room. Isaac greeted his nephew, Joseph, whom he had not seen in several years. When he put down his luggage, Isaac assured himself that he was home now, home with his family. But they were all speaking English, and he couldn't understand a word. He felt isolated, displaced, discouraged. His brother had a good job, a devoted wife, a son about to reach bar mitzvah age, and had just finished his third novel, *The Brothers Ashkenazi*, which was to become a classic in its time. Isaac had not even seen a copy of *Satan in Goray*, which had been published in Warsaw just after he left. Nor could he imagine what he might do in this strange land with its alien tongue. He looked around him at Sea Gate, a private community with a lock on the gates to keep out riffraff, and it seemed to him that the lock had been meant to keep him out too.

Isaac felt just as alienated among Joshua and Genia's friends, who showed up frequently in large gatherings at the house—Maurice Schwartz and other Yiddish actors, Yiddish writers such as Ludwig Satz, the playwright John Wechsler, author of *The Last Mile*. Isaac felt he had little in common with them. And his attempts to get a job on the *Forward* resulted only in Abraham Cahan's agreement to consider Isaac's work on a free-lance basis. In fact, he was to continue working for Cahan as a free-lance journalist until 1942, when he was hired as a staff member.

Feeling like an intruder in Joshua's home, Isaac soon moved to a boarding house nearby, where he spent his first winter in Brooklyn for about sixteen dollars a month. From a landing outside the house he would stare for hours at the big steamships coming into New York harbor. After a while he met a woman who rented out rooms to Yiddish writers and moved into her establishment. This was a big building a millionaire had left to a girlfriend before Isaac's landlady took it over. The landlady also doubled as Isaac's lover. He used to rendezvous with her late at night in the rooming-house hallway, where he also recalls a bookcase crammed with "seventy-year-old books," some of them best-sellers in their day. He wondered if he would ever write a book himself that would be a best-seller, or even wind up in somebody's home library. In recent years he has revisited that house, once with a New York *Daily News* reporter and photographer at his side.

There was another woman "from the old country" whom he continued to see on and off for years. And he made a number of other friends, including Mona Shub, the sister-in-law of Elizabeth Shub, who later became one of his translators and editors. Mona Shub helped him learn English; one day he was thrilled to find that he could read Blake's "The Tiger" all the way through, though as yet he could not quite manage Poe in English.

In those days Isaac also had a girlfriend who loved the movies. "She took me to the movies on Mermaid Avenue—in the daytime, which made me feel particularly wicked and irresponsible. You paid ten cents and they showed three features." Isaac hated the movies, which he remembers as uniformly terrible, but he went to humor his friend. Occasionally he took her to the Yiddish theater, which was in the last days of its glory on Second Avenue. They would see overwrought melodramas, musicals, Ansky's classic *The Dybbuk*, sometimes Shakespeare, the characters rebaptized with Jewish names and relocated to Jewish neighborhoods for the delectation of Jewish audiences.

For a time Isaac reviewed Broadway plays for the *Forward*. He would be sent on the second night after an opening, when the play has already been reviewed in English in other papers and everyone in town knew pretty much whether it was a hit or not.

"They seemed to send me only to bad plays. I got the impression that all American plays were bad. I never really knew the names of the actors, but I seldom wrote about the acting, anyhow. It seemed to me that if there were faults, it was to be blamed on the play, not on the actors."

In the spring of 1936 Isaac moved away from Sea Gate, to a rooming house on East Nineteenth Street in Manhattan, where he paid four dollars a week for rent. Then he lived for a brief period in a house near Croton-on-Hudson that belonged to Leon Crystal, the Sunday editor of the *Forward*. "I had a room in his house," Isaac says, "a room he gave me for nothing. I was almost without any money at all." Later Isaac lived for a time in Sheepshead Bay, in another cheap furnished room.

All this time Isaac was able to write nothing except an occasional essay or review for the *Forward*—sometimes under pen names, such as I. Warshawsky and D. Segal, which made him feel freer, "more able to play with my pen." (The inspiration for this practice came from Joshua, who had sent his dispatches from Poland signed G. Kuper.) These pieces, he says, were "half essays, half stories." The editors of the *Forward* did not always share his apolitical point of view. "Crystal, my editor, and Abe Cahan, the editor-in-chief, tended to look at things from the perspective of social beliefs. I felt they really didn't want my work. I considered myself a complete failure in every respect and kept away from the Yiddish journalists who would gather at places like the Café Royal. I didn't think I had anything in common with them." Isaac couldn't even bring himself to show his face in the offices of the *Forward* and would send his manuscripts in by mail.

Isaac ate his meals in cafeterias. He remembers one place where he was able to get "two steaks for fifty cents." Isaac's total income averaged about twelve dollars a week. He did a lot of reading. "And I took walks—long walks. There was talk of war, and there was a feeling of desperation in the air. Everybody felt that if Hitler achieved his goals we were all goners. They took the attitude, 'Well, as long as you live, you live.' " In Isaac's case the grim news that filtered across the seas about unemployment and increasing anti-Semitism in Europe reinforced his feelings of impotence and isolation. Isaac, who has so often talked of the writer's need for roots, felt himself at that time utterly without them. He often thought about suicide.

"I lived through a terrible disappointment. I felt then—more than I believe now—that Yiddish had no future in this country. In Poland, Yiddish had been very much alive when I left. When I came here it seemed to me that Yiddish was finished; it was very depressing. The result was that for five or six or seven years I couldn't write a word. Not only didn't I publish anything in those years except for the pieces in the *Forward,* but writing became so difficult a chore that my grammar was affected. I couldn't write a single worthwhile sentence. I became like a man who was a great lover and is suddenly impotent—knowing at the same time that ultimately I would regain my power. I shouldn't even have tried to write anything then, but I did try, again and again, without success."

One of those attempts Isaac now considers a failure was inspired by a correspondence with Aaron Zeitlin, his Warsaw friend and collaborator on the magazine *Globus.* In 1935 Isaac had written Zeitlin, saying that he had made a mistake in coming to America and should have gone to Palestine instead. Zeitlin wrote back, counseling Isaac against the idea of settling in Israel. "At this time, Eretz Israel is not ready for creative literature. . . . The writers sit in Tel Aviv and write stories in Hebrew about Galicia. . . . For me, the country is too holy, too beautiful—literature can grow only where God does not compete with man." He urged Isaac to stay in America, to concentrate on getting his work translated from Yiddish into English—for only with translation, he felt, would success as a writer come to Isaac.

In 1936 Zeitlin wrote again, urging his unhappy friend to get back to writing fiction: "My God, why are you silent? Why don't you polish your novel about the sinning Messiah? (I feel from afar that you are not working, although you have received so much encouragement from me.) Heed my advice and resume this work if you have not done so up to now. You know surely that my aim is for you to prepare this novel for translation."*

Isaac decided to follow Zeitlin's advice, to return to the manuscript of *Messiah the Sinner*, which he had begun before leaving Poland. Like *Satan in Goray*, the story dealt with a false messiah—not that ill-fated aspirer of the Orient Sabbatai Zevi but a man named Jacob Frank, an eighteenth-century Polish Jew who founded a heretical sect based on Zevi's brand of mysticism. Despite its fascinating subject matter, *Messiah the Sinner* was a literary flop—although it ran not only in the *Forward* but in the *Varshanahaint*, a Yiddish newspaper in Warsaw, and in the *Pariser Haint*, whose editor Isaac had gone to see during his stopover in Paris. Isaac himself is the chief disparager of *Messiah the Sinner*. "Instead of describing the environment of the story," he says, "I made the mistake of trying to concentrate on Frank himself. But he was a Sephardic Jew, and I knew about Sephardic Jews as much as I knew about Turkish Catholics. The book was a complete failure—never translated, God forbid."

The parallel between Isaac's loss of faith in the future of Yiddish and his inability to write during this period, and Joshua's disillusionment with Yiddish after *Steel and Iron* was published and his ensuing difficulties with writing is striking. Yet, if Isaac felt Yiddish literature was dead and that he was "in a cemetery," it was in that cemetery that Joshua had managed to write, soon after his arrival in New York in 1933, his Yiddish masterpiece, *The Brothers Ashkenazi*.

❀

Set in Lodz at the turn of the century, this epic novel depicts the vicissitudes of the Jews in that city as it grows from a village to an urban center of industry. Dominating the foreground is the story of twin brothers who are as different as brothers could possibly be. Simcha, the first born, a weak, mean child, grows up accustomed to insults and rejection but makes the most of a carefully cultivated imperviousness to cruelty and an aptitude for study. His extroverted brother, Jacob, is highly popular, good at games, but a rotten scholar. Vaguely one glimpses in Simcha the lineaments of the frail and introverted young Isaac, in Jacob those of the athletic, outgoing Joshua. The

---

* Zeitlin was to come to America in 1939, just in time to escape the Nazis, although his wife and children perished in Poland in the Holocaust. He died in New York in 1974.

resemblances really end there—even though, at the end of the tale, when Jacob becomes Simcha's rescuer, as Joshua in some sense was Isaac's, one might be tempted to read in a kind of parallel.

Simcha makes an advantageous marriage to Dinah, the girl next door who has been pining away for his attractive brother, Jacob, and through guile and painstaking application rises from accountant in his father-in-law's mill to partner to head of the business. Now a merchant prince and a war profiteer, he divorces Dinah and marries a rich widow. Eventually he moves his business to Petrograd, where he is trapped by the Russian revolution, his business is confiscated, and he is sent to jail.

Meanwhile Jacob, who makes his way lightheartedly and without apparent effort, has married a sickly girl named Pearl and gone to work for a mill that is a rival of his brother's. Later he divorces Pearl, becomes the lover of the mill-owner's wife, and makes a fortune. The climax of the tale comes with Jacob's arrival in Russia, where he frees Simcha from prison. As the brothers try to reenter Poland they are stopped by border guards who jeer at Simcha because he is visibly a Jew. Infuriated, Jacob loses control, strikes the captain of the guards, and is shot to death.

Simcha escapes. He gets to England, where he borrows enough money to rebuild his factory in Lodz. But a depression comes, and Simcha is reviled as a pariah by the other merchants in town for using English money to rescue his business. The book ends somberly.

We have met these brothers before. They are Cain and Abel (although one would be hard-put to judge which one is Cain, which Abel); they are Shem and Shaun, the eternal Janus-faced dream-world pair of brothers in *Finnegans Wake*. And they embody certain traits of Isaac Bashevis and Israel Joshua. But *The Brothers Ashkenazi* is really less about Simcha and Jacob than about the changing fortunes of their people in Poland.

Through scenes as vivid as those in an epic movie Joshua once again fills in his giant 643-page canvas with the realistic details that somehow breathe life into the places and people in his sprawling saga. As in his previous books, everything is shown in mercilessly sharp focus, and there are few pretty moments. The Poles are pig-faced, avaricious, primitive, and insensitive; the Jews, petty, parochial, and capable of much meanness. Yet there is no doubt as to who the real victims are in the struggle of the Jews to hold on to their hard-won corner of comfort and security amid the shifting fortunes of Lodz. In the end, at the burial of Simcha, who has come to symbolize both the burgeoning and the death of obsolescent industrial Lodz, the mourners mutter, with heavy but apt symbolism, "Sand . . . everything we have built was built on sand."

The Brothers Ashkenazi, published in 1936, is justly considered Israel Joshua Singer's magnum opus. With its masterly, muscular translation into English by Maurice Samuel, which appeared the same year, Joshua's international literary reputation rose higher than ever (it is ironic that although almost all his books are available in English nowadays, this one is not). For behind the machinery of the tale it is impossible to ignore the meticulously chronicled, inexorable motion of history, the rise and fall of a city as indifferent as any natural disaster to the pains and pleasures of its inhabitants. It is history, and the waste men make of its opportunities, that matters to Joshua. Tears are wrung from the eyes of the characters and laughter sounds from their lips on cue, but to Joshua the historian catastrophes are communal; what happens to individuals is only illustrative of what happens to men *en masse.*

Whereas the streets in one of Isaac's novels will twist and dissolve beneath the feet of characters who wander in terror through them, Joshua's cityscape is caught in the lens of a strictly reportorial objectivity. Each episode is a life study in the strictest realist tradition, where distortion of perspective is unthinkable. This does not mean that irony and humor are absent from Joshua's prose—he uses them over and over to convey, for example, his scorn for the stifling, petty rituals that drive ultra-Orthodox Jews to self-defeating extremes of piety, whereby the purity of a square of matzoh, for instance, becomes more important than the miracle it is intended to commemorate. But Jacob, his Gulliver, his natural, spontaneous, generous man, is as doomed as the Lilliputians who surround him. The indifferent lava of events spares nobody, big or small.

The Brothers Ashkenazi's unsparing depicting of brutality and its portrait of the victims of that brutality could hardly fail to move even a cold-hearted reader, and every scene is woven through with its author's implicit outrage against injustice; yet it nonetheless portrays a world revealed by the camera eye of realism. It would remain for Isaac to distort the lens, freeing the figures in the landscape from their bondage to the rigid laws of perspective. He too would show that he could sit patiently before the *camera obscura* of realism and set down all he might see as a scrupulous observer, but his pen would probe beyond appearances to the seething world of the psyche where motivations are perhaps less logical than those that animate Joshua's characters, but somehow, for that, all the truer.

❀

May 6, 1976

Joseph Singer, Joshua's son and Isaac's principal translator in recent years, is a big-framed, intense man with thinning gray hair who speaks with a rapid-fire, staccato fluency. Although he seems to have inherited his father's talents as a painter and writer, he says he has no serious literary ambitions and thinks of himself as mainly a translator and journalist. Yet he too writes books and has studied art.

Joseph remembers his Uncle Isaac in the days when he first came to live in his father's house in Brooklyn. In fact, his memories go all the way back to childhood days, when Isaac would visit the family in Warsaw.

"My uncle was always rather playful," Joseph says. "He used to run through the house, barking like a dog and quacking like a duck—probably for my benefit. The whole family shares a tremendous love of animals. Isaac may be a little nervous about them, but he really loves them. Horses were my father's favorite, and I emulate him in this to a ridiculous degree. I'm a little *meshugah* about dogs. I have a St. Bernard and am capable of no resistance where animals are concerned. And Isaac, of course, with his birds and his sentimental ideas about living creatures and his vegetarianism . . . yes, it seems to run in the family."

Joseph was struck from the first, however, by the contrasts in personality between his father and his uncle. Joshua was "a gregarious type, outgoing, social. Isaac is more withdrawn, always has been.

"The whole Jewish world of books and the theater used to come to visit us in Sea Gate. There were so many parties at our house, and there my Uncle Isaac would be, off by himself, sitting and listening. I am always surprised when I go to an auditorium and see him lecture; as a young man he was so shy—quiet, bashful. Otherwise, in fact, he doesn't seem much changed to me over the years. He's the same Isaac. He was one of the youngest in the crowd usually, but he always looked old."

Joseph hates it when Yiddish journalists try to tell him his father was more of a writer than his uncle. "It's a foolish comparison. You don't compare writers." In recent years Isaac has been apt to get more space in the encyclopedia listings and biographical dictionaries than his brother, but Joseph points out that his father "also had his share of fame. What with the popularity of *Yoshe Kalb* as a book and a play, his friendships with the literary lights of the day—including Sholem Asch—and the wide respect he commanded, he was hardly an obscure figure. He was interviewed too, and went on the radio. He traveled, he was a man of the world. He saw and he did, as the saying goes. And after all, he died young.

"My father was bigger and huskier than Isaac. He worked with his hands, while Uncle Isaac, with all his fame, remains the quintessential yeshiva *bocher*. My father looked like a one hundred percent Kraut. He used to go to those Nazi rallies in Yorkville—to gather material for a piece he was doing on the American Nazi movement in the thirties—and he could go out with these guys and talk to them. I mean, he knew German and drank beer with them, and they never caught on. If Isaac had tried that they would have spotted him right away and lynched him."

And what of the world that the Singers had left behind? In Warsaw, according to Joseph, Poles and Jews lived so far apart that "the Yiddish literary world became a tightly knit family where everyone knew everyone else. There was the Writers' Club, where they all hung around, where they ate their meals, made their assignations, even slept—did everything and really led a lively, busy, active kind of life. They had their theaters, their cafés, their clubs. I don't think they made much money, any of them, and you would think they might have been unhappy, because it was all hopeless, they were all doomed. But there was a kind of spirit of hope and gaiety which cannot be explained by any logical theory. It was the gaiety and the hopefulness of people who had lost hope."

This nephew of Isaac's, who feels not at all sentimental about the Warsaw of his childhood and can scarcely remember the months spent with his father and mother in Paris before they came to New York, has fond memories of Sea Gate. "Sea Gate was a kind of never-never land as a place to grow up. When I was a child there, the beaches were wild—you could jump out of the window in our house and be on the beach and go swimming. There were no lifeguards. I remember going out in boats and fishing. It was like Maine, or like what Fire Island used to be before it became crowded. And just beyond us was Coney Island, still fairly old-countryish, with a large Jewish population, rustic really—a part of New York City, yet a world all its own."

Joseph was going on thirteen when his family moved to Sea Gate, but he was not bar-mitzvahed. "I was raised in a house with great Yiddishkeit but absolutely no religion. I wouldn't even have been circumcised if it hadn't been that my mother insisted on it." At home Joshua spoke to his wife in Yiddish. He had spoken Polish to his son in Poland; in Brooklyn he spoke to him in English. In Warsaw Joseph had been enrolled in a segregated Jewish *gymnasium*. In Brooklyn he attended a public grade school, then Abraham Lincoln High School. From high school Joseph went directly into the Marine Corps.

Joseph has forgotten both the Hebrew and the Polish he learned in Warsaw, but he does speak Yiddish, which he picked up in childhood by "osmosis." In fact, he knows the language well enough to translate directly from his uncle's original manuscripts, as he did from his father's with novels such as *Steel and Iron* and *The Family Carnovsky*.

"When my uncle came to see me about this kind of work, I remember I was living in some little town in New Jersey. It was around 1950, and I had just come back from Miami Beach, where I had spent a couple of years trying to earn a living. My uncle wanted me to translate a story into archaic English. That didn't work out too well. Later I tried my hand with some of his short stories and translated *The Manor* and *The Estate*. He has had many translators, of course, but none of them except Mirra Ginsburg has worked directly from the Yiddish text the way I do. When I do translate one of his books, I get very excited about the project. I admire his talent enormously.

I'm so anxious to read on from one page to the next. It's a pleasure to work with my uncle's prose because the construction is so good that the material naturally lends itself to good translation."

Joseph, who has converted a good many of his uncle's works into apt if not always soaring English, is the only one of Isaac's translators whose credit line in *The New Yorker* does not list Isaac as a co-translator.

Isaac goes over Joseph's translations when they are completed and makes changes, but they seldom discuss the manuscript. "When it's handed in to the publisher, that's usually the last I see of it." When the translation appears in print, Joseph never reads it. "Once I've done with it, I put it away."

Whenever a new piece by his uncle is making its debut in the *Forward*— and almost all Isaac's novels have been serialized there—Joseph buys the paper (Isaac's work usually appears on Thursdays and Fridays) and automatically goes to work on an English version. He says he has worked on five or six of his uncle's novels that have not yet seen print. He believes that Isaac harbors a whole trunkful of untranslated and as yet unpublished material.

To Joseph, as to Irving Howe and a number of critics who have written about Isaac's work, his short stories are his forte. And Joseph prefers the stories about Poland to those with American settings. He particularly admires "The Gentleman from Cracow."

Joseph, who turned fifty-six in 1978, lives what he calls a secluded life with his wife, June, in a small New Jersey town. (He says he plans to move to California soon and may give up working as his uncle's translator.) His children—Sharon, Brett, Ian, and Valerie—all in their twenties, have left home. Sharon is married and has a child. Valerie teaches English. Joseph is fond of his sons and daughters: "I'm involved with them. When they were growing up, I used to shout and sometimes I hit, but I'm into my family like nobody's business. You see, my own childhood was kind of strange. My brother died before I came here. I grew up ambivalent—the Yiddish background and with that, baseball. And I was always around adults. I wanted to really care about my kids."

Joseph looks at his watch. He wants to be as helpful as he can but really would rather not talk about himself. "I like to keep a low profile," he says. Like all the Singers, he is a private person and truly a modest one.

"I have no illusions about myself," Joseph says. "I'm a craftsman. That's all I am and all I intend to be."

❀

In Isaac's collection of stories *A Crown of Feathers* there is a tale called "A Day in Coney Island," translated by the author and Laurie Colwin, which sheds light on Isaac's life in Brooklyn in those first days in New York. In it

Isaac describes himself as living in a rented room in Sea Gate writing "almost nothing." A Yiddish editor has told him that no one wants to read about demons, dybbuks, and imps in Poland two centuries ago. "At thirty, a refugee from Poland, I had become an anachronism. As if that were not enough, Washington had refused to extend my tourist visa. Lieberman, my lawyer, was trying to get me a permanent visa, but for that I needed my birth certificate, a certificate of morality, a letter saying that I was employed and would not become a public charge, and other papers I could not obtain. I sent alarmed letters to Poland. They never replied. The newspapers were predicting that Hitler would invade Poland any day."

In this story we come upon Isaac looking through his bathroom window at the big liners arriving from Europe, then staring despairingly at himself in the mirror: "Already, my red hair was gone, I had watery blue eyes, inflamed eyelids, sunken cheeks, a protruding Adam's apple. Although people came from Manhattan to Sea Gate to get sunburned, my skin remained sickly white. My nose was thin and pale, my chin pointed, my chest flat. I often thought that I looked not unlike the imps I described in my stories."

Isaac is having a love affair with his landlady, a divorcee whom he here calls Esther, getting letters from a girl in Warsaw, and being taken to the local ten-cent movie house on Mermaid Avenue by yet another friend he calls Sylvia, who "translated for me in broken Yiddish what the gangsters in the films were saying."

As usual, even in this tale of a past recalled decades later (the story was written in the seventies), nothing escapes Isaac's powers of observation. Here is his description of a morning stroll down the Coney Island boardwalk:

"The sun poured down like fire. From the beach came a roar even louder than the ocean. On the boardwalk, an Italian watermelon vender pounded on a sheet of tin with his knife and called for customers in a wild voice. Everyone bellowed in his own way: sellers of popcorn and hot dogs, ice cream and peanuts, cotton candy and corn on the cob. I passed a sideshow displaying a creature that was half woman, half fish; a wax museum with figures of Marie Antoinette, Buffalo Bill, and John Wilkes Booth; a store where a turbaned astrologer sat in the dark surrounded by maps and globes of the heavenly constellations, casting horoscopes. Pygmies danced in front of a little circus, their black faces painted white, all of them bound loosely with a long rope. A mechanical ape puffed its belly like a bellows and laughed with raucous laughter. Negro boys aimed guns at metal ducklings. A half-naked man with a black beard and hair to his shoulders hawked potions that strengthened the muscles, beautified the skin, and brought back lost potency. He tore heavy chains with his hands and bent coins between his fingers. A little farther along, a medium advertised that she was calling back spirits from the dead, prophesying the future, and giving advice on love and marriage."

Isaac sits down on a beach near a group of angry men, who he imagines never eat or sleep, who do nothing but debate about Hitler, Stalin, Norman Thomas, and the plight of the workers. He wonders whether the world will succumb to the Nazis and he will perish in a concentration camp. What good, in that case, would it be to add more novels or stories to the world's store? He stops for lunch at a cheap cafeteria and considers applying for a job as a Hebrew teacher—or even a messenger—before he gets down to his last dollar. He is already contemplating the idea of becoming a vegetarian—or maybe saving money by fasting. With one of his last coins he phones the Sunday editor of a Yiddish newspaper and learns that they have just accepted one of his pieces. When he hangs up, coins begin to pour out of the pay phone as out of a Las Vegas slot machine: "dimes, nickels, quarters." He hesitates at first to take them but then thinks of all the times he has lost money in phonebooths and finally walks away feeling rich with this newfound little fortune. He remembers that he has forgotten to pay his check at the cafeteria and goes back, but the cashier is talking to his boss and refuses to accept the money for fear of being compromised by his oversight. With so much luck all at once, Isaac feels he is being tested by higher powers. He goes off for cheesecake and coffee at a café, where he meets a Yiddish journalist. The scene offers a glimpse of Isaac as a "greenhorn" immigrant: "I never thought of myself as short, but among the American giants I became small. . . . My Warsaw suit looked outlandish, with its broad lapels and padded shoulders. In addition, it was too heavy for the New York heat." His well-dressed associate tells him that the only way for him to get a visa is to marry an American citizen. Just then Esther happens to walk into the café. Isaac blushes when he sees her. ("I had become pathologically bashful in America. My boyish blushing had returned.") Esther is embarrassed too that they are meeting in public and acts like "a provincial girl from Poland." Isaac's table companion calls Esther over and tells her of the advice he has just given Isaac: Marry an American girl, become a citizen. Esther's comment is "Why not?" Isaac, unable to think of something clever at the moment, says, "I wouldn't marry to get a visa." His journalist friend puts in, "I'm not a matchmaker, but you two would make a fitting pair." Esther looks at Isaac "questioningly, pleading and reproachful." He's hot, his shirt is wet, he can't think of a word to say. Abruptly Esther gets up; she must keep an appointment, she says. Isaac feels the coins in his pocket. Lucky in gambling, unlucky in love. "As my game with the powers on high stood now, I seemed to have won a dollar and some cents and to have lost a refuge in America and a woman I really loved."

The story "Schloimele," which appears in the collection A *Friend of Kafka* in a translation by Elaine Gottlieb and Alma Singer, offers another revealing glimpse of those early days. Here we find Isaac in one more furnished room, trying to learn English with the aid of the Bible and a dictionary. A "pink-cheeked young man with cherry-dark eyes" comes to see him, a fellow he calls Sam Gilbert, who was brought to America from a village in Poland at the age of five and still goes under the nickname of Schloimele. Schloimele has sought out Isaac because he wants to turn Isaac's story "Yentl the Yeshiva Boy" into a play. Schloimele, a hustler if there ever was one, says he is currently producing a script by his girlfriend, Sylvia Katz, and now he wants to put on "a Jewish show" in English. He sees Sylvia in the role of Yentl. Nothing comes of this plan, but Isaac keeps meeting Schloimele in Broadway cafeterias and at his apartment in the Village. Each time, Schloimele is living with a different girl (each perfect, he insists, for the part of Yentl) and full of grandiose plans, inveigling Isaac into attending bohemian parties and plying him with transparent promises. Years pass, and Isaac and Schloimele keep running into each other. Schloimele grows older and fatter but still dreams of glory on Broadway or in Hollywood. Isaac offers this portrait of himself as he approaches middle age, still unable to write: "Around my bald spot the hair had turned gray. . . . I lost all desire to write. My fingers grew sluggish. The fountain pens sabotaged me, either leaking or withholding ink. I couldn't read my own handwriting. I skipped letters, left out words, made ridiculous mistakes, wrote long, stilted sentences. Often I said the opposite of what I intended, as if a literary dybbuk had gotten into me. My notebooks, even my manuscripts vanished. My nights were sleepless. I stopped receiving mail, wasn't called to the telephone. The moment I put on a shirt it was wet with perspiration. My shoes hurt. I cut myself when I shaved. Food spotted my ties. My nose was clogged; I could barely breathe. My back itched and I developed hemorrhoids. . . ."

One summer Schloimele and Isaac go off to a resort in the mountains. Schloimele, wearing a straw hat, a pink shirt, and a bow tie, is "gray-haired, bent, with a yellow complexion, a wrinkled double chin, and sad eyes." When he and Isaac board the bus for the country, Schloimele is still babbling on about having met the perfect girl to play Yentl, this time a "Yemenite actress" who is "delirious" about the prospect. Isaac never dreamed in those days that one day there would actually be such a play on Broadway.

❀

A shivery December evening in 1975. Isaac is having dinner at Dvorah and Abraham's apartment on the top floor of a battered old tenement on Manhattan's Lower East Side. To get there Isaac has come by taxi all the way from Eighty-sixth Street and climbed six flights of stairs. Dvorah and Abraham have done wonders with the cramped rooms of their East Fifth Street railroad flat. They have covered the walls of the narrow front room with burlap, painted the rough plaster ceiling sky blue, furnished the place with painted wooden chests and comfortable vinyl-covered chairs. The shelves are crowded with books on photography. Photographs and paintings and a woolen rug with a design of animals, birds, and leaves adorn the walls. One end of the room has been converted into a kind of lounging area decked with huge oriental cushions, a curving upholstered backrest as wide as the room, a red strip of carpet. Dominating the area is a hundred-gallon fish tank, constructed by Abraham and filled with underwater plants and red platties, all descendants of the handful with which the tank was originally stocked. A small color television set and a compact amplifier and record player complete the scene. There's also a darkroom where Abraham develops and prints his photographs, a tiny kitchen, a cozily furnished little bedroom.

There is no problem about what to serve Isaac, since he has managed by now to convert both young people to vegetarianism. After dinner he is drawn to the brightly lighted fish tank. For a while he watches the newborn platties darting in and out of the thick green underwater plants. Then he sees a male pursuing a female. "Look how she pretends to put up a resistance," he exclaims, "just to make sure that something will happen." Nothing can lure him away from the tank.

Dvorah suggests that since Isaac enjoyed The Bronx Zoo so much, she and Abraham ought to take him someday to the aquarium out at Coney Island. Isaac is all in favor of such a journey; he has his own memories of the area.

In the weeks that follow, Dvorah brings the matter up several times, but always there is some reason to postpone the trip. Whenever she and Abraham do manage to pin Isaac down to a day, it usually rains and the trip is called off. Spring comes, and once again they agree on a time. But when the morning for the trip arrives, Isaac phones to say, "It looks like rain. Let's forget it." Dvorah talks him into going anyhow.

It's a sticky morning late in May when Dvorah and Abraham call for Isaac and Alma in their car. As it's drizzling, Isaac brings along an umbrella. When they get to the aquarium, he stands in front of a big tank containing huge white whales, holding his open umbrella over his head and staring fixedly at these huge sea mammals. Then, carefully, Isaac proceeds from tank to tank, deliberating over the printed legends, the names in Latin and English, wanting to know the habits of the various species—what they eat, how they mate.

When they pass the seals, Alma tells of her horror on learning that these beautiful creatures are beaten to death for their coats. Isaac is overjoyed when the keeper comes to feed the seals and they leap into the air to catch their lunches.

When lunchtime comes around for the human visitors, the four go to an indoor shed where there are picnic tables and spread out a treat Dvorah has prepared—soup, imitation chopped liver made of vegetables, a Thermos of tea.

After lunch they leave the aquarium and get into Dvorah and Abraham's car for the drive home to Manhattan. They have gone a little way when they come to the resort called Sea Gate. Isaac makes Dvorah stop the car. He wants to show them a house on a side street where a "woman friend" of his in the days soon after his arrival in America once lived. They peer out the car windows, through the rain, at a dilapidated Victorian house covered with scalloped clapboarding, the paint scaling from its long-neglected facade. Isaac tells them about the woman who used to live here. She was the one who rented out rooms to Yiddish writers, he says, and used to meet him secretly, late at night, in the hallway of this old rooming house.

Now Isaac is feeling lively. He asks Dvorah to drive down to the sea. He wants everyone to get out of the car and take a walk with him. He leads them out to a jetty where gulls are circling and crying in the light rain as they dive for prey. Then Isaac runs down to the beach. "See you, folks, see you, folks," he calls out, giving his best imitation of an American accent.

Late in the afternoon the four stop at a dairy restaurant for refreshments. Over coffee and cake the talk turns to one of Isaac's favorite topics—the impossible demands of monogamy. Isaac predicts that the practice will soon be completely outmoded. "If you have one candle," he says, "with the flame from that candle you could light fifty others." But he also expresses the idea that there should be sex only when there is real feeling, real love. There must be boundaries of some kind. Real love enhances life, mere lust destroys it. An expense of spirit destroys the people having the affair and even those around them.

Abraham says he can't imagine having any sort of relationship outside his marriage with Dvorah unless there were real love between himself and some other woman.

Dvorah adds that if there were such love, and she and the other woman were both involved with Abraham, then there would have to be some kind of empathy and understanding among the three of them—not anything sexual between Dvorah and the other woman, but some feeling that bound them all together.

Alma is horrified. She says she is trying hard to understand all this talk, but in fact why should a man and a woman who really love each other have to look anywhere else for love?

Dvorah gets up and buys Abraham some apple pie, which he insists on sharing with the others.

The afternoon draws on. It's beginning to get dark and raining harder. Driving home, nobody talks much at all.

❀

Six months after his arrival in New York, Isaac wrote to the New York headquarters of the Hebrew Sheltering and Immigrant Aid Society of America (HIAS) requesting help in obtaining the government's permission to remain another year. On October 3, 1935, an answer arrived from the general manager of the organization, quoting a report from their Washington office: "The case having reached the Department, we took it up with the proper official today who has agreed to recommend an extension of six months on the understanding, however, that Mr. Zynger severs his connections with any American newspapers, will not write for them for pay, and will be remunerated solely by the foreign paper [*Pariser Haint*] which he represents in this country."

This would not do at all, and Isaac turned for help to the editors of the *Forward*. Meanwhile, on September 11, 1935, Harry Rogoff, at that time the *Forward*'s managing editor, had written to the Commissioner of Immigration on Ellis Island, asking that "Mr. Icek-Hersz Zynger of Warsaw, a novelist and writer" be permitted to remain in the United States to write an "extensive serial" to be published in the *Forward*. "The serial," Mr. Rogoff explained, "will require Mr. Zynger's presence in this country for about one year for the purpose of research work and the preparation of copy. His special training and outstanding gifts in this field make his services to us indispensable. We therefore would greatly appreciate it if you would grant Mr. Zynger an extension of one year so that he may be able to fulfill this assignment."

This respectfully requested permission was granted.

In 1937 two things happened that changed the course of Isaac's life. The first of these was that he decided to become an American citizen. Two years after he came to New York, Isaac was still living on the visitor's visa by which he had entered. He was told that to get a permanent visa he would have to go to Cuba or Canada. Since he couldn't get into Canada legally with a Polish passport, it was arranged for him to travel to Detroit and walk across the bridge to Windsor. "What actually happened," Isaac says, "is that a friend met me and smuggled me into Toronto. There I was able to obtain a card that paved the way for me to become an American."

Six years passed before Isaac was able to obtain his first citizenship papers. "I remember they asked me who makes the laws, and I told them 'Congress.' In 1943 I got my final papers. This was a big event in my life. For years as a Jew in Poland I had known I was a second-class citizen—maybe even third class. They didn't really want us there. There was no place for us. They couldn't feed their own non-Jewish peasants, who had to emigrate to other lands to make a living. Why keep a minority, strangers in your house? Now I was where I was wanted. When I came back to New York from Toronto with that little card from the consulate which was my permanent visa, I put my hand in my jacket pocket over and over to make sure it wasn't lost. My American citizenship means a lot to me. I would not trade it for all the money in the world."

The second significant thing that occurred in Isaac's life in 1937 was that he met Alma Wasserman, who would become his wife.

❀

It's an icy evening in December 1975 with a bitter wind blowing through the streets of New York, the kind that blasts the winter boulevards of Warsaw in Isaac's stories. Isaac is at the American-Israel Friendship House on East Thirty-ninth Street tonight to receive the Maggid Award for contributions to Jewish journalism from the American Jewish Public Relations Society, a small group of organizational public relations people working in the Jewish field. Considering the bad weather, the society has expected maybe a dozen of its members to show up tonight, but with Isaac as the attraction nearly a hundred people are on hand. There's a bit of a crisis at first, since the planners have forgotten that Isaac is a vegetarian, and there is chicken on the menu for the buffet dinner. But a can of pea soup is hastily purchased from a nearby grocery, a salad is put together, and the guest of honor doesn't have to go hungry. He has a heavy cold, though, and looks especially chalk-faced and frail this evening. Even so, he and Alma are soon involved in spirited conversation over cocktails with the members of the society, and he even grants an interview to an intense women from an Anglo-Jewish weekly newspaper published in Washington.

Sam Levenson, last year's Maggid recipient (a *maggid* is a man respected for his wisdom), is here to present the award at the long head table set up before draped·American and Israeli flags and photographs of Jewish life in various lands. Levenson, long a schoolteacher and famed as a humorist, says, "I'm not going to try to match poetry or prose with you, Mr. Singer. . . . This man has transplanted to the American scene the cedars of Lebanon, somehow keeping their aroma and their greenness and their loveliness alive. . . . If you will give me whatever it is I'm supposed to turn over to him I will do it now on behalf of all of you gathered here . . . when it gets here I'll turn this over to you, and I guess you are supposed to make a speech for two hours after this. . . ."

Isaac accepts the award with smiles and nods of gratitude. He apologizes, saying that because of his cold he will make only half of the speech he has prepared. "I was supposed to give a speech about what makes a Jewish writer, and before that what makes a writer altogether. I will talk only about what makes a Jewish writer." Isaac then advances his theory about the value of roots, that a writer must have an address, that a Jewish writer in particular must be "both a child of his people and its stepchild," with a conscience never immune to shock at God's injustices or man's. A Jewish writer must write about the aspects of Jewish life familiar to him. He must understand his heritage. "It is not by chance that the great Jewish writers come from places where the Jews spoke their own language and lived their own life. . . . The richer the soil, the stronger the plant. . . ."

What Isaac enjoys most about the evening is a program of Jewish folk songs from Eastern Europe. He applauds loudly and even puts in a couple of requests. Then he and Alma don their hats and heavy coats and hasten into the snow-smudged street to hail a taxi. Nights like this make him long for his place in Florida, where he and Alma will head tomorrow. They leave behind a group of exhilarated public relations men and women, who agree that their choice this year was a good one. Who else would have shown up with a heavy cold like that on a night like this to accept a minor award from a small uninfluential group of colleagues? Once again, like the trouper he is, Isaac has sacrificed his own comfort so as not to disappoint people who have counted on him.

PART 3

"Why Does a Woman Choose a Man?"

In North Miami Beach, in the prosperous neighborhood known as Seaside, Isaac and Alma spend several months every winter in their condominium apartment at Surfside Towers on Collins Avenue high above the Atlantic. The apartment, which has the look of a high-priced hotel suite, is carpeted wall to wall in a dusky yellow, furnished with overstuffed chairs and sofas, and decorated impersonally throughout in shades of yellow and gray. There is little of the feeling of a long-shared home that invites the visitor to relax in their Upper West Side place in New York; here all is neat and new. Alma is planning, however, to fix up the place—which they bought in 1973—and make it more homelike. What Isaac likes best about the Florida apartment is the big terrace where he can stand and look out at the skyline of high-rises to the north, the sweep of spectacular beach, and the warm green sea below.

The Singers spend their days quietly here. Isaac seldom takes on speaking engagements. He doesn't do much visiting, although Alma goes to see people she knows, sees movies when she can, visits museums and galleries, responds to dinner party invitations. (Alma is not a vegetarian, though she cheerfully accommodates Isaac when she cooks for him.) Her favorite pastime, like Isaac's, is taking long walks, usually in the afternoons, especially when the Florida sun is beaming down. Isaac spends a few hours of every day here writing. To him Seaside represents a retreat from the hectic schedule he follows in New York. The telephone rings less often—although it does ring, and the callers' voices sometimes come from great distances. An aspiring writer in New York calls for advice on how to get a story published; would Isaac take a look at it? Agents, publishers, producers, phone to discuss business. Friends ring him up to find out how he is and when he's coming back to the city. Lecture bureaus seek his services. Isaac talks to them all calmly and patiently, replying softly to every question, doing his best, as always, not to disappoint anyone.

Alma has many friends here in the area, some of them in the same building, and on this day in January 1976 they have arranged a birthday party in her honor. She is sixty-eight. They have brought sandwiches and home-made cakes to the celebration, which has lasted through most of the after-noon. Alma is a little flushed and tired but agrees to keep her promise to talk about herself and her years with Isaac, who retires to the bedroom "so you won't feel inhibited."

"We met," Alma recalls, "on a farm in the Catskills. It was called Porter's Farm. We were both vacationing there. We got into long conversations and complicated discussions, and we liked one another so much that it devel-oped into a courtship.

"Why does a woman choose a man? I fell in love with him. It was a tense and strange relationship. I was married. I was not free. I had two children— little children—and a husband. We had only arrived recently from Ger-many, my husband and I, and we had to count our pennies, and Isaac had no money either. This was not an expensive farm. But I remember there was a little lake, and I took the children on a boat ride on the lake, and that was where I met Isaac. And then when we got back to the city, we started to write to each other, and this went on for some time. And then we broke off because I didn't see how I could leave the children, my boy, Klaus, and my daughter, Inga. I really didn't know what to do. I was just past thirty when I met Isaac. But everything about him attracted me."

Alma is a handsome woman, her pale face somewhat ravaged by time, her hair a reddish blond, her bright pale-blue eyes at once keen and gentle, her body kept rigorously from stoutness by careful dieting and exercise. A snapshot of her, taken on the farm where she met Isaac, shows a lithe and lovely young woman with handsome features, her hair longer than it is now. She is wearing a long summer gown, lolling on a grassy lawn in the dappled shade of a tree—an altogether appealing woman, as indeed she still is.

Although they both grew up in Europe at the turn of the century, Alma's background is entirely different from Isaac's. "I was born in Munich, Ba-varia, the oldest daughter of Paul and Lena Bach Haimann. My father's family had lived in Germany for three generations. His father in turn had been a judge who dealt with commercial cases—a *Handelrichter*. That was considered an exceptional position for a Jew. My mother came from a fam-ily I suppose you would have to call nouveau riche. Her father and his brother had made the family fortune, so in a way I suppose you could call her an heiress.

"We lived on the Princeregestrasse, opposite the English Gardens. Our house was five minutes from the Hofgarten, where they held many of Mu-nich's most important concerts. We had three servants—one for the chil-dren, one for the household, and a cook. There were eight rooms in our apartment. Even before I started going to school I had a governess, an Englishwoman who taught me English. We never spoke Yiddish at home, only German. My father spoke Swedish, Dutch, Italian, and French as well as German. He was a well-read man and completely informed about world affairs. My grandfather used to bring me clothes from Paris, the latest fashions.

"My father's business was textiles—silks and velvets, retail. He was an expert weaver. He was an outgoing, good-natured man, very popular, with many friends. He was tall, with an erect bearing. My mother was a pretty women with milk-white skin and brown hair and blue eyes.

"There was one other child, my sister, who is still alive. We were not raised in the Orthodox Jewish fashion—in fact, the only time I recall going to synagogue was on the High Holy Days. In school, however, the children were obliged to take religious courses, two hours a week, so my sister and I took the Jewish course. We learned how to read the Hebrew letters and studied the Bible and some Jewish history. My father wanted us to know we were Jews. He would have been unhappy had either of us married a non-Jew. He would dress up when we went to the synagogue, which was a Conservative congregation, but he refused to wear the customary top hat. What he liked best was the sermons, delivered by a rabbi who would thunder out brimstone and fire."

After attending public school in Munich, Alma went to a university in Switzerland. She became an avid reader, especially of the classics. She loved concerts and the theater. In the summers the family traveled widely through the capitals of Europe—Geneva, Paris, London, Rome.

"Shortly after I came home from Switzerland, I married a businessman, Walter Wasserman. He owned a state agency for spirits and alcohol, and he was also involved in the stock market. We married in 1927. He too came from money, but the family fortune was lost after World War One, and Walter rebuilt it. Walter was an only child. We met during a hike in the countryside, but it turned out that our two families were acquainted.

"My family approved the match, but later they felt I had made a mistake, that Walter was not a romantic enough companion for me. But when I married Walter, he was a good-looking young man. Tall, like my father. His face had those chiseled features, and he had light brown hair and brown eyes.

"In 1936 we got out of Germany. It was no place for Jews. We came to New York with Klaus and Inga. My husband had enough money to support us without any serious financial problems, but we could no longer live on quite as high a scale as we had in Germany.

"We went to live in a comfortable apartment on Seaman Avenue in the Inwood section of Manhattan. Since we lived in what was then predominantly an Irish part of town, and we wanted to raise our son and daughter as Jews, we used to take them all the way to Temple Emanu-El on Fifth Avenue on holidays. We sent them to Sunday school.

"When we came here, most businessmen didn't want to touch the market so soon after the Great Depression, but Walter bought U.S. Steel and Bethlehem Steel stocks for practically nothing and rode the crest of the wave to prosperity. But he never read a book unless it was about business, he didn't enjoy theater or concerts. About the only thing we shared in common was our love of nature and our enthusiasm for hiking.

"And then I met Isaac. For several years we went on seeing each other and breaking off and starting up again, and all that time I said nothing to my husband. Finally I had to tell Walter. And then I left him. In 1939 we were divorced."

Isaac almost didn't marry Alma at all. He wasn't sure he wanted to be tied down. Moreover he was not in a particularly good frame of mind. The year 1939 was a bitter one for him in terms of news from abroad. With the Hitler-Stalin Pact and Hitler's invasion of Poland, Isaac's mother and brother Moishe were deported in a cattle wagon from Dzikow. Isaac had heard a rumor that Moishe had starved to death—was given a piece of bread on the Sabbath but refused to carry it home, because one is not allowed to carry things on the Sabbath, or to eat it on the spot, since it wasn't kosher. ("He was a saint. I am the very opposite.") After the war he was to discover that the Russians had taken Bathsheba and Moishe to Kazakhstan in a cattle train and that they had frozen to a death in a forest with a group of prisoners who were ordered to build themselves log cabins in the depths of winter. But in 1939 he had no idea what had actually become of them and the news from abroad depressed him. He began to miss his son. He wrote to Runya in Palestine asking her to come to America and bring the nine-year-old boy with her. She replied that she could see no point in such a voyage unless they were to live together again. She would not send her son to New York to be brought up by some other woman. It was up to Isaac to decide what to do. Isaac made the decision—and as a result did not see Israel again until the young man came to New York in 1955.

In 1940 Alma and Isaac were married at a civil ceremony in Manhattan.

"When I married Isaac," says Alma, "you must understand that he wasn't yet Isaac Bashevis Singer. I mean to say, we had nothing. The first thing I did was to go to work in a factory—a friend got me the job—sewing sweatbands into men's hats. Then for a while I got a job sewing ladies' hats together. I even took a course in how to make such hats—but apparently I wasn't cut out for that career. I took all kinds of jobs. I mean, Isaac always worked as a journalist and was independent and supported himself, but for the comforts of life I wanted, it was necessary for me to work too."

Alma went on working while her ex-husband supervised the upbringing of Klaus and Inga. She would take sales jobs at women's clothing stores such as Lerner's for Christmas. Later she worked five and a half days a week at Arnold Constable, at a starting salary of fifteen dollars a week, which, after four years, went all the way up to thirty-six. By this time she had been promoted from the rank of salesperson to that of personal shopper. "You must understand that being a personal shopper actually meant shlepping merchandise from one department to another, writing up the sales checks, and sending the purchases on to the customers. But at least on this job my taste came into play, because I was the one who would make the selection for a customer—the blouse or sweater or whatever she wanted. And this was a little better than sewing hatbands. All this time Isaac was writing articles and making some money as a journalist, but I knew he had a more important contribution to make than that."

In the summer of 1947, when Isaac and Alma decided to go off to Europe, Alma was informed by her superior at Arnold Constable that if she could afford to travel overseas she probably didn't need the job, and she was let go. When the Singers returned, she worked as a buyer for a Brooklyn clothing firm ("They liked refugees because the owners had gone through all the horrors in Poland and understood what it meant.") In 1955, after a second trip abroad with Isaac, Alma took another department store job, at Saks Thirty-fourth Street. She remained there until 1963, when the store failed. Then she went to work for Lord and Taylor on Fifth Avenue. A few years ago she and Isaac agreed that it was time for her to retire.

During her working years Alma was up and out early every morning. Usually she didn't see Isaac until evening. "He used to say to me, 'You stand on your feet all day. I don't want you to come home and have to start cooking. I want you to be able to sit down with me somewhere and have your dinner in peace.' He would work on his writing, and I would work on my job, and at night we would have dinner out most of the time."

When Alma was working full time, she always took care of their home, cleaning, sweeping, dusting, and trying to keep Isaac's books and papers in some kind of order. Sundays she did the washing and attended to practical and domestic arrangements.

The Singers lived on Ocean Avenue in a sparsely furnished apartment in Brooklyn from 1940 to 1941. After that they moved to a five-story walkup on West 103rd Street in Manhattan. A year later they "graduated to Central Park West," renting two rooms and a kitchenette—a small apartment with a fine view of the park. In 1959 they moved to larger quarters on West 72nd Street. Since 1962 they have rented their spacious apartment on West 86th Street.

Was Isaac a difficult man to live with? "I want to tell you something," Alma responds. "When we first got married, Isaac was an absolute doll. He was the easiest man in the world to be around, nothing was complicated. Today he's under so much pressure it's hard for him to go on being as easygoing as he was in those days. But at the same time, life today is much easier for me."

In recent years Alma has occasionally accompanied Isaac on lecture assignments to such places as St. Louis and Kansas City and on his trips to

Israel. But the two do spend time apart. "We have our own interests and our own lives," Isaac says.

Alma is aware of Isaac's difficulties in adhering to the traditional requirements of monogamy but feels that they have both invested so many years in their marriage that parting would be unthinkable. She has never forgotten the emotional upheaval that followed her separation from her first husband and does not ever want to go through such an experience again. She herself has no wish to experiment with adventures outside her marriage; the whole idea is numbing to her. "And I must remind you," she adds, "Isaac is basically a very conservative person." She doubts he would accept infidelity on her part.

Alma's daughter, Inga, is today a woman in her forties with two children. She lives in New Jersey. Alma sees her daughter—"not regularly, but we are in constant contact." She is on good terms with both her children. Her son, Klaus, born in 1934, is still a bachelor. Like his father, he is interested in the stock market, finance, and real estate. He lives near his mother in an apartment on the Upper West Side of Manhattan and owns a country house as well.

Does Isaac share his ideas and his work with Alma? Sometimes. He will show her the first draft of a chapter written in Yiddish (Alma understands Yiddish though she doesn't speak it), and once in a while they discuss the contents. "I might have a small criticism about something he writes. But in general I think his writing is beautiful. I love his clear, precise sentences. Even a child can understand his writing." Alma is credited as co-translator on some of his recent stories.

She herself wrote a story once, but the publisher she sent it to asked for a different ending, and she never got around to supplying one. The *Jewish Exponent* in Philadelphia reported in January 1977 that Alma was working on her autobiography and quoted her as saying, "I'm about as far as the first hundred pages." Isaac doesn't think she is going to finish it.

The telephone rings, and Isaac comes hurrying in from the bedroom to answer it. The caller is a woman who is writing a book about making jewelry out of bagels; she wants Isaac to supply an endorsement for the jacket. He tells her he's sorry, his publisher does not permit that sort of thing—he has signed an agreement about it. Anyhow, she should go after movie stars and best-selling glamorous authors to endorse her book, not Isaac Singer. An agent? No, his own agent is too much of a big shot for her at this stage of her career. She should find someone with a smaller clientele who can devote more attention to her manuscript. "But send me the book to read, and I wish you luck with it."

Putting down the phone, Isaac welcomes a cup of tea and some cake left over from the birthday party. Outside, the winter dusk deepens quickly. Alma lights the lamp. Husband and wife look the picture of contentment sitting there on the sofa in the soft lamplight, eating cake and sipping tea.

❀

April 6, 1978

Hanna Desser is a tall, handsome woman with a fair complexion, brown hair worn short, and keen, probing brown eyes. She recently retired as executive editor of *Present Tense*, the American Jewish Committee quarterly, but continues to work as a consultant for the magazine, which recently carried a section of *A Young Man in Search of Love*. Over lunch at a French restaurant in midtown Manhattan Hanna talks about her friendship with Alma Singer.

Alma and Hanna met about seven years ago at a penthouse party on Central Park West given by a mutual friend. "I remember that Alma impressed me particularly that evening," Hanna says, "because she was so elegantly dressed—more so than most of the other guests. She had on a pale blue satin dress that was quite striking. Alma cares about her clothes and her appearance. She always is sure to be wearing the right hat and gloves and shoes. To me she is a very European woman. She is much put together. Not informal. The only place I've ever seen her really relaxed and careless of her appearance was poolside at the building where she and Isaac have the condominium in Florida."

The friendship between the two women developed when *Present Tense* asked Isaac to contribute articles and stories to its pages. "I went to visit them, and suddenly Alma and I were going places together, to concerts, museum exhibitions, and so forth."

How deep are Alma's cultural interests? "She has a feeling for art and music. She once told me that I was opening up a new world for her, which rather surprised me, since in a long lifetime she has certainly seen much of the world. On the other hand, she worked for many years and kept to a busy schedule which prevented much by way of leisure activities. When we go to the Frick Museum for a concert of chamber music or to a gallery, her reactions to what she sees and hears are invariably intelligent and discriminating, and her interest in these pursuits is really quite genuine. But of course all of our excursions haven't been on a cultural plane. I live in the same area, and we've gone to some dreadful neighborhood movies together as well.

"After my retirement from *Present Tense*, she called me and said that since I would have more time, we must get together more often. I have been to dinner at the Singers' apartment on quite a few occasions, and I'm always surprised by the formality that Alma brings to the event. She puts out her best silver and crystal and loves to hark back to the days when she lived with her family in Munich and everything was done in style. Once I visited her in Florida with my daughter and granddaughter, and she served us a fabulous lunch."

Even when Alma joins Hanna for lunch at a cut-rate coffee shop on upper Broadway, she will treat the occasion, Hanna says, as if it were a gala event, dressing for the appointment and displaying her excellent old-world manners.

One of Alma's interests, Hanna learned, is money. She dabbles in the stock market, and despite her long-standing habits of economy, left over from more stringent times, she loves to shop for antiques and furniture. "She is always careful to point out that Isaac has his money, but she also has hers and is firm about being mistress of the ways she spends it."

Hanna has found Alma deeply loyal to Isaac. As others have observed, if he gets a bad review she takes it personally and seems more upset about it than he does. "When people who disapproved of the nudity in *Yentl* on Broadway started calling in the middle of the night, she was terribly upset. She told me once that after a performance she had attended a woman stopped her in the aisle and started to scream at her that her husband's play was obscene. Alma was shattered."

Alma, Hanna believes, would fuss more over Isaac, especially over his health, than she does if he did not detest that kind of attention. "At the same time Isaac, who claims to be so contemptuous of doctors and medicines, once arrived with Alma in Florida all upset about a bag that was discovered missing when they got to their apartment. And the bag, it turned out, was completely filled with his medicines! Alma frets about his health constantly. She wishes he would cut down on the lecture tours and spend more time resting. Only occasionally does she accompany him on his trips. She worries about the way he says yes to anybody who wants to interview or visit him and feels that he allows too many people to intrude on his privacy. Of course when she's there, she always comes out with tea and cakes or a cordial, but she wishes he would make himself less accessible. On the other hand, she is thrilled when a celebrity comes to the house. I was there one afternoon for tea when a well-known English writer arrived, and Alma really responded to that situation."

Hanna has noticed that Alma finds ways to protect Isaac from his public despite himself. One night when Hanna was there a young woman representing a publishing firm was trying to get Isaac to show her his old family photographs. Alma managed to prevent her from seeing any pictures at all that evening.

It has not escaped Hanna's attention that Isaac is sometimes irritable with his wife and does not hesitate to put her down when she voices some opinion he doesn't agree with or calls him by some nickname that annoys him. "Yes, she's upset about Isaac's brusqueness sometimes, but I think she accepts this as a part of being married to a genius, knowing that it's not easy to live with a genius. She has long considered him one of the great writers of our time. She's been pleased when he's invited her to work with him on translations. She considers *The Slave* his finest book but wasn't so happy about *Enemies, A Love Story*, which she felt was written on a cruder level.

"Alma never hesitates to tell Isaac what she thinks of something he has written. She has persuaded him to rewrite articles and book reviews, for example, when she declared that a particular effort was not worthy of him. She takes Isaac and his work very, very seriously. She has also been doing some writing of her own—working on her autobiography, she says, but hasn't shown any of it to me."

Hanna attributes Alma's reluctance to hire servants to her ingrained sense of economy. A cleaning woman does come in about once a week when the Singers are in New York, but Alma is seldom satisfied with the job any cleaning woman does. Alma herself takes the laundry to a local Laundromat, cooks all the meals, and attends to the household.

How does all this square with her risking money in the stock market? "It fascinates her. It brings out another side of her, an adventurous side. I asked her once if she had made any money on the market. She paused for a minute to think and then replied, 'Well, I think I came out even.' So it must be the excitement of the thing. I went with her once to a brokerage office in Miami. She sat there talking as knowingly as any big wheel from Wall Street."

Even so, Alma cannot bear to throw things away. Her closets are filled with clothes from years back, shoes with stiletto heels, ancient fur coats, dresses long out of style.

"As she grows older," Hanna says, "Alma is getting more interested in life rather than less so. More than ever she wants to go places, to experience things, to enjoy music and paintings and good books and parties. She wishes Isaac would work less and spend more time enjoying the fruits of his achievements. She respects his vegetarianism, but she herself loves all kinds of good food and wine. But most of all, she loves Isaac. She sees him plain, with all his faults and foibles, but she deeply loves him."

PART 4

"Slowly I Turned

Back to Writing"

Isaac did not start to write fiction again until he was nearly forty and he and Alma were living on Central Park West. By that time Joshua and his family had left Sea Gate for Riverside Drive in Manhattan and were living in an apartment in the same building with the managing editor of the *Forward*, so the brothers were virtually neighbors.

"I knew," Isaac says, "that by the age of forty many writers, including my brother, had composed great masterpieces. And at almost forty I hadn't accomplished anything, except for one small book—*Satan in Goray*. I felt a complete failure. Then slowly I turned back to writing."

His attempts at that time to draft large works came to nothing, but he was able to complete a number of short stories. Important among these was "The Destruction of Kreshev." The plot, as in *Satan in Goray*, involves the possession of an entire village by Satanic forces. Satan himself narrates the story: "I am the Primeval Snake, the Evil One, Satan. The Cabala refers to me as Samael and the Jews sometimes call me merely, 'that one.' " In the course of the tale the Evil One arranges some peculiar marriages. The story, in fact, is like a grim rendering of the scene in Gilbert and Sullivan's comic opera *The Sorcerer* in which each of the villagers, after swallowing a love potion, falls passionately in love with the first person of the opposite sex he or she happens to see on awakening. "The Destruction of Kreshev" ends with the heroine, a rabbi's daughter, deciding, after her corruption by Satan, to take her own life—just as Isaac had often thought of doing during his first days in America.

The *Forward* editors did not care much for "The Destruction of Kreshev," or for the stories that followed—"Diary of One Not Born," "Zeidlus the Pope," and "Two Corpses Go Dancing." But all these appeared in 1943, the year Isaac got his citizenship papers, in *Shoten an Goray un Anderer Dertailungen* (*Satan in Goray and Other Tales*), published in New York by Farlag Matones.

Speaking of the stories he wrote in the early forties, Isaac told Irving Buchen, "In the Yiddish circles, this kind of writing was strange. I remember my editor telling me, 'Why do you write about things the readers have already forgotten? These things might have been valid two hundred years ago, but not today.' But you know, writers are sometimes very stubborn. I kept on writing in the same way and I didn't listen to my editor. In any case, he fought me, tried to convince me to be what he wanted me to be, a social-conscious writer, to write about the situation of tailors in New York, how badly they live and how they fight for their existence. Somehow these things did not appeal to me."

Total royalties from the sale of *Satan in Goray and Other Tales* in Yiddish (a thousand copies were printed): ninety dollars.

❀

By 1937 Israel Joshua Singer had completed his fourth novel, *Khaver Nakhman (Comrade Nachman)*, published in Yiddish by Farlag Matones; a year later, in 1938, it was issued by Alfred A. Knopf in a translation by Maurice Samuel as *East of Eden*. (It was reprinted by the Vanguard Press in 1967.)

The hell on earth that the Soviet system imposed on its victims has never been more unsparingly documented than in the pages of *East of Eden*. The story chronicles the hardships endured by Nachman Ritter, a naive worker for the Communist party in Poland who risks his life to cross the Polish border into the Soviet Union only to undergo unspeakable deprivations and later imprisonment, beatings, and torture rivaling anything set down decades later by Solzhenitsyn in *The Gulag Archipelago*. Nachman is drawn as the perfect victim, a Jewish lightning rod for all the world's unfairness and cruelty. Reporting on what he had witnessed in the Soviet Union with the merciless, obsessed precision of a disenchanted convert, Joshua calls the shots on what the builders of the New Society in Russia were up to at a time when many intellectuals all over the world were still starry-eyed about Russian communism. But *East of Eden* is a kind of agit-prop novel turned upside down—Brecht in reverse—without the distancing and largely without the laughter. It throttles its characters in its merciless tabulation of injuries. One leaves the last page of *East of Eden* feeling like a hunted creature emerging in the nick of time after a long punishing chase through a smothering sewer. No doubt it all happened just this way, but perhaps even a novel of Jewish suffering has to reveal more than suffering.

In 1938, in addition to *East of Eden*, Alfred A. Knopf published a collection of I. J. Singer's short stories entitled *The River Breaks Up* (reissued in

1976 by the Vanguard Press). Translated into stark, unvarnished English by Maurice Samuel, these tightly constructed stories—including "Pearls," which first attracted a readership for Joshua when it appeared in Warsaw in Yiddish in 1922—are again overwhelming in their power. It is as if the author did not know his own strength; relentlessly, like a man shouting into the wind, he deals out episode after episode of greed and cruelty illustrating man's ingenuity at inflicting pain on his fellows. The title story is about an ox-driver who attempts to carry his newly acquired goat across the Vistula on an ice floe so that he might return to his village in time for Passover. But the ice is breaking up; man and animal perish in a roaring flood. In "Pearls," Moritz Spielrein, a hypochondriacal gem merchant, exploits his tenants in a Warsaw slum, piles up wealth on the jewelry exchange, and foils the undertaker eager to bury him. In this tale and in "Old City," the story of an eccentric antique-shop owner who rules a menagerie of pets with an iron hand, there is a richness of detail and a depiction of decadence that leads the reader into a hothouse world resembling that of Carson McCullers's *Reflections in a Golden Eye.* Had Joshua pursued this bent, he might have bequeathed an entirely different body of work to Yiddish literature. But in many of the stories the author goes too far in setting down the gruesome particulars of ugly events. Raw, gossiping, shrill housewives and surly, selfish husbands shout and brawl and scrabble for subsistence through pages dense with squalor. One puts down the book with a sense of relief that there are no further horrors to man or woman or beast to be endured, no more stenches to suffocate one, no more blood or battered heads to contemplate.

In 1943, the same year that *Shoten an Goray un Anderer Dertailungen* was published, I. J. Singer's last novel, *De Mishpokhe Karnovski* (*The Family Carnovsky*) appeared in Yiddish, published by the same firm. Again the scope is wide, encompassing three generations of a Jewish family seeking assimilation in Germany, and the technique is cinematic (Joshua would have made a marvelous screen writer.) David Carnovsky, a son of the Enlightenment and the scion of the Carnovskys of Greater Poland, scorning the narrow-minded ways of the Polish Hasidim, takes his wife, Leah, to Berlin, where he seeks to live his life "as a Jew among Jews and a German among Germans." He names his son after the unorthodox Jewish philosopher Moses Mendelssohn. Leah misses the old ways and turns to Jews from Poland for friendship, but David works as an importer of lumber, trims his beard, wears a derby (on the Sabbath, a top hat), orders a frock coat with silk lapels, and raises the apple of his eye, his son, Moses Georg, to be a surgeon and a German. Georg does become a famous surgeon and marries his gentile nurse. Then trouble begins. The Nazis are on their way to power, and Georg's ill-fated, frail son, Jegor, bears the brunt of his family's futile efforts to assimilate. Egged on by a militaristic, Nazified uncle on his mother's side, Jegor turns into an anti-Semite. Although the family escapes the fate of the concentration camp, which seems so sure, and is able to start a new life among the Jewish refugees of New York City's Washington Heights, Jegor, after suffering traumatic humiliations at school, grows up hopelessly neurotic. He fails even in an attempt to become an undercover agent for the Nazis in Yorkville and shoots himself after bludgeoning to death his corrupt homosexual employer, who lusts after him. Will Georg be able to save his son's life? The outcome is left ambiguous.

As a chronicle of what happened to the Jews of Berlin in this century *The Family Carnovsky* is a vivid document. We know that this is how it must have been for those Jews who wanted only to exist quietly among their neighbors and follow their faith without flaunting external differences of dress and behavior. And the reader who pursues this novel to its bitter outcome learns that their travails did not end when they escaped to America. The arrogance of some Jewish refugees from Germany brought a new kind of scorn and ostracism from their neighbors. The Depression forced men like Georg, respected doctors, distinguished members of other professions, to grasp at any straw, to return to abandoned—and now humiliating—ways of eking out a living as laborers and peddlers.

Writing *The Family Carnovsky* when he did, it was impossible for the author to maintain any kind of Brechtian distance between himself and the ordeals that befall his Jewish characters or to draw three-dimensional portraits of their oppressors. How could a man like Joshua be expected to maintain a serene objectivity during the rise of Hitler (whose name he would not so much as mention in his pages) when incredibly ugly reports of the all too real suffering of the Jews in Europe were reaching this country daily?

As in so many old-fashioned epic movies, the book's figures, although drawn in illuminating, persuasive detail in the earlier chapters, later seem to forget to breathe and petrify into frozen symbols, types. By the time we get to Jegor and his problems, the characters have started to turn into the stock figures of a morality play. Jegor is too pat an example of the fate of children of intermarriages; he would feel all too at home in blackface in one of those militant homemade plays of the sixties about the half-white hero who doesn't know where he belongs. Sometimes the book reads for pages on end a little like the screenplay for the TV series *Holocaust*. Yet Joshua's stereotypes are never the prettified portraits that were trotted out to represent Jews in Hollywood treatments of the period. In fact, both the Jews and the gentiles in *The Family Carnovsky*'s mammoth cast are depicted much of the time as greedy, selfish creatures. Only a few of them are lovable in their humanity, or display much of it. Waste is another theme that runs through the book, as it does through all Joshua's fiction. People long for the wrong things, buy what they don't need, squander their substance, swathe their vanity in impractical and ostentatious finery, hiding their simian natures behind improbable, extravagant airs. Yet there is a saint dwelling among all these simian creatures: old Ephraim Walder, sealed off from the turmoil of German life around him, surrounded by his holy books and manuscripts, which are crumbling to dust due to the depredations of mold and mice. It is Reb Ephraim who sums up the message of the tale: "Life is a terrible prankster, Reb Carnovsky. It loves to play tricks on people. German Jews wanted to be Jews in the house and gentiles in the street, but life turned this ambition completely topsy-turvy. The fact is that we have become gentiles in the house and Jews in the street." The model for Reb Ephraim might have been old Pinchas Mendel Singer himself.

For all *The Family Carnovsky*'s weaknesses, the novel's master-plan is drawn up with such skill and the sweep of much of the action is so gripping that it stands even today with a classic solidity that is impressive.

The Family Carnovsky did not appear in English until 1969, when Vanguard published it in a translation by Maurice Samuel. A paperback edition was published by Harrow, the paperback division of Harper and Row, in 1973.

What effect did all this crushingly graphic prose have on the mind and spirit of Isaac Singer? He was always overwhelmed by the power of Joshua's pen and felt that his own early work was trivial and inconsequential compared to his brother's. Yet he had already proved in *Satan in Goray* that he could match that power while leavening the cruelty with humor, irony, and fantasy. Even so, he emulated the structure and realism of his brother's family novels in his next three novels, *The Family Moskat*, *The Estate*, and *The Manor*. In his later work he would come more and more to temper the grimness, not denying for an instant the pain of existence but offering our sensibilities the anodynes of pleasure and fantasy, permitting us to hear a subtler laughter than the howls of boors. Although he would never question the sanctity of structure (every story must have "a beginning, a middle, and an end" or by Isaac's yardstick it is not a story), he would manage to elude the most dangerous trap of "realism"—the notion that a clear-eyed view of reality can reflect only a landscape of unrelieved ugliness peopled mainly by monsters. Yes, Isaac's landscapes are often enough abodes of the grotesque, but even his freaks are capable of experiencing pleasure as well as sorrow, of sharing with us the ecstasies of existence along with its despairs.

In some ironic and elusive way Isaac Singer's pessimism was to prove more exhilarating in the long run than what he regarded as his brother's more positive outlook on life. He has brought back no valentines from hell, but he has reported hearing laughter on his visits there; even if it is only the Devil's over the anguish of his victims, and the rest is tears, it is a reassuring sound. Isaac shares little of T. S. Eliot's Anglican puritanism, but like Eliot, he long ago came to realize that "humankind cannot bear very much reality."

There was one more book from Joshua's pen. This was *Of a World That Is No More,* which had been serialized in the *Forward* as *Fun a Velt Vos Iz Nishto* but did not appear in book form until 1946, posthumously, when it was published in Yiddish by Farlag Matones. It was issued in English in 1970 by Vanguard, in an excellent translation by his son, Joseph. These reminiscences of growing up Jewish in Leoncin and Bilgoray during the reign of Czar Nicholas II are similar in spirit and subject matter to Isaac's first book of memoirs, *In My Father's Court.* The story of how the rabbi's eldest son chafed under the yoke of cheder and the Torah and became a friend of the town's most disreputable and colorful elements, finding the road from the confining village to the great world beyond, is among the most engaging of Joshua's literary efforts. *Of a World That Is No More* is suffused with a gentler humor than are Joshua's novels and stories, and yet it is informed by the unflinching view of reality that characterizes all his work; the vanished world he describes is painstakingly portrayed in all its ugliness—but there is beauty there too. Joshua, the master of the family novel, never wrote about a family better than he did when he described his own.

Israel Joshua Singer died in 1944 in New York. "He had a heart attack," his son Joseph explains. "All his life he'd suffered from a clot in one of his legs. About three weeks before his death the clot moved, and this apparently led to the attack. I believe there is some kind of history of arterial sclerosis in the family. My grandfather died of heart trouble, and one of my aunts, and then my father—at the age of fifty-one, at the height of his powers as an author. It was a real tragedy, a loss I was only to come to understand fully as I grew older."

To Isaac, Joshua's death was "the greatest misfortune of my entire life. He was my father, my teacher. I never really recovered from this blow. There was only one consolation—whatever would happen later would never be as bad as this." Yet the shock of that passing seemed somehow to galvanize Isaac, to free him to develop his powers as an author. Could it be that awe of Joshua's success had immobilized him? Or that he was moved to speak again because his brother's voice was silenced, and it was now up to him to take up where Joshua had left off?

On the dedication page of the English version of his own first family novel, *The Family Moskat,* Isaac wrote, "I dedicate this to the memory of my late brother, I. J. Singer, author of *The Brothers Ashkenazi.* To me he was not only the older brother, but a spiritual father and master as well. I looked up to him always as to a model of high morality and literary honesty. Although a modern man, he had all the great qualities of our pious ancestors."

Irving Buchen has put forward the opinion that Singer's preoccupation in his works with "the supplanting of Esau by Jacob and his equally strong determination to persist in his demonic work and appear in translation suggest the possibility that Singer was working in the shadow, not the light of his older brother. To be sure, the influences were there, and without I. J. Singer, Singer probably would have remained in Warsaw and, like Asa Heshel of *The Family Moskat*, perished in the Warsaw ghetto. Still, a strong brother and his influence may obscure more than it nourishes. Besides, by coming into his own literary birthright, Singer has been able to pay his brother the most lasting tribute."*

Before he could fling open the tight-shut windows of Yiddish literature and let in the air of his unique originality, Isaac had first to put himself through an apprenticeship that was a kind of homage to the memory of his older brother and his achievements—the fabrication of mammoth family novels that in length, if not in power, would rival those monuments to the sufferings of Poland's Jews erected by Joshua. Only through these agonizing exercises could he free himself for a leaner and lighter form of literary architecture—to produce, along with numerous masterworks in miniature, such unique achievements as *The Magician of Lublin, The Slave,* and *Enemies, A Love Story,* novels that owe little to the Russian tradition, or to Knut Hamsun, or to anyone's genius but his own. He had already given his readers a provocative glimpse of what he might do in the fevered, phantasmagoric *Satan in Goray.* But before he returned to that terrain, he would face and resurrect the immediate past he had fled, in *The Family Moskat* and later in *The Manor* and *The Estate,* books that provided maps of obliterated worlds populated by believable living beings.

❊

Isaac walked the streets of Manhattan's Upper West Side in 1944 and brooded on his brother's death and on the world he had left behind in Poland a decade before. He made lists of the people he had known, recasting and combining them into the characters he would bring to life in his prose. He had made an earlier attempt to write a novel about the fortunes and misfortunes of a Polish-Jewish family named Moskat. Now he felt ready at last to cope with such a project. He plotted his chapters carefully. He did research in libraries. He combed through the files of old Warsaw newspapers, accumulating incidents, anecdotes, even old weather reports and glimpses of half-forgotten history. Most of all, he searched and re-searched his own memory until everything that had happened shone with the luminosity of experience not only recalled but comprehended. Then, about a year after Joshua's death, Isaac Bashevis Singer opened a cardboard-covered com-

---

* *Isaac Bashevis Singer and the Eternal Past.*

position book with lined pages and, in a tiny, precise Yiddish script, started writing the story down.

The Family Moskat, published by Alfred A. Knopf in 1950, is a turbulent, fevered, sprawling saga drawn on a huge canvas—in English, even with the original final chapter eliminated by the author's own decision, it runs to more than six hundred pages. For three years, even as he wrote it, the novel ran chapter by chapter in the pages of the *Jewish Daily Forward*. And the feeling that one is reading a serial story persists when one reads it in book form.

The Family Moskat concerns three generations of Polish Jews during the years 1912 to 1939. The book boasts a huge cast of characters, among them the pious, prosperous, thrice-married Jewish patriarch, Meshulam Moskat; his children, grandchildren, and great-grandchildren, who cannot match him in business acumen, energy, integrity, or devotion; Rosa Frumetl, the widow old Meshulam meets at a spa and brings back to his fancy apartment in Warsaw; her daughter, Adele; his granddaughter, Hadassah, a fragile, sensitive, intelligent girl; his daughter, Leah; his fat, self-indulgent, lustful but lovable son-in-law, Abram Shapiro, who could have been played to perfection by the late Zero Mostel; his caretaker, Koppel, who manages to steal some of the old man's fortune and control the rest after his death and to run off to America with Leah.

"All my books are about me," Isaac has confessed. "They are myself. The events in my stories are not always what did happen but always what might have happened." And this is true especially of *The Family Moskat*, where his hero, Asa Heshel Bannet, is the son of the rabbi in a provincial town called Tereshpol Minor, which bears a striking resemblance to the Bilgoray of Isaac's adolescence. The worldly watchmaker of Isaac's youth, Todros, turns up as Jekuthiel, who guides Asa Heshel into the byways of scientific knowledge and secular philosophy. And Isaac is certainly the model for Asa Heshel himself—not only his pallor, his physical fragility, and his relationships with women, but his very dreams and the questions he asks as a child: "How high is the sky? How deep is the earth? What's at the other side of the end of the world? Who made God?" Asa Heshel comes to Warsaw with a copy of a book by Spinoza in his pocket. He is at once worldly and unworldly, enlightened and ignorant, boldly amorous and abjectly shy.

If Asa Heshel's personality is akin to Isaac's, Asa Heshel's experiences are of the kind Isaac might have had if he had pursued a different course. In this sense *The Family Moskat*, like the novels that follow it, is an autobiography in the "What if . . ." category.

The story begins when the Jews of Poland are turning away from the old Orthodoxy and becoming more and more assimilated into the ways of a country that doesn't want them. Reb Meshulam Moskat brings his third wife, Rosa, whom he has met at a spa, back to Warsaw along with her daughter, Adele. A family gathering is celebrated. Enter Asa Heshel Bannet, fresh from the provinces. Asa Heshel marries Moskat's crabbed, acidulous stepdaughter, Adele, but leaves her for the old man's granddaughter, Hadassah, who runs off with him for a holiday in Switzerland. (Once they profane the Day of Atonement, the holiest day of the year, by making love.) Later he leaves her.

There are scenes in the book involving the Hasidim of Bialodrevna, a village close to Warsaw. In Bialodrevna, as in Warsaw, we are given to understand that the winds of change are blowing. Youth are "running away from the study house, shaving off their beards, eating the unclean food of the gentile."

Reb Meshulam grows sick. "All is vanity," he says. He knows his family cares nothing for the religious values he lives by. Meshulam dies. His caretaker, Koppel, steals the estate and seizes power. Asa turns more and more to secular literature and science. But his life is a failure; unlike Isaac, he had no vocation; his abilities never jell into anything productive; he feels useless. In fact all those in the novel who try to live modern lives meet with disillusionment. As Meshulam's gluttonous, carousing son-in-law Abram tells Asa, "Ah, the Exile, the Exile, it's demoralized us."

Asa Heshel joins the army and goes through the hell of senseless war, projecting all Isaac's fears as to what might have happened to him if the military in Poland had got hold of him. Isaac's single day in jail is carried to its logical conclusion when Asa Heshel is arrested and has to spend time behind bars.

The Moskats continue to pursue the ways of assimilation. At a family Passover *seder* some of them can no longer believe the words they repeat about how God has rescued the Jews in each successive generation from the cruelty of the tyrants who persecuted them.

Toward the end of *The Family Moskat* there is a masked Chanukah ball, heralded as "A Ball of all Balls! A thousand attractions. A hundred prizes. Voting for a beauty queen and seven princesses. Jazz band. Buffet of the finest food. Oriental dances. Salon decorated by the greatest painters. Special review by distinguished stars. Recitation of modern and classical poets. A Jewish magician, Mr. Trick of America, in a performance which has baffled the greatest scientists. A Jewish strongman, whose name must be kept secret for the present, rending chains and breaking irons, as well as female hearts. Each guest will automatically participate in a lottery and may win such gifts as a Chanukah lamp, an alarm clock, a lorgnette, a Japanese fan, a bonbonnière, and the finest gift that any Jew might wish—a set of the works of Mendele Mocher Sforim, in a deluxe binding. . . ."

The ball itself is no festive experience for the protagonists. Hadassah has a sore throat and a fever and nearly faints in her finery. Asa broods through the whole affair. Abram, older, fatter, and more lustful than ever, is planning a sordid little escapade with a servant girl that will lead him straight to a heart attack. In the swirling, crowded, febrile confusion, Hadassah sees "a bewildering variety of masked figures . . . Russian generals with epaulets, Polish grandees in elegant caftans, Germans in spiked helmets, rabbis in fur hats, yeshiva students in velvet skullcaps, sidelocks dangling below their ears. It was some time before Hadassah realized that these were merely masquerade costumes."

This ball is really a bizarre rehearsal for a final dance of death. A few pages later the Nazis are on their way to Warsaw. Asa tries to take flight with Barbara, a newly acquired Marxist girlfriend (shades of Runya), but it is too late. The bombs are falling.

The books ends when a character named Hertz Yanovar, the vessel for Isaac's interest in the occult, says to Asa Heshel, "The Messiah will come soon." Asa Heshel looks at him in astonishment and asks what he means. "Death is the Messiah," is the reply. "That's the real truth." In the Yiddish version there are additional pages in which all the Moskats, including Asa Heshel himself, return to Judaism as the Nazis converge to effect their destruction.

The theme of *The Family Moskat* is the dissolution and ultimate destruction of Warsaw's Jews. The events of the plot symbolize decline and deterioration; as Irving Malin points out in his book *Isaac Bashevis Singer,* there is a breakdown of communication "within the same family and the same religion"; even Meshulam's funeral has symbolic connotations, as though the Jewish way of life itself were going to its grave. But these symbols are never thrust upon us; they remain implicit, between the lines. And Isaac, ever the storyteller rather than the historian, pursues his account through the details of daily existence, of personal aspirations, appetites, desires, struggles, and defeats. The story itself unfolds mechanically; the book is a mosaic of episodes as contrived as any in a soap opera. But no soap opera was ever peopled with such lifelike characters pursuing their lives in so realistic an environment. The members of the Moskat family are in some ways almost larger than life; in their relentless emotionality, for example. They rail at one another, give one another no quarter; even love scenes are riddled with bitter exchanges and recriminations. But beneath this surface truculence we see them for the vulnerable, susceptible characters they are. We know, when they walk down a boulevard, how precarious their very safety is because they are Jews. The women are victims of masculine selfishness; the men grapple blindly with entangling nets of guilt. Only the old and the pious—Asa's father, Rabbi Dan Katzenellenbogen, in his *shtetl* prayer house in Tereshpol Minor, the rabbi of Bialodrevna, and the old man Meshulam himself—are able to transcend their own petty lusts. By the time we are through with him Asa Heshel, staggering through the streets of Warsaw after a bombing, with the Nazis about to invade, has become somewhat preposterous as well as oppressive in his melancholy, mumbling about Spinoza and making lists of philosophical notions while he neglects his wife and son, wrangles with his mistress, and deserts them both to join the army. Asa's wintriness and Warsaw's ubiquitous snowscape eventually numb us. (No one describes the physical sensation of cold more effectively than Isaac.) And it is not only the reader who suffers from the pervasive, chilling bleakness of the book; the characters themselves, as in *The Family Carnovsky*, seem overcome, even as they cling to the promises of the Enlightenment, by the unrelieved tragedy of their lives. In this respect Isaac's family novels have somewhat the same effect as Joshua's. Only later would he temper his tragedies with wit and joy—though even in *The Family Moskat* scenes of festivity abound; his characters knew how to laugh as well as kvetch. They are complex, multidimensional people, and the penetrating descriptions of their psychological states enable us to identify with their emotions as well as their circumstances.

In *The Brothers Ashkenazi* Israel Joshua had surveyed his Warsaw Jews with a cool regard, expressing, as critic Max F. Schulz had pointed out, "the Jewish community's obsession with social standing; its eager collaboration in the transformation of rabbis from students of the sacred Law into sharpers at home . . . and its easy sanction of the employer class's economic exploitation of the worker in combination with a hypocritical concern for his morality . . . contradictions between old-fashioned *shtetl* piety and enlightened commonsense." Isaac, in *The Family Moskat*, goes further, without ever losing his compassion. His characters, driven to insanity by the constricting hold of their faith, fall prey to their own lusts and ambitions—even more the victims of their own humanity than the mere symbolic figures who people the Gothic scenery of *Satan in Goray*. They all are punished by their own passions, while the tide of history pushes them ever closer to death.

Isaac never allows a public event, be it battle or bombing, to obtrude into the foreground, yet the reader is always conscious of the backdrop of the historic events that jostle the lives of individuals as would the callous, earthshaking footsteps of an indifferent giant. And Isaac knows better than any of us that this giant must catch up with these fleeing pygmies and crush all the desire and hunger and selfishness out of them. For they have deserted the ways of their fathers, which, for Isaac, are the only source of strength in adversity. Over the Moskats, to the very moment of their doom, hovers the spirit of their progenitor, Meshulam, rebuking them for abandoning the values that gave him strength. It is as though old Lucinda Matlock of Edgar Lee Masters's *Spoon River Anthology* had risen from her grave to say again, with a Yiddish accent this time, "Degenerate sons and daughters, life is too strong for you."

One ingredient is conspicuously absent from *The Family Moskat*: the extra dimension of the fantastic with which the author had experimented in *Satan in Goray* and which would later free his writing from the tyranny of nineteenth-century realism. For if Joshua had been the Eisenstein of Jewish letters, Isaac was to become its Chagall.

The Family Moskat would bring fame to Isaac Bashevis Singer at long last. Yet after the first chapters appeared in the *Jewish Daily Forward* Abraham Cahan, then in his eighties, wanted the serialization stopped. He had his own ideas about how the story ought to develop, and some older members of the staff tended to agree with him, but Isaac refused to take their advice. However, other editors at the paper sided with Isaac, and the serialization continued until the book was completed in 1948. It was published in Yiddish in two volumes by Morris S. Sklarsky in 1950.

The Yiddish reading public, including the critics, was pained by the book's frank depiction of sexuality and the unrestrained realism of its description of Jewish life in Warsaw. Adultery on Yom Kippur! Why, even the rabbis were portrayed as prone to the urgings of the flesh. What a way to present Jews to the world!

Isaac summed up his attitude to this sort of criticism once in an interview with Richard Elman and Joel Blocker (*Commentary*, November 1963): "My judgment is that good does not always triumph, that this is far from the best of all possible worlds. That's why my Jews are not all good Jews. Why should they be different from anybody else?"

Alfred A. Knopf, who planned to publish *The Family Moskat* in English, wanted Isaac's friend Maurice Samuel to do the translation, as he had done with several of Joshua's books. Samuel, however, called in his friend Abraham Gross, who needed the work more than he did, to do the job. Gross died before he finished the translation, so the work was completed by his daughter, Nancy Gross, in collaboration with Maurice Samuel and Lyon Mearson. Meanwhile Isaac, who had received a five-hundred-dollar advance from Knopf, began to work on the manuscript himself, changing and cutting sections of it.

"This actually was a kind of precedent for what I do with all my books which appear first in the *Forward*," Isaac says. "First I write them. Then, during the process of translation, much of the real editing is done. While the translation is going on I come to see which sides are stronger and which are weaker, and where it's weak I try to correct it. In the case of *The Family Moskat*, these changes were later incorporated into the Yiddish text when it was reprinted."

Both Alfred A. Knopf and Herbert Weinstock, the editor Knopf had assigned to *The Family Moskat*, had asked for a number of cuts and changes. On May 29, 1949, Weinstock wrote to Isaac, calling the book "a remarkable achievement" but adding that "in our view the manuscript is by no means in a satisfactory form."

"It seems to us," Weinstock wrote, "to need several kinds of cutting and tightening. We feel that it could be improved by the removal of very numerous sentences, phrases, and single words. The book seems to lag in interest in its second half, where certain passages are repetitious." He suggested that "several of us sit around a table at your convenience and discuss what must be done." On June 15 Weinstock sent Isaac a specific list of suggested cuts and alterations. On August 19 he wrote Isaac that he was "disturbed to learn that you have accepted very few of the cuts suggested" and "have in effect restored between two-thirds and three-quarters of them."

"We do not wish," Weinstock also stated in that letter, "to cut out any material that adds largely to the picture of a vanished way of life. Our desire is to cut repetitions and passages so extraneous to the line of the story as to be almost certain to bore the English reader and persuade him to put the book down." He invited Isaac to come to his office or go over the manuscript with him at Isaac's apartment on Central Park West. On August 25 Knopf himself wrote to Isaac:

Dear Mr. Singer,

I must confess that I am greatly disturbed by Mr. Weinstock's report of his last conversation with you following your receipt of his long letter of August 19. Four of us have now read carefully the manuscript of THE FAMILY MOSKAT and I am one of the four. I agree heartily with everyone that this book is likely to have a very poor chance indeed with the American bookseller if it is not substantially cut. I realize how painful an author finds such surgery and how easily and freely his blood flows; and sometimes I am very reluctant to press my point. But in your case there is such unanimity of opinion and I am, myself, so sure that my advisors are correct in their judgment, that I must beg of you to give weight to my judgment in a matter of this kind.

As a matter of fact, when we made our agreement with you for this book, it was my understanding that the question of cutting would be decided finally by Mr. Gross and that there would be no appeal from his decision. I had just such an arrangement with your dear brother in the case of THE BROTHERS ASHKENAZI. There Maurice Samuel was the judge. Of course one cannot guarantee results in advance of publication, but certainly your brother had no reason in the end to feel that he had made a mistake in following our advice and Samuel's in cutting very considerably THE BROTHERS ASHKENAZI.

There is no reason at all why THE FAMILY MOSKAT should not be made from the point of view of the American reader into a very much better novel than it now is. And this without destroying the quality which you seek to preserve in it and which I respect as being a sort of monument to a life that has ceased to exist and will never exist again.

Yours faithfully,
Alfred A. Knopf

On August 27 Isaac replied that he would be "glad to meet with anyone you think advisable to have your specific suggestions and recommendations about the manuscript." He pointed out that it was "in the very nature of such a work for there to be many details and subplots. It is my feeling that the reader will expect them. I am afraid that too much slickness and smoothness may do much harm to the character of the novel. I hope that the editor with whom I meet will bear this in mind."

On September 16 Knopf wrote, "I am afraid that we are not advancing very fast toward a meeting of the minds." He denied that "slickness" was the publisher's objective.

Eventually there *was* a "meeting of the minds," and Isaac cut ninety pages from the manuscript, writing to Knopf on November 8 that he estimated "an additional one hundred pages have been eliminated by cutting parts of the pages themselves." Knopf wrote back the next day expressing thanks for the "good news."

Even so, when the English version appeared in 1950, Isaac was not happy over the cuts to which he had agreed. According to Roger Straus, Jr., although *The Family Moskat* made the Book Find Club, Isaac "vowed he would never publish with Alfred again."

Isaac's resentment extended to Knopf's failure to spend what he regarded as sufficient sums on the promotion of his book. The company had widely advertised John Hersey's *The Wall*, a novel about the Warsaw ghetto uprising, when it was published earlier that year. But *The Wall* had been a best-seller and a Book-of-the-Month Club selection. As far as Isaac was concerned, however, *The Family Moskat*, which was a product of his own experience, deserved at least as much attention as *The Wall*, which was based on secondhand information. He decided to leave Knopf and find another publisher.

Even so, 1950 was a banner year for Isaac. At forty-six he saw *The Family Moskat* appear in Yiddish, in English, and at the same time in Hebrew in the two-year-old state of Israel.

Today Alfred Knopf feels that perhaps he made a mistake with Isaac and tended to underestimate his talent: "I was devoted to his brother, I. J. Singer, and because I felt then, as I still do, that it is best not to publish for two close members of the same family, I opted, so to speak, in favor of the author of *The Brothers Ashkenazi*. Looking back, this was, of course, a publishing blunder of the first order, but then, I could not foresee . . . the brilliant future of his brother."

When Knopf released *The Family Moskat*, Joshua Kunitz, in the New York *Herald Tribune*, praised the translation and said that "this sprawling, heaving, churning, lustful narrative [was] very effective" despite its "great length, panoramic sweep, multiplicity of interwoven plots, and bewildering variety of bizarre characters, locales and situations." In *The New York Times* Richard Plant stressed that "the scene he depicts is gone forever" and that

The Family Moskat might turn out to be "one of its lasting monuments." Plant was delighted with Isaac for not "glossing over its gory sides, and for never trying to romanticize Hasidic and Polish-Jewish life into something quaint and folkloristic." To him, the novel recalled Turgenev and Balzac with its "narrative qualities, its completely credible characters, its throbbing vitality—even if the events and incidents sometimes threaten to overflow the shores." In *The New Yorker*, where the author's work would begin to appear some years later, *The Family Moskat* was consigned to the "Briefly Noted" list, where it was dismissed as "a collection of folk customs and habits and attitudes rather than a novel about human beings." The *Forward* gave the book a favorable but brief review.

The novel sold 35,000 copies, including the Book Find Club sales. The Yiddish edition brought Isaac $250. Royalties from the English edition came to $2000 net (the translation fees were deducted).

Even while it was running in the *Forward*, *The Family Moskat* began a second life as a radio serial over WEVD, the New York station that specializes in ethnic programming. There was a chapter on the air every Sunday. Isaac himself wrote the scripts, and when *The Family Moskat* came to an end, he wrote more scripts based on later novels and memoirs. He kept this up for five years.

"I used to mail them in to the station," he recalls. "They paid me about twenty dollars a script. Later the fee went all the way up to fifty dollars, but there was also inflation. The programs were in Yiddish, and some of the greatest actors of the day performed in them."

Zvee Schooler, who is still with WEVD, producing and directing programs, is able to throw further light on this chapter in Isaac's life.

Zvee is a stage actor and film director whose career in the theater stretches back to 1921, when he made his debut in *The Dybbuk* at the Yiddish Art Theater. For the past forty years he has been the "Grammeister," or Rhyme Master, on WEVD's *Forward Hour*, offering rhymed commentaries in Yiddish on the news. Zvee was one of the people involved in putting on the radio versions of Isaac's books and stories.

"Our director was Ossip Dymow," he recalls, sitting in one of the WEVD cubicles on an autumn day in 1977. "Henry Greenfield, who was the producer, brought Dymow in to direct these episodes, which were on every Sunday between eleven and twelve. The dramatizations would last about ten minutes. Isaac wrote all of them himself. When we did *In My Father's Court*, I played Isaac's father, Pinchas Mendel. What actors we had! There was Murray Schwartz, the son of the famous Maurice, and the late Jacob Ben-Ami and Miriam Kressyn—the great ones."

The Singer scripts were performed live on the air with large, distinguished casts, music provided by a full orchestra, and a liberal use of sound effects. Many of the shows were recorded but, alas, nothing is left. Only Isaac has saved a few samples of individual scripts. When the station changed hands some years ago, according to Schooler, "there was no room, and they threw all that stuff out."

Zvee recalls an incident concerning an actor who had a part in one of the series for twelve weeks but needed to be on for a thirteenth in order to collect unemployment insurance. When this problem was called to Isaac's attention, he said, "Don't worry about it" and simply revised the ensuing segments to include the actor's character in an additional episode.

"I remember meeting Isaac," Zvee says, "when he'd come here to the station. I stood in awe of him." Zvee doesn't think Isaac has changed much over the years. "I saw him recently at the Famous Restaurant up on Seventy-second Street. Alma was eating fish, and I wondered about this. I thought they were both vegetarian, but evidently she isn't. I asked about this, and Bashevis told me Alma feels that if it's right for fish to eat fish it's all right for her. He looked the same to me—no younger, but not much older either. But then, he was seventy-two and I'm seventy-seven, so how old could he look to a man my age?"

❁

A chilly, cloudy November noon in 1976. Isaac is again lunching at one of his favorite dairy restaurants in the West Seventies. It's a homey place, not big on atmosphere but known for its wholesome food. The author is greeted cordially in the back room, half a flight below the main part of the establishment, where there are rows of tables and a take-out counter. He is settled comfortably with his guests in the corner of the back room, where the walls are painted in bright colors, the table tops are shiny Formica, and the lights are brutally fluorescent.

The announcement of Jimmy Carter's election has come a few hours earlier, and Isaac is in high spirits, but he says the election is not the reason. He is noncommittal on the subject of both Ford and Carter. As a matter of fact he hasn't even voted: He has recently become an official resident of Florida, and he never got around to filling out his absentee ballot. He hopes that "with God's will" Carter will prove an effective president but doesn't seem inclined to pursue the subject. He concentrates instead on giving his order to the waiter, a heavy-set fellow who seems to be left over from the glorious era of kosher restaurants where the word of the waiter was law and you didn't get your dessert unless you finished all your vegetables. Isaac says he is going to indulge himself today by ordering both potato pancakes and blintzes. He exhibits his wrist watch; something has happened to the buckle, and the straps are being held together by a safety pin. He is pleased to hear that there is a theory that the more complicated the man, the simpler his watch. Isaac's old watch is totally devoid of ornaments or gadgets. At the moment it isn't ticking. He says he has forgotten to wind it.

Talk of wrist watches leads to comments on Switzerland. Isaac declares that his three favorite places in the world are Israel, New York, and Switzerland. The weeks he and Alma spent in Wengen last summer were particularly serene. Since then he has spent some time in Florida working on a new novel and the play *Old Love*. The play, in his opinion, is not yet in good enough shape to be seen by anyone.

Dvorah is supposed to be coming to lunch, but she's already late; Isaac keeps looking at his nonfunctioning watch and wondering where she is. Meanwhile he recalls a story about a woman who was asked how she felt about Switzerland and said, "It's very beautiful, but you can't really see it on account of the mountains getting in the way." He says he made a special visit to Switzerland in 1947 when he was writing *The Family Moskat* to make sure that the background for the elopement of Asa Heshel and Hadassah to that country was authentic. Indeed, the passages describing the Swiss scenery are particularly vivid and detailed, and it is not surprising to learn that they, like so much in Isaac's books, were based on firsthand observation.

Dvorah arrives, an event that raises Isaac's spirits even higher. He wants her to order some lunch, but she says she has already eaten and will just have some tea. Isaac extols the virtues of both the pancakes and the blintzes—"The richest lunch I have ever eaten in my life"—but Dvorah will not be persuaded. He urges a plate of prunes on her, but she won't eat them. "If you won't eat these prunes," Isaac warns her, "I will pronounce certain words from the Cabala, and the entire world will be destroyed." Dvorah pays no attention to this grandiose threat. She says he's looking wonderful today—younger than ever.

"They always tell that to an old man," Isaac retorts. "Whenever they meet you on the street, they tell you how young you're looking. And you know very well that it isn't true and they know it isn't true also, but they always say it."

He points to his balding head, on which the remaining white hairs are yet a little sparser than they were a year ago. "Once a year I go for a haircut," he says, "mostly to help keep the barber in business."

He tells about running into a man on the street many years ago in Warsaw, a chap he hadn't seen since his childhood. "In those days," Isaac recalls, "for some reason I often used to shave the hair off my head. So I looked practically bald, the way I do now. And I said to this fellow, 'How did you recognize me after so many years?' And he answered, 'I last saw you at your circumcision, and you looked just about the same as you do today.' "

Isaac is asked about the uncannily vivid descriptions of weather in his fiction, particularly of cold winter days and snowstorms. He affirms that all his life he has detested cold weather and hates feeling chilled, which is one of the reasons he bought the place in Florida.

The waiter, who has overheard the talk about the cold, takes the opportunity to serve Dvorah her tea and trot out an old joke about the sinking of the *Titanic:* An anti-Semite assures a friend that the Jews were to blame for the disaster. "How could that be?" asks the friend. "Everybody knows it was an iceberg that sank the *Titanic.*" The Jew-hater replies, "Iceberg, Goldberg, what's the difference, it was the Jews!"

Isaac points out that Roald Amundsen, the Norwegian explorer who was the first man to reach the South Pole, once said that in his opinion the coldest place in the whole world was the city of Seattle. This brings him to a story about a cold night in Warsaw on which a prostitute is picked up by a sadist who offers her twenty zlotys if she will let him beat her while he has sex with her. Business is so slow that night that she agrees, but she wants to know how long the beating will go on. "Until the twenty zlotys are spent," the customer replies.

Isaac is worried about Dvorah's appetite. "Are you sure you don't want anything?" She's sure.

"I am deeply suspicious of anybody who doesn't want anything."

Again Isaac tries to persuade Dvorah to eat the prunes. When she resists, he finishes them off himself.

Asked why he was so reluctant to cut *The Family Moskat* at Alfred Knopf's behest, Isaac says that as a matter of fact he did make some cuts, but not precisely the ones the publisher suggested. "Plenty of people would like to cut the Ten Commandments," he adds, "even though they take up less than a page."

Isaac has finished the blintzes, the pancakes, and the prunes, and Dvorah is nibbling on a cookie in between sips of her tea. One feels that this cozy session could go on forever. Perhaps it is not only Isaac's watch that has stopped, but time itself.

Somehow the talk turns to hypnotism. Isaac discloses that nobody has ever been able to hypnotize him, although he was willing to undergo the experience. "If my father was unable with all his efforts to hypnotize me into being a devout Jew," he concludes, "how could anybody else expect to do the job? He made me immune."

At length the check arrives. Dvorah helps Isaac on with the old black overcoat he refuses to put into retirement, the battered hat he won't trade in for a new one.

"That's the novelist," a waitress explains matter-of-factly to a customer as the Singer party leaves. "Sure, he comes here sometimes. He likes blintzes and potato pancakes. What can I tell you?" Automatically Isaac checks out the watch that has stopped, becoming aware as he reaches the street that time has not. He intends to put in a full afternoon's work. For all his relaxed demeanor, time is precious to Isaac. There are projects to complete, pleasures to be savored. He doesn't intend to waste a single minute.

❀

In the 1940s Isaac was dividing his time as a writer between producing fiction and working at the *Jewish Daily Forward*. He went on spending his afternoons at the paper for many years. His relations with others on the staff were not always cordial. "They brought up their own children to speak English while they preached about Yiddish." When Isaac pointed out such things or expressed his contempt for organizations like the Workmen's Circle, with its Socialist tinge, it did not help to make him popular with his fellow journalists.

The *Forward*, as Isaac remembers, was run in those days by a board of directors called the *Forward* Association. Many of their sessions, he says, were devoted to discussions of his intransigence. "I was in danger every week of being thrown out. Somehow I could just not make peace with them."

Yet Isaac wrote countless features for the paper, and every Thursday the latest episode of whatever book he was working on at the time would appear. To this day he continues his association with the *Forward* and maintains a close friendship with its editor, Simon Weber.

❀

March 28, 1977

The offices of the *Jewish Daily Forward*, located today on East Thirty-third street, exude nothing at all of the old-fashioned, dingy atmosphere one would have found in the paper's old quarters in Chinatown before it moved a few years ago. The new offices are modern, almost austere. In the office of Simon Weber, the editor of the paper since 1970, walnut bookshelves extend along one wall from floor to ceiling. The shelves are crammed with Jewish encyclopedias, bound volumes in Yiddish, Yiddish-English dictionaries, books in English. A large globe sits atop a modern filing cabinet. There are plastic-covered armchairs, a comfortable sofa with orange-and-green-striped upholstery, a coffee table—all in Scandinavian style. Awards from the United Jewish Appeal and other Jewish organizations adorn the walls. About the only old-fashioned object in the room is Weber's capacious desk, covered with papers and galley proofs, rulers and containers of pens and pencils. Weber, a short, wiry, alert man with gray hair and twinkling brown eyes, sits in a swivel chair looking younger than his sixty-four years. Behind him there's a large portrait of his predecessor, Abraham Cahan, and a woodcut of Sholom Aleichem's fiddler perched on a barnyard roof. Staring at him from the opposite wall is a framed photograph of Isaac Loeb Peretz.

"I didn't want to have Cahan looking right at me," the editor explains in a mild voice tinged with a Polish-Yiddish accent. "I preferred him to look down over my shoulder and to have Peretz placed where others can look at him, in direct view, for literary inspiration."

Weber himself was born in a little Polish town not far from the city of Kielce, known for its pogroms of old as well as for recent riots by Polish workers over inflationary food prices. In 1928 he went to Argentina. In 1936 he came to the United States, where he worked for a time on a Yiddish newspaper in Detroit, then as a city editor on the New York Yiddish newspaper *Freiheit*. *Freiheit* had a Communist orientation, and after the anti-Semitic trials in Moscow, Weber decided to quit. In 1939, after a brief stint on still another Yiddish paper in Philadelphia, he accepted an offer from Abraham Cahan to return to New York as a newswriter on the *Forward*. He met the Singer brothers soon after that.

"We had a large room in the old building where people gathered from their cubicles to kibitz. Israel Joshua was always holding court there. He was one of the best storytellers I ever met. I couldn't get over the fact that this revered author was standing right there, so unassuming, exchanging gossip with us aspiring green journalists. That same year I met Isaac. . . . I wasn't so impressed with him at first as with his brother, but when they started running *The Family Moskat* in the *Forward*, I was enchanted. I had only read his light pieces before that, mostly written under those pseudonyms, like Warshawsky and Segal. Here he was writing a book with characters as memorable as in the great Russian novels. Who can forget Abram, the lusty, greedy, larger-than-life uncle who lived it up in *The Family Moskat*!

"Bashevis wasn't married then but lived alone, a boarder in a rooming house. We would have lunch sometimes. Later, after I got married in October of 1939, my wife and I used to have him over to dinner. He'd sit there, so pale, his head already almost completely bald where the red hair had been, and talk about women and tell jokes and stories. He was an arch-conservative even then—against Roosevelt, against social progress, especially against anything that sounded like communism or even socialism. But he had an awful lot of charm. He has always been wonderful company."

Simon Weber and Isaac Singer have spent considerable time together and have traveled together, making lecture appearances.

Weber recalls a summer vacation he spent with Isaac in the late forties.

With their wives they set out in Weber's car, having no particular destination in mind. "We went up along U.S. One, and when we got to Portland, Maine, we stopped at the state tourist office to ask for a place where we might stay. We never made advance reservations anywhere. At the tourist office they advised us to drive back twelve miles to Orchard Beach, because along the rockbound coast of Maine they weren't so anxious for Jewish tourists. We went back the twelve miles and came to a place called Coney Island. And Isaac said, 'For this we had to come all the way to Maine? To arrive in Coney Island?'

"Well, we were hungry, and somehow I remember we found a place where you could actually order a plate of chopped liver. Then we drove all the way to Camden, arriving finally at a village called Lincolnville Beach. There were twelve houses in the whole town and also a beautiful restaurant. We decided to try the first house in view. The landlord wasn't Jewish, but he accepted us as tenants. There were four rooms available upstairs, and we rented three of them. A couple of days later we saw a car with a New York license drive up and watched our landlord, a Mr. Morris, go out and turn them away even though there was still a vacant room. When we asked him about it, he said, 'I didn't want to take in strangers. You people are together, after all.' Imagine! We found out later that Mr. Morris was so sympathetic with us because as a Catholic he knew from personal experience about prejudice.

"But Bashevis, you know, has his own prejudices—especially about women. One time we were trying to decide where we should go next on our trip, and Alma made a suggestion. Right away Isaac jumped on her. Who had asked her to mix in? He told me later when we were walking alone that the Germans had trained Alma for a thousand years to be an obedient wife, and he wasn't going to undo all that training."

On other trips Isaac and Simon spent time in Quebec, at Lake George, and on Martha's Vineyard.

"Bashevis was always writing, usually on pads of lined paper. He could sit anywhere and write. In a car, in a crowded room—anywhere. One time we were on the Vineyard, driving to Oak Bluffs. When we got there, I stopped the car in front of the local chamber of commerce office to pick up folders and literature about Martha's Vineyard. I came back to the car and handed these over to Bashevis, reminding him about his assignment. 'What are you talking about?' he retorted. 'I not only wrote it, I mailed it already.' Sure enough, some scribbling I had noticed him doing earlier on a pad that afternoon in the car was an article on the island, which he had long since deposited in some mailbox along the route. And what had Bashevis written? The most accurate, detailed, carefully observed description of the island, down to the tiniest fly. The color of the grass, the trees, the sand, the sea, the ferry-ride over—everything.

"The ground that man covered! In those days he was writing four pieces a week for the *Forward*, a weekly script for *The Family Moskat* soap opera for WEVD, articles, short stories, and novels that will outlive us all."

Isaac, in Weber's view, "has reconstructed the Yiddish which has been almost completely forgotten in the United States—the Yiddish of the *shtetl* of Eastern Europe, spoken there for more than three centuries. This is a treasure that will remain because of his writings. It's not that he has created the language, of course, but that he remembers it.

"The *Jewish Daily Forward* was a major institution of the whole immigrant culture in America, from the time it was founded in 1897. Today it is the principal Yiddish newspaper remaining in this country. It has always printed ordinary journalism along with some distinguished prose. And much of the distinguished prose has been contributed by Isaac Singer. Where else would it appear? There are not that many literary periodicals appearing in Yiddish."

From the first, many readers of the *Forward* disapproved of the sexual element in Isaac's fiction. Weber has been asked frequently why some of the franker scenes in the installments of his books aren't edited out.

"Nobody ever stops reading them," Weber points out. Recently an eighty-year-old rabbi approached Weber at a yeshiva banquet and showed him a passage in a recent piece by Isaac that he said had really shocked him. "Tell me," Weber retorted, "if you are so appalled by it, why do you read it?" And the rabbi had no answer. "When people make inquiries of that kind, I suggest that they start reading modern literature in English. Then they will see how meek and tame is the work of Bashevis by comparison . . . I call him Bashevis, by the way, because that is the name he used in Yiddish before he started using Singer. You see, he didn't want to trade on the reputation of his brother, I.J. It was only after his brother died that he started signing his name Isaac Bashevis Singer. At any rate, they would ask me why his stuff wasn't edited—they meant censored—and I replied that I would be as likely to make changes in a manuscript by Bashevis as in a text of Tolstoy's or Dostoevsky's. If he writes an article and there's an error in it, that's corrected. But one does not tamper with literature on that level."

Despite objections from readers, most of the mail that comes to the paper about Isaac's work, according to Weber, is approving.

Why aren't Isaac's works published in Yiddish in book form any more? "You must understand," Weber answers, "that today there is no publishing house in a position to underwrite such books. If you want to publish a book you have to invest your own money. It's like a vanity press. And Isaac doesn't have that type of vanity.

"But one must not get the impression that Bashevis's books are read in Yiddish only by a minuscule group of people. Everything he writes is published by us—that's fifty thousand readers—and in the Yiddish newspaper in Buenos Aires. About half a dozen of his books have appeared in Yiddish in

Israel, the rest in Hebrew. *The Mirror and Other Stories* came out there in Yiddish a year ago. And of course his books are read all over the world in other languages—in French, Swedish, Finnish, Dutch, Spanish, Italian, Norwegian. *Enemies, A Love Story* was even published behind the Iron Curtain in Hungary. And in Japan they publish everything, including his children's books."

Weber doesn't think Isaac has changed much over the years—"only to the extent that he has improved, matured. And his work has matured. There is tremendous growth, for example, from *The Family Moskat* to *The Slave*. And in the writing of short stories he has no peer."

Weber feels Isaac's work inevitably suffers in translation, "but if you don't know the original you can't possibly tell." He misses the flavor of the Yiddish in the English versions. "Some Yiddish writers say when they read his stories and novels they are actually relearning a language they have almost forgotten how to use. He has so many synonyms for things—items of clothing and women's jewelry and objects of furniture. . . . He has brought the archaic aspects of the language and modern usage and melted them into one idiom. If he were a composer he would probably write marvelous music because he hears so precisely the exact sound of everything. When you walk with him, when you ride in a car with him, you think this man is seeing nothing and hearing nothing. Maybe he's completely absorbed in some story or article he's planning. But later you find out he missed nothing, not the buzz of an insect, not the look or the scent of a flower. And this is perhaps what helps make him such a virtuoso of language."

For all Isaac's success and his accessibility, Weber feels that he is "a man alone. All by himself. Not really a sociable person, not a man who makes friends easily. People who meet the celebrity never really get to know him. He shakes hands, but next time he may not even recognize the same individual. It's understandable. He meets thousands of people, how could he possibly remember them all? His friends are few; I consider myself one of them. He does cherish a few close friends."

Twice a week, on Thursdays and Fridays, the *Forward* publishes seven or eight columns of Isaac's prose. Sometimes it is a short story or a memoir or an essay, sometimes a chapter of a longer work. Much of this material has yet to appear in English.

What does the *Forward* pay its star author? "Not as much as he deserves," Simon Weber replies. "We pay him the same that we pay a contributor who works a full five days a week on the paper. It's really not enough."

Where does Weber feel Isaac belongs in the total spectrum of Yiddish writing? "He is unique. He's so industrious and productive. He doesn't preach in his stories. He writes about life, never propaganda. He never confuses a novel with a treatise on sociology, which some Yiddish writers have done. We certainly have had other Yiddish writers of distinction on our staff. But they take six months off to devote themselves to literature. Isaac never stops except for a month in the summertime. He is always in the paper, with a short story or a long story in four installments or a novel that runs for many months on end.

"Above all, Isaac's prose is supremely readable. He charms the reader. In print as in life, he's good company. And he is a master of the Yiddish language, second to none. His brother could be more economical with language, get more out of a sentence than Isaac does; he was a master at creating characters—yet who can forget Isaac's characters? If he has any weakness it is only perhaps that he writes too much. I know that in English his work is rigorously edited, but in Yiddish the editing is not always severe enough. Even so, there is nobody writing in Yiddish who can compare with him."

❀

When a novel starts germinating in Isaac's head, he often makes lists of the characters and sometimes of the people he has known in real life who are to serve as models for these characters. He jots down ideas for incidents, prepares an outline of the action. But when he is actually writing a book, he finds that "the characters will often go their own ways, quite apart from my plans for them, and the book will develop as it wishes, no matter how many lists I have made or outlines I have previously put down on paper." Although he believes that any story, from a vignette to an epic, must have a plot, he also believes that a work of fiction must be allowed to evolve, that a writer must not cling to his original conceptions or organizational plans.

Isaac says that much of the research he does for his books consists of rummaging for memories inside his own head. The places in Poland where he grew up are still vivid in his memory in surprising detail. He has a hard time remembering dates, he says, but people and incidents from the world of his past are still there somewhere in his mind, to be summoned back as he needs them.

Still, Isaac does not rely entirely on memory for the background and historical information in his books and stories set in Poland. When he was writing his family novel *The Manor*, he relied on old newspapers as a source. He found yellowing journals dating back to the 1890s, some in a library, others in a bookstore on the Lower East Side. "Even the advertisements and the editorials in newspapers were of help to me—what people were discussing, what was for sale in a certain time."

Isaac also keeps notes in tiny notebooks and on scraps of papers. He is a keen observer of details, noting without seeming to the telling elements of any environment he enters as well as the people he encounters, and all this is raw material for his work.

The rest is imagination, insight, seemingly inexhaustible energy, and the indefinable talent of a born storyteller.

❀

The influence of Joshua's work was still strong in 1952, when Isaac began work on the longest of all his books, another family novel, entitled *The Manor*. The two-thousand-page manuscript, written in Yiddish, took Isaac three years to complete. Once again, the novel appeared chapter by chapter in the *Forward*. When *The Manor* finally reached the English-speaking world, it had turned into two books collectively entitled *The Manor*, published in 1967, and *The Estate*, which did not appear until 1969. The publisher was Farrar, Straus and Giroux. (A one-volume paperback containing both *The Manor* and *The Estate* was published by Avon in 1979.) The translation is credited to Joseph Singer and Elaine Gottlieb. In his foreword Isaac expresses gratitude for the editorial contributions of Cecil Hemley, Elizabeth Shub, and Robert Giroux.

The whole project, in Isaac's words, is "in a way a continuation of the same saga as *The Family Moskat*, but it portrays an earlier period—the epoch between the Polish insurrection of 1863 and the end of the nineteenth century. . . .

"It was the era of gas lamps," Isaac wrote in his introduction to *The Manor*, "the time when the Poles had finally become resigned to their loss of independence and turned to a kind of national positivism. Poland now began to emerge as an industrial country; railroads were built, factories were opened, and the cities grew rapidly. The Jews, who until 1863 for the most part lived in a ghetto atmosphere, now began to play an important role in Polish industry, commerce, the arts and sciences. All the spiritual and intellectual ideas that triumphed in the modern era had their roots in the world of that time—socialism and nationalism, Zionism and assimilationism, nihilism and anarchism, suffragettism, atheism, the weakening of the family bond, free love, and even the beginnings of Fascism."

The Manor has a vast cast of characters, but its central focus is on the family of a pious businessman named Calman Jacoby. Jacoby is an industrious, thrifty, enterprising grain merchant who seizes his opportunity when the Poles rebel against their Russian oppressors. Taking advantage of the ensuing economic expansion, Jacoby leases the lands of Count Jampolski, recently banished to Siberia, sells the timber from the estate for railroad ties, develops a limestone quarry, and amasses a fortune. But this does not prevent his children from rebelling against the Judaic taboos that circumscribe their lives. One of his daughters, Miriam Leba, elopes with a *sheigetz*, the count's dissolute, alcoholic son, Lucian, and converts to Christianity—an act for which she is to pay bitterly.

When Jacoby's wife dies, he marries a scheming, sophisticated woman named Clara, whose particular combination of passion, willfulness, and common sense is so often found in the women in both Isaac's books and his life. Clara's self-indulgence leads her into the beds of other men, among them a petulant student named Zipkin. In the final pages of *The Manor* Jacoby, now old and abandoned but uncorrupted, retreats even further from worldly concerns but finds a link with the future in his friendship with his son from his second marriage, Sasha.

When *The Estate* opens, at the end of the nineteenth century, Sasha, now grown, has abandoned his faith and devotes himself to managing his father's estate. His mother, Clara, is abroad, having an affair with a Russian Jew she encountered in Monte Carlo, while her father lies dying. Her former lover, Zipkin, has gone to New York, where she eventually pursues him. Miriam Leba's husband, Lucian, freed after serving a jail sentence, embarks on a Dostoevskian course of disintegration that leads to theft, murder, and finally suicide. Ezriel Babad, the character in whom we identify Isaac himself—or rather the man Isaac might have been had he decided to become a psychiatrist instead of a writer—has abandoned his yeshiva studies to pursue a medical career and begun to ponder the enigmas of the "universal mystery" that have haunted Isaac all his life: "Why are some people poor and others rich? What was there before the universe? Does a goat have a soul? Was Adam a Jew?" In *The Estate* he pursues a career in psychiatry and becomes a pioneer in the field.

"Below the level of these characters," as L. E. Sissman was to sum it up in a review in *The New Yorker* (February 7, 1970), "there is a sizable supporting cast of wives, suitors, lovers, sisters, sons, and brothers, who are rendered in the round and at almost equal length. Below *them* is a small army of minor but memorable characters." To Sissman, it began to seem as if "the entire population of Poland in the nineteenth century" had been crowded into this "panoramic mosaic of a place and period." But one by one the author rather precipitously kills off his principals. Only two of them, who have adhered to the precepts and practices of Judaism, seem prepared for the end—Rabbi Jochanan, a saintly man who dies an ascetic's death with a celestial vision dancing in his brain, and Calman Jacoby, who clings to his Orthodoxy and expires with a pure heart, watched over by his Creator.

Because the cast is so huge and the misfortunes pile up so relentlessly, *The Manor* and *The Estate* are at times trying books to read, but the storyteller's art is so skillful that one is compelled to go on reading to find out what happens next. And the novels' brilliantly illuminated scenes tend to stick in the mind like real memories, as do certain episodes from *The Family*

Moskat. The novels are less memorable for their telling philosophical conversations or their skillful juxtaposition of episodes than they are for the life that Isaac breathes into his scenes and the characters who people them. Witness Clara's first impressions of New York:

> God in heaven, from her earliest childhood, Clara had heard about the wonders of America. But it was a city like all cities. The sky was above, not below. Clara sat at the window looking out. Lifting the lorgnette that hung around her neck, she looked through it at this once-distant country. Clara thought that if there was a life after death it would be like this—different and yet the same. Who was that giant carrying a sign? Oh, he was walking on stilts. He wore a red-and-white striped top hat. A clown from a circus? A peddler hawked his wares in a loud singsong. A crowd gathered around him. Was he giving things away? People grabbed up something, laughing. They were all so quick, so active, dressed garishly in bright colors or checks. Across the street, the entire window of a clothing store was filled with mannequins, dressed in silk, velvet, fur coats and stoles somehow different from the ones one saw in Warsaw. The crowds of women in front of the windows wore dresses and hats that looked new. Good God! There was a girl riding a bicycle! Why was everybody carrying so many boxes and packages? Yes, it was different. . . .

Then, when Clara's affair with Zipkin has begun to sour:

> Later that winter there was snow such as Clara had never seen before. It fell heavy as sand. The tracks of the streetcar that led to Zipkin's house were buried. As soon as the snow was shoveled away, another storm came, to be measured in inches by the newspapers. The days grew as dark as during an eclipse, the nights dense and black. The city was disease-ridden. Zipkin's wife and child became ill. He suddenly found himself with more patients than he could handle. Clara's disenchantment with America increased. There were no cafés where ladies could sit down and read. The theaters were far from where she lived. Clara had nothing in common with the neighboring German women. In the evenings, no light could brighten the city's murkiness. Clara's only consolation was an occasional letter from Sasha. But even these were delayed by storms. . . .

Later Clara gets lost in the snowy night, and the description of the scene fuses poignantly with the pain and loneliness of exile:

Usually Clara knew which streetcar to take home, but she was in an unfamiliar neighborhood. It was evening and it had grown colder. People walked rapidly, emitting vapor from their mouths and nostrils. Horses slipped on the ice and the teamsters shouted. Five wagons went by in a blasting uproar. Clara stopped various people and asked for directions, but they all contradicted each other. She had come out on the Bowery and was advised to take the El. She climbed the stairs and waited for the train. The wind lifted her hat and she had to hold it by the brim with both hands. The cold penetrated her heavy clothing. Her forehead smarted, her nose felt wooden, and her eyes teared. There must have been an accident. She waited fifteen minutes and when no train arrived went down to the street again. She had to warm herself somewhere. Her hands were stiff. Her eyebrows prickled. The snowflakes on them made everything rainbow-colored. Suddenly Clara caught sight of a jewelry store. It was still open. She decided to go in and get warm. She might even purchase a trifle. A dense fog formed before her eyes. Men were standing behind counters under bright lights: One man was fussing with a jewelry box. Another was looking through a magnifying glass. Clara wanted to say something in English, but she seemed to have forgotten the little she had learned.

Such scenes linger in the mind when the complex plot, the rush of events, in *The Manor* and *The Estate*, like those in *The Family Moskat*, have been long forgotten.

Isaac says that his writing bears no message: "If we would stick with the Ten Commandments we would have enough messages for the next ten thousand years." Perhaps that is the message. *The Family Moskat, The Manor,* and *The Estate* all seem to be warning that the more Jews try to flee from their faith and their Jewishness, the more worthless they find their freedom. Life, to be fulfilling, must have boundaries, which only traditional Judaism can satisfactorily supply for Jews. In his later novels Isaac would carry this idea even further. In *The Magician of Lublin* the hero is to find consolation from the life of a libertine in confinement as a penitent. In *The Slave* escape from slavery leads to worse than slavery when life is lived without form or pattern.

Time magazine thought *The Manor* might turn out to be "the breakthrough book to gain Singer the wider audience he deserves." The reviewer found in it, as in "all his fiction . . . a subtle form of autobiography projecting the author's own sense of exile. Yes, [the author] seems to say, change is king. And yes, life goes on, about as bad and as good and as endlessly fascinating as always. No other novelist today can balance this double truth so well." John Wain wrote in *The New York Review of Books:* "At a time when every critic can prove that the novel is 'finished,' Singer's very old-fashionedness becomes a virtue. . . . Not that he is indifferent to form; technically, he is a master. It is just that he is satisfied with the novel as it is and has been, and he is well able to justify his satisfaction." Robert Alter, in the *Saturday Review*, found *The Manor* "a transitional work, bridging the social realism of . . . *The Family Moskat* and the demon-ridden world of his later, more characteristic stories." Alter was impressed by the "full spectrum" of life among Eastern European Jews conveyed in the book. He marveled at the author's ability to convey character in "a few quick visual strokes. . . . a broken cap-visor, a wart on the nose . . . are made to stand in the mind for a detailed rendering of the whole image, and thus the narrative, despite its panoramic expansiveness, begins to move forward with something of the compelling swiftness of Singer's shorter fiction. With so many groups of characters, sustained character development is not really possible, but the novel does present an interrelated series of striking vignettes, and certain scenes attain a measure of the hallucinated dramatic power that marks Singer's best short stories."

Two years later, when *The Estate* appeared in English, Alter, again in the *Saturday Review*, complained that the novel "too often reminds us of the conventions of soap opera with its sentimental delectation of troubles for their own sake." But he added that "impressively, Singer manages to make this into a thoroughly readable book because, whatever he does, he remains a gifted storyteller." And yet, symptomatically, the repeated questions asked by the protagonist about the meaning of life in the face of such suffering seem abstract and a little hollow, less the articulation of a philosophical quest through the medium of fiction than a naked expression of craving for belief." In *The New York Times Book Review* for November 5, 1967, Gerald Jonas said, however, that Isaac's "unfaltering stylistic control" keeps the book from "disintegrating into an anthology of melodramatic episodes. . . . there is nothing fragmentary about it." He found "the second volume . . . just as exhilarating to read as the first." He added, "It is only as one approaches the end of *The Estate* that the true dimensions of Singer's imaginative achievement become apparent."

In a long essay in *The New Yorker* L. E. Sissman expressed profound disappointment in the English translations of *The Manor* and *The Estate*. After praising the author for offering "a full conspectus of Polish daily life, down to the last details of dress, speech, manners and food" and doing so "brilliantly," Sissman went on to condemn the translation as "pedestrian." He found it "copybookish" as well as "unidiomatic, or just careless and clumsy." "This translation," he wrote, "reduced people and actions of the utmost complexity to a kind of simplistic literalness. Yet every attempt was made to insure success: in 'The Manor,' Mr. Singer credits two translators and three editors. Perhaps it should have been a one-man job."

In 1967 *The Manor* was nominated for the National Book Award.

❀

Isaac was never to revert to the huge canvasses of the ambitious, complexly plotted, and thickly populated family novels—epics he might never have assembled save for the example set by his older brother. For one thing, in 1953, the same year he undertook to chronicle the sprawling saga of the Jacoby family, he paused to write what is generally agreed to be his finest short story, "Gimpel the Fool." For another, he was already planning novels on a more intimate scale, where the stories of individuals stood on their own, without the scaffolding of history. In these novels the imps and demons confined to the shadows since the writing of *Satan in Goray* would emerge to mingle at will with the earthbound cast of characters. No longer were the rampagings of Satan's minions to be confined to dream sequences or moments of fever-induced delirium; now there was to be night in broad daylight in Isaac's pages. His apprenticeship to Russian realism was almost at an end, and with that leap forward was to come at once his liberation and his greatness.

During 1956 and 1957 Isaac worked on two long novels, which up to this time have not appeared in translation.

The first of these was *Shadows on the Hudson*, the story of a group of refugees who arrive in the United States just after World War II. They settle on the Upper West Side—a neighborhood Isaac, by then, knew intimately—resuming their lives and pursuing their loves, but the past constantly intrudes on the present; they have brought the Old World with them, their indiscardable mental and spiritual luggage. Irving Buchen describes *Shadows on the Hudson* as a "kind of transmigrated ship of fools."

The novel that followed was *A Ship to America*—another "What if?" tale about how things might have been for Isaac had he lost his passport en route from Poland and been forced to live as an alien in a land where he had no official right to be. The book ends as World War II approaches and the hero marries the woman he loves and brings his son by an earlier marriage to America to live.

Both novels were serialized in the *Forward*—as all Isaac's novels have been except for *Satan in Goray—Shadows on the Hudson* in 1957, *A Ship to America* in 1958.

Speaking of this serialization process, Isaac told Buchen, "It's a delight. You have to work. You can't come up with excuses. It is true that your control cannot be perfect—but that's not really possible anyway in a novel, only in a short story. Besides, you can't write a novel of a thousand pages without serialization. It's too frightening."

A third novel Isaac contemplated in those days but never put down on paper was to be called *The Builders of Zion*. "I never wrote it," he says, "because I was never there."

PART 5

"To Make a Long Story Short"

I prefer the short story," Isaac Singer has said, "because only in a short story can a writer reach perfection—more than in a novel. When you write a novel, especially a long novel, you are never the ruler of your writing, because you cannot really make a plan for a novel of say five hundred pages and keep to the rules or keep to the plan. While in a short story there is always the possibility of being really perfect."

In 1953 Isaac wrote the short story that many critics regard as the capstone of his achievement. This was "Gimpel Tam" ("Gimpel the Fool"), which appeared in the May 1953 issue of *Partisan Review* in a stunningly idiomatic if slightly slangy translation by Saul Bellow.

Isaac has often said that he himself is Gimpel, a statement that should not be taken too literally. Gimpel is also everything Isaac is not—victim, cuckold, *shnorrer*, butt of the world's jokes. Gimpel is a baker who lives in the little Polish town of Frampol. He doesn't regard himself as a fool, but that's how he's known to everybody in town. "I had seven names in all: imbecile, donkey, flax-head, dope, glump, ninny and fool. The last name stuck."

Gimpel is the perfect mark for every prankster in Frampol. He believes anything anyone tells him. One day he decides that he's had enough. He takes a vow "to believe nothing more." This doesn't work out, and he goes to the local rabbi, who informs him, "It is written, better to be a fool all your days than for one hour to be evil. You are not a fool. They are the fools. For he who causes his neighbor to feel shame loses Paradise himself." Even so, before he leaves the rabbi's house, the rabbi's daughter manages to put over a little joke on Gimpel.

The biggest joke of all is played on him when the townspeople persuade Gimpel to marry a reputed virgin named Elka, who devotes herself over the years to deceiving him and bearing children that aren't his. During a busy week when he has to sleep at the bakery, the oven stops working and he goes home—to find Elka in bed with another man. The rabbi advises Gimpel to move out, but Gimpel can't bear to be away from her.

On her deathbed Elka confesses all her infidelities to Gimpel. That night he is visited by the Evil One, who urges him to revenge himself on the townspeople by urinating on the dough for the next day's bread. But Elka appears to Gimpel in a dream and assures him she is paying in the next world for her sins in this one. He goes out and buries the defiled bread. He gives away all he has to Elka's children, leaves Frampol, and becomes a wanderer:

"I wandered over the land, and good people did not neglect me. After many years I became old and white; I heard a great deal, many lies and falsehoods, but the longer I lived the more I understood that there were really no lies. Whatever doesn't really happen is dreamed at night. It happens to one if it doesn't happen to another, tomorrow if not today, or a century hence if not next year." And he decides, "No doubt the world is entirely an imaginary world, but it is only once removed from the true world."

The story itself is Isaac's world in microcosm, containing the lowly lie that turns out to be a higher truth; caricature as characterization; the critical moment when a man must decide whether to take the false step and forfeit Paradise; the mockery of the mob; the untrustworthiness of women; the deception that is so often the portion of those who love. Like so many of Isaac's short stories, it is set down with supreme economy and all the seemingly artless art of a folktale.

Why does Isaac say that he is Gimpel? Perhaps he is being ironic; perhaps he is only trying to convey in other terms what Picasso meant when he said, "Art is a lie that tells the truth." Or maybe, as the symbol-hunters are only too ready to agree, Gimpel is the quintessential Jew, taunted and dispossessed but preferring to wait for his reward in the next world rather than seek revenge on his tormentors in this one.

Soon other stories by Isaac were appearing frequently in several American magazines. *Partisan Review* followed "Gimpel the Fool" with "From the Diary of One Not Born" (1954); "The Gentleman from Cracow" and "Fire" appeared in *Commentary* (1957), "The Wife Killer" in *Midstream* (1955), and "The Mirror" in *New World Writing* (1957). In 1961 *Mademoiselle* paid Isaac four hundred dollars for a single story, "The Shadow of a Crib," almost twice as much as he made from the Yiddish edition of *The Family Moskat*. A few months later *Esquire* published "The Beggar Said So" and, before the year was out, "The Spinoza of Market Street." Before long *Harper's*, *The Saturday Evening Post*, *Playboy*, and *The Reporter* joined the list. Mass-circulation magazines were now publishing stories that a few years before would only have appeared in publications few of their readers had ever heard of (and in a language even fewer could understand). At the same time the *Herald Tribune* and *The New York Times*, *Midstream*, *American Judaism*, and other journals were publishing Isaac's essays while articles about him were beginning to appear almost as often as articles by him.

"Gimpel the Fool" first came out in book form in *A Treasury of Yiddish Stories*, published in 1954 by The Viking Press, then in the collection *Gimpel the Fool and Other Stories*, published by Noonday Press in 1957, the first book of Isaac's short stories to appear in English. It did not appear in a Yiddish collection until six years later, in *Gimpel Tam un Anderer Dertailungen*, published by the Central Yiddish Culture Organization—the last of Isaac's books to be published in this country in Yiddish. The Noonday Press volume was reprinted in paperback by Avon Books in 1965 and by Farrar, Straus and Giroux in 1979.

Gimpel the Fool and Other Stories is a remarkable collection, containing some of Isaac's finest, most fascinating stories, and most of them in excellent translations. In addition to Saul Bellow, the translators include Martha Glicklich, Elaine Gottlieb, Nancy Gross, Norbert Guterman, Schlomo Katz, and Isaac Rosenfeld.

The collection contains "The Gentleman from Cracow," the story of a rich young man from the big city who arrives in a small Polish village— Frampol again—to tempt the populace with gold. He also pairs off all the single folk in town in a lottery held at an orgiastic ball, winding up himself with Hodle, the girl with the loosest morals in the district. In the end the gentleman turns out to be no gentleman at all but "none other than Ketev Mrir, Chief of the Devils."

"The Little Shoemakers," one of Isaac's most memorable fables, first appeared in this collection. Here, the patriarch of a family of shoemakers in Frampol sees his eight sons go off to America one by one until he has to close up shop. As a very old man, when German planes bomb Frampol, he crosses the sea to join his family. They welcome him warmly, but he languishes—until his now prosperous sons build him a cobbler's hut, where they all join him on Sundays, "cuttng soles and shaping heels, boring holes and hammering pegs, as in the good old days."

The collection also includes "The Mirror," the story of an imp who lures a bored housewife through the looking-glass in her boudoir with promises of ecstasy that prove instead to be a passport to the tortures of Gehenna. "The Mirror" was later produced as a play by the Yale Repertory Theater. Making an imp or a devil or a gossipy old aunt the narrator of one of his tales was already one of Isaac's favorite devices. "From the Diary of One Not Born," written in the early forties and included in the Noonday collection, is the first-person memoir of a devil born from a drop of spilled semen who proudly recounts the highlights of his career as a tempter and malefactor. Another story, "The Unseen," is also recounted by an "evil spirit," who arranges for the seduction and downfall of a good husband.

The collection contains a dozen tales in all, including "By the Light of Memorial Candles," an eerie winter evening spent with beggars in a study house sharing stories of their misadventures; "The Wife Killer," in which an old woman tells how a local Bluebeard outlives all his wives and his enemies and is left penniless and alone in the world; "Joy," the story of a pious rabbi saved from apostasy through the intervention of his dead daughter's ghost; "Fire," a story of circumstantial evidence, in which a young man is reviled by his family for a crime he only intended to commit. When the family mill burns down, he rescues his brother, whom he hates, and his brother's family from the flames. Since he is discovered at the scene with a tinderbox and a bag of shavings, he is naturally accused of setting the blaze—which he did not do. The story raises a tricky moral point that comes up frequently in Isaac's work: Should a man be judged by his deeds or by his intentions?

One of the stories collected in the book had been published in Warsaw back in 1933. This was "The Old Man," the story of a rich old man, Reb Moshe Ber, who loses everything when he is forced to flee from Warsaw during World War I. He is obsessed by a tale of a wonder-working rabbi in the town of Turisk and goes through all sorts of hardships to find him. The Hasidim of Turisk reward his pilgrimage by building him a house and arranging a marriage for him with a deaf-and-dumb spinster who, like Sarah in the Bible, surprises the old man by bearing him a son.

The rest of the stories in this collection were written in New York between 1942 and 1957. Isaac has since written hundreds of short stories; at least a hundred have so far been translated into English and published in five collections—*The Spinoza of Market Street, Short Friday and Other Stories, The Seance and Other Stories, A Friend of Kafka and Other Stories,* and *Passions and Other Stories.*

Increasingly the critics were praising Isaac's work. Irving Howe called him a genius. *The Times Literary Supplement* said "Gimpel the Fool" was the greatest story ever written about a shlemiel. Milton Hindus praised Isaac as one of the best Yiddish writers in America. Henry Miller, in *Life* magazine, termed him "a writer to drive one crazy if one has the ear for the underlying melody, the meaning behind the meaning." Isaac, he exclaimed, was "afraid of nothing." Miller, the master of the subject, particularly admired Isaac's treatment of sex, "always full-bodied like a rich wine." "Above all," Miller wrote, "there is love, a bigger, broader love than we are accustomed to reading about in books."

Recently, in an appearance with Norman Mailer on an NBC News Show, Miller asked Mailer to admit that Isaac Singer was a greater writer than either of them, or anyone else around. Mailer said he agreed.

❀

August 8, 1976

Elaine Gottlieb Hemley is a serious, intense woman of middle age, the mother of two sons and the widow of Cecil Hemley, the poet and translator. In the 1950s both of them played a significant part in the next stage of Isaac Singer's career.

Mrs. Hemley wears her dark-brown curly hair short. Her brown eyes peer out solemnly through dark-rimmed glasses. Dressed informally in a purple T-shirt, lavender slacks, and white summer shoes, she relaxes on a sofa bed in the living room of her mother's home in Long Beach, Long Island.

Elaine Hemley is an associate professor of English at Indiana University, where she has been teaching and directing writers' conferences and workshops since 1972; she is also the author of dozens of stories published in *Partisan Review*, *The Kenyon Review*, *Southern Review*, and other literary magazines, as well as critical articles and essays—including feature interviews with Isaac Singer and a piece published in the *Southern Review* called "Singer and Hawthorne, a Prevalence of Satan." (It was the critic Stanley Edgar Hyman who nicknamed Isaac "the Yiddish Hawthorne.") Her novel, *Darkling*, was published in 1947. She also worked with Joseph Singer and Isaac on the translations of *The Manor* and *The Estate*.

The room is cozy, crowded with simple, old-fashioned, comfortable furniture. It's a rainy Sunday afternoon. Beyond the porch outside the sky is dark, and the air is heavy and strangely still. A hurricane warning, in fact, has been announced for the New York area, and drops of rain have begun to fall.

Mrs. Hemley frowns as she tries to recall the circumstances in which she and her husband first became involved with Isaac.

"My husband and Arthur A. Cohen founded the Noonday Meridian Press, and they were on the lookout for quality writers. One evening in 1953 Cecil went to visit Dan Talbot, who later became manager of the New Yorker Theater, where they show all those first-rate movie revivals. . . . In the course of the evening Dan read to us Saul Bellow's translation of "Gimpel the Fool"—the story which had just been published in the May issue of *Partisan Review*. We were all mad for it. I think another of Cecil's partners, Bill Webb, was there that night and heard the story too. The next thing I knew we were meeting with Jacob Sloane, who was translating *Satan in Goray* into English at the time. He told us Singer was unhappy over the cuts Knopf had made in *The Family Moskat* and was interested in finding a new publisher. Sloane brought Singer up to the Noonday office, and my husband and I immediately took a shine to him. I remember he looked like a little rabbi and had those twinkling eyes. He was so modest it was hard to believe he was the author of that fierce story *Satan in Goray*. He spoke English with an accent, but he spoke it well.

"The translation we received from Jacob Sloane was rather rough. My husband and I worked very hard on it. Sloane was very cooperative. Singer also went over every chapter in English quite carefully. The only thing we never changed was the archaic language in the last pages, which seemed to be an appropriate equivalent to the Yiddish.

"We were terribly excited about *Satan in Goray*. In those days fantasy was kept on the fringes of fiction—it was something you read in *Argosy* magazine. And here was Singer writing so imaginatively, so fantastically about the supernatural. I think he started a whole new trend."

It was the goal of the Hemleys, along with Noonday editor Dwight W. Webb and associate editor Elizabeth Pollet, to make the world aware of Isaac Singer's work in translation. In 1955 Noonday Press issued *Satan in Goray* in English.

Irving Howe, in *The New Republic*, found Isaac's first novel, in its exceptionally careful English translation, "a remarkable book, brilliant, enigmatic, and deserving of the attention of anyone interested in modern literature." Meyer Levin, in *The New York Times Book Review* (March 13, 1955), said the book had been "beautifully written by one of the masters of Yiddish prose, and beautifully translated." Levin considered the novel "folk material translated into literature." Cachine Rainer, in the *Saturday Review*, found the translation "lyrical" and said the "whole work manages to capture that barbaric, Oriental flavor that one associates with Eastern Jews of the period."

"After the book came out, Singer was on a television interview program and was asked about the translation," Mrs. Hemley says. "He told the interviewer that he worked closely with his translators but never mentioned any of us. We were upset by this, although we never said anything about it to him."

Mrs. Hemley recollects a huge party at the Singers' apartment on Central Park West, attended by the staff of the *Jewish Daily Forward*. "There was a huge spread—somebody had brought a magnum of champagne—it was like a banquet. Later we invited Isaac and Alma to our place in Riverdale and to our apartment on Riverside Drive when we moved to New York. Alma was a handsome woman, but she had a rather melancholy look at times. I used to wonder whether this was because of the way Isaac sometimes spoke to her—rather gruffly!"

The Hemleys hoped to get more of Isaac's stories published in *Partisan Review* and other magazines through their friendships with editors, and in 1957 Noonday issued *Gimpel the Fool and Other Stories* in English. Its publication prompted Irving Howe to write the first extensive essay on Isaac's fiction. The Hemleys also ran several of Isaac's short stories in their own periodical, *Noonday Magazine*.

After *Satan in Goray* was published in English, Mrs. Hemley started to work with Joseph Singer on the English version of *The Magician of Lublin*. Noonday published the book in 1960. Then Cecil Hemley started work on the English version of *The Slave*.

"He worked on it tirelessly," Mrs. Hemley recalls. "He was a poet himself, after all, and he used to read every line aloud to try to capture the cadences. He really made himself sick over it. Cecil and I were back in New York, and Isaac would come over to our house or we would go over there. No translation was ever worked on more intently."

Cecil Hemley was suffering from severe hypertension at the time, and the Noonday Press was not doing well. With the help of a friend, author and editor Stanley Burnshaw, Hemley was able to take over the direction of a small publishing house in Ohio, where there would be less pressure. But in 1966, just past the age of fifty, he died of a heart attack.

Back in New York, Mrs. Hemley continued to work with Isaac after Cecil's death. She translated several of his stories, taking down his rough English versions directly on the typewriter and later refining them. She did most of the translation, she says, of *In My Father's Court*, although others, including Channah Kleinerman-Goldstein and Isaac's nephew, Joseph, are credited for it. She would go to Isaac's apartment and type up chapters while he translated for her directly from the pages of the *Forward*.

As has been his arrangement with other translators, Isaac paid Elaine Hemley a specific sum for each job rather than a share of the royalties.

"I loved *Satan in Goray*," Mrs. Hemley says, "and I thought *The Magician of Lublin* was wonderful. I think his short stories are just preludes to his novels. I really don't care as much for the family novels—*Moskat, The Estate, The Manor*—as for the more imaginative and daring books. I had an awful time working with Joseph on the English version of *The Manor* and *The Estate*. I had practically to be strapped to my chair to finish the job. And I didn't care so much for *Enemies, A Love Story*. I disliked it, for one thing, because of his attitude toward women. I don't think it's a fair attitude. Yet in a story like 'Yentl the Yeshiva Boy' he seems to understand so much. He has Yentl say that she wants to live her own life, that she won't be any man's footstool. But he's full of surprises that way. He's always entering new territories, doing the unexpected, even though sometimes in some ways he does repeat himself.

"Of all that Singer has written," she says, "I think my favorite is the story 'The Little Shoemakers,' which was translated by Isaac Rosenfeld. And it's funny about these stories. They are so self-contained. They leave you with little to say. It's all there. I tried to teach something of Isaac's in one of my classes. It was so simple, so complete in itself, the students were at a loss for words."

Mrs. Hemley tries to recapture some of her memories of Isaac in the fifties. Once, she recalls, her daughter Nola (who died several years ago) tried to hypnotize Isaac. "She was fifteen at the time. She made him stretch out his legs and arms and go through the whole thing. She came back home quite proud of her achievement. When I asked Singer about it later, he said he had only been pretending."

Mrs. Hemley found Isaac's celebrated vegetarianism to be no more orthodox at first than his Judaism. She recollects an occasion when she and her husband were still living in New York: "I had bought a turkey on sale at the local store. It turned out to be a big one, too much for our family, so we called up Alma and Isaac and invited them over for dinner. He said, 'I'm just on my way to becoming a vegetarian. But since you cooked the turkey, I wouldn't want it to go to waste.' And they came over, and he certainly ate his share." Later, though, when Isaac visited the Hemleys in Ohio, Mrs. Hemley was always careful to prepare vegetarian dishes for him.

Although Mrs. Hemley admires Isaac's stories for children, she doesn't think he's really too fond of children. "One time we were visiting the Roger Strauses up in Westchester, and our son Robin was with us—he was about three. He was wandering about the grounds, and he found a little frog, and he was just delighted with it. Then Isaac saw the frog in Robin's hand and took it away from him and tossed it into the pool. He said, 'The animal must remain with nature.' So he defended the frog, but he hurt the child."

❊

"If a man builds a house," Isaac says, "he will know how to build ten houses. But in writing this is not so. He may write six books and not know how to write the seventh, which may turn out to be a terrible failure. Every book is a problem in itself. Every book demands a different form, a different technique. And so you never really learn your profession. Every time you write a book it is a miracle if it comes out right."

Isaac feels that the trouble with many writers is that "they have only one book. They have only one thing to say, and after they say it, they have nothing more to say. It is a tragedy, but it is in the nature of many writers."

Isaac is in no sense a one-book writer. Each of his novels represents a tremendous leap forward from the last, a daredevil's attempt to accomplish what he has never accomplished before, to explore new territory, always matching the form of his work to the demands of its subject. Yet his subject remains the same—the lives and experiences of Polish Jews. He will go back through time to the sixteenth century or as far forward as the day before yesterday. He will write about the lives of his people in Poland or trace their migrations to Israel or the Americas, but his characters are always Polish Jews, whether they are kibbutzniks in Beersheba or refugees in The Bronx.

By the time he wrote *The Magician of Lublin* Isaac had already stepped out of Joshua's shadow and was speaking in a voice entirely his own. He had freed himself of the restrictions of the sprawling "family" novel and begun to adapt this form successfully to his own literary needs.

In *The Magician of Lublin,* written in 1958 and serialized in the *Forward* in 1959, we are presented with Isaac in the guise of Yasha Mazur, a man of forty, respectably married to a pious woman in a suburb of Lublin while he carries on a secret, precarious second life in the Warsaw underworld that involves him with four other women. These interlocking affairs are strikingly reminiscent of the complex romantic network Isaac would describe years later in *A Young Man in Search of Love.* Like Isaac, Yasha is really two people—the respectable, conservative, conventional husband of Esther, who knows nothing of his hidden powers or his adventures, and the magician, the Houdini who can open locks, escape from closed trunks and demanding mistresses, practice hypnotism, and read minds, and at the same time walk in the fear of God and the consequences of his deeds in this life and in the next. So in this novel, and in those that will follow, the focus is on a single life rather than an entire village or clan; the action takes up a few weeks, rather than decades. And all is seen through one man's eyes—Yasha's.

The plan is carefully drawn. We find Yasha first surrounded by domesticity; Esther is serving him a hearty breakfast after he has returned from a trip and recovered from earlier adventures by sleeping for two days. The Mazurs have no children, but their household is crowded with animals—a chattering monkey, a shrieking parrot, trilling canaries, even a pair of mares nicknamed Dust and Ashes. Yasha is prosperous and respectable, yet his neighbors have little use for him. He doesn't wear a beard, attends synagogue only on the High Holy Days, smokes on the Sabbath, consorts with musicians. A magician by profession, he can "walk on a tightrope, skate on a wire, climb walls, open any lock." His neighbors in Lublin suspect vaguely but correctly that if Yasha had chosen crime as a career "no one's house would be safe."

Yet Yasha is a personable and good-hearted fellow, whose scruples somehow keep him honest in spite of every opportunity, and he continues to be likeable even as we follow him on his philandering from the arms of one woman to another. Yasha is patently the perennial artist, the poet careening through a world of prose, who, among other things, can "never understand how other people managed to live and spend their entire lives with one woman without becoming melancholy." Such a hero should have hidden powers, and Yasha assuredly does. When his wife loses her wedding ring, he is able to lead her unerringly to a water barrel, where the ring lies gleaming at the bottom. Esther sees the very tricks of her husband's trade as sorcery— and no doubt they are.

Only a few pages into *The Magician of Lublin* Yasha is off, driving his wagon through fields where he can almost hear the crops growing under the moon. In one little town he stops to visit Magda, a former assistant, a flat-chested Christian girl with pimply skin. They sleep together and in the morning are served tea by her mother, the widow of a blacksmith. Both mother and daughter are spellbound by Yasha. But this Icarus of Eastern

Europe dreams, in more ways than one, of flying, and even while staying on with Magda and her mother takes time out for a rendezvous with the motherly Zeftel, a deserted wife and lapsed Jew who envies Yasha's freedom but always welcomes him: "Always a new one. A sniff here, a lick there and . . . you buzz away. . . . It would be worth surrendering my last pair of drawers to be a man." Yasha appeases Zeftel with a coral necklace and tells her about his latest conquest, a professor's widow named Emilia who wants him to convert. Zeftel wants Yasha to take her to Warsaw with him, but she is wise enough not to insist or hold him back.

After an encounter with a colleague who has brought a new pick-proof lock for Yasha to open—which of course he does—the magician and Magda are off for Warsaw. There Yasha's downfall awaits him, in the form of a dangerous dual love affair with the aging Emilia and her adolescent daughter, Halina, and a final temptation that becomes the familiar climactic moment of a Singer tale, "the one false step" by which a man can "lose Paradise." Yasha plans to climb the balcony of a wealthy man named Kazimierz Zuriski and break into his safe. He fails; he is unable to open the safe. He jumps down from the balcony and sprains his foot. To escape pursuit he hides in a synagogue. There it occurs to him exactly how he could have broken the lock, but it's too late. Too late, that is, to become a thief—not too late to become a Jew again. For on this night a number of lessons are brought home to the magician of Lublin. He comes to realize that each affair has come complete with its own set of domestic problems and needy relatives—an endless succession of proliferating responsibilities. But now, in the synagogue where he takes refuge, all becomes clear to Yasha: "He had broken or contemplated breaking each of the Ten Commandments! He had even lusted for Halina, already woven a net in readiness to ensnare her. He had plumbed to the very depths of iniquity. How had this come about? And when? He was by nature good-hearted. In winter he scattered crumbs outside to feed the birds. He seldom passed a beggar without offering alms. He bore eternal hate against swindlers, bankrupters, charlatans. He had always prided himself on being honest and ethical."

Now Yasha, whose ambition it has been to perform his magic before the princes of Europe, this back-country sensualist whose appetites have seemed insatiable, realizes he has "reduced others to dirt and did not see—pretended not to see—how he himself kept sinking deeper into the mud" while only "a thread restrained [him] from the final plunge into the bottomless pit." Yasha turns to prayer and comes to believe again in God—"a God who sees, Who hears, Who takes pity on man, Who contains His wrath, Who forgives sin, Who wants men to repent, Who punishes evil deeds, Who rewards good deeds in this world and—what was even more—in the other." Yasha tells himself, "I must be a Jew! A Jew like all the others."

The final pages of *The Magician of Lublin* are devoted to Yasha's prolonged atonement. He locks himself in a cell where he is to stay until he feels that he is worthy again to live in the world with the pious woman who loves him. Meanwhile, however, he has driven Magda to suicide and hastened Zeftel on her way to life in a brothel.

Merely to sum up what happens to Yasha is, of course, to do the book an injustice, for in *The Magician of Lublin* Isaac has portrayed the inner life as well as all the adventures of a man in trouble. As with most fables, the energy of the tale relieves the austerity of its moral. Yasha may ride his horse and wagon through a gaslit land of the past, yet he is a thoroughly twentieth-century hero, a bright fellow whose mind is full of windows open to the world, a Faust with whom we can easily identify today—even as we are hard-put to identify with Joshua's idealistic, long-suffering, embattled noble peasants. Still, in the end, Isaac leaves Yasha to suffocate in a stifling cell. But the endings of Isaac's novels are seldom satisfactory, and this is not merely a matter of construction. The fact is, Isaac's protagonists, with so much of Isaac in them, are always so large, so alive, and so awake to the world that their repentance and atonement are merely disappointments for us. If this is redemption, the Gehenna in which they serve out their sentences would probably be a better place to spend eternity than that institutional heaven where the pious reside in celestial study houses.

To Irving Buchen the lesson of the book is that "in slavery Yasha will find his true freedom." But for the modern reader it is the hero's magical escape from the box of his little world that is exhilarating; his self-administered punishment in the end seems gratuitous, tendentious. Such a magician should be allowed to climb back on his tightrope and once again astound his audience—as Isaac, the magician of West Eighty-sixth Street, continues to do. True enough, in real life any man who attempts to deal with five women at once, to live five lives at once, as Isaac himself learned to his sorrow, is bound to be worn out sooner or later by the accompanying complications—but how brave of Yasha even to try! A man with that kind of courage deserves a better fate than a bowl of rice and milk in an airless cell, a boring wife, and the mindless admiration of superstitious mediocrities. This is too much like those Hollywood gangster pictures that were intended to prove that crime doesn't pay. The moral is the only unbelievable element in *The Magician of Lublin*.

The Magician of Lublin, translated by Joseph Singer and Elaine Gottlieb Hemley, appeared in 1960. Milton Rugoff wrote in the New York *Herald Tribune* that the book "casts a spell"; he described it as "a mixture of realism and fantasy" with "a power to evoke the people and places of nineteenth-century Polish Jewry that loads every page with rare pleasures and unexpected rewards." In *The New York Times Book Review* Milton Hindus praised Isaac's strengths even though he expressed some reservations about whether Isaac had realized his aim: "The author evidently intends this tale . . . as a parable of the modern Jew's reaction against the rude temptation to cut himself off from the ancestral tradition where his morality has its source. It is a great weight that Singer has undertaken to lift in 'The Magician,' and even if upon rereading his book we are not convinced that he has succeeded, it is clear that he is a writer of far greater than ordinary powers." Christopher Driver, writing in *The Guardian*, found *The Magician of Lublin* "a touching and fantastic tale." In *The Nation* Richard Elman declared that "this is the stuff of literature and it is as distinct from the stuff you find in novels which merely catalogue sensations and events as it is from works of propaganda or hagiography." *Time* rhapsodized over the author's "clean and sun-washed optimism, a sense of human uncertainty in the face of divine certainty." Francis King, in the *New Statesman*, caught the novel's spirit accurately when he wrote that "the apparent tranquility" of its surface, "shining with optimism and good humor," actually concealed "an inner chasm of violence and despair." King summed up the book as "at once a parable and a novel of suspense."

It is that "chasm of violence and despair," that European preoccupation with the dark night of the soul that imbues Isaac's novels with both their power and that curious pessimism that seems somehow at odds with the author's own ebullient nature. Perhaps, in his books as in his life, he is just as he says, "a pessimist, but a happy pessimist."

Asked if he identifies himself with Yasha Mazur, Isaac has this to say: "I'm not completely the magician of Lublin, but at the same time I am. I write either of what has happened or of what might have happened—if I think it was possible."

With the publication of *The Magician of Lublin* something happened in Isaac's career that has happened to very few writers. The book was serialized in Yiddish in the *Forward* and published as a book in English, but it never appeared in book form in the language in which it was written. And this was a pattern that was to be repeated with Isaac's novels from then on. Isaac's finest prose of the last two decades, although widely available in hardcover and paperback editions in English and in many other languages all over the world, is today unavailable in Yiddish.

The Slave, Isaac's next novel, was written in 1960—his best novel thus far. A year later the book was serialized in the *Forward*; in 1962 it was published in English by Farrar, Straus and Cudahy (later Farrar, Straus and Giroux). In this translation Cecil Hemley's poetic sensibility, combined with the infinite care he took over every page, preserves the flavor of Isaac's Yiddish style and the essence of the story's pastoral, impressionistic beauty.

"When I wrote a family novel, like *The Family Moskat* or *The Estate* or *The Manor*," Isaac has said, "my goal was to recreate an epoch, not just a single human being. But when I wrote a novel such as *The Magician of Lublin* or *The Slave*, I tried to concentrate on a single character. It is a ques-

tion of what my purpose is. In writing *The Manor* and *The Estate* I wanted
to give in a way the history of Jewish people, the literary history of Jewish
people in Poland in the second half of the nineteenth century. And since
this was my aim, I used different methods than I use in a short story or in a
short novel.

"When you go by plane from New York to Los Angeles, you don't try to
see everything on the way. A superficial way of looking is necessary in this
case. But when you take a horse and buggy, or even a car, and you go from
village to village, you see differently. In literature it is the same thing."

In *The Slave* Isaac was able to concentrate even more closely on the relations between individual characters, calling into play all his powers of observation to bring the little world around them to vivid life.

The plot of *The Slave* is relatively simple, at least at the outset. The action begins at dawn with the call of a single bird. Jacob is a Jew living in a
barn in the primitive mountains of Poland, a setting that is almost Biblical
in atmosphere. But this is actually the middle of the seventeenth century,
shortly after the bloody depredations of Bohdan Chmielnicki and the wholesale slaughter and dispersion of Polish Jewry. Jacob has been a lucky es-
capee, hiding out in the mountain country, the slave of a brutish, almost
Cro-Magnon overseer. Here Jacob has managed somehow to keep track of
the seasons and observe the Jewish holidays. But he has also fallen in love
with Wanda, the daughter of the man who holds him in bondage. She is a
blue-eyed, fair-skinned, flaxen-haired creature—playing Lilith to his Adam
in this infertile Eden. In comparison with the savage creatures all around
them, Wanda "seemed city-bred. She dressed in a skirt, blouse and apron,
and wore a kerchief on her head; moreover, her speech could be understood. A bolt of lightning had killed her husband Stach and from then on
she had been courted by all the bachelors and widowers of the village. . . .
In the village she had been nicknamed 'The Lady.' As Jacob knew very well,
according to the law he must avoid her, but if it had not been for Wanda he
would have forgotten that he had a tongue in his head. Besides, she assisted
him in fulfilling his obligations as a Jew."

Even as Jacob longs to make love to Wanda, he knows that all this has
been "contributed by Satan." But in the barn where Jacob lives, surrounded
by mountains "as deserted as in the days of the Creation," Jacob and Wanda
consummate their love—at the holy time of the Jewish New Year. Their
idyll is interrupted by the arrival of an expedition searching for pogrom survivors. They redeem Jacob from his bondage and take him back to Josefov,
the village of his birth, whose population has been decimated by Chmielnicki's Cossacks. In a pilgrimage to the places of his past Jacob learns the extent of the horror.

"Alas, poor Dinah, they ripped open her stomach and put a dog in. You
could hear it barking."

"They impaled Moishe Bunim, and he didn't stop groaning all night."

"Twenty Cossacks raped your sister Leah and then they cut her to pieces."

But the author, although he never flinches from describing the inhuman cruelties of war and persecution, is not one to dwell too long on horror for its own sake. Jacob still longs for Wanda, and after he learns that his wife and family have been wiped out, he goes back to find her.

Dressed like a peasant, carrying a sack over his shoulder with bread and cheese, phylacteries and a prayer book, and presents for Wanda, Jacob returns to the primitive mountains. He goes by dangerous roads, where the night teems with witches and demons lurking behind trees, deeper and deeper into the woods, "as solitary as the original Adam, with no sign anywhere of man and his works." Passing bubbling streams under crowds of stars, Jacob asks himself questions Isaac asked as a boy: "Suppose we had wings and flew in one direction forever, would we come to the end of space? But how could space end? What extended beyond? Or was the material world infinite? But if it was, infinity stretched to the east and west, and how could there be twice infinity? And what of time? How could even God have had no beginning? How could anything be eternal? Where had everything come from? These questions were impertinent, he knew, impermissible, pushing the inquirer toward heresy and madness."

At length, his mind fixed on the story of Ruth and Boaz instead of these heady speculations, Jacob finds Wanda. "Suddenly clutching him, she let out a wail that made Jacob shudder. Crying, she kissed his face, licked his hand. A howl tore itself from her throat.

" 'Jacob, don't leave me again, Jacob.' "

The second part of *The Slave* seems almost to belong to another book. Eden has vanished. In its place appears the square of a village where the scarred pogrom survivors are trying pathetically to repair their lives. Jacob becomes involved in the affairs of a pair of lazy and profligate Polish aristocrats. Wanda is Sarah now, a convert to Judaism. She pretends to be a mute, and she and Jacob move to another town called Pilitz, where he will not be recognized. There follows a turbulent operatic scene in which a Polish squire exults in his power over a helpless throng of Jews, and Wanda-Sarah almost gives herself away by crying out at his cruelty. Jacob and Sarah must endure the slanders of malicious townspeople (here again is that comic-operetta chorus of unfeeling gossips waiting in the wings). Sarah becomes pregnant and makes ready "to summon a Jewish soul from the Throne of Glory" while Jacob ekes out a living teaching school.

Awaiting the birth of his child, Jacob goes out one night under the stars, like the ancient Rabbi Akiba, to see signs everywhere: "The summer night throbbed with joy; from all sides came music. Warm winds bore the smells of grain, fruit and pine trees to him. Itself a cabalistic book, the night was crowded with sacred names and symbols—mystery upon mystery. In the distance where sky and earth merged, lightning flashed, but no thunder followed. The stars looked like letters of the alphabet, vowel points, notes of music. Sparks flickered above the bare furrows. The world was parchment scrawled with words and song." (It is in this passage that the high poetry of Hemley's translation proves itself equal to the lyricism and descriptive precision of Isaac's Yiddish.)

The novel ends rather prosaically and by no means happily. Sarah cries out in the agony of prolonged labor, and this time her identity is discovered. The women of the village believe that Sarah, like Rechele in *Satan in Goray*, is possessed by a dybbuk. The baby, a boy, survives, but Sarah dies; the hovel they have been living in burns to the ground; Jacob finds himself alone and homeless, the wandering Jew once more. Twenty years later, we are told, Benjamin, the son of Jacob and Sarah, has become a lecturer in an academy in Jerusalem. Jacob has returned to Pilitz and dies in the local poorhouse. He is buried beside Sarah's grave, beneath a headstone that reads, "Lovely and pleasant in their lives, and in their death they were not divided."

In *The Family Moskat* Isaac portrays himself as a man in search of political truth who finds no answer in politics; in *The Magician of Lublin* he casts himself as the wordly Yasha, the artist who seeks salvation in illusion and self-gratification but is transformed into the penitent Jacob, humbling himself before God; in *The Slave* another Jacob seeks fulfillment in romantic love with a Christian woman, but he also can find redemption only in piety and finally surcease in death.

From the sprawling complexity of the family novels to the harrowing nocturnal suspense of *The Magician of Lublin* to the silken lyrical beauty of *The Slave* there is a constant stylistic and thematic progression, and in some curious way, an increasingly modern expression of sensibility. The coarse, vital women, the greedy sensual men, who dominate the earlier books are gradually replaced by more reflective characters more attuned to mystery and wonder. Although *The Slave* has its full share of meddling minor characters, and the brutish mountaineers of its early pages are truly terrifying monsters, Jacob and Wanda are not grotesques, not caricatures, not freaks, but sensitive innocents in a harmonious natural setting, far removed in space and time from the teeming, hectic cityscapes of *The Manor* and *The Estate*. Jacob and Wanda do not waste their substance in bickering or self-pity. They do not lust for wealth or knowledge or power over others, but only for each other. Their story is tragic, but it is a tragedy of submission, not defiance. If "all stories are love stories," as Isaac insists, then *The Slave* is the apotheosis of the romantic tale of love.

How did American critics react to *The Slave*? Jean Stafford, in *The New Republic*, found it "surprising and wonderful to be convinced and engrossed altogether by a contemporary using an archaic form that is half tale and half morality. . . . In the hands of another writer, lacking Mr. Singer's genius at spinning a yarn, this story of torture and forbidden love . . . would be preposterous. But he is a spell-binder as clever as Scheherazade." Milton Hindus wrote in *The New York Times Book Review* that Isaac had composed "a story stripped down to almost Biblical simplicity while trying not to violate the contemporary reader's expectations of fiction too radically." Although Hindus felt that Isaac had imposed too heavy a burden of "allegorical suggestiveness" on his characters, he praised the book's "lovely lyricism," which reminded him of "expressionistic paintings." In the *Saturday Review* the late David Boroff found *The Slave* "distinguished and memorable" because "Singer is able, as few writers are, to transmute metaphysical ideas into pure emotion. What the novel really says is that one way or another we are all slaves. . . . Few writers since Shakespeare have been able to evoke so harrowingly the nightmare world of savage animals . . . and man's kinship with them." Boroff went on to describe *The Slave* as "a brilliant portrayal of a tumultuous society and a poignant account of a man who while wrestling with God found his soul." Others have probed *The Slave,* as they have all Isaac's books, for symbols, hunting allegories of the Jewish experience. Buchen speaks of the book as an illustration of a paradox: In some ways Jacob is freer as a slave than when he must make his own way. It is this and more—a vivid documentation of the gruesome anti-Semitic cruelties that sets the stage for the Nazi Holocaust still centuries away, and a portrayal of enslavement itself—Jacob enslaved by Wanda's father, his people by Polish landowners. But above all *The Slave* is a superb love story that evades its own net of subtly interwoven symbols to shimmer and sing.

❀

In the mid-fifties Isaac began to be invited to lecture at colleges and universities, a prospect which at first terrified him. "At meetings of the Yiddish P.E.N. Club in Warsaw I hated even to ask if somebody would close a window when there was a draft. I had always been shy. How could I make speeches? I thought, This is impossible. Then I thought it over. I wrote a speech called 'My Philosophy as a Jewish Writer.' I wrote it in Yiddish, and Mr. Hemley translated it for me into English. I must have repeated that speech about a hundred times since. But the first time was agony for me."

After Isaac made his first speech at Harvard, Edmund Wilson wrote him, saying the evening was one of the most rewarding he had ever spent. (Isaac has since lost the letter.) "So I said to myself, If I can entertain Wilson, I suppose I can entertain anybody. For years after that I took trains to Jewish centers and synagogues and universities all over the country. When I came to these colleges, it was really my first real contact with gentiles. I found out they liked me best when I gave humorous answers to questions, so that's what I've been doing ever since. This talent must have been hidden in me somewhere. At first I would make my speech, answer as few questions as possible, take my check, and leave. In recent years I have found lecturing much more fun, although Alma thinks I tire myself out doing too much traveling and lecturing. But I enjoy it."

The lecturing led to invitations—which he accepted—to serve as writer-in-residence at Oberlin in 1966, at the University of California in 1967, and at Bard in 1974 and 1975. Through the years he has also continued to lecture all over the country and abroad.

In addition to "My Philosophy as a Jewish Writer" Isaac regularly delivers five or six lectures, including "The Cabala and Modern Man," "The Autobiography of Yiddish," and "Why I Think Yiddish Is Richer Than English."

❀

Los Angeles, a Friday afternoon in November 1976. The sun shines down on a winding road that leads to the sea. Rabbi Alfred Wolf is driving Isaac to a country retreat, Hess-Kramer Camp, in the woods not far from the Pacific. After a five-hour plane ride from New York Isaac should be tired, but his blue eyes shine with enthusiasm. Here in the woods are cabins, a rustic lounge, a mess hall, a clearing where there are an altar and benches for a congregation. The first thing Isaac wants to do is take a walk in the woods. He follows a leafy trail almost to the end before he turns back to the camp site.

At sunset the couples taking part in the retreat, ranging in age from thirty to sixty and dressed in bluejeans, country-style shirts, sweaters, and hiking boots, gather in the mess hall for an informal Sabbath eve service. The Reform service conducted by Rabbi Wolf, a "creative" variation on the traditional prayer-book ritual, intersperses readings of modern poetry and music with the Hebrew and English prayers. Isaac seems rapt, caught up in the mood of the service, praying quietly in Hebrew, in the traditional way he learned as a boy.

After services the couples dine in groups at wooden tables. There is a twist—a *challah*—for the Sabbath, gefilte fish, and for Isaac a plate of eggs, a dish of carrots, celery, and olives, with a portion of Jell-O for dessert. Then Isaac delivers his lecture, "The Cabala and Modern Man." Everyone brings a chair and the group forms a circle around him, listening devotedly. After the lecture there are the usual questions. Relaxed and good-humored in this informal Sabbath atmosphere, Isaac talks to them quietly about his experiences in Radzymin and Warsaw.

Back in the bungalow, Isaac sleeps soundly. He is happy to be awakened the next morning by birdsong and is on time at the mess hall for a hearty breakfast.

Sabbath services are held outdoors in the clearing where benches face an ark built into mountain rock. When the Torah is removed from the ark, Isaac is called upon to read the portion for the day—an honor in any Jewish congregation. Today's portion is the story of Noah, and there is an extra treat in store for these congregants among the trees: Isaac is going to read his children's book *Why Noah Chose the Dove*.

Back at the mess hall for lunch, Isaac feels he is among old friends. Whenever a little group clusters around him there is the sound of laughter. There is time after lunch for another walk along one of the trails. Then a couple who are going back to the city take Isaac to a modest hotel, where he is to spend the night. He goes up to his room for a nap. In the evening he dines quietly, goes to bed early.

The next day another young rabbi and his wife call for Isaac in their car to take him to a Sunday brunch at Wilshire Boulevard Temple, a rather grandiose Hollywood house of worship presided over by Rabbi Judah Magnin, a venerable leader of the Jewish community now in his eighties. This is "the rabbi of the stars," the man who arranged Elizabeth Taylor's and Sammy Davis, Jr.'s conversion to Judaism. They meet before the lecture Isaac is to give and talk comfortably together. Then everyone enters the sanctuary, a cathedrallike interior with stained glass windows, elaborate decorations, solid rows of carved benches—in every way the opposite of the rustic retreat in the woods.

One woman in the congregation expresses her concern that by doing all this traveling Isaac will wear himself out, but he doesn't look the least bit tired. Suddenly along comes an old friend—Leo Fuchs, the veteran Jewish actor, who still appears in Yiddish plays on the Los Angeles stage. Isaac is overjoyed. Leo and his wife, Rivkeh, offer to take Isaac out after his next lecture that evening at another congregation; he heartily accepts.

Isaac's Wilshire Boulevard Temple lecture is on literature and folklore. Once more he answers the familiar questions—where does he get his ideas and does he really believe in demons? When the session is over a Sunday brunch is served in a meeting room—bagels, lox, and cream cheese. Isaac munches happily as he exchanges anecdotes with Rabbi Magnin, his assistant, and members of the congregation. He finishes up with several bites of cake and a cup of coffee. Then he's driven back to the hotel.

Isaac stands before the window of his room, looking out at a parking lot, where a blue Volkswagen is parked close to a red one. Are the two cars having an affair? When nobody is looking, do they nestle close and touch radio antennae? Except for a few palm trees in the distance, the cars seem to be the only creatures in sight. No owners appear to call for them. Are they orphans, or brother and sister, or truly lovers?

Around seven that evening a well-dressed Orthodox rabbi driving a shiny Cadillac calls for Isaac and takes him to his home in Beverly Hills, where the *rebbitzin* has prepared a handsome dinner that includes a carrot soufflé. The house is spacious and decorated in an old-fashioned style that brings out all Isaac's geniality. He is also pleased to be surrounded at dinner by the rabbi's good-looking daughters. The *rebbitzin* tells Isaac that she has aspirations as a writer. She would like to write a book of her experiences, to be called *The Mad Story of a Mad Rebbitzin*. The *rebbitzin* is a substantial blond woman with a strong personality—the sort of woman who attracts Isaac and is likely to turn up in his books and stories. Isaac sits there quietly, next to the rabbi, doing his best to attend to the conversation, which is about religious matters, but aware the entire time of the *rebbitzin*, her remarks, her laughter, her feminine presence. When dinner is over, Isaac leaves the table reluctantly. It's time for another public appearance.

Members of the party get into the rabbi's Cadillac and proceed to Congregation Beth Jacob for the after-dinner speech. Isaac delivers once more his lecture "The Cabala and Modern Man." This time the whole presentation is a bit more formal. Then come the questions. The Cabala is left hanging while Isaac tries to deal with such matters as what is going to happen to the sons and daughters of Jewish families who go off to join the Reverend Moon or shave their heads and go around chanting Hare Krishna or join the Jews for Jesus movement. Isaac tries to tell the troubled parents that in a modern industrial society where science is worshipped as a substitute for religion young people are bound to look somewhere for the spiritual sustenance they need. This doesn't seem to be the sort of answer his questioners had hoped to hear. But at the end they applaud him heartily anyway.

Isaac finds his old friends Leo and Rivkeh Fuchs waiting for him. Their car is not a Cadillac. It's little and old, and Isaac likes it. He lounges in the backseat, looking more relaxed and at home than ever. Now he can talk Yiddish with friends who speak his language in every sense of the word. Even though it is a number of years since they last saw one another, they trade old memories, laugh at private jokes, share the special frame of reference of a long, long friendship. They drive to a coffee shop called Nibbler's, where they sit and lounge for hours in one of those Hollywood-style fake-leather-upholstered booths. They fill one another in on the events of their lives like true *landsleit* rejoined after half a lifetime of wandering and separation.

Late that night Leo and Rivkeh drive Isaac back to his hotel. He smiles and waves to them for a long time as their car disappears into the Los Angeles traffic and smog.

The next morning yet another car, this one crowded with children's toys and miscellaneous battered objects, drives up to Isaac's hotel. A deferential young man goes up to Isaac's room and helps him out with his luggage. They drive to the airport. The flight home is smooth.

❀

In the late 1950s lack of money and personal difficulties between Arthur Cohen and Cecil Hemley were speeding the decline of their publishing firm. The company's future was in doubt. Then in 1960 Farrar, Straus and Cudahy acquired the Noonday Press and turned it into a paperback house, and Isaac had a new publisher.

❀

December 4, 1975

Roger W. Straus, Jr., is a handsome, gray-haired man who looks younger than his sixty years and every inch the German Jewish patrician, Guggenheim heir, and successful publisher he is. He recalls, "I can't remember exactly the first time I met Isaac, but I know that for years he addressed me as Mr. Straus. I had been publishing his work for ten years when we finally got to a first-name basis. I know I thought he was the most marvelous little gnome I had ever seen in my life. He was so sweet and seemed so innocent and was terribly shy. I remember, even when he had to go to the home of his own relatives or in-laws for dinner, he would be shy about that. He was poor. And although he was certain enough about the quality of his own work, he was insecure about its commercial possibilities. He never quarreled about the amount of an advance on a manuscript. He has developed a lot of confidence since those days. And confidence about the reception of whatever he has to say." Yet, from the beginning, Straus says, when Isaac lectured at places such as Harvard, "he wowed them."

In those days Isaac didn't have an agent; his publishers represented him, at first with Paula Diamond and later with Lila Karpf handling subsidiary rights. With Farrar, Straus and Cudahy (later Farrar, Straus and Giroux) as his publishers Isaac's fortunes began to prosper. The money began coming in. Yet even though his American readership was growing, Isaac's reception overseas was less encouraging. At first his books didn't sell well in Germany. They were read in Yiddish in Poland and other Eastern European countries, but they never appeared in the languages of those countries. In Israel sales only began to grow gradually. Today his books and stories appear in a score of languages everywhere, and sales are high.

"He was a late starter," Roger Straus observes, "but he's been so prolific. So many of his books appeared, one after another. Now I'm told that he's high on the list for a Nobel prize. Each year has been better for him than the last."

In addition to printing his new novels, Farrar, Straus published *The Slave* in English in 1962 (it became a best-seller), *The Manor* in 1967, and *The Estate* in 1969, and reissued *The Family Moskat* in 1965 (in hardcover and paperback). They have printed most of the short-story collections, starting with *The Spinoza of Market Street*, and the book of memoirs *In My Father's Court* (in 1979 many of these books were reissued in paperback after Isaac did win the Nobel prize). A *Little Boy in Search of God* and A *Young Man in Search of Love*, however, were published by Doubleday. A number of the children's books have been brought out by Harper and Row, others by Scribner's, but most of them by Farrar, Straus.

As his publisher, Roger Straus talks to Isaac about once a week on the telephone, and they occasionally visit each other's homes for dinner. "Alma is a real old-fashioned German-Jewish kind of hostess," Straus says. "There's always too much food, but it's always very, very good. . . . You know, Alma worries a lot about the public appearances Isaac makes, the lectures and the TV shows and the autograph-signing at bookstores and the parties and the trips all over the country. A few years ago he wasn't too well, and she asked me to try to persuade him to cut down. I told him one day I thought he was overdoing it, but he said to me, 'Roger, this is what gives me my lift.' And I think I understand. I think all the attention and the public appearances are really very good for him. I think it's his life's blood. When I met him, there was very little of this. The only people who knew him were on the staff of the *Jewish Daily Forward*. He was vaguely known as an odd-ball who fed pigeons and kept parakeets. When Cynthia Ozick published her short story called 'Envy; or, Yiddish in America,' with a portrait that was obviously a caricature of Isaac, a lot of people who knew Isaac were up-tight about it—quite disturbed—but Isaac wasn't. He always was sure of his work; now he's sure of himself. Fame was a long time coming to him. I've never known anyone who enjoyed it more, or let it affect him less."

❀

Cynthia Ozick's "Envy; or, Yiddish in America" first appeared in *Commentary* in November 1969 and was later published in 1970 by Shocken Books in her collection *The Pagan Rabbi*. The hero, Edelshtein, a sixty-seven-year-old widower from the Ukraine who has been living in America for forty years, is a Yiddish poet who hates American-Jewish novels but reads them all. Edelshtein's envy and spleen find a special focus in the person of Yankel Ostrover, a pallid author with an uncanny resemblance, at least on the surface, to Isaac Singer. Ostrover is everything Edelshtein is not. He writes in Yiddish, but in translation his books have won him a worldwide reputation. Starting as a "columnist for one of the Yiddish dailies, a humorist, a cheap fast article-writer, a squeezer out of tales," Ostrover has graduated to *"The New Yorker,* to *Playboy,* to big lecture fees, invitations to Yale and M.I.T. and Vassar, to the Midwest, to a literary agent, to a publisher on Madison Avenue. . . ." Seething with rage over Ostrover's success and still smarting from the memory of an affair Ostrover had thirty years before with his wife, Edelshtein writes to Ostrover's publisher demanding that he too be provided with a translator. He is turned down but persists in the search. He writes to a "spinster hack" who has worked for Ostrover; in her reply she accuses Ostrover of underpaying and maltreating her, but she refuses to work for Edelshtein. Accompanied by friends who share his distaste for Ostrover's success, the poet goes to a Y (obviously the Ninety-second Street YMHA where Isaac often lectures) to hear the great man deliver a dissertation, read a story aloud, and answer questions from the floor. Edelshtein even conducts an imaginary dialogue with his nemesis, who patronizes him even in his own fantasy and advises him to "stop believing in Yiddish."

Yet Edelshtein consents to meet Ostrover when he gets the opportunity and even masochistically mumbles compliments on the story his rival has read. He later phones Ostrover by mistake and engages in a strange conversation, which Edelshtein breaks off, screaming, after Ostrover tells him that "envy sounds the same in all languages." Even when Edelshtein thinks he has finally found a woman who will translate his poems and pleads with her to "help out an old man," she turns him down cold: "You don't interest me." Dialing a wrong number once more, he is subjected to an anti-Semitic tirade from a stranger. Edelshtein shouts back, "On account of you I have lost everything, my whole life! On account of you I have no translator."

"Envy," like so much of Ozick's caustic prose, is delivered from some unspecified but lofty moral plateau, yet it is nevertheless a fascinating tale and, not unlike one of Isaac's own stories, builds ingeniously to its fevered denouement. It is impossible not to pity Edelshtein. But Ozick's view of Isaac-Ostrover is curiously myopic. The story Ostrover reads at the Y, while it serves the plot of "Envy" well enough, is a dimensionless fable lacking the wit, charm, and flashing illumination of detail that distinguish the real thing. Where Isaac's exchanges with his audience are penetrating and hilarious, Ostrover's are gross, mindless, and unamusing; his quips could only be equated with Isaac's by a humorless parodist impervious to the vitality of his style, distracted from his profundity by the deliberate lightness of his approach. It is on history that Edelshtein should blame his failure, not on Ostrover's jokes. How many great Jewish writers, after all, could a single generation of Eastern Europe's Jews, so many of them dead in concentration camps, be expected to produce? Ozick is asking us to squirm, as she often does, for the wrong reasons—to feel embarrassment we haven't merited, nor Isaac either—since he is far from being the person he is made out to be in "Envy." Yet, viewed in the light of its own moral laws, the tale is a strong one.

❀

December 11, 1975

Dorothea Straus, the wife of Roger Straus, Jr., began working as one of Isaac's translators in the 1960s. Born Dorothea Liebmann, she married Roger in 1938; they have one son, Roger W. Strauss III.

Looking relaxed and poised on a long sofa in the living room of their townhouse on Manhattan's Upper East Side, she talks about working with Isaac as a translator: "He could do his own translations, really. Those of us who have our names down as his translators are not really doing that at all. We function more like copy editors. He goes over and over things, and believe me, he knows a great deal. Sometimes he has worked with me directly from the *Forward* with the newspaper in his hands. Other times he will read from bits of a manuscript covered with tiny Hebrew letters. He sits in his chair, always the same chair in his living room, and I sit on the same sofa with the stripes, and I try to keep up with his reading aloud in English, writing everything down in longhand. But he's so quick it's almost impossible to keep pace with him. He is really translating the story as he goes.

"Every once in a while he will grope for an idiomatic English phrase. He'll ask, 'What is that word for getting red in the face?' and I'll answer, 'You mean *blush*.' And then he'll say, 'What would I do without a translator?'

"He really knows what he's after—the ring of that folkloric language he uses reflected in the English. And as often as not he finds the right phrase himself before it is out of your mouth. His ear is so perfect that if you only approximate what he is looking for he will tell you, 'It doesn't sound right.' And it doesn't."

Working with Isaac, says Dorothea, is a lesson in mental agility, the ability to do any number of things seemingly at the same time, and to do them all well. "He interrupts his reading aloud to answer the telephone, he does twenty-seven other things, and he goes right back to where he has been and doesn't even lose his place. Sometimes he does lose the manuscript he's been working from, but even then he doesn't get too fussed."

After Isaac has finished reading aloud in English, Dorothea, usually suffering from writer's cramp by that time, goes home and writes it all out again in longhand. Sometimes, if a word has been overused, she supplies a synonym. "That kind of thing. And after I'm finished smoothing out the English, the piece is typed up, and off it goes to him, and I don't usually see it again until it's published."

One of the things that has impressed Dorothea about Isaac is that he seldom gets irritable over a job, at least with her. "He's quick, but he's also careful and at the same time remarkably patient. And you know, he's such a born storyteller that even when he's working with you on a translation he just has to keep you in suspense. He'll say, 'Now, that's enough for today,' and I'll ask, 'But how is it going to end?' And he won't tell me. Sometimes it takes two or three sessions to complete the dictation of a single story, and I'm kept in suspense the entire time."

Dorothea is particularly fond of the stories dealing with aging journalists from Warsaw trying to maintain their dignity in a world they are still not used to—stories such as "The Cafeteria," of which Isaac has written a good many in recent years. She also likes the many stories that describe a man who is leading a double life, going back and forth from the unworldly world of his wife to the all too worldly world of his mistress, entangling himself in lies and deceptions.

To Dorothea Isaac's basic theme is: " 'When you desert the standards of faith of your fathers, you're in Gehenna. You have to cling to the old values.' And the number of variations he has rung on that simple premise!"

According to Dorothea Isaac has quite recently tried writing several stories directly in English but has not been too happy about the results. "Perhaps he's too quick. He could never spend a whole day on a sentence like Conrad. He has a mind that speeds ahead like lightning. He is so anxious to get it all down on paper—not like some writers who fear that their ideas will dry up, but more like Keats, fearing that his pen will cease to flow before he's gleaned his teaming brain."

Dorothea got to know the Singers socially when her husband became Isaac's publisher in 1960, and they were friends before she began to work with him.

"He's always been such marvelous company—at dinner, for example. A first-class performer, always holds everybody spellbound."

Dorothea also played one scene with Isaac in Bruce Davidson's film *Isaac Singer's Nightmare and Mrs. Pupko's Beard.*

"In one of the scenes I was supposed to ring the doorbell and then walk in. We did this over and over, the way it's done for a movie. And then Isaac just couldn't stand it anymore. He said, 'I'm not going to keep my friend standing outside my door a whole morning.' He came to the door and let me in—at the same time disrupting the shooting of the scene. But he just couldn't see having me wait outside over and over like that. As a matter of fact, he wanted to be sure we didn't waste our time while Mr. Davidson was doing all the things people do to prepare for filming, so we translated a whole story while the lights and cameras were being set up in different positions and the filmmakers were going through all the various motions Isaac could only regard as squandering the hours."

Dorothea Straus feels she gets more satisfaction from reading the note Isaac always encloses with his check, which almost invariably reads, "Thank you for a job well done," than from the arrival of the check itself.

Not all Isaac's translators feel that way. There is a story about a woman who was invited to work with him on a translation and never got a check at all, let alone a note of gratitude. When she reminded Isaac about it, he is said to have reproached her with some remark such as 'I thought you were my friend.' Much of the gossip about him makes him out to be reluctant to acknowledge the contributions of others, from translators to collaborators on plays. His champions defend his attitude by pointing out that Isaac, who worked so long and so hard to get where he is, cannot help feeling that others are exploiting his originality for their own profit and that there must be a limit to the claims they can make for work that would not even exist except for the effort and imagination he himself put into it.

Dorothea believes that Isaac sometimes makes provocative statements out of a sheer love of mischief. One time he assured her that he thought "any woman who commits adultery should be hanged." This struck her as so retrogressive that she remembered it and brooded about it for a long time. Finally she told him, "Isaac, I just haven't been able to get over that statement you made about hanging women who commit adultery. Do you still believe it?" "I will tell you," was Isaac's characteristic response, "I don't really believe it—but I wish I did."

In *Prisons and Palaces* (Houghton Mifflin, 1976), a book in which she describes the exceptional people she has known and the places they have lived in, Dorothea Straus offers two sketches of Isaac, one in his neighborhood on the Upper West Side, the other in his Miami Beach condominium. Deftly she pencils in a picture of Isaac coming to meet her for lunch at the old Tip Toe Inn, once a favorite eating place in the neighborhood where he lives.

"Who is this crossing the wide avenue? He is of small stature, fair-complexioned, and is wearing a long dark winter coat, although it is spring and the weather is warm. From under a felt hat his large pale blue eyes peer out, as darting as his gait. He is clutching a brown paper bag. It is Isaac Singer."

Isaac hopes he isn't late. He has stopped on the way to buy bird food, to feed "God's creatures" out of a paper bag. From the *landsleit* café they walk up eleven blocks to his apartment, Dorothea sprinting to keep up with Isaac's "scuttling pace." When they get there, they work on a translation of his story "The Son from America."

To Dorothea the building where Isaac lives, with its shadowy courtyard, seems "a fortress, or perhaps, a converted prison." Isaac has told her that he chose the place because it reminded him of his childhood home on Krochmalna Street. He picks up his mail—the periodicals in Yiddish, the journals on extrasensory perception, the fan letters. In his paper-crammed study, with the parakeet Matzi, who "would alight on Singer's bald pate" when Isaac spoke to him, Dorothea finds herself transported to the old world of Isaac's characters, the Yentls, the Getsls, the "youths in their study houses, the women in the ritual bath"—a world that she, with her prosperous, upper-class American Jewish background, never knew. Isaac sits with a few pages clipped from the *Forward* in front of him, dictating a rough translation of his story. At the end of the session he teasingly refuses to tell her what is going to happen next. While talking with Isaac she perceives the "small boy's curiosity" peering out through the "prominent sharp eyes of the adult."

Later Dorothea visits Isaac in Miami Beach to work on a translation of another story. "Broadway has yielded place to Collins Avenue and a new bright white condominium, heavily carpeted, with a plastic sculpture in the lobby. It was a strange home for him and I felt nostalgia for the shabby rectangular fortress and its sunless courtyard. The elevator mounted to dizzy heights and my husband and I were disgorged into a compact, light apartment, the entire dwelling no larger than the obscure foyer at 86th Street. It was sparsely furnished and I wondered what we would use instead of Singer's armchair and the bright sofa. After a hospitable coffee klatch with rich cakes, served by Alma in elaborate Munich style, Singer, always impatient to return to his stories, said, 'Now we get to work.' "

They moved out onto that balcony of his, perched high above the sea, and Isaac—with his back to the spectacular view—began to dictate rapidly from the pages of a manuscript "covered with his small illegible writing in Yiddish" while Dorothea jotted down what he said.

"As usual, I rushed to keep pace with him. But my eyes kept straying to the extravagant sea spread over his shoulder below until his tale took possession of me. Once again I was back among the pious rabbis, the *landsleit* in the cafeterias, the Yiddish journalists, the yeshiva students, the housewives baking the Sabbath loaves, the miracles, the dybbuks—reaching me through the lips of the immortal storyteller. The courtyard that had reminded Singer of his boyhood Warsaw home was, after all, an unnecessary stage set, no more vital than the beach in Miami. Isaac Singer's world, the world of the historic Jew, does not have its true existence among the perishable phenomena of things in space. From biblical recording to the events of contemporary days, the Diaspora, enacted again and again, has made the Jew a transient in all places of the earth. Yet he endures. Singer is a link in a chain celebrating in words the continuation of a people in abiding Time."

It is a convincing summation, a lot easier to accept than some of the convoluted analyses of his plots presented by the more solemn critics who have probed Isaac's works for symbolic systems and secret meanings while ignoring their chief and altogether accessible beauty—that they are what they are and mean what they say.

❀

May 27, 1976

Lila Karpf came to New York from California in the late 1950s and, after a stint at Doubleday, went to work at Farrar, Straus and Cudahy in the subsidiary rights department. After two years she became director of the department. At that point she met Isaac and began to handle the subsidiary rights to his books and pretty much acted as his literary agent.

Behind her desk at Reader's Digest Books, where she works today, Lila Karpf, a youthful-looking, earnest woman, allows her essentially noncommittal expression to grow even more so as she recalls her relationship with Isaac. "I really don't remember exactly when I first met him," she says, "but it was very pleasant and professional. Of course he called me Lila and I called him Mr. Singer, and my main concern was that his income should be high enough and that his reputation be built on a wider and wider level. You have to build an author. When I first began offering his stories for placement in magazines, he was not yet known, and it was a difficult job. Then he was published in *Playboy* and *Mademoiselle* and several times in *Esquire,* and the job grew easier. I remember in those days we tried several times to sell stories to *The New Yorker,* but they had a policy at that time of not taking anything in translation. Then I came back from abroad after a vacation, and there were several stories on my desk for me to look at. I read one of them called "The Slaughterer," and I felt that if *The New Yorker* didn't take *that* one we ought to stop sending them his stuff altogether. But they took it, and Isaac acquired a whole new audience, certainly not the one he originally set out to write for in Warsaw."

Lila Karpf was handling the rights for a number of other authors as well, but she spent a lot of time on Isaac's work. "I'm a meddler," she confesses, "because I believe everything concerning an author's career—the look of a volume and the advertising promotion and the rights and all—should mesh. And so I was interested not only in the matter of rights but in what went into the collections of his short stories and just about everything else connected with the publication and promotion and sales.

"From the beginning there were people interested in turning Isaac's books and stories into plays and films and even operas. I handled all of that. There were a number of early option deals. Often nothing came of it, as when Barbra Streisand expressed an interest in acquiring the story 'Yentl the Yeshiva Boy' as a starring vehicle; some stories and books, like *The Magician of Lublin,* were spoken for with options which may still be held." (*The Magician of Lublin* has finally been made into a movie.)

Lila Karpf feels Isaac is "probably the master short-story writer of our time. There is almost no one who can realize characters and situations in short fiction form to the degree that Isaac can today. In his novels he does something different—and it's not something that many other novelists do. He is a traditional writer, a natural writer, and in each of his books he creates a whole world. Everything in his life is material for him. He takes a trip to Canada on a train, and it turns into a story, a marvelous story. Once he went on a trip to Portugal, and I gave him the names of some people I thought he might want to look up. The next thing I knew, there on my desk was a story about that experience."

Lila Karpf calls Alma "a lovely woman, an extremely patient and forbearing woman. She helped support the two of them during the years when so little money was coming in from his writing. Very little of that is done these days."

Lila Karpf rejects the view of the women in the literary world who feel that Isaac is unfair in his treatment of women in his work. To her his fiction only reflects the attitude toward women that was considered normal in the world of the *shtetl* and that immigrants from that world brought along with them. "After all," she points out, "all his characters are flawed; that's where their fascination for him lies."

When Lila Karpf left Farrar, Straus in 1972, Isaac acquired Robert Lesher as his agent, and she has not seen him since. "Ours was essentially a friendly business relationship," she says. "We saw each other often on that basis, and I enjoyed working with him. My role in his working life was really not very important. I don't believe editors and subsidiary rights people and others in publishing should be in the foreground or seek publicity for themselves. It is the author who counts. And this is especially true in the case of a great author like Isaac Singer. I think we're in a pretty strange period of history, and it's hard to say what people will look back on as significant, but I feel certain that Isaac Singer's work is going to endure."

❀

The publication of *The Spinoza of Market Street* by Farrar, Straus and Cudahy in 1961 marked another step in Isaac's acceptance as one of the great short-story writers of our time.

Except for "The Destruction of Kreshev," which had first appeared in Yiddish in 1943, these were all new stories, written between 1958 and 1961. "The Man Who Came Back" and "Shiddah and Kuziba" first appeared in *Commentary*; "The Shadow of a Crib," in the March 1961 issue of *Mademoiselle*; the title story and "The Beggar Said So," in 1961 in *Esquire*.

The array of translators again was impressive—Joel Blocker, Shulamith Charney, June Ruth Flaum, Martha Glicklich, Mirra Ginsburg, Cecil Hemley, Gertrude Hirschler, Elizabeth Pollet.

The dozen stories in *The Spinoza of Market Street* are set in Poland; Isaac has not yet crossed the Atlantic in his imagination. But the Polish landscape offers plenty of variety and a cast of caricatures as fascinating as any in the

Singer gallery. There is the Spinoza of Market Street himself, Dr. Nahum Fischelson, pacing his garret room in a Warsaw tenement, poring over Spinoza's *Ethics*, haranguing the insects who share his quarters, and peering up at the stars through his telescope, and down at the "rabble" in Market Street below. Dr. Fischelson, a retired librarian now living on his quarterly pension, suffers from stomach trouble. He has never married because he took to heart Spinoza's dictim that a man ought to be independent. One day Black Dobbe the bagel-seller comes to Dr. Fischelson's room to get a letter from America translated and finds him lying unconscious in his bed. She takes care of him, marries him, and finally, as Spinoza's *Ethics* drops from her bridegroom's hands, contrives the consummation of their marriage. Peering up at the stars on his wedding night, Fischelson murmurs, "Divine Spinoza, forgive me."

In the long story "The Destruction of Kreshev" the narrator is the Devil himself, who explains that his particular delight is arranging incongruous marriages: "an old man with a young girl, an unattractive widow with a youth in his prime, a cripple with a great beauty, a cantor with a deaf woman, a mute with a braggart." In this story he outdoes himself with a particularly disastrous marriage that brings about the virtual annihilation of an entire Polish town. The narrator sets the scene—Kreshev, near Lublin, where the houses are "half-sunk into the earth and have patched roofs," and the windows "are stuffed with rags or covered with ox bladders"—and introduces his principal victims—Lise, the refined, well-educated, and beautiful daughter of Reb Bunim, one of Kreshev's few wealthy men; Shloimele, a Talmudic scholar and prodigy, a secret follower of the false messiah Sabbatai Zevi, and Lise's chosen bridegroom; and Mendel the coachman, a lusty, simple fellow, an unbeliever and the chosen instrument of a perverse cabalistic stratagem that Shloimele devises to speed the coming of the Messiah.

The plot unfolds in a masterly way. Lise has been brought up to be "half Polish lady, half pious Jewish maiden," but she is in any case a woman, "and women, as it is well known, bring misfortune." Lise also has a strong masculine component to her nature. As she is being led to the altar her father thinks to himself, "It's a shame she's not a boy. What a man she would have made." (Yentl's father makes the same observation in "Yentl the Yeshiva Boy.") Shloimele believes that the Messiah will come only when his generation is utterly sunk in depravity—as was Rechele's in *Satan in Goray*. He prevails on Lise to sleep with Mendel the coachman. Lise, who adores her husband and is anxious to oblige him in everything, puts up little resistance. Mendel is what is called in Hebrew an *am ha'aretz*, a "man of the earth" or "ignoramus," the Talmudist's contemptuous term for an unlearned peasant; he is delighted to fall in with Shloimele's scheme. The narrator, the only one who stands to profit from all this, is the best pleased of all.

Schloimele confesses his sins during the services in prayer house, and the wretched folk of Kreshev, whose "burning faith" has only made them sullen and bigoted, concoct an elaborate punishment for these three sinners. Mendel is beaten, hooted at, and driven out of town; he nevertheless remains an arrogant unbeliever to the end. Lise, with a pudding pot on her head, garlic cloves and a dead goose around her neck, her loins girdled with a straw rope, is led through the village and doused with slops, spattered with chicken entrails, insulted and mocked; in desperation she hangs herself. Schloimele has repented, and the villagers offer him a reprieve from punishment, but he refuses it. So he too is paraded through the village, taunted, shouted and whistled at. Finally a fire, believed to have been set by Mendel, destroys most of Kreshev, and "to this day the town has remained small and poor; it has never been rebuilt to its former size . . . And this was all because of a sin committed by a husband, a wife, and a coachman." Although the Devil may seem rather too compassionate as the narrator to have been the author of all these calamities, "The Destruction of Kreshev" is nevertheless a powerful fable of sin and repentance, of the arrogance of learning, and of the fury that transforms pious and conventional people into a vengeful mob. It is also a warning to mere mortals not to tamper with the laws of nature.

"Caricature" is the story of Dr. Boris Margolis, an ailing scholar working on a manuscript he considers a failure and knows he will never finish, since he is sixty-nine and no longer feels "the need to see his name in print." He comes home from a meeting to find his wife, Mathilda, sitting at his desk, asleep. She is wearing his dressing gown and has been smoking one of his cigars. When he awakens her, Mathilda pronounces his manuscript a masterpiece, a work of genius. "Evidently she wished to convince herself that the book was worth publishing." But the image of Mathilda in her husband's dressing gown, a grotesque replica of the man she loves and has grown to resemble through the years, is chilling and unforgettable.

"The Beggar Said So" is an ingeniously plotted story about a Jew who has come to a village looking for work, simply because a beggar he met on the road has told him that they needed a chimney sweep. He is mocked for his credulity, but through a complicated chain of circumstances the beggar turns out to have been right, and the town does acquire a chimney sweep just when it most needs one.

"The Man Who Came Back" tells of a rich man whose wife is so determined not to let him die she literally shakes him back to life while he lies on his deathbed. No good comes of it.

"A Piece of Advice" is a disarming story that says a great deal in a few pages, not only about Jewish life in Poland but about the Jewish religious outlook in general. The narrator is the son-in-law of a Mitnagged who "called the Hasidim 'the heretics' and was not ashamed to speak evil of the saintly Baal Shem himself." Yet this Mitnagged father-in-law, "a

dealer in timber and a mathematician of sorts," a rationalist and intellectual par excellence, has a temper he can't control and is finally persuaded
against his better judgment to visit the wonder-working Hasidic rabbi of Kuz-
mir to rid himself of this affliction. Rabbi Chazkele advises him to go around
flattering people for eight days—not to give his temper any opportunity
to assert itself. "How can one convey the rabbi's lesson? Pearls fell from his
mouth and each word burned like fire and penetrated the heart. It wasn't so
much the words themselves, but his gestures and tone. The evil spirit, the
rabbi said, cannot be conquered by sheer will. It is known that the Evil One
has no body, and works mainly through the body of speech. Do not lend
him a mouth—that is the way to conquer him. Take, for example, Balaam,
the son of Beor. He wanted to curse the children of Israel but forced himself
to bless them instead, and because of this, his name is mentioned in the
Bible. When one doesn't lend the Evil One a tongue, he must remain
mute." The Mitnagged exorcises his terrible temper and even comes to
admit that the rabbi "is a great man." There is one twist that makes this tale
remarkable, revealing that the rabbi is giving not a lesson in civility but a
lesson in faith: "The rabbi commented on the law. And what he said was
connected with what he had told my father-in-law at their meeting. 'What
does a Jew do if he is not a pious man? The Almighty does not require good
intentions. The deed is what counts. It is what you do that matters. Are you
angry perhaps? Go ahead and be angry, but speak gentle words and be
friendly at the same time. Are you afraid of being a dissembler? So what if
you pretend to be something you aren't? For whose sake are you lying? For
your Father in Heaven. His Holy Name, blessed be He, knows the intention
behind the intention, and it is this that is the main thing."

In this second collection of stories Isaac proved his power to transmute the
stuff of provincial folklore and simple faith into works of art of great beauty
and universal appeal. This was the collection that prompted Irving Howe
in *The New Republic* to call Singer a genius. Howe went on to say that Isaac
had "total command of his imagined world; he is original in his use both of
traditional Jewish materials and his modernist attitude toward them; he provides a serious if enigmatic moral perspective; and he writes Yiddish prose
with a rhythmic and verbal brilliance that can hardly be matched." He
added a word of caution: "Singer seems to be mired in his own originality.
There are times, as in some of the lesser stories in *The Spinoza of Market
Street*, when he displays a weakness for self-imitation that is disconcerting."
Herbert Kupferberg, in the New York *Herald Tribune*, said the stories were
of the kind that "haunt the memory, for many of them are concerned with
the spectral, the occult, and the demonic. . . . But it is the everday life of
his people, rather than his demons, that makes Mr. Singer's stories so unforgettable." Milton Hindus, in *The New York Times*, found these stories
"very satisfying as entertainment, and provocatively deep in their implica-
tions." Eugene Goodheart, in the *Saturday Review*, pronounced Isaac "per-

haps the greatest Jewish writer of all time" and praised his "freedom from parochial pieties." But the most incisive critical appraisal was offered by J. W. Smith in *Commonweal*, who spoke of the "irony and earthiness and wild humor" of these stories, which is where their real strength lies. Isaac has always considered himself fundamentally an entertainer, and to overlook that "wild humor" is to miss the point of so much of what compels and delights us in his fiction. Even in describing the darkest moments of suffering, Isaac is himself a kind of demon whose blue eyes seem to burn and twinkle in the very gloom of the poorhouse; he can be a Prospero who conjures up fantastic shapes and terrifying worlds of illusion, but he is also a Puck who always sees the joke in "the wisest aunt telling the saddest tale."

❁

It was in 1962 that Isaac decided to become a vegetarian—although he is not a strict vegetarian. He will eat eggs and could never deprive himself of the luxury of blintzes.

"For years," he said, "I had wanted to become a vegetarian. I didn't see how we could speak about mercy and ask for mercy and talk about humanism and against bloodshed when we shed blood ourselves—the blood of animals, of innocent creatures. I had never allowed myself to own a coat with a collar made of fur."

In an article on Jewish vegetarians that appeared in *The New York Times* Living Section on September 14, 1977, Isaac was cited, along with Martin Buber, as one of the "famous and well-respected Jews who had given up eating meat." Isaac was quoted as saying: "Early in my life I came to the conclusion that there was no basic difference between man and animals. If a man has a heart to cut the throat of a chicken there's no reason he should not be willing to cut the throat of a man." Stories such as "Blood" and "The Slaughterer" are expressions of this idea. Isaac stopped observing the traditional rules of *kashruth* many years earlier, "the minute I left my father's house." He concluded: "It took me a long time to come to the decision to be a vegetarian because I was always afraid I'd starve to death. But never did I have a moment in these fifteen years when I regretted that decision."

❁

April 15, 1977

A pleasant apartment on the Upper West Side. Early spring sunlight filters through windows that look out on backyards where trees are beginning to bud. Plants thrive everywhere in the sunlight that splashes into the living room in the early afternoon. There are many books and classical records on the shelves. The scatter rugs have cheerful patterns, the furniture is made of light-colored wood. On a couch, hands clasped, sits an olive-skinned, older woman with long, straight black hair showing glints of gray, and keen black almond-shaped eyes. This is Mirra Ginsburg. Many people who know Isaac have said, "You really ought to see Mirra Ginsburg." She is wearing a dark blue blouse set off by a handsome metal pendant, a bright skirt with a flower print. She is a slim, poised, concentrated sort of person.

Mirra, who has known Isaac for more than twenty years, began working with him as a translator in the 1950s. Her family left Russia when she was a child, and Mirra lived briefly in Latvia and Canada before she came to this country in her teens. Her grandparents spoke Yiddish and Russian at home, and she learned both languages. Mirra got into translating when she was going to college. Her father was sick, and she had to go to work to earn money. She started with the prose of immigrants the family knew from Europe. For a number of years she worked for Radio Liberty in New York as a scriptwriter. She has translated works by a number of Russian writers, including Yevgeny Zamyatin and Isaac Babel, several anthologies of Soviet science fiction, plays and novels by Mikhail Bulgakov, the Bantam edition of Dostoevsky's *Notes from the Underground*, Andrey Platonov's *The Foundation Pit*, and numerous Russian stories for children and young adults. One of her translations, a book of essays by Yevgeny Zamyatin, was nominated for a National Book Award. She has written several articles about the problems of translation and some poems and stories of her own, but she has never had very strong ambitions, she says, as a writer. She feels that the work of a translator is extremely important in itself and should never be belittled.

Mirra was collaborating with Raymond Rosenthal on a translation of *Sunset*, a play by Isaac Babel, when Cecil Hemley first brought Isaac to meet her. She was living in the East Bronx at the time.

"Our meeting was very funny," Mirra recollects. "I spoke to Isaac in Yiddish, and he would answer me in English. When we started to work together, I agreed to translate only those stories I thought were really excellent. We worked on one called, I believe, 'A Dead Fiddler.' It was one of those stories of Isaac's where the narrator is a small-town woman who skips around from one point to another. In real life an Aunt Yentl *does* skip around when she tells a tale. I was not happy with the way Isaac allowed himself to be swayed by editorial judgments in these matters, reorganizing continuity when it should have been left sounding haphazard and spontaneous. He seemed willing to make changes in order to please others. He's a marvelous craftsman but perhaps an unconscious one. I was vexed when he would give in so easily to suggestions for changes."

Mirra was the only one of Isaac's translators, apart from Joseph Singer, who refused simply to take down his rough English versions in dictation. She would work directly from the manuscripts. "The only problem I ever had was with his Hebrew, with some of the unusual words he used. My mother would help me with those. Isaac would always be saying a word in Yiddish and then telling me what it meant in English, although I knew well enough what it meant.

"One time when we were working together I told Isaac he was not a man but a witch. He enjoyed this, although I understand Alma was not too happy when the remark was repeated to her."

During the long hours they spent together Mirra used to get Isaac to go out for walks in the fresh air so they could clear their heads. She believes that he might once have been mugged while living on Central Park West but never admitted it to anybody, for he always hesitated to go on these walks.

"I'd say, 'Come on, Isaac, let's go down for a walk in Riverside Park.' I mean, this was years ago and it was broad daylight and the sun was shining. 'Come on,' I'd say. 'If anything happens, I'll defend you." And finally he would come along.

"We would often stop while Isaac fed the pigeons in the area. And then one time I was watching a news feature on NBC about the aged—how helpless and lonely and desolate they are—and on the screen all of a sudden I saw Isaac standing there feeding pigeons and then walking back toward home along Broadway, and I thought, Is this the most lonesome and desolate and helpless old man they can find? I even wrote to them about it, that they ought to be more careful how they chose their examples."

Mirra knew Isaac when he first became involved with his celebrated parakeets. "I think Isaac does not really love animals," she says, "no matter what he thinks or says about it, but he did love those birds. The first of them was a little yellow parakeet who flew into his house. He was tremendously touched by the bird's acceptance of him and affection for him. I really think he competed with Alma for that parakeet's love. He called the bird Matzi, which I resented—I mean, matzoh is something you eat. And finally he went around to a pet shop and got a mate for Matzi. Later there were others, but these were the first two. And it is true that it was the parakeets that helped lead to Isaac's decision to become a vegetarian."

Mirra enjoyed teasing Isaac about his vegetarianism. " 'It's really sacrilege,' I'd tell him. 'You're taking it upon yourself to be better than God, to improve on God's design. If you're religious, you know that God created us carnivorous—and you're trying to improve on Him.' And he answered me, 'Do you think He did that?' 'Of course,' I'd reply, 'we're animals—created to eat meat.' And Isaac said, 'Well, then, to the Devil with Him.' "

Mirra feels that there is a marked difference between Isaac's fantastic novels and Joshua's realistic novels—except for *Yoshe Kalb*, which she thinks really should have been written by Isaac; she also feels that perhaps Joshua should have written Isaac's realistic family novels *The Family Moskat*, *The Manor*, and *The Estate*.

Mirra has never worked on any of the translations of Isaac's books, only on his stories, but her favorites among the longer works are *The Magician of Lublin*, *The Slave*, and *Satan in Goray*. "The Little Shoemaker" is her favorite of his stories; she also liked "Teibele and Her Demon," as well as "The Key" and "Alone." Mirra agrees with many of Isaac's critics that he has difficulties with his endings.

Mirra recalls that Isaac never particularly tried to exercise his charm on her. "He was himself. Sometimes he was brilliant, other times he was dull. We treated each other as equals." But she feels that Isaac should not be judged by ordinary human standards. "He's not an ordinary human being. He really is like a creature from somewhere else in the universe who just drops down here in the dark on trips between worlds from heaven knows where. He can be big and generous and at the same time terribly petty— sometimes about money. He would pass up one pet food shop where he felt prices were too high and walk more than a mile to another to save a few pennies on pigeon food.

"I mean, I've seen him agonize in a restaurant over a dime. Should he add it to the tip or not? He'd put it down, pick it up, and put it down again. And yet when people tried to persuade him to apply for a Guggenheim when he badly needed money, he'd refuse. He considered it begging to apply for a fellowship, and he wouldn't beg. At the same time he never did pay his translators enough. When the stories I worked on were published in book form, Isaac would take the attitude that I had already been paid my share on magazine publication. Well, I finally stopped working with him, but he kept after me. Then he drew up an agreement about payments, but that didn't work out either. I don't consider myself a greedy person, but I did expect more for my efforts. . . .

"He would get very impatient with me if I were late," Mirra recalls. "Of course I think he likes the women in his life to be submissive."

Mirra is anything but submissive. She is outspoken about her likes as well as her dislikes, one of which was the play *Yentl*, which she felt was a betrayal of the story: "I think they mutilated and vulgarized it, and he let it happen. He is too willing to let others influence him in changing his work."

Mirra enjoyed working on Isaac's prose "because I loved fantasy, I loved wit, and I found it easy to translate him, which is what I feel when there is an affinity between me and the writer.

"Isaac's Yiddish is so rich, so marvelous. I translated one of his tales into Russian, which I found even easier than trying to get his prose across in English. The rhythms are closer. And the ways of thinking and feeling."

To Mirra Isaac is "completely unique and absolutely original both as a Jewish writer and a world writer. I don't know of anyone else who has done what he has done. If he had lived a thousand years ago he would be one of the creators of folklore. He has opened up a new world. But he has done it all naturally—he is a natural. Sometimes when I was working with him, he would ask me to read him one of the reviews that had come in the mail. He had little patience with these critics; he felt they were going out of their way to try to be profound when they wrote about him and impress the reader by trying to fit him into a particular framework. And he paid no attention. He didn't seem to care what they said about him. He ignored the attacks by other Yiddish writers too. And he was right most of the time."

Mirra noticed that whenever Isaac read one of his own stories he seemed as fascinated and surprised as if somebody else had written it. Once he came across a phrase in which a woman is being tickled by the devil and her laughter can be heard "all the way to Madagascar." Isaac was particularly delighted by this phrase. "It was the delight of an intuitive artist in seeing what he has created through his own intuition."

Mirra made several attempts to introduce some of her favorite writers to Isaac. She lent him a number of books in English while they were writing together, which he seldom got around to reading—including the stories of Isak Dinesen and several of her own translations, which he never read at all, as far as she remembers.

Once Mirra chided Isaac about his attitude toward money. "You have enough to live on," she told him. "You've earned enough to last you a lifetime. Why do you have to be so careful?" Isaac's reaction, she says, was usually to shrug off the criticism, but this was apparently too much for him. "Oh, yes, when he gets angry that white skin turns sort of purple and his nose gets sharp and his eyes get sort of pointed like pins. And that time he said, 'How do you know? Maybe I do secret charity.'

"Well, he can't be judged by the standards you would apply to other people. He's simply not human in the ordinary sense. He's extraterrestrial."

Mirra admits quite frankly that, with the possible exception of Cecil Hemley, she considers herself the best translator Isaac ever had. "Cecil felt that Isaac should be treated not as a Jewish writer, a man writing in Yiddish, but as a man writing in English. I don't agree with him. I felt that some of the original flavor and color, some of the nuances and tonalities, should be preserved—there is a good deal of value in them."

❀

Ruth Whitman, the poet and essayist, has also described her experiences working as Isaac's translator. In an essay called "Translating with Isaac Bashevis Singer" published in Irving Malin's *Critical Views of Isaac Bashevis Singer*, she tells of sitting with him in her living room in Cambridge, Massachusetts, "I sat at the typewriter, Bashevis at my side with scraps of Yiddish in his hand." They had just come to a passage in his story "Three Tales" that would eventually read, "The rabbi looked at the wall to make sure that Zeivele was casting a shadow. Demons don't, you know." Just as they were struggling with those sentences, "we both looked up at the window in time to see the sun slide behind a cloud. Then both of us glanced down at the floor beside his chair where there was—no shadow. We laughed, but only half humorously. He had cast the thought into my mind like a spell and he knew it." Ruth Whitman describes working with Isaac as "a kind of enchantment." She speaks of Isaac's world, "charged with sex and the supernatural as it is," as being a place illuminated with "the authenticity of poetry."

A translator who has the right rapport with Isaac, Ruth Whitman found, cannot help seeing him as a character in one of his own stories. He often quoted to her the line from Spinoza that inspired the title of his 1975 collection of stories: "Anything can be a passion." She found that he has an insatiable appetite for information. "A luncheon conversation with him leaves one stripped of one's history." She was amazed at the speed of his writing and compares the years when his pen was idle to his recent productivity, observing that today Isaac himself "can hardly keep up with the flow."

In her essay Ruth Whitman grows lyrical about Isaac's "lovable, singable Yiddish" and quotes him as saying, when he received a National Arts Council grant of ten thousand dollars in 1967, that he would devote the money to publishing all his work in Yiddish, a language he regarded as "sick, but not dead." (This has not yet happened.) She observes correctly that many of his translators do not know Yiddish and adds that some "have been incompetent in both languages." She and Isaac generally worked through the material together, "phrase by phrase, sentence by sentence." She is particularly proud of her translation of the story "Cockadoodledoo," which she feels was a success because for once she was able to see the original text for herself and take it home to work on. Readers later assured her that this time her translation had "the real *nigun*"—melody, lilt—of the original. She predicts that with courses now being given in Yiddish at Queens College and other schools the language will become increasingly important "for students and lovers of literature." Isaac hopes so too, but he has his doubts.

❄

In 1964 Farrar, Straux and Giroux (by that time Sheila Cudahy had left the firm, and Robert Giroux, who would offer Isaac much valuable editorial advice over the years, had joined it in 1955 and been made a full partner in 1963) published *Short Friday and Other Stories*, Isaac's next collection of stories. The book contains his first stories of Jewish life in America, although stories set in Poland (and the other world), concerning witches and demons, pious and impious Hasidim, study houses and slaughter houses, still predominate. If occasionally he had started to repeat himself, as some of his critics complained, these "self-imitations" were often simply variations on a favorite theme, each subtly different in mood and texture.

All these stories had been written between 1960 and 1964. Three of the sixteen tales had appeared in *Commentary*—"Yentl the Yeshiva Boy" in 1962, "Teibele and Her Demon" in 1963, and "A Wedding in Brownsville" in 1964. Four others—"The Fast" (originally "The Faster"; 1962), "The Last Demon" (1962), "I Place My Reliance on No Man" (1961), and "Big and Little" (1961)—had been published in Yiddish in *Gimpel Tam un Anderer Dertailungen*. All the stories—as has been the case with virtually all Isaac's prose—had first appeared in Yiddish in the *Forward*. "Blood" had been published in English in *Harper's* (1964), "Esther Kreindel the Second" in *The Saturday Evening Post* (1964), "Cunegunde" in *Esquire* (1964).

After a quarter of a century in America and countless hours spent walking the streets of New York, feeding pigeons on the traffic islands on Broadway, lunching with newfound friends at Steinberg's (once his favorite restaurant uptown, but now gone), riding the subways and getting to know the look of the city and its people ever more intimately, Isaac had begun to write about Jews who, like himself, were creatures of the Old World transplanted to the New.

In "A Wedding in Brownsville" a successful doctor from Poland, married and living contentedly with his wife in Manhattan, goes off on a snowy night, against his better judgment, to attend a wedding deep in Brooklyn, only to be confronted by the ghost of a girl he had loved long ago. Like Dr. Margolin, we scarcely know by the time the story ends whether we have been visiting a Jewish ghetto in old Poland or a wedding hall in modern Brooklyn; distinctions blur—of time, of place, between the real and the imagined, between the living and the dead.

Even more powerful is the story called "Alone," which foreshadows some of Isaac's more harrowing travel tales. The narrator is staying at a hotel in Miami Beach that suddenly closes. The atmosphere of the place is rendered with as much power as the Lido and the resort hotels in *Death in Venice*. And the story itself, though neither as complex nor as profound as Thomas Mann's, has the same delirious quality. The narrator finds another room in a rundown seaside inn, aimlessly rides by bus through the humid city, returns in the midst of a storm to his damp, suffocating room, where he spends a strange and sexless night with a witchlike hag from Cuba. While the rest of the world seems to be tranquilly sunning itself, the hero's thoughts are still with the Cabala, with Spinoza, with truths "impossible to grasp in a northern climate: the eternal questions tapped in my brain: Who is behind the world of appearance? Is it Substance with its Infinite Attributes? Is it the Monad of all Monads? Is it the Absolute, Blind Will, the Unconscious? Some kind of superior being has to be hidden in back of all these illusions."

"Teibele and Her Demon" rings a change on the demonic motif. An unfortunate widow turns in her loneliness to a teacher's helper, who maliciously takes advantage of her kindness by pretending to be the demon Hurmizah, lord of darkness. "Blood" lives up to its name—a powerfully sanguinary fable about the passion between a ritual slaughterer named Reuben and a lusty lady named Risha, who revels with her lover in the killing of animals and eventually takes over the business of bloodshed herself, wallowing in a red world where "the passion for blood" and "the passion for flesh" orgiastically mingle.

"The Fast" is a kind of antidote to "Blood." In this tale a "small eater" named Itche Nokum goes one step beyond Isaac's vegetarianism. "Even bread, potatoes and greens were too much. It was enough to eat just to sustain life. And for that, a bite or two sufficed for several days." Itche practices an equally rarified form of sadism on his ex-wife, Roise Genedel; he has a strong emotional hold over her and contrives to torment her—telepathically.

Rounding out the collection are "Yentl the Yeshiva Boy," the original perfectly crafted tale from which the play was adapted, and of course the title story, "Short Friday," one of the sweetest and simplest of Isaac's tales, about a man and wife who love the Sabbath so much that their happiest Sabbath Eve is the longest one of the year. They are almost the only really good people in this entire gallery, and they end up, as they deserve, being led by an angel into Paradise.

A glance at the names of the people who worked with Isaac on these stories is enough to indicate how fortunate he has been in his translators. Among them were Joel Blocker, Mirra Ginsburg, Cecil Hemley, Elizabeth Pollet, and Marion Magid. Joseph Singer is listed as one of the translators of the title tale. Others who worked with Isaac on these crisp, clean English versions were Channah Kleinerman-Goldstein, Martha Glicklich, Roger H. Klein, and Ruth Whitman. Blocker's translation of "Alone" is, as anyone who knows that author's work might have expected, especially outstanding.

The collection is dedicated to "the blessed memory of my brother, I. J. Singer, author of *The Brothers Ashkenazi*, *Yoshe Kalb*, etc., who helped me to come to this country and was my teacher and master in literature." Although the dedication concludes, "I am still learning from him and his work," Isaac has by now emerged almost completely from the shadow of Joshua's influence, speaking ever more clearly in his own voice.

Playwright Paddy Chayefsky, reviewing *Short Friday* for *The Reporter*, praised the author as "a bold and skillful writer, a superb storyteller, unafraid of frightening emotion and with the ear and eye of a poet. And as with that rye bread whose name I've forgotten for the moment, you don't have to be Jewish to enjoy him." He called Isaac's characters "passionate in their imperfections. As individuals they reach the depths and they achieve the heights. Singer, in point of fact, portrays characters very few authors have dared to deal with. . . . I've read all sorts of accounts of the early eremites; Singer writes of the ascetic experience better than any."

Jonathan Baumbach, in the *Saturday Review*, pointed out correctly that the stories in the collection, "for all their similarity of occasion and concern, are impressively various, though one is forced to add that they are not all equally successful." He continued: "As one might expect from a religious moralist, Singer is at his strongest in dealing with the proliferation of evil. . . . That Singer can be very bad on occasion ("Jachid and Jechidah," for example, is an extraordinary clinker) is an indication—a valuable one, I think—of the stature of his gifts." He found a number of the tales "deeply memorable."

In *The Nation* Warren Miller drew a different conclusion from the un-evenness of the stories in this collection: he observed that "new bottles interest him not at all. Content is everything for him, and when the wine is right all is well; but often it is not and we have to do with the thin fare of anecdote and cautionary tale. It is not Singer who is an anachronism, but, for better or worse, it is the tale, which has ceased to be for us a valid literary form. All surface, lacking in reverberations, it is, even in Singer's hands, the copy of a copy. It grows ever more remote from art, and descends toward something which at best is merely charming." Perhaps charm is in shorter supply these days than it was in 1965; in any case, although repetition is always a danger for any writer as prolific as Isaac, why condemn the cobbler for sticking to his last? It is not likely that the tale will die out as a literary form as quickly as all that.

In fact William Barrett, in the *Atlantic*, turned this argument around to Isaac's advantage: "Mr. Singer, regardless of language, had again proved himself one of the best writers of fiction now in America. . . . At present, we have many short-story writers in this country, but few tellers of tales. This distinction is cardinal in understanding Mr. Singer's unusual qualities. Because his work is rooted in a people, he is a superior kind of folk artist who brings narrative back to the original meaning a story had: a tale passed on by word of mouth from one person to another. His style—spare, energetic and lyrical—has the rhythm of spoken language. Moreover, his people, whatever their language, are not alienated from their community . . . nor are they estranged from a deep religious view that gives meaning to life. These are formidable advantages for a writer, however remote the places and times he deals with may seem."

In 1965, when Isaac was sixty years old and had been in America thirty years, Richard Elman went to visit him, first in his offices at the *Jewish Daily Forward*, and later several times at his apartment on West Eighty-sixth Street. Elman told of those meetings in an article called "The Spinoza of Canal Street," which appeared in the August 1965 issue of *Holiday* magazine. The piece contains a fascinating portrait of Isaac in those days when he still had his parakeets and had just been nominated by his West German publishers for the Prix Fomenter:

"Singer is the most cordial of men but also the most intensely scrutinizing. As with so many of his characters, there is something birdlike about his stare. . . .

"My visits to his home have always borne a remarkably similar character. Singer always greets me formally, dressed in a severe blue or black suit with a vest, a starched shirt, a dark tie. Once, when he came to the door in his shirt-sleeves, he excused himself and returned a moment later fully dressed. If I called on him at dusk, after a day's work, the rooms would be heavy with shadows, and Singer's voice appropriately subdued, as if there were others nearby, likely to overhear. Unlike [Isaac] Luria, Singer does not claim to understand the chirping of birds. But occasionally one of his pet parakeets will chirp and he will quiet it with a few soft words in Yiddish or English. Sometimes he excuses himself formally, goes into the next room, and comes back accompanied by one of these gaudy green and yellow birds, which eventually settles down with him upon an ancient couch, cooing against his knee, his hand or even his forehead—a vivid streak of color and sound in otherwise subdued surroundings.

"Singer's extremely fair skin and extravagantly blue eyes seem especially stark against such a background. If he ever had much hair, it was as red as fire. Now he is almost completely bald, but his features are so finely cut, his eyes so widely set, the crown of his head so marvelously sloped and shaped, you get the impression that hair could never have been essential to his appearance. Singer's is the face of a saint in porcelain or tinted marble; smooth lids, a slender jaw, a high forehead, a nose of bone delicacy. But this is a saint who has suffered torments and known temptations; the thin-lipped mouth is wide and slightly sensual when he declares, 'I am possessed by my demons, and they add a lot to my vision and my expression.' A thousand ironies seem hidden in every one of Singer's smiles, even those that come upon him most spontaneously."

Elman also described how Isaac had first acquired his parakeet, Matzi, had bought a mate for her, and was desolate when she flew away:

"Singer spent many hours wandering through Riverside and Central parks, hoping to find his pet bird. He advertised in the newspapers; he followed up every response, but Matzi was never found. Singer then bought his female parakeet another mate, but was never again the same without

Matzi. Perhaps that is why Singer began to spend more time among the pigeons along Broadway."

When Matzi Number Two drowned in a vase of water, Isaac gave up on owning birds. That was also when he decided to become a vegetarian. "When I saw a creature dead I said to myself that I would never eat meat again. I haven't had a single moment when I regretted or doubted this decision." As for the birds, "They were a lot of joy, but they were also much trouble. I suffered so much when they suffered, when they got sick, got lost or fell down, that in a way I am happy I don't have them anymore."

Isaac's next triumph after becoming an internationally celebrated author lionized by the public, praised by the critics, nominated by Edmund Wilson for a Nobel prize, and elected in 1964 to the National Institute of Arts and Letters—the only American member of the institute to write in a language other than English—was to have a story accepted by *The New Yorker*. Lila Karpf had sent the manuscript of "The Slaughterer" directly to William Shawn, editor of the magazine. "The Slaughterer" appeared in the fall of 1967; Rachel MacKenzie and William Maxwell, both highly respected writers themselves, became Isaac's new editors.

Isaac remembers getting a call from Rachel MacKenzie shortly afterward: "She said, 'I'm going to be your editor. Would you like to come over to the office, or should I come to you?' The idea that *The New Yorker* was going to send an editor to my house sounded unbelievable. At the same time I felt kind of bashful about going there, so she came to my apartment. Since then she's not only my editor, she's a good friend. I admire her highly."

❀

January 26, 1976

The corridors of *The New Yorker* editorial offices on West Forty-third Street twist and turn like the passages in a Luna Park funhouse. Just now, on a cold, windy morning in January 1976, the offices are in the process of being redecorated, and a number of the walls are being torn down. One passes a network of cubbyholes and partitioned cubicles where the doors and most of the walls are painted the cream color once favored by Brooklyn landlords. Grim windows afford haphazard views of other office buildings. A few of the offices are comfortably appointed in a homey way. Others are ramshackle. It certainly doesn't look like one of those skyscraper magazine headquarters in a Hollywood movie.

Rachel MacKenzie sits behind a desk that has seen better days in a spacious, light-filled office—temporary quarters until her new office is ready to receive her. She is a mature woman with long gray hair tied at the back with a red bow. Her friendly eyes crinkle, smiling out through rimless spectacles. She is a rather frail person, who has survived open-heart surgery, described in her book *Risk*, and long hospitalizations a number of times since then.*

She dispatches a young woman assistant to round up the exact publication dates of Isaac's stories, starting with "The Slaughterer," which appeared in the November 25, 1967, issue. A poodle scampers up the hallway past the office. Rachel says this is not at all unusual. She herself used to bring her schnauzer to work with her.

With a mixture of warmth and caution Rachel settles down to talk about her role as Isaac's editor: "He's a joy to work with. He knows instantly when something you suggest is an improvement, and he knows just as quickly when he doesn't want something you suggest. He'll say, 'If you'll just tell me what's wrong, I can take care of it.' And he can. His relation to the language is sure. It's a colloquial language that he writes. I've often asked him why he doesn't write in English—I'm sure many people have—but he says because it isn't his native tongue, he would only write dictionary English." Yet when it's a question of a word, "invariably he'll be able to choose from among words you suggest or himself offer the exact word. And he's so inventive. In a story we were going over not long ago he was writing about a rabbi going to bed with a long knife under his pillow. And I said, 'Well, what kind of a knife?' I thought maybe a carving knife. 'No, no,' he said. 'It's a knife such as a pregnant girl would have used to ward off the evil spirits that might harm the unborn.' So of course that went into the story."

Rachel MacKenzie often wishes she knew Yiddish herself so that she could come still closer to Isaac's intentions, but when a problem comes up, she turns to one of Isaac's translators for help in straightening it out. Sometimes she meets with Isaac and Joseph to go over points that puzzle her. But she is interested in more than Isaac's English vocabulary. Occasionally she urges cutting to bring out the "shape" of a story: "I will ask him to take a minute to think about it, and sometimes he will say, 'I don't need a minute. I know you're right.' " On the other hand, she recalls that in a broadcast interview Isaac once said, "I have a very fine editor, but when she's wrong, I override her."

Although *The New Yorker* is notoriously finicky about punctuation, Rachel says fiction writers are allowed somewhat more latitude. She tries, for example, to respect Isaac's aversion to an overabundance of commas.

The job of preparing an Isaac Bashevis Singer story for publication in *The New Yorker* can be a complex task. Rachel and Isaac go over every story, line by line. She recalls a whole series of phone calls back and forth between them about the final line in one story. William Maxwell wanted it changed; Isaac wanted it changed back. She can't remember now who won.

* In 1978 Rachel MacKenzie resigned as fiction editor of *The New Yorker* due to ill health.

Once, when illness kept Rachel away from the magazine for an entire year, William Maxwell took her place as Isaac's editor. "I sent Bill a two-page memorandum on the subject of dealing with Isaac's prose. Rule number one was to make three Xeroxes of every page."

The New Yorker has "first refusal rights" to Isaac's fiction—that is, a story can't be sent anywhere else until the magazine has turned it down. In recent years such agreements with authors have generally been terminated. Isaac is one of the few whose work is still treated on this basis.

Over lunch at the Algonquin Hotel, Rachel tells how her editorial relationship with Isaac developed into a personal friendship: "When I've been in the hospital, he has always come to visit me. He'd bring a big paper bag filled with fruit and sit there and talk to me for hours. He's a warm and generous friend. When people say, as some do, that he is not generous, that he is not thoughtful of other people's feelings, I can't believe they are talking about the person I know. Always I have found him unfailingly sensitive and generous."

Sitting at a nearby banquette that used to be reserved for *The New Yorker*'s founding editor, Harold Ross, is Brendan Gill, whose book *Here at The New Yorker* has just hit the paperback best-seller list. He scribbles a note and passes it to Rachel. The note is a joking apology for being caught at Ross's banquette. He is well aware, the note says, that he is not Harold Ross or William Shawn—only Brendan Gill.

Rachel MacKenzie smiles, waves at Gill, and returns to the subject. Like so many others, she has been struck from the beginning by the contrast between the air of absent-minded innocence that Isaac projects and the enormous range of his knowledge and experience. "He plays the role of a man who doesn't read anything, an uncultivated man. Of course, he doesn't play any roles with *me*."

Rachel recalls that on one evening at the Singers' Alma served a cheese that Rachel found particularly delicious. When she left, she took the package with her. Isaac, who really *does* notice everything, remarked at their next meeting, "And you steal cheese too."

Before she met Isaac, Rachel had read and admired *The Family Moskat*. It remains her favorite among his books, along with *Enemies, A Love Story*, which she believes is revealingly autobiographical.

Shortly after *Enemies* appeared in print, Rachel, who had done some editorial work with Isaac on that book, received a phone call from Alma expressing her displeasure with it. Indeed, she felt this book was a disaster and an embarrassment. Rachel assured her that it was a fine piece of work. (Alma has since revised her opinion of *Enemies*.)

Rachel says she admires Isaac not only as one of the supreme storytellers of our time, but for his "grace and courtesy," the way he bows when he shakes hands with new acquaintances, hurries out to answer the door, rushes back to his living room after a phone call so as not to keep a visitor waiting. Above all she treasures their mutual respect as editor and author: "I respect his story, he respects my taste."

❀

Isaac's short stories have always been published in collections, after appearing in Yiddish in the *Forward* and later in various American periodicals in English. These collections usually include the stories written during a particular period. But Isaac's tales can also be divided into certain categories. Although he says they are all "love stories," some take place in Poland; a number of them—especially the recent ones—concern Jewish immigrants in the United States, usually in New York. There are stories about the mischief created by dybbuks, imps, and demons, especially in the Old Country, although some of these are set in places as far apart as Brooklyn and Rio de Janeiro. Sometimes these evil creatures—or Satan himself—are cast as narrators. Then there are reminiscences of his childhood and youth in Poland, which are usually in the first person and are really memoirs. There are the stories put in the mouth of Aunt Yentl and other cronies from his Krochmalna Street days, with their deliberately mixed-up chronology, their earthy wisdom, and their period settings. There are whole books of stories for children. Even some of the tales written for adults are simple fables, while others are well developed, suspenseful, complex chronicles of adventure. Some feature those unmistakably vigorous Singer women as protagonists. And some, told in the first person by a narrator who is—and at the same time is not—Isaac, deal with his travels in various parts of the world.

Consider one category of Isaac's stories—the travel tale. As in all his writing, what really happened and what might have happened on these journeys are indistinguishably intertwined. These particular stories tell us a great deal about the traveler as well as the world seen through the storyteller's eyes, eyes that seem to notice nothing when you are with him, but that actually take in everything, as a number of his friends have observed.

"When I was a young man," Isaac says, "I longed to travel, but I never got beyond Lublin, Cracow, and a few Scandinavian cities. Now when I would like to rest, I have to travel all the time." Yet Isaac really enjoys his travels, as is evident from his stories based on them. He has used every area he has visited to provide the background and atmosphere for adventures that invariably make for enjoyable reading. Some of them are among his most distinguished works of short fiction. As in his other tales, most of the principal characters are Jews from Eastern Europe. A colorful lot they are.

One of the most revealing of Isaac's tales of his travels is "Hanka," published in *The New Yorker* on February 4, 1974, translated by the author and

Blanche and Joseph Nevel, and later reprinted in the short-story collection *Passions*. The narrator is Isaac the traveling lecturer. He has accepted an invitation to spend two and a half months in Argentina on a tour. On a hot day in October he boards a ship called *La Plata* and spends eighteen days at sea in luxury and loneliness. Most of the passengers are Latin Americans who speak no English; the narrator wonders "if by some magic I had become one who sees and is not seen."

Arriving in Buenos Aires, the narrator is met by a Señor Poliva and a woman named Hanka, who claims to be a great-granddaughter of the narrator's Aunt Yentl by her first husband but is really related to him only by marriage. Conducting him through the city, which, as usual, is in the throes of a political crisis and a power shortage, Hanka, "petite, lean," and with a "head of pitch black hair," tells him she is a dancer who was hidden away in Warsaw when the Nazis came; the lover who brought her to Argentina has deserted her. Since her arrival in Buenos Aires she has been a "fugitive and wanderer"—what is called a *nay'nad* in Hebrew—and is "hungry" for relatives. The narrator hopes to have a short affair with Hanka, but she rebuffs his advances—like so many Jewish refugees in Isaac's tales, she is really a walking corpse—and persuades him instead to come with her to visit another ostensible relative, a young man named Jechiel. Hanka and Isaac walk down an endless boulevard to a tacky neighborhood where they find Jechiel and his wife in a shabby apartment. Jechiel answers all questions with *Sí* or *No* or *Bueno*, yawns and dozes. His wife too is numb and inarticulate. "They're both sick," Hanka explains when they leave the moribund couple. "He suffers from asthma and she has a bad heart. I told you, they became acquainted in Auschwitz. Didn't you notice the numbers on their arms? . . . Those who stood at the threshold of death remain dead."

At the end of the evening Hanka embraces the narrator and disappears. He goes to his hotel and looks out on the city from a balcony strangely resembling the Krochmalna Street eyrie of his boyhood.

The next day the sun is shining, and springlike breezes remind the narrator of the Vistula. Señor Poliva congratulates him for shaking himself free of Hanka, actually, he is searching for her. Looking up at the southern sky one night he sees consonants and vowels in the constellation (as does Joseph in *The Slave*). He calls out in his mind to Hanka: "You are an eternal letter in God's scroll." And he does indeed see her again—in a lecture audience one evening. She smiles at him and winks, then vanishes.

"Hanka" uses a locale where Jewish life is moribund as the setting for a realistic tale that is at the same time a ghost story about Jews whose spirits have departed to leave them walking zombies, sundered from their roots and the Jewish past. After reading "Hanka" we also have the feeling that we ourselves have made the journey to Argentina. We know exactly what Buenos Aires was like for Isaac—the walls of his hotel, the neighborhood in which it was located, the Jewish community centers and societies where he delivered his lectures, the history of the Jewish immigrants. But in "Hanka," as in Isaac's other travel tales, there is an eerie, supernatural aspect to the journey itself: It is as though the narrator's traveling companion were the past. In a lecture hall he sees "so many familiar faces that I could scarcely believe my eyes. True, I did not remember their names, but they reminded me of friends and acquaintances of Bilgoray, Lublin, Warsaw. Was it possible that so many had been saved from the Nazis and come to my lecture? . . . I wanted to go down into the audience and greet these resurrected images of my past." He represses this impulse. Travelers can only observe and then return home to try to make sense of what they have seen. Jechiel and Hanka, after rising like ghosts in their graveclothes to greet him, have returned to their graves; for Jews, Buenos Aires, like Warsaw, is only another cemetery.

Did Hanka really come to Isaac's lecture? Apparently not. "It had been a hallucination. It lasted only one instant. But I will brood about this instant for the rest of my life."

"The Colony," which appeared in the collection A *Friend of Kafka* in a translation by the author and Evelyn Torton Beck, is another story based on Isaac's trip to Argentina. Here Isaac tells of a visit to the old Yiddish colony in Entre Rios in the company of a Yiddish poet named Sonya Lopata, who is to read her poems on the same program with Isaac. On a Sunday in spring they journey from Buenos Aires over a dusty road past vast wheat fields and ranches where untended oxen graze, riding in a car driven by a chauffeur who speaks only Spanish, which Isaac cannot understand. They stop at an inn for lunch. They reach the Jewish colony by ferry in the afternoon. Sonya, who has spent the day pressing her leg against Isaac's and caressing him, tells him as they pass an empty synagogue that the Jews in the district are "all assimilated." There is nobody there to meet them at the hotel where they are going to stay. Inside Isaac notices that there are barrels of unpacked books, many of which he read in Warsaw. Once there had been a library here and visiting lecturers and Yiddish theater troupes, but no more. Isaac feels "overcome by sadness and longing."

A group of "boorish men and fat women" attend Isaac's speech on Yiddish literature and Jewish history that evening, but they don't seem to understand a word he says. Insects fly through the hall, a dog walks in and barks. These colonists, it seems, have grown fat and rich and now have servants to do their work while they go off on trips to Buenos Aires. Many of them have intermarried. It was once the dream of the German philanthropist Baron Maurice de Hirsch to establish these colonies as a refuge where Jews persecuted in Czarist Russia could till the soil; now they are simply deteriorating. To these people "there should have come a prophet, not a writer of my kind."

That night Sonya comes across Isaac poking around in the abandoned barrels of books and asks him what he's doing. "I am visiting my own grave," he replies.

Later Sonya tells Isaac about her life—her attempts to be a journalist in Buenos Aires, the miserable climate, the editor who promised to publish her work if she would sleep with him, her marriage, their poverty, their pseudo-intellectual friends, her husband's impotence, her hapless affairs with married men.

One afternoon Sonya and Isaac visit an old man dressed in gray, in an outmoded Warsaw fashion, who rocks back and forth as he reads from a prayer book. The old man denounces the fat, complacent Jews of the colony. He invites Isaac to dinner and then tells his own story—of a wife who has died, children who have "wandered off," and the Jews who arrived with high hopes and were trapped by debt, by the hatred of their gentile neighbors, by the very charity that brought them to this strange land. Isaac, Sonya, and the old man go to visit a cemetery where the toppled headstones are overgrown with weeds. Sonya and Isaac walk among the graves, reading the inscriptions. The old man sleeps, looking "stiff as a corpse." Once more it is driven home that for Jews Argentina is a land of death and desolation. This is what has become of "Baron de Hirsch's grandiose dream to turn Russian Jews into Argentine peasants."

Another of Isaac's tales with a South American setting is "One Night in Brazil," which appeared in *The New Yorker* of April 3, 1978. Here the narrator's unsettling adventures in a suburb of Rio de Janeiro provide a kind of tropical mirror image of an earlier story called "The Lecture," which takes place in Montreal. Paltiel Gerstendrescher, a Yiddish writer living in Rio de Janeiro, has sent Isaac a copy of one of his books, a turgid conglomeration of autobiography, metaphysics, and theosophy published by a vanity press called Myself Publications. This leads to a rather one-sided correspondence and finally an invitation to Isaac to visit the author of *The Confession of an Agnostic* when Isaac's ship stops over in Santos on his forthcoming voyage to Argentina. The ship is delayed by a hurricane, however, and when Isaac arrives in Santos, Paltiel is not there to meet him, as arranged. He takes a bus to Rio and a taxi to a forsaken part of town that the driver had never heard of. There he is greeted by an old acquaintance from Warsaw, Lena Stempler, a former actress, singer, monologist, and painter—and a onetime habitué of the Writers' Club. Isaac remembers hearing that Lena has gone through four husbands; she now is living with Gerstendrescher. Lena has turned into a wrinkled apparition with dyed hair, too much makeup, a cigarette dangling from her lips, wearing slippers and a flimsy kimono. She begins to tell Isaac that she is possessed by a dybbuk, the spirit of her dead lover, who has ensconced himself in her stomach. Paltiel arrives (he and Isaac simply missed each other in Santos), seems disappointed by his guest's appearance, talks about literature, and speculates that perhaps God himself is seeing a psychiatrist. Paltiel and Lena begin to argue in Portuguese, and Paltiel walks out of the house in a rage, leaving Isaac alone with Lena and her dybbuk. She takes him out into one of the lushest tropical gardens in all literature, an enclosure thronged with banana trees, wildflowers, crickets, croaking frogs, and mosquitoes, under a low sky sprinkled with Southern constellations. In this humid Eden, Lena places the narrator's hand on her stomach, so that he can feel her dybbuk's nose, tells him that Paltiel seems to be trying to turn himself into a Yiddish Joyce, then goads him into seducing her. He determines to have none of it, but even as he makes this decision he finds himself embracing Lena. As always, he is fascinated by those who doom themselves—pursuing failure relentlessly, thriving on its vicissitudes, martyring themselves to its falsehoods. But while they are making love the hammock they are lying in gives way, and they fall into a swamp. A swarm of mosquitoes attacks them, biting them viciously and finally driving them back into the house. Lena interprets the attack as a sign of God's love: He has been good enough to send the punishment before the sin, she says. Paltiel returns abruptly, and the next day he and Isaac drive back to Santos in silence. Paltiel hands Isaac an envelope filled with more of his manuscripts and tells him that both he and his wife have profited greatly from Isaac's visit: Paltiel now has a true reader, and Lena has a true dybbuk. In a kind of coda to the tale we learn that Lena has died of cancer and that Paltiel has been locked up in a mental institution. Spiritually, of course, they were both already dead—displaced, misguided wanderers—before Isaac ever arrived in their Brazilian house of exile.

In the collection *Passions* there is a similar story called "Sabbath in Portugal" (translated by the author and Herbert R. Lottman). An editor in New York has asked Isaac to look up a man named Miguel de Albeira when he passes through Lisbon on his way to France. "If you need something he will be glad to help you." Isaac wonders what it is he could possibly need in Lisbon. He has his passport, his traveler's checks, his hotel reservation.

In Lisbon Isaac finds himself at a hotel surrounded by "compatriots from New York and Brooklyn." The wives have dyed hair and wear heavy makeup; they smoke, play cards, chatter, and laugh. The husbands study the financial pages of the *International Herald Tribune*. "Yes, these are my people, I said to myself. If the Messiah is to come, he will have to come to them because there are no others."

Any reader familiar with Isaac's travel tales is certain that something harrowing is about to happen to him. And sure enough, he finds out that his room has been reserved for only two days, and he will have to move out to make room for another American tourist. He tries to call Senhor de Albeira, gets several wrong numbers, then finally reaches him, and ends up being taken to lunch by a stranger who has interrupted his business day merely on the strength of a note from an American editor. Albeira helps Isaac find another hotel room and shows him around the city.

The following Saturday Albeira brings his guest home to meet his wife and adolescent children. There Isaac is surprised to see a "braided loaf" next to the carafe of wine on the table. "The Sabbath I had desecrated for years had caught up with me in a gentile home in Lisbon." Albeira asks Isaac about his religion, about the difference between Ashkenazic and Sephardic Jews, whether there are any Israeli Christians, then suddenly pounds a fist on the table and announces, "I am a Jew." He brings in a tiny cabinet of dark wood containing a Hebrew book written by one of his ancestors, he says, six hundred years ago and asks Isaac for a translation. The little book proves to be a volume of *responsa*—rabbinical answers to questions of law, containing cases much like the ones Pinchas Mendel used to judge in his study on Krochmalna Street.

Senhor de Albeira, in sum, is a descendant of Marranos—Spanish and Portuguese Jews who publicly espoused Christianity and practiced their Judaism in secret. "We are not pure Jews. We come from generations of Catholics. But the Jewish spark remains in us."

The story ends on a spooky note. As the visitor looks at his host's wife he thinks he sees in her his "old love" Esther. "Esther had returned. Only now did I grasp why I had decided to stop in Portugal, and why Senhor de Albeira had accepted me with such fervor." Isaac can barely restrain himself from "running to her, falling on my knees, covering her with kisses." Esther speaks, asking Isaac a question in Portuguese but in a voice with "the tone and tremor of Esther's Yiddish." What she wants to know is whether he believes "in the resurrection of the dead." He hears himself answer, "They never died."

It is a curious tale, different from the others in that, for once, the survivors are not living Jews whose spirits are already dead but seemingly dead Jews who turn out to be still alive.

One of the finest of Isaac's travel tales, "The Lecture," first appeared in *Playboy* in December 1967 and was later reprinted in the story collection *The Seance*. In this nerve-wracking chronicle Isaac leaves New York for a midwinter lecture engagement in Montreal on a train, dressed for "an expedition to the North Pole" in a heavy overcoat with two sweaters. His manuscript is in his pocket; his train seat is comfortable; his citizenship papers accompany him ("a naturalized American gets out his citizenship papers and studies his own photograph, as if trying to convince himself that the document is not a false one"). Basking in comfort, he considers his good fortune in contrast to the hardships of his Polish past: "The prompt arrival of American trains and the ease in boarding them have always seemed like miracles to me. I remember journeys in Poland when Jewish passengers were not allowed into the cars and I had to hang on to the handrails. I remember railway strikes when trains were halted midway for many hours and it was impossible in the dense crowd to push through to the washroom.

"But here I was, sitting on a soft seat, right by the window. The car was heated. There were no bundles, no high fur hats, no sheepskin coats, no bosses, and no gendarmes. Nobody was eating bread and lard. Nobody drank vodka from a bottle. Nobody was berating Jews for state treason. In fact, nobody discussed politics at all. As soon as the train started, a huge Negro in a white apron came in and announced lunch. The train was not rattling. It glided smoothly on its rails along the frozen Hudson."

A heavy snow starts falling. The train no longer races but crawls. The heating system breaks down. The train halts in a forest. The stewards and conductors suddenly turn rude. People strike up conversations, but Isaac is left alone. Disaster seems imminent. The train arrives late, and there are no taxis. But a lame, wrinkled old woman ("like an old woman in Poland") and her slovenly daughter are waiting on the platform for the visitor; they have been waiting for hours. The women refuse to let their guest go to a hotel; they insist he spend the night in their apartment. They have lost the name of the hotel anyhow. The daughter insists on carrying his luggage. The old woman talks on and on about her past in Poland, her hard labor in a concentration camp, her rheumatism, her admiration for the visitor's books. They arrive by taxi in a suburban street "reminiscent of a small town in Poland; murky, narrow, with wooden houses." The sick woman insists on paying the fare, loses her cane, has to be helped upstairs.

What a night it turns out to be! Isaac spends comfortless hours on a folding cot in a freezing room with barred windows. He can't find his manuscripts; he can't sleep; his nose is stuffed; the air is icy; he's afraid to cough or even move for fear of bringing the cot crashing to the floor. During the night the old woman dies. The daughter comes into the room hysterical, screaming for a doctor. She tells Isaac how her mother loved him and his work, never stopped talking about him, lived for his arrival.

Left alone with the corpse of the mother while the daughter goes out to seek help, Isaac thinks of New York and his comfortable life in America as "memories of a previous incarnation." Suddenly he wonders if he has lost his citizenship papers too, along with the text of his lecture. He searches again, feels the stiff papers in his pocket. "This document was now testimony that my years in America had not been an invention." From the paragraph that follows we learn what it means to this man to be an American citizen:

"Here is my photograph. And my signature. Here is the government stamp. True, these were also inanimate, without life, but they symbolized order, a sense of belonging, law. I stood in the doorway and for the first time really read the paper that made me a citizen of the United States. I became so absorbed that I had almost forgotten the dead woman."

In the frigid dawn Isaac puts his arms around the frightened daughter,

Binele, trying to comfort her. "We stood there midway up the stairs and rocked back and forth—a lost Yiddish writer, and a victim of Hitler and of my ill-starred lecture. I saw a number tattooed above her wrist and heard myself saying: 'Binele, I won't abandon you. I swear by the soul of your mother. . . .' "

And so even here, on a Jewish street in a Montreal suburb, the author encounters the scarred, the displaced, and the unutterably lonely victims of old traumas and persecutions they can never escape—even as Isaac himself can never really escape his people's history, even with his citizenship papers comfortingly in order and all the conveniences of a fulfilled, successful, ordered life awaiting his return.

"The Briefcase," which ran in *The New Yorker* on February 23, 1973 (Shulamith Charney was co-translator) and appears in the collection *A Crown of Feathers*, is another chronicle of the sort of adventure that Isaac encounters—real, imagined, or a superbly realized combination of the two—whenever he sets foot out of New York City. Like the others, this account opens quietly enough: "That winter I worked on a newspaper, wrote books, went on lecture tours, and also agreed to be visiting professor of creative literature at a Midwestern university." Isaac was also involved with Reizl, another of those intense Singer women as recognizable as a breed by now as the Thurber women in their day—passionate, jealous, hating to have him out of her sight: "The doorbell rang three times. That must be Reizl. She always arrived in turmoil. She brought with her the tensions of ghetto life, of secret frontier crossings, of the D.P. camp. She was blond, blue-eyed, and slim and, though almost forty, looked like a girl in her twenties. A dressmaker by profession, she had been asked to be a model. But she knew no English. Besides, in the ghetto she had developed the habit of drinking.

"Before she closed the door, she was shrieking, I won't ever go anywhere by subway again! I'd rather die."

The hero goes off to lecture in the Midwest, and Reizl makes a scene about it. After his lecture he meets a woman he recognizes from the past, Rosalie Kadish, who invites him to her apartment, tries to persuade him to smoke a reefer, serves him tea and cookies. Back in New York Reizl is still furious, but it seems likely she will get over it. So far, no nightmare. Then Isaac takes a train to the next midwestern town on his agenda, loses his briefcase, goes to the wrong hotel—a fleabag instead of the first-class place where his sponsors have reserved him a room. Cut off from the world, frightened, alone, and uncomfortable, he rediscovers what poverty is like, what hunger is like. Finally both women arrive on the scene to take care of him, and he returns to the security of New York a wiser man. "The Briefcase" is typical of those "What if?" stories Isaac develops so expertly, projecting himself into circumstances in which he is stripped of all the

comforts and conveniences of his life and is reminded how close to the abyss
we all live, walking our private tightropes above the chasm of oblivion.

These stories about Isaac's journeys have certain elements in common.
Usually it is Isaac in the persona of the itinerant lecturer who narrates—the
passive observer of nightmare experiences that befall him unexpectedly in
all extremes of climate and situation. Whether the scene is a midwestern
campus or Buenos Aires in spring or Montreal in the grip of a blizzard, the
characters do not change—they are Jews without roots, homeless, stranded
in an alien world, fixated on the past, living in a dream that the arrival of
this visiting *landsman* causes to flare briefly into nightmare, only to subside
again into death or a kind of cultural narcolepsy. When the scene is Israel,
there is the turbulence of war or alienation of another kind even in the
midst of Jewish life in a Jewish state.

"The Mentor," first published on March 21, 1970, in *The New Yorker*
and included in the collection *A Friend of Kafka*—it was translated by the
author and Evelyn Torton Beck—is set in modern Israel, which the narrator
visits on a lecture tour in 1955. There he meets two kinds of people he has
known in the past—those who knew him as a young writer in Warsaw and
those who remember him from his days as an adolescent tutor in a town
that in this tale he calls Jadow. The Jadowers want to know what has happened to his red hair; they themselves have "changed beyond recognition."
Many Jews from Jadow, he learns, died in the ghettoes of Poland and the
concentration camps or perished of starvation, typhoid, and scurvy in Russia. Some lost sons in the 1948 war with the Arabs.

The story focuses on Isaac's reunion with a woman called Freidl, about
ten years his junior, one of the pupils he tutored in Jadow. As a girl she was
pretty, with green eyes, black hair, and white skin. "She promised to marry
me when she grew up. Actually she married a local boy named Tobias
Stein, a fervent Zionist who brought her to Palestine." Tobias and Freidl
have raised an adolescent daughter, but now they are separated. Freidl is a
successful neurologist, speaks eight languages, and has published a book.
She looks younger than she is, wears tweeds and a ring with a large emerald.
"Worldliness, energy and resolution emanated from her." Isaac can no
longer keep up with her Hebrew—a language he taught her in the first
place. At the gathering where they meet, the others from Jadow listen to
their conversation "with awe." But Freidl is not the person she seems to be.

When she offers to drive Isaac back to his hotel, the ride turns into one of
those fantastic nightmare journeys. Instead of going to the hotel, they drive
through a *chamsin*—the hot, dry desert wind of Israel—into a red sunset,
past fields and orchards and orange groves—all night, in fact—to the kibbutz in the north where Freidl's sixteen-year-old daughter, Rina, lives. On
the way Freidl tells him about her failed marriage, her atheism, her lovers.

With all her energy and sophistication, she proves to be as lost and forlorn as the dying old woman in Montreal: "Once, I had a passion for my work; now even this isn't what it used to be. I would like to write a novel, but no one is waiting for my fiction. Besides, I am actually left without a language. Hebrew is not my mother tongue. To write in Yiddish here makes no sense. I know French fluently, but I haven't used it in years. My English is quite good, but not good enough for writing."

Freidl claims that as soon as she gets rid of one neurosis, another springs up to take its place. Her latest involves her daughter. "What is it that you want of her?" Isaac asks. She answers, "That she should love me."

At dawn Isaac and Freidl arrive at Rina's kibbutz. Tobias, Freidl's estranged husband, greets her with the information that the journey has been in vain; Rina has spent the night with her boyfriend, her "mentor," and has not come home yet. Freidl is furious. Isaac thinks of asking Freidl whether she isn't using a double standard here—one for herself and a different one for others—but he stops himself. For suddenly in Freidl's face he recognizes the features of his own mother. "I knew that her contradictions were also my contradictions. The powers that rule history had brought us back to the land of our ancestors, but we had already defiled it with abominations." Beneath the veneer of sophistication, the smart talk, the brashness, the eight languages, and the knowledge of psychiatry, Freidl is just one more displaced soul in exile—a disconsolate Jewish mother, homeless and rootless even in her own motherland.

Another of the Israeli stories, "The Psychic Journey" (*The New Yorker*, October 18, 1976), describes a rather bizarre interlude that begins on the Upper West Side in New York and ends in Israel in the midst of the Yom Kippur War of 1973. This is a marvelous tale. It has everything in it that a first-rate Singer story should have—pigeons, a temptress, the supernatural, and a vegetarian dinner.

The story opens in New York on a hot summer day. The narrator is feeding pigeons on upper Broadway when a fellow pigeon-fancier strikes up a conversation. She is Margaret Fugazy, daughter of a half-Jewish doctor and a faithful reader of *The Unknown*, a magazine devoted to the occult, to which he also subscribes. She explains that she had heard an astral voice ordering her to feed these pigeons at six in the evening, even though they're not usually hungry at that time. Because of this she is convinced that her meeting with the narrator is preordained. Oh, she has read his work and knows all about him. She has, in fact, been in telepathic communication with him for some time and has paid several astral visits to his apartment. She takes him home and feeds him an indigestible supper of raw carrots, molasses, and sunflower seeds. He goes back to his own apartment at one in the morning, blaming the whole incident on his wife, Dora, who has taken off to visit her daughter in Israel. But this is only the beginning.

Margaret Fugazy begins to call him up and makes further astral visits to his flat; she even persuades him to sign up for a package tour of Israel that is to combine culture and zionism with lectures on psychic research; both of them will serve as guides. Surprised at his own docility, Isaac goes along as co-host of the tour. He gives lectures on the Cabala; Margaret's talks are concerned with more practical matters: health, sex, and money; harnessing the powers of the subconscious while placing bets with your bookie or your stockbroker; techniques for landing a job or a husband. She sprinkles her lectures with gibberish borrowed from esoteric Buddhism, esoteric Judaism, and biofeedback, and explains how to open the pineal eye and how to find the Lost Continent of the Theosophists. Most of the subjects at her hypnosis sessions are obliging enough to go to sleep—or at least to keep their eyes closed. She finally confronts Isaac with the revelation that his mother has appeared to her in a vision and asked her to keep a close watch on him—as a Sagittarian he faces real danger from an impending collision with a Scorpio.

Margaret Fugazy and Isaac don't have a love affair in this story; they don't have time. First they have to find a restaurant where they can have a last meal before the Day of Atonement fast. Then they are caught in the Yom Kippur War. Their adventures, as well as the blackout in Tel Aviv, the mobilization of Israel's civilian army, and an air-raid alert are narrated with a control that keeps the reader constantly in suspense and on the verge of both tears and laughter.

The narrator's wife never does find out that he was in Israel at the same time that she was. Later, when he attempts to tell her, half jokingly, about the whole episode, she doesn't believe him. Isaac actually was in Israel when the Yom Kippur War broke out and says that a number of the events, though not all of them, really occurred. As for Margaret Fugazy we are left in doubt as to whether she was a real woman or a witch. In either case hers is one of the most sharply drawn in the gallery of Isaac's portraits of the ladies who have enlivened his travels.

"The Bus," published in *The New Yorker* on August 28, 1978, finds the narrator in Spain, on a twelve-day motor-coach tour, recovering from a love affair. He boards the bus in Geneva and scarcely a paragraph has gone by when the driver seats him next to a woman with red hair, a heavily rouged face that fails to conceal her wrinkles, and deep blue eyeshadow on her eyelids. Another Singer woman! Her name is Selina Weyerhofer, and she wears a cross but soon discloses that she is Jewish—a former concentration-camp inmate who survived, married a Swiss bank director, and converted, at her husband's behest, to Christianity. The husband, in fact, is sitting across the aisle from her, and when the narrator asks her why, she says it's because he hates her. The narrator, who before long has his hands full with the overwhelming Mrs. Weyerhofer, then meets a Mrs. Metalon from Istanbul, whose adolescent son is determined to find her a husband. Because the routine of the bus requires passengers to exchange seats every day, the narrator also gets to know the Swiss banker, characterized by his own wife as a pathological liar and latent homosexual. After a few pages our traveler is embroiled in a typical set of complications.

When the bus gets to Spain he is assigned a hotel room without a bath, but Mrs. Metalon's son extends an invitation to him to come over and use theirs. Looking for the Metalons' room, he knocks on the wrong door and ends up in Mrs. Weyerhofer's room instead. She warns him that the Metalon woman is only using the invitation to bathe as a pretext for seducing him. By the time the narrator does get to Mrs. Metalon's room the hot water is no longer running, but she detains him to tell him the story of her unhappy marriage and divorce and her troubles with her son, a genius who could do logarithms at the age of five, but who is scheming to get her married again.

As the tale proceeds it grows even more bizarre. Mrs. Weyerhofer keeps delaying the bus, failing to return on time from shopping trips. She insists that her husband is trying to get rid of her, makes a scene on the bus, denounces him to all the passengers as a Nazi, a sadist, and a homosexual.

Although it has been only a week since he left Geneva, the narrator feels as if he has been on the road for months. He is beset with lust for Mrs. Metalon, yet when he is left alone with her in Seville, his passion cools. He never does get a hot bath. One day he decides to quit the tour. He takes a train back to Geneva, agreeing to lose two hundred dollars to the bus company rather than become embroiled in further complications. But when he goes to the dining car aboard the train, who should be there worrying a cooked chicken but the ineluctable Mrs. Weyhofer. She persuades him to join her, says she has left her husband, congratulates him for escaping the trap of an affair with Mrs. Metalon. Taking over the evening, she orders a vegetarian dinner for him. The waiter says it's time to close the dining car, but Mrs. Weyerhofer instructs her friend not to rush. Unlike their harried bus driver, she assures him, the demons that threaten to rob them of their sanity are infinitely patient.

"The Bus" is a long story, but it never drags. Within its confines the author creates a web of unrelenting suspense and a story line that could have served a less inventive writer as the plot for a full-length novel. The characters, the action, and the background of Spanish scenery are unusually well fleshed out. For through the corner of the author's eye, despite the distractions of seething personal relationships in the foreground, one manages to catch glimpses of a hot summer landscape where the Patriarchs might have wandered and the shocks of harvested grain in the fields recall Joseph's dreams of plenty.

Seville or Lisbon, Rio or Buenos Aires, Montreal or Tel Aviv, Isaac's pen transforms the cities he passes through in his travel tales into timeless realms of his own devising, apt settings for allegorical adventures that leave him shaken but essentially unscathed.

❀

The April 1967 issue of *Harper's* Magazine carried an article by Isaac about the Hasidic Jews in the Williamsburg section of Broadway. Entitled "The Extreme Jews," it begins with Isaac's comments on the photographs by Nancy Rudolph that accompanied the text—of "fur-edged rabbinical hats, long gaberdines, big beards, sidelocks, women in wigs and in bonnets that were already obsolete in my youth in Warsaw." Why did modern Jews have to dress that way? It still amazed him, especially when he saw pictures of Hasidim driving trucks, carrying bundles, delivering merchandise. It reminded him of how puzzled he was when he first saw nuns in their habits or photographs of Gandhi "in a sheet." He came to the conclusion that "a style of dress, of hair, and of every kind of external nonconformity represents a sort of language." The Hasidim, the nuns, "Gandhi in his sheet, Tolstoy in his peasant's smock" were all protected by their clothes, he decided, from succumbing to worldliness.

Isaac goes on to explain how the Jewish style of dress in Poland set the Jew apart and strengthened his identity. "If the gentile wore a short coat, he, the Jew, would wear a long one. If the gentile's hat was round, his would be pointed. According to the Talmud, the book of Jewish religious law, the Jew dared not even tie his shoelaces in the same way as his gentile neighbor. These laws were established not out off enmity toward the gentile but rather as a reminder for the Jew to adhere to certain conditions if he wanted to retain his identity for hundreds if not thousands of years." Along came the Enlightenment and the Jew took off his gaberdine, but with emancipation a "new type of Jew" evolved, one "who could renounce the laws of his religion yet remain a Jew." But this "so-called worldly Jew was a riddle to himself and the Christian world. If he disobeyed the Jews' laws, of what elements did his faith consist?" Zionism was one answer, "common interests, character and personality" was another. To the end "the modern Jew's identity may not be defined in any dictionary, but it exists nevertheless." For the pious, though, a Jew without a religion is "an enigma, a mass of contradictions," and he must "enforce ever-stricter and more religious measures in order to retain his historical role and to raise a generation that will follow in his ways." These ultra-Orthodox Hasidic Jews, these "extremists," number perhaps 100,000 in all the world; many of them do not recognize the state of Israel; they refuse to speak modern Hebrew but "stick to the Yiddish of their grandfathers and great-grandfathers"—and are convinced that they alone will be left to receive the Messiah when he arrives. "Are they right or do they represent an ossified sector of the Jewish community, an anachronism that time will disperse?" Isaac does not presume to answer: "Only history will tell." Their way of life, "based on a profound religious logic and a historic reason," is aimed toward "one purpose only—complete segregation from the gentile" and even from the rest of Jewry, whom these Hasidim regard as "heading toward ultimate disappearance." "This segregation," the article concludes, "is as old as Jewish exile itself and has maintained the Jew through the two thousand years of his existence in the Diaspora."

The same text, in a slightly altered form, made up the introduction to the book *The Hasidim*, published by Crown in 1970. Instead of photographs of the Williamsburg Hasidim, this volume contains some seventy-five drawings, etchings, and lithographs by Ira Moskowitz, who later illustrated Isaac's *A Little Boy in Search of God*. These illustrations catch the spirit of the Hasidim, not in Williamsburg but in the European milieu in which they once flourished and in the Hasidic neighborhoods of Jerusalem and Safed, where the artist visited and sketched them from life. Here they are as of old, studying, meditating, praying; a community celebrates the holidays of Succoth and Simchas Torah, wearing their traditional gaberdines, their prayer shawls, their fur-trimmed hats; a family sits down to a modest Sabbath meal; a rabbi guides a young boy through a page of the Torah. The drawings reveal the essential strength that enabled the sect to survive alienation and pain through two centuries of self-imposed isolation.

To the original essay Isaac appended a chapter, "The Spirit of Hasidism," in which he traces its origins to the upheavals that shattered the stability of the Jewish community in the twelfth century and its development as a movement, emphasizing the emotional aspects of the Jewish faith that swept over Europe, while the Maskilim, "the enlightened ones," demanded that Jews "take off their gaberdines and become Europeans." In this chapter Isaac offers brief portraits of the prophetic leaders—the Baal Shem Tov, who founded the Hasidic movement; his great-grandson, Rabbi Nachman of Bratzlav; Rabbi Isaac Luria, the cabalist on whose ideas Hasidic leaders drew—and describes the struggle between the Maskilim and the Hasidim for the minds and hearts of Poland's Jews, a kind of bloodless war between rationalism and the folk beliefs of the devout. Eventually, he says, the stand against the Hasidim softened; today even the Reform Jews are searching for the emotional elements in worship and belief. But it was only when the Maskilim, who sided with the Enlightenment, felt that it was "safe" to study Hasidism, since it was no longer a "force to contend with," that the thinkers and writers of European Jewry begin to admire the "mysticism" and "high spiritual temperament" of the sect they had so long opposed and scorned.

"The Haskalah [the Enlightenment]," he sums up, "could persuade people, convince them with its logic, but it could never produce the juices that nourish creativity. . . . The Haskalah lacked the warmth and the exultation to really lift up the spirit. It could promise nothing but worldly gains. Willingly or unwillingly, Judaism's finest writers and painters had to return to the life of the ghetto that the Haskalah despised, to its pious ancestors, and to the joys that only Hasidim in its early stages could bring to the Jew. There is not a single true Jewish work of art that glorifies the Haskalah and its movement. The true artist is never inspired by sociology or politics."

PART 6

"Every Story
Is a Love Story"

By the time *The Seance and Other Stories* was published in 1968, it was possible to perceive certain subtle changes in Isaac's style, at least as far as the English versions of his short stories were concerned. These tales and many that were to follow were also more polished and ordered than their predecessors. Perhaps as a result of Rachel MacKenzie's influence, perhaps because he himself was playing an increasingly greater role in translating, his prose was becoming more fine-grained, his plots less pat and more ingeniously organized, his characters less like caricatures hastily sketched in charcoal and more like delicately drawn and shaded portraits—though the point of his pen was as sharp as ever.

Although "Two Corpses Go Dancing" had first been published in Yiddish back in 1943, most of the stories in this collection were written between 1964 and 1968. Some had been printed originally in *Chicago Review*, *Harper's*, *Cosmopolitan*, *Vogue*, *Esquire*, *Encounter*, *Playboy*, *Cavalier*, and *The Saturday Evening Post*, while others first reached English-speaking readers in magazines of Jewish interest: *Hadassah Magazine*, *American Judaism*, *Commentary*, and *Israel Magazine*. Two—"The Slaughterer" (November 25, 1967) and "The Letter Writer" (January 13, 1968)—had first appeared in *The New Yorker*. Women dominated the ever-growing group of Isaac's translators in those days, though the title story was translated by Roger H. Klein and Cecil Hemley, and the list includes J. M. Last and Joseph Singer, who would later take over most of the translation for *The New Yorker*.

Whereas "Blood" had dealt with the bloodlust of the slaughterer Reuben and the insatiable Risha, "The Slaughterer" deals with Yoineh Meir's reluctant acceptance of the role of ritual slaughterer in the town of Kolomor after he is turned down for the post of village rabbi. In a moment of rebellion he drops all the instruments of his profession into an outhouse pit and eventually throws away his prayer shawl and phylacteries, since these religious objects—like the very scrolls of the Torah itself—are made out of the skins of animals. Finally Yoineh turns to God and cries out, "Father in Heaven, Thou art a slaughterer! . . . The whole world is a slaughterhouse!" It is a bloodcurdling tale, summing up all Isaac's attitudes toward the horrors of casual cruelty.

The title story in the book, which appeared in *Encounter* in 1965, reveals the fine hand of Cecil Hemley in its glowing English prose. The story itself deals with the supernatural, this time with the immigrant Dr. Zorach Kalisher's visits to a charlatan medium named Mrs. Kopitzky on Central Park West. Dr. Kalisher renounces rationalism when his mistress, Nella, is lost to the Nazis, and turns for comfort to Mrs. Kopitzky, whose spirits have an odd way of duplicating her errors in syntax and pronunciation. One night the doctor falls ill at a seance and on his way to the bathroom stumbles across Mrs. Kopitzky's confederate. He wets his pants and is altogether miserable, but Mrs. Kopitzky, fake though she is as a spiritualist, proves to be the real thing as a woman and saves the poor man's life.

By now Isaac was striving more than ever for economy and compression in his tales. A character in one of them says, "If I were to tell you all the stories I know, we'd be sitting here seven days and seven nights." Another: "If I wanted to tell you everything we spoke about that day, I would have to sit with you until tomorrow morning." Characters relating their experiences are always promising to "make a long story short." The device turns up in tale after tale; Isaac makes sure that his characters themselves—like his readers—are never bored.

"Henne Fire," one of Isaac's many stories relayed by a town gossip, is about a creature who is the apotheosis of the I. B. Singer female, a fiery woman who constantly flies into rages. Henne is so inflammable that her very presence is enough to start a series of conflagrations in the village where she lives, and the fire within her ultimately consumes her. "The Needle"— about the test used to weed out prospective candidates by a mother seeking the perfect wives for her sons—has all the virtues of a first-rate fairy tale. In "Two Corpses Go Dancing" we come upon a couple who have cheated the grave, who walk and even wed among the Jews of Poland, who never realize that they are dealing with the living dead. These Poe-inspired protagonists are prototypes of the zombielike survivors Isaac frequently describes in his travel tales.

The longest story in the book and one of the best realized is "The Letter Writer," about the strange salvation of an aging editor in a New York Yiddish publishing house. The man's job collapses and he comes close to death through hunger and illness, but he is rescued through the circuitous workings of Providence when a lady from a far-off city, whom he knows only through their correspondence in a periodical devoted to the occult, comes to his rescue. Here Isaac is at his sly and humorous best, mixing farce and pathos in a tantalizing fictional brew. When the pathetic refugee Herman

Gombiner is lying half-dead of pneumonia, his principal worry is that the
mouse he has been feeding will go hungry for want of cheese and crackers.
Isaac has admitted that, as usual, there is much in this fantasy that is based
on reality: Not only is he himself an avid reader of occult publications; he
actually did know a man who always left food out for the mouse in his apartment and worried incessantly about what would happen if he wasn't there
to keep the creature alive.

In these stories Isaac continues to offer his readers pictures of *shtetl* life
shorn of prettification, and characters who are vulnerable mortals rather than
personages too good to be true: lechers, lesbians, thieves, and murderers as
well as God-fearing Hasidic rabbis and their devoted wig-wearing wives.
Even so, the wisdom of the past, albeit mingled with lust, superstition, and
madness, illuminates every page. Still, it is no wonder that apologists who
wanted the past retouched and represented through a sentimental haze re-
coiled from these bold, brilliantly realized tales.

The Seance and Other Stories was greeted somewhat coolly by Curt Leviant in the *Saturday Review*, with the complaint that the locales of some of
the stories were becoming so familiar that they exuded "a faint aura of déjà-
vu." Yet the collection as a whole, he felt, added "to its author's well-
deserved reputation as one of our major creative artists. When a man writes
as well and as prolifically as Isaac Bashevis Singer, we need not expect
supremacy in every single piece."

Newsweek's reviewer thought that the stories in the new collection varied
"widely in quality—as widely as the magazines of origin. The best of these
stories, while they don't always attain the level of his finest previous work,
are very fine indeed; the less successful ones are sometimes curiously fragmentary and cursory, glittering pages of a major writer which have not been
woven into seamless wholes." As Leviant observed, however, "discovery of
even one gem is cause for rejoicing." The collection that contains "The
Seance," "The Slaughterer," "The Lecture," and "The Letter Writer" could
be said to contain more than one.

Isaac's introduction to his next book of tales, *A Friend of Kafka and Other
Stories* (Farrar, Straus and Giroux, 1970), succinctly sums up the contents:
"The stories in this collection were all written in my later years, some of
them quite recently. About one third are about immigrants in the United
States, where I have now lived a longer time than in the country of my
birth, Poland." With respect to the translations he says: "I have translated
these stories with the assistance of collaborators, and I find that I do much
revision in the process of translation. It is not an exaggeration to say that
over the years English has become my 'second' language. It is also a fact that
the foreign-language editions of my novels and stories have been translated
from the English."

Over the years Isaac has come to play an increasingly important role in the translation of his books and stories. He still writes everything in Yiddish, since, he says, "Yiddish contains vitamins that other languages don't have." But more and more his work is revised in the process of translation, so that the Yiddish version of an opus is treated somewhat like an experimental draft and receives considerable alteration and polishing before it is published in English.

"My translators, whose names appear at the end of each story in this book, are not only my first readers but also my first constructive (I hope) critics. I have been a translator all of my adult life and I consider translation the greatest problem and challenge of literature. The 'other' language in which the author's work must be rendered does not tolerate obscurity, puns, and linguistic tinsel. It teaches the author to deal with events rather than with their interpretation, to let the events speak for themselves. The 'other' language is often the mirror in which we have the chance to see ourselves with all our imperfections and, if possible, to correct some of our mistakes."

Since stories by Isaac Bashevis Singer were by now appearing regularly in *The New Yorker*, half of those collected in *A Friend of Kafka* had been edited by Rachel MacKenzie before publication; the collection as a whole was edited by Robert Giroux. The book, in fact, was dedicated to Isaac's editors and translators. These "collaborators" included Elizabeth Shub, Dorothea Straus, Evelyn Torton Beck, Elaine Gottlieb, Mirra Ginsburg, Channah Kleinerman-Goldstein, Elizabeth Pollet, Ruth Schachner Finkel, Rosanna Gerber, and Alma Singer—most of them old hands by now at working on translations with Isaac.

But what of the tales themselves? More and more they become revealing of Isaac—less as the detached narrator than as an actual participant in modified treatments of his own adventures. The title story is an amusing yet touching vignette about a former actor in the Yiddish theater who claims to have known Franz Kafka, in fact, to have discerned the Czech writer's genius before anybody else had ever heard of him. Set in the Writers' Club in Warsaw in the thirties, "A Friend of Kafka" provides pungent caricatures not only of the aging actor with his monocle and threadbare pretensions, his dubious though vividly detailed anecdotes about love affairs with countesses and wrestling matches with the "tough angel" who is his heaven-sent adversary, but also of the other habitués of the club, with their woolly ideas on philosophy, literature, sex, and the danger that man might end up as a "word machine" who will "eat words, drink words, marry words, poison himself with words."

"Guests on a Winter Night" is a memoir of Isaac's childhood on Krochmalna Street and might well have served as a chapter of *In My Father's Court*. There is a telling little sketch of his parents. "My father was fair, his sidelocks dark, his beard red like tobacco. He had a short nose and blue eyes. A strange thought occurred to me—that he resembled the czar whose picture hung in our cheder. I knew well enough that a comparison like that was a sacrilege. The czar was a vicious man, and my father was pious and a rabbi. . . .

"An open book lay on the table in front of my father, and he put his sash in it as a sign that he was interrupting the study only for a short while. On his right stood a glass of tea, half full. On his left lay his long pipe. Opposite him sat my mother. My father's face was almost round, and my mother's face, her nose, her chin, were angular. Even the gaze of her large gray eyes was sharp. She wore a blond wig, but I knew that under it her hair was fiery red, like mine. Her cheeks were sunken, her lips thin. I was always afraid that she was reading my mind."

The story proper is about a ritual slaughterer who wishes to divorce his disagreeable wife and about a visit from a distant relative. But its charm lies less in the plot than in the recollection of the vanished sites of Jewish Warsaw.

"The snow covered the poverty of Krochmalna Street, and it looked rich now. I imagined that Warsaw had in some strange way moved deep into Russia—perhaps Siberia, where according to my brother Joshua the winter is one long night and white bears travel on ice floes. The gutter became a skating rink for boys. Some of the stores were closed, their windowpanes framed in ice and covered with frosty palm branches, like the ones used in the Feast of Tabernacles. In others, customers were let in through the back doors. The delicatessen was brightly lit. Long sausages hung from the ceiling. . . .

"It was even more interesting to look into Chaim's coffee shop. Many couples sat there, all of them emancipated, not Hasidic. The place was frequented by thieves and 'strikers'—the young men and girls who only a few years before were throwing bombs and demanding a constitution from the czar. What a constitution was I had not yet learned, but I knew that on Bloody Wednesday scores of these young people fell before bullets. Still, many remained alive, and some of those who were put into prison had later been released. They sat in Chaim's coffee shop, ate rolls with herring, drank coffee with chicory, sometimes took a piece of cheesecake, and read the Yiddish papers. They tried to learn about other strikers deep in Russia or abroad. The strikers were dressed differently from the thieves. They wore collarless shirts closed with tin studs. The visors on their caps were not pulled down so far over their eyes. The girls were poorly clothed, their hair caught up in combs. The thieves sat at one large round table, and their girls wore summer dresses in the middle of winter—red, yellow, some with flowers. Their faces looked to me as though they had been smeared with borscht; their eyes, rimmed in black, shone uncannily. My mother said that these sinful creatures had lost both this world and the world to come."

In this story there is a glimpse of Hinde Esther shortly before her marriage: "She was dressed like a lady, in a hat fastened with rhinestone pins, a fur collar trimmed with the little head of an animal, and a muff. She was already engaged and her trousseau was being prepared." And one of Joshua: "Joshua wore a long gaberdine and a small cap. He had sidelocks, too, but they were trimmed. Joshua had become enlightened—'spoiled,' my father called it. He refused to study the Talmud, he read secular books; he was opposed to the use of a matchmaker. Almost every day my father had a discussion with him. Joshua insisted that the Jews in Poland lived like Asiatics. He mocked their sidelocks, their gaberdines down to their shoe tops. How much longer were they going to study the law concerning the egg that was hatched on a holiday? Europe, my brother said, had awakened, but the Jews of Poland were still in the Middle Ages." And of Isaac himself: "I listened to him [Joshua] dispute with my father, and I was always on his side. I wanted to cut off my sidelocks, put on a short jacket, study Polish, Russian, German, and learn what makes a train go, how to build a telephone, a telegraph, a balloon, a ship. I never dared to take part in these arguments, but I knew very well that men in long gaberdines and women in wigs and bonnets were not allowed inside the Saxony Gardens. My father kept promising me that when the Messiah came those who studied the Torah would be saved and the unbelievers would perish. But when would the Messiah come? Perhaps he would not come at all."

We see the Singers gathered in their apartment in those days on a winter evening. Isaac, Bathsheba, Hinde Esther, and Joshua are sitting in the kitchen. Water is boiling for tea. Bathsheba is rendering goose fat for Chanukah while Joshua tells stories about the Black Hand bandits in America, who rob only millionaires. Hinde Esther turns the pages of a Yiddish newspaper. She is reading a serialized novel—a forerunner of those later to be devised by her brothers. Joshua pronounces the stuff she is reading trash—for greatness one has to look to Tolstoy, who has just been offered a quarter of a million rubles by a publisher for his manuscripts. Bathsheba brings up the theft of the Mona Lisa, which sent all France into mourning, "as though it were Tisha ba'Av," the holiday commemorating the destruction of the Temple in Jerusalem. She thinks the French must be mad idolaters to take on like that over a picture. Joshua disagrees. "In Europe, they want beauty, not the Torah of an old man who recites the Psalms and has a rupture." Hinde Esther, described here as a girl with brown hair, large bright eyes, and a rosy face, informs her mother that women are wearing pants in Paris. But Hinde Esther has "sick nerves." "One moment she laughed, the next she cried. One day she covered Mother with kisses, another day she accused her of being her enemy, of trying to send her into exile. One day she was overly pious, the next she was blasphemous. She often fainted. She had even tried to throw herself out of the window. . . .

"To me and my younger brother, Moishe (who was asleep in the bedroom), she was always good. She brought us candy. She told us stories."

Hinde Esther is about to tell one of those stories when there's a knock on the door and an old woman named Itte Fruma (she turns out to be one of Pinchas Mendel's aunts from the country) intrudes on the scene. Interesting as are her stories (which Isaac will someday make his own) about demons disguised as yeshiva boys, hobgoblins, werewolves, imps, and dybbuks, her arrival scatters the focus of a vivid and revealing episode.

The next story in the book, "The Key," is one of Isaac's best. It is a compassionate portrait of a suspicious old lady who locks herself out of her upper west side apartment and has to spend the night on the sidewalk. There seems to be more than a hint of Hinde Esther in the character of Bessie Popkin who, in her paranoid fantasies, suffers from the depredations of both human tormentors and demons and imps. As is always the case in the strongest of Isaac's tales, pathos and comedy mingle in these pages to keep the reader teetering on the thin boundary between tears and laughter.

"The Cafeteria" sheds light on Isaac's life during the 1960s. It begins, "Even though I have reached the point where a great part of my earnings is given away in taxes, I still have the habit of eating in cafeterias when I am by myself. I like to take a tray with a tin knife, fork, spoon and paper napkin and to choose at the counter the food I enjoy. Besides, I meet there the *landsleit* from Poland, as well as all kinds of literary beginnings and readers who know Yiddish. The moment I sit down at a table, they come over. . . ."

The greeters chat with Isaac about Yiddish literature, about the Holocaust, about Israel. The next thing he knows, one or another of them is dead. "Since I seldom read a paper, I learn this news only later. Each time, I am startled, but at my age one has to be ready for such tidings. The food sticks in the throat; we look at one another in confusion, and our eyes ask mutely, Whose turn is next? Soon we begin to chew again. I am often reminded of a scene in a film about Africa. A lion attacks a herd of zebras and kills one. The frightened zebras run for a while and then they stop and start to graze again. Do they have a choice?"

By now Isaac knows his neighborhood on the Upper West Side as well as he knew Krochmalna Street as a lad: "I have been moving around in this neighborhood for over thirty years—as long as I lived in Poland. I know each block, each house. There has been little building here on uptown Broadway in the last decades, and I have the illusion of having put down roots here. I have spoken in most of the synagogues. They know me in some of the stores and in the vegetarian restaurants. Women with whom I have had affairs live on the side streets. Even the pigeons know me; the moment I come out with a bag of feed, they begin to fly toward me from blocks away. . . . Almost every day on my walk after lunch, I pass the funeral parlor that waits for us and all our ambitions and illusions. Sometimes I imagine that the funeral parlor is also a kind of cafeteria where one gets a quick eulogy or Kaddish on the way to eternity."

The tale finally focuses on the experiences of a woman named Esther

who lives in the neighborhood with her crippled father, whose legs were
frozen in one of Stalin's Siberian labor camps. Isaac is smitten with her and
returns to the cafeteria where they met to seek her out, but the place has
burned down. After the cafeteria is rebuilt, he sees Esther there again, and
she tells him a strange tale: She had gone to the cafeteria in the middle of
the night that it burned and found a Nazi meeting going on, with men
in white robes and swastikas on their sleeves, and Hitler himself presiding.
Their friendship continues intermittently until Esther simply disappears.
Perhaps she has committed suicide. The narrator never finds out what really
happened to her. But it is plain enough that once again we are dealing with
survivors who have not survived. "Yes, corpses do walk on Broadway."

"Pigeons" is about a Jewish professor in Warsaw with Isaac's penchant for
feeding pigeons in the street. The tale takes place at the time when nazism
is on the rise, and the professor, who is something of a pigeon himself, is
stoned to death by hoodlums. The pigeons he has befriended escort his
hearse, "a winged host" above the funeral procession, accompanying "their
benefactor to his eternal rest."

"The Son" is the moving story described earlier of Isaac's reunion with his
son Israel in 1955. "Fate" tells of a woman so plagued by bad luck that it's
dangerous to sit too close to her at a party. The collection concludes with
"Something Is There," a yarn about a rabbi who abandons *shul* and *shtetl* in
a determined effort to be evil and godless in Warsaw. Protected by his own
simplicity, the rabbi is beyond temptation. Even the prostitute who tries to
seduce him arouses his compassion rather than his lust. Despite all his efforts to turn himself into a sinner, he finds his way, still innocent, back to
God.

During lunch at one of his favorite vegetarian restaurants on upper Broadway shortly after A *Friend of Kafka* was published, Isaac was asked whether
he thought the pieces in that collection shared a common theme. He had
just returned from Europe and Israel and was in excellent spirits after learning that one of them, "The Key," had been chosen by Martha Foley for the
latest edition of *Best American Short Stories*.

Isaac pondered the question before he replied with a counter-question:
"Do they all have to be related with a theme?" Then he allowed that there
might possibly be an idea, if nothing so solemn as a theme, linking the tales
in the book. The idea, he said, was that even in the most commonplace setting—even in matter-of-fact upper west side Manhattan—the same
demons might lurk that had crowded the Polish ghettoes. And even when
there are no demons on the scene, his characters still must wrestle with the
personifications of temptation and evil in one guise or another. Sometimes
the adversary is within, and Isaac's protagonists are their own worst enemies.
So it is that the deranged woman in "The Key," for example, locked out of
her apartment and forced for once to stare up at the sky instead of down at

the street, learns to her amazement that the neighbors she thought were her enemies really are not, that life need not consist entirely of misery, and that even the Puerto Rican superintendent who terrifies her would rather help than harm her. The situation is timeless, but the manner of Bessie Popkin's redemption from paranoia is startlingly up-to-date.

Of *A Friend of Kafka*, Sarah Blackburn wrote in *The New York Times Book Review* that "the effect is inspiring and depressing, and often both at once; those [stories] which are not actually set in the ghetto are set in its parallel, the ghetto of the mind. Some of the characters are liberated from it, others destined to enter it still more deeply and to remain there forever. . . . All of his tales are unfailingly entertaining, but Singer's reputation as a master storyteller rests on his ability as a teacher, in the real sense of the term: he establishes our trust in him by his open trust in us as readers, and we follow the narratives of his knowledge with a sense of personal discovery and delight at our own new perception about the news he has to tell us. . . . The translations from the Yiddish . . . are consistently fine—contemporary and colloquial." Indeed they are—in each successive collection less stilted, more plausible, idiomatic, and graceful on the whole than in the last, as he himself has had an ever greater hand in their preparation. But Curt Leviant, reviewing *A Friend of Kafka* in the *Saturday Review*, was still complaining that the author's "prolifigacy is showing. . . . The creative concentrate that once had been synonymous with Singer's fiction is now thoroughly watered down. . . . Nevertheless, Singer still manages to produce a few good stories, and there are some fine passages in the bad ones." "The Key," "The Son," "The Cafeteria," "The Colony," "A Friend of Kafka," "Pigeons," all in one collection. "A few good stories" indeed!

❀

In 1966 the *Forward* serialized a novel by Isaac Singer called *Sonim, di Geshichte fun a Liebe* (*Enemies, the Story of a Love*); Farrar, Straus and Giroux published the book in English in 1972 as *Enemies, A Love Story*. Aliza Shevrin and Elizabeth Shub were credited with the translation. Shub, along with Rachel MacKenzie and Robert Giroux, are acknowledged in the author's introduction for their editorial assistance. There is also this prefatory word from the author: "Although I did not have the privilege of going through the Hitler Holocaust, I have lived for years in New York with refugees from this ordeal. I therefore hasten to say that this novel is by no means the story of the typical refugee, his life, and struggle. Like most of my fictional works, this book presents an exceptional case with unique heroes and a unique combination of events. The characters are not only Nazi victims but victims of their own personalities and fates. If they fit into the general picture, it is because the exception is rooted in the rule. As a matter of fact, in literature, the exception *is* the rule."

Herman Broder is a refugee from Poland whose entire family has been annihilated in the Holocaust. Out of gratitude to Yadwiga, a Polish woman who hid him from the Nazis in a hayloft in her village, he agrees to live with her in Coney Island. Herman makes a living ghostwriting for a pompous and fraudulent New York rabbi. However, he tells Yadwiga that he is a book salesman, as a pretext for his prolonged visits to a neurotic, overwrought divorcee named Masha Tortshiner, who shares an apartment in The Bronx with her mother, an embittered concentration-camp survivor. Suddenly, as if life weren't complicated enough for poor Herman, he finds out that his real wife, Tamara, who he thought had perished in Poland along with their children, is living in New York. This complication elevates Herman's normal state of anxiety to fever pitch and sets in motion this tragi-comic tale of love and hate.

Although Herman has endured the hardships of life in a D.P. camp, he is completely unable to come to terms with his survival. He wears no tattoo on his arm, yet he is as surely a marked man as if he had endured the horrors of Auschwitz. Merely imagining what might have happened to him has left him in a permanent state of apprehension: "Even if he never had a large appetite, the hunger of the Nazi years had left Herman with a sense of excitement at the sight of food. Sunlight fell on crates and bushel baskets of oranges, bananas, cherries, strawberries and tomatoes. Jews were allowed to live freely here! On the main avenue and on the side streets, Hebrew schools displayed their signs. There was even a Yiddish school. As Herman walked along, his eyes sought hiding places in case the Nazis were to come to New York. Could a bunker be dug somewhere nearby? Could he hide himself in the steeple of the Catholic church? He had never been a partisan, but he often thought of positions from which it would be possible to shoot. . . ."

Herman is fashioned very much in the image of his creator. He feels that "phrases like 'a better world' and 'a brighter tomorrow' " are a "blasphemy on the ashes of the tormented." Herman is fascinated by the occult and spends spare moments away from his women in the Forty-second Street library reading up on dybbuks, poltergeists, extrasensory perception, and clairvoyance. "Since formal religion was as good as bankrupt and philosophy had lost all meaning, occultism was a valid subject for those who still sought the truth." Herman acquires two parakeets, which he brings home to Yadwiga on her name-day. Herman also likes to visit the zoo and the botanical gardens in The Bronx.

The reactions of the other survivors to their reprieve from death is less equivocal. Tamara, drained by the horrors she has experienced, constantly speaks of herself as a walking corpse. Masha, on the other hand, who has also survived the camps, is as fierce and passionate a creature as Isaac has ever drawn, a woman of wild, irrational moods, hating Herman as much as she loves him: lover and enemy. Shifrah Puah, Masha's mother, never stops bewailing her plight and despairing over her volatile daughter. Yadwiga only wants to hold on to Herman; she converts to Judaism and in the end bears him a daughter. Yet for all the life in them and the lust that courses in their blood, these people are as dead as the creatures in "Two Corpses Go Dancing"; they haunt the landscapes of Brooklyn and The Bronx and the Upper West Side like restless ghouls who can find no peace in their graves.

"In the beginning was lust," Herman Broder tells himself, and he proceeds to act out a kind of New World sequel to the Lublin magician's escapades. After his years in the hayloft, enduring rat and insect bites, frights and fevers, Herman has "likened himself to the Talmudic Sage Choni Hamagol, who according to legend slept for seventy years and when he awoke found the world so strange that he prayed for death—a Jewish Rip Van Winkle." He begins to envy the simple lives of animals and tells Masha, "I don't want to live." But it is Masha who dies of an overdose of sleeping pills.

Herman disappears, and Tamara searches for him in vain. Yadwiga lives on; when she gives birth to Herman's child, she names her Masha. The baby, in fact, is born in Tamara's apartment, for she has arranged for Yadwiga to move in with her. She works in a store so that Yadwiga can stay home and take care of the child. But Tamara refuses to marry again, saying half-jokingly that she will be content to be reunited with Herman in the next world.

Although once again in *Enemies* there seem to be too many fatalities in the final pages and Herman's *weltschmertz* seems to vacillate uneasily between self-pity and cosmic despair, the book hangs together uncommonly well. Isaac has not shrunk from describing the horrors of the Holocaust and its legacy of despair, yet he never permits history to detain the progress of his story for long. History lives in the very marrow of his characters' bones. Above all, *Enemies* is a love story. And, at sixty-one, Isaac had learned to pare away all digressions and concentrate on the lines of force that bond his characters together, ironically, angrily, passionately, even though life has done everything to deprive them of their illusions and their appetites.

Are they all frauds and fools, these heroes of Isaac's? Frauds in the sense that they lie and scheme to evade the consequences of their selfishness, certainly. *Satan in Goray* is the story of a spurious messiah. Asa Heshel in *The Family Moskat* deceives his wife and deserts his mistress. The pages of *The Manor* are thronged with bounders and deceivers of both sexes. Yasha the Magician lives his whole life by sleight-of-hand chicanery. Jacob in *The Slave* compels his wife to live a life of silence and deceit. Herman Broder of

Enemies has to disappear in order to disentangle himself from the net of dishonesty he has woven. Yet how sweet they are, deep down, each of these prodigal sons who has "wasted his substance with riotous living" but in the end desires only to return to his father's house and atone for his sins until he is forgiven. They seek to give pleasure to others, they lie to spare the feelings of their women, and they often wound themselves precisely through their involved efforts to avoid causing others pain.

It must be remembered that Isaac is a comic tragedian. To look at his characters without humor, without appreciation of the ironic jokes played on them by their invisible, silent God, is to miss the point of all their agonies. Yes, they are all fools—all Gimpels as well as frauds—stumbling into the elaborate snares they set for others, punishing themselves for the evil deeds they have not committed, converted by their own passions, seduced by their own lusts on dark empty streets that lead nowhere, driven by their mortal hungers and thirsts into comic cul-de-sacs of disappointment and frustration. The deceivers are themselves deceived, the worldly repent in dust and ashes, the thinkers are betrayed by their own thoughts, and the lovers by those they love most. Only the patient ones who avert their eyes from the vanities of life—the innocent sages, the pious, all whose ways are the ways of prayer—escape the mocking, grotesque images that appear in the impious man's mirror. In each of Isaac's novels there comes the pivotal moment. And almost invariably the false step is the one taken, and Paradise is lost. Isaac's heroes may evade Chmielnicki or Hitler or the Warsaw police with exquisite cunning; they are still pursued by the laughter of God.

"I am all my characters," Isaac has said. "And since I am a storyteller, and all storytellers are liars, you have to watch out for me." Isaac has also said often that it is "the freak, the exception" that interests him, and so each of his heroes, from Gimpel the Fool to Herman Broder, is indeed an exceptional individual of one kind or another. The author insists that he is not interested, even in his children's books, in conveying "messages," yet every tale he tells is a fable—a fable, if shrewdly read, that frequently subverts its own ostensible moral. The Jewish ethic, like the conventions of all religious art, sets certain restrictions. The outrages and excesses committed by one of Isaac's heroes may land him in a penitent's cell, or back in the stifling bondage of his family, but it is for his sins rather than his repentance that we remember him; his hungers and follies are what make him believable; his blasphemies and deceptions endear him to us.

When *Enemies, A Love Story* appeared in English, L. E. Sissman, who had expressed such misgivings about *The Manor* and *The Estate*, had nothing but praise for it in his review in *The New Yorker*. He found "this tight-knit novel . . . not a solemn requiem but, at least in the beginning, almost a Feydeau farce." He said it was "a measure of its author's art that we are carried along by the vigor of the plot for scores of pages before we realize that this is to be a tragi-comedy, in which the opposing elements are delicately balanced." "All the people in this book," Sissman summed up, "are suffering from, are under the unrelenting influence of, the ineradicable experience of the Holocaust. In America, where all things are suddenly inverse, where peace and plenty are at hand, these people no longer have the strength to manipulate their destinies. One death in a life is enough; two are one too many." To Sissman, Herman Broder at first seemed "a common, garden nebbish, a simple dupe of his own desires who drifts fecklessly and helplessly through life. But it is soon apparent that his character and circumstances are formed by something sterner than the mere ground rules of farce. . . . And so this cunning novel, with its funny confrontations, its comic turns of fate, its multiplication of conjugal beds, becomes at last—in a slow, artful modulation—a tragedy. Herman, who in his sleep has dreamed of 'an eclipse of the sun and funeral processions,' becomes part of a drama in which, like the people of the cortege in his dream, he is 'both the dead and the mourners,' of whom he asks, 'Can a condemned tribe lead itself to its own burial?' "

Newsweek's anonymous reviewer agreed: "In his first novel set in America, Isaac Bashevis Singer works out this bizarre plot with perfect naturalness and aplomb. The book has the surface gaiety, ribaldry and surprises of a medieval fabliau. Yet the New York subways, telephone calls, Bronx Zoo, bus trips to the Adirondacks are solidly, meticulously real. Herman's three women expand into mythic dimensions. . . . It's hard not to feel that *Enemies, A Love Story* goes haywire in its last ten pages, when fate sweeps down and shatters the comic mode. But we were warned. . . . Whether or not you accept its ending [*Enemies, A Love Story*] is a brilliant, unsettling novel."

Lore Dickstein, in *The New York Times Book Review*, however, felt that the book dealt with "mutilated psyches, but little else. The paucity of felt life, surprising in a Singer work, makes the novel seem curiously clinical and removed, despite its relentlessness. Singer's marvelously pointed humor has turned black and bitter, the sex is flat, and there is little irony or self-consciousness." *Enemies*, she said, was a "bleak obsessive novel that offers neither release nor hope," and seemed "an odd book to come from so accomplished and brilliant a writer." For the most part, though, the book was well received and remains a favorite among many of Isaac's admirers, including several of his translators.

❀

What is reality? What is illusion? How do you tell the difference between the two? Why do men allow lies and false values to lead them to their destruction? That is a theme that runs through many of the twenty-four tales in *A Crown of Feathers and Other Stories*, the largest collection yet of Isaac Singer's short stories, published by Farrar, Straus and Giroux in 1973 (a paperback edition was issued by Fawcett Crest in 1974). The book was a main selection of the *American Journal* Book Club, the *Saturday Review* Book Club, and the *Commentary* Library Book Club, and it won the National Book Award.

By now Isaac had developed a following in every country where his books were permitted to be published. Fifteen of the stories, all written in the 1970s, had appeared first in *The New Yorker*. Others had come out originally in the *Southern Review, Intellectual Digest, Hadassah Magazine, Nimrod, Present Tense, Union Seminary Quarterly Review*, and a publication simply called *Yiddish*.

Isaac's translators included Laurie Colwin, whose own abilities as a first-rate writer of fiction are reflected in the tales on which she collaborated in translating with the author, Ruth Schachner Finkel, Herbert R. Lottman, Dorothea Straus, Shulamith Charney, Rosanna Gerber, Evelyn Torton Beck, Joseph Singer, and Alma Singer.

In his introduction to *A Crown of Feathers* Isaac notes that "there are in this collection as many stories dealing with life in the United States as stories about pre-war Poland." He points out that he has now lived in the United States longer than in Poland and has therefore developed roots in the United States too. "Just the same," he continues, "my American stories deal only with Yiddish-speaking immigrants from Poland so as to ensure that I know well not only their present way of life but *their* roots—their culture, history, ways of thinking and expressing themselves." Yet, he says, the field of his interest was growing large and "my responsibilities even larger." He reminds his readers that some of the people he was writing about "helped to build Warsaw and New York and are now helping to build Tel Aviv. They lived in the midst of almost all the social movements of our time. Their illusions were the illusions of mankind. The vandals who murdered millions of these people have destroyed a treasure of individuality that no literature dare try to bring back." He also mentions his own increasing role in the processes of editing and revision and adds "I do not exaggerate when I say that English has become my 'second original language,' paradoxical as these words may sound." But with reference to his editors and translators he exclaims, "God bless them all." The book is dedicated to his late friend and former colleague on the *Jewish Daily Forward*, Maurice Winograd, who also wrote poetry and, like Isaac, considered himself a "psychic researcher."

"The Beard" is the story of an incompetent writer whose bearded wife insists that the narrator write a complimentary piece about his work; the tale was the basis for Bruce Davidson's movie *Isaac Singer's Nightmare and Mrs. Pupko's Beard*. "The Son from America" is a fable about a man who comes back to his Polish *shtetl* in his old age to share with his parents the wealth he has acquired in America but discovers that they are content with the little they have, that in their serene and pious world his hard-won dollars are worthless. Although the demons take a backseat in this collection, they pop up occasionally, as in "The Lantuch," a tale related by garrulous Aunt Yentl concerning a familiar spirit of a settled variety who does household tasks efficiently enough but exacts a sinister price from his hostesses.

The title story in this collection is one of Isaac's finest—and most complex. It is a strange tale about a grandfather and a grandmother, both saintly seeming souls who after their deaths are impersonated by evil spirits that attempt to corrupt their granddaughter, Akhsa. They cause her to reject her suitor, Zemach, and to read the forbidden New Testament. One morning the girl wakes to find a crown of feathers beneath her pillow. Who braided it? How did it get there? This magical object leads Akhsa to visit a priest, and she converts to Christianity, shocking the whole Jewish community in her village. When she marries a squire who has inherited his uncle's estate, the evil spirits at last cease to taunt her. Akhsa goes to live in comfort with her squire in another town, but, still in her thirties, she comes suddenly to feel old. She hears that the synagogue in her native village has burned down, that there have been epidemics, that the Jews there have become paupers forced to beg for their bread. Akhsa cannot go back, but she thinks she knows what has happened to the Jews in her town—they are the victims of the "black powers" that rule the entire universe. She begins to suspect that the crown of feathers she found under her pillow was woven by the Devil himself, and she summons the Evil One, ready to give herself to him. Satan, though, seems more interested in confusing her with paradoxes: "The truth is that there is no truth." In the end Akhsa goes off to look for Zemach. She will give up the comforts and security of her life with the squire for the man she should rightfully have married in the first place. Zemach and Akhsa wed and live in poverty in a hut with a dirt floor, but Akhsa is at peace because she has overcome all temptations and given up worldly comforts to be a proper Jewish wife. Never again can she be confused by deceitful advice offered by creatures of illusion.

"Lost" is another story in this collection dealing with the depredations of demonic powers who, in this case, cause a woman to lose her money, her possessions, even her fiancé, by means of their mischief. Yet in this tale there is a deliberate, almost Jamesian ambiguity: Was it really the demons who ruined Anna Barzel, or something self-destructive in her own nature?

"The Captive" is set in modern Israel, but the theme is medieval, involving the widow of a dead painter from Poland who holds a living artist captive as a forger of canvases by her late spouse. In the end Isaac himself becomes her captive too, as the ghostwriter of his late friend's memoirs. In "Property," a strongly ironic tale, Isaac draws on his experiences as a Yiddish journalist on the *Forward* to describe the efforts of a literary anarchist named Max Peshkin to apply his theories about the immorality of owning property to the realm of sexual relations.

Another story with a similar setting is "The Cabalist of East Broadway," one of Isaac's cafeteria tales, this time about Joel Yabloner, an emaciated Yiddish cabalist, the victim of innumerable misfortunes, who at last finds love, honor, and esteem as a literary lion after he moves to Tel Aviv. Some time later Isaac sees Joel again, sitting alone, disheveled and broken, in a cafeteria on East Broadway.

Why did Yabloner give up his worldly success in Israel to return to a life of obscurity and deprivation on New York's Lower East Side? Where do these demons come from who drive people, like Akhsa in "A Crown of Feathers," to reject wealth or fame or the "good life" to chase after a different kind of salvation? Do we invent our own downfalls, or does the Devil drive us to them? Is it really the truth that there is no truth, or is this just one of Satan's diabolical sophistries? More than one tale in the collection has a Rashomon-like quality; it's difficult to know what to believe even after the evidence of witnesses is presented: Did Morris Terkletaub in "Neighbors" really have an affair with Isadora Duncan, or was he the outrageous liar his friends suspected he might be? Are Mathilda and her son Izzy in "The Dance" incestuous lovers, or is Izzy simply her brute of a husband reincarnated? Is Max in "The Third One" (another cafeteria tale) really a homosexual, or is he just playing the part in order to get the woman he is after into his bed?

In Isaac's stories the motivations behind people's actions are more often than not veiled in mystery. Why does the heroine of "The Bishop's Robe" join a Christian cult in Los Angeles, lose her fortune to charlatans, and drive her husband and herself to suicide? Why does the impractical publisher in "The Magazine" found journals that are doomed to failure?

Sometimes Isaac's irony alone sustains a tale, as in "Her Son," in the course of which a Yiddish writer finds himself adopted by the son of his own dead mistress and the man she has married. Isaac's skill at exposing pretension is employed when the writer telling him the story moves with breathtaking ease from the cosmic to the mundane—a trick of deflation at which Isaac is particularly adept:

" 'I'm not a scientist, but I've read some science. I know the theories and all the babble about evolution. It's a big lie. The universe happened in one second. God alone, if he exists, simply became. There was nothing. Suddenly it all was there—God, the world, life, love, death. Oh, here are our blintzes.' "

Is it all a "big lie"? And if so, how did we get here, and what are we doing on this curious planet where passions push us to folly and the most plausible things deceive? Never mind. Better to enjoy a good meal. And yet:

" 'The blintzes didn't come all of a sudden,' I remarked.

" 'Eh? Not at Sholum's Café. If this cook were God, we would still be in Genesis.' "

A Crown of Feathers is a rich stew, a *tsimmes* of characters comic and pathetic, all pursuing the eternal questions, trying to distinguish good from evil, truth from lies, reality from fantasy, in a hopeless battle where the human mind is outmatched by hidden powers and where once again only the devout can make peace with the pain of existence.

Despite the power of the stories in this book, the thoughtful, balanced order of their appearance, the excellence of their translations, and the distinguished award it won, *A Crown of Feathers* did not please everyone. "No single story in this new collection," wrote Seymour Kleinberg in *The Nation*, "good as many of them are, meets the standard set by 'Gimpel the Fool,' 'Blood' or 'The Slaughterer.' It seems to me that the more worldly the author becomes, the more private, idiosyncratic and self-indulgent the fiction grows. Again, Singer's delightful obsession with the supernatural, which in his earlier fiction could be taken as symbolic of humanity's essential irrationality, now seems less metaphoric, peculiarly literal. *A Crown of Feathers* is the least rewarding of Singer's short-story collections." Yet even Mr. Kleinberg hastened to add that it was "only in comparison with his past achievements" that the new book fell short.

Crawford Woods, in *The New Republic*, disagreed. Although, as he noted, the tales came to us through the mediation of translators and co-translators, "The singular thing about these stories . . . is that they speak with one voice—clear, direct and uncolored, the cozy drone of a natural storyteller . . . a kind of chant soon fills the reader's ears. . . ." Woods noted that the tales took joy in paradox and found them "often tragic but never sad." "If their resemblance to each other," he concluded, "makes the book seem long, it also makes it cut deep. What might be a sign of limitation in a lesser writer in Singer must be seen as wisdom."

Peter Prescott, in *Newsweek*, expressed unqualified praise for the collection: "I believe that Singer in his short and humorous tales drawn from an old tradition celebrates the dignity, mystery and unexpected joy of living with more art and fervor than any other writer alive."

❃

March 1, 1977

Laurie Colwin is a good-looking young woman with long, tawny blond hair and gray eyes. She lives in a spacious garden apartment in the Chelsea district of Manhattan's West Side. There's a huge, friendly kitchen, a fireplace, a luxuriance of plants, a cat.

Laurie was born in New York City but spent the first seven years of her life in a small rural community on Long Island. Later the family lived in Chicago and in Melrose Park, Pennsylvania. Her mother was Jewish. Her father, who was not, worked for many years as a fund-raising executive for the United Jewish Appeal. Laurie went to Bard College and Columbia University. Many of her short stories have appeared in *The New Yorker* as well as in *Redbook*, *Mademoiselle*, and *Antaeus*. A collection of her stories, *Passion and Affect*, was published by Viking in 1974. A novel, *Shine On, Bright and Dangerous Object*, appeared in 1975. In 1976 her story "The Lone Pilgrim" won the O. Henry Short Story Award. In 1978, *Happy All the Time*, another novel, published by Alfred A. Knopf, was widely praised.

Laurie first met Isaac at a literary party in 1969, given in New York by his German publisher. There she asked Lila Karpf to introduce her to Isaac Singer "because I thought he was a great writer." It turned out that they shared *The New Yorker* editor Rachel MacKenzie. The following week, when Laurie went to see Rachel about a story of hers—her first to be accepted by *The New Yorker*—she told the editor how much she had liked Isaac's story "The Key," which had recently appeared in the magazine. "Write him a letter about it," Rachel suggested.

"I did too. I sent him a fan letter. I was working at Viking at the time, in the foreign rights department. The phone rang on my desk, and a voice said, 'Miss Colwin?' I had no idea who it was until he told me. I said, 'Oh, Mr. Singer!' And he said he wanted me to come and talk to him. I asked, 'What about?' and he answered, 'About translation.'

"I met him up at the old Tip-Toe Inn on Broadway near Seventy-fifth Street. He told me he would like me to work with him as a translator. I warned him I didn't know Yiddish, and he answered that wouldn't matter as long as I knew English. How did he know I was good enough? Well, Rachel had said I was a good writer, so I must be a good writer."

Laurie, then twenty-five, was the youngest translator Isaac ever employed. They began work soon after their first meeting on a story that later appeared in *The New Yorker*. Sometimes they would meet on Saturdays for lunch at the Famous on West Seventy-second Street or the Tip-Toe Inn or the Sterling Cafeteria. But usually Laurie would go to Isaac's apartment direct from work at Viking and work late. One night she came home to find that her cat had given birth to six kittens. She called them the Isaac Singer Memorial Litter.

Laurie was surprised by the variety of mail that piled up outside Isaac's door, especially from *The Republican Monthly*, which he was receiving from the Republican Party. How could a man like that, she wondered, get involved with those Republicans? Isaac's answer to this is that after all he had witnessed and read of the suffering Jews endured in the name of socialism, he tended to retreat more and more to a conservative political view. Besides, he has explained, when he voted for Nixon, it was because he was sure if Nixon were president it would be good for Israel.

Translating with Isaac was a revelation to Laurie. Like Dorothea Straus, she watched with amazement as he answered every phone call, then took up exactly where he had left off as though there had been no interruption.

"I would sit on the couch," she recalls, "he would sit on his striped chair, the parakeets would fly in and out. I would sit there and take everything down in longhand, until one day I said, 'Mr. Singer, I don't want to write in longhand anymore. I want to use your typewriter.' " Isaac said the noise would disturb him, but Laurie got her way and translated four more stories for him on a Smith Corona electric portable.

Laurie worked with Isaac for about two years. She translated a number of the tales that appeared in *The New Yorker*, including "The Magazine," "The Third One," "A Day in Coney Island," and "A Crown of Feathers." As for "A Crown of Feathers," she had suggested, " 'Let's do a story from the old country.' And he came up with that one."

Laurie's own literary heroes and heroines, she says, are Charles Dickens, Jane Austen, John Cheever, and Mavis Gallant—storytellers all. "Like Isaac's, their work is translucent. There's nothing obscure about their writing. But Isaac—well, he's one of a kind. He's the last of the Mohicans—and he knows it. Here is this fellow who grew up in a medieval tradition—where the men wore long dresses and the women wore wigs, and it's gone—all gone. It will never be again. Those stable roots that took five centuries to build were wiped out. And Isaac grew up with all that. And then he went to Warsaw and said, 'Oh, my God, there are guys here who don't wear gaberdine coats, and girls who show their own hair, and they smoke cigarettes and drink wine and whiskey'—like a country bumpkin, you know, on his first visit.

"I have many feelings about him when I look back. He was always full of himself, and so proud of his awards, but at the same time he would sit there with his Mont Blanc fountain pen and go over the pages—over and over— and I would see the precision and clarity as he struggled after the right word—the absolute ruthlessness of the way he went over his own prose. He wanted it right. He taught me one of the most valuable lessons as a writer— treat your own work as if somebody else wrote it. Don't fall in love with your own words. Make sure it comes out absolutely right. . . ."

"Working with him as a translator, I wished so many times that I knew Yiddish. When it came to some phrase like 'nest egg' and he would say 'egg nest,' why, that was easy, but sometimes I'd ask him to read me some sentences in Yiddish just so I'd get an idea of the rhythm. . . .

"When I think of it—that man doesn't have *any* language anymore. Unless it's your own language, you can never really be fluent in it."

Of Isaac's novels Laurie's favorite is *Enemies, A Love Story*. "It's a gem.

It's like Nabokov's *Laughter in the Dark*—just perfect." On the whole, though, like many others, she considers Isaac more a master of the short story than of the novel. She shares his admiration of clarity and his lack of enchantment with Joyce ("Graduate schools are invented for guys like Joyce"). "I'm not crazy about trail-blazers," she says. "I like basic old traditional storytelling. I guess that's why Singer and I were able to work so well together."

❁

Passions and Other Stories (Farrar, Straus and Giroux), the latest collection of stories by Isaac Singer, appeared in the fall of 1975. Many of the twenty tales in the book had first been published in *The New Yorker.* The translators listed include Blanche and Joseph Nevel, Joseph Singer, Herbert R. Lottman, Ruth Schachner Finkel, Dorothea Straus, Rosanna Gerber Cohen, Hanna Koevary, and Marion Magid. Seven of the English versions are attributed to Joseph Singer. One tale, "The Adventure," is "translated by the author."

"As the reader can see," Isaac writes in his preface to *Passions*, "many of these stories were translated by me in collaboration with those whose names are given at the end of each story. I have worked on these translations with my editors, Rachel MacKenzie, Robert Giroux, and lately also William Maxwell, to all of whom I am grateful."

He continues: "While obscurity of content and style may now be the fashion, clarity remains the ambition of this writer. This is especially important since I deal with unique characters in unique circumstances, a group of people who are still a riddle to the world and often to themselves—the Jews of Eastern Europe, specifically the Yiddish-speaking Jews who perished in Poland and those who emigrated to the U.S.A. The longer I live with them and write about them, the more I am baffled by the richness of their individuality and (since I am one of them) by my own whims and passions. While I hope and pray for the resurrection, I dare to say that, for me, these people are all living right now. In literature, as in our dreams, death does not exist."

The *mise-en-scène* in *Passions* shifts from Argentina to Portugal to Miami to New York to Warsaw. The collection opens with "Hanka," that eerie story of a visit to the Jewish quarter of Buenos Aires in the company of a living ghost who is a survivor of the Holocaust in Poland. "Sabbath in Portugal" is a tale that describes an encounter with a latter-day Marrano—a crypto-Jew who admits his faith to Isaac on a spooky Sabbath afternoon in

Lisbon. "Old Love," which Isaac has since been trying to turn into a play, takes place in an eleventh-story apartment in a Miami Beach condominium much like Isaac and Alma's. Here, Harry, a lonely Polish-born widower of eighty-two, bereft of wife, children, and grandchildren (they live in Canada), derives little comfort from the money he has accumulated until he meets a neighbor, an emancipated widow, as displaced and lonesome as himself. They talk of traveling around the world together and settling in Israel; but it is really too late for either of them. Melancholy over the indifference of her daughter, who has gone off to live in British Columbia, the widow does away with herself, and Harry is left alone again in his fine apartment high above the sea. "Errors" brings us back once again to the Polish past, this time in a fable narrated by a glazier in a little village who deplores society's growing leniency in tolerating errors. The plot concerns the consequences suffered by a squire who protests too loudly when a princess gets his name wrong, and the punishment meted out to a scribe by a rabbi who finds a mistake in a holy book. The fable questions whether, in a world where "everything comes from divine sources," there really can be such a thing as an error. One memorable literary aphorism of Isaac's appears in "Errors": "An author doesn't die of typhus, but of typos."

"The Admirer" finds Isaac in a situation common enough in his life—in an encounter with an admiring reader. But the visit from Elizabeth Abigail de Sollar proves to be a shattering experience. The woman—who is obviously mad—starts out by claiming to be distantly related to the author and by having an epileptic fit on his living-room floor. Before the nightmare is over, the narrator has received threatening phone calls from his admirer's husband, her mother-in-law, and her lawyer and, seeking help for the patient, has locked himself out of his own apartment.

"The Yearning Heifer" is an anecdote about the days in 1938, when Isaac was writing a column of facts for the *Forward* and living in a furnished room on the fourth floor of a New York walkup. He sees an advertisement for a "room on a farm with food, ten dollars weekly." Having just broken up with a girlfriend, he takes the next bus to a country town in the Catskills called Mountaindale. The pastoral retreat proves to be a ramshackle country house presided over by a harsh-sounding couple straight out of *Cold Comfort Farm*—except that the proprietor reveals himself to be a Polish refugee who is in the habit of reading his visitor's newspaper column faithfully every week. Before the first day is over, Isaac decides to stay on with Sam and Bessie, who manage to engineer a reconciliation between their guest and his estranged girlfriend. How the heifer got into the title is another matter, one resolved winningly before the final page. The farm in the tale, incidentally, sounds a bit like the farm in the Catskills where Isaac met Alma.

In "The New Year Party" the scene shifts to New York and an evening with a group of "Yiddishists" in the home of a Jewish poet. Isaac displays his talent for caricature in his portraits of the guests: the poet, Pearl Leipziger, a short woman with "a high bosom, broad hips, a round forehead, a hooked nose, and large black eyes" whose bosom "glitters with a golden Star of David," who "wears a diamond ring and long earrings," and whose living room and life "are cluttered with bric-a-brac"; Mira Royskez, an eighty-year-old writer from Warsaw with "innumerable wrinkles" and lively eyes; Matilda Feingevirtz, a poet with a huge bust and the face of a peasant who brings along syrup for the Chanukah pancakes to be served at the party; Bertha Kosotzky, who has carrot-colored hair and writes pulp novels for the Yiddish press; Comrade Tsloveh, a "midget of a woman" alleged to have played a key role in the 1905 Revolution in Russia; Harry, a tall Jew with freckles who looks like an Irishman—and has forgotten to bring the duck for the dinner party; and, most memorable of all, the rich real-estate operator keeping Pearl Leipziger. In the course of the tale we meet Boris Lemkin, high-spirited patron of Yiddish writers and artists, who occupies an apartment on Park Avenue with Harry, who serves as his cook and butler. Before the night is over Boris has denounced his mistress and her poetry and has been revealed by Harry as a lecherous old miser. When he dies, Boris leaves the devoted Harry nothing. Yet Harry, who still loves him, is concerned that Boris has no headstone and is last heard of trying to raise the money to put one up at his grave.

"The Sorcerer" is about a Polish squire with occult powers and the "court Jew" who handles his business affairs, tends to his needs, and even brings him his own wife to sleep with on request. The squire's lust for the ideal woman impels him eventually to build one piecemeal, a sort of female Golem.

Set in Poland, "Three Encounters" is a memoir of the time when Isaac was seventeen, rebelling against becoming a rabbi, entering into a marriage arranged by a matchmaker and wearing gaberdines and earlocks. Isaac recalls how his brother summoned him to Warsaw to become a proofreader. Before leaving the little town in Galicia where he is staying with his father and mother, he is paid a farewell visit by Rivkele, the local shoemaker's daughter, who has just become engaged to her father's apprentice. Isaac tells her about his literary ambitions. He shows her a copy of the magazine on which he'll be working, tells her the Middle Ages are over, this is the twentieth century, the "world has awakened!" "I told her about Warsaw, Zionism, Socialism, Yiddish literature and the Writers' Club. . . . I showed her pictures in the magazine of Einstein, Chagall, the dancer Nijinsky, and of my brother." Isaac tries to persuade her to forget her engagement, go off with him to Warsaw, become an actress, travel with him all the way to California. Rivkele listens to everything but assures Isaac that such behavior would break her mother's heart: "The outcry would be worse than if I converted." But Rivkele turns up later in Warsaw—pregnant by a visitor from America. Now, too late, she wants to run away with Isaac, who first planted all these modern thoughts in her head. Years later, poor and lonely in New

York, he comes home one night to find Rivkele waiting for him. She has converted; her family has "sat shiva" (spent a week in mourning) for her—the fate of converts in devout Jewish families. The child she bore years ago has been put in a foundling home. She came to America with one man, split up with him, then married a Catholic from Chicago who has stabbed a fellow in an argument and gone to jail. She is working as a waitress in an Italian restaurant while she waits for him to be released. But she is ready to leave him—and marry Isaac. She wants to be a "Jewish daughter again." "You are responsible," she says, "for what happened to me." Was there really a Rivkele in Isaac's life? There's no use asking him. In these tales facts fuse with fiction at such white heat that the two become inseparable.

The narrator of "The Adventure" is David Greidinger, a Warsaw magazine editor who is invited to dinner by Morris Shapiro, the owner of the printing shop where the magazine is published. David meets Morris's wife, who confides to him that her husband has become "impotent toward her" and her doctor has advised her to have an affair to prevent a nervous breakdown. She has chosen David since she is an admirer of his writings (David bears a strong resemblance to Isaac). David agrees to let her have an answer in three days. By the time the three days are up, he is a nervous wreck. He gives up his job on the magazine and goes to work on another, and tells the woman he cannot accept her proposal. Years later he meets Mrs. Shapiro, now a widow, who thanks him for saving her from her "downfall."

Passions ends with the title story, which illustrates the book's theme most dramatically. Once more the narrator, Zalman the glazier, tells three tales, the first about a village peddler in Poland named Leib Belkes who decides he is going to build an exact model of the ancient Temple in Jerusalem. His wife resents the attention he gives to this project and either destroys it or encourages the firemen in town to destroy it as a hazard: Zalman isn't sure which. In any case the peddler's temple, just like the original it was modeled after, is demolished. Leib goes into a decline. He disappears, only to turn up after five years, announcing that he has been in the Holy Land. He has gone there on foot and returned by boat.

In the second tale a tailor with the same name as the richest man in town is called up by mistake to carry the scroll of the Torah through the synagogue on Simchas Torah, the holiday of Rejoicing over the Law. Discovered and denounced as an ignoramus with no right to this honor, he swears that within the year he will become the greatest scholar in the district. The local usurer says that if that happens he will build the tailor a house in the marketplace free of charge. The tailor replies that if it doesn't he will make an ankle-length coat of fox fur for the usurer's wife. The whole town takes sides in the matter while the tailor gives up his tailoring and apprentices himself to a Talmud teacher. The tailor wins the wager, and the following year is once more given the honor of carrying the scroll through the synagogue on Simchas Torah. The usurer has to build him a house—which the tailor wants not for himself, as it turns out, but as "an inn for yeshiva boys and poor travelers."

The third tale of obsession is about a cabalist named Rabbi Mendel who likes to fast, immerse himself in cold baths, and generally abuse his body, which he regards as an enemy. In his old age Rabbi Mendel announces to his dwindling followers that from now on his life is going to be one long Day of Atonement—"except for the Sabbath and Feast Days!" And he makes good his promise. Rabbi Mendel, it seems, is one of the "hidden saints for whose sake God spares the world from destruction." He dies in the midst of a Day of Atonement prayer. "Everything can become a passion, even serving God," Isaac writes in a statement of the book's implicit theme.

The appearance of *Passions* prompted a critic who signed himself J.L.C. in the *Saturday Review* to say that Isaac was "among the greatest storytellers of our time" and to praise him for continuing to focus, "with unwavering clarity," on the Jews of Poland slaughtered by Hitler as well as those who escaped. "For all their diversity," he wrote, "Singer's stories are animated, in one way or another, by a religious imagination with the same moral vision, stubbornly struggling to come to terms with the enigmatic relationships between the Jews and their God."

Alfred Kazin, writing in *The New Republic,* found the collection "uneven" and felt the stories often had "the effect of anecdotes." He said, "Singer, like the ever-dwindling Yiddish audience for whom he writes directly in the *Jewish Daily Forward,* is endlessly fascinated by Jews . . . from the Bible to the 20th-century apocalypse. Singer portrays himself in these stories as a Jew also baffled by the convolutions of Jewish existence, and the exalted claims made for it. . . . The problem with this book . . . is that Singer's naturally dry, matter-of-fact, laconic wit shines somewhat artificially in translation. The more anecdotal stories, which depend on the dramatic polarities of Yiddish speech, read as if the translations had been energized to cover up some unavoidable Yiddish intonation."

Newsweek noted that in the collection "passion takes many forms." W. R. R. Branca, writing in a publication frankly called *Best Sell,* extolled Isaac's "disarmingly clear and direct" style, noted the increasing use of his own experiences in these stories, and praised their "quality of mystery, of the unexpected." The book as a whole gave Mr. Branca "the unsettling feeling that behind our veneer of civilization lies the primitive beast seeking to emerge. At evoking this feeling Singer is a master craftsman."

❀

Since the publication of *Passions* in 1975 new stories, meticulously edited by Rachel MacKenzie, have appeared at fairly frequent intervals in *The New Yorker*. Most of the translations are credited to Joseph Singer. These tales continue to explore the by now familiar landscapes of Isaac Singer's world— the Warsaw of old, the Israel where he has lectured and passed many summers, upper Manhattan, where he still walks and window shops, feeds pigeons, and entertains admiring readers.

Some of Isaac's less ardent admirers, often readers who pursue his work only in *The New Yorker*, complain of disappointment over the familiarity of themes and characters. And it is true that these shorter works of fiction represent only one aspect of his talent. Just the same, every one of them reflects his remarkable ability as a storyteller, some break brand-new ground, and a number of them, including some of the travel stories discussed earlier, can be counted among his outstanding achievements.

"Elka and Meir" (*The New Yorker*, May 23, 1977) is set in the underworld of Warsaw, the terrain of his recent *Yarma and Kayle*. Meir is a thief and safecracker, a tough Samson of a man whose answer to being arrested is simply to wrench open the handcuffs or break down the door of the patrol wagon. Meir goes straight, gets a job at the Warsaw Benevolent Burial Society, which supplies burial plots and shrouds for penniless Jews in the city, and marries a beautiful woman named Beilka Litvak, who works as a cook in a wealthy home. When Beilka fails to become pregnant, loses her looks, and becomes quarrelsome, Meir leaves her for a girl named Red Elka, who looks after the female corpses at the society. Although Beilka won't give Meir a divorce, he spends more and more of his time with Red Elka, helping to bring in the corpses of Jews, first while Warsaw is occupied by the Russians and later when the Germans take over. Meir dreams of going to America with Elka and opening a funeral parlor. He refuses to listen when his wife tells him Elka is really a Krochmalna Street prostitute. When Beilka dies, Meir and Elka are free at last to be together. But they are so busy bringing in corpses that they scarcely have time to make love. When Elka finds out that she is going to die of cancer, she picks her successor, a cousin named Dishka, as Meir's lover and co-worker in the burial society. But Meir and Dishka die before Elka when a hearse crashes. In her last days, however, as she lies moribund in a hospital bed, Elka is serene in the thought that when the Messiah comes, she and Meir, with a branch of myrtle, will at last find their way to the Promised Land. A sweet, strange, touching tale.

The story "Two" (*The New Yorker*, December 20, 1976) belongs in the same category as "Yentl the Yeshiva Boy" and "Zeitle and Rickel," with their lesbian overtones. But in "Two" the theme of homosexuality is for the first time explicitly drawn (no Shakespearean misconstruals, no confounded identities): A pair of gay Hasidim in turn-of-the-century Poland come out of the closet. Zissel, whose parents really wanted a girl, goes off to yeshiva and falls in love with the handsome, worldly Ezriel from Lublin. They are both married off to women but leave their wives and fall into each other's arms. For years they live together, but when they fall on evil times, Zissel must disguise himself as a girl and go to work as a bath attendant to earn their keep. There, suddenly smitten by a beautiful, rich bride-to-be of seventeen, Zissel realizes he is bisexual. Before the story is over, Zissel and the girl drown in a ritual bath, and Ezriel is murdered by a gang of ruffians. Bizarre events, yet essentially the tale rings true.

"Yachne and Shmelke" (*The New Yorker*, February 14, 1977), set in old Poland, concerns a pampered Jewish daughter who marries a yeshiva student so religious that bride and groom have to interrupt the consummation of their marriage to search for the skullcap that has fallen off his head. Yet they are wildly happy—until Shmelke dies during a journey when a bridge collapses in a storm. But there is a consolation: Yachne is pregnant and will have a child to remember Shmelke by. A sentimental sketch but, again, a touching one. Both these tales would seem to indicate Isaac's growing fear of sudden death.

"Two Weddings and One Divorce" (*The New Yorker*, August 29, 1977), translated by Isaac and Alma Singer, takes us back once more to Krochmalna Street, where a shoemaker has killed himself because his fiancée went off and married someone else. The event is being discussed in a study house by Zalman the glazier, an uneducated man who recites fifty pages of the Zohar every day although he does not understand a word of Aramaic; old Levi Yitzchak, who is afflicted with trachoma and must wear sunglasses night and day; and Meyer the Eunuch, who is lucid for two weeks of every month and strangely incoherent for the other two. The men regale one another with tales of other incidents brought to mind by the recent tragedy—stories of marriages that ended in death for one or both of the partners.

Zalman tells of a young student who pretends to be stupid so he won't have to marry the girl his father has picked out for him. Instead he marries a girl with fins in place of hands and feet. She bears him five perfectly normal daughters but dies after turning into a fish.

Levi Yitzchak counters with the example of a dying man who divorces his own wife to spare her from having to go all the way to America after his death to ask his brother for permission to remarry. According to Jewish law a widow must marry her late husband's brother if he wants her. But in one of those reversals so common in Isaac's work the husband doesn't die. The wife, who can no longer share her former husband's life, renounces the world in her distress and goes off to the poorhouse to live as a pauper. But when they die, they are buried next to each other. Separated in life, they are united in death, for, Isaac says, only bodies are governed by the law of divorce; souls cannot be divorced.

It is Meyer the Eunuch who has the last word. He tells of a prodigy, a *yenuka*, in the city of Praga before the Hasidic movement was founded, who is regarded as a wonder rabbi. The *yenuka* is androgynous, yet he decides to marry. The bride he chooses is also androgynous, and the two of them appear at their wedding in strange garb—he in a white robe and cowl, that look like a winding sheet, his bride in a white gown that shimmers with the hues of lightning. When she lifts her veil, the wedding guests see two *yenukas*, their faces pale and shining, their eyes glowing with love. The groom dies on his wedding night. Meyer the Eunuch never explains what happens to the bride. It is the time of the full moon and Meyer's confusion is upon him; he can't continue coherently.

"Tanhum" (*The New Yorker*, November 17, 1975) is about a Hasidic scholar in Poland who wants to emulate his prospective father-in-law, at once a man of learning and a prosperous lumber merchant. But Tanhum isn't cut out for the practical life. Instead of proceeding with the marriage and making good, he wastes his time pondering the questions that haunt him: If God is merciful, and surely He is, then why are innocent children and dumb beasts allowed to suffer? Why is man condemned to die? Why have God's miracles stopped? Why have God's chosen people had to endure exile for two thousand years? Tanhum can't find the answers to his questions in any of the sacred books. Finally he abandons his fiancée along with all worldly ambitions and flees to an obscure yeshiva, where he gives up meat and wine, puts pebbles in his shoes, and lives as a total ascetic, sleeping on a bench behind a study-house stove.

"The Power of Darkness," (*The New Yorker*, February 2, 1976) takes us back to Number 10 Krochmalna Street. There are interesting glimpses here of Isaac's mother (when she was excited, Isaac says, her blond wig would fly into disarray, as though a strong wind had caught it) and of Isaac at eleven, characteristically eavesdropping on adult conversations while pretending to read a storybook. The boy visits a tailor named Selig, a man whose exposure to Enlightenment has filled his head with heretical ideas. He gives vent to these notions in Isaac's presence, questioning the teachings of the boy's parents and even suggesting that perhaps there is no God—or, if there is, that maybe He's a gentile, not a Jew. Isaac covers his ears when he hears this, knowing that his father despises such talk.

The focus of the story, however, is on Henia Dvosha, who is making herself die because she wants her husband to marry her sister—to Isaac's utter bafflement. After Henia Dvosha wills herself to death, Isaac personally encounters the primal scene—catching a glimpse of his parents in bed—and finds this situation confusing as well. The thought of his pious and holy father in bed with a woman is almost unthinkable. If his father can commit such an act, is there anything that *can't* happen? In the end the dead Henia Dvosha has her way from the grave, and her husband marries her sister, Tzeitel. Soon after the wedding Henia Dvosha's spirit takes up residence in Tzeitel's left ear and begins to torment her with renditions of religious songs, recitations of laments for the Destruction of the Temple, and even threnodies for the victims of the *Titanic*. Word spreads through Krochmalna Street that a dybbuk has settled in Tzeitel's ear, and a nerve specialist is called in. But World War I breaks out, and there are other things to think about. Then news arrives that the marriage so strangely planned by Henia Dvosha is breaking up. Isaac's mother is astonished, for supposedly the couple were very much in love when they wed. The explanation, it seems, is that every night the spirit of the dead Henia Dvosha comes and gets into bed between her former husband and her sister. This Isaac's mother understands. The living die so that the dead may live, she murmurs.

In "A Cage for Satan" (*The New Yorker*, May 24, 1976) we find a holy rabbi obsessed with the idea of capturing Satan himself. He even constructs a cage for the Evil One. Late one night he awakes to discover the intruder he has so long anticipated. He struggles with the figure in the dark, throws it to the floor, and chokes it—only to learn the next day that the demon he has murdered was merely an orphan boy, a young burglar. The rest of the holy man's days are devoted to remorse and atonement. He deems himself unworthy of being buried in the Jewish cemetery. The elders of the town disagree: The rabbi's intentions were honorable, although his objective was futile. Satan can never be caged or killed. He will exist for as long as the world itself exists.

One of Isaac's recent tales, "The Boy Knows the Truth" (*The New Yorker*, October 17, 1977), is the story of Rabbi Gabriel Klintower, a spiritual leader much respected in his Polish home town. Rabbi Klintower will not pray for women as his father and grandfather did before him, because he doesn't consider himself pure enough to accept the petitions of females. He is a sensual, hotblooded man, prone to the temptations of lust, assailed by venal thoughts even when he is in the midst of prayer, and he doesn't trust himself. His susceptibility is heightened by the circumstance that his wife, although she has borne him a whole family of children, is now ill and has closed her bedroom doors to him. Temptation enters the scene in the form of a widow, a female relative he doesn't even want to let into his study. She gets in anyhow and later comes to haunt his dreams, until he begins to wish his ailing wife would leave as soon as possible for the next world so he can marry her. When his shameful wish is granted, he is overcome with guilt. It is a relief to be able to report that, although he resigns from his post, he ultimately recovers his senses. How? His late wife appears in a dream, as radiant as an angel, and talks him out of marrying his attractive cousin; chastened, he returns to his vocation.

"The Boy Knows the Truth" (the title comes from a scene in which the rabbi asks one of his own young students for advice) is like an entire Singer novel in miniature, complete with imps and Satanic temptations. The pietistic ending is somewhat counterbalanced by the skeptical assertion that God never did answer Job's questions, that all He did was boast about his

own powers. Yet the message is that a man, particularly a man whose vocation is the rabbinate, must continue to be a Jew even if he has lost the world
to come, as Rabbi Klintower apparently has.

Only a few of Isaac's *New Yorker* stories are credited solely to the author,
and this is one of them. Isaac notes, however, that both Rachel MacKenzie
and his Doubleday editor, Eve Roshevsky, visited him while he was sum-
mering with Alma in Wengen and helped him polish the English prose so
that this story, too, was actually the product of collaboration of a sort.

"Not for the Sabbath" (*The New Yorker*, November 27, 1978) is one of
Aunt Yentl's tales, told on a Saturday afternoon to her neighbor Chaya Riva
and their friend Reitze Breindels while eleven-year-old Isaac eavesdrops
from a storage room behind the porch—after being dismissed by the
women, who regard the subject matter as unfit for his young ears. Chaya
Riva's grandson has been slapped by a teacher, which reminds Aunt Yentl of
the transgressions of another teacher, Fivke, a sadistic fellow who used to
terrorize his charges and administer fierce whippings to them at a cheder in
Lublin. Backing and filling in her own inimitable non-sequitur style, Aunt
Yentl tells how Dosha, the mother of one of Fivke's victims, came to the
school to protest but, being a masochist, fell in love with the cruel Fivke.
Aunt Yentl's tale—which she has to be urged to continue since she keeps insisting it's not a fit story to tell on the Sabbath—grows more convoluted with
every sentence. Fivke is dismissed from his post, becomes a teacher of the
children of thieves in a town called Piask; becomes a thief himself and a
leader of thieves—their rabbi, in fact; is arrested along with a group of them
in another town they have come to rob. Dosha hires a lawyer to help free
Fivke, sleeps with the local governor to get the other thieves off; turns to
prostitution; runs a brothel where Fivke is her procurer; and eventually is
whipped to death by him. By the time Aunt Yentl's story is over, so is the
Sabbath and it's time for the evening prayers.

❀

In Isaac's later novels even as in his short stories and memoirs it becomes increasingly difficult to disentangle autobiography from fiction. In *Shosha*, his
latest book to appear in English (Farrar, Straus and Giroux, 1978), the narrator is a struggling writer named Aaron Greidinger who has returned to
Warsaw to take a job as a proofreader and translator after teaching in
"muddy villages" in the Polish countryside; in terms of his character and experiences, it is impossible to separate the invented Aaron from the real
Isaac. The title character is the same Shosha who appears in *In My Father's
Court* and several earlier stories, Isaac's childhood companion at Number

10 Krochmalna Street. "She was my first love and actually these kinds of love never die." Set in the 1930s, when Poland was on the brink of the Nazi invasion, *Shosha* is one of those "What if?" tales—this time what if Isaac had stayed in Poland until the Nazi invaders were already on their way to Warsaw?

In the novel Aaron becomes involved shortly after his return with Dora Stolnitz—another woman we can recognize from Isaac's past—"whose goal was to settle in Soviet Russia, the land of socialism," and whose "hollow slogans and bombastic clichés" have already begun to get on Aaron's nerves. Aaron also has encounters of various kinds with Sam Dreiman, an American producer who has come to Warsaw to produce plays and has given Aaron an advance on a play in which Dreiman's wife, Betty, is to star; the prosperous Haim Chentshiner and his wife Celia, who cuts her husband's hair, trims his nails, and has love affairs behind his back with other men; and Morris Feitelzohn, a lusty philosopher whose love of life and fondness for complacent women and elusive philosophical concepts recalls Abram Shapiro in *The Family Moskat*. Celia and Betty are vigorous, fiercely opinionated women of the classic Singer type, and Aaron finds time in the course of the tale to go to bed with both of them. But the book isn't really about these worldly creatures or about the disastrous production of Aaron's play. The book is mainly and most significantly about Shosha herself and the world of Krochmalna Street to which Aaron is impelled to return after many years of absence. What did the street look like in those days? Isaac tells us in detail, describing a walk back into his past with the actress Betty:

> . . . the stench I recalled from my childhood struck me first—
> a blend of burned oil, rotten fruit, and chimney smoke. Every-
> thing was the same—the cobblestone pavement, the steep gutter,
> the balconies hung with wash. We passed a factory with wire-lat-
> ticed windows and a blind wall with a wooden gate I never saw
> open in all my youth. Every house here was bound up with mem-
> ories. No. 5 contained a yeshiva in which I had studied for a term.
> There was a ritual bath in the courtyard, where matrons came in
> the evening to immerse themselves. I used to see them emerge
> clean and flushed. Someone told me that this building had been
> the home of Rabbi Itche Meir Alter, the founder of the Gur dy-
> nasty generations ago. In my time the yeshiva had been part of the
> Grodzisk house of prayer. Its beadle was a drunk. When he had a
> drop too much, he told tales of saints, dybbuks, half-mad squires,
> and sorcerers. He ate one meal a day and always (except on the
> Sabbath) stale bread crumbled into borscht.
>
>   No. 4 was a huge bazaar, Yanash's Court, which had two
> gates—one leading into Krochmalna and the other into Mirowska

Street. They sold everything here—fruit, vegetables, dairy, geese, fish. There were stores selling secondhand shoes and old clothes of all kinds.

We came to the Place. It always swarmed with prostitutes, pimps, and petty thieves in torn jackets and caps with visors pulled down over their eyes. In my time, the Boss here had been Blind Itche, chief of the pickpockets, proprietor of brothels, a swaggerer and a knife carrier. Somewhere in No. 11 or 13 lived fat Reitzele, a woman who weighed three hundred pounds. Reitzele was supposed to conduct business with white slavers from Buenos Aires. She was also a procurer of servant girls. Many games were played in the Place. You drew numbers from a bag and you could win a police whistle, a chocolate cake, a pen with a view of Cracow, a doll that sat up and cried "Mama."

I stopped with Betty to gape. The same louts, the same flat pronunciation, the same games. I was afraid that all this would disgust her, but she had become infected by my nostalgia. "You should have brought me here the very first day we met!" she said. . . .

I didn't know what to show her next—the den in No. 6 where the thieves played cards and dominoes and where the fences came to buy stolen goods; the prayer house in No. 10 where we used to live, or the Radzymin study house in No. 12, to which we later moved; the courtyards where I attended cheder or the stores where my mother used to send me to buy food and kerosene. The only change I could observe was that the houses had lost most of their plaster and grown black from smoke. Here and there, a wall was supported on logs. The gutters seemed even deeper, their stink was stronger. I stopped before each gate and peered in. All the garbage bins were heaped high with refuse. Dyers dyed clothing, tinsmiths patched broken pots, men with sacks on their shoulders cried, "Ole clo's, ole clo's, I buy rags, ole pants, ole shoes, ole hats, ole clo's, ole clo's." Here and there, a beggar sang a song—of the *Titanic*, which had gone down in 1911, of the striker Baruch Shulman, who had thrown a bomb in 1905 and been hanged. Magicians were performing the same stunts they had in my childhood—they swallowed fire, rolled barrels with their feet, lay down bareback on a bed of nails. I knew it couldn't be, but I imagined that I recognized the girl who went around shaking a tambourine hung with bells to collect coins from the watchers. She wore the same velvet breeches with silver sequins. Her hair was cut like a boy's. She was tall and slim, flat-chested, her eyes were shiny black. A parrot with a broken beak perched on her shoulder. . . .

On Krochmalna Street, as the end of Jewish life in Poland looms on the horizon, Aaron finds Shosha and her mother, Bashele, living in abject poverty in a tenement. Shosha's little sister, Yppe, has died in an epidemic; her older sister, Teibele, has gone to school and works as a bookkeeper. But Shosha lives at home with her mother, doomed to eternal childhood. She has neither grown nor aged; she is the soul of all that is innocent and uncorrupted. "Her figure had remained childlike, although I detected signs of breasts. Her skirt was shorter than those in style and it was hard to tell by the gaslight whether it was blue or black. . . . Everyone in Warsaw wore sheer, gloss, colored stockings, but Shosha's appeared to be made of coarse cotton." Shosha is a dull and artless girl, as the other women in Aaron's life never tire of pointing out to him, but she is superbly drawn as a creature of innocence, and her fascination for Aaron is made utterly credible. She is the Virgin of Krochmalna Street, drawing Aaron inexorably back into his own past. He marries her, although we know from the start that he will abandon her at last; everything in her character and in her circumstances seem to make this betrayal inevitable. Shosha exists at the still point of a world spinning toward extinction—an unforgettable, fey creature with, at the same time, a kind of peasant canniness that roots her, like all Isaac's best fantasies, in the rich loam of reality. In the end Shosha is on her way to seek escape in Bialystok across the Russian border. But she weakens and can't go on. "She cannot even walk anymore," Isaac explained one day, outlining the plot before the English version had been completed. "She just sits down and dies."

How petty and self-indulgent the other characters in the book appear next to Shosha's almost eerie simplicity! And how pitiful they are, these enlightened ones, gratifying their routine appetites and enthusiasms in the face of the horror that is about to consume them. There is an epilogue set in modern Israel, where Aaron, visiting the country as a famous author,. finds his former friend Haiml alive, but it is all really finished for the cast of *Shosha* by this time.

Aaron's struggles to find himself as a writer parallel Isaac's own early failures. Aaron even writes a novel about the false messiah Jacob Frank that sets him on the road to literary achievement. When Aaron marries Shosha, Isaac's mother, Bathsheba, and his younger brother, Moishe, turn up (under their own real names) for the celebration, and there are some vivid glimpses of both of them. Moishe's innocence is almost a mirror of Shosha's. And in the last pages of *Shosha* Aaron describes what was apparently the actual fate of Moishe and Bathsheba:

"After 1941, the Russians saved them by taking them in a cattle train to Kazakhstan. The trip took two weeks. I met a man who was with them in the same train, and he told me the details. They are both dead. How my mother could last several months after the experience of this trip, I still don't grasp. They were taken to a forest in the middle of the Russian winter and told to build themselves log cabins. My brother died almost immediately after he arrived."

Yet in his introduction to *Shosha* Isaac states, "This novel does not represent the Jews of Poland in the pre-Hitler years by any means. It is a story of a few unique characters in unique circumstances." To make that uniqueness believable Isaac has borrowed liberally from the past that is still alive in his own remarkable memory.

Shosha appeared first in the *Forward* in 1974 under the title *Soul Expeditions.* It was translated into English by Joseph Singer. "A number of chapters," Isaac reveals in his introductory note, "I dictated to my wife, Alma, and to my secretary, Dvorah Menashe. The entire work was edited by Rachel MacKenzie and Robert Giroux." He adds characteristically, "My gratitude and love to all of them."

Shosha had a difficult delivery, but with considerable editorial work on the translation by Rachel MacKenzie and others, its birth into English proved worthy of the pangs. *Shosha* is a powerful and important work. The minor characters are emancipated Jews of Warsaw who have left the ghetto to live out the last days that remain, like bright ephemeral mayflies. They are familiar enough from earlier books, but *Shosha* casts a fresh light on them, making their story one of the most poignant Isaac has ever written. In his seventies, he proves himself here to be still at the height of his powers. To the old ironic tone has been added a certain calm perspective that it might not be too much of an exaggeration to call wisdom, so that even in its blasphemies the voice of Isaac talking through his characters in *Shosha* remains devout:

"The conversation turned to occultism, and Feitelzohn said, 'There are unknown forces, yes, there are, but they're all part of the mystery called nature. What nature is no one knows, and I suspect that she doesn't know herself. I can easily visualize the Almighty sitting on the Throne of Glory in the Seventh Heaven, Metatron on His right, Sandalphon on His left, and God asking them, "Who Am I? How did I come about? Did I create Myself? Who gave Me these powers? After all, it couldn't be that I've existed forever. I remember only the past hundred trillion years. Everything before that is hazy. Well, how long will it go on?" ' "

After such a flight no writer knows better than Isaac how to land comfortably on earth again. Feitelzohn continues without pause, "Wait, Mark, I'll get your cognac. Something to nibble on? I have cookies as old as Methuselah."

Reviewing *Shosha* in *The New York Times Book Review* for July 23, 1978, Alan Lelchuk called the novel "a record of Jewish ghetto life in Poland in the 1930's" as well as a "chronicle of the swarming literary-political life in Warsaw, with pagan Communism battling Torah laws in young Jewish minds." In the end Lelchuk found the book "a kind of elegy for the dead."

He felt that *Shosha* at its best contained "charming scenes, moving moments, flares of chaos" and praised "the variety of characters." He was disappointed, however, in the book's "tidy formulas of description." In *Newsweek* J. N. Baker, commenting on the humor in *Shosha*, asked, "Why do people write so rarely about how funny Singer can be?" Baker praised Isaac's "wonderful gift for having his characters discuss great issues—the meaning of life, good versus evil, the plight of modern man, death and immortality—and making the reader chuckle only when the author wants him to." A. C. Kempf, writing in *Library Journal*, stated that *Shosha* once again proved "the universality of I. B. Singer" and was struck by how the characters, on the very eve of the Holocaust, were able to "transcend their ethnic and national background. . . . While Hitler is in everyone's thoughts and conversation, the characters continue to intrigue and love, to be concerned with the mundane, such as the next meal, and the philosophical, such as the political ideal. That the humanity of individuals cannot be crushed is beautifully affirmed in this story of a world no longer with us."

In *The New Yorker* Lis Harris called *Shosha* "more evocatively otherworldly" than many of Isaac's books, perhaps "because many of the people in it are, in part, reincarnations of characters in Singer's earlier works or because any description of the lives of Warsaw Jews in the period just before most of them were killed is so fraught with pathos that it is inherently a bit ghostlike." On the other hand, she said that "if the ghetto and all other manifestations of Polish Jewry have vanished, the forty-odd years that separate Singer from the life he is writing about have happily not dimmed his memory of it. His descriptions of the shabby street he grew up on and the cheder he studied in are as precise as pins. Even if Singer were not the superb writer that he is, one would be grateful for the privileged view of history that he continues to pass on to us." She felt that the original title, *Soul Expeditions*, was more apt than *Shosha*, since Shosha, although "central to the story," is "only one of many characters who step forward, reveal their natures, and then recede into the background behind the narrator—the familiar skeptical young writer who drifts in and out of many of Singer's best tales." "Singer," she pointed out, "has always kept his stories about pre-Second World War European Jews matter-of-fact and unsentimental, and this factual tone gives his work an emotional force that is unequaled, I think, by any other writer who has taken on the subject. He has an extraordinary gift for letting large matters seep into small events, and for making ordinary gossip, or, as his characters call it, schmoozing, into an art." She found it refreshing that in his work "obsessive passions are meant to be self-explanatory" and that "neither the mystical-romantic nor the Freudian viewpoint can gain even a toehold" in Isaac's fiction.

❀

Isaac at eighteen in Warsaw.

Isaac (*far right*) in his early twenties with friends and
colleagues. *Left to right*: Yiddish writers Melech Ravich,
Joseph Kerman, Kadie Molodowsky, and Samuel Jacob Imber,
nephew of Naphtali Herz Imber, who wrote the words of
Israel's national anthem, *Hatikvah*.

Isaac in the twenties when he was working as a proofreader on the magazine *Literary Pages*.

Isaac with Yiddish journalists at the resort town of Shvider in the late twenties. *Left to right*: Joseph Heftman, Helen Edela, Isaac, a woman whose name Isaac cannot recall, and a writer named Zach.

Isaac was in his early thirties when he posed for this picture at a photographer's studio in Warsaw.

Isaac at the Writers' Club in Warsaw with Yiddish writers
Joseph Kerman *(left)* and Joshua Perle *(right)*.

Isaac as a young man.

Maurice Kreitman (now Maurice Carr), Hinde Esther's son, at the age of twelve in Warsaw.

Yiddish journalists in Warsaw, about 1930. *Left to right*: Rachel Korn, Isaac, Israel Joshua, Aaron Zeitlin, and Melech Ravich.

Isaac's passport issued by the P.E.N. Club in Warsaw in 1932.

Membership card issued to Isaac by the P.E.N. Club in Warsaw in 1932.

Press card issued to Isaac in 1935 by the French-Yiddish newspaper *Pariser Haint*.

Isaac's son, Israel, and his
mother, Runya, just before
they left for the Soviet
Union in 1935.

Above: Isaac's nephew Joseph (*left*), his mother, Genia, and his
father, Israel Joshua Singer, in the mid-thirties, shortly after Isaac's
arrival in America.

Facing page: Alma Singer at the time of her meeting with Isaac at
a farm in the Catskills.

Alma and Isaac on Central Park West in 1955.

Isaac with Elizabeth Shub, who persuaded him to write his first book for children, *Zlateh the Goat*, when he was past sixty.

In Isaac's absence Alma Singer accepts the Newbery Medal of Honor for *Zlateh the Goat* in 1966. *Left*: Raymond C. Harwood, president of Harper & Row, who published the book; *right*: illustrator Maurice Sendak.

Isaac with Raphael Soyer, who illustrated his books of memoirs, *A Young Man in Search of Love* and *A Lost Man in Search of Himself*.

Isaac sometimes works with a translator directly from an episode in one of his books after it appears in Yiddish in the *Jewish Daily Forward*.

Isaac in front of a photograph of himself in a study where the walls are covered with framed awards and doctorate certificates.

Isaac addresses a group of children from the altar of a synagogue in Israel in the seventies.

Isaac enjoys a vegetarian breakfast in the kitchen of his West 86th Street apartment. (*Photograph by Abraham Menashe for the filmstrip* Meet the Newbery Author, *courtesy Miller-Brody Productions.*)

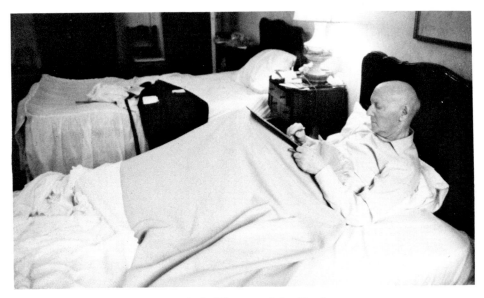

Isaac sometimes enjoys writing in bed. (*Photograph by Abraham Menashe from the filmstrip* Meet the Newbery Author, *courtesy Miller-Brody Productions.*)

Isaac answers questions from his young audience.

Israel Zamir in the dining room at Kibbutz Bet Alpha.

At the library (*left to right*): Paul Kresh; Isaac; Simon Weber, editor of the *Jewish Daily Forward*; and Swedish author Knut Ahnlund. (*Contact Press Image.*)

Following his Nobel lecture Isaac autographs copies of his books. (*Photo courtesy* Jewish Daily Forward.)

At the Concert Hall in Stockholm Isaac receives his Nobel prize
medal, certificate, and monetary award from Swedish King Carl XVI
Gustaf. (*Photo courtesy* Jewish Daily Forward.)

Isaac examines his award. (*Photo courtesy* Jewish Daily Forward.)

Above: On the eve of the Nobel banquet, December 10, 1978,
(*left to right*): Isaac's son, Israel; Alma; Isaac; and Simon Weber.
(*Photo courtesy* Jewish Daily Forward.)

Following page: Isaac enters the Banquet Hall in Stockholm with the
Princess Christina, sister of King Carl XVI Gustaf.
(*Contact Press Images.*)

Isaac's latest novel, serialized in the *Forward* in 1977 and scheduled for publication in English in 1979, is *Yarme and Kayle*, which deals with the Jewish underworld in Warsaw in the days when Isaac was growing up in his father's house. The prostitutes he saw on Krochmalna Street, the stories he heard about pimps and thugs and swindlers, served as the raw material for a novel of extraordinary frankness and power. In these pages Isaac goes further than ever before in exploring that half-world that figures in *The Magician of Lublin*.

The story begins in 1911 on Krochmalna Street (Isaac was seven years old then). It is six years after the first workers' revolution. Nicholas II has granted Poland a constitution, but one government after another has failed. In Russia there are pogroms, in Poland Jews are still persecuted. The newspapers predict war in the Balkans; some even envision a war between Russia and Germany. Hundreds of thousands of Jews are smuggling themselves across the border, some into Prussia, some into Galicia. From there, a good many are going to seek the legendary life they have heard about in America.

Kayle is twenty-nine, a red-headed whore who was worked in three houses of prostitution. Now she considers herself the "luckiest whore in the world" because she has just married Yarme. He is Yarmehu Eliezer Holzman, who, at thirty-two, has served four jail terms for theft, has been arrested on a number of occasions for trafficking in "live merchandise," and is, like Yasha Mazur in *The Magician of Lublin*, proud of his reputation as an expert lockpicker.

Yarme and Kayle swear eternal fidelity and are happy together until "lame Max" comes into their lives. Max Levitas is an old friend of Yarme's who has just returned from the New World, where he has been operating a successful white slave network. He sports a diamond ring on one finger, a signet on another. Max takes the couple to a drunken party where Yarme, incensed by Kayle's attentions to Max, punches her in the nose and sends her sprawling. Later, however, Yarme, Kayle, and Max team up and the two men send Kayle out on missions of seduction. Soon they are all living together. Yarme tells Kayle of his homosexual relations with Max when they were both in jail and says they must live now as a trio with one body, one soul. But Kayle, in an unexpected access of piety, goes off on Succoth to the local synagogue, where she sobs and weeps and begs God for forgiveness for her life of sin. She runs upstairs to the rabbi's house to ask him for advice. There she meets the rabbi's son, Bonim, who advises her to go to America and get away from her evil companions.

Bonim, who bears a vague resemblance to Joshua Singer, is studying to be a sculptor; he brings Kayle to his studio, where she gets drunk and seduces him. Meanwhile Yarme's feelings toward Max have cooled, and he no longer wants to go to bed with him. Bonim has a Socialist girlfriend he hasn't told Kayle about; the girl is arrested for her political activities. It snows heavily, as it must in one of Isaac's novels about Warsaw, and the complications pile up with the snow. One minute Kayle is threatening to go off with Max to South America and become the madam of a whorehouse for millionaires; the next she is swearing she will chop a hole in the ice of the Vistula and drown herself in the river.

Eventually Bonim and Kayle elope to America. She becomes a servant in an old man's house and later a bagel-seller. Bonim finds work first as a presser in a clothing factory, then as a teacher in a private religious school. They rent an apartment on Attorney Street on the lower east side of Manhattan—which Bonim thinks of as another Krochmalna Street: There is even a brothel across the way where the whores hang out the windows trying to attract customers.

Bonim teaches himself English in the same way that Isaac did when he first came to America, printing an English word on a piece of paper with the Yiddish beside it and trying to memorize the English. He writes home to his family, but his sister writes back that his parents speak of him as though he were dead. At night Bonim and Kayle lie in bed, and she regales him with tales of her adventures as a whore. They are happy together.

One day, however, Max Levitas turns up in New York—like a Jewish Sportin' Life, twirling a cane and wearing a big pearl stickpin, and things become complicated again. Max tells Kayle that Yarme will never give her a divorce. Yarme loves her and wants her back. In fact, Yarme too has come to New York.

It would not be fair to tell how the story comes out, but even this much of the plot shows clearly how Isaac has used his unexpected knowledge of the Jewish underworld in this most profound and least inhibited of his investigations of human passions. Other elements in the story are more familiar—the Jewish customs, holidays, superstitions, and aspirations that make up the common past that all the characters are struggling to escape.

The Yiddish reading public has not taken kindly to this latest foray into the seamy side of Jewish life. One editor at the *Forward* was heard to remark that maybe there were pimps and prostitutes among the Jews of the Warsaw ghetto, but certainly never pederasts! The book represents Isaac's biggest offense yet against those who believe that Jews must portray themselves in books (or on the stage and screen) as lovable, innocent, good-hearted folk who ask only to worship God in their own way and to be let alone to pursue their blameless lives.

❋

There is one novel of Isaac's that has been translated into English but published only in Yiddish in the pages of the *Forward*. That is *The Penitent*, written in the early seventies and translated by Joseph Singer.

The Penitent opens at the Western Wall in Jerusalem, where the narrator has come in 1969 to watch the crowds gather at the site of the ancient Temple. There he encounters a little man in a long gaberdine and a velvet hat; he is not terribly old, but his beard has turned white prematurely. This man is Joseph Shapiro, a Jew from New York, who says that he used to attend the narrator's lectures. Now he lives in Israel and has enrolled as a yeshiva student. The next day he visits the narrator at his hotel and tells him his story. It takes two days for Joseph's story to unfold. As it does it becomes evident that here again we have a "What if?" story: What if Isaac had renounced the world for the life of a fervently pious Hasidic Jew in the Holy Land? For although Isaac is clearly the narrator who hears out Joseph's tale, Joseph, under his gaberdine and ritual fringes, is very much like Isaac Singer. But the book itself doesn't seem to have been written by Isaac at all. It is as though the manuscript had been dictated by his father Pinchas Mendel, as a fable of dissolution with the moral that the modern Jew should renounce all worldly things and return to a life of strict orthodoxy.

Like Isaac, Joseph is a descendant of rabbis. Joseph believes he can trace his ancestry back to King David. When the Nazis bombed Warsaw in 1939, he fled on foot to Bialystok. He wandered through Russia, suffered "the whole gamut of troubles," and in 1945 was able to escape back to Poland. There, in Lublin, he met his old girl friend Celia, a former Communist, who had been "cured" by events in the Soviet Union. Joseph and Celia go to Germany, have an affair; they are married in a D.P. camp. They are planning to go to Israel but get visas to the United States instead. In New York Joseph finds a job in a drygoods store and prospers. Celia finishes college with honors. They have an apartment on West End Avenue and a summer house in Connecticut. Celia is forced to undergo an operation, which prevents her from having children. Eventually Joseph grows bored with her and takes up with a divorcee named Liza. She is an avaricious woman who lets him pay her rent, take her to the theater, buy her clothes. Celia begins to suspect the truth when Liza breaks all the rules and phones Joseph at home. Liza expects Joseph not only to support her but also to give money to her radical daughter, Micki, and even to pay for an abortion for Micki after she is made pregnant by her loutish left-wing lover. They begin to quarrel, and Joseph becomes impotent. Finally Liza and Micki have a violent argument; Micki hits her mother so hard that she almost kills her. Liza grabs a knife and has to be restrained from stabbing her daughter. Joseph rushes out, only to return home and find his wife in bed with another man. This is the last straw for Joseph. He decides to give up his life of sin and turn his back on the "Sodom" of his American existence. He will go to Israel and become a penitent. At the same time he decides to become a vegetarian. No more licentiousness—which must lead by one route or another to the GPU and the Gestapo. "If you don't want to be a Nazi you must become his opposite." He heads for the nearest Hasidic prayer house. Later, without even going home for his clothes, he boards a plane for Israel.

On the plane, while leafing through a book of pious maxims, he is engaged in conversation by an attractive woman smelling of eau de cologne who attempts to seduce him under the blanket they are sharing. This doesn't quite happen, but the episode makes Joseph feel that his journey has become spiritually meaningless. Even so, Joseph manages, after a number of minor adventures in Israel, including a brief stay on a kibbutz, to get to Jerusalem. There he is taken in by a Hasidic family in the ultra-Orthodox neighborhood of Mea Shearim. Eventually Joseph obtains a divorce from Celia and marries Sarah, the sweet and innocent daughter of his Hasidic mentors. He lets his beard and earlocks grow, renounces "everything that had to do with modern man, with modern Jewry." Joseph and Sarah have three children, and he enrolls as a student of the Torah in a Jerusalem yeshiva.

That, in sum, is the story of *The Penitent*, but the book is also devoted largely to denunciations of twentieth-century life in all its forms. One of the characters is an "Evil Spirit" who constantly tries to tempt Joseph back into the maelstrom of modernity. Singer lashes out like an old-fashioned fundamentalist preacher against promiscuity, greed, the indulgence of the senses, novels without plots, paintings without scenery, and the eating of flesh. Break one of the Ten Commandments and you'll soon be breaking them all. Even to read a newspaper is to contaminate the soul with stories of war, murder, rape, and corruption. "According to the paper, if the nation would only choose the president it recommended and put into effect this or the other reform, all would be right in the world. Even the obituary page was made to seem somehow optimistic. It listed all the accomplishments of those who had died and displayed their photographs. A theatrical producer had died and the obituary enumerated all the trashy plays he produced, all the smut he had presented on stage. The fact that he had died young was glossed over. The emphasis was on the fact that he had accumulated a big estate that he left to his fourth or fifth wife.

"That day, too, a murderer was arrested, one who had been charged with the same crime several times before but each time been freed on bail or paroled. His photograph was printed too along with the name of his lawyer, Horowitz or Freedman, whose function it was to teach this murderer how to avoid punishment so that he could kill more innocent people. . . ."

The world is truly wicked, and Jews who try to emulate its wickedness are even worse. The penitent must return not just to Judaism but "to the Jewishness of [his] grandfathers and great-grandfathers." He must renounce everything, from alcohol and adultery to movies and popular magazines. Like Yasha in *The Magician of Lublin*, he can be saved only by paying the price that T. S. Eliot has called "not less than everything."

Joseph starts without faith, but observance leads to belief. "Deeds must come first. Long before the child knows that it has a stomach it wants to eat. Long before you feel a total faith you must act in a Jewish way. Jewishness leads to faith. I know now that there is a God. I believe in His Providence. . . ."

Isaac has decided so far to go along with the advice of some of his literary counselors and not have this sermonic novel published in English. Yet clearly there exists, somewhere in Isaac himself, this vegetarian penitent who really believes that the world is as wicked as his father warned him it was, that indulgence of the senses and attempts to achieve Utopia through political change can lead only to sorrow. And certain passages in *The Penitent*—such as the following one—might make even the most exasperated reader feel that maybe the book should have been published after all: "If someone found a watch on an island and said it had been made by itself or that it developed through evolution, he would be considered a lunatic. . . . But according to them, the universe evolved all on its own. Is the universe less complicated than a watch?"

PART 7

"Too Many Partners"

I don't have strong feelings about the theater," Isaac says. "I never have been stagestruck. To me, the theater is a sideline. I like art to be pure. A book is written by one man. In the theater you have too many partners—the director, the producer, the actors, the writers. In a way it's already a collective. I don't go to the theater often. But when I do go, it's for enjoyment. I don't want to go to a play where they try to solve all the problems of humanity. A work for the stage has to entertain."

Despite his lack of enthusiasm for the theater, Isaac has been involved in a number of theatrical adaptations of his stories over the years, some staged by the Yale Repertory Theater and small professional groups around the country. And movie options have been taken on several of his tales and books, though most of them have not been exercised.

In 1957 the Folksbeine Theatre on East Broadway on Manhattan's Lower East Side performed a dramatized version of passages from *In My Father's Court* in Yiddish. The late Jacob Ben Ami, one of the great figures of the Yiddish stage, also produced a revival of *Yoshe Kalb* at the Folksbeine during the same period.

In 1963 Isaac granted Theater à la Carte, Inc., a repertory touring company, rights to dramatize any of his short stories they chose for production. Co-producers Peninah Schram and Lenore Janis picked "Gimpel the Fool," and Richard Hall adapted it as a one-act play. Isaac personally approved the script and was delighted with the showcase production given at the Mermaid Theater in New York in May of that year. Later this version of "Gimpel" was performed at synagogues and Jewish community centers in several cities on the East Coast. Two composers have also written operatic scores for "Gimpel the Fool"—one in English, the other in Yiddish.

Isaac has written about the Yiddish theater and his own experiences with the world of the stage. In "Once on Second Avenue There Lived a Yiddish Theater," which appeared in the Sunday *New York Times* Arts and Leisure

Section on April 17, 1966, Isaac traces the history of that theater back ninety years to "a wine cellar of the Rumanian city of Jassy" where a play by Abraham Goldfaden first attracted a Yiddish-speaking audience. Recalling that when Goldfaden died in New York in 1908 his funeral cortege was followed by seventy-five thousand people, Isaac deplores the absence of Yiddish theater in New York, which once was able to fill twenty playhouses in the area of lower Second Avenue. He attributes this decline to the facts that even Yiddishists no longer sent their children to Yiddish schools (though studying Yiddish has since become popular among Jewish college students) and that Yiddish theater was suffering from the "same malady as the theater in English—almost no good plays are being written. Yiddish literature is still producing good novels, short stories and poems, but no very good dramatic works have been written in Yiddish in recent years." *Landsleit*—neighbors who hailed from the same *shtetls*—were still buying out benefit performances where they could meet old friends, but the only "dynamite" that could keep them quiet during a performance was a wedding scene or a recital of the *kaddish*. (Isaac's *Yentl* was to include both.) These *landsleit* also took their families to Yiddish plays at the Folksbeine and the Yiddish Village Theater on Second Avenue, where they could be heard, frequently louder than the actors, explaining the action to their offspring. "A few hundred such translators can kill the best play," Isaac comments. The *landsleit* did tend to display better manners on Broadway, but for Isaac Broadway musicals like *Fiddler on the Roof* and *The Zulu and the Zayda* were only "ghosts" of vintage Yiddish drama. He did not see a future for Yiddish theater (he still doesn't) but wanted to remind his readers of its history and its role for America's Jewish immigrants as "a remarkable mixture of university and place of amusement." Yiddish theater, he writes, had made them aware of their past, and the heroics of that past had slaked their thirst for music and dancing, and for some had even taken the place of attending a synagogue, with its "cantors singing and reciting the old Jewish prayers." While every production offered a love story, the sacred institutions—the family, marital fidelity, respect for the old and infirm—were "never mocked," and the audience "had to leave the theater with the feeling that God was on the side of justice. Only then could they enjoy the fresh bagels and the tasty egg cookies which the restaurants on Second Avenue offered the after-theater crowds." The children and grandchildren of those audiences, Isaac felt, still looked for the same values in the theater, and non-Jewish ticket-buyers seemed to find the same sort of enjoyment in *Fiddler* as they did in trying out matzohs and blintzes. Middle-class audiences were still looking for "comparatively clean entertainment" on the stage—even though the Yiddish intelligentsia had long ago made up its mind that everything the Yiddish theater ever put on was kitsch.

In this piece for the *Times* Isaac did not lose the opportunity to heap scorn on playwrights who dabbled in obscurity or symbolism, for whom entertainment was a "dirty word," and who set out to shock by portraying overt sexuality on the stage—or to exhort the playwrights of the future to search for their "roots" rather than their personal identity. Isaac, at once the audacious experimenter and the implacable conservative, felt that though the Yiddish theater might not hold its own in the future, it would give life to other kinds of theater that could absorb its values and virtues and in which "dramatic entertainment" would in the end prevail over "case-history excitement."

❀

February 18, 1976

Bruce Davidson, a photographer in his early forties, sits in a large, restful living room crowded with plants and furniture upholstered in leather and worn velvet, talking about the making of his movie *Isaac Singer's Nightmare and Mrs. Pupko's Beard.* The half-hour movie was based on "The Beard," which appeared in *A Crown of Feathers.*

"The Beard" is a story about an impoverished Yiddish writer in New York named Bendit Pupko, with one blind eye and a game leg, who makes a fortune from cheaply bought stocks and real estate, and bribes a critic to publish an essay hailing him as a genius—thus proving the Talmudic quip that money purifies a bastard. Pupko also asks the narrator of the tale, Isaac himself, to write favorably about him but is turned down. When Pupko is dying of cancer, his wife, a cigar-smoking woman with a full beard, comes to see the recalcitrant narrator and accuses him of trying to kill her husband by refusing to praise him in print; he must, she says, atone by writing an essay lauding Pupko's prose. This is the only thing that can save Pupko's life. The narrator relents and writes the piece, but by the time it appears in print it is posthumous: Pupko is dead.

Davidson's movie roughly follows the plot of the story—which he had read before it was published—but it introduces new elements. There is a cocktail party, filmed in Isaac's own living room, where the author's admirers jabber fatuously of literature and the fate of Yiddish. There are scenes shot at the famous Garden Cafeteria near the old *Forward* building, where Yiddish writers used to hang out and harangue one another about journalism and politics over glasses of tea and plates of rice pudding. There's even a dialogue between the narrator and a translator—Dorothea Straus, played by herself, in a classy cocktail dress and a huge black picture hat. We see Isaac writing in bed, which he sometimes does in real life, feeding his parakeets, and feeding pigeons near the Museum of Natural History, under a sign that says Pigeon Feeding Prohibited. While feeding the pigeons Isaac meets a student (played by Carol Hill), who accompanies him on a walk in one of the film's loveliest interludes. Alma is in the movie too, playing herself, dressed in a bathrobe that she agreed to wear only when the director insisted that it constituted the only proper costume for the scene. Both Pupko and his wife are portrayed in caricature by the same actor, Jack Weiner, a dance teacher who was chosen for the role partly because he can speak Yiddish.

There is a free-wheeling, casual quality about this film, unpolished and scarcely fussed over, yet cleverly reflecting the caricature in Isaac's work. There are hints of profundity too beneath the comic antics of the action, into which Isaac enters with the zest he has so often revealed in his platform appearances.

Davidson made *Isaac Singer's Nightmare* in 1971 with a grant from the American Film Institute in association with the Corporation for Public Broadcasting. There wasn't much money to spend, but by keeping to a certain rough-hewn style he managed to make something of a virtue of the economies he had to impose. The film was well received when introduced the following year on Channel Thirteen in New York, and other educational stations have since repeated it. In 1972 it won first prize in its class at the American Film Festival. It is distributed by New Yorker Films.

Bruce is a plump, heavy-set fellow. Today he is dressed casually in a sport shirt and jeans, a costume in keeping with his relaxed, genial manner—offset only by a certain wary look in his alert, attentive eyes. He grew up in the Middle West, in Oak Park near Chicago, and came east to study at the University of Rochester and later at Yale. He was ten when he decided to become a photographer ("about the same age," he says, "that Isaac discovered he wanted to be a writer"). Bruce has been married some ten years. The Davidsons have two young daughters, who get a lot of affection and attention from their father.

Bruce had already photographed Isaac for *Time* and done a portrait of him for *Holiday* when he got the grant that led to the production of *Isaac Singer's Nightmare*. The Davidsons were living in the Village then, and Bruce was set on finding an apartment in the huge stone fortress where the Singers live. With Isaac's help he was able to do so; the capacious quarters where the Davidsons live now, with blowups of his photos on the walls and light pouring in from numerous windows, is a few floors directly above Isaac's.

What made Bruce Davidson choose "The Beard"? And why did he decide to ask Isaac to play himself in the movie?

"I had read a good many of Isaac's stories. The grant was to do a documentary on a leading writer. It could have been Arthur Miller or Norman Mailer. The way it worked out, I actually integrated a documentary into a fictional film. It's a combination of the two forms, and "The Beard" was ideal for that. It was short enough.

"Why Isaac? First of all, bringing him into it took care of the documentary aspect. He was open to the idea from the beginning, although he wasn't too sure what making a film meant. But aside from that Isaac's whole life has really been theater. His father the rabbi, pronouncing judgments on divorces and disputes, was himself a kind of performer. That rabbinical court of his was a theater. And, you know, Isaac himself reminded me so much of my own grandfather from Warsaw. They even looked a bit alike. My grandfather was a tailor whose sons took over his business. When the family came here we were all what they call 'assimilated.' But you reach a certain stage in your life when you start to look for your roots. Isaac turned me on to my past. I wanted to make this movie about him and with him."

Before making the film Bruce spent a month with Isaac, following him to the Garden Cafeteria, to lectures at Brandeis, to meetings, and through his daily routine. These experiences led to the publication, several years later, of "The Cafeteria," a feature that appeared in *New York* magazine on October 15, 1973, illustrated with Davidson's own excellent photographs. The photographic essay describes his visits to the Garden, long known as the "Jewish Oasis" on East Broadway. While there Bruce interviewed survivors of the Nazi camps, elderly storekeepers recalling the past over bagels and coffee, a man who was once a contender for the featherweight boxing title, an assistant cashier who used to earn her living singing and dancing, and a waiter in his eighties who boasted that he could sing *Pagliacci* in Italian.

"During the weeks I visited the Garden," Bruce recounts in the text, "I found more than the survivors of the Nazi Holocaust. I found the remains of the Jewish life my grandparents knew—the food, the faces, the gestures and words—living on in a blend of memories, cream cheese, and old age."

One of the habitués Bruce met at the cafeteria called the place "Heaven . . . where you could sit all day with friends, eating, and never pay the check." Not the least of the Garden's attractions that day was Isaac himself. He was greeted like a returning warrior. "When we got to the Garden to check out the location," Bruce says, "all sorts of people who knew him crowded around our table. By the time we went down to light the area for shooting the scene in the movie that takes place there, we knew everybody by name." As one of the Polish journalists on the scene explained to Bruce, the Garden was "a place where everybody could come in. A literary man could come in, a writer or a longshoreman could come in, as long as he's a *mensch.*"

Returning to the story of how the movie of "The Beard" was made, Bruce says, "When we flew up to Brandeis, Isaac was writing—little notes, observations, all the way. On the train coming home too. When he heard we were going to shoot scenes in New York with pigeons, he insisted on a certain kind of bird seed—it had to be exactly the right stuff." Isaac took Bruce to a special store he knew about to buy the pigeon food. When they were filming in front of the Museum of Natural History, Isaac would spread the feed on the ground. "Then he would tell us to wait, because it takes time for the first pigeon to become aware of the food. 'When one starts eating,' he explained to me, 'the others follow.' So each time we'd wait some fifteen minutes for a crowd of pigeons to gather. They assembled by the hundreds. Then I would place the clapstick with the scene number on it in front of our single camera and snap it so we could find the scene and match it with the soundtrack later when we went to edit it. And each time I did this the noise from the clapstick would set the pigeons flapping off frightened in all directions. After this happened a few times, Isaac came running over to ask what was wrong. When I told him, he shook his head. 'Listen, Bruce,' he said, 'you may know, God bless you, about films, but about pigeons you know nothing.' We had to forget the clapstick."

Isaac could never get used to the idea that the same scene had to be shot over and over for a movie, first from one angle, then from another. He couldn't understand why he had to repeat the same line of dialogue three or four times. "What if they were making a film when God was creating the world? He would have had to say 'Let there be light' four times."

When it came time to dress up actor Jack Weiner as the bearded Mrs. Pupko, the crew made an expedition to the Lower East Side to find the right costume. The clothes and makeup were so convincing, and Weiner, a dancer, was able to imitate a woman's movements so well, that on Mrs. Pupko's first appearance he fooled even the crew.

Isaac loves surprises, and he got a real one during the shooting of *Isaac Singer's Nightmare* when Jack Weiner showed up in his apartment in his Mrs. Pupko outfit. "With so striking a personality to deal with, my, Isaac was real good that day," Bruce says.

Shooting the movie with one camera in nine days was so harrowing that on the second day the sound-man erased the entire soundtrack by mistake. He was so rattled that he quit the company, and everything had to be shot all over again.

Bruce Davidson was especially pleased by Isaac's cooperation. "You see him writing, and he's really writing. You see him the way he is with Alma, curt sometimes but often tender and charming too. You see him being comic one minute, serious the next. Oh, he's sharp—he can defend himself in any kind of debate. He's like a bird—a survivor—a pigeon—a Yiddish pigeon."

Isaac liked the movie when he first saw it in the editing room, was pleased with it when he saw it again on television, and told everybody in the neighborhood to go to see it when it was playing at the New Yorker Theater on upper Broadway.

Recently Davidson has been trying to raise money for the production of a more ambitious film—a full-length version of *Enemies, A Love Story*, to which he has the screen rights. The screenplay, by a South African short-story writer named Barney Simon, has been revised by Isaac and further revised by Bruce. Bruce would also like to make a movie of the short story "Pigeons." One can see why.

❀

On January 19, 1973, the Yale Repertory Theater in New Haven, Connecticut, presented the world premiere of *The Mirror*, a play by Isaac Bashevis Singer. Billed as an "erotic fable," *The Mirror* was based on a story that first appeared in English in *New World Writing* in 1955 and was subsequently published by the Noonday Press in 1957 in the collection *Gimpel the Fool and Other Stories*. The play tells the story of Zirel, a woman bored with her impotent husband and beset by erotic fantasies. She is tempted to enter the mirror in her boudoir by a handsome demon from Sodom. But Zirel learns that it is easier to go in through the looking glass than to come out again.

The production, heightened by music and dance, was staged by Michael Posnick, with scenery and costumes by Stephen Rubin, choreography by Carmen de Lavellade—who also played a temptress in the story—and original music by Yehudi Wyner, a member of the faculty at the Yale School of Music. Zirel was Marcia Jean Kurtz, and Richard Venture was the demon who leads her astray. Her husband, Schloimele, was portrayed by Nicholas Herman, who doubled as Asmodeus, the King of the Underworld.

The staging by the Yale group, who had previously performed *Gimpel the Fool* in a story theater format, prompted the *New Haven Register* to recommend that "the whole mixed-up world should get on a bus and go to New York and visit Isaac Bashevis Singer before it's too late for all of us." The reactions from correspondents of *The New York Times* and other major newspapers were restrained (though the *Times* did call Isaac "a welcome addition to the ranks of young playwrights," and the *National Observer* described *The Mirror* as "a richly satisfying play, funny and wise by turns"). *The Mirror* played in repertory for several months and was a popular attraction at Yale.

Discussing the play with Irving Howe, editor of *Dissent* at the time a tape of their conversation was broadcast over the Yale campus station, Isaac said its theme was "more or less that we run away from boredom into wickedness, and there is almost nothing in between." Howe saw the behavior of the king of Sodom, who demands instant gratification ("Give me natural love in five minutes because we in Sodom have no time"), as rather American. "Yes, exactly," Isaac replied, "we have no time. And when she says that it has to take time, he becomes very angry, and he gives her a pill; they have special pills for natural love. . . . So, in a way, it reflects our time."

Howe went on to speak of "the Faustian impulse of human beings to be active, to do things, and then, afterward, misery follows." Isaac agreed.

Later, in a local press interview, Isaac summed up *The Mirror* as being about "a person who cannot be happy with God and cannot be happy with the Devil. God—the way the Jews understand it—is too boring, too dogmatic, too stagnant. So Zirel thought the Devil—let's call it the secular life—would be good. But the play shows that the secular life is also full of dogmas, also full of silly duties, also full of checks, not of assets—and a lot of cruelty in addition.

"The idea is that a person who cannot live with the religious dogma and cannot live with the worldly dogma is a lost person, and there's nothing left except to remain in the mirror. In other words, to remain suspended between two worlds. In a way it means death. . . .

"Sodom is not for me hell. Sodom is the secular, the atheistic notion of pleasure—the man who denies God and wants to create a hedonistic way of life. It is ruled by Satan, because from my point of view, if you give yourself completely to pleasure you are in Satan's realm.

"In a way demons express the human subconscious. But to me the demons also symbolize a life without any faith altogether. I call people who have decided that there is no God—that the world is nothing more than a physical or chemical accident and all men have to do is find as many pleasures as they can—I call such people demons. Not because of their viciousness but because of their utter mistake. Such a life cannot exist. It becomes the very opposite of pleasure, it becomes sheer misery."

The evil of the king of Sodom, to Isaac, is his very desire for speed, for instant gratification. "You cannot compress pleasure, you cannot compress love."

Isaac planned to rework *The Mirror*, which he had written in English with the help of director Posnick, but what with other projects has not yet got around to it.

The following year, on April 12, 1974, the Yale Repertory Theater presented the "first production anywhere" of *Shlemiel the First*. Billed as "a comedy with songs," this next play dealt with the power of illusion. Based on incidents in Isaac's book of children's tales *The Fools of Chelm and Their History* and on his story "The First Shlemiel," the plot follows the adventures of a superdolt, a beadle named Shlemiel who works for the "wise man" in Chelm—the mythical town of fools—Gronam Ox. Shlemiel sets out to spread the wisdom of Chelm to the entire human race. On the way he meets a beggar who sets him off in the wrong direction, so that he ends up back in Chelm. Gronam and his sages hold a meeting and decide that since Shlemiel would never have returned home without completing his mission, this must be somebody else—Shlemiel the Second, in fact, while Shlemiel the First must still be out there somewhere, sharing the sagacities of Chelm with a grateful world.

Shlemiel the First was actually produced as a substitute for a treatment of Dostevsky's *The Possessed*, which had to be canceled when the director was called off to fulfill a film commitment in Europe. Like most of the plays at Yale, it was presented in rotating repertory with other productions. Staged by Isaiah Sheffer, who worked closely with Isaac on the script, *Shlemiel* featured Anthony Holland in the title role. Kurt Kazner was Gronam Ox, Chelm's head wise man; Norma Brustein—the wife of Robert Brustein, who heads the Yale Repertory Theater—played Gronam's shrill, addlepated spouse, Yenta Pesha.

Like *The Mirror*, *Shlemiel the First* received only qualified compliments from the visiting critics and never made it beyond Yale.

❀

March 5, 1976

Robert Brustein, the author and critic, and director of the Yale Repertory Theater,[*] sits in his sun-flooded office on the New Haven campus and talks about Isaac Singer and the theater. Brustein, a tall, darkly handsome man who measures his words and metes them out in quiet, level, frosty tones, ventures the thought that Isaac's problem as a playwright is that "he tends to write narratives rather than plays. The plays move in a linear fashion, whereas most plays move both forward and up and down.

"When we did *Gimpel the Fool* in story-theater style, the script did not move very far from the original. The narrative and all the dialogue were the same as in the story. We had produced this, by the way, as part of a double bill called *Two Saints*. The other saint was Flaubert's *St. Julian*. So we had a Jewish saint and a Catholic saint, and the two together had some success. Making the other Singer stories into full-length plays presented more of a problem—transforming fiction into drama. But the later plays had enormous charm, enormous color."

The script of *The Mirror*, written in New York, arrived in New Haven by mail. Brustein went down to see the playwright in Manhattan to discuss the production with him, "but Isaac did not come up to see the production until it had jelled and was ready to open." The same thing happened with *Shlemiel the First*. Isaac stayed away until the opening. But in the meantime Brustein did get to know Isaac, had dinner with him and Alma at their apartment in Manhattan, and says he hugely enjoyed their company. "A charming, lovely person . . . the warmest, funniest man I ever met," is how Brustein describes Isaac. "I'm a great admirer of his work. Ever since I

---

[*] Brustein left this post in 1978.

first read 'Gimpel' I was certain we were in the presence of a great writer."

Robert Brustein compares Isaac's preoccupation with demons to Yeats's belief in automatic writing. "I don't think Yeats ever really believed in Rosicrucianism. He used it as a metaphor in his writing, and I think Singer with his demons does the same thing.

"I miss not seeing him lately," Brustein says. "He always tells such wonderful stories. He told me once of complaining about the vermin in a room where he was staying—cockroaches or bedbugs or something. This was not too long after he arrived from Europe. He registered his complaint, and then he heard a knock on his door and opened it to encounter a big black fellow in the doorway. Singer wanted to know who he was. 'I'm the exterminator,' the man said. Singer was sure, he claimed, looking at him, that what the man had come to exterminate was himself and promptly dove under his bed."

As far as the theater goes, Brustein feels that Isaac might have learned more about adapting his work for the stage "if he had worked more in the rehearsal process and hung around the actors more, so that he might have begun to write with actors in mind. He has a great sense of character but thinks about characters in terms of fiction rather than as a dramatist. I think it would be an easy step for him to improve his playwriting technique, since he is already head and shoulders in his gifts above most playwrights. His dialogue is juicy and ripe. The *shtetl* atmosphere in the plays is exotic and attractive. And there is a sweet philosphy that radiates from his work. But he needs a better firsthand acquaintance with the problems of turning a story into a play."

❀

Isaac spent many months gaining just the sort of experience Robert Brustein prescribed when the Chelsea Theater of Brooklyn produced *Yentl*.

Isaac did not believe that "Yentl the Yeshiva Boy" could be made into a play until, some years back, a man by the name of Valsheri ("He was in love with a girl that I knew years ago") sent him a note saying he would like to buy the rights to the story and make a movie out of it. Isaac agreed to write a screen treatment and was paid a modest sum for that and for the screenplay. There was talk of Barbra Streisand being interested in playing the lead. Then the rights were sold to somebody else, and the project petered out. This was an old route as far as Isaac was concerned. Various companies had taken movie options on his novels *The Slave* and *The Magician of Lublin*, and nothing had ever come of it. Isaac had put aside thoughts of a *Yentl* movie when, in 1974, Robert Kalfin, the founder of the Chelsea Theater Center in Brooklyn, came to see him to talk over the possibilities of a stage version.

Isaac wrote an outline treatment in Yiddish of *Yentl* as a play, first in longhand, then on the Yiddish Remington portable typewriter he has been using since 1945. (Speaking of this machine, Isaac once told Kenneth Turan of *The Washington Post* during an interview, "I have a Yiddish typewriter which is very capricious and highly critical. If this typewriter doesn't like a story, it refuses to work. I don't get a man to correct it since I know if I get a good idea the machine will make peace with me again. I don't believe my own words saying this, but I've had the experience so many times that I'm really astonished. But the typewriter is forty-two years old. It should have some literary experience, it should have a mind of its own.")*

Leah Napolin, a young author of poetry and short stories who had spent a three-year apprenticeship directing the school's Young People's Theater, worked in summer stock, and served for a while as manager of the Jewish Theater for Children in New York, was later brought in to collaborate with Isaac on the script. Mrs. Napolin was thrilled with the assignment.

❀

December 18, 1975

Leah Napolin arrives for lunch at the Russian Tea Room wearing a navy stocking cap, a leather coat, and black boots. An unpretentious, plain-spoken young woman, she stares unwaveringly across the table through hexagonal, metal-framed glasses as she toys with a mushroom omelette, talking in even tones about the whole experience.

"Robert Kalfin and I had been undergraduates together at Alfred University in upstate New York. I was having dinner with him one evening when he asked me if I had ever read the story. Although I had been a Singer fan for some years, this particular tale had escaped me. I looked it up in the collection *Short Friday*. I felt immediately that I was the right person to do it. I called Robert the next day and told him the story was fantastic, and I was ready to take on the assignment. He warned me that he couldn't guarantee an option on the script as yet from the Chelsea Theater since he had never read anything I'd written. Could I prepare a couple of scenes for him? I went to work, and in about ten days the scenes were ready. He loved it, and I went on to sketch a first draft of the play based on Isaac's Yiddish outline without ever meeting Mr. Singer at all." (Leah says she has learned to call Isaac by his first name when she's with him but prefers "Mr. Singer"

---

* "Isaac Bashevis Singer: I Walk on Mysteries." *The Washington Post*, December 28, 1976.

the rest of the time, as she doesn't wish to be assumed guilty of name-dropping.)

By the fall of 1974 Leah Napolin's script was ready. Isaac was down in Seaside. Leah flew to Miami with her husband, Bob, to meet him at his condominium apartment and show him what she had done.

"I was terrified. I had never come face to face with one of my literary idols before. It was a tense situation for me. Would he like it? Would he hate it? Well, he liked it. But that was only the beginning of my job. I spent three days down in Miami Beach and about four or five hours of each of them working with Isaac. We went through the script line by line. We would break for dinner and start again the following afternoon."

Leah speaks no Yiddish, but her husband does, and he was on hand to help out in matters of translation.

What sort of changes was Isaac after? "I felt at the time that his main concern was with cultural accuracy. He wanted to be sure that we made no mistakes in portraying these Polish Jews of the nineteenth century, that we were correct in all matters pertaining to rituals and customs. And for me, that was just fine. We talked a lot about life in the small towns of Eastern Europe, about what the Jews who lived in that time and that place were permitted to do, to say, to feel. Isaac was extremely sharp in matters of language and translation. In one narration I had described Avigdor's wife as snoring like a buzz saw. Isaac objected. At first I couldn't understand why. The phrase appeared in the English version of the story itself. But Isaac said this should never have gone through—there were no buzz saws in the *shtetl* then. We cleared up a number of such anachronisms.

"By the time Bob and I left Miami we felt we were living in Bechev in 1873 and not in America in 1974. We also felt good about the script. There were a number of further drafts, but essentially the play had taken the shape it would have."

❀

The choice of an actress to play Yentl was crucial, and Robert Kalfin picked a tiny, pretty actress named Tovah Feldshuh. Born in New York, raised in Westchester, and graduated from Sarah Lawrence, this young performer served her apprenticeship in regional theaters from Cleveland to Seattle. When she got the offer to play the title role in *Yentl*, she had just won the 1974 Outer Critics Circle Award for best supporting performance on Broadway, in *Dreyfus in Rehearsal*, which also took place in a Polish ghetto.

On stage, in her sideburns and yarmulke and black gaberdine, her green eyes hidden behind rimless lenses, Tovah, as Yentl, looked every inch the girl who should have been born a boy and whose passion for learning had impelled her to disguise herself as one in order to enter a yeshiva in a Polish village.

❀

May 12, 1976

On a warm afternoon, dressed in a white suit with a bold blue tie, Tovah looks more like a rising young star than a yeshiva boy.

"I almost didn't go into the theater at all," Tovah says. "I was on the waiting list for Harvard Law School when I changed my mind and decided to become an actress instead of a lawyer. I came to New York in June of 1973 after playing some twenty parts as a journeyman—in the Guthrie Theater in Minneapolis after getting my master's degree out there at the University of Minnesota.

"I was supposed to play a food-seller in a musical version of *Cyrano,* but the play folded, and I began doing repertory all over the country. I was understudy for Bernadette Peters in the musical *Mack and Mabel* when David Merrick introduced me to Garson Kanin, and I got the role of the young girl in *Dreyfus in Rehearsal.* After that I was supposed to go into another musical, so when Robert Kalfin offered me the part as Yentl, I said, 'No way.' At thirteen I was bas-mitzvahed, and I had been to Israel, but I didn't want to become stereotyped. I was going to find myself a nice Episcopalian role. I felt I was spending all my time with my great-great-grandfather in Europe. I was on my way to my agent's to return the script without opening it. Then somebody who was supposed to meet me for lunch didn't show up, and I started reading the script. I couldn't put it down. I called up to find out if it was too late to still audition for the part. It wasn't, and I got it."

In preparing for the role Tovah underwent an experience strikingly similar to that of the character in the tale, who disguises herself as a boy to get into a yeshiva. Tovah and Irishman John Shea, a former student of Robert Brustein's who was making his New York debut as Avigdor, actually succeeded in getting themselves smuggled into a Hasidic yeshiva in Brooklyn, where they could study the looks and manners of the boys in the classroom.

"I will never forget the white faces of those kids," Tovah says. "They spent so much of their lives indoors. My mother and father came from an Orthodox background, but they belong to a Conservative synagogue, and I never really had any contact with Hasidic Jews until that summer of 1974. If Avigdor and I were convincing yeshiva *bochers*, it was because we studied the originals at first hand. Their lives were completely immersed in those religious books. I was struck by the way they would touch the books, kiss the books and hug them—it was almost a sexual thing."

Tovah never perceived Yentl as a girl with lesbian tendencies. "If she had such tendencies, they were unconscious. Her libido was bound up with the Torah. Her passion was for learning. Her sexual inclinations were toward Avigdor. And this is how I tried to play the role."

The weekend before rehearsals started, director Bob Kalfin invited Tovah to go along with him and his costume designer, Carrie Robbins, to meet Isaac. "Alma answered the door," Tovah recollects, "and there stood this man with gleaming blue eyes and pointed ears and white skin with a kind of aura about it. He had an impish look, and I thought, In this man, with his wit and his devilishness and his lightness, lies the real key to the character of Yentl.

"Isaac was very concerned throughout rehearsals that the ritual details be exactly right. I asked him all sorts of questions about body movements in prayer and gestures and specific matters of business to project the character. During rehearsals he came to my dressing room several times and was always promising to take me out and buy me the best blintzes in New York City. This didn't happen, but long afterward, when *Yentl* was on Broadway and he had turned up at what I felt was one of the worst performances I had given, I wrote him a letter apologizing for my acting and telling him I had not forgotten about the offer of the blintzes."

Isaac wrote back:

Dear Tovah,

I was happy to receive your most kind letter. I found your name in the Manhattan telephone book and tried many times to call you. I haven't forgotten you, your kindness to me and your great talent. Neither have I forgotten the blintzes which I've promised and which have gotten cold from waiting so long. However, God creates new blintzes and new angels every day so we still have a chance. I'll try to call you again, but if I don't get you, do me a favor—call me. . . .

Isaac has yet to treat Tovah to a plate of blintzes, but they did discuss the problems of the play and the character a number of times. When Tovah learned she was expected to remove all her clothes in the scene of the ritual bath when Yentl is preparing for marriage with the beautiful Hadass, she balked and was ready to quit the cast. It was Isaac who persuaded her to stay and go through the nude appearance.

✿

In deference to Isaac's concern about cultural accuracy, Robert Kalfin hired Rabbi Leonard Cohen, a Hasidic rabbi from Brooklyn, as a technical advisor, and the cast was taken on tours of Jewish neighborhoods in Brooklyn. Looking over the designs for the costumes, Isaac would ask for changes in the length of a skirt or the color of a pair of shoes. He would correct the way the performers put on their prayer shawls and phylacteries. Leah Napolin remembers that Isaac felt that *Yentl* was concerned more with "the divine androgyny of the soul" than with homosexuality.

When the Chelsea Theater production of *Yentl* opened at the Academy of Music in Brooklyn on December 17, 1974 (a hundred and one years later than the time of the story), the play ran nearly four hours. Yet *Yentl* was so successful and the press reports so glowing that it played for forty-eight performances, and it was decided to bring the tomboy yeshiva girl and her adventures to Broadway. This time Isaac involved himself more personally in the process of getting the play into shape, but not always with constructive results.

After promising several times to attend try-out rehearsals in Philadelphia, Isaac turned up one day in September 1975 to see how things were going. He sat in the audience complaining to playwright Napolin about the performance, then went backstage and upbraided the cast. He had said a number of times that the humor ought to be played down, that he didn't want *Yentl* to be another *Fiddler on the Roof.* Now he shouted that the comedy ought to be played up—that the whole thing was too serious. *Yentl*, after all, was a folktale; it could not be solemn!

Isaac's sudden appearance and contradictory suggestions confused the cast. Instead of going to the director to discuss the production, as is considered proper in the theater, he had gone over Kalfin's head, directly to the players. Leah Napolin wondered what had happened to Isaac's feeling that *Yentl* dealt with the "divine androgyny of the soul."

❈

A crisp, blustery October evening in 1975. After a week of previews *Yentl* opens tonight at the Eugene O'Neill Theater on West Forty-ninth Street. An early curtain, of course, to accommodate the critics.

"Cheryl Crawford, Moe Septee, The Chelsea Theater with Mrs. Victor H. Potamkin present The Chelsea Theater Center of Brooklyn Production of *Yentl*," announces the *Playbill* program, "a play by Leah Napolin and Isaac Bashevis Singer." Production "conceived and directed by Robert Kalfin."

Not exactly a black-tie audience but well-dressed enough and definitely bustling. Clive Barnes of the *Times* is standing down front, oversized and benign, saying how much he admires Isaac and is hoping the play will be wonderful. Down front sits Walter Kerr, who will write his own opinion of *Yentl* in the *Times* next Sunday. Yes, the critics are all there, from *Time*'s Ted Kalem to Howard Kissel of *Women's Wear Daily*, and reviewers from the *Jewish Daily Forward*, *The Jewish Press*, and *Jewish Week*, and the TV and radio reporters who will be delivering their capsule verdicts over the tube scarcely moments after the play is over.

Isaac has spent an agreeable afternoon autographing copies of his latest collection of short stories, *Passions*, at a bookstore on upper Broadway. At the theater now, dressed in one of his dark suits, a white shirt, and a particularly sober tie, he half sits, half stands in his seat down front while Alma, rigged out attractively but not gaudily, beams at his side. A constant stream of well-wishers comes down the aisle to pay them homage. Friends, editors, representatives of Jewish organizations, the producers, the director, the cast, the co-author, and paying members of the theater-going public who like to be on hand for openings—they're all here too.

There is no curtain. The house lights go down, and the stage lights come up on a set decorated with copies of drawings suggesting Jewish life in Poland a hundred years ago. There's a revolving stage, where sparse props and articles of furniture represent in turn a rabbi's study, a prayer house, a study house, the exterior and interior of a yeshiva, the dining room of a prosperous Jewish home, a ritual bath, a hotel room in a Polish town.

When Tovah Feldshuh comes out in her yeshiva-boy costume to narrate the opening lines of the tale, it is easy enough to mistake her for the real thing. The lighting and the revolving set work well as the action shifts from the villages of Yanov to the towns of Zamosc, Bechev, and Lublin in the year 1873. Tovah has the audience in her grip as she raises her voice in the little prayer house to insist that she as a woman has a right to say *kaddish* for her dead father. The action is paced swiftly at first but slows down as the play proceeds. Even though the running time has been cut from four hours to less than three, in a format of two acts with a single intermission, some episodes still drag. The play never quite recovers momentum again in the second act, which seems overlong. (Perhaps *Yentl* should have been a three-act play, although Kalfin considered that idea and rejected it.)

There is plenty of humor, and during the major wedding scene one is reminded, just as Isaac had feared might happen, of *Fiddler on the Roof*. The jokes bring guffaws, while the frontal nudity elicits gasps from some sections of the audience and seems to constitute the main topic of conversation during the intermission. Tovah Feldshuh's Yentl is the sensation of the evening. John Shea too is uncannily authentic as the yeshiva student who is loved by Yentl but loves the conventional Hadass, portrayed with serene charm by a beautiful blond actress named Lynn Ann Leveridge. The supporting casts plays broadly but authentically enough.

There are some lovely stage pictures in *Yentl*, especially during the episode in the ritual bath (although some found the boys peeping into the bath an offensive touch). Avigdor's wedding, where Yentl shocks everybody by breaking all the rules, getting smashed, and dancing with a woman, makes a spectacular first-act finale. When Avigdor is henpecked by the ugly shrewish woman who takes him for a husband and makes him manage her shop, sighs from the audience begin to mingle with the chuckles. And when Yentl's thwarted love can find no fulfillment, even alone at last with Avigdor in a hotel bedroom, a few sniffles can be heard.

The world of the *shtetl* is drawn in *Yentl* in the broad strokes of operetta, much as in some of Isaac's stories, with the inevitable chorus of gossips and yentas, the scathing sarcasms about the incompetence of physicians, the spitting to ward off the Evil Eye. The atmosphere is authentic, and the situations and dialogue almost always seem credible, though occasionally a false note is struck, as when Yentl asserts to Avigdor that she did it all "for love of the Torah," which sounds specious after all the mischief she has managed to create. When the lights go up at the end, there is plenty of applause—even cheers—but neither Isaac nor Leah Napolin are called to the stage. Suddenly everyone is on the way out through the lobby to West Forty-ninth Street.

At Sardi's a few blocks down, the opening night party is already underway. In fact there are several parties for *Yentl* being held on various floors. Isaac enters the restaurant with Tovah Feldshuh. They are cheered and applauded. Isaac is so embarrassed by the storm of greeting that he wants to go out again and come in by a side entrance. Tovah tries to get him through the clapping throng of admirers, but he won't go with her.

Over supper Alma says that she had asked the ticket agent for fifty tickets for her friends and he wanted to know, "Do they all have to come on opening night?" She is confident that the play will succeed. She thinks the production is "brilliant" and has felt good about the show since the first preview (before the run is over she will see *Yentl* six more times). The scene she likes the most is when Yentl says *kaddish* for her father. Her only misgiving is about Yentl's use of her religious devotion as a pretext for everything, even marrying Hadass and deceiving her in bed. "A weak reason," Alma calls it.

When Isaac is asked whether he is going to stay up all night and wait for the reviews, he is astonished at the idea. Amidst the drinking, the laughter, the banter and introductions, he and Alma fade out of the picture early and go home.

❀

What did the critics think of *Yentl*? All of them, even the adder-tongued John Simon, had praise for Tovah Feldshuh (Simon called her "delightful"). The capsule reviews on the TV news shows were less than ecstatic about the play but effusive about Tovah's performance. In the *Times* Clive Barnes praised the "undeniable sweetness" of the play but found the Broadway version, although "well-focused" compared with its Brooklyn predecessor, faster paced, and "rather less garrulously anecdotal," less charming. He called it a kind of *Fiddler on the Roof* "without a fiddler," saying that its virtues were "perhaps more subtle, if less theatrical." He lauded Tovah Feldshuh as "far more touching on Broadway than in Brooklyn." He praised the "splendid Avigdor" of John Shea, the "imaginative scenery," and the costumes, which he thought suggested "old photographs, even in their color and texture." "The power of the play," he wrote, "is very much in its evocation of a culture and a time." But he concluded with a Yiddish lilt, "So it has charm, but drama it lacks." In the Sunday *Times* Walter Kerr praised Tovah Feldshuh but dismissed the play as irritating. He considered its situation to be "one that will not work . . . a fabulist may persuade us of something unreasonable in a typed paragraph or two on a page; the stage is too literal, too graphic, to tolerate such elision." Some other critics too were less than friendly. In the *Daily News* Douglas Watt wrote that he had found *Yentl* a "hard story to follow" and one that "never really made it to the stage." In the *New York Post* Martin Gottfried called Tovah's performance "overpowering" but felt the play had not lived up to the "potential" even of the flawed Brooklyn production and wound up with the verdict that "for all the fable and soul of *Yentl* it is too erratic and finally disappointing." Agreeing with Kerr, he said: "It isn't the first time a Singer story has proved elusive for the stage and he may well be unadaptable." But *Newsweek*'s Jack Kroll declared that *Yentl* was "one of the wisest of feminist works," and Harold Clurman, in *The Nation*, judged its charm to be "more than superficial." *Variety* compared *Yentl* to *Fiddler*, scored the show for "lack of pace and romantic excitement," and predicted "a moderate run." In *Time* Ted Kalem wrote: "*Yentl* may not be pure theater but it is a delightful stage experience, one delight being the realization that the seventy-one-year-old Singer has written one of the wisest of feminist works."

How did Jewish newspapers and periodicals react to *Yentl*? Not all of them favorably, to be sure. *The Jewish Press*, an Orthodox weekly, called the play "offensive to Jews, an embarrassment and a disgrace as an alleged representation of traditional Judaism and Yeshiva life. It makes a sham of family sanctity and is basically a bad, dull play." An editorial, signed by Arnold Find, branded the play as "pornography" and expressed the hope that "in the future when producers present a show on Broadway with a Jewish theme they will show better taste." In the *Jewish News* of New Jersey Edith K. Schapiro evaluated the play as "slightly flawed" but "very good theater." She added that "the few fleeting moments in the production that could have been rated 'X' might have been handled a bit more discreetly, but they definitely follow from the artistic expression of the plot and cannot be branded sensationalism." For Esther Blaustein in the *Jewish Community News*, *Yentl* was "hard-hitting, honest, beautiful theater. . . . With *Yentl*, the Jewish play has finally come of age." The *Jewish Daily Forward* carried a picture of Tovah Feldshuh in her Yentl costume and another of Isaac Singer that must have been taken when he first came to this country, if not while he still lived in Warsaw (he isn't sure). The review by Yitzchak Perlov described the story as "a pearl of Yiddish literature" and praised the acting, scenery, costumes, lighting, and music. "Today's women libbers," he wrote, "should have Yentl's courage, arguments and longings to carry with them on their protests and demonstrations. . . . There came from the stage the feeling of good Yiddish literature as well as great theater which captured and held one's attention." Comparing *Yentl* with *Fiddler on the Roof,* he delivered the verdict that "*Yentl* is even better—more meaningful, more impressive." Writing in *Jewish Week*, though, Eleanor Lester complained that "what was wry humor in the narrative turns out to be burlesque on the stage. . . . the conclusion of Singer's fantasy suggests that something demonic has been unleashed by Yentl's unholy crossing of sex lines. Three lives have been blasted and the community is in turmoil with speculation running to Satanic intervention. This element is cut to a cute chicken-plucking scene among three gossips and we are left with an upbeat ending that strangles the tale." Even so, she writes, "the play is entertaining. . . . Feldshuh's performance has rocketed her to stardom, and director Robert Kalfin's meticulous attention to authentic details of gesture, costume and accent makes for a great deal of nostalgic charm. And feminists will delight in Yentl's fierce determination to create the life she wants." A few days later, along with Kerr's review, the Sunday *Times* carried a feature by the same writer in which she reported that Isaac saw himself "as still only on the threshold of playwriting and . . . eager to learn more about the craft." " 'Playwriting is the most difficult art,' " she quoted Isaac as saying, " 'the greatest challenge to a writer. A great play should be from the beginning written as a play. But since there are very few great plays, and many people who want to go to the theater, it becomes the custom to make a play from a story. So I, too, try my hand at it.' " Isaac told Eleanor Lester that when he first heard about Robert Kalfin's idea of staging the story, it did not strike him as particularly promising. Yet he felt that the work was still "ninety percent mine—the language is all mine and the construction is mostly as I had it."

This sort of talk upset Leah Napolin when she overheard it at a gathering shortly after the opening. She reminded Isaac that she, after all, had had something to do with the writing of *Yentl*. Isaac made a joke of it. Others who have worked with him, to be sure, have voiced similar complaints about his reluctance to share credit. One gets the impression again that Isaac feels he is surrounded by people who have tried to capitalize on his talents and his lifetime of effort; when it comes to sharing credit, in perhaps almost every case "ninety percent of it," as he estimates, should go to him after all.

The reception of *Yentl* on the part of both critics and public had been mixed, but *Yentl* later went on tour in other cities in the United States and Canada. Tovah Feldshuh was nominated for a 1976 Tony Award as best actress of the year for her performance in *Yentl*. She didn't win it, but her career was safely launched. Her return to the Brooklyn Academy of Music as Irina in a production of Chekhov's *The Three Sisters* in the spring of 1977 brought her further critical acclaim, as did her TV appearance in *Holocaust*. Tovah feels that if *Yentl* had been pruned down more and sharpened up a bit it might have run for years instead of months. Isaac later talked to her about doing the lead in Eva Friedman's adaptation of *Teibele and Her Demon* if and when it was ready for the stage. Tovah is still waiting for him to take her out for that plate of blintzes.

❀

In the spring of 1978 the play on which Isaac collaborated with Eve Friedman, based on his story "Teibele and Her Demon," opened at the Tyrone Guthrie Theater in Minneapolis. A reporter in *Variety* described the new play as "a drama of significant substance" and "a major, enduring work of art." The reviewer judged *Teibele and Her Demon* to be the "best original work staged" at the Guthrie. "The humor is warm and at times incisive," he wrote, expressing some misgivings over the change of mood that overtakes the play at the end, when "the humor turns bitter . . . and gives way to tragedy." *Teibele*, he assured *Variety*'s readers, was "no *Fiddler*." Reporting in from Minneapolis, Richard Eder sent *The New York Times* a mixed review. "The sad and delicate irony of an Isaac Bashevis Singer short story," he began, "has been captured briefly and then flooded out in its staging at the Guthrie Theater here." He judged the production, under Stephen Kanee's direction, "at its best . . . humorous, poignant and sometimes quite beautiful" and "at its worst . . . heavy and bombastic." To Eder the heart of the story about the cabalist who pretends to be a dybbuk in order to possess the woman he yearns for is "a riddle" rather than a tragedy, with a climax that is "paradox, not purgation." He found the early scenes "pithy and meditative," with F. Murray Abraham effective as the shy, pedantic student Alchanon, who drives poor Teibele mad with his pranks, and Laura Estherman (Tovah Feldshuh was busy elsewhere) "affecting" as Teibele. He called the marriage scene between Alchanon and Teibele "extraordinary."

But Eder scored as inappropriate the ending of the play, culminating in
Teibele's madness and death, which, he said, turned the drama, "with por-
tentous lighting, music and smoke, and disembodied voices, skipping about
overhead while Teibele flops and gibbers," into "foolish medodrama."

The week Eder saw *Teibele* both Isaac and Alma were in Minneapolis to
see it for themselves, and discussions were under way about bringing *Teibele*
to Broadway.

❁

July 27, 1978

"When I. B. Singer goes," says actor Lou Jacobi, "and he should live for
many years yet, the mold will be broken, the die destroyed. He is the last
link with the Jewish past in Poland, the only one who really remembers and
knows how to bring it all back to life, detail by detail." Jacobi, who has
played countless Jewish roles over the years, is leaving tomorrow to play the
role of a Polish non-Jew in the movie that is finally to be made of *The
Magician of Lublin*. Shooting starts next week in Berlin, where the producer
is setting up locations. The film will be called *The Magician* and is described in the screenplay as "based on" the novel. The story has been
simplified and a new ending supplied—a kind of mini-holocaust, foreshadowing the Nazi barbarism to come. The producer is Menahem Golan
(*Trunk to Cairo, Sallah*), an Israeli filmmaker who has spent several years
trying to raise money for this project while preparing various versions of the
screenplay, for which he shares writing credits with Irving S. White and
Joseph Gross. Golan, who will also direct the movie, runs Golan-Globus
Productions, Ltd., with offices in Hollywood, New York, and Israel. There
is said to be Israeli as well as American and European money in the enterprise.

In *The Magician* Jacobi is to play the part of the philandering Yasha
Mazur's "impresario," who is always trying to hold his client's career
together and keep his mind on his magic. It is a part built up from a mere
paragraph in the book, and Jacobi is enthusiastic about its possibilities. He is
the first of the principals to speak in the opening scene, which takes place in
the town of Piask, where Yasha is seen walking a tightrope for the diversion
of the crowd below. The role of Mazur has gone to Alan Arkin. Portraying
the women in the magician's complicated life will be Shelley Winters as his
loyal, provincial spouse, Esther, Louise Fletcher as the impoverished
countess Emilia, and if plans remain as they are, Valerie Perrine and Carol
Kane as others whose beds Mazur shares. Since there are no more *shtetls* in

Warsaw, Golan intends to recreate the ghetto scenes by shooting in other cities in neighborhoods that still retain a turn-of-the-century look.

Jacobi is taking with him as many books of Isaac's stories as he can round up in paperback editions. "I have always thrilled at the magic Isaac Singer can create in a couple of paragraphs," he says. "I have admired his brother's books too. I will never forget seeing *Yoshe Kalb* in the Yiddish theater on Second Avenue when I was a boy. What a role! The past those men described is gone now—Hitler did a good job—but it all comes alive again in their pages. I play the magician's agent, a very grandiose fellow. I start right in disparaging the town where he's appearing—'Where am I? I overslept. I'm looking for a stinking little place called Piask. This is Piask?' " Instantly Jacobi has transformed himself into the "fat, energetic, nouveau-riche" type he is to enact on the screen. He praises the choice of Arkin for the starring role, calling Arkin the possessor of a "healthy madness" that is sure to come into play to the film's advantage. Then he looks at his watch. Time to go home, where his wife is packing. "It's very exciting," he says. "So many years of talk about making a movie from this book and now, finally, it's going to be done, and I'm so happy to be a part of it."

PART 8

"I Can Remember
When Nobody Asked Me"

hat kind of living does Isaac Bashevis Singer make from his writing?

Isaac remembers getting a letter from Roger Straus, Jr., in the early days of their association predicting that someday his income would amount to twenty thousand dollars a year. "It looked to me like a joke. I thought, well, this is wishful thinking." The wish has fulfilled itself many times over, yet only one of Isaac's books—*Shosha*—has ever hit the best-seller list in *The New York Times* (although *The Manor* was listed as a best-seller in the *New York Post* for some weeks, and the Penguin edition of *The Slave* did become a best-seller in England).

In an October 1965 article in *Harper's* entitled "What's in It for Me?" Isaac discusses his income:

"How does a Yiddish writer exist? How does he make a living? Who publishes his books and who reads them?"

He then proceeds to deliver what he calls "a few dry facts." Of the first American publication in Yiddish of *Satan in Goray and Other Stories*, in 1943, he writes: "To the best of my recollection, one thousand copies were printed and my royalties totalled $90. And this sum I was only able to collect several years after the book had been published, and following much haggling with the publisher."

Of "Gimpel the Fool": ". . . the Yiddish magazine in which it appeared paid me $20."

Of the Yiddish edition of his novel *The Family Moskat*: ". . . I received $250. The bulk of this sum I had to lay out for author's corrections. Naturally, I proofread the manuscript without payment."

Of the Yiddish edition of *In My Father's Court*: ". . . I got $300."

Of the Yiddish edition of *Gimpel the Fool and Other Stories*: ". . . I got $400."

Isaac asserts that he was better paid by the *Jewish Daily Forward* for his stories and the serialization of his novels than by Yiddish book publishers and magazines.

After Isaac's work began to appear in English the rates went up, but they were still on the modest side. He collected two thousand dollars in royalties from Alfred A. Knopf for *The Family Moskat,* which was a selection of The Book Find Club. "The reason the royalties amounted to so little was that the publisher deducted the translator's fee from the total. It happened that the translator, A. Gross, died before he could finish it and it cost me additional time and money to complete the job."

For *Satan in Goray* Noonday Press offered Isaac an advance of three thousand dollars. Similar advances were paid for the English-language editions of *Gimpel the Fool and Other Tales* and *The Magician of Lublin.* For stories in *Partisan Review, Commentary,* and *Midstream,* he got about three hundred dollars apiece. Later, with Paula Diamond and Lila Karpf looking out for his share of subsidiary rights, "better things began for me." Isaac asked rhetorically, "Just how good are they?

"Not good enough so I can make a living from my books and stories alone. My main source of income is still derived from my journalistic work for the *Jewish Daily Forward.* I also write sketches for radio station WEVD and lecture—a lot of work for a man of sixty. I couldn't have managed all these years if my wife, Alma, didn't hold a job as a saleswoman."

Yet: "I don't know of a single writer more satisfied with his lot than I. When I began to write, I was fifteen and I never heard of anybody making a living from writing. I am still surprised every time I get a check for a story or even for lecturing. I was brought up with the idea that the Torah is not to be used as a means of livelihood and that spiritual work is its own reward." He found out that his only literary problem in America would be trying to find a publisher to print his books in Yiddish. "I hope one day to find a Yiddish publisher who will not ask for an advance from *me.*"

In the decade that followed, Isaac's fortunes changed for the better. In addition to the motion-picture options held on *The Magician of Lublin,* options were taken on *The Slave* and "Yentl the Yeshiva Boy." The run of *Yentl* on Broadway brought him a substantial sum. Demands for his services as a lecturer and teacher have proliferated. *The New Yorker* pays far more than three hundred dollars for a story. His children's books sell well. His advances on his novels from Farrar, Straus and Giroux and on his recent books of memoirs from Doubleday, with his agent, Robert Lesher, doing the negotiating, have been high. In fact, these days, Isaac Singer is not as open as he was back in 1965 in discussing his income, although in 1978 he did tell a *Time* interviewer that he estimated his income as approximately one hundred thousand dollars a year. It is rumored that Farrar, Straus and Giroux has decided to ration Isaac's annual receipt of funds so that all his money will not go to taxes. Isaac has come a long way since the days when he sold his masterpiece "Gimpel" for twenty dollars. Even so, he often allows Jewish publications to print original work at prices far below what they could command on the commercial market.

Isaac wrote at the end of that disarmingly honest *Harper's* article, ". . . there is a possibility that when this article appears, things will look better for me. One of the editors of *Harper's* suggested that they would put a footnote saying that the author has in the meantime become rich. I am glad the footnote isn't here. We already have too many rich writers, many of them poor writers."

Isaac feels that success has not spoiled him. Except for the condominium apartment in Miami Beach, the summer trips to Switzerland and Israel, and a few additional comforts, he doesn't believe that his life-style has been affected by his bank account. "I live today as, most likely, by and large I would be living anyhow, even if my books and lectures had not made money for me."

"It's almost impossible," says Alma, "to persuade him to go out and buy new clothes when he needs them. He will wear a hat until it falls apart. He likes to shop, but it seldom gets further than window shopping."

Isaac continues to prefer modest eating places where he feels at home to glamorous restaurants, and simple surroundings to ostentation of any kind; luxuries make him uncomfortable. Fame came to him so late that it has not gone to his head.

"I always am happy to sign an autograph," he says, "because I can remember when nobody asked me to sign one."

❀

The December 1975 issue of *Esquire* carried an essay headlined "If you could ask one question about life, what would the answer be?" The two people invited to respond were Eugene Ionesco and Isaac Bashevis Singer. Ionesco's answer was "No." Isaac's answer was "Yes."

In the essay Isaac speaks about his discussions with his father and brother about whether or not there was a God who had created the world: "In our home the most pressing questions were the eternal ones; there the cosmic riddles were not theoretical but actual. . . .

"The world that was revealed to me," he continues, "was not rational. One could as easily question the validity of reason as the existence of God. In my own spirit there was chaos. I suffered from morbid dreams and hallucinations. I had wildly erotic fantasies. Hungry children, filthy beggars, refugees sleeping in the streets, wagons of wounded soldiers did not arouse admiration in me for human or divine reason. The spectacle of a cat pouncing on a mouse made me sick and rebellious. Neither human reason nor God's mercy seemed to be certain. I found both filled with contradictions. My brother still clung to the hope that in the end reason would be victorious. But young though I was, I knew that the worship of reason was as idolatrous as bowing down to a graven image. . . .

"My childish hope was to discover the truth and through the discovery to give sense and substance to my life. But, finally, my conclusion was that the power of philosophy lay in its attack upon reason, not in the building of systems. None of the systems could be taken seriously; they did not help one to manage one's life. The human intellect confronted existence, and existence stubbornly refused to be systematized. I myself was the insulted and shamed human intellect. Many times I contemplated suicide because of my intellectual impotence."

Later, Isaac writes, he evolved a philosophy of his own, that "the basic substance of the world was potentially as seen as a whole." This brought him to the concept that God is "an eternal belle-lettrist," yearning "throughout all eternity to perfect his creation. . . . All His worlds are nothing more than states and experiments in a divine laboratory. I quoted to myself that passage from the Midrash that says God created many worlds before He created this one. Like my brother and myself, God threw His unsuccessful works into the wastebasket." ("The wastebasket," Isaac has said, "is a writer's best friend.") And like all writers, "the Almighty has His critics. We know that the angels have nothing but praise. Three times a day they sing: 'Sublime! Perfect! Great! Excellent!' But there must be some angry critics, too. They complain: Your novel, God, is too long, too cruel. Too little love. Too much sex. They advise cutting. How can a novel be good when three fourths of it is water? They find it inconsistent, sensational, antisocial, cryptic, decadent, vulgar, melodramatic, improvised, repetitious. One keeps on reading it day and night. The fear of death is nothing but the fear of having to close God's book. We all want to go on with this serial forever. The belief in survival has one explanation: we refuse to have any interruptions in reading. As readers we are burning with a desire to know the events of the next chapter, and the next, and the next. We try hard to find the formula for God's best seller, but we are always wrong. The heavenly Writer is full of surprises. All we can do is pray for a happy ending, but, according to the Cabala, God's novel will never end. The coming of the Messiah will only be the beginning of a new volume. Resurrection will bring back some characters the reader, but not the Writer, has already forgotten. What we call death is but a temporary pause for purely literary reasons. . . .

"God creates continuously, and continuous creation is man's destiny, too. God, like the artist, is free. Like the artist, His works cannot be predetermined. Continual change is their very essence. Beauty is their purpose.

God's fantasy is their limit. God, like the artist, never knows how his work will develop. Only the intention is clear: to bring out a masterpiece and improve it all the time. I once called God a struggling artist. This continual aspiration is what men call suffering. In this system emotions are not passive as in Spinoza's philosophy. God himself is emotion. God thinks and feels. Compassion and beauty are two of his endless attributes."

This is Isaac saying "Yes."

❀

Enjoying lunch on a May Sunday in 1977 at his favorite eating place on West Seventy-second Street, Isaac points out with pleasure an excerpt in *The New York Times Book Review* from a forthcoming volume called *The Book of Lists.** Among the lists are "Henry Miller's 10 Greatest Writers of all Time." They include Proust, Dostoevsky, Rabelais, Nietzsche, Lao-tzu, Tagore, Walt Whitman, Élie Faure, Marie Corelli—and Isaac Bashevis Singer. Another list is entitled "28 Writers Who Could Have Won the Nobel Prize in Literature—But Didn't." The nominees are Tolstoy, Spencer, Chekhov, Ibsen, Hardy, Conrad, Twain, Rilke, Meredith, James, Swinburne, Brandes, Strindberg, Gorky, Brecht, Valery, O'Casey, Proust, D'Annunzio, Dreiser, Croce, Freud, Woolf, Fitzgerald, Wells, Cather, Maugham, and Mao Tse-tung. Isaac says he is proud to be in their company.

❀

Dvorah, who comes in at eleven in the morning and doesn't leave until six in the evening, has organized Isaac's files and is hoping to make order out of his correspondence. Isaac gets letters from all over the world, in Yiddish, Hebrew, and English, from admirers and detractors, relatives, editors, publishers, filmmakers, producers, aspiring writers, new acquaintances and half-forgotten ones from long ago, students looking for help with term papers or theses. Writers send him stories, poets send him poems, playwrights send him plays, screenwriters send him scenarios. The mail piles up outside his door—newsletters, magazines, books for comments to be used on their jackets, invitations to speak, love letters from directors of organizations

* David Wallechinsky, Irving Wallace, and Amy Wallace, *The Book of Lists*. New York: William Morrow, 1977.

thanking him for speeches he has already made. There are publications devoted to Judaism, vegetarianism, Republicanism, socialism—every ism in the world. There are periodicals devoted to the occult. There are reviews of his work, letters from prisoners; long, thoughtful missives from professors and university presidents, questionnaires from the editors of *Who's Who*.

Here is a letter from a doctor in Chicago expressing appreciation for Isaac's sketches and stories in the *Forward* and at the same time irritation over a phrase in one of them: Isaac has attributed an event to "fickle Providence." Providence, the doctor feels, is not "fickle."

A woman friend writes to inquire how Isaac is faring with his hay fever, from which he suffers every summer, and to report on the birth of a new baby. She would love to accept his proposal that she come and work as his secretary, but, alas, she cannot type. Maybe he should go to the Gaspé in Quebec, which, she hears, is a place free of hay fever.

The executive secretary of the American Jewish Congress in Winnipeg is offering a fee of two hundred dollars plus traveling expenses if Isaac will come up and address a meeting on the anniversary of the Warsaw Ghetto uprising.

A prospective translator thanks Isaac for entrusting him with the original manuscript of "Gimpel the Fool," which he promises to guard with his life, and returns the manuscript of a novel he is not sure he is equipped to transform into English commensurate with the language of the original.

Who's Who in World Jewry sends a copy of Isaac's biography for correction; a critic forwards excerpts from an introduction to an anthology that will contain several of Isaac's stories; an admirer requests an autograph on the flyleaf of his copy of *The Family Moskat*; a publisher wants Isaac's signature on two copies of a contract; a radio producer wants the rights for the adaptation of a story to be broadcast.

A five-page letter from Washington Heights discusses a piece Isaac once wrote about a Yiddish translation of the Bhagavad-Gita. As a student of the esoteric teachings, this correspondent would like to establish contact with Isaac. She describes herself as a woman of sixty-five who all her life has been striving for "mental and spiritual advancement." She outlines her life story (born in Rumania, suffered from typhoid fever at nineteen followed by a nervous breakdown, arrived in America in 1910, married a man who died young, turned to Eastern philosophy for solace). She would like to place at Isaac's disposal certain valuable books on the occult that might prove of extraordinary interest to his work. If he will drop her a note arranging an appointment. . . .

An "ardent admirer" reports an "unfavorable opinion" of a recent series in the *Forward* on the subject of the Writers' Club in Warsaw that Isaac has signed with the pen name Warshawsky. He cautions Isaac to inquire into the opinion of "others" before proceeding with the series.

The editor of a children's magazine writes to thank the author for a recent article on the Jews of South America.

An Argentine importer whose son is about to be appointed Portuguese Consul in Argentina (this was in 1958) asks if Isaac can help arrange for the young man to serve as an ad-honorem correspondent of the *Forward*.

From the University of Notre Dame a history teacher writes to ask whether Isaac has published any new stories—and whatever happened to a proposed novel about Jews who returned from "Turkish captivity."

From Czechoslovakia comes a poignant missive from a man who has been translating pieces into Czech from Yiddish, Hebrew, and English. He would appreciate a Yiddish text of the story "The Little Shoemakers" so that he can translate from the original.

An editor of a syndicate circulating features of interest to the English-Jewish press encloses an unfavorable review of one of his own books in *The New York Times Book Review*, along with a reply that was never printed, and wonders why "Gimpel the Fool" was not translated as "Gimpel the Simpleton," since the word *"nar"* in Yiddish "has a nuance beyond the dry English word 'fool.' "

From Los Angeles comes a characteristic request, from a graduate student in the theater arts department of the University of California, to adapt *Satan in Goray* for the stage; a later report describes progress on the script.

A rabbi thanks Isaac for taking time out to evaluate the text of a sermon.

A publisher sends a small check as "permission payment" for reprinting "Gimpel the Fool" in a collection of short fiction.

Isaac reads them all, answers them all; invites admirers he has never met to visit him; offers advice to poets, playwrights, and writers of fiction; grants permission for stories to be turned into dramas and operas; autographs books; accepts requests for luncheon appointments, personal consultations, sittings for photographic portraits, lecture trips, reprints, interviews, psychic exchanges. He thanks a fan for her "touching letter" and advises her that "in literature, death does not exist" and that for him, even in real life, "everything which ever existed, from a microbe to the greatest of men, is alive and eternal." He thanks a poet in Canada for a poem she sent him, adding, "If I ever come to Paradise and the Almighty would ask me what I would like, I would answer him, to spend eternity with all my good readers—if they will be there too." He thanks Mayor Teddy Kollek of Jerusalem for an invitation to visit that city, assuring him that "your treatment of writers and spiritual people in general is adding glory both to you and to the great city which is the symbol of the Eternal Spirit." He thanks Louis Nizer for sending him a copy of *My Life in Court* and hopes that someday soon they can share a vegetarian meal. "Even though my wife wasn't at the Lotos Club dinner, she was delighted to hear about our meeting and she liked very much the portrait you drew on the napkin." To a Ph.D. who has attended a lecture on mysticism at the Jewish Museum and is worried about the potential dangers of mystical beliefs, Isaac replies: "The fact that people use mysticism to hurt other people does not make mysticism unkosher." He sends a contribution to the New York Public Library and with it a letter recalling what the library in Warsaw meant to him as a child when he went there to find warmth and shelter and the nourishment of books.

Nobody goes unanswered. Nobody is ignored, put down, patronized, or dismissed with formula phrases. Permission is granted, encouragement expressed, time made somehow for all who ask for it. Isaac fills out the forms, signs the contracts, takes the checks to the bank, and goes back to whatever manuscript he is working on, managing somehow never to lose the thread of the story he is writing or to neglect to feed the pigeons in the neighborhood or to answer the next call on the telephone—which is ringing away even now.

❄

Over the years, as interest in his work has widened, Isaac has made himself increasingly available to photographers, interviewers, feature-writers, and journalists. He has welcomed into his home a seemingly unending procession of visitors, some of them simply curious to meet the author whose work has provided them with so many hours of diversion, others dispatched by editors who have felt that an interview with Singer would make stimulating copy. He has also appeared from time to time as a guest on television and radio talk shows, including Jewish religious programs in New York and in other cities.

One of the most significant of these interviews was conducted by two outstanding authors and critics on the American Jewish scene—Joel Blocker and Richard Elman. Their piece on Singer first appeared in *Commentary* in November 1963 and has been reprinted in several collections, including Malin's *Critical Views of Isaac Bashevis Singer*.

Blocker and Elman arrived for their interview better prepared than most, and Isaac responded with his usual good humor, and sometimes shrewdly, to their searching queries. Asked, for example, how he felt about writing in Yiddish after the "decimation" of the Yiddish reading audience during the Holocaust, he responded that although he expected the number of Yiddish writers to get "smaller and smaller," he didn't feel the language would ever die out completely. The *Forward*, he estimated, has "eighty or ninety thousand readers," and most of them follow his fiction. The *Forward* has a tradition of publishing good fiction, and its readers consider the inclusion of stories and serialized novels in the newspaper "a must." Yet Isaac could not help but see the future of Yiddish as black, for "if a Yiddish reader dies, there is no one to replace him." He quoted Abraham Cahan, the guiding light of the *Forward* for so many years, as saying that the first generation of American Jews would speak Yiddish, but the second generation would not.

When he writes, Blocker and Elman asked, does Isaac think about his readers? The truth is, Isaac answered, he doesn't. "The only audience I'm conscious of—you may laugh at me—is myself. I have to please myself." A writer who thinks of his readers when he is writing is liable to get "all mixed up." Insofar as an author writes for any audience at all besides himself, he "must feel that he writes for people who know everything he knows—not for the stranger. It's only when you write for your own people and when you don't think about anybody else that the other people reading in a foreign language will appreciate your work and like it." His Yiddish readers, he added, are a "peculiarly sensitive group." They are seldom neutral; they either love him or hate him. Some think he is a heretic; others consider him "too Jewish."

It was in the *Commentary* interview that Isaac first discussed his well-known theory of "as if" in connection with the writing of fiction. Not to be confused with Isaac's invention of alternative lives he might have led had things gone differently, this has rather to do with the presumption of good fortune, even of immortality, that sustains the human spirit. Blocker and Elman wanted to know, "Would it be fair to say that you are actually writing in a somewhat artificial or illusionary context, as if none of the terrible things that happened to the Jewish people . . . really did occur?" He replied, "Yes, very fair. There was a famous philosopher, [Hans] Vaihinger, who wrote a book called *The Philosophy of 'As If,'* in which he showed that we all behave 'as if.' The 'as if' is so much a part of our life that it really isn't artificial. After all, what could be more artificial than marriage? When a man marries a woman, he assumes that she's going to be devoted to him, and he acts as if his wife will treat him in this fashion. And so on and so on. . . . Every man assumes he will go on living. He behaves *as if* he will never die. And I wouldn't call my attitude artificial. It's very natural and healthy. We have to go on living and writing."

Isaac also told Blocker and Elman that he considered himself part of the *Jewish* tradition but not part of the *Yiddish* tradition. He went on to say he had learned much from his brother Joshua about construction, about avoiding "Thomas Mann's habit" of interspersing a story with comments. "When I tell a story, I tell a story. I don't try to discuss, criticize, or analyze my characters." He said he was surprised Irving Howe had described him as a "modernist" and wasn't sure what Howe meant by it.

Isaac explained his use of pseudonyms to distinguish his less serious work from "the stories which I take very seriously." Only after he had carefully "cleaned up" the manuscript of *In My Father's Court*, which first appeared in the *Forward* under the name Warshawsky, did he sign it Isaac Bashevis Singer.

Isaac also characterized his stories as tales constructed "around a moral point of view" rather than morality tales. Finally, admitting to a life-long skepticism about religious as well as political dogmas, he tried to explain—despite the fact that he is not "an observant Jew"—what he means when he says that he believes in God: "I believe in God but not in man insofar as he claims God has revealed Himself to him. If a man comes to me and tells me he has been to the planet Mars, I would call him a liar, but I would not stop believing in the existence of the planet. I believe that the Higher Powers do not reveal themselves so easily; you have to search for them. Consequently I have no faith in dogmas of any kind; they are only the work of men. Man is born to free choice, to believe, to doubt, or to deny. I choose to believe. I also believe in the power of personal prayer. While I shun organized prayer and religion, I would call myself a religious man. The Higher Powers, I am convinced, are always with us, at every moment, everywhere except, per-haps, at the meetings of Marxists and other left-wingers. There is no God there; they have passed a motion to that effect. . . ."

In Malin's collection there also appears an essay by Marshall Breger and Bob Barnhart called "A Conversation with Isaac Bashevis Singer." These two, undergraduates at the University of Pennsylvania, interviewed him in 1964 for their college literary magazine, *The Handle*, and many of his responses on that occasion covered the same ground as the piece in *Commentary*. He did elaborate, though, on some of the problems he had after coming to America in trying to adjust to a new land and a new language: "I will give you an example: in my country, where I lived, all the spoons are not round, but are longish—elongated. When I saw for the first time in this country a round spoon, I said to myself, 'Oh, what is this?' For my business, for literature, it is good if things are steady, if they don't change. For ex-ample, in our country, a drugstore was a store where they sold drugs. Here, when I saw a drugstore and people were eating sandwiches, it was for me a kind of catastrophe. Not a spiritual one, but a kind of literary catastrophe because then the word 'drugstore' has another meaning. When you write in Europe 'drugstore,' the reader gets a feeling what it is, he knows already with what it is connected. But when you see a different drugstore and they serve food, it means that the word has changed. I have a feeling that this is what people would say if they ever reached the planets or the moon. The whole dictionary would have to be changed."

Asked if he thought literature in general was deteriorating, Isaac told his interviewers that old men talk that way in every generation, so when he gets to feeling that he read all the good books when he was young, he reminds himself that twenty thousand books are published every year in this country

alone. How then can he claim to be well acquainted with the world's literature, much less judge it? "The only thing I can say is that I have not seen
for the last twenty years any books about which I could say here is another
Tolstoy or Dostoevsky or Gogol."

Isaac denied being influenced by American writers, since he hadn't read
enough of their work for such an influence to be possible. He confessed to a
preference for reading nonfiction rather than fiction and to an excitement
over new scientific discoveries, especially in the field of space travel.

When the subject of translation came up, Isaac said, "It is true that in
every translation the author loses—you do not gain in translation. Once in a
while you may gain in one sentence, but as a rule you keep on losing. This
is true in all translations, because translation is a kind of compromise. . . .
Poetry loses almost everything; you just can't translate it. The same thing is
true about humor, especially when it is connected with folklore. In my case
I lost a lot, but since I myself take care of the translation, I know that I am
not losing everything."

(In a 1968 interview that appeared in the *National Jewish Monthly*
Isaac added that translation might have damaged him as an author, but it
hasn't yet "killed" him. A writer, if he's really a good one, "will come
through even in translation. I have seen it in my own case. Also translation
helps me in a way. I go through my writings again and again while I edit the
translation and work with the translator, and I see the defects of my writing
while I am doing this. So I would say that in many cases translation has
helped to avoid many pitfalls.")

Asked by Breger and Barnhart how he felt about Poland, Isaac responded,
"The truth is . . . I am still living there. I lived there my first thirty years;
and you know that your experiences in childhood are the most important for
a writer. So for me the Poland of my youth still exists." As for America: "I
begin to feel I am also here a citizen. I mean in a literary sense. In the first
fifteen or twenty years I just couldn't understand American people. Naturally I understood from an emotional point of view. I didn't know what
made their minds work. Today I have a feeling that, when I sit with two
young people like you, I know more or less what you think and how you
feel, just like the human beings in Poland."

When asked what he meant when he wrote in "Gimpel the Fool": "No
doubt the world is entirely an imaginary world—but it is only once removed
from the real world," Isaac referred his interrogators to Bishop Berkeley,
who said that the world is only an aggregation of ideas and concluded,
"When I say 'a table,' I know it is nothing but a name; behind this word
there is a thing in itself of which I have no idea. This feeling is in every
writer, and because of this feeling there is a kind of skepticism in writing. In
other words, even though you say things, you say them with your tongue in
cheek. There is a kind of almost playing around with ideas."

Asked to describe his concept of God, Isaac waded valiantly into a speculative dissertation about God as "the plan of the world" and said that demons and angels were possible because, after all, microbes "were living for millions of years, and we did not know about them." His demons, he said, came partly out of folklore and partly from his own imagination. He also told his visitors that his vegetarianism was sincere and that he really did love animals, inviting his earnest visitors to go into the next room and meet his parakeets, where they could see for themselves that he didn't keep them locked in a cage.

At sixty-four Isaac was interviewed by Dick Adler of *Book World*, the Sunday literary section of *The Washington Post*, which published the results on October 29, 1967, in a piece called "The Magician of 86th Street."

Isaac told Adler that only a short time back he had been worried that the *Jewish Daily Forward* might close down—and how would he earn a living? "I dreamed one night I was running an elevator and I was so happy. Then I found out it isn't easy to get a job like that. You first have to belong to the union."

"Such worries have since faded away," wrote Adler, "and Singer now uses an accountant to prepare his income tax."

About his success Isaac said: "I would be a liar if I said I ever desired failure. I know many writers say that making money from literature is a disgraceful thing, but I don't agree. If a man sits down to write a book with the idea that he is going to make $100,000 and sell it to the movies, such a writer is degrading himself; he will never write a good book. When you sit down to write a book, you have to think about the theme, the topic, the characters, the descriptions—not how much money you are going to make. I must say such thoughts don't cross my mind when I sit down to write a book; I only think about what I should write. But once the book is written, I enjoy very much seeing it sold. When I began, I never heard of anybody making a living from literature. I am still surprised every time I get a check."

Isaac told Adler, "To be a Yiddish writer in America is to be like a ghost: you see others but are yourself unseen." Discussing the inevitable topic of translation, he related that he had advised "a friend of mine, also a Yiddish writer" that he "must be prepared to lose at least forty percent in translation, and to make sure that the other sixty percent has some value. Or, better still, write something that was one hundred and forty percent good."

On April 27, 1968, shortly after the paperback edition of *The Slave* appeared, Haskel Frankel reported on an interview with Isaac in the *Saturday Review*.

Isaac showed Frankel the lined composition book in which he wrote in Yiddish, discussing the virtues of describing one little village rather than "the whole of humanity," praised animals for not being "so silly as people," and concluded: "To me, in my work, the religious question and the eternal question—why do we live, why do we exist?—are identical. I am not completely a religious writer, but neither am I secular. In my writing religion is always there—even when I write sexy.

"One thing. I never sit down to write a slice of life. There is always a real story when I start to write, or I don't start."

On March 15, 1970, in Tucson, Arizona, Isaac was interviewed by Paul Rosenblatt and Gene Koppel* of the university faculty. Isaac's children's book, *A Day of Pleasure*, had just won the National Book Award, and he was in particularly good form that day. He promised to try to give "different answers" to questions he had been asked before, and it must be granted that, by and large, he kept his promise. He spoke of writers who fear that journalism might be detrimental to creative work and said that had not been his experience at all. A writer, he said, must be a good reporter, even if he is reporting fantasies. Fiction must sound as probable, as real, as fact. "Actually," he summed up, "a fiction writer is a reporter of a higher kind."

The interview was a long one, covering many aspects of Isaac's life and views. Unavoidably he had to go over a certain amount of familiar ground, but he also made provocative, populist comments on a number of subjects.

On explaining works of fiction: "The moment explanation enters, literature becomes bad. Sometimes when I read Nabokov and he tries to be his own critic or to tell us what we can learn from him, I see that he is spoiling the story.

"Nonetheless: If I were to become for a moment a critic of my own writing, I would say that it always stresses the power of the spirit over the body in one way or another. I don't feel that life is nothing but a kind of chemical or physical accident, but there is always a plan behind it. I believe in Providence. I believe in spiritual powers, good and evil. The supernatural is always in my writing and somehow I always wanted to say to the reader that even though life looks to us chaotic, it is not as chaotic as we think. There is a scheme and a design behind it."

On pessimism: "I will tell you that I am a pessimist as far as our small world is concerned, but I am not a pessimist as far as the universe is concerned. I am sure that the creator of the universe had a plan in it and that this plan was not a vicious plan. . . . I have two parakeets. They fly around free. But if I want to move from one apartment to another and it's winter, I have to put them in a cage and cover the cage in the middle of the day so that they don't catch a cold. But these parakeets don't know it. They see only cruelty. . . . I have enough imagination to know that God may be much cleverer than I am. And since there is such a huge difference between

---

* *A Certain Bridge, Isaac Bashevis Singer on Literature and Life.* Tucson: University of Arizona Press, 1970.

the intelligence of a parakeet and mine, how huge is the difference between my intelligence and God's? In other words, I am both a pessimist and an optimist."

On keeping notes: "I write out in my notebooks topics of stories. . . . I will never write down, let's say, that the lake looks in the sunset like copper. These are things which I will remember anyhow. I tried once when I traveled abroad to write down these things but somehow I lost the notebook and I never made use of it. Also, images are valid only if they fit into the story. The same image may be right in one story and completely false in another. So by writing down just images, you gain very little."

On the search for identity in fiction: "On this I say, identity—shmidentity. Give me a good book. I will identify myself. If I would have been looking for my identity all my life I wouldn't have read Tolstoy, Dostoevsky and Gogol. What kind of identity would I find there? I was looking for a good story. Identity I got at home."

On other Jewish American authors: ". . . wherever I come people ask me, 'Do you think that Bellow and Malamud are Jewish writers, or that they are writers who happen to be Jews?' So once when I met Mr. Bellow I asked him this question. I said, 'What do you think?' He said, 'I consider myself an American writer who happens to be a Jew. I don't consider myself a specific Jewish writer.' As a matter of fact, even *I* don't consider myself a Jewish writer. I am a Yiddish writer, not a Jewish writer. A Jewish writer I would call a man like my father who wrote all the time about religion. The expression 'Yiddish writer' fits me better than Jewish writer, because sometimes I write things of which religion would not approve altogether.

"Another thing, to be a Jewish writer you need more than to know just the Jewish people in the United States or in Chicago. It is necessary to know also more about the tradition. I would say that to be really a Jewish writer you have to know Hebrew, you have to know Aramaic, you have to know the Talmud, history. In other words, it's not enough to know your hero. You must know the hero's father and grandfather and how they thought and how they behaved. Writers like Philip Roth and others know only one dimension. They cannot know their hero in depth, and this is the reason why some of them write such things as they do write. In my case, I know the American Jew's grandparents, but I don't know enough about the American Jews because I haven't been brought up in America. So all these are shortcomings but time will cure them. There will be an American-Jewish writer who will know both the present and the past and the languages and the tradition. I am sure there will be such a writer."

On his own novels set in America: ". . . the heroes of these novels are always immigrants. I never write about people who were born here. . . . I am very careful not to write about things of which I don't know or about which my knowledge is superficial. It is the worst thing a writer can do."

On loving one's own characters: "If I would give only love, the writing

would be monotonous. I have to see only the facts, just like a father sometimes loves his child, but at the same time he'll say, 'My older boy is somehow not completely normal.' I have to see my people in the way I see them
and I know they are not all saints, they are not all geniuses, they are not all
completely sane. Some will think that because I write this way, because I
describe bad Jews, I help the anti-Semites. Actually, the reader of literature
knows that a writer cannot just keep making all people good. If you do this,
you falsify literature and you make the reader suspect that you are a liar altogether."

On symbolism: "Yes, some of the critics love to find symbolism in everything. I once told a tailor in Poland to make for me a coat with crooked
pockets. The tailor said to me, 'You don't have to say "crooked pockets";
you say "straight pockets," they will come out crooked anyhow!' If you sit
down to write a good story it will be symbolic, but if you sit down and you
begin to search your mind for symbols, there will be no story and no symbolism. . . . Literature was not created to heap millions of symbols one on
the other. . . . It is nothing but a fashion which passes. The critics of the
future will find out that this is not the only goal of literature. But they will
create some other fad which I cannot foresee now."

On his "favorite child" among his books: "Actually, if I would have the
time and the energy and the power, I would rewrite all of them. But I'm not
even so sure if this would be good because the tomorrow is not always
cleverer than the yesterday."

Shortly after the appearance of *Passions* in 1975 an English journalist
named Morris Lurie interviewed Isaac for the Sunday Magazine of the *London Daily Telegraph*. Lurie asked for the appointment after meeting Herbert
Gold, who had told him, "Certainly you must see Singer. Oh, he'll see you.
He sees everyone. He's a lovely man. A gossip. He loves to talk."

When Lurie called Isaac, he agreed to see him at four o'clock the following Saturday afternoon. "I was an hour early," Lurie recounts. "I sat in
Central Park. I had doubts. What business did I have, I asked myself, interrupting Isaac Bashevis Singer? He is an old man, seventy-one or -two. What
could I possibly say to him?"

Lurie, who himself had grown up in Poland, sat so long brooding in the
park that he was late for his appointment—which Isaac had completely
forgotten. But Isaac welcomed him nevertheless, put down his papers and
his pen, insisted that he sit in a comfortable armchair while he went off to
find a straight-backed chair for himself.

Lurie found the apartment on West Eighty-sixth Street "more French
than New York, upper-middle-class Parisian" with "a casual elegance." He
told Isaac, who had spent the afternoon dictating scenes for a screenplay of
Enemies, A Love Story to a young couple, how "indebted I was to him for
furnishing me with a past" through his stories.

Isaac was in a mood to talk about government aid and foundation grants for writers and artists. "Do you know," he said, "I was offered money by the Rockefellers, the Fords, to go to Switzerland, to go to Japan. It would be good there for my writing, they said, I would write better. They offered me a lot of money." Isaac threw his hands up in the air and said, "What do I want with Switzerland? What do I want with Japan? If you want to write, you will write. It is something inside you. You have it or you don't. That's all there is to it. If it's inside you, it will come out."

Shortly afterward Isaac excused himself and went back to work on his screenplay.

The September 1976 issue of the magazine *Moment* carried an interview with Isaac by Isidore Haiblum, a science-fiction writer and Yiddishophile; Adrienne Joy Cooper, a fellow at the Max Weinreich Center for Advanced Jewish Studies; and David Neil Miller, who teaches Yiddish at Queens College. When this youthful trio arrived at Isaac's apartment, he was busy dictating to Dvorah and once again had obviously forgotten all about the appointment, but "was most gracious" and talked to them in Yiddish for a while. He assured Adrienne that for a girl like her he would get a divorce, saying, "You will provide for me." Then he settled down to the routine of answering their queries in English.

He assured them that "the Jewish novel has not yet been written" because Jewish life is too rich and adventurous to be contained within the pages of any book or even series of books. "To know the Jews is really to know the universe. So whatever a writer does is really almost nothing."

The history of humanity, he said "is the history of unbelievable things." If chapters in the works of Solzhenitsyn, for example, seem incredible, the things he describes "are unbelievable because of Russia, not because of his writing."

He talked of changing fashions in writers, saying, "I may be fashionable today, and tomorrow they may say somebody else is fashionable."

He explained that he uses narrators like his Aunt Yentl in his tales because "when an old woman sits down and tells a story, she doesn't worry about style. Or repetition, or anything else except the story. . . . Since I rarely would write myself in such a mixed-up style, I sometimes let my aunt or some other person tell a particular story. Women are especially good at telling stories, and telling about unusual things. In other words, I would say, in literature, like in sex, the less you make an effort, the more you succeed."

Asked about a revival of Yiddish, he replied, "If we would be normal people, I would say it's impossible. . . . But with the Jews—anything can happen. Because they are so meshugeh." What other people would have revived a language like Hebrew after two thousand years?

He congratulated his interviewers on their Yiddish and told them that in his own writing he actually combines three languages, Yiddish, Hebrew, and Aramaic—which creates additional difficulties for his translators.

Isaac also said he didn't take seriously his nominations by Edmund Wilson and Rebecca West for the Nobel prize.

"No writer writes for prizes. The great writers don't always get prizes. Tolstoy was nominated for the Nobel prize, another man got it, nobody knows who he is. Proust, Joyce, didn't get prizes. When a writer sits around and waits for a prize, it is a very miserable situation. Although I got a few prizes."

In an interview in *Time* magazine for July 3, 1978, accompanying Paul Gray's review of *Shosha*, Isaac, who had just gone through a winter of illness, was described as "a slightly stooped, nearly bald host with fine, parchmentlike skin and strikingly pale eyes. He looks frail until he talks or moves, scuttling between sofa, telephone, and front door with the vitality of a chipmunk."

"Those who come to ask questions," *Time* continued, "are surprised to find themselves being interviewed instead. 'I take from everything,' he says of his writing, 'like a little bird building a nest.' Thus visitors often bring him gifts—a fact, a mannerism, a speech habit—that later appear in his fiction. Says Singer: 'Many writers believe that they can make real experiments by word combinations. The real experiments are the combinations made in nature. We should look inside this laboratory. I never fear that there will not be enough material. I got more than I can use. . . .'

". . . 'a writer is not a god,' he insists. 'He is someone with the talent to write a story that will entertain. It is not for us to explain life. Fiction can entertain and stir the mind; it does not direct it. If a preacher like Tolstoy could not help his people, we are not going to be helped by a lot of little preachers.' Singer is reluctant, outside the area of his work, to suggest behavior to others. A vegetarian for the past sixteen years, he refuses to proselytize. Asked if he took up the diet because of his health, he says, 'I did it because of the health of the chickens.'

"Despite earnings of about $100,000 a year, Singer lives much the way he did when Alma clerked at Lord & Taylor to supplement their income. He points proudly to the typewriter outfitted with Yiddish characters that he has used for forty-three years. He is also concerned that the flow of Singer works will make his readers grow tired of him. 'I'd like to build up a little bank of literature,' he says, 'but not publish anything for a while. Keep quiet at least two years . . .'"

In the summer of 1978 Isaac's former translator Laurie Colwin came back into his life to interview him for *The New York Times Book Review*. The results appeared alongside Alan Lelchuk's review of the novel *Shosha* on the front page of the July 23 issue. As usual Isaac took the occasion to disparage

experimental writing by authors of less talent than Kafka or Joyce, depre-
cated his own popularity, emphasized that he was "before everything else a
writer, not just Jewish." He assured Laurie that he never makes up a plot:
"the plot comes to me." Discussing his own reading habits, he said, "I love
to read a story with real suspense. I mean, not that there should be only
suspense—I don't read detective stories—but if it has a literary value and it
has suspense." Laurie asked Isaac what elements interested him in a book—
"Love? Treachery? Sex?" "Yes," he replied, "love and sex more than anything else." "Treachery is second?" Laurie wondered. "If there's love," came
the answer promptly, "there is treachery." Isaac stressed the advantages of
having a built-in audience through the pages of the *Forward*. Once, he told
her, he had made a mistake in an episode in one of his books, writing that a
prayer for the dead was recited on precisely the High Holy Day when it
wasn't, and hundreds of letters poured in to point out the error. Having a
world of such alert and informed readers, even if it is a dwindling world (he
estimates that about half of the forty thousand subscribers to the *Forward*
read his work), keeps him on his toes and in touch with reality. He also
pointed out, as he so often has, that if it is true, as she put it to him, that he
was "preserving a last part of a vanished culture," it was not because he deliberately sets out to do so when he writes. "I wouldn't be a writer if I would
sit down to preserve the Yiddish language, or make a better world or bring
peace. I don't have these illusions. I know that my story will not do anything
else but entertain a reader for half an hour. And this is enough for me."

In *The New York Times Book Review* for February 13, 1977, accompanying Cynthia Ozick's review of *The Street of Crocodiles*, a novel by Bruno
Schulz, a Polish-Jewish writer who died in the Holocaust and whose book
had just been issued for the first time in English, there appeared the text of
an interview with Isaac by Philip Roth. The subject was supposed to be
Bruno Schulz, but as the conversation between Isaac and Roth proceeded
the subject veered closer and closer to Isaac and further and further from
Schulz.

When Isaac told Roth that he had spoken Polish in his youth "with an accent" and that "as a matter of fact I speak all languages with an accent,"
Roth commented, "Not Yiddish, I take it." Isaac replied, "Yes. The Litvaks
say I speak Yiddish with an accent."

The Jewish authors who wrote their books in Polish in the thirties, Isaac
told Roth, were "kind of leftist" and were viewed with suspicion by Polish
Jews, who found things in their work that they felt sounded anti-Semitic.
"I did not agree that it was anti-Semitism, because some critics said the
same thing about me. Although I wrote in Yiddish, they said, 'Why do you
write about Jewish thieves and Jewish prostitutes?' And I said, 'Shall I write
about Spanish thieves and Spanish prostitutes? I write about the thieves and
prostitutes that I know."

Attempting to explain to Roth why Jews in Poland in the thirties resented Jewish writers who wrote in Polish more than Jewish lawyers, for example, who changed their names and tried to assimilate into intellectual circles, Isaac said: "No writer here would say to Saul Bellow or to you, 'Why don't you write in Yiddish, why don't you go back to East Broadway?' Yet some small part of that still exists. I would think that there are some conservative writers here, or critics, who would say that people like you are not really American writers. However, here the Jewish writers are not really ashamed of being Jewish and they don't apologize all the time. There, in Poland, there was an atmosphere of apologizing. There they tried to show how Polish they were. And they tried of course to know Poland better than the Poles, in which they succeeded. But still the Poles said they would have nothing to do with us." Isaac asked his interviewer to imagine what it would be like "if we would have, now, here, a goy who would write in Yiddish." If the goy failed he would be "left in peace; if not, we would say, 'What are you doing writing in Yiddish, why don't you go back to the goyim, we don't need you.' "

Roth asked, "A Polish Jew of your generation writing in Polish would have been as strange a creature as that?" And Isaac answered, "Almost . . . if there would be many such people, let's say there would be six goyim who would write in Yiddish, and there would come a seventh one . . ." Roth got the point.

Toward the close of the conversation Roth recalled the "major Jewish authors" of Isaac's generation—Schulz in Poland, Babel in Russia, Jiri Weill in Czechoslovakia, who were destroyed "either by Nazism or Stalinism," and asked Isaac how he had the prescience to escape the same fate. "After all, to be exiled from one's native country and language is something that the majority of writers would dread and probably be most reluctant to accomplish voluntarily. Why did you do it?"

Isaac has been asked this question frequently in one form or another, but his answer on that occasion was unusually cogent. "I had all the reasons to leave. First of all I was very pessimistic. I saw that Hitler was already in power in 1935 and he was threatening Poland with invasion. Nazis like Goering came to Poland to hunt and to vacation. Second, I worked for the Yiddish press, and the Yiddish press was going down all the time—it has been ever since it has existed. And my way of living became very frugal—I could barely exist. And the main thing was that my brother was here—he had come about two years before. So I had all the reasons to run to America."

Roth's last question dealt with the fears Isaac may have had on leaving Poland "about losing touch with your material." The reply, an immaculate sample of Isaac's spontaneous skill in mixing wisdom with a disarming combination of pathos and hilarity, deserves to be quoted in full: "Of course, and the fear became even stronger when I got to this country. I came here and saw that everybody speaks English. I mean, there was a Hadassah meeting, and so I went and expected to hear Yiddish. But I came in and there was sitting about two hundred women, and I heard one word, 'delicious, delicious, delicious.' I didn't know what it was, but it wasn't Yiddish. I don't know what they gave them there to eat, but two hundred women were sitting and saying 'delicious.' By the way, this was the first English word I learned. Poland looked far away then. When a person who is close to you dies, in the first weeks after his death he is as far from you, as far as a near person can ever be; only with the years does he become nearer, and then you can almost live with this person. This is what happened to me. Poland, Jewish life in Poland, is nearer to me now than it was then."

In the mid 1970s Isaac's own work was published for the first time behind the Iron Curtain, in Hungary. Not long afterward the Polish weekly journal *Tyogdnik Powszechny* published his story "The Sacrifice" in its January 30, 1977, issue, marking the first time to Isaac's knowledge that his work appeared in his native land in the Polish tongue.

"Isaac Bashevis Singer Talks . . . About Everything" was a two-part series by Richard Burgin that ran in *The New York Times Magazine* on November 26 and December 3, 1978. Handsomely illustrated with a full-color cover drawing and sketches by Raphael Soyer, the piece, in question-and-answer form, lived up to its title, ranging over a wide area of topics Burgin had brought up in the course of some fifty interviews taped with his subject during a two-year period.

Isaac alluded briefly to his beginnings, recalled his first impressions of America following his arrival in 1935 ("My first impression was that Yiddish was not going to last in America more than another five or six years") and his efforts to expand his English vocabulary from the three words "Take a chair" by writing down words on cards and repeating them every night before he went to sleep. He talked of the conflict he has always experienced between the part of him that dreams of "going away somewhere to an island and hiding" and the part of him that wants to "accept people, talk to them." He said he was far more interested in books than in their authors, that "if Tolstoy would live across the street, I wouldn't go to see him. I would rather read what he writes." Asked to define "what makes one a Jew," he stressed "restlessness and eagerness to do things" as the qualities that had prompted him to write in *The Family Moskat* that the Jews are "a people who can't sleep themselves and won't let anybody else sleep." He denied the accusation by some women that he disliked women ("The liberated woman suspects almost every man of being an antifeminist"). Questioned about his attitude toward writers such as Faulkner and Joyce, he told Burgin that the "stream of consciousness is really a way of avoiding a story, of avoiding describing characters. Also it's a very easy method. You let a character think for 300 pages." Once again he asserted that he felt it was "unhealthy" for writers to commit themselves in political or social matters. He spoke at length about roots and the dangers of assimilation ("No assimilationist can be a great writer"). He talked proudly of his son, Israel, and his life as a kibbutznik. He predicted that the novel would endure, called the form "only a larger story," and commented that a short story "is a lot easier to plan" and that the longer a novel is the more likely it is to be flawed. Asked how he came to write *The Family Moskat,* he explained, "I said to myself, 'Warsaw has just now been destroyed. No one will ever see the Warsaw I knew. Let me just write about it. Let this Warsaw not disappear forever.' " He predicted a healthy future for the novel: "For me, if I would be sentenced either to ten years in prison with books or to five years without them, I would rather take the ten with books."

In the second part of the series Isaac discussed the theme of passion in his work, saying that the "very essence of literature is the war between emotion and intellect, between life and death. When literature becomes too intellectual—when it begins to ignore the passions, it becomes sterile, silly, and actually without substance." He went on to talk of other motifs in his fiction: betrayal—by men of their fellows as well as of themselves; error—"Error is a human conception. We would never say that a storm makes an error because it didn't howl in the right way"; free will and fatalism—"The truth is that the belief in free will is a categorical imperative. We cannot live a moment without believing in it"; keeping the Commandments—"No novel, no poem, and no short story can take the place of the Ten Commandments. It is not enough to read the Commandments, you have to practice them. So literature will not do the job. Religion becomes literature when people don't take it seriously anymore. . . . If you read the Bible as just a good book, as poetry or prose or history, then you are not anymore a religious person."

Isaac also told Burgin that he feels man in general hasn't made much progress through the centuries nor have the Jews in a moral or spiritual sense: "When Moses gave the Torah, he believed it was possible to create a nation of spiritual people, a kingdom of priests, a whole nation which would live according to moral codes. This never became a reality." Asked how he reconciled this view of Jewish history with his own belief in God, Isaac explained: "I believe in God, but I have my doubts about revelation. I have no proof whatsoever that God reveals Himself or tells us how to behave, what to do, what He wants. I believe God is a silent God. And He must have a very good reason why He is silent. If He would begin to talk, He would have to speak in 3,000 languages and in all kinds of accents. God speaks in deeds. But the language of deeds is so large—its vocabulary is as large as the universe, perhaps—so we only understand a very small part of His language." That language, Isaac added, he himself understood like "a child of three years" with a vocabulary of a few words. Several times he reiterated his belief that the universe is not an accident, that "nature is not blind." Did he envision God in any material form? "I'm inclined to believe that God and the world are actually identical. God is everything, a spirit, all matter, what is, what was and what will be, as Spinoza conceived him." He pointed out "how little we know" with all our science. He himself, he emphasized, is still interested in "the eternal questions"—and so are the protagonists of his novels. He has come to the conclusion, however, that there are no answers to these questions. "Those writers who imagined that they found the final answers were sooner or later a disappointment to others and often to themselves."

The interview concluded with Isaac's admission that for all the fulfillment life has granted him, "human blindness" and God's "permanent silence" give him no rest. "I feel a deep resentment against the Almighty. My religion goes hand in hand with a profound feeling of protest. . . . I often say to myself that God wants us to protest. He has had enough of those who praise Him all the time and bless Him for all his cruelties to man and animals. . . . Yes, I am a troubled person but I am also joyful when I forget (for a while) the mess in which we are stuck. It may be false and contradictory in many ways, but I am a true protestor. I would picket the Almighty with a sign, 'Unfair to life.' "

On the same day, December 3, 1978, the *Times*, referring to the 911 suicides in Guyana the week before, offered, by way of an "antidote" to counteract the "poison" of the bad news from Jonestown, "the quiet reflection of Isaac Bashevis Singer" in the following quotation from the *Times Magazine* piece: "I always feel that God was very frugal, very stingy in bestowing gifts on us. He didn't give us enough intellect, enough physical strength. But when He came to emotions, to passions, He was very lavish. He gave us so many emotions and such strong ones that every human being, even if he is an idiot, is a millionaire in emotions. . . . There is nothing in life which cannot become a passion. The man who collects stamps can become so passionate about them that he would endanger his life to get some silly stamp from some faraway country. . . .

"We don't know what life is. We speak about electrons and we know how they work, more or less, but not what they are and how they came to be. Actually, our knowledge is a little island in a great ocean of nonknowledge. The supernatural is like the ocean, while the so-called natural is only a little island on it. And even this little island is a great riddle."

"I sometimes think I give too many interviews," Isaac says. "But just the same, I say things that I didn't say before."

❋

Both Isaac and his work have also been heard and seen on radio and television. He is a frequent guest on the Jewish Theological Seminary's program, *The Eternal Light*, on NBC TV. He has read his stories aloud, talked about his childhood, expressed his opinions about the Cabala and other aspects of the Jewish religion and Jewish life on *Adventures in Judaism*, a weekly radio series presented on various stations around the country by the Union of American Hebrew Congregations, the central congregational body of Reform Judaism. He has been interviewed on ABC's Sunday religious television series, *Discovery*, and on numerous other shows.

Occasionally Isaac balks at traveling to broadcasting studios. When *The New Yorker* presented its authors in a series of readings over the Mutual Broadcasting System, he insisted that the engineers come to his home to record his voice. But most of the time he is a willing guest who has bar mitzvah suit, will travel.

On December 12, 1976, *The Eternal Light* offered "A Conversation with Isaac Bashevis Singer." Since the interview took place during Chanukah, Isaac talked about the Chanukah celebrations he had enjoyed as a child. "Chanukah," he said, "was, so to say, a half-holiday. The people were allowed to buy things. You went to the cheder only half a day. It was a holiday with many pleasures and with few duties. So we children loved it especially."

The interviewer, Rabbi Jules Harlow, observed that in Isaac's stories for children there were often pleasant things and happy endings. Why not in his stories for adults? "I would say," Isaac replied, "that if I had to torture someone, I'd rather torture an adult than a child. . . . . I feel that a child should feel in the first years of his life that good is rewarded and bad is punished. . . . Later we may discover that's not always so. . . . Since I love children, I just want to spare them these disappointments. I think they will experience plenty of them in later years."

Isaac told the rabbi that he had grown up in an area of Poland not far from Chelm, known in Jewish folklore as the city of fools. He talked of his father's rejection of secular literature, his older brother's influence as a mentor and teacher, the dual influence on his work of his mother's rationalism and his father's mysticism. "I don't feel like boasting, but I would say that I have tried to take what was good in my father and what was good in my mother. . . . We wouldn't have reached the moon just by mysticism or by intuition. We needed logic and mathematics and the laws of nature. At the same time I am against those people who think by logic and mathematics they'll really discover the secret of Creation."

Reminded once again of the questions concerning the ultimate nature of things, which plagued him as a child, Isaac confessed that he had never found an answer to any of them. "I will tell you, rabbi, since none of these questions have been answered, I keep on asking them, again and again today as I asked them when I was six years o¹ ' ᵀʰen I still had some hope that my mother would answer them, or my father, or my older brother. Today I am resigned. I know that the so-called eternal questions are not to be answered in my lifetime. But just the same, the urge for asking is still with me."

Appearing on the Dick Cavett show over educational television on the evening of July 17, 1978, Isaac went over much of the same ground he had covered in earlier television and radio interviews but managed, just the same, to score some fresh points and to deliver a few sharp observations in the course of a lively half-hour conversation.

After emphasizing his own role in working with translators, he told Cavett—who described himself as a "recent convert" to Isaac's writing—that some of his work really gains in translation because "I sometimes see my own defects better than I would have seen it in my own language. And I will try to correct it." He defined the supernatural as "all the things we don't know." He cited a dream that his otherwise skeptical mother once had about someone winning money in a Polish lottery, which actually came true, as she often pointed out. "I would give half my royalties," Isaac declared at one point, "to see a ghost." He admitted that even as a vegetarian who considered all life sacred, he has more than once squashed a mosquito that bit him. But he confirmed that he disapproved of the late Vladimir Nabokov for hunting and killing butterflies. He praised Henry Miller for fighting against censorship, adding that even though he could not bring himself to employ the kind of language Miller has in his fiction, "I am glad that a writer who wants to use [such words] is free to use them—there's no policeman or governor who tells him not to use them." When Cavett wondered in what respect Isaac considers himself a Jew, he replied: "If you ask me really how I am a Jew I would say that it's a great problem to me, but since I get up in the morning a Jew and I go to sleep a Jew, I dream like a Jew, I speak like a Jew, I suspect that I must have some Jewish blood in me." Responding to a question about his story "The Briefcase," in which a visiting lecturer strongly resembling the author gets lost in a Chicago suburb, misplaces his notes, and undergoes a series of misadventures, Isaac assured Cavett that there was an element of autobiography in the story, since he himself often loses things because "the demons are after me all the time." He confessed that he buys the lined notebooks he writes in at Kresge's five-and-ten-cent stores, but he disclosed too that he is nonplussed by the red lines running down the margins of the pages, which always stop him in his tracks since he writes in Hebrew script, which runs from right to left. "If there wouldn't be this red line, I might really have become a genius."

Isaac defended his pessimism on the grounds that pessimists are realists and "if you keep on saying that everything is going to be bad, you have a good chance of being a prophet." When Cavett asked him whether he believes in life after death, Isaac answered, "This is wishful thinking. . . . But I would say that the Almighty is torturing us now, and there's a good chance that he will continue to do it in another way." Asked why he goes on writing in a dead language, he replied that "nothing in Jewish history ever dies." He also assured Cavett that he always plans every book and story in advance, "but in the process of the writing the plan goes to pieces. Just the same, I always make a plan just as I have been making programs all my life. I will get up at seven o'clock and at eight I will sit down to work—and in fifty years I never kept to this program." A few minutes later Cavett looked up at the clock and expressed surprise that the half hour was already over.

❀

In addition to his novels, stories, essays, plays, lectures, and reviews, Isaac has for some years now been writing his memoirs. The first collection of these, *In My Father's Court* (Farrar, Straus and Giroux, 1966), was based on the sketches of his childhood published under the pen name Isaac War-shawsky in the *Forward*. In his introduction Isaac called the book "in a certain sense a literary experiment . . . an attempt to combine two styles—that of memoirs and that of *belles-lettres*—and its approach to description and its manner of conveying situations differ from those used in my other writings."

"The idea," he explained, "had been with me a long time; when still very young, I had actually thought of writing my recollections of the *Beth Din*. It was only after the newspaper publication of the series that I decided to release them in book form under my own name, because they portrayed a life and environment that no longer exist and are unique."

This "elegy to the past," as a *Newsweek* reviewer called it, covers the years in Warsaw—Isaac's boyhood, the hardships that beset the Singers during the First World War, and the events that led to Isaac's return to Bilgoray. It is regarded by many as a classic of its kind by now. Alfred Kazin, writing in *Book Week*, said Isaac had "turned the tables on his ancestors" by converting "piety into fable." In the *Saturday Review* A. H. Friedlander called Isaac "one of the great literary artists of our time." He praised the book for preserving "the foundations of a unique world that no longer exists." He stressed that "these memoirs confirm the grotesqueries of his novels and short stories. . . . Nevertheless, it is not the grotesque that stands out as the chief element in the world of Isaac Bashevis Singer but its moral quality." In an article called "Isaac's Nominal Case" published in 1969 in Irving Malin's collection of essays, *Critical Views of Isaac Bashevis Singer*, Edwin Gittleman cautioned that the reality of *In My Father's Court* was "the psychological reality of Isaac Singer"; that the "method used is the journalistic memory of Isaac Warshawsky, but only after that memory has been adapted, and thereby transfigured, by the sacralizing imagination of Isaac Bashevis.

Therefore, whatever the original journalistic intentions of Isaac Warshawsky in the pages of the *Jewish Daily Forward*, the book has become a self-conscious literary experiment in the form of a fictional biography. . . . *In My Father's Court* subverts conventional distinctions between real and non-real events."

In his subsequent books of memoirs, also reworked from sketches written for the *Forward*, Isaac continued to subvert these conventional distinctions, casting his autobiographical memoirs in "fictional" form—remolding events, changing names, ordering and refining his memories—walking what Jules Chametzky, reviewing *In My Father's Court* for *The Nation*, called his "literary magician's difficult tightrope" to achieve "the miracle of art."

The second volume, *A Little Boy in Search of God*, lavishly illustrated with full-color sketches by Ira Moskowitz, was published by Doubleday in the fall of 1976. Farrar, Straus and Giroux had planned to issue this volume, but when Roger Straus, Jr., saw the Moskowitz illustrations, he was disappointed. *A Little Boy in Search of God* was less well received than the first book. Edward Grossman complained in the Sunday *New York Times Book Review* that the book "does not break much ground. . . . Again the reader meets young Singer as Singer-the-famous-writer wishes him to be encountered, an impressive lad with red earlocks trying to puzzle out the mysteries of being by smuggling Spinoza and Schopenhauer into his Orthodox home, a voracious observer taking in all and everything around him, fascinated by animals and pain and sex, and beginning to scribble." The writing style, Grossman granted, comes through "even in translation . . . a rapid, declarative flow full of tangible allusion, at once homely and sly, artfully exploiting a pretense of artlessness." He even allowed that "the last few pages where the hero is no longer a child with earlocks, but a young man who has rejected the outward signs of piety, and is living a bohemian existence in a Warsaw that smells of doom," are strong stuff, and that the final chapters, with their revelations of his early experiences as a young journalist in Warsaw, make his novel *The Family Moskat* "more accessible." "But as an autobiographer," he concludes, "Singer does not really give away much, and the reader is mostly left to wonder what his personal experiences were and how he apprehended them as they were happening."

An anonymous reviewer in the magazine *Choice* wrote that "the book's value lies more in the insights it provides into Singer's temperament than in its contribution to the literature of religious experience. Like much of Singer's fiction, *A Little Boy* leaves the reader with the illusion of listening to the clear prose of an enigmatic teller of tales who knows more than he tells." *The Christian Century* asserted that "the Moskowitz illustrations raise the price on what otherwise would be a rather slight book." The reviewer added, "Little that Singer, a master storyteller, writes is overlookable, and this story of his search for God holds the attention, but it leaves less in the memory than we might have imagined." But in *Library Journal* N. K.

Fenenbock praised Isaac for once again being able to "breathe life into the past."

Isaac went right on improving on life in his memoirs, working as much fiction into them as he deemed necessary to make literature of it. Even so, the frank descriptions of youthful love affairs in Isaac's third volume of memoirs, *A Young Man in Search of Love* (published in 1978 by Doubleday, with illustrations by Raphael Soyer), should have helped to satisfy Mr. Grossman's curiosity about the "personal experiences" he found missing in *A Little Boy in Search of God*.

A Young Man in Search of Love begins when Isaac returns to Warsaw in his twenties. It covers his attempts to stay out of the army, his evenings at the Writers' Club in Warsaw, and his involvements with a number of young women—from the time when it was "enough for a woman to merely glance at me to make me blush deeply and grow distracted" to his vigil at the side of the woman he calls Gina as she lies dying in a rented villa at a summer resort.

A capsule review in *The New Yorker* quoted Isaac's description of *A Young Man in Search of Love* as "a kind of spiritual autobiography," and continued: ". . . among the fringe benefits one recieves while enjoying the rich past of this unfailingly robust spirit are glimpses of the pre-Second World War Polish-Jewish literati (heavy battles between Stalinists and Trotskyites), a peek at the loutish anti-Semitism of the Polish army, and a privileged look at the first glimmerings of what might crudely be called the generation gap between pious old Jewish parents and their emancipated children. Raphael Soyer's lush, sympathetic drawings and paintings perfectly complement the wonderful text." *Time* found "the one truly requited affair in the book" to be the one that came of Isaac's "passion" for writing, which "makes every page shine with a wit and vigor that belie the author's 73 years."

Isaac's next book of memoirs, *Lost in America*, also illustrated by Raphael Soyer, is scheduled for publication by Doubleday in 1979. The book describes Isaac's life from the time of his arrival in America up to the year 1940. After it comes out, Isaac says, he thinks he would like to take a little vacation from autobiography for a while.

❈

July 1977

Isaac and Alma are about to take off once more for a month in Wengen, Switzerland. Isaac has just returned to New York from a series of lectures in far-flung cities around the country. He has been having a little trouble with an ear infection and has had to do some of his traveling by train instead of plane. The doctor wanted to work on the ear and clear it out, but Isaac preferred to let nature take its course. The ear is better now, but as he approaches seventy-three one of Isaac's eyes (he'd rather not say which one) is bothering him. He's not seeing well out of it. Perhaps that is why he is experimenting these days with a tape recorder Alma picked up for him as a bargain somewhere. Up to now Isaac has stayed as far from all such machines as he could. He has never listened to records of his own stories, owning no phonograph and not wanting to own one.

Earlier in the summer Isaac and Alma went to Toronto, where they saw a new production of *Yentl.* Isaac has also been to St. Michael's College in Vermont, where he received another honorary doctorate. "When they gave it to me," he relates, "I was surrounded by Catholics—bishops and cardinals—imagine!" He brings out the certificate, which has not been framed yet. "Author of over twenty-five books," it reads, "twice winner of the National Book Award. You are the son and grandson of rabbis and like your father and grandfathers you have continued to confront the mysteries of life and scripture. Your writing enables us to enjoy and endure life. In your stories we face our neighbors and learn not to despise them but to love and to have compassion. Your stories live forever—for who is there like you? It is for all of your life's work that we confer upon you the degree of doctor of letters, *honoris causa.*"

Rachel MacKenzie has come into town from her country home to work on the novel *Shosha,* soon to be published. *Shosha* has already appeared in Yiddish in the *Jewish Daily Forward,* but there are some problems with the English version. The book is to undergo some serious editing, and Isaac is writing a prologue and a new chapter to add to the text. It will be a big novel, he says, about four hundred pages.

Meanwhile Isaac's latest novel, *Yarme and Kayle,* is running serially in the *Forward.* Eve Friedman has finished her stage treatment of *Teibele and Her Demon,* but Isaac is not too sure about the merits of the script at this point. Soon there will be another collection of Isaac's children's stories. He's been digging up old Yiddish stories for adults too, working on the English versions himself, then going over them with Rachel MacKenzie.

Lately Isaac has been trying to learn more American slang, to make his English more idiomatic. He has asked Dvorah to teach him a couple of new phrases every day until he gets them right. "It doesn't go down right," he'll repeat after Dvorah, or "You got it." At the same time Dvorah has been trying to learn Yiddish. She hopes to work with him on future translations. Recently she and Isaac had a discussion about the relative advantages of growing up knowing the Talmud and growing up knowing about baseball. Dvorah had always assumed Isaac knew nothing about baseball. Then he opened to the sports page in *The New York Times* "and it turned out," Dvorah reports, "that he knew everything that was going on . . . the tennis champions, the baseball scores. I think he was surprised himself to see how much he knew."

PART 9

"One Kafka Is Enough"

By and large, Isaac has been fortunate in his critics. Alfred Kazin wrote of Isaac Bashevis Singer: "He was born in 1904, but thousands of years of Jewish history are embodied in him, thousands of ghosts." Ted Hughes wrote: "He has to be considered among the really great living writers. . . . his writing . . . is blazing with life and actuality." The late Stanley Edgar Hyman called Isaac "the Yiddish Hawthorne." Irving Howe has called him "above and beyond everything else . . . a great performer, in ways that remind one of Twain, Dickens, Sholom Aleichem." But Ben Siegel, after bracketing Isaac's name with Gogol's for "sharp kaleidoscopic detail" and Flaubert's for "disciplined detachment," pointed out in "Isaac Bashevis Singer," a pamphlet published by the University of Minnesota Press in 1969: "Ironically, Yiddish critics do not rate Singer as high as do the English-speaking. American readers find appealing his offbeat themes and rejection of social philosophies—in short, his existential stance; Yiddish readers, however, often view him with an uneasiness akin to suspicion. Several Yiddish critics have attacked his tales of 'horror and eroticism, his distasteful blend of superstition and shoddy mysticism,' and his 'pandering to non-Jewish tastes.' What merit these criticisms may have is vitiated by the obvious resentment accompanying them—a resentment that develops in some literary corners whenever a writer wins recognition beyond the Yiddish pale. Sholem Asch proved a similar target."

Siegel in particular has shown an excellent grasp of Isaac's aims and methods. He quotes Isaac as saying that for him realism and fantasy are only "two sides of the same coin," that "the world can be looked at one way or another, and the theme of a story determines its style." In *The Family Moskat*, for example, the narrative is "direct, realistic," while in *Satan in Goray* demonic and psychological elements are introduced to heighten the fantastic dissolution of a community on the edge of chaos. Yet both approaches have as their purpose the exploration of "men's moral fibers under testing circumstances and their varied stratagems as they withstand or succumb to temptation." Speaking of Isaac's knowledge of "the Jewish psyche and culture," which is "deep and ancestral," Siegel says: "One of the few writers to have mastered the entire Judaic tradition, he can enter and articulate it at any point without a discordant note. So true are eye, ear, and verbal touch that tone and mood are often the major conveyors of meaning. Viewing traditional concepts and values with an ambiguous mixture of love, pride, and doubt, he finds no easy answers to the eternal questions. What few answers there are, he makes clear, each must glean for himself. His refusal to champion group, philosophy, or commandment bothers many. For Singer all mankind constitutes the human reality; hence he spares neither Jew nor Christian code nor attitude. Singer [does distinguish] between the true pietists (rabbis primarily) and those pious pretenders (cabalists frequently) who corrupt their learning for material ends. Still he has no quarrel with cabalist or other ideas sincerely held and moderately espoused. Common sense, discipline, occasionally learning, and always luck are needed to avoid personal disaster. Calamity may result from the lack of any one. If compassion is missing, for instance, piety, asceticism, and intellectualism are useless. Even his pietists recognize worldly rewards as more likely for the strong or lucky than the weak or unlucky, but for no one is reward certain."

Siegel takes seriously Isaac's oft-quoted comment that "One Kafka in a century is enough," that "a whole army of Kafkas could destroy literature." He underlines Isaac's respect, as a "veteran journalist," for "the hard fact and objective report." He perceives Isaac's names for his demons, drawn from Jewish mystical lore, as elements in a "spiritual stenography" for demonstrating how thin a line separates truth from appearance.

Siegel recognizes that Isaac "is essentially his own man as individual and artist. His dignity, compassion, incisive intelligence, and originality are as evident as is his deep dedication to his craft. His unique vision gives to Jewish tradition, history, and lore new meanings and applications."

Alas, Isaac's critics are not all as perceptive as Mr. Siegel. Irving Malin's monograph *Isaac Bashevis Singer* is an attempt to come to grips with Isaac's work through a thoughtful analysis of the early memoirs, of what Malin calls the "open novels," including *The Family Moskat, The Manor,* and *The Estate,* and of the "closed novels," such as *The Slave, The Magician of Lublin,* and *Satan in Goray,* which he refers to as "tight, claustrophobic and concentrated" since they "insist upon the detailed, symbolic event, not the comprehensive sweep of history." Tracing the motifs in Isaac's books with an earnestness that occludes their mischief and their humor if not their irony, Malin offers summaries that point up the "recurring themes of freedom and slavery" and "the nature of Jewishness" in the novels. He grasps their patterns and their paradoxes, grants that Isaac is a great storyteller if "not an innovator," and admires his ability to "relate the most extraordinary, unbelievable events in a matter-of-fact tone." The trouble is,

Malin's own approach is too often matter-of-fact, and when he comes to a subtle tale like "The Key" or pursues too academically his quest for "dream stylization and parable," he can be insensitive to the magic of Isaac's tales. He finds revealing clues to mysteries but fails sometimes to respond with wonder and perceptivity to the mysteries themselves.

Reviewing another Malin book, *Critical Views of Isaac Bashevis Singer*, Robert Alter, writing in the *Saturday Review*, offers this guideline for how "criticism should begin to approach Singer: not as an explorer of theological and philosophical profundities or as an 'epic' portrayer of a vanished world, but as a magical teller of tales, who, through alternating or intermingled qualities of canny observation and uninhibited invention, has managed to develop a unique imaginative response to the reality that troubles us all."

While it remains true, despite Alter's remarks, that Isaac *has* attempted to be precisely the "epic" portrayer of a vanished world in emulation of his brother Joshua, what this critic has to say about the Malin collection applies equally well to another roundup of essays, Marcia Allentuck's *The Achievement of Isaac Bashevis Singer*. Here eleven critics discuss the themes in Isaac's work and subject them to rigorous, long-faced literary examination.

William H. Gass, a novelist, professor of philosophy at Purdue University, and reviewer for *The New York Review of Books*, talks solemnly about the "ontological quality" of Isaac's fiction, comparing its "fine solidity" favorably with the lack of solidity of Joyce's work "though he [Joyce] uses up a city of details" and with the "vaporous" nature of the characters in Henry James. Eli Katz, who teaches Yiddish at Berkeley, points out, as Isaac so often has himself, that Isaac's work is not truly in the "classical" Yiddish tradition and that his inability to "reconcile his *shtetl*" with the *shtetl* in the minds of his Yiddish-speaking readers makes them wonder at times which side he is on. Maximilian E. Novak, an English professor at the University of Southern California in Los Angeles, feels Isaac's world is more comparable to Hieronymous Bosch's than Dostoevsky's. Max F. Schulz, chairman of the English department at the University of Southern California, compares *The Brothers Ashkenazi* with *The Family Moskat* and concludes that both books "manage to be at once thematically consistent with their own versions of reality, and yet cognizant of the linear endlessness of time." And so it goes, through earnest examinations of one novel after another, until we get to Paul N. Siegel's revelation that Gimpel is really the archetype of the wandering Jew in Yiddish fiction—"the ecstatic wanderer, hopeless in this world because so profoundly committed to the other."

In an article entitled "The Other Singer," published in *Commentary* in March 1966, Irving Howe points out that Isaac's public, unlike Joshua Singer's, "is composed of third-generation and semi-assimilated Jews, as well as some gentile fellow-travelers, whose nostalgia or curiosity about Jewishness is decidedly limited but who find in the author of *Satan in Goray* and *The Magician of Lublin* a congenial voice." While a certain misunderstanding exists between Isaac and his readers "which neither takes pains to remove" (Isaac is not quite the "swinger" his American readers might think he is), "they are right in feeling that he is closer to them than any other Yiddish writer they are likely to encounter." Whereas Joshua Singer wrote in the "rationalistic and humanistic" tradition of nineteenth-century Yiddish literature, Isaac moved "backward to a pre-Enlightenment sensibility" and "forward to modernism." What his Yiddish-reading public finds strange, his English-speaking readers find "attractive." "He brings together esoteric Judaica, which requires no commitment from the reader, and a sophisticated modern tone, which allows for immediate recognition; and this mixture speaks to highbrow readers as no other Yiddish writer, and few American writers, can."

In his introduction to the Random House collection *Selected Short Stories of Isaac Bashevis Singer* Howe praises the "verbal and rhythmic brilliance" of Isaac's Yiddish. He quotes the critic Eliezer Greenberg, who collaborated with him on the *Treasury of Yiddish Stories* (Viking, 1954), as saying that "Singer has to be heard to be believed." "Behind the prose," Howe emphasizes, "there is always a spoken voice, terse, ironic, complex in tonalities, leaping past connectives." When Howe heard Greenberg read "Gimpel the Fool" aloud, "with a fluency and pith I could never capture in my own reading of Yiddish, he recognized immediately "that here was the work of a master. The story came as a stroke of revelation, like a fiction by Babel . . . encountered for the first time."

❁

September 7, 1977

How does Irving Howe sum up the achievement of the Singer brothers today? The critic, author of the best-selling book about the Jewish immigrants to America, *World of Our Fathers*, published by Harcourt Brace Jovanovich in 1976, sprawls comfortably in an armchair in his Manhattan apartment in the East Eighties and ponders the question. The living room is large, with cheerful yellow walls, a sofa and chairs upholstered in warm colors, a comfortable, old-fashioned oversize desk, stereo equipment, a whole wall of books, framed prints—just the sort of room Howe might have dreamed of working in when he was a City College student in New York years ago, staunchly anti-Stalinist left-wing and with ambitions as a literary authority that have since been more than fulfilled. A large-framed man with a rather pink face and white hair, which he tends to twirl with the end of his fingers when he is searching for the right words in which to frame the reply to a question, Howe seems to measure his words as he responds: "Israel Joseph and Isaac Bashevis Singer are very different writers. I would not want to say that one is a better writer than the other. But their styles are completely different. Anyone able to read Yiddish could tell immediately. I would say that if somebody wanted to learn to write Yiddish well, the older Singer would be a marvelous model; the style of the younger Singer is much more idiosyncratic—and I am not using the word as a putdown, only descriptively."

Howe feels that Israel Joshua was a master of construction, of the *bildungsroman* of the nineteenth-century tradition, where a whole world is presented as in *The Brothers Ashkenazi*. Isaac, on the other hand, he regards as primarily a master of the short story. (Indeed, it was Howe who first recommended "Gimpel the Fool" to the editors of *Partisan Review* for translation and publication in English. He still regards Saul Bellow's translation of the tale as one of the best ever provided for a Singer story.) He considers Singer's "family novels" largely failures and the later books, *The Slave* and *The Magician of Lublin,* for example, simply extended tales, "not novels if by a novel we mean a book that opens an entire world for our inspection."

Howe says he wonders whether Isaac is not being appreciated for the "wrong reasons" and is simply too delighted with his success to admit it. "Bashevis," he says, "has never been all that popular with Yiddish writers or readers, and he is not quite the kind of modernist his admirers may think he is. He is really a sport in the evolution of Yiddish literature. The tradition out of which he sprang was called *edelkeit*—nobility, refinement. Bashevis has nothing to do with that tradition. He belongs with the medieval past or the immediate, post-Enlightenment present, but not with the nineteenth century, whose great writers influenced his brother's work. Bashevis is concerned with the grotesque. His style is leaping, rapid, and vivid—though much of this is lost in English. He sees things from his own unique angle." Isaac's emphasis on sexuality and the irrational further place him, Howe feels, in the modern literary mainstream.

Isaac and Irving Howe have appeared together over the years at lectures and symposiums and in TV and radio interviews. Howe has always been impressed by Isaac's platform manner and ability to think on his feet. He remembers a lecture during which one woman in the audience kept quoting things she attributed to a nephew of hers until her listeners grew noticeably restive—at which point Isaac broke in with the remark, "Lady, if you have a nephew, I have a niece." "That brought the house down," Howe recalls.

Back in the fifties, when Howe was referring to Isaac as a genius and he and Eliezer Greenberg included several of Isaac's short stories in the 1954 collection *A Treasury of Yiddish Stories*, he and Isaac used to meet for lunch at Isaac's favorite haunt, the now vanished Steinberg's Dairy Restaurant on upper Broadway. Once Howe asked Isaac over their blintzes if he wasn't really a secret follower of the messianic pretender Sabbatai Zevi, who figures so importantly in *Satan in Goray*—a book Howe regards as one of Isaac's best. Isaac, he recalls, was delighted at the idea.

Howe is skeptical of the pietistic, traditionalist morality explicit in Isaac's work, believing that in Isaac "there is a strong streak of antinomianism—a wish to break down laws, to favor instinct." If Isaac is really religious, he thinks, it is not a conventional kind of religiosity, however much Isaac may express his admiration for the strictly observant Polish rabbis of earlier times.

Since moving to the East Side, Howe says, he has somewhat lost track of Isaac. He has found the tales with American settings disappointing, even though the cast of characters is always made up of Polish Jewish immigrants. He has not looked into recent books such as *Enemies, A Love Story* or followed Isaac's stories in *The New Yorker* with any particular devotion. In fact, he has his reservations now about the ultimate reputation of this man he once called a genius. He does, however, still regard Isaac as a rather amazing phenomenon. "There's nothing in the Jewish immigrant culture to account for him. He has this hunger for sensation and then—almost like Dostoevsky—he spits out the forbidden fruit he has tasted. I think he enjoys the vogue he has among younger readers even though these readers may misunderstand what he is trying to do. At the same time I think he still regards the world as a place of enmity—just as the Jews of the *shtetl* did—as his own father did. A dangerous place, where today things may go well but tomorrow you may be out on the street. But he has a fantastic gift as a storyteller, and he's a marvelous performer."

❀

The most thorough study of Isaac's life and work to date is surely Irving Buchen's *Isaac Bashevis Singer and the Eternal Past*. The book begins with a brief factual biography, then takes up in turn—with many illuminating notes and references at the ends of chapters—the novels, short stories, and memoirs in thoughtful detail. Many times in the course of these carefully constructed chapters Buchen seeks to peer beyond what Irving Howe called the "expressionist clamor" of Isaac's fictional world to ponder the ultimate meaning of his work. He finds plausible symbols everywhere: the tortured heroine of *Satan in Goray* is the personification of Jewish suffering through the ages; Asa Heshel, the pursuer of "secular knowledge" in *The Family Moskat*, is the epitome of the "homeless wanderer between heaven and earth and the past and the present" who "sums up the terrible freedom of being broken off from God." In the lyrical pages of *The Slave* Buchen perceives the futility of man's quest for freedom: Jacob, the hero, is seen as truly freer during the first part of the book when he is a slave than after his liberation, and to Buchen the book as a whole is an allegory of the Jewish Biblical experience, with Jacob's enslavement in Poland equated with the slavery of the Jews to "pagans in Egypt." In the magician of Lublin's penitence for his excesses Buchen finds a "metaphor for the Jewish journey from the circumference of freedom and self-expression to the center of slavery and inhibition." Yet, paradoxically, only after he has "entombed himself" can Yasha-Jacob, the erstwhile hedonist, "breathe." In a final chapter Buchen comes to the somewhat spooky conclusion that by "all the standards of literature, Isaac Bashevis Singer is a ghost and his work should not exist." His "fictional world is so jammed with the dead that there does not appear to be any room for the living." Yet he sees Isaac's goal in constructing a cemetery of words as an attempt to project "his vision of the eternal past" as a route that could lead to the truth and to the future. His "archaically primitive and sophisticated modern premises" provide a double insight into the enigmas of existence.

Though the symbols Buchen finds in Isaac's work are plausible and his insights frequently ring true, the price he pays for approaching his subject in this way is a kind of airless solemnity, so that what he sometimes discerns as a gleam of Judaical wisdom in Isaac's eyes, as often as not, is the mere twinkle of a storyteller's natural taste for literary mischief—and quite as indefinable.

An Italian critic named Vittorio Saltini, writing in the journal *Nuovi Argumenti* in the fall of 1977, compared Isaac to Dante himself. "Every so often," Saltini avowed, "I repeat that which is clear and little known—the best writer living is the Jewish storyteller Singer." For Saltini the best of Isaac's novels is *The Family Moskat*, but greater still is the first book of memoirs, *In My Father's Court*. He praises Isaac's writings, particularly the memoirs, for their tact and brilliant subjectivity. He extols "Gimpel the Fool" for its objectivity, impersonality, and power. For this champion "Singer dropped into our century as from heaven" and recreated a "destroyed people" in a moribund language; Isaac is "epic" and "biblical" and wraps all he describes in a "sacred halo"; he is a part of the Jewish community and apart from it; he is the author of Ecclesiastes, speaking at once out of faith and out of disillusionment, a believer and a nonbeliever writing with "diabolical irony." Saltini quotes a "specialist in Hebrew and oriental literature" named Claudio Magris as saying that in Isaac's world chaos and cruelty are the norm; tenderness is perverse. Reading the story "Blood," Saltini is reminded of Dante—and of Rembrandt's paintings. Some of the stories make him think of the worlds of Bosch and Breugel, as indeed they might. He mentions Chagall too, and Hoffman and Gogol. And he ends by quoting Henry Miller: "None know so well how to sing, how to dance, or how to weep."

PART 10

"Children Don't Care
What the Critics Say"

Isaac was sixty-two years old and already world-famous as an author for adults when he sat down to write his first published children's book, *Zlateh the Goat and Other Stories,* for Harper and Row.

The stories he heard from his mother as a child, tales of goats and cows and Chelm, are the stories he has tried to write down in his own way for children. He writes them in longhand, on lined paper or in big composition books, in Yiddish.

"I like to write for children," Isaac says. "You can't be a faker when you write for them. Children don't care how famous you are or what the critics say about you. If you can't hold their attention, if your work is boring, you simply lose them."

In an introduction to an edition of Aesop's Fables published by Doubleday in 1968 Isaac praised the "brevity, directness and clarity of the fable," virtues he has striven to achieve in his own tales for children as in every story he ever set down. Indeed, it is difficult to distinguish Isaac's stories for children from those for adults (the jacket flaps of his children's books usually bear the message "for all ages"). Although Isaac's Sodom in the children's story "The Wicked City," for example, is a sexless place, the world of his children's books is inhabited by as many demons and agents of Satan as are his most fantastic adult tales and novels, and the lovers in his children's books *Joseph and Koza* and *Alone in the Wild Forest* are almost as passionate in their own ways as their counterparts in adult books such as *The Slave.* Isaac, in fact, tells of meeting a woman at a party shortly after the publication of *Zlateh the Goat* who asked him to autograph a copy for her. "Who is the child?" Isaac inquired. "It's for me," the woman confessed. "I am the child."

What Isaac has to say about Aesop's Fables in his introduction throws some light on the fables he has made up for children: "In a sense the fable may have been the first fictional form. Ancient man believed that his tales and myths were true. When it came to conversations between wolf and sheep, man and ape, fox and crow, bull and goat, even primitive man could not accept them as reality. A child understood that these stories were not to be taken as facts. The fable taught man that there is sometimes a deep truth behind an obvious falsehood. . . . The fable taught wisdom and morality mainly through the portrayal of character. In this sense as well, it represented a basic element of fiction. One might say that the fable created its own philosophy: the character of a being is its fate. Though the wolf may speak sweetly, he remains a wolf with all his wolfish attitudes and appetites. The fox remains sly. The cat always persecutes mice. The lion is forever strong and majestic. The fabulists knew that although circumstances play their part, they cannot change nature. In no fable does the wolf become permanently merciful, the cat a true friend of mice, or the hare believably courageous. It is a fact that the writers of fables used clichés, but these were not clichés of style but symbols of eternal character. . . .

"If Aesop were alive today," Isaac concludes, "he might have written a fable about a skunk who was psychoanalyzed to lose his stench, or about a hare who preached the dictatorship of hares. However, in essence, the fable remains the same. It is as constant as the types of human character. Art in general has much to learn from Aesop, because art as a reflection of human character can never undergo radical changes. When art begins to ape science it becomes exactly that—an ape. It appears just as ridiculous when it tries with its limited powers to retard or push forward the wheels of history.

"There is no reason why some modern fabulist should not deal with jet planes, rockets, and in the not too distant future, even animals that may exist on one of the planets. But he will never be able to escape from the age-old truths of Aesop."

It may be deduced from these comments that Isaac has been more conscious of what he was about as a storyteller for children than those who credit him with simply an inborn "natural" ability as a spinner of yarns might realize.

Elizabeth Shub, who persuaded Isaac to write his first children's book, has known Isaac for almost as long as he has lived in the United States. In a memoir about him that appeared in the 1975 spring-summer issue of *The Calendar,* the newsletter of the Children's Book Council, she tells how "by sheer chance" she had "the good fortune to meet Isaac Singer during what was probably the very week he arrived in this country."

"I remember," she recalls, "how excited my brother and I were when we were told that our parents' dinner guest one Saturday evening was to be a young writer who had just arrived from Poland. Our father referred to the newcomer by his middle name of Bashevis to distinguish him from his already well-known novelist brother. We were cautioned to speak only Yiddish since our guest did not speak English.

"We were intrigued by the idea of someone coming all the way from Warsaw, Poland, but the key word for us was 'young.' A *young* Yiddish writer? As far as we were concerned, Yiddish writers were born old. We knew quite a few, and even had our favorites among them, but it seemed to us that 'Yiddish writer' and 'old' were synonymous. Certainly the ones who visited us were at least as old as our parents, in their doddering forties, and some were even older."

Isaac arrived late at the Shubs' house in Brooklyn; he had lost his way, which somehow endeared him to the family from the first. Libby (as she's known to her friends) Shub remembers the sparse carrot-colored hair that grew from the top of his head, the crooked teeth, the "very fair skin," the dark, foreign-looking suit. She feels that even if she and her brother had not been able to speak Yiddish, "there would not have been a language barrier. There was no generation gap. There was immediate rapport." As has been the case with many others, the Shubs felt that they were dining with an old friend. Jokes and anecdotes were bandied about the table. "There was no stiffness, no formality. . . . It was an unforgettable meeting, happily repeated on many future occasions, and the beginning of what can best be described, in the old-fashioned phrase, as a lasting friendship. There have been gaps, of course, and long periods when we did not see one another, as well as the usual ups and downs of lifelong friendships."

After one of these gaps Libby, then married and living on Central Park West, invited Isaac to dinner. She describes the scene: "We have eaten. Singer is not yet a vegetarian. He is, however, already an ardent bird lover and the proud owner of a parakeet who often sits on his shoulder as he works. There is still always a room in Singer's apartment in which whatever birds he happens to have (for a time there were two canaries) fly free.

"We catch up on what has been happening, make a date to go for a walk the following day, during which I will accompany him on his daily stint feeding street pigeons. The pigeons know and expect him. He rarely disappoints them. As usual, we are laughing a lot, when suddenly he says, 'I don't want to go home yet, but I have to write an article for the *Forward*. Will you excuse me a few minutes? I'll go into your husband's study. I won't take long.' "

In less than fifteen minutes Isaac is back from the study. "Are you going to write the article?" Libby asks. "If you have an envelope and a stamp," he answers, "I'll just put it in the mail chute."

At that time, as Libby recalls, Isaac was contributing quite a few articles to the *Forward* written under various pseudonyms, as well as signed short stories and serialized novels. "His subjects ranged from science to, at one time, I believe, a column of advice to the lovelorn."

Libby persuaded Isaac to write his first children's book after she started work at Harper and Row as a children's book editor. "He responded enthusiastically, but it was some time—almost a year—before he sat down to write a story for children. In the memoir Libby describes their meeting when Isaac had finished the story: "He reads it to me in a vegetarian restaurant he frequents on Seventy-second Street. The story somehow doesn't work. We are both unhappy. But only a day later he calls me up. He has written *another* story. I know from his voice that he is satisfied. The story is 'Zlateh the Goat.' "

Isaac wanted Elizabeth Shub to translate the story. She was "both flattered and petrified." But when she learned that Isaac would be at her side, ready to "say it differently, always brilliantly, and never quite the way she might expect" if something seemed untranslatable, she began looking forward to the experience.

❀

January 2, 1977

Today Libby works as a children's editor at Greenwillow Books, a division of William Morrow and Company, and lives in Manhattan Towers near Lincoln Center in a handsomely decorated apartment that is as neat as a pin and has a breathtaking view of the Hudson. Libby herself is an attractive woman with hazel eyes and auburn hair. Her voice is low, her manners flawless. Hands folded in her lap, she talks of her enduring friendship and working experiences with Isaac Singer.

When she first met Isaac, she was in her teens. She never expected to become one of the midwives assisting at the rebirth of his work for the English-speaking public. She met Joshua Singer too and recalls him as a "large man" with blondish hair and blue eyes. Several summers before Joshua died, Libby's parents shared a bungalow in the Catskills with him, his wife, and Joseph, who was still a little boy. Libby's father, a literary critic who wrote for the *Forward* under the name of S. Niger, was considered the dean of Yiddish letters back in those days. He favored the work of the older Singer, and Libby feels he was right as far as technical proficiency is concerned. "But I think Isaac at his best is a greater writer," she ventures.

In her youth, in the East Flatbush section of Brooklyn, Libby, who reads Yiddish only haltingly, came to know the works of Sholem Asch and the other reputable Yiddish authors of the day in translation, "but I didn't think of them as writers. To me they were friends of the family who happened to write novels."

"I became a children's editor," she says, "almost by accident. I had been divorced and I needed a job. Literary connections helped. Harrison Salisbury sent me up to see a friend at Harper's about an opening. There wasn't anything in the trade department, but how about children's books? I

couldn't imagine why they would want to hire me, since I knew nothing
about children's literature, but they did—at first as an outside reader, later as
an editor. It occurred to me, knowing his stories, that Isaac would probably
make a wonderful writer for children. I simply called him up one day and
suggested it. We were both still living on Central Park West then, about half
a block away from each other. At first, nothing came of the suggestion, but
then the head of our department, Ursula Nordstrom, wanted to follow up
on the stories in the beautiful *Nutshell Library* series with a Chanukah tale.
And so I asked Isaac if he could do a Chanukah story for us. And he asked
back, would I translate it? After one false start, a really disappointing first
try, 'Zlateh the Goat' came to be.

"The manuscript for 'Zlateh' was sitting on Ursula Nordstrom's desk
when Maurice Sendak, the *Nutshell Library* illustrator and one of the best
artists for children in the field, happened by one day. The name Singer
leapt to his eyes. He asked if he could illustrate the book—and so he did."

Libby Shub has since translated all but a few of Isaac's tales for children—
more than a dozen have appeared in English and in other languages all over
the world. She has also worked on the translations of three of Isaac's novels
for adults—*The Manor, The Estate,* and *Enemies, A Love Story.*

Libby feels that Isaac has not changed much with the years. "He seems to
be a bit more poised and sure of himself than when I met him in my teens"
but still fundamentally "a shy man." He understands people in a way that
she finds "uncanny." Like others who know him, she has observed that "everything is grist to his mill. He will use any and all experiences—adapt them
to his needs. And that facility! He can write with his eyes closed almost. He
can write on subway trains, in little black notebooks with lined pages. He's
so wonderful with names for his characters too. And you know, those names
always mean something."

Working with Isaac was a little different for Libby than for his non-
Yiddish-speaking translators. Often he would dictate a draft to her half in
Yiddish, half in English. But she too found it amazing how he always could
find "exactly the right word" in English to express what he meant. And yet
Libby and Isaac have had their disagreements, mostly over particular words
in his tales. When she felt something was wrong, she would look up at him,
and he'd say, "How do you expect me to continue if you make a face like
that?" "Then," she recalls, "suddenly he would pull everything together
with a single sentence."

Libby believes that Isaac's strength in writing for children is "the same
strength he has as a writer for adults. He is a natural storyteller. He never
editorializes. He can delineate an entire character in a phrase. Everything is
alive—a child, a goat, a supernatural creature." Not that she has liked all
his stories for children. She considers *The Topsy-Turvy Emperor of China,* a
book he wrote for Harper and Row, a weak effort. But she feels that readers
who know him only from his pieces in *The New Yorker* are acquainted only

with the tip of the iceberg as far as his talent is concerned. Still, she likes his short stories and his shorter novels better than his longer ones. Of his children's books she likes *Zlateh the Goat* best, and next to it *A Day of Pleasure*.

One time Harper and Row tried to get Chagall to illustrate one of Isaac's tales. Libby feels there is a great affinity between Isaac and the French master and encouraged the idea, but Chagall did not take up the offer.

Libby looks at her watch. "I must say," she concludes, "that as an editor working with Isaac Singer, I learned a tremendous lot: how to construct a story; the importance of a specific viewpoint; what originality really means. As a writer, he's totally aware of what he's doing. He's not a stylist like Flaubert. He's simply a great spinner of tales, and he understands the essence of human beings."

❀

"Zlateh the Goat" takes place in a Polish village much like Leoncin or Radzymin during the Chanukah season one unusually warm winter around the turn of the century. This means bad business for Uri the furrier because nobody wants to buy a fur coat in such weather. Since Uri's family doesn't have enough money to make the holiday a festive one, they decide to sell their twelve-year-old goat, Zlateh. Uri's son, Aaron, who is also twelve, is to take her to a butcher to see what he can get for her. His father, mother, and two sisters say farewell to Aaron as he sets out in his cap with earflaps and padded jacket on this unpleasant errand. When a fierce snowstorm blows up, Aaron and Zlateh seek shelter in a haystack. There the goat feeds the boy with her milk, they comfort each other, and he comes to understand how useful, lovable, and faithful old Zlateh is. He also learns patience and resignation from her, for she seems by her example to be telling him, "We must accept all that God gives us—heat, cold, hunger, satisfaction, light, and darkness." Aaron and Zlateh are marooned in the haystack for three days and three nights. It seems as though they will never be able to leave and that winter will never end. One night Aaron dreams of summer, of "green fields, trees covered with blossoms, clear brooks, and singing birds." When he wakes up he digs his way out of the shelter and looks with wonder on the world of snow in the moonlight: "It was all white, quiet, dreaming dreams of heavenly splendor. The stars were large and close. The moon swam in the sky as in a sea." When the storm ends, boy and goat are able to get home at last, in time for the family's Chanukah celebration. The family learns how Zlateh has saved Aaron's life, and none of them ever speaks again about selling her. Then the weather turns cold and things start looking up for the furriers.

Zlateh is an enchanting tale, and not the least of its merits is Elizabeth Shub's flawless, sensitive translation. But there is also Isaac's way of bringing Zlateh's character to life without ever resorting to anthropomorphism, his tender description of the love between child and animal, his ability to make the winter cold penetrate a reader's bones. At the same time he evokes for children as he has so well for adults the atmosphere of a Polish country town in the early 1900s and the customs of a Jewish family living just then and just there.

The other stories in this first of Isaac's children's books represent a cross-section of the themes he has explored in writing for the young. There are love stories; stories of scolding wives and their henpecked husbands; stories of the town of Chelm, that Mecca of fools who pride themselves on their wisdom; stories of imps and devils and goblins. In "Fool's Paradise" a young man named Atzel falls ill and imagines he is dead. A great specialist cures him in eight days by getting Atzel's parents to decorate a room for him so that it looks like Paradise, with satin hangings and costly rugs and attendant servants decked out with angel's wings on their backs. Atzel becomes so depressed by these surroundings that he is delighted when he learns, after the week is up, that he is to be evicted and brought back to earth. He is over-joyed to find that he is alive, and marries Aksah, the girl he loves, in one of Isaac's favorite forms of finale—an elaborate wedding. "Grandmother's Tale," like "Zlateh," is a Chanukah story, this time about a stranger who visits a group of children on the holiday, beguiles them, and nearly destroys them. The visitor appears to be a delightful companion, sharing the children's pancakes and their *dreidl* game, but turns out to be a demon who casts no shadow, and they are saved from his wiles in the nick of time. In "The Snow in Chelm" the Chelmites imagine that the new-fallen snow sparkling on their streets consists of precious jewels that will make them rich. They stay up all night making plans for spending their treasure, but morning brings melted wealth and disillusionment. "The Mixed-up Feet and the Silly Bridegroom" is set in East Chelm, a suburb of the village with rival claims as a center of wisdom and sophistication. Here Yenta, Pesha, Trina, and Yachna, the four daughters of the farmer Shmelka and his wife Shmelkicha, get all tangled up in bed one night and can no longer figure out whose feet are whose. A whack on their quilt resolves the problem, and all ends merrily. Chelm is also the setting of "The First Shlemiel," the story of a fellow who gets into all kinds of trouble when his wife leaves him to mind the baby while she goes off to sell vegetables in the marketplace. (This story about the lazy Mr. Shlemiel was the basis of the play "Shlemiel the First," staged by Robert Brustein for the Yale Repertory Theater.) "The Devil's Trick" is another Chanukah tale, liberally sprinkled with snow, peopled with goblins and devils, and featuring the heroism of a boy named David who thwarts the kidnapping of his parents by threatening to cut off the Evil One's tail.

The seventeen pictures by Maurice Sendak are at once the most realistic and most fantastic renderings imaginable of the world of Isaac's stories and the creatures who inhabit them.

Zlateh the Goat and Other Stories, published by Harper and Row in 1966, brought high praise for its author, and its publication did not make him any poorer. In *The New York Review of Books* Alison Lurie advised her readers, "If you have no older children on your list, buy this book for yourself." Hugh Nissenson, writing in *The New York Times Book Review,* found in the stories "an expression of a great religious sensibility." The book also had its detractors: Irving Feldman, in *Book Week,* found these rich pages, except for the title story, "thin and perfunctory."

Zlateh the Goat was a Newbery Honor Book. In Czechoslovakia Gene Deitch made a film of "Zlateh the Goat" with a real goat as the heroine (Isaac didn't care for it much). Miller-Brody, an audio-visual firm that turns Newbery Award Books into filmstrips and recordings, has converted "Zlateh" and other children's tales by Isaac into sound filmstrips and records narrated by Eli Wallach (Isaac liked their version of "Zlateh," illustrated by Penrod Scofield, far better than the movie).

Isaac's next two books for children appeared in 1967. In one, *Mazel and Shlimazel; or, The Milk of a Lioness* (Farrar, Straus and Giroux), two spirits—Mazel, which means good luck, and Shlimazel, which means bad luck—make a bet about their powers—much like the bet God makes with Satan at the start of the Book of Job. Mazel says he can make anybody happy. Shlimazel replies that he can "destroy in one second" what Mazel takes a year to accomplish. Their Job is Tam (the Yiddish word for "zest"), a boy who lives in the poorest hut in the humblest of villages. Mazel arranges for him to be whisked away to a king's palace. All goes well until the king's life is in danger and can only be saved by milk from a lioness. With Mazel's help Tam goes and milks a lioness, but nobody believes there is real lion's milk in the jug he brings to the king. The king's Haman, Prime Minister Kamstan, hungry for power, does his best to incite suspicion about the authenticity of the milk. The king gets to drink the milk just in time, though, and Tam escapes hanging, if just barely. Shlimazel has lost his bet; the forfeit is to keep his "red nose" out of Mazel's affairs for fifty years. Tam gets to marry the lovely crown princess, Nesika, and the story ends: "Actually, Tam no longer needed Mazel, excepting once in a while. Tam has learned that good luck follows those who are diligent, honest, sincere and helpful to others. The man who has these qualities is indeed lucky forever." Margot Zemach's full-color illustrations are nothing less than enchanting.

The Fearsome Inn (Charles Scribner's Sons) is a scarier piece of work. It opens with one of those Polish snowfalls that are Isaac's specialty, taking us to an inn "on a hill overgrown with thistles, by a windmill with a broken vane and a smithy whose forge had long been cold." The inn is run by a witch named Doboshova and her half-man, half-devil husband, Lapitut. Together they ensnare helpless travelers who stumble on the inn as they search for shelter. For servants, this evil landlord and landlady employ three pretty girls—Reitze, Leitze, and Neitze, who are really their slaves. During the snowstorm three young men—Herschel, Velvel, and Leibel, the last a student of the Cabala—arrive at the inn. They are administered herbs in their food that cause nightmares, and potions that deprive them of all will. In the end, however, the witch and her husband are banished to the "wastes of the netherworld," the good young men free the three Cinderellas of the inn and wed them, and the inn is transformed into a haven for travelers who lose their way. It is a gripping fable for readers of any age, and Nonny Hogrogian's innocent color drawings offset some of its scarier scenes.

Isaac's next book for children was *When Shlemiel Went to Warsaw and Other Stories* (Farrar, Straus and Giroux, 1968). He dedicated the volume to "the memory of my father and mother—great and enthusiastic storytellers, persons of deep faith and love of man, especially of all Shlemiels, old and young."

"Some of the stories," he wrote in his introduction, "my mother told me. These are folktales she heard from her mother and grandmother. I have re-told them in my own fashion, totally recreating them in plot, detail and perspective." Others, he disclosed, came out of his own imagination, and all were "products of a way of life rich in fantasy and make-believe." He went on to say that in his work "there is no basic difference between tales for adults and for young people. The same spirit, the same interest in the super-natural is in all of them. I even mention the same villages and towns. In our time, when literature is losing its address and the telling of stories is becoming a forgotten art, children are the best readers."

It is true enough that the eight stories in the collection can delight the hearts of adults as well as children. The title story itself, set once again in Chelm, is the strongest and funniest. Shlemiel is a man who would like to see the world, but when he sets out for Warsaw, he gets lost and winds up in Chelm again. When he is greeted by a family exactly the same as his own, he decides that he must have started out in Chelm I and has now arrived in Chelm II.

Two other Chelm stories appear in the collection—"Shlemiel the Busi-nessman," which finds the same character off on his travels again, trying to make good in business, and the perfect target for swindlers of every kind; and "The Elders of Chelm and Genendel's Key," in which a wife who tries to stop her husband from talking foolishness is defeated by the other elders—all fools—who serve with him on the community council. "Utzel and His Daughter Poverty" is a more serious fable about the consequences of laziness and procrastination. "Tsirtsur and Peziza" is a brief gem about an "orphan imp" and her friendship with a cricket. In "Rabbi Leib and the Witch Cunegunde" a peaceful rabbi who spends his days praying, caring for the sick, and being kind to animals in the forest tangles with an evil witch. She offers to marry him so that they can combine their powers of good and evil, but he turns her down. Furious, she determines to destroy the rabbi, but his powers prove mightier than hers.

"Shrewd Todie and Lyzer the Miser" is set in the Ukraine, where poor Todie has all he can do to support Shaindel, his wife, and their seven children. Once more, the season is winter, and a hard winter it is, complete with heavy snow. With no money even to buy wood, Todie goes to the town miser, Lyzer, for a loan. When he's turned down, Todie borrows a silver spoon from Lyzer and deceives him into thinking the spoon has given birth to a baby spoon. Eventually the town rabbi catches up with Todie, but it is Lyzer the Miser who is brought to shame for his gullibility.

In "Menaseh's Dream" the hero is a young man of intense curiosity who, like so many of Isaac's heroes, asks the sort of questions that plagued Isaac as a little boy: "How high is the sky? . . . How deep is the earth? . . . What is beyond the edge of the world? . . . Why are people born? . . . Why do they die?" Menaseh's only possession is a children's storybook called *Alone in the Wild Forest*—which happens to be the title of a book by Isaac that would appear a few years later. An orphan who lives with his uncle, Menaseh gets lost one day in the forest outside Lublin and dreams about a castle where his own portrait hangs on the wall and he discovers all his relatives dressed up as though for the High Holy Days. He wants to speak to his parents, but his grandfather tells him he will have to wait many years before that will be possible. In one of the rooms of the castle Menaseh finds the clothes he wore as a child; in a second room, the toys he played with; in another, the soap bubbles he blew from his pipe; in still another, sounds of talk and laughter, and the songs he used to sing when his parents were alive. In a fifth he encounters the heroes and heroines of *Alone in the Wild Forest;* in a sixth room, the shapes of his own dreams; and in a seventh, a girl his own age with long golden braids, surrounded by strangers who, his grandfather explains, are the people he will meet in his future. Menaseh wakes up in the woods to find the girl with the braids stretching out her hand to help him to his feet.

This generous assortment of *bubah meises* (roughly, "tales my grandma told me") was well received. The review in *The New York Times* was typical: "In this book children are getting what they deserve—some of the most imaginative stories that have been available in recent years. . . . All of them have the ease and simplicity of great folk literature."

It was Isaac's next book, *A Day of Pleasure* (Farrar, Straus and Giroux, 1969), that won him his first National Book Award. The citation declared in part: "At a time when in children's literature the power of the imagination is frequently lost sight of or diluted, it is fortunate that we can honor a great storyteller. Mr. Singer has created out of remembered fragments of his own childhood a place instantly familiar, where life is not neat and orderly, where the adventures of a boy throw into sharp and recognizable focus those resistant elements of the ever-troubled human condition."

A Day of Pleasure, subtitled *Stories of a Boy Growing Up in Warsaw*, is made up largely of chapters from *In My Father's Court*, and illustrated with photographs taken by Roman Vishniac of Jewish Warsaw between 1933 and 1939. "The world portrayed in these photographs," as Isaac points out, "is essentially the same as the one in the stories, even though the stories take place a generation earlier." The chapters—fourteen selected from *In My Father's Court* and five new ones—all deal with the first fourteen years of Isaac's life. The first of the additional episodes, "Who I Am," tells of Isaac's earliest years, his curiosity, his alertness to the world of grownups, his awareness of human suffering in a land "torn and divided" among Russia, Austria, and Germany. Other added chapters deal with the Singers' trip from the tiny town of Radzymin to Krochmalna Street in Warsaw; with Itchele the grocer and his overworked but good-hearted wife Shprintza; and with Isaac's attempt to convince his boyhood friend Mendel that he knew the Cabala, could create pigeons, make wine flow out of a wall, fly in the air, turn invisible, change pebbles into pearls, and utter spells. Here too one finds the story of Shosha, the nine-year-old girl who was Isaac's first love, and the subject of his novel *Shosha*. In the story he comes back to visit Shosha just as he is about to leave Warsaw for the United States and discovers a child who looks exactly the way Shosha did when he was a boy. The girl proves to be Shosha's own daughter, Basha. Isaac tells her a story within the story about the kidnapping of a beautiful blond by a demon—a plot he dreamed into being in his boyhood.

When Isaac received the National Book Award for *A Day of Pleasure*, he told the audience in Boston's Symphony Hall that "there are five hundred reasons why I began to write for children, but to save time, I will mention only ten of them.

"Number one: Children read books, not reviews. They don't give a hoot about the critics.

"Number two: They don't read to find their identity.

"Number three: They don't read to free themselves of guilt, to quench the thirst for rebellion, or to get rid of alienation.

"Number four: They have no use for psychology.

"Number five: They detest sociology.

"Number six: They don't try to understand Kafka or *Finnegans Wake*.

"Number seven: They still believe in God, the family, angels, devils, and witches.

"Number eight: They love interesting stories, not commentary, guides, or footnotes.

"Number nine: When a book is boring, they yawn openly without any shame or fear of authority.

"Number ten: They don't expect their beloved writer to redeem humanity. Young as they are, they know that it is not in his power. Only adults have such childish delusions."

In the 1970s Isaac continued to turn out books for children, sometimes at the rate of two a year. Both *Joseph and Koza* and *Elijah the Slave* (Farrar, Straus and Giroux) appeared in 1970. *Joseph and Koza; or, The Sacrifice to the Vistula* takes place in pagan Poland, where barbarous tribes who believe in devils and witches sacrifice a maiden to the river Vistula every summer. But the wandering Jew Joseph arrives on the scene to prove that the one God is mightier than all devils and witches put together and to save Koza, the daughter of the tribe's chieftain, from being sacrificed. The book is illustrated with drawings in sepia by Symeon Shimin. *Elijah the Slave* is a biblical tale in which Elijah, God's messenger, sells himself into slavery in order to help a poor scribe named Tobias. Elijah earns his own freedom by building a magnificent palace with the help of a skilled band of angels. The full-color illustrations by Antonio Frasconi are perfect complements to a sparse and pristine text.

The following year saw the publication of *Alone in the Wild Forest* (Farrar, Straus and Giroux, 1971), in which the hero—like the boy in "Menaseh's Dream" who carried this very book about with him—is an orphan who meets an angel in the woods. The angel supplies him with an amulet that can fulfill all his wishes. Joseph wishes for a prayer book, delicious food, and an eagle, which flies with him to the kingdom of King Maltuch, where the lad falls in love with the Princess Chassidah, who had actually loved him "in a former life" but was prevented from marrying him. In order to win her, Joseph has to overcome the wicked tricks of still another of those evil prime ministers refurbished from the Book of Esther, this time a monster named Bal Makane who is out to have Princess Chassidah for himself. There's lots of action in this tale and a noble Talmudic moral.

In *The Topsy-Turvy Emperor of China* (Harper and Row, 1971) Isaac takes another opportunity to lampoon the grotesqueries of the avant-garde in art and literature, this time for the delectation of young readers. The story, in a translation by the author and Elizabeth Shub and exotically illustrated by William Pène du Bois, concerns the Emperor Cho Cho Sang of China and his mean wife, who turn all the values of their country upside down. Being ugly himself, Cho Cho Sang issues a decree: *Attention! Be it understood that from this day forward everything called just and beautiful is declared unjust and ugly and everything that is considered mean and hideous is declared fair and lovely.* Women are ordered to wear fur coats in summer and bathing suits in winter. Thieves are transformed into policemen who arrest the innocent. The scent of a skunk is prized as perfume. Love is banned. Ignorance and injustice become the noblest of traits. Everything Isaac scorns—obscurity in literature, the difficult and the experimental in art and music—is exalted by the Topsy-Turvy Emperor: "Students were taught that facts were not of value in science. The job of the scientist was to invent complicated words and fancy names. There was no higher praise for a scholar than that his work was so deep he could not understand it himself. . . . The more difficult the books were to read, the more profound they were considered to be. The libraries of China were soon filled with manuscripts no one could stand to read. . . ." And the only poetry published, of course, is the kind "that made people yawn."

In the emperor's land, where men worship monkeys and two and two make five, there is no hope for the traditional standards of beauty that Isaac admires—until, after a palace revolution, Cho Cho Sang's own handsome and sensible son, Ling Ling, assumes the throne. Then there's a big wedding for Ling Ling and his bride, Min Lu, a carnival, and general rejoicing.

For all its twinkling humor and the surface wisdom of its basic premise, *The Topsy-Turvy Emperor of China* is too much a catalogue of Isaac's own intellectual and esthetic prejudices to rank with his more colorful adventure stories for children, and the absence of a Jewish theme seems to deprive the story of the dimension that lends depth to his tales of Chelm and the memoirs of his childhood. As anti-intellectual propaganda, this fable should have delighted the hearts of Philistine parents and teachers. Actually it attracted little attention and soon went out of print. In any case, what kind of a China could it have turned out to be under Ling Ling, who presumably would abolish dissonant music, abstract art, esoteric poetry, and "difficult" books? After all, Joyce and Proust, Eliot and Pound, Picasso and Mondrian, Schoenberg and Stravinsky, Beethoven for a while, indeed, even the stories of Isaac Bashevis Singer, have been banned until recently in the real China, and there is some question as to whether the cultural climate there has been any the better for it.

In 1972 came *The Wicked City* (Farrar, Straus and Giroux), a retelling of the story of Sodom and Gomorrah. In Isaac's version Lot is a lawyer who goes to Sodom, where he makes a fortune defending criminals since there are so many of them in town. Accompanied by two angels, Abraham comes to visit his nephew but refuses to eat the *tref* meal that is served to him. Lot's wife is embarrassed by this provincial behavior. Lot himself is disturbed by Abraham's prediction that a catastrophe is about to befall Sodom and loads up a hamper with pork and flees from the pagan city with his family. His wife looks back because she's worried about her house and her jewels and so turns into a pillar of salt largely because of her materialistic preoccupations. Lot still isn't convinced that God exists and attributes the destruction of Sodom to the eruption of a volcano. In the end Lot finds another corrupt city and again becomes "the champion of murderers, thieves and swindlers" while Abraham goes off to join Sarah, who is about to bear Isaac. *The*

Wicked City is a delight and is especially interesting since, for children, Isaac has reversed his usual approach and managed to tell the entire story without the slightest hint at sexuality among the Sodomites. Leonard Everett Fisher's drawings are artful if a measure too formal for the tale.

The book that followed was devoted entirely to Chelm. In *The Fools of Chelm and Their History* (Farrar, Straus and Giroux, 1973) we find out how Chelm came to be, how the Chelmites first became "civilized," and about the woes that followed. With civilization comes war, revolution, a treasury devoid of coin. Gronam Ox and his sages—Shmendrick Numskull, Berel Pinhead, Shmerel Thickwit, and our old friend Shlemiel, secretary of the town council—seek ways to rescue Chelm from default, but each new program only plunges the town deeper into trouble. Chelm ultimately gives up its military ambitions against the neighboring *shtetls* of Gorshkov and Mazelborsht and is saved by the simple virtues of industry and application. Yet the town never does abandon its dream of glory. As Gronam Ox tells the citizens at the unveiling of the latest monument in his honor, "We do not wish to conquer the world, but our wisdom is spreading throughout it just the same. The future is bright. The chances are good that someday the whole world will be one great Chelm." As indeed it seems at times to have become.

In 1974 Isaac's gift to children was *Why Noah Chose the Dove* (Farrar, Straus and Giroux), with bright, poster-color pictures by Eric Carle. Noah chose her, we find out, because all the other animals talked too much and only the dove knew how to keep quiet. The text of the tale is especially succinct and at the same time especially witty. This story too was turned into an educational filmstrip.

A Tale of Three Wishes (Farrar, Straus and Giroux, 1976) is a charming fairy tale with strong religious overtones. The story opens on the last night of the Feast of Tabernacles, when "the sky opens" and everyone watching can make a wish that will come true. Three children, Shlomah, Esther, and Moshe, slip out to the local synagogue, each ready with a wish. Shlomah wants to be as wise and rich as Solomon. Moshe yearns for the learning of Maimonides. Esther would be as beautiful as the queen whose name she bears. The sky indeed opens, revealing fiery chariots and Jacob's ladder and choirs of angels, but the children's wishes do not come true. And an old man they encounter on the way home tells them why: "No one can become wise without experience, no one can become a scholar without studying. As for you, little girl, you are pretty already, but beauty of the body must be paired with beauty of the soul. No young child can possess the love and the devotion of a queen who was ready to sacrifice her life for her people. Because you three wished too much, you received nothing."

But in later years, when the children grow up, their wishes are fulfilled indirectly. Shlomah becomes adviser to the King of Poland, Moshe a great scholar, Esther the wife of a rabbi who often must intercede for her people with the rulers of the land. Irene Lieblich's full-color illustrations, summoned from her own memories of a Polish childhood, enhance the text.

One of the loveliest of Isaac's children's books is *Naftali the Storyteller and His Horse, Sus, and Other Stories* (Farrar, Straus, and Giroux, 1976). Margot Zemach is back again this time as illustrator, with evocative black-and-white drawings marked by economy of line. Eight of the stories were translated by Joseph Singer, who also figures as a character in one of them. "Dalfunka, Where the Rich Live Forever" was written in English by Isaac and first appeared as an endpaper in the magazine section of the Sunday *New York Times*.

Three of the stories are return visits to Chelm. In "Dalfunka, Where the Rich Live Forever" the treasury of Chelm is empty once again. The wise men of the city are sitting around trying to figure out what to do about it when they receive a visit from Zalman Typpish, the richest man in town. He wants to live forever, and if the sages of Chelm can work this out for him he promises to pay two thousand gold pieces from his fortune to rescue the community. But Zalman is already eighty years old, and the matter requires deep thought. The advice the wise ones hit upon is that Zalman should go and live in Dalfunka, a Chelm suburb where everybody is poor and no rich man has ever died. Zalman takes their advice; for five years he enjoys a comfortable life in Dalfunka. But he still wants to "live forever" before he will pay out the two thousand gold pieces. Meanwhile he is living high and earning no money. It is decided in the end that Shlemiel, whose suggestion it was that the rich man move to Dalfunka, should stop giving advice and just keep quiet.

"The Fools of Chelm and the Stupid Carp" concerns the punishment of a fish who proves to be neither as smart nor as good as the wise men of Chelm had been led to believe. They decide to drown him by dropping him in a lake, and a decree is posted in the official town gazette that if he ever comes back he will be sent to jail for the rest of his life. "Lemel and Tzipa" is about a pair of foolish Chelmite lovers who nevertheless manage to marry, make ends meet, and bring more fools—but good-natured fools—into the world. "The Lantuch," one of Aunt Yentl's Sabbath tales about a house demon, was reprinted here from the collection *A Crown of Feathers*, showing how easily some of Isaac's stories can be moved from the adult to the children's category without the slightest revision. "A Hannukah Eve in Warsaw" brings us back to Krochmalna Street in the grip of a cold spell, during which Isaac, in his cheder days, really did get lost in a snowstorm.

"Growing Up" is another memoir about dreams, Isaac's childhood dreams of the Holy Temple in Jerusalem, the Messiah, and the Resurrection. "I knew full well," the author explains, "that all this was just in my head. Actually I was in Warsaw, my father was a poor neighborhood rabbi, the land of Israel belonged to the Turks, the Temple lay in ruins, David, Solomon, Bathsheba and the Queen of Sheba were all dead. My friend was not a prince of the Kingdom of Israel but Black Feivel, whose father was a porter in Janash's bazaar and whose mother sold crockery in the market-place. Until just a few weeks ago I had attended cheder on Twarda Street, but I had stopped going because my father couldn't afford the two rubles a month tuition." But there is one dream young Isaac clings to: He himself will become a writer, Feivel a printer. They will bring out Isaac's first book, "all of sixteen pages long," to be priced at two kopecks. Then they'll be able to open their own printing shop, publish their own books, and with the profits, board a ship for Israel. Feivel turns up one day with a case of rubber type and an inkpad. The boys set up shop in a Hasidic study house that's empty during the day. Feivel publishes the title page of Isaac's first book— *Alone in the Wild Forest*. But Isaac, eleven at the time, has trouble with the plot. He can't decide whether the hero should wind up a hermit, die of longing, or marry the daughter of a magnate. "I had just launched my writ-ing career and already I had fallen into a literary dilemma." The boys abruptly decide to give up the publishing business and open a yeshiva where the students can study the Cabala in secret. Joshua turns up in this reminis-cence too, making skeptical comments when a visitor regales the family with tales of his travels—including a visit to Shushan, the capital of ancient Per-sia, no less, with a stopover at Mt. Ararat to see Noah's Ark.

Then there's "The Cat Who Thought She Was a Dog and the Dog Who Thought She Was a Cat" (the dog, like all Isaac's storybook dogs, is named Burak, the cat Kot), a brief morality tale. But the most enchanting story in this landmark collection, and the most revealing about Isaac, is the opening piece about Naftali, who loves stories so much that he can't wait to learn how to read. After he grows up, he acquires a horse named Sus and goes from town to town in a wagon that is a Polish Parnassus on Wheels, selling storybooks to children and gathering them in the wagon to listen to his tales. Then he meets the rich and goodhearted Reb Balik, who builds him a house big enough for a library and a print shop, as well as a stable for Sus. Later Naftali writes down the stories he has told, sets them in type, and makes many journeys to nearby towns "to sell his storybooks or give them away to those who couldn't afford to buy them." The parallel with Isaac's own career is plain enough. Naftali and Sus ultimately die and are buried side by side, "but this doesn't end the story of the world. The whole earth, all the stars, all the planets, all the comets represent within them one divine history, one source of life, one endless and wondrous story that only God knows in its entirety."

"An old man is nothing but a little boy," Isaac has said.

But how does the seventy-four-year-old author with the little boy still alive inside him feel about other children? As with animals, his love for them is perhaps more literary than actual; he has, after all, been known to grow restless after too many hours on his son's kibbutz in Israel surrounded by his own grandchildren. Yet those who have seen him reading his tales on a rainy morning to a jampacked audience of parents and children at the Ninety-second Street YMHA and then answering their questions, to their wild delight, as wittily as any he has fielded from an adult audience, have seen the magic of his personality work on children as surely as it does on grown-ups of any age at all.

Isaac's stories for children have been translated not only into English from Yiddish and into Hebrew from the English but into French, Spanish, Italian, Japanese, and a dozen other languages. They have elicited praise from most critics, disgruntlement from a few. They have even prompted the kind of psychoanalytical criticism generally reserved for introspective novels. Isaac had only published his first three books for children when a writer named H. R. Wolf—an English teacher at the State University in Buffalo with an interest in psychology as well as literature—published an essay dealing with *In My Father's Court* and Isaac's early stories for children. In his essay, ominously titled "Universalism and the Rankian Hero," Mr. Wolf applies his Rankian stethoscope and jargon to "Zlateh the Goat," *Mazel and Shlimazel*, and *The Fearsome Inn*, finding in them "Rankian paradigms" (Isaac's more solemn critics can't get through a whole essay without using the word *paradigm* somewhere) not to mention all sorts of Freudian symbols. Wolf's prose is matched in impenetrability only by William Empson's psychoanalysis of *Alice in Wonderland*—and in the parody of it, wherein *Winnie-the-Pooh* undergoes similar scientific treatment in the full dialect of the trade, in the funniest pages of Frederick C. Crews's *The Pooh Perplex*.

Mr. Wolf (whose essay appears as a chapter in Marcia Allentuck's 1970 collection *The Achievement of Isaac Bashevis Singer*) characterizes *In My Father's Court* as a "centrifugal journey out of enclosure." He then rolls up his intellectual shirtsleeves for a dissection of the "Rankian motifs" in *Mazel and Shlimazel*, which derive from the fact that Tam was raised by humble parents and therefore might be regarded as an abandoned child who goes on to fulfill "the promise of nobility that the Rankian pattern outlines." After listing the ways in which the story differs from the "Rankian paradigm" (Tam is not really the king's son, though he becomes his son-in-law, and there is no queen in the story), Wolf forges on to discover that Mazel and Shlimazel are really "father surrogates" for Tam's "divided self" (or Isaac's divided self, and admittedly, there is plenty of evidence for this in his own life and opinions). The wicked Prime Minister Kamstan is unmasked as "a further reduplication of the father Shlimazel."

But now the paths of Wolfian prose become even more densely overgrown with words. Wolf makes much (as what analyst wouldn't?) of a slip of the tongue of Tam's when the lad tells the king he has brought him the milk of a "dog" when he means to say "lioness." Suddenly comparisons are being made between *Mazel and Shlimazel* and Henry James's huge novel *The Golden Bowl*. Wolf then combs the story for phallic elements, unearthing a "tripartite analogy . . . between head, foot and penis" as well as the symbol of a male genital organ in the peaked hat Shlimazel wears. Before his brave essay is finally over, Mr. Wolf has found not only oedipal rivalry in Tam's adventures but "intra-psychic conflict" and "the battle between the generations." Mazel proves to be the symbol of Eros and further embodies Thanatos, while Shlimazel symbolizes Thanatos but also embodies Eros. At length: "If we, imaginatively, set Tam against the sanctified father in *In My Father's Court* and God the Father of the same court, it will not seem surprising that the implied father-son conflict in *Mazel and Shlimazel* can be expressed only in the context of an elaborate defensive structure. Theoretically, we would expect that longing for the mother would be repressed equally, but Singer seems, in this particular story, to have unconsciously portrayed the mother, in part at least, at an earlier stage of the child's development; and the history of literature suggests that the loss of the nurturing mother can gain access to consciousness more readily than can be an imagined loss from the oedipal period. If one thinks, as example, of *Jane Eyre* and *Sons and Lovers*, it becomes clear that. . . ." Ah, but it never does become clear at all.

And yet there is a statement in this essay of Wolf's that perhaps provides the crucial key to a more commonsensical assessment of Isaac's makeup as a person and as a writer: "The world that Singer knew growing up was a divided one: Jew and gentile, Satan and God, empirical mother and mystical father, experienced brother and virginal hero. Such bifurcations of sensibility and value lead easily into class divisions of the myth, low and high born, and the double parentage that structures this class division."

The very divisions in Isaac's world, the contradictions within himself, what Buchen has called the "duality" of his nature, make him a hard man to sum up. The longer one knows him, the more difficult it becomes to pin him down, to get him in focus. Even so, it is perhaps time to ask: What is Isaac Bashevis Singer?

He is a writer who looks at reality unflinchingly but whose most realistic tales are leavened with fantasy and whose fantasies are firmly rooted in the world of fact. His stories and novels are interwoven with the real experiences of his life; his memoirs revise reality to heighten experience and make the story of his own life readable. His most pragmatic characters are susceptible to the occult, while even his imps and demons and witches have a practical streak in their makeup. He is indeed, as Picasso defined the artist, a liar who tells the truth.

He is an American with a European turn of mind, a citizen who preserves the objectivity of a foreigner, a Jew who regards himself as a full member of the human race but never lets himself forget that he is fundamentally an outsider.

He is an iconoclast who has broken all the traditional taboos of Yiddish fiction—and an innate conservative who believes that traditional Judaism and traditional politics offer greater rewards in life than rebellion and self-indulgence; an atheist who believes in God; a religionist who resents the dogmas and closed systems of organized religion; a mystic with a healthy respect for science; a philosopher with strong reservations about the value of cold philosophy. He is the most suspicious and the most trusting of men.

He is a sensualist with an ascetic turn of mind, a sophisticate who still retains a singular innocence—an aging man who knows that inside he is still "a little boy." He is at once the most provincial and the worldliest of men, a creature of vanity with the modesty to disparage his own importance, a private man who loves the public, a loner with a thousand friends, a shy man who will speak to anyone, a man of secrets impatient with secrecy, a man who talks much but also knows well how to listen, in whom strangers confide and in whose company his friends delight, a teacher who learns from his pupils. He is an experimenter wary of experiments, a modern man who mistrusts modernity, a charmer not taken in by charm, a money-conscious man who can drive a hard bargain with a dollar but who at the same time is generous with his money and willing to interrupt whatever he is doing to offer advice, answer a telephone call or a letter requesting help, comfort a friend in trouble. He is a traveler who likes best to stay home, a lover who knows how to hate, a timid man who can be extraordinarily brave, a man of intense concentration who welcomes the distractions and surprises an adventurous life still brings.

He is a man of many paradoxes and contradictions, yet withal a man, like Whitman's poetical self, large enough to "contain multitudes," reconciled to the war of forces within himself and somehow at ease with himself.

He is a splendid man and a great writer, certainly the greatest Jewish writer of our time, a Janus-faced observer with antennae tuned to the past as well as to the present and the future—which he turns, by the alchemy of his prose, into the lasting stuff of literature.

❀

When Isaac Singer talks about the future, it is usually in terms of the past. "My future is my past," he has said, and his work certainly bears the statement out. At the same time, he does not regard the ways of the past as ways "to be passively accepted and slavishly followed." The past must serve as a framework on which to build the future, shedding light on the road but not determining its direction. For Isaac a hero is not a man who submits blindly to tradition but who, through the small revelations that come to him in the course of his life, finds a way to create his own tradition and, as it were, to collaborate with God in determining his destiny.

Will his books endure? Isaac says he doesn't care. "Either people will read *The Family Moskat* or *The Slave* one hundred years from now or they will not read them. Whatever they do is all right with me." He talks objectively about the importance of his work. "I don't think that these novels will redeem the world or help humanity get rid of sickness or of suppression or of any other things." If he has a hope, he says, for his writing, it is that "I have given the children who were born in assimilated houses a certain bridge between themselves and old Jewish life."

❉

November 21, 1977

Isaac is seventy-three years old today. To celebrate, lunch with Dvorah at the Famous. (Alma is down at the Miami Beach condominium, recovering from a siege of phlebitis that confined her to a Florida hospital for a while.)

Which is Isaac's real birthday? July 14, 1904, as it says in his passport, or November 21? "I was born in the third week of the month of Heshvan on the Jewish calendar—which is roughly equivalent to the month of November. But when I was a little boy, and we moved from Leoncin to Radzymin, I asked my parents when my birthday was. It was then the month of Tammuz, which usually corresponds to July. 'Today is your birthday,' they told me, to cheer me up. So I have usually celebrated on Bastille Day. But actually, as I found out later, the November date, as far as I have been able to figure out, is more or less the correct one."

Isaac wants to treat Dvorah to lunch, but she would rather treat him; he won't hear of it. The waiter at the Famous greets Isaac as "Dr. Singer" and has all kinds of recommendations to make for what "the doctor" should order. Isaac ignores them and orders pea soup and a kasha dish. So does Dvorah. She wants her kasha served with milk. Isaac predicts she'll never get it. The waiter explains that kasha with milk is served only in the summertime; she settles for *kasha varnishke,* Isaac's choice.

Saul Bellow is to receive the Nobel prize in literature next month. How does Isaac feel about Bellow getting it instead of himself? "Nobel, Shmobel, I have a wall of prizes," he says, "all kinds of plaques and certificates. I don't think I have room for any more." If there is a slight tinge of green in those white cheeks as he says this, his smile does not betray him, although he doesn't seem sorry when the subject is changed.

Just yesterday Anwar el-Sadat, the President of Egypt, addressed the Israeli Parliament in Jerusalem and met with Prime Minister Menachem Begin, an unprecedented event telecast by satellite all over the world.

Dvorah watched; Isaac didn't. She wants to know how he feels about this development. Isaac says he sees little hope that the "historic meeting" will lead to peace in the Middle East. "When a husband and wife have been separated a long time, they suddenly begin to develop hot feelings toward each other and insist on getting together, but as often as not soon afterward they are at each other again and a divorce follows. I think it is better to be skeptical about the outcome of such things, since they usually turn out badly. A skeptic is never as disappointed as an optimist, at least most of the time. Politicians are cold people, anyhow. They can smile and shake hands, but inside they are always cold and calculating." Half the bloodshed in the world, he says, has been caused by religious fanatics, the other half by politicians, especially those "who consider themselves reformers."

Dvorah says the lighting in the back dining room at the Famous brings out the blue in Isaac's eyes.

Dvorah dips into her purse to bring out a letter that has arrived from a medium who would like Isaac to write an introduction for her forthcoming book on the occult. Isaac says he would be willing to supply a quote but not a whole introduction. He is too busy at the moment making revisions requested by Rachel MacKenzie on the manuscript of his novel *Shosha*. And he has not yet handed in the epilogue to his novel *Yarme and Kayle*, which currently still runs in the *Forward*. He cannot make up his mind whether Yarme should commit suicide or not in the end. He really doesn't know yet how the story will turn out.

The conversation gets around to age. Isaac insists that he has always looked old. He has seen photographs of himself surrounded by people who were in their seventies when he was in his fifties. "I looked older than they did. Now they have only caught up with me." He talks about his forthcoming book of memoirs, *A Young Man in Search of Love*, especially about Raphael Soyer's illustrations. Soyer has done a cover for the book full of embracing figures. Isaac considers this rather daring, especially for a conservative artist like Soyer. He is quite excited about the drawings. "He has outdone himself," he says.

Now Isaac wants Dvorah to order some prunes for dessert, but she says she would rather have the fruit salad. He assures her that the kind of fruit she will get will be impossible to chew. He turns out to be more or less right about this, but Dvorah goes on chewing bravely anyhow.

Isaac has just sold another story to *The New Yorker*, another tale of his travels in South America, called "One Night in Brazil." He is pleased at the prospect of seeing the new story in print but distressed by the spate of recent illnesses—his, Alma's, his son's (Israel was recently in New York for some medical tests). Isaac spoke to Alma only this morning though, and she seems to be coming along nicely. Isaac shrugs off his gloom, changing the subject to keep the conversation lighthearted and upbeat.

"Without a little nonsense," Isaac says, "I don't understand how people can get through life." He recalls accepting an invitation some time ago to have dinner with the members of a "gay synagogue" in Greenwich Village. There were only two women at the dinner party, the rest were gay men, but he couldn't find anything gay about the evening in the traditional sense of the word. Everybody was terribly earnest, he recalls. All the men had just finished reading *Satan in Goray* in the original Yiddish and were anxious to discuss the novel in detail with him. "I finally got them," he says, "to talk about themselves. It was much more interesting."

The waiter brings the check. Once more Dvorah offers to pay it. Isaac stuffs her money back into her purse. It's his birthday, and *he* will treat. He thanks her warmly for not allowing the waiter to bring in one of those cupcakes with a candle in it and sing "Happy Birthday" to him. He says every time that occurs in a restaurant he thinks to himself, "Thank goodness it isn't me." He's ready to get back to West Eighty-sixth Street, back to work. Dvorah waits until he stands up to put on his raincoat, then stuffs a couple of dollar bills between the sugar dispenser and a flower vase for a tip. Isaac wants her to put the money away in her purse and let him leave the tip too, but she insists on this one small gesture to mark the occasion.

Isaac and Dvorah go out into a rainy afternoon, walking very fast. Isaac's head in his battered old gray felt hat bobs as he talks; Dvorah's is thrown back in laughter that echoes down Seventy-second Street as they turn up Broadway.

PART 11

"I'll Take It Like a Man"

On Thursday morning, October 5, 1978, Alma answered the telephone at the Singers' condominium apartment in Seaside, Florida, where she and Isaac were spending the High Holy Days. She was told on the phone that the Swedish Academy had just announced that the Nobel prize for literature was to be awarded to her husband. Isaac had gone out for a walk and was waiting for Alma to join him for breakfast at a drugstone on Collins Avenue, growing more and more impatient as she didn't show up. Finally she came running in. Isaac wanted to know where she had been and why she was so late. She explained that she had been on a long distance call—and told him the good news.

Isaac's first words when he heard about the prize were, "Are you sure it's true? It must be a mistake. They must be confusing it with a nomination for a Nobel prize." Then he said, "In any case, let's eat breakfast. What do you think—we can stop eating because of happiness?"

After breakfast Isaac and Alma returned to the apartment house, where they found a battalion of reporters and cameramen waiting for them. The phone kept ringing all day. Every editor in the country seemed to be after an interview.

"No writer writes for prizes," Isaac told an Associated Press reporter. "Tolstoy was a candidate and some other writer got it . . . so the prize, while it's pleasant to get, it doesn't prove, really, so much. I am sorry that writers greater than I did not get it. . . . I am nothing more than a storyteller."

When he heard that the cash award to go with the Nobel prize would add up to the equivalent of $163,000, Isaac said, "I don't think anyone owes me anything. But since it came, I will take it like a man." He also said, "It's money, but I'll try not to take all of it for myself. I'll try to give it to others who need it more than I do."

The Swedish Academy of Letters, which awards the Nobel prize for literature on behalf of the Nobel Foundation, cited Isaac for his "impassioned narrative art which, with roots in a Polish-Jewish cultural tradition, brings the universal human condition to life." Lars Gyllenstein, the permanent secretary of the Swedish Academy, added that Isaac's experiences in the Warsaw ghetto had helped to shape his character and provided him with "the ever-vivid subject matter for his inspiration and imagination." In his statement Gyllenstein called Yiddish "the language of the simple people and of the women, the language of the mothers who preserved fairytales and anecdotes, legends and memories for hundreds of years past, through a history which seems to have left nothing untried in the way of agony, passions, aberrations, cruelty and bestiality, but also of heroism, love and self-sacrifice."

As the day wore on, Isaac gave out dozens of interviews to television, radio, newspaper, and magazine reporters. He answered phone calls from Stockholm, Israel, South America, Paris, and New York. One call that day was from President Carter. Isaac told him that call would make it a day to remember. He doesn't remember, however, what Carter said to him—just that it was something "kind and clever." Isaac told *Newsweek* that demons were still stealing his books, his glasses, and "sometimes even my checkbook." He told *Time*, "Everything will remain the same—same typewriter, same wife, same apartment, same telephone number, same language. I am thankful, of course, for the prize and thankful to God for each story, each idea, each word, each day." Asked if he would go to Stockholm to accept the prize on December 10, he answered, "What can I do? I will go and I will make a little speech. It will not shake the world."

When Cathy Grossman Keller, a reporter for the Long Island newspaper *Newsday*, arrived at the apartment for an interview, she heard Isaac saying to one caller, "Yes, now you've got the bigshot on the phone." She found him propped up in bed wearing blue slacks, a light-blue shirt, and suede shoes. On his bedroom dresser lay a copy of a story about Chanukah that he had just completed. He talked about his work with her, commenting that he would "still strive, as always, to entertain the reader." As for the prize, "It will not make me an optimist. It will not cure human misery or human tragedy." At the same time he felt that the award meant a "victory and recognition for all the Yiddishists. I share it with all the Yiddish-speaking world and my English readers."

Alma finally urged the throng of reporters out of their white-and-yellow living room so Isaac could eat a proper dinner, but when Isaac saw them waiting in the hallway, he called them back. At length they all left, and Isaac and Alma sat on the bed in their bedroom sharing a piece of honey cake, a traditional Jewish High Holy Days food that is supposed to symbolize a sweet year ahead.

That night, for the first time in his life, Isaac found it necessary to turn off the telephone so he could get some sleep.

The day after he heard about the new prize, Isaac called Dvorah from Seaside and asked to speak to her husband, Abraham. "I just wanted you to know," he told Abraham, "your friendship means more to me than all the prizes in the world."

The three major newspapers in New York City—the *Post*, the *Times* and the *News*—were still on strike at the time, but one of the interim publications, *City News*, carried a big picture of Isaac on the front page the very next day. "Pole wins Nobel," said a headline in the *Los Angeles Times*. Dick Cavett taped a new introduction to the interview he had done with Isaac during the summer, and the show was rerun on educational television. Wherever one switched on the dial, there was Isaac, answering questions, his eyes twinkling as he said things like "No writer stops writing because he gets a prize. . . . what else is there to do, a man of my age? We writers never stop. . . ."

Actually Isaac had stopped writing and would find it difficult to resume his craft for several weeks.

At the *Jewish Daily Forward* there was special rejoicing over Isaac's award. Simon Weber, the editor, said that the moment of the announcement that Isaac was the Nobel laureate in literature was "the proudest moment for the *Forward* and myself." He called the prize "the greatest thing to have happened in Yiddish literature" and predicted that it would give a boost to the sales of books in Yiddish. Isaac had already told one interviewer that he hoped to use some of the prize money to help get all his own books published in Yiddish editions.

A week after the award was announced Isaac returned to New York for a few days.

Before that week was out, Isaac also spoke to Israel's Prime Minister Menachem Begin. They met for half an hour at the Regency Hotel in New York. Isaac reported later that it had been more of a monologue on the Prime Minister's part than a conversation, with himself saying rather little. He did, however, manage to tell the Prime Minister that he felt Yiddish had too long been looked down upon by Israelis as a mongrel tongue and ought to be accepted in Israel as a second language after Hebrew.

Immediately afterward Isaac went to Washington, D.C., for television and radio interviews, and after that kept a lecture commitment in Richmond, Virginia. The October 14 *Washington Post* carried an interview with him in the course of which he was quoted as saying, 'Before the prize, of course, I did not give every week fifty interviews, but it's more or less the same—I think about the books and plays I will write, the people I will put in them. I think my friends are more excited about this prize than I am." He admitted that he had not done any writing "for a whole week. I was so busy, people calling, interviews. I decided it's not a misfortune if I don't write for a week." He told Joseph McCellan, the *Post*'s interviewer, that if he had his entire life to live over he would only do so if it would be full of surprises, "if I couldn't know what was going to happen next."

On October 12 John Leonard, *New York Times* columnist and former editor of *The New York Times Book Review*, had declared over the WNET Reports Special Edition program on Channel Thirteen in New York that for a long time he had been "one of the stiffs in the so-called New York literary community who was asked every year to fill in a postcard nominating some writer for the Nobel prize for literature" but had never recommended Isaac. Over and over he had filled in "two names on my postcards: Vladimir Nabokov and Doris Lessing. Other names came to mind, of course: Bellow and Borges, John Cheever and Gabriel García Márquez. But I was stern and firm. Bellow obviously didn't need my help. But, alas, Nabokov died without a prize, like Tolstoy and unlike Pearl Buck.

"Perhaps," Leonard continued, "the name of Isaac Bashevis Singer should have occurred to me. It did not. This might have been because we are forever being told that Singer can be appreciated only in the original Yiddish, a dying language, by readers with some historical experience of an almost-vanished European Jewish culture with special reference to the demonism of the seventeenth century. 'Gimpel the Fool' is brilliant, but is it *central*? Hasn't Singer somehow finessed the Holocaust?"

Now, said Leonard, he wanted to apologize for failing to recommend Isaac for the prize. "A week of the witty Singer has consoled and refreshened. Not only has he been the sort of grandfather, wise and modest, that we all wanted when we were young enough to have a grandfather, but a dying language and a vanished culture are, perhaps, the conditions of literature, castles of words in the kingdom of the imagination. 'Listen,' says Singer, and he sings of the Devil in a twitchy time of self-pity and self-aggrandizement. He is not, like so many of our writers, a media brat, a cracker-barrel full of poisoned candy. In any language, he celebrates and mourns. The Swedish Academy could have done better, but usually does worse."

When *The New York Times* resumed publication on Monday, November 6, 1978, after an eighty-eight day strike, the paper carried a photograph of Isaac with a boxed story about the award in which Christopher Lehmann-Haupt commented that Isaac had long been credited by his admirers with having "made of the East European Jew, especially the Hasid, an exemplar of the suffering modern man who has been exiled from his divine inheritance." Lehmann-Haupt added that "if influence and appeal are standards of Nobel excellence, then Singer is a worthy choice. For he has carried on the tradition of such Yiddish storytelling masters as Mendele, Aleichem, Peretz and Asch, and he has influenced a generation of American-Jewish writers now thriving in his wake. As for his appeal, one need only note that any writer who can command a following in such disparate publications as the *Jewish Daily Forward*, *The New Yorker*, *Commentary* and *Playboy* can scarcely be accused of cultural parochialism."

The announcement of the Nobel prize came as the capstone of a whole year of eventful turns in Isaac's life. The winter in Florida had been a bad one, with a prostate operation that left him weak for months. Alma too had not been well. But in the spring they were both up and around again. Farrar, Straus and Giroux had published *Shosha*, and the reviews had been glowing. Isaac's latest book of memoirs, *A Young Man in Search of Love*, had been well received too, and he had started work on another book in the series, *Lost in America*, with Joseph Singer translating each installment into English as soon as the Yiddish version had appeared in the *Forward*. Farrar, Straus and Giroux had announced that the firm would publish Isaac's novel about the Warsaw underworld in the 1930s, *Yarme and Kayle*, the latest collection of his short stories, *Old Love*, and a new book for children, *Eight Hannukah Stories*. Meanwhile, Moshe Mizrahi, who produced *Madame Rosa*, announced that he was planning a film of *The Slave*. Isaac had seen his name twice in one month on the front page of *The New York Times Book Review*, and the same day that the Nobel prize was announced shooting was completed in Europe on the movie version of *The Magician of Lublin*.

❀

November 4, 1978

Back from Berlin after the shooting of Menahem Golan's film of *The Magician of Lublin*, Lou Jacobi tells how, with the aid of a large subsidy from the West German government, company set-builders recreated, on the streets of West Berlin, the Jewish quarter of the city of Lublin as it looked at the turn of the century. "And the town of Piask too, where much of the action takes place. We had extras, German extras, wearing beards and caftans." After a while the company ran out of false beards and sidelocks and Hasidic costumes. "Imagine the irony," the actor says, "in Berlin! There are no more than six thousand Jews living there today." It cost hundreds of thousands of Deutsch marks to turn Berlin streets into Lublin streets.

Earlier scenes were shot in Munich. For four days that Bavarian city, where Hitler's rise to power began, was the site of an effort by "an Israeli director, an Israeli producer, and an Israeli crew" to shoot scenes for a movie about the Jews of Poland. "When we got to Berlin," Jacobi says, "we turned the cellar of a building which had once housed the Gestapo into a synagogue."

The movie, which is reported to have cost about six million dollars, was originally supposed to have been made in Lublin, but that would have meant obtaining visas for some thirty Israelis, and the Polish government turned the producers down. Additional scenes were supposed to be filmed in Israel, but, Jacobi explains, "we ran out of money and had to finish the job in Germany."

Director Golan hoped to have a final cut of *The Magician* ready, Jacobi says, "by the time Isaac collects his Nobel prize in Stockholm," with the official opening to take place at the Cannes Film Festival.

"It was quite an experience making a movie about Poland in Germany," Jacobi concludes. "I only wish the author could have been there himself to see how we did it." Isaac, who has said he will never go back to Poland even on a visit, refuses to set foot on German soil as well.

❀

Now that he was so sought after, it became necessary to install an answering device for Isaac's telephone in New York (he picked it up every time it rang anyhow, and has since had to resort to an unlisted number). Isaac's doctor advised him to give up his lecture commitments and to spend more time resting, but he soon went back to writing every day and agreed to keep a promise to lecture at Congregation B'nai Jeshurun in New York after the woman running the lecture series actually got down on her knees to beg him not to cancel.

In October 1978 *Shosha* had hit the best-seller list and become a Book-of-the-Month-Club selection, and Isaac continued to be besieged by requests for personal appearances and endorsements of books by other authors. Into Isaac's New York apartment came television and radio interviewers representing networks and stations from all over the world. Alma complained that they tracked up the house with their equipment, moved furniture, left so much debris that it took days to get the place cleaned up again. Every reporter in the country seemed to want to interview him, every photographer to take his picture. It finally became necessary for Alma to rent a hotel room where Isaac could work on his Nobel acceptance speech and do his other writing away from the incessantly ringing telephone and the never-ending procession of visitors.

The Swedish Jewish community announced that it planned a special gathering in his honor when he arrived in Stockholm during the first week in December.

❀

November 6, 1978

The sanctuary at Congregation B'nai Jeshurun, the synagogue on West Eighty-ninth Street in Manhattan that Isaac attends, is filled to overflowing this Monday evening. Outside the huge auditorium a thousand people are gathered to hear the Nobel laureate over loudspeakers. Isaac is here as the latest personality in a "Dialogue" series being conducted by the synagogue's spiritual leader, Rabbi William Berkowitz, but no event in the series has attracted a crowd of these proportions. The starting time set for the program was 8:30 P.M.; people have been lining up in front of the Eighty-eighth and Eighty-ninth street entrances to B'nai Jeshurun since well before eight.

Isaac is in high spirits. He reaffirms his belief in God. He deplores what he calls a "historical mistake" on the part of the Jewish people when they kept "our women" from fully participating in religious rituals or serving in the rabbinate. He talks about how Jewish women were alienated from Jewish learning in the Poland where he grew up, encouraged to read silly Polish novels and to look down on the Yiddish tongue. He talks about his relations with his own parents, recalling that he was often scolded and criticized but never doubted for a minute that both Pinchas Mendel and Bathsheba deeply loved him. When Rabbi Berkowitz asks him about the institution of marriage, Isaac cites his oft-repeated belief that monogamy is not for everybody and that there are sound reasons why divorce is easy to obtain under rabbinical law.

Asked, once again, about love and sex in his novels, Isaac defends the importance of these subjects but reminds Rabbi Berkowitz that he has never used four-letter words or indulged in pornography.

Rabbi Berkowitz wants to know if Isaac would ever consider running for office. "I have plenty of trouble without being a politician," he says, adding that when he heard Norman Mailer was running for mayor of New York City, he "didn't know whether to laugh or cry."

Was his Nobel prize intended as a recognition of the importance of Yiddish as well as his own literary achievements in that language? Not at all, "because Yiddish has been around for hundreds of years." Was the prize meant to pay respect to the millions of Yiddish-speaking Jews who died in the Holocaust? "Perhaps subconsciously. In any case great numbers of Jews have died, but Yiddish remains alive." Is Yiddish sick? "In Jewish history, the distance between sickness and death can be a long, long time."

How would Isaac like best to be remembered? As an "honest writer" who always wrote what he really believed.

At the close of the dialogue Rabbi Berkowitz announces that Columbia University has just established an I. B. Singer award to be given to a student who excels in Yiddish or Yiddish literature.

❧

November 10, 1978

In the Low Memorial Library at Columbia University, where a table in a large, cheerful room has been set out with drinks and hors d'oeuvres, Isaac is shaking hands with well-wishers and signing autographs between sips of the tea Dvorah has several times tried to get him to drink before he enters the Rotunda to deliver the Jacob and Anna Blauder Memorial Lecture. Isaac appears to be in good health and high spirits. His cheeks are pink, his eyes especially blue, and he greets his friends and admirers with much cordiality. Dvorah is worried that he will tire himself out at this reception and fetches him a chair, where he sits happily chatting with the people surrounding him while his tea grows cold.

At 8:30 P.M. Isaac goes onstage in the Rotunda, a high-ceilinged, impressive hall dominated by pillars and stone statues of ancient Roman luminaries. He is greeted by a standing ovation. Then he sits down at a table provided for him on the platform, takes off his glasses so he can see the pages better, and reads into a microphone his sketch "Sabbath in Gehenna" to appreciative chuckles from an audience of many hundreds who completely pack the auditorium. An unusually large percentage of tonight's crowd consists of students. Following the reading, questions are invited from the floor. Isaac moves from the table to a lectern to answer them.

One student wants to know whether Isaac has trouble because he writes in Yiddish and all his work must be translated. Isaac responds, "I've had troubles all my life, and if there should be one day without troubles I wouldn't know what to do with myself. . . . So I say, my answer to you is, somehow I manage. And if I don't manage, I go to sleep without managing."

One woman who says she is Irish wants Isaac to know how much she appreciates the fact that his works are translated into English, since if they weren't she wouldn't be able to enjoy them. Isaac tells her that "just as you read me, I read Irish writers."

Asked why he doesn't translate his own works into English, Isaac replies that the way things are he can always blame any failures on his translators; if he did his own translations he would have to take the blame himself.

Asked if he is planning to make his Nobel prize acceptance speech in Stockholm in Yiddish, Isaac says, "I will say a few words in Yiddish; I will begin in Yiddish. But since no one understands Yiddish there, I will continue in English. I certainly will not make it in Swedish! But since my English is almost like Yiddish, I can almost say that my speech will be more or less in Yiddish."

After fielding a few more questions Isaac returns to the table to read a piece in Yiddish about how there are more synonyms to describe a poor man in that language than in any other. At first he has trouble finding the manuscript among the papers on the table and confides to the audience, "I want to tell you that if there would be a Nobel prize for misplacing things I would get not one but two or three." Then he finds the essay and proceeds with a reading punctuated by roars of laughter from those who understand and even from some who don't. After that he says he is going to read a story in English—"The Needle"—but changes his mind and reads "The Son from America" instead. Then he gets up to answer more questions: Since childhood plays such a big part in his writing, what about his own? Isaac reminisces a bit, tells about growing up on Krochmalna Street. He recalls an incident when his father visited him in Warsaw in the 1920s and asked him how his newspaper business was going, because he had told Pinchas Mendel he was making a living selling newspapers rather than admit he was a writer. But he loved his parents. It wasn't the fashion to blame all your troubles on your parents in those days. He tells of meeting a friend in New York who was going to an analyst and asking him how he was making out. The friend replied that the analysis was going fine. What was so fine about it? "And he told me, 'I go to him only six months and I already hate my father!' "

To a question about his interest in the supernatural Isaac replies with an anecdote about a man who brought him a terrible manuscript to read. Isaac was afraid to tell him what he thought of it for fear the man would kill himself. But shortly afterward the writer claimed that he had met his dead father on a bench in Central Park and his father had told him never to publish his work. "Many years were added to my life," Isaac says. "I told him, 'Your father was right.' " How fortunate, adds Isaac, that this would-be writer believed he could meet his own dead father in the park and was willing to follow his advice.

Asked about his own son, Israel, Isaac speaks proudly of Israel's career as a farmer on a kibbutz and more recently as a journalist and translator. He points out that Israel has translated a number of his books into Hebrew, disclosing that when news of the Nobel award reached the Jewish state, so many reporters came to interview his son that after a while Israel began to imagine that he himself was getting the prize.

❀

Although Isaac's performance at Columbia University was supposed to mark his last public appearance before his trip to Stockholm, he spent the night of his seventy-fourth birthday, November 21, with New York's Mayor Koch attending a reception at the mayoral mansion in Gracie Square. He was now getting almost as many telephone calls at the midtown hotel where he was supposed to be hiding out as he usually got at home.

Meanwhile Isaac's son, Israel, had arrived in America to spend several days with him and Alma over the Thanksgiving holiday.

On November 29 the "Notes on People" column in *The New York Times* reported that Isaac was complaining about the calls and the correspondence, which seemed to be getting completely out of hand. "I decided to always have my home phone listed so my readers can keep in touch, but this time it's become a mass movement." Even so, he had accepted invitations to appear at a number of receptions arranged in his honor, including a big one on Monday evening, November 27, sponsored by the *Forward* and attended by eighteen hundred people at the High School of Fashion Industries in Manhattan, and another arranged by the American Jewish Committee, which sponsors the publication *Commentary*, where "Gimpel the Fool" first appeared in English a quarter of a century ago. It was all beginning to get to him, though. He told the *Times*, "Sometimes I think of Mr. J. D. Salinger, who in his wisdom has gone somewhere and does his work."

Writing about the new Nobel laureate in *The New Republic* for October 21, 1978, Maureen Howard had said she was certain that after Isaac got to Stockholm there would be reports "that cufflinks were lost, that Singer's black shoelaces snapped at the last moment in his hotel room, or that the sleek flight attendant on his jet from Kennedy served drinks with the inky fingers of a yeshiva boy and asked an impertinent question of our hero instead of mouthing a polite phrase." What she really looked forward to, she wrote, was "the story that will come, for there will be a story shortly, not so much about a trip, wining and dining, Swedish blondes and a befuddled, bright old Jew from New York—but about some small pluck of misfortune, that instance of the broken shoelace, which will reverberate like the sounding string, Chekhov's mysterious thread of civilized continuity, which snaps at the end of *The Cherry Orchard*. . . . There's no telling what Singer will say in Stockholm, but my guess is that there will not be any false rhetoric nor high oration. He will speak as he writes . . . as a man who is in touch with his language and his people—the living and the dead."

❈

December 5, 1978

At Kennedy Airport in New York, in a large, luxuriously appointed, softly lighted private departure lounge provided by Scandinavian Airlines for the VIPs among its first-class passengers, Isaac and his party are sipping drinks from the bar and chatting away as they wait for flight SK912 to bear them aloft at 5:05 P.M. on the journey to Stockholm. In addition to Isaac, cheerful and dapper in the inevitable dark blue suit, white shirt, and unobtrusive tie, the party includes Alma, wearing a jacket made of tan-and-white squares of some thick fur; Roger Straus, Jr., looking informal and at the same time distinguished in a light brown suit and tan turtleneck; his wife, Dorothea, swathed in gray; Robert Giroux, a tall, ample, genial man with a ruddy face and a shock of white hair; Simon Weber, editor of the *Jewish Daily Forward*, debonair in dark slacks and a gray-and-white patterned sport jacket; and Mrs. Weber, who has come down to see him off. Also with the group are two of Alma's close friends, Sally Frank and the painter Mildred Simonson, known to her intimates as Simone. Alma's son and daughter were supposed to be coming along but couldn't make it, so Sally and Simone are standing in for them. In Alma's purse is said to be a top-secret itinerary listing every appearance Isaac is scheduled to make—every press conference, lecture, reception, luncheon, huddle with foreign publishers, and banquet he is due to attend, every interviewer he has consented to see in Stockholm. It is rumored to be a long list.

Dorothea congratulates Isaac on a recent statement attributed to him about biographers, to the effect that he can't understand why people should want to eat "stale bread" when they can get the fresh product straight from the baker himself. He nods in acknowledgment of her praise, then springs up to pose for a cameraman with various members of the traveling entourage in various combinations. "They give me all kinds of instructions, these photographers," Isaac says affably. "Look this way, look that way, move over a little here, move back, move forward, don't look at me, look over my shoulder. Finally they say, Just look natural. How else can I look?"

An SAS representative arrives to guide the group down to the gate to board the 747. Here the party is split up—Isaac, Bob Giroux, and the Strauses proceed to first class, Alma and her friends and Simon Weber to economy; the Singers, with their strong sense of thrift, just couldn't see squandering money on a first-class fare for Alma. Isaac's, of course, has been paid by the Nobel Foundation. On board, Isaac, seated next to Bob Giroux, turns the pages of the current issue of *People* magazine, pausing to scrutinize a photograph of himself. This week there are enough stories about and pictures of him being printed all over the world to keep him busy reading about and looking at himself for weeks on end.

In the economy-class section of the plane Simon Weber pulls out the page proofs of a new story Isaac has submitted for publication in a special Chanukah supplement of the *Forward*. Twenty-two years ago, Simon recalls, he put out a huge jubilee edition of the *Forward* in which he ran the story "The Gentleman from Cracow." The new one is called "The Betrayal of Israel," and it's one of those Krochmalna Street pieces. It's about a man who comes to Pinchas Mendel for advice after a career as a quadrigamist— he has married four women, three of them with rabbinical sanction. These unions have resulted in a total of six children. Isaac's father reproves the visitor, who proceeds to defend himself on grounds of historical precedent:

Didn't Jacob have several wives and Solomon a thousand? Despite such arguments, Pinchas Mendel hands down a decision: The man can't keep all these wives; bills of divorcement must be drawn up. In the end the client chooses the youngest of his brides and takes off with her for America— because where else would a scoundrel go?

Still vigorous at sixty-seven, Simon says he has to eat often to ward off the return of a now-dormant ulcer that used to plague him. There's no problem on SAS, with the frequent snacks, a generous dinner, a breakfast that has to be served while you can almost still taste the after-dinner coffee. Up in first class the Strauses and Bob Giroux have just dined on an excellent meal and a fine wine. Roger is stretched out under a blanket snoozing, Bob is reading; Isaac, having enjoyed a specially prepared vegetarian collation, decides to go back to the economy-class section to visit his wife and her friends and see how Simon is doing. Arriving at Simon's seat, he is twitted mischievously by the *Forward* editor for a sloppy job of proofreading "The Betrayal of Israel." He calls himself a proofreader? All those years reading proof in Warsaw on *Literary Pages*? And now, just look at these errors. Simon waves the Yiddish galleys in front of the author. It's a disgrace. Isaac laughs and says he's sorry, he's had a lot on his mind lately. They talk for a long while in Yiddish. Then Isaac goes back to the first-class area. The plane has to land for a stopover in Copenhagen. As the group assembles to leave the aircraft Isaac looks up to see Alma approaching. "Ah," he exclaims, "a familiar face!"

Back on the plane, breakfast is served. Dorothea, finding Isaac in the economy-class section again on her way forward, says she had been wondering where he had gone. "With your supernatural powers," she tells him, "I thought you'd gotten off the plane." Soon there is a hint of dawn in the Scandinavian sky, and snow can be glimpsed on the ground as the gigantic plane descends. When the captain announces that it's 12 degrees Farenheit in Stockholm, a low moan goes up among the passengers.

❀

December 6, 1978

In a gray dawn at Arlanda, Stockholm's international airport, a group from the Ministry of Foreign Affairs is advancing rapidly on Isaac's party. An energetic young woman named Ruth Jacoby, who describes herself as the only Jew in the Foreign Ministry, takes Isaac firmly by the arm. She will let go of that arm only rarely for the rest of the week as she guides Isaac and company through the intricacies of Stockholm's complex series of plans for him. She and her associates personally relieve the tired travelers of passports

and luggage stubs, introduce the laureate and his retinue to various representatives of the Foreign Ministry and the Nobel Foundation, as well as to the
economics laureate, Professor Herbert A. Simon (who looks rather left out of
things), then whisk everyone upstairs to a VIP lounge thronged with reporters and cameramen for a scheduled press conference—the only one
Isaac has agreed to in Stockholm.

The spokesman for the reporters and media people (it later turns out he
was self-appointed) is a journalist named Peter Dragadze, representing, of all
publications, *Town & Country*. As bulbs flash and microphones are held
in Isaac's face, it looks like a scene out of Fellini's *La Dolce Vita*, but Isaac,
even though he hasn't slept, beams from a sofa and fields all questions with
his usual aplomb. How does he feel about the prize? "Many writers before
me, great writers, lived out their years, and they never got any prize. Of
course I'm very happy about it." For which of his books does he feel he's
earned the award? "If you would have six children and someone would ask
you, 'Which child do you love best?' you would be as embarrassed as I am. I
have to love them since I've already published them. Of course, if I could, I
would rewrite all of them." For one reporter Isaac consents to "speak Yiddish" in his Warsaw accent; he assures another that Yiddish may be sick, but
it isn't dead yet. On the subject of Prime Minister Begin's trip to Oslo to receive the Nobel peace prize and the chances for peace in the Middle East:
"I'm going to say something very original. And this is, I hope there will be
peace. Have you ever heard of such a profound idea?" On "What is a Jew?":
"My own answer is that there is such a thing as a maximum Jew and a
minimum Jew. My father was a maximum Jew. He got up in the morning a
Jew, went to sleep a Jew; he ate like a Jew, he slept like a Jew, he dreamed
like a Jew. . . . I'm somewhere in the middle." On the fact that the year
brought a Polish Pope to the Vatican and a Polish Nobel prize winner for
literature: "I would say that it's far-fetched to make a kind of partnership between the Pope and myself. . . . All I can say is, I'm very happy that a Pole
became Pope." Would his prize be "an injection for Yiddish?" "It would be
an injection but not a cure." Whom would he recommend for the next
Nobel prize in literature? "I would say that if I would have to choose five or
six people, not one, Henry Miller would be one of them. You'd be surprised. Even though I don't write in the way he writes, I think that he has
done many good things for literature. He fought against censorship, and I
would give the prize even for this fight alone. In addition, I think he's a
very talented writer."

The members of Isaac's party agree that he has acquitted himself with his
usual showmanship and pile into dark blue limousines, in which they are
whisked along immaculate roads past snow-covered fields in cold but blazing
sunshine to the Grand Hotel, which is grand indeed—all gold and rich
brown leather and crystal chandeliers, with casements looking out on the
harbor, where the icebreakers await deep winter in the northern provinces.

Inside the Venetian-red building the members of Isaac's group are conducted upstairs to the various compartments of an eight-room suite for a
well-earned rest. By three in the afternoon night has fallen on Stockholm.
The group members are allowed to recuperate for several hours, then conducted, at six, to an official reception for the laureates and their families.

❀

December 7, 1978

Isaac is on the front pages of both the *Svenska Dagbladet* and the *Dagens
Nyheter* in Stockholm this morning. The *Dagbladet* features right in the
headline his suggestion that Henry Miller be a Nobel candidate. The Singer
group is scheduled for an early tour of the city with Janina Billner, a cultural attaché from the Foreign Ministry, a woman of considerable poise and
beauty whose long Russian coat has caused her more than once to be mistaken for a princess. Isaac has to stay at the hotel to be interviewed by NBC
correspondent Al Simon. This is one of the innumerable interviews to
which Isaac has agreed to submit, in addition to meetings arranged by the
Strauses with various representatives of his foreign publishers from England,
France, and Germany, as well as the firm of Bromberg right here in Stockholm. Soon he'll be a familiar face on television screens all over Scandinavia.

Stockholm is like a movie dubbed in English in the most magical way.
Ask nine out of ten citizens a question, and the reply is given in your own
tongue, phrased and pronounced more clearly than by most New Yorkers.

A taxi driver this morning wanted to know if the rest of the world really
takes the Nobel prize as seriously as they do in Stockholm. A hotel porter
commented that this was the first time in years he himself had read a book
by one of the winners; he just recently finished *Enemies, A Love Story*.

In front of the Grand, horse-drawn carriages of monarchic opulence are
starting to disgorge diplomats and statesmen in formal livery. In addition to
the line of Christmas trees atop the hotel marquee, workmen are putting up
three metal braziers to shed torchlight through the long December nights of
the Nobel festivities. This Nobel week is like a city-wide holiday for the
Swedes.

When the group assembles for the city tour, the Strauses are absent, having overslept, but a new member turns up: Israel Zamir, Isaac's son, who
has flown in from London and is covering the story of his father's honor for
Al Ha-Mishmar. Israel, still fit in his late forties, his hair looking redder
than ever, joins the tour with enthusiasm, listening, fascinated, to the statis-
tics about Stockholm's miles of waterways, architectural glories, one

hundred and thirty parks, and staggering prices (a cup of Irish coffee costs thirty Swedish crowns—about seven American dollars—and dinner for one, with a single cocktail, is hard to find for less than the equivalent of twenty-five dollars).

Shortly before noon the bus returns its sightseers to the Grand. Next the Singers and their friends are to be taken to a luncheon for the laureates at the Swedish Academy. Up in the spacious drawing room of Isaac's suite almost everybody (with the possible exception of goodhumored Bob Giroux) looks tired or tense or worried about something. Roger Straus comes in holding up a new French paperback edition of *Shosha* with a particularly ugly cover and the words PRIX NOBEL splashed across it. "Real class," he says with a sigh.

Ruth Jacoby, mastermind of the week's schedules, is clearly anxious to get everybody down and into the limousines, but Isaac refuses to be hurried or made anxious about anything. Wherever he is, he spreads an aura of benign sunshine all about him. He admits that all these interviews are getting pretty boring (nobody says the word quite like Isaac—it becomes a musical phrase of three descending notes), and he's tired of answering the same questions with the same answers. Yet his self-possession is remarkable, and this entire city is falling in love with him. They call him *Tomtegubben*—a little elf, a Santa Claus—in the newspapers. They call him the Magician of Lublin too, and "a little man with big dreams." He always has a quip on his lips, and when he can't think of a new one offhand, he borrows (from himself) one of the sure-fire lines that has served him in the past. He is a kind of Yiddishist Will Rogers here in Stockholm. His stooped, slightly tremulous, fragile figure becomes the focal point of any room as soon as he enters. Isaac has aged noticeably in the past year, but the blue eyes twinkle as engagingly as ever, the pink head with its thinning aureole of white hair nods attentively, the frail voice makes itself heard, and his comments are invariably cogent and penetrating.

Over a lunch of small open-faced sandwiches at a charming restaurant called the Fem Små Hus in the medieval-looking quarter of the old city, Israel Zamir talks about his father. He mentions the embarrassment he felt when every journalist in his own country seemed to want to take his—Israel's—picture and interview him as though *he* had won the prize. He says he was about to publish a book of his own short stories in Hebrew when news of the Nobel prize came. He decided to withdraw his own book from publication at that point—he didn't feel it was worthy enough. He worries about the fact that his father doesn't take time to read his contemporaries and still goes on talking about Tolstoy and Dostoevsky as though no great fiction had been written since their day, putting down Joyce and Faulkner and the moderns, whose work he does not really know. Speaking of his father's fiction—and Israel includes the books of memoirs pretty much in this category—he points out how over and over again, whenever one of the women in one of Isaac's stories turns out to be too much for the hero, he simply cuts loose and walks out on the situation. The women are invariably left behind; the man moves on and in a new direction. Israel feels that this method of escaping from trouble throws light on his father's own way of extricating himself from tight situations. He is also concerned that there has been no chance since the award was announced for his father to do any real writing and hopes that the ink will soon flow from Isaac's pen for something more significant than autographs, that inspiration will not be paralyzed by fame. He agrees with Alma's reaction to *Shosha*—that perhaps this novel should have been rewritten yet again (it got three rewrites in all) before it was published in English. Israel says too that he wants nothing from his father but his friendship.

Israel misses his wife and children and wishes they could be with him. He plans after lunch, in response to a request from one of his sons, to go looking for a jockey cap—even though he is distressed over the high prices in Sweden and intends to make up for the expense of this lunch by having a hamburger for dinner at the local Wimpy's.

❦

December 8, 1978

Isaac gives his Nobel lecture today at the Swedish Academy. The large, light room, all gray and gold, is thronged to capacity. There are four hundred people waiting to hear him. He is introduced by Lars Gyllenstein, who speaks of the "richness and diversity" of Isaac's stories and novels, and actually uses the phrase "existential epiphany" in connection with Isaac's work. Unruffled, Isaac, in his blue suit and blue shirt, sits down at a table decorated with a bowl of spectacular red roses, moves the microphone closer to him like the true professional he is, takes off his glasses so he can see his manuscript, and begins—in Yiddish—a language that has probably never been spoken in these halls before—the Nobel prize lecture that will be quoted tomorrow in countless languages in the press all over the world.

„דער גרויסער כבוד, וואָס די שוועדישע אַקאַדעמיע האָט מיר
אָנגעטאָן, איז אויך אַן אָנערקענונג פֿון אידיש, אַ לשון פֿון גלות,
אָן אַ לאַנד, אַן גרענעצן, נישט געשטיצט פֿון קיין שום מלוכה".

    Der groyser kovad vos di Shwedishe Academie hot mir ongeton
    is oich an anerkenung fun Yiddish—a loshon fun golus, ohn a
    land, ohn grenitzen, nisht gshtitzt fun kein shum meluchoh.

He then translates the Yiddish phrases into English while his audience follows on mimeographed texts, which rustle noisily as each page is turned:

> The great honor that the Swedish Academy has afforded me is also a recognition for Yiddish, a language of exile, without a country, without frontiers, that is not supported by any government. . . .

Isaac continues in English: "The storyteller and poet of our time, as in any other time, must be an entertainer of the spirit in the full sense of the word, not just a preacher of social or political ideals. There is no paradise for bored readers and no excuse for tedious literature that does not intrigue the reader, uplift his spirit, give him the joy and escape that true art always grants. Nevertheless it is also true that the serious writer of our time must be deeply concerned about the problems of his generation." Isaac sums up these problems as the weakening hold of religion, the loss of a "spiritual foundation" for family life, the "disappointment of modern man," despite every technological advance, "his loneliness, his feeling of inferiority, and his fear of war, revolution and terror."

Our society, which has lost confidence in its leaders, now looks to its writers: "I am not ashamed to admit that I belong to those who fantasize that literature is capable of bringing new horizons and new perspectives— philosophical, religious, esthetical, and even social. In the history of old Jewish literature there was never any basic difference between the poet and the prophet. Our ancient poetry often became law and a way of life."

Isaac recalls that his cronies on the *Forward* used to call him a "pessimist" and a "decadent" but says "there is always a background of faith behind resignation. I found comfort in such pessimists and decadents as Baudelaire, Verlaine, Edgar Allan Poe, and Strindberg." He also found solace, he says, in Swedenborg and Rabbi Nachman of Bratzlaver, and mentions the friend of his youth Aaron Zeitlin as a source of inspiration to him. The pessimism of a creative person "is not decadence but a mighty passion for the redemption of man."

Isaac speaks of the ghetto where he grew up as a "great experiment in peace, in self-discipline, and in humanism. . . . My father's home on Krochmalna Street in Warsaw was a study house, a court of justice, a house of prayer, of storytelling, as well as a place for weddings and Hasidic banquets." He asserts that the world can learn much from the conduct of the kind of Jews his parents were. And the Yiddish tongue reflects that conduct. Like Yiddish, "the Yiddish mentality is not haughty. It does not take victory for granted. It does not demand and command, but it muddles through, sneaks by, smuggles itself amidst the powers of destruction, knowing somewhere that God's plan for creation is still at the very beginning."

Nor has Yiddish had "its last word. It contains treasures that have not been revealed to the eyes of the world. It was the tongue of martyrs and saints, of dreamers and cabalists—rich in humor and in memories that mankind may never forget. In a figurative way, Yiddish is the wise and humble language of us all, the idiom of a frightened and hopeful humanity."

A storm of applause greets Isaac's address.

❀

Back at the Grand this evening, Isaac stops off to visit Simon Weber in his suite. He sits down to read Simon's story in Yiddish covering the day's events, which the *Forward*'s editor is about to send over the wires to his paper in New York. Isaac nods and seems pleased with the prose, some of which Simon reads aloud with relish. Isaac then reiterates his weariness with the demands of fame. He goes so far as to imagine himself in a room without a telephone, granting no interviews, posing for no pictures, returning again to his composition books and his writing and the privacy of a life that would belong to him rather than to the public. He says he wishes there were some way that you could get a Nobel prize and they would just send it to you in the mail, without all this pomp and ceremony.

A little later the Singers are off to a dinner party being tendered for them by Rabbi Morton H. Narrowe, spiritual leader of Stockholm's Great Synagogue—a private affair but not private enough, in Isaac's mood, for Isaac.

❀

December 9, 1978

Isaac and Alma and their party are scheduled to attend Sabbath services this morning at the Grand Synagogue a few blocks from the Grand. Isaac hasn't been particularly anxious to go, since he feels that it's somewhat hypocritical of him to attend services on the Sabbath after so many years of truancy, but the other Jewish laureates are going and how would it look?

In front of the synagogue a number of teen-age congregants in knitted skullcaps are waiting for Isaac, so that even here, as he enters the building, flashbulbs go off in his face. Photographs on the Sabbath would never be permitted in an Orthodox institution in New York, but this is not an Orthodox institution; neither is it Conservative or Reform. Swedish Jews do things their own way. The prayers are recited in Hebrew, with some interpolated passages in Swedish; the men wear hats and the women are segregated up in the balcony. But there is also an organ accompanying the choir as in a Reform temple in America.

The service is already in progress as the Singer entourage enters, but there is a murmur of recognition from the congregants as the laureate in literature is seated in a row with two of the three other laureates of his faith—Arno Penzias and Daniel Nathans (Professor Simon is not present). When the ark is opened for the reading of the day's portion from the Torah, the three are invited up for the honor of reciting the blessing that precedes the chanting of the portion. Rabbi Narrowe has chosen to deliver his commentary in English today, and his sermon, about Jacob's dream in the desert, brings him somehow to the prize winners and their accomplishments and the pride of the Jewish community in what they have done.

The president of the congregation introduces each of the laureates in turn, and each says a few words. Isaac talks about how honored he feels to be here—and to be accompanied by Simon Weber, whose newspaper has kept Yiddish alive and provided him with a readership through the years.

Following the service there is a reception in the library. Like fans at an Academy Award ceremony in Hollywood, the congregants throng the room to capacity, men and women holding their children aloft to get a glimpse of Isaac, straining forward to shake hands with the author. Since it's forbidden to write on the Sabbath, at least he doesn't have to autograph books this morning. A lavish post-service *kiddush* has been spread out for everybody, and Isaac joins with the others in sipping a cordial and eating a piece of sponge cake. Then it's back to the Grand for a brief rest; and after that, lunch with the United States ambassadors, Mr. Rodney Kennedy-Minott and Mrs. Kennedy-Minott, at their residence. Alma gets her friends Sally and Simone added to the ambassadors' invitation list at the last minute and brings them along.

In the afternoon there is a reception at the Nobel Library of the Swedish Academy. Here is another immense room, and by three thirty in the afternoon (it's been dark for some time now) it is packed with the laureates and their guests—diplomats, reporters, artists, scientists, authors, publishers, the cream of Sweden's intellectual society and overseas visitors connected with the week's events. One side of the room is devoted to a display of Isaac's books in many language, old photographs of his family, memorabilia, pictures of life in the Warsaw ghetto, and other material on Isaac's life and work. On hand this afternoon is Dorothea Bromberg, Isaac's attractive young publisher here in Stockholm, and the author Knut Ahnlund, who recently visited Isaac in New York by arrangement with Farrar, Straus and who has just published a monograph about Isaac in Swedish called *Isaac Bashevis Singer—Hans språk och hans värld* (*Isaac Bashevis Singer—His Language and His World*). Everyone is drinking champagne and munching on Scandinavian hors d'oeuvres. Alma beams. Isaac goes off to a private room away from the noise and confusion, where he sits autographing still more books—every guest here seems to have brought along a book by Isaac for his signature. Isaac is amiably relaxing with a few admirers when the photographers find him. "One more!" he comments wryly. "I think from now on that's what I'll say about my novels—one more, just in case!"

This evening, at the Judiska Center on Nybrogatan, the combined organizations of the Jewish community, including the Jewish Youth Fund and the Swedish Family Society for Yiddish and Yiddish Culture in Sweden, hold a huge reception for their "*Jiddisch Nobelfesten.*" There's a slide lecture on life in the *shtetlakh* of pre-Hitler Europe. Jeanette Meyer sings Yiddish and Hebrew songs. Judith Arnow reads a chapter from *In My Father's Court—* "The Vow"—in Yiddish. A choir of the local Hillel Day School, which has just decided to change its name to the Singkoren, or Singer Choir, in honor of the laureate, sings more songs. Isaac reads an essay in Yiddish, the one in which he points out that there are more ways to describe a poor man in that language than in any other. Fritz Hollander, a local leader and philanthropist, even reads his thank you speech in Yiddish. (Later tonight, Israel Zamir will report the whole thing over the phone to *Al Ha-Mishmar* in Tel Aviv—in Hebrew.)

In the fever of enthusiasm over Isaac's presence nobody has remembered to introduce Dr. Nathans and Dr. Penzias, but Isaac steps in himself to correct the oversight. Dr. Penzias, the award-winning physicist who fled Munich in 1940 and now teaches at City University in New York, tells of trying to get fitted for a tuxedo for a TV appearance in New York right after learning he had won the prize. The tailor couldn't see why he had to have the suit the same night or understand what prize he was talking about—until Penzias mentioned Isaac Bashevis Singer. Then he got service.

There's a picture of Isaac and Alma on the front page of *The New York Times* today, looking slightly done in. The *Times* also carries Isaac's Nobel lecture, including the Yiddish opening set into type by the *Jewish Daily Forward*. In *Dagens Nyheter* there's a photograph of Isaac's Yiddish typewriter. Isaac has complained to the press about his Yiddish typewriter. It seems there are no more Yiddish typewriters, only Hebrew typewriters, and the characters are not exactly the same. When Isaac gets his prize money, he intends, he says, to go on television and ask if anybody has an old Yiddish typewriter he can buy. "And maybe from all the Yiddish typewriters together I will get one good one!" The one he has now, he declares, is forty-three years old and sometimes stops functioning in the middle of a story. "I used to take this typewriter to a mechanic and ask him to correct it. But I've learned that this typewriter doesn't care about mechanics." Evidently the machine considers itself a literary critic, and what Isaac wants is a type-writer, "not a critic."

In the New York *Daily News* Pete Hamill will suggest next Monday that when Isaac comes home, the city "should throw him a parade. We've had parades for baseball champions and prizefighters, for cheap politicians and foreign kings. We dropped the confetti on Charles Lindbergh and John Glenn. We brought the bands for Douglas MacArthur and Dwight D. Eisenhower. But Isaac Singer is from New York. And it's not every day that somebody from New York winds up with the Nobel prize in literature. That demands a celebration. The biggest *simcha* in the city's recent history.

"Singer, an old man who will live forever, would probably object. Parades are not his style. But maybe the route could be changed and the right people chosen to ride in the limousines, and Singer would go along with it. They could start out at Sea Gate in Brooklyn, where Singer lived when he arrived from Poland in 1935; they could move along Ocean Ave., where he lived with his wife Alma after they were married, and they could take the cars through Williamsburg, where he also lived, before crossing the bridge to join the marching bands."

❀

December 10, 1978

Simon Weber's 55,000 Yiddish-speaking readers in New York are a little disappointed today. To save cable costs he had left behind a basic article with a Stockholm dateline, including the headline "Isaac Bashevis Singer Begins His Nobel Lecture in Yiddish" to warm their hearts, and even a sentence, written in advance, describing the ovation Isaac received after delivering it. But much of the material had to be cut to make room on the same page for news of Golda Meir's death.

Isaac has certainly won the allegedly cold heart of the city of Stockholm, conquering all Scandinavia, apparently, with his wit, his charm, his presence of mind. The stooped little man in the black overcoat is a strange sort of hero for this land of the Vikings. And he is entirely conscious of the mythic quality of his popularity here—the cheder boy from a Krochmalna Street tenement who made it all the way to the foremost literary honor in the world and soon will be dining with royalty at a banquet table.

This morning John Vanocur of *The New York Times* asked Isaac how he felt about the peace prize going to another Polish Jew. He got an answer that will be quoted all over the planet tomorrow: "Begin's award has no meaning to me. It has no connection to my prize. I want peace for Israel whether Begin gets an award or not. I say, Let there be peace. I got the Nobel prize for something I've done already. He and Sadat got the prize for something they still intend to do."

So far, the demons Maureen Howard of *The New Republic* predicted would get to Isaac in Stockholm, snap his shoelaces and make off with his cufflinks, have pretty much let him be. He only wishes more and more that people would do the same. The boxes have arrived from the tailor shop with the sets of white tie-and-tails outfits for the award ceremony this afternoon and the gala banquet tonight, and Isaac's seems to be all in order. The 11 A.M. rehearsal at the Concert Hall has gone smoothly. In fact, over in his son's room this afternoon Israel is already dressed, and he and Bob Giroux are taking pictures of one another. Then there's more picture-taking in the big drawing room where everybody is gathering, all dressed up and ready to go to the Concert Hall for the award ceremony. The women—Alma and Dorothea and Alma's friends Simone and Sally—look particularly attractive in their evening gowns, Alma in beige with a large aquamarine pinned to her bosom. And here comes Ruth Jacoby, the vigilant schedule-keeper from the Foreign Ministry, all dressed up too and ready to herd the entire party down to private buses. These will be available all evening, first for the Concert Hall event, then for the banquet at the old Town Hall. Waiting in the bus to issue reassurances and last-minute instructions over its public address system is Janina Billner, the cultural attaché who had conducted the Singer group on a city tour. She looks especially beautiful tonight in a long red coat over a glittering gown. The bus maneuvers through the city, which is also dressed up in twinkling lights for the Christmas season, and in a matter of minutes arrives at the hall on Hotorget Street at 4 P.M. promptly.

What a beautiful hall it is, blindingly bright now, gold and white, under photoflood lamps set up for the convenience of the news photographers and television cameramen. On the stage sit the members of the Nobel Academy; behind and above them in a balcony overhead are assembling the players of the Stockholm Philharmonic, who will perform the musical parts of the ceremony. The orchestra plays "Trumpet Voluntary." Carl XVI Gustaf, young and fresh-faced, a blue ribbon across his chest, enters with the beautiful Munich-born Queen Silvia in a dark blue gown and a crown of diamonds, along with Prince Bertil, Princess Lilian, and Princess Christina. The laureates take their seats stage right on massive thronelike chairs. Professor Sune Bergstrom, Chairman of the Board of the Nobel Foundation, makes the opening speech, which winds up: "Nobel Prize Day plays more and more the role of an annual reminder to those in power in the world of the quickly exhausted and irreplaceable assets which people of the calibre of our prize winners represent. They must be granted the conditions they require to develop and exploit their intellectual capacity and industry in their constant search for further knowledge. Allow me to conclude by illustrating this point with Isaac Singer's suggestive image: 'If there is such a thing as truth, it is as intricate and hidden as a crown of feathers'—to which I would simply like to add: What is more enticing or important than seeking that crown wherever the search may lead."

Each winner is introduced by a speech and an appropriate musical selection. Each goes to the center of the stage, gets his diploma, a gold medal, and a check for his share of the $163,000 awarded in each category. Peter L. Kapitsa, Arno A. Penzias, and Robert W. Wilson accept awards for physics after a speech by Professor Lamek Hulthen; Peter Mitchell is presented with the award for chemistry after a speech by Professor Lars Ernster; Werner Arber, Daniel Nathans, and Hamilton O. Smith are given the awards in physiology of medicine after Professor Peter Reichard speaks. (All the speeches are in Swedish, but a booklet of translations has been distributed to everyone in the audience.) Now the orchestra plays Hilding Rosenberg's "Journey to America" in Isaac's honor. Professor Lars Gyllensten, who introduced Isaac when he gave his Nobel lecture the other day, begins his address on the literature prize with a quotation from "The Spinoza of Market Street": "Heaven and earth conspire that everything which has been, be rooted out and reduced to dust. Only the dreamers, who dream while awake, call back the shadows of the past and braid from unspun threads nets. . . ." He talks of Isaac's origins, of his books, where "the saint and the rogue are next of kin," and of his greatness as a "consummate storyteller and stylist." Then Isaac goes up to get his medal and diploma and his $163,000; bows to the king; goes back to his own throne; violates protocol by sitting down before the king does; gets up; sits down again. The orchestra has struck up the overture to George Gershwin's *Of Thee I Sing* in honor of the American laureates. The piece sounds incongruous in this formal setting, as Isaac must feel in this company of scientists and the royal household—a seventy-four-year-old Yiddishist and spinner of yarns about a persecuted people, now a matinee idol among the Nordics. Next the Bank of Sweden Prize in economic sciences is presented to Herbert A. Simon. The musicians play the Swedish National Anthem, "*Du gamla, du fria.*" The guests retrieve their overcoats and don them against the cold wind of the Northern night.

Buses whisk their well-dressed passengers to the Town Hall now for the banquet in the Blue Hall, which looks like an open-air Venetian courtyard but is actually a vast enclosure with a high ceiling and a curved staircase leading down from a ballroom above. Of the twelve hundred guests here tonight, four hundred are students who have won their tickets by lottery. They wear white hats that look like yachting caps. ABC anchorman Howard K. Smith is on hand, facing a color-TV camera as he rehearses the final narration of an hour-and-a-half documentary about this year's Nobel awards, being prepared for public television in the states next Saturday and for viewing by satellite throughout the world. "The King, the Queen, the laureates," he says in his suave voice, "the audience, the reporters, have been moved, in toto, from the Concert Hall, where the awards were given, to the Town Hall, the old Town Hall, for this banquet." But there's something wrong with the sound, and Smith has to say the whole thing again. Then he goes on: "The laureates now, after the toast to the King and Queen, have nothing to lose but their dignity—which they may well do, in front of flowing wine, tables groaning with food, and later, serenading students. But those who do will be forgiven because this has been a strenuous formal affair, and this is almost too relaxing a close."

Smith tells how the crew has tracked down each of the laureates, including the Russian Peter Kapitsa, to his home habitat for filming in the course of preparing this television special. Isaac was documented in his New York apartment, strolling around the Upper West Side with Alma and lunching at his favorite restaurant, the Famous, on West Seventy-second Street. Rachel MacKenzie was taped too, praising Isaac's prose to the skies.

The guests have taken their seats in the Blue Hall by this time, and Karl Neilheim leads the orchestra in the "Entrata" from Hilding Rosenberg's *Taffelmusik*. The guests of honor descend the stairs, Isaac escorting the beautiful Princess Christina, whom he will regale with his wit at the royal table throughout the evening; Alma escorted by a diplomat. Professor Sune Bergstrom proposes a toast to the king, who in turn proposes one to the memory of Alfred Nobel. Then the banqueters consume cold Parisian lobster and braised duck, champagne and three other kinds of wine, and, for dessert, "Glace Nobel," decorated with a big N—the insignium of the Nobel Academy. (Isaac sticks to vegetables.) Coffee is served, and each of the laureates makes a short speech. Isaac begins his, "His Majesty, ladies and gentlemen; People are asking me often, why do you write in a dying language? And I want to explain it in a few words. First, I like to write ghost stories, and nothing fits a ghost better than a dying language. The deader the language, the more alive is the ghost. Ghosts love Yiddish; they all speak it. Secondly, I believe in resurrection. I'm sure that the Messiah will soon come, and millions of Yiddish-speaking corpses will rise from their graves one day, and their first question will be, 'Is there any new Yiddish book to read?' Thirdly, for two thousand years, Hebrew was considered a dead language. Suddenly, it became strangely alive. What happened to Hebrew may also happen to Yiddish one day, although I haven't the slightest idea how this can ever happen. There is still another, minor reason why I write Yiddish, and this is because Yiddish is the only language I really know well. Of course it's a minor reason, but it is a reason." He goes on to recite the ten reasons why he writes for children—the same ones he enumerated when he got the National Book Award for *A Day of Pleasure*. The applause is thunderous.

Following the speeches student singers from the University of Stockholm offer a group of songs—including a lullaby by the composer Maurice Karkoff to a text drawn from the pages of *Enemies, A Love Story*. The chairman of the student body delivers a summary address, and Dr. Penzias responds. At 10 P.M. the celebrants proceed upstairs to the great green-and-gold ballroom, where they are soon waltzing away to the strains of "The Blue

Danube." Isaac and Alma join a group of special guests in the Green Room, where more flashbulbs pop and distinguished hands exchange shakes. Half an hour later the Singers sneak out quietly for a night of well-earned rest. Tomorrow they will attend another banquet—at the Royal Palace, given by Their Majesties the King and Queen. The following week Israel's ambassador to Sweden will hold a reception at his residence for the Jewish laureate, Isaac will get still another honorary degree for his collection from the University of Uppsala, and the Singer party will leave for Paris, where there will be more meetings with publishers, more press conferences, more interviews, more receptions, and a lecture by Isaac at the Sorbonne. When he gets home, he will learn that the members of the city council in Seaside, Florida, where Isaac own his condominium, are hoping to change the name of the street where it stands—Ninety-sixth Street—to Isaac Bashevis Singer Boulevard. Meanwhile, here in the ballroom the guests who have assembled in honor of the prize-winners are dancing. They will go on dancing—and drinking—until two in the morning.

Selected Bibliography

WORKS BY ISAAC BASHEVIS SINGER

Novels

Shoten an Goray (*Satan in Goray*). Warsaw: P.E.N. Club, 1935.

Di Familie Mushkat (*The Family Moskat*). New York: Morris S. Sklarsky, 1950.

The Family Moskat. Translated by A. H. Gross. New York: Alfred A. Knopf, 1950.

Satan in Goray. Translated by Jacob Sloan. New York: Noonday Press, 1955.

The Magician of Lublin. Translated by Elaine Gottlieb and Joseph Singer. New York: Noonday Press, 1960.

The Slave. Translated by the author and Cecil Hemley. New York: Farrar, Straus and Cudahy, 1962.

The Manor. Translated by Joseph Singer and Elaine Gottlieb. New York: Farrar, Straus and Giroux, 1967.

The Estate. Translated by Joseph Singer, Elaine Gottlieb, and Elizabeth Shub. New York: Farrar, Straus and Giroux, 1969.

Enemies, A Love Story. Translated by Aliza Shevrin and Elizabeth Shub. Farrar, Straus and Giroux, 1972.

Shosha. Translated by Joseph Singer and the author. New York: Farrar, Straus and Giroux, 1978.

Yarme and Kayle. New York: Farrar, Straus and Giroux, 1979.

Unpublished Novels

Shadows on the Hudson (serialized in the *Jewish Daily Forward,* 1957).

A Ship to America (serialized in the *Jewish Daily Forward,* 1958).

The Penitent (serialized in the *Jewish Daily Forward,* 1974).

Collections of Short Stories

Shoten an Goray un Anderer Dertailungen (*Satan in Goray and Other Stories*). New York: Farlag Matones, 1945.

Gimpel the Fool and Other Stories. Translated by Saul Bellow, Isaac Rosenfield, and others. New York: Noonday Press, 1957.

The Spinoza of Market Street. Translated by Martha Glicklich, Cecil Hemley, and others. New York: Farrar, Straus and Cudahy, 1961.

Gimpel Tam un Anderer Dertailungen (*Gimpel the Fool and Other Stories*). New York: Central Yiddish Culture Organization, 1963.

Short Friday and Other Stories. Translated by Joseph Singer, Roger H. Klein, and others. New York: Farrar, Straus and Giroux, 1964.

Selected Short Stories of Isaac Bashevis Singer. Edited and introduced by Irving Howe. New York: The Modern Library, 1966.

The Seance and Other Stories. Translated by Roger H. Klein, Cecil Hemley, and others. New York: Farrar, Straus and Giroux, 1968.

A Friend of Kafka and Other Stories. Translated by the author, Elizabeth Shub, and others. New York: Farrar, Straus and Giroux, 1970.

An Isaac Bashevis Singer Reader. New York: Farrar, Straus and Giroux, 1971.

A Crown of Feathers and Other Stories. Translated by the author, Laurie Colwin, and others. New York: Farrar, Straus and Giroux, 1973.

Passions and Other Stories. New York: Farrar, Straus and Giroux, 1975.

Old Love. New York: Farrar, Straus and Giroux, 1979.

Memoirs

Main Tatn's Beth-Din Shtub (My Father's Beth-Din Court). New York: Kval Publishers, 1956.

In My Father's Court. Translated by Channah Kleinerman-Goldstein, Elaine Gottlieb, and Joseph Singer. New York: Farrar, Straus and Giroux, 1966.

Isaac Bashevis Singer and Ira Moskowitz. *A Little Boy in Search of God; or, Mysticism in a Personal Light*. Garden City, New York: Doubleday, 1976.

A Young Man in Search of Love. Illustrated by Raphael Soyer. Garden City, N.Y.: Doubleday, 1978.

Lost in America. Illustrated by Raphael Soyer. Garden City, N.Y.: Doubleday, 1979.

Children's Stories

Zlateh the Goat and Other Stories. Translated by Elizabeth Shub and the author. Illustrated by Maurice Sendak. New York: Harper and Row, 1966.

The Fearsome Inn. Translated by Elizabeth Shub and the author. Illustrated by Nonny Hogrogian. New York: Scribner's, 1967.

Mazel and Shlimazel; or, The Milk of a Lioness. Translated by Elizabeth Shub and the author. Illustrated by Margot Zemach. New York: Farrar, Straus and Giroux, 1967.

When Shlemiel Went to Warsaw and Other Stories. Translated by Channah Kleinerman-Goldstein, Elaine Gottlieb, and others. Photographs by Roman Vishniac. New York: Farrar, Straus and Giroux, 1969.

Elijah the Slave. Illustrated by Antonio Frasconi. New York: Farrar, Straus and Giroux, 1970.

Joseph and Koza; or, The Sacrifice to the Vistula. Translated by the author and Elizabeth Shub. Illustrated by Symeon Shimin. New York: Farrar, Straus and Giroux, 1970.

Alone in the Wild Forest. Translated by the author and Elizabeth Shub. Illustrated by Margot Zemach. New York: Farrar, Straus and Giroux, 1971.

The Topsy-Turvy Emperor of China. Translated by the author and Elizabeth Shub. Illustrated by William Pène du Bois. New York: Harper and Row, 1971.

The Wicked City. Translated by the author and Elizabeth Shub. Illustrated by Leonard Everett Fisher. New York: Farrar, Straus and Giroux, 1972.

The Fools of Chelm and Their History. Translated by the author and Elizabeth Shub. Illustrated by Uri Shulevitz. New York: Farrar, Straus and Giroux, 1973.

Why Noah Chose the Dove. Translated by Elizabeth Shub. Illustrated by Eric Carle. New York: Farrar, Straus and Giroux, 1974.

A Tale of Three Wishes. Illustrated by Irene Lieblich. New York: Farrar, Straus and Giroux, 1976.

Naftali the Storyteller and His Horse, Sus, and Other Stories. Translated by Joseph Singer, Ruth Schachner Finkel, and the author. Illustrated by Margot Zemach. New York: Farrar, Straus and Giroux, 1976.

Eight Hannukah Stories. New York: Farrar, Straus and Giroux, 1979.

Translations

Stefan Zweig. *Romain Rolland.* Vilna: B. Kletzkian, 1927.

Knut Hamsun. *Die Vogler.* Vilna: B. Kletzkian, 1928.

Knut Hamsun. *Victoria.* Vilna: B. Kletzkian, 1929.

Erich Remarque. *All Quiet on the Western Front.* Vilna: B. Kletzkian, 1930.

Knut Hamsen. *Pan.* Vilna: B. Kletzkian, 1931.

Erich Remarque. *The Way Back.* Vilna: B. Kletzkian, 1931.

Thomas Mann. *The Magic Mountain.* Vilna: B. Kletzkian, 1932.

Leon Glaser. *From Moscow to Jerusalem.* New York: Max Kankowitz, 1938.

Essays and Reviews

"The Everlasting Joke." *Commentary,* 31 (May 1961): 458–60.

"The Poetry of Faith." *Commentary,* 32 (September 1961): 258–60.

"A New Use for Yiddish." *Commentary,* 33 (March 1962): 267–69.

"Realism and Truth." Translated by Adah Auerbach Lapin. *The Reconstructionist,* 15 (June 1962): 5–9.

"Why I Write in Yiddish." *Pioneer Woman,* 38 (January 1963): 13.

"What It Takes to Be a Jewish Writer." Translated by Mirra Ginsburg. *National Jewish Monthly.* 78 (November 1963): 54–56.

"Sholom Aleichem: Spokesman for a People." *The New York Times,* 20 September 1964, Section 2, pp. 1, 4.

Introduction to *Yoshe Kalb,* by I. J. Singer. New York: Harper and Row, 1965.

"Rootless Mysticism." *Commentary,* 39 (January 1965): 78–79.

"Indecent Language and Sex in Literature." Translated by Mirra Ginsburg. *Jewish Heritage,* 8 (Summer 1965): 51–54.

"The Ten Commandments and the Modern Critics." *Cavalier,* June 1965, p. 30.

"A Phantom of Delight." *Book Week,* 4 July 1965, pp. 2, 7.

"What's in It for Me." *Harper's,* 231 (October 1965): 166–67.

[Review of *Pan,* by Knut Hamsun] *Holiday,* 38 (December 1965): 166–67.

"Peretz's Dream." *American Judaism,* Spring 1966, pp. 20–21, 60–61.

"Once on Second Avenue There Lived a Yiddish Theater," *The New York Times,* 17 April 1966, Section 2, p. 3.

Kafka's Trials." *Book Week,* 1 May 1966, pp. 16–17.

"Hagigah." *American Judaism,* Winter 1966–67, pp. 18–19, 48–49.

"The Future of Yiddish and Yiddish Literature." *The Jewish Book Annual,* Vol. XXV. New York: Jewish Book Council of America, 1967, pp. 70–74.

"The Extreme Jews." *Harper's*, 234 (April 1967): 55–62.

"Civilising the Shtetl." *Jewish Chronicle*, 8 December 1967, pp. i–ii.

Introduction to *The Adventures of One Yitzchok*, by Yitzchok Perlov. New York: Award Books, 1967.

Introduction to *Hunger*, by Knut Hamsun. New York: Noonday Press, 1968.

"The Writer of Inborn Goodness." *Book World*, 17 March 1968, p. 4B.

"Editor's Prize." *Playboy*, 15 (May 1968): 18.

"The Fable as Literary Form." Introduction to *Aesop's Fables*. Translated by George Fyler Townsend. Garden City, N.Y.: Doubleday, 1968.

"Roth and Singer on Bruno Schulz." *The New York Times Book Review*, 13 February 1977, pp. 5, 14, 16, 20.

Nobel Lecture. New York: Farrar, Straus and Giroux, 1979. (English and Yiddish)

Uncollected Short Stories

"Hail, the Messiah." Translated by Morris Kreitman [Maurice Carr]. *Jewish Stories of Today*. Edited by Morris Kreitman. London: Faber and Faber, 1958, pp. 35–51.

"Sacrifice." Translated by Hannah Goldstein. *Harper's*, 228 (February 1964): 61–64.

"Converts." Translated by Joseph Singer. *Commentary*, 38 (December 1964): 46–48.

"One Day of Happiness." *Cavalier*, September 1965. pp. 19, 78–84.

"The Strong." *American Judaism*, Winter 1965–66.

"The Prodigal Fool." Translated by the author and Elizabeth Shub. *The Saturday Evening Post*, 26 February 1966, pp. 64–66, 68–69.

"The Boudoir." Translated by the author and Elizabeth Shub. *Vogue*, 1 April 1966, pp. 148–49, 214.

"My Adventures as an Idealist." Translated by Aliza Shevrin and Elizabeth Shub. *The Saturday Evening Post*, 18 November 1967, pp. 68–73.

"Peephole in the Gate." Translated by the author and R. S. Finkel. *Esquire*, 75 (April 1971): 124–27.

"Escape from Civilization." Translated by the author and R. S. Finkel. *The New Yorker*, 6 May 1972, pp. 34–36.

"Tanhum." *The New Yorker*, 17 November 1975, pp. 41–45.

"The Power of Darkness." Translated by Joseph Singer. *The New Yorker*, 2 February 1976, pp. 31–35.

"Dalfunka Where the Rich Live Forever." *The New York Times Magazine*, 28 March 1976, p.111.

"A Cage for Satan." Translated by Joseph Singer. *The New Yorker*, 24 May 1976, pp. 38–40.

"The Psychic Journey." Translated by Joseph Singer. *The New Yorker*, 18 October 1976, pp. 38–44.

"Two." Translated by Joseph Singer. *The New Yorker*, 20 December 1976, pp. 37–42.

"Yochna and Shmelke." Translated by Joseph Singer. *The New Yorker*, 14 February 1977, pp. 39–42.

"Elka and Meir." Translated by Joseph Singer. *The New Yorker*, 23 May 1977, pp. 36–42.

"Two Weddings and One Divorce." Translated by the author and Alma Singer. *The New Yorker*, 29 August 1977, pp. 28–33.

"The Boy Knows the Truth." Translated by the author. *The New Yorker*, 17 October 1977, pp. 48–53.

"One Night in Brazil." Translated by Joseph Singer. *The New Yorker,* 3 April 1978, pp. 34–40.

"The Bus." Translated by Joseph Singer. *The New Yorker,* 28 August 1978, pp. 30–51.

Books About Singer

Allentuck, Marcia, ed. *The Achievement of Isaac Bashevis Singer.* Carbondale: Southern Illinois University Press, 1970.

Buchen, Irving H. *Isaac Bashevis Singer and the Eternal Past.* New York: New York University Press, 1968.

Malin, Irving, ed. *Critical Views of Isaac Bashevis Singer,* New York: New York University Press, 1969.

Malin, Irving. *Isaac Bashevis Singer.* New York: Frederick Ungar, 1972.

Rosenblatt, Paul, and Koppel, Gene. *A Certain Bridge: Isaac Bashevis Singer.* Tucson: University of Arizona, 1971.

Siegel, Ben. *Isaac Bashevis Singer.* Minneapolis: University of Minnesota Press, 1969.

Critical and Biographical Articles

Alter, Robert. "Shosha." *The New Republic,* 16 September 1978, pp. 20–22.

Blocker, Joel, and Elman, Richard. "Interview with I. B. Singer." *Commentary,* 36 (November 1963): 364–72.

Burgin, Richard. "Isaac Bashevis Singer Talks . . . About Everything." *The New York Times Magazine,* 26 November 1978, pp. 24–26, 32, 36–38, 42–48.

———. "Isaac Bashevis Singer's Universe." *The New York Times Magazine,* 3 December 1978, pp. 38–40, 44–46, 50–52.

Chametzky, Jules. "The Old Jew in New Times." *The Nation,* 30 October 1967, pp. 436–38.

Colwin, Laurie. "I. B. Singer, Storyteller." *The New York Times Book Review,* 23 July 1978, p. 1.

Elman, Richard. "Singer of Warsaw." *The New York Times Book Review,* 8 May 1966, pp. 1, 34–36.

———. "The Spinoza of Canal Street." *Holiday,* 38 (August 1965): 83–87.

Feldman, Irving. "Fools' Paradise." *Book Week,* 30 October 1966, p. 4.

———. "The Shtetl World." *The Kenyon Review,* 24 (Winter 1962): 173–77.

Fenyvesi, Charles. "A Dybbuk in DC." *The New Republic,* 21 October 1978, pp. 17–18.

Fiedler, Leslie. "The Circumcized Philistine and the Unsynagogued Jew." *American Judaism,* 16 (Fall 1966): 30, 33–36.

Fixler, Michael. "The Redeemers: Themes in the Fiction of Isaac Bashevis Singer." *The Kenyon Review,* 26 (Spring 1964): 371–86.

Flender, Harold. "Isaac Bashevis Singer." *The Paris Review,* 11 (Fall 1968): 53–73.

Frank, M. Z. "The Demon and the Earlock." *Conservative Judaism,* 20 (Fall 1965): 1–9.

Goodheart, Eugene. "Singer's Moral Novel." *Midstream,* 8 (September 1962): 99–102.

Hemley, Cecil. "Isaac Bashevis Singer." In *Dimensions of Midnight: Poetry and Prose,* edited by Elaine Gottlieb. Athens: Ohio University Press, 1966, pp. 217–33.

Hindus, Milton. "The False Messiah." *New Leader,* 28 November 1955, pp. 24–26.

———. "The Family Moskat." *The New York Times Book Review,* 14 March 1965, pp. 4, 44–45.

————. "Isaac Bashevis Singer." *Jewish Heritage Reader,* edited by Morris Adler. New York: Taplinger Publishing Company, 1965.

Howard, Maureen. "Isaac the Fool." *The New Republic,* 21 October 1978, pp. 15–17.

Howe, Irving. "Demonic Fiction of a Yiddish 'Modernist.' " *Commentary,* 30 (October 1960): 350–53.

————. "I. B. Singer, Storyteller." *Encounter,* 26 (March 1966): 60–70.

————. "In the Day of a False Messiah." *The New Republic,* 31 October 1955, pp. 20–22.

————. "The Other Singer." *Commentary,* 41 (March 1966): 78–82.

————. "Stories: New, Old and Sometimes Good." *The New Republic,* 13 November 1961, pp. 18–19.

Hughes, Catharine R. "The Two Worlds of Isaac Singer." *America,* 18 November 1967, pp. 611–13.

Hughes, Ted. "The Genius of Isaac Bashevis Singer." *The New York Review of Books,* 22 April 1965, pp. 8–10.

Hyman, Stanley Edgar. "Isaac Singer's Marvels." *New Leader,* 21 December 1964, pp. 17–18.

————. "The Yiddish Hawthorne." *New Leader,* 23 July 1962, pp. 20–21.

Jacobson, Dan. "The Problem of Isaac Bashevis Singer." *Commentary,* 39 (February 1965): 48–52.

Jonas, Gerald. "People with a Choice." *The New York Times Book Review.* 5 November 1967, pp. 1, 52.

Kahn, Lothar. *Jewish Horizon,* 30 (November–December 1966): 16, 18.

Kazin, Alfred. "His Son, the Storyteller." *Book Week,* 24 April 1966, pp. 1, 10.

————. *"Passions and Other Stories* by Isaac Bashevis Singer." *The New Republic,* 25 October 1975, pp. 24–25.

————. "The Saint as Schlemiel." *New Leader,* 4 August 1958, pp. 21–23.

Kibel, Alvin Charles. "The Political Novel." *The Reconstructionist,* 31 October 1957, pp. 27–32.

Kolateh, Mollie. "With Singer in the Shtetl." *Jewish Life,* 33 (November–December 1965): 51–54.

Kresh, Paul. "An Early Masterpiece by I. B. Singer." *Hadassah Magazine,* 49 (December 1967): 18–19.

————. "A Master Storyteller." *Hadassah Magazine,* 50 (October 1968): 24.

————. "Singer's Demons Move to New York Streets." *Hadassah Magazine,* 52 (January 1971): 15.

————. "A Jewish Pixie." *Hadassah Magazine,* 60 (February 1979): 10–12, 25–26, 28.

Ludwig, Jack. "The Two-Fold Nature of Truth." *Midstream,* 4 (Spring 1958): 90–93.

Madison, Charles. "I. Bashevis Singer: Novelist of Hasidic Gothicism." *Yiddish Literature, Its Scope and Major Writers.* New York: Frederick Ungar, 1968, pp. 479–99.

Miller, Henry. "Magic World of Imps and Villagers." *Life,* 11 December 1964, pp. 14, 20.

Pinsker, Sanford. "The Isolated Schlemiels of Isaac Bashevis Singer." In *The Schlemiel as Metaphor.* Carbondale: Southern Illinois University Press, 1971, pp. 55–87.

Pondrom, Cyrena N. "Isaac Bashevis Singer: An Interview and a Biographical Sketch." *Contemporary Literature,* 10 (Winter, Summer 1969): 1–38, 332–51.

Prescott, Peter. "Singer the Magician." *Newsweek,* 16 October 1978, pp. 97–98.

Reichek, M. A. "Storyteller." *The New York Times Magazine,* 23 March 1975, pp. 16–18.

Rosenthal, Raymond. "The Darkness of the Glass." *New Leader,* 9 May 1966, pp. 13–14.

Schulz, Max F. "Isaac Bashevis Singer, Radical Sophistication and the Jewish-American Novel." Paper read at the MLA Convention, December 1967.

Shenker, Israel. "Isaac Bashevis Singer Scoffs." *Atlantic Monthly* 226 (July 1970): 98–100.

Siegel, Ben. "Sacred and Profane: Isaac Bashevis Singer's Embattled Spirits." *Critique*, 6 (Spring 1963): 24–47.

Sontag, Susan. "Demons and Dreams." *Partisan Review*, 29 (Summer 1962): 460–63.

Straus, Dorothea. "The Courtyard and the Waiting Room." *Palaces and Prisons*. Boston: Houghton Mifflin, 1976, pp. 130–43.

Sundel, Alfred. "The Last of the Yiddish Mohicans." *New Leader*, 11 December 1961, pp. 20–22.

Teller, Judd L. "Unhistorical Novels." *Commentary*, 21 (April 1956): 393–96.

Turan, Kenneth. "Isaac Bashevis Singer: 'I Walk on Mysteries.' " *The New York Times*, 28 December 1976, pp. C1, C3.

Wachtel, Nili. "A Portrait of Isaac Bashevis Singer: Freedom Through Slavery." *Midstream*, 23 (May 1977): 75–80.

Wincelberg, Shimon. "Proving a Vanished Past." *New Leader*, 26 February 1968, pp. 26–29.

Discography

Isaac Bashevis Singer Reading His Stories
"Gimpel the Fool," "The Man Who Came Back" (Translated by Cecil Hemley)

Caedmon TC 1200

Isaac Bashevis Singer Reads in Yiddish

קליין און גרויס • שידה און כוזיבא • דער צוריקגעשריגענער

"Klein un Grois," "Shiddah un Kuzibah," "Der Zurickgeshriggener"
"Big and Little," "Shiddah and Kuziba," "The Man Who Came Back"

Caedmon TC 1202, cassette CDL 51202

Isaac Bashevis Singer Read by Eli Wallach
Directed by Paul Kresh
"The Seance," "The Lecture"

Spoken Arts SA 1153

Eli Wallach Reads Isaac Bashevis Singer
From *Zlateh the Goat:* "Fool's Paradise," "The Snow in Chelm," "The First Shlemiel," "Zlateh the Goat"

From *When Shlemiel Went to Warsaw and Other Stories:*
"Shrewd Todie and Lyzer the Mizer," "Rabbi Leib and the Witch Cunnegunde," "When Shlemiel Went to Warsaw"

Newbery Award Records (two discs) NAR 3063/64, (two cassettes) NAC 3063/64

Index